Community
Building

Community Building: Renewal, Well-Being, and Shared Responsibility

Edited by

Patricia L. Ewalt
Edith M. Freeman
Dennis L. Poole

With a foreword by

John B. Turner

NASW PRESS
National Association of Social Workers
Washington, DC

Josephine A. V. Allen, PhD, ACSW, *President*
Josephine Nieves, MSW, PhD, *Executive Director*

Jane Browning, *Executive Editor*
Christina A. Davis, *Senior Editor/Project Manager*
Donald Delauter, *Senior Editor*
Marcia D. Roman, *Staff Editor*
Sarah Lowman, *Staff Editor*
Bill Cathey, *Typesetter*
Chanté Lampton, *Acquisitions Associate*
Heather Peters, *Editorial Secretary*
Beth Gyorgy, *Proofreader*
Bernice Eisen, *Indexer*

©1998 by the NASW Press, Inc.

Library of Congress Cataloging-in-Publication Data

Community building : renewal, well-being, and shared responsibility /
    edited by Patricia L. Ewalt, Edith M. Freeman, Dennis L. Poole ;
    with a foreword by John B. Turner.
        p. cm.
    Includes bibliographical references and index.
    ISBN 0-87101-292-8 (pbk. : alk. paper)
    1. Community development. 2. Human services. I. Ewalt,
    Patricia L. II. Freeman, Edith M. III. Poole, Dennis L.
    HN49.C6 IN PROCESS
    307. 1'4--dc21   98-12183
                                                              CIP

Printed in the United States of America

Contents

    Communities: School-Linked, Family Resource Centers   306
    David R. Dupper and John Poertner

28 Creating Family-Centered Integrated Service Systems and
    Interprofessional Educational Programs to Implement Them   316
    Dean Corrigan and Kathleen Kirk Bishop

29 An Interagency Collaboration Strategy for Linking Schools
    with Social and Criminal Justice Services   331
    Donna Tapper, Paula Kleinman, and Mary Nakashian

30 School-Linked Comprehensive Services: Promising Beginnings,
    Lessons Learned, and Future Challenges   343
    Katharine Briar-Lawson, Hal A. Lawson, Connie Collier,
    and Alfred Joseph

31 Establishing School-Based, Collaborative Teams to
    Coordinate Resources: A Case Study   355
    Cynthia Lim and Howard S. Adelman

PART VII: COMMUNITY HEALTH PARTNERSHIPS

32 Building Community Capacity to Promote Social and Public
    Health: Challenges for Universities   369
    Dennis L. Poole

33 The SAFE Project: Community-Driven Partnerships in Health,
    Mental Health, and Education to Prevent Early School Failure 380
    Dennis L. Poole

34 Partnerships for Improved Service Delivery:
    The Newark Target Cities Project   390
    M. Katherine Kraft and Janet E. Dickinson

35 An Empowerment-Centered, Church-Based Asthma Education
    Program for African American Adults   398
    Marvella E. Ford, Gloria Edwards, Juan L. Rodriguez, Rose C. Gibson,
    and Barbara C. Tilley

36 Retooling for Community Health Partnerships in Primary
    Care and Prevention   407
    Dennis L. Poole and Mary Van Hook

37 Addressing At-Risk Pregnant Women's Issues through
    Community, Individual, and Corporate Grassroots Efforts   411
    Judy Balsanek

38 Social Support Networks of Confidants to People with AIDS   420
    Stephen Jankowski, Lynn Videka-Sherman,
    and Karen Laquidara-Dickinson

    About the Editors   431

    About the Contributors   433

    Index   439

Foreword

Americans' identification with the often-quoted African proverb "it takes a village to raise a child" is but one example of why there is so much interest in the quest for community. Many of the objectives of physical and social well-being, if they are to be realized, require community support and action, both formal and informal. In the village of the past, face-to-face relationships dominated. There were no strangers. There was a closely knit group. Life situations required a high degree of interdependency. Village members knew what behavior represented their best interests and how to teach and discipline wayward members. They could count on each other for support. They related to internal and external situations as a group.

A cursory review of chapter titles in this book makes it clear to the reader that at least in social work, the day of community has arrived. It appears that there is some mystique about community. Professionals in many fields are in search of more effective means in their efforts at social betterment. They seek the holy grail of community and neighborhood.

Few American population centers approximate village communities of the past, yet the properties of community are as necessary as ever. If we cannot return to the days and times of village America, how can structures and processes be determined that will enable disadvantaged citizens to more effectively define and advance their own life chances in a society that is increasingly nonresponsive to their status? This book is about the authors' experiences in efforts to guide the building and maintenance of communities, families, and children.

Practitioners, students, and teachers will find this collection of articles an invaluable resource. They reference the range and depth of strategic and tactical action situations that confront those who seek to intervene in community. Although not a how-to-do-it guide, this book broadens and deepens our understanding about the properties of community and well-intentioned behavior of agencies and ways of working with them.

At the center of community work is the science of identifying, focusing, and activating different sources of social influence sufficient to accomplish the relevant objective. The editors have selected 38 articles covering a variety of topics, but each discusses issues of strategy and tactics. Of equal importance for institutions, communities, individuals, and families is the science of human motivation—the question of how to initiate and maintain change.

Among the practice issues dealt with are

- Efforts to achieve cohesion between policy and its implementation at national and state levels with community action at the local level. Clearly this is an important area of concern, for in many cases policy established in larger political arenas is needed to facilitate reaching goals and objectives of local communities.

- Criteria for selecting a single issue, such as prenatal health versus improving communication about a variety of health problems in the community. Frequently, success on the first issue may require a parallel action around the second. When agencies seek to undertake collaboration on one issue they must understand and be prepared to assist with another. Whose definition of the problem or issue is to guide the action?
- Approval of the worker's role and mission, especially when it involves accountability to multiple communities. Crucial to the credibility of the program is the perception that the professional legitimization maintains accountability to the service consumer group or community.
- Most, if not all, of the communities discussed in the articles are by definition impoverished in a major way. What does honesty of partnership require with respect to the overwhelming visual and experiential facts about the socioeconomic status of their lives and place of residence? This is not to question the wisdom of current approaches, but it demands that we ask what else is needed.

There is one other group that can benefit from the learnings of this book. One would hope that agency boards and staffs would use this book as a resource in planning and evaluating their work with communities in regard to decision making about program and finance.

John B. Turner, DSW
Chapel Hill, NC

Introduction

In welfare reform and other cost containment policies, self-sufficiency is emphasized as a goal. Yet it is clear that self-sufficiency can be achieved only in the context of a facilitating community. People acting alone do not acquire economic security, education, health, housing, and cultural sustenance; they acquire these necessities through networks of mutual interdependence in communities. When community resources and decision-making capacities are impoverished or when social institutions fail to meet their share of responsibility in caring, the well-being of communities and their members is threatened.

The new era of community renewal has dramatically changed the role of social workers in community practice. Social workers once assumed the role of change agent, mobilizing community members through locality development, planning, and social action. Today, greater emphasis is placed on encouraging community members, including youths, to participate and assume leadership roles in all phases of community capacity development. This realignment of roles is sometimes characterized as a shift from "community organizing" directed primarily by professionals to "community building" directed primarily by community members.

In community building, community members should have opportunities and supports to

- define community interests
- define assets that already exist
- define assets that are required
- develop community capacity in governance
- strengthen mutual helping processes toward shared responsibility
- identify and strengthen local leadership capabilities
- improve participation of all populations, including youths, women, and people of color, in decision-making
- reform oppressive structures that are harmful to community well-being.

Within this framework, community members identify and determine improvements needed in the physical environment, housing, economic opportunity, safety, education, and health care.

In the past, community programs in such areas tended to be conducted as independent initiatives. Emphasis is now on broader, more comprehensive programs such as those sponsored by community development corporations and comprehensive community initiatives. The federal government, charitable foundations, and other entities have indicated through funding investments that more effective and meaningful outcomes for communities can be achieved through multifaceted approaches than with singular modes such as economic development or social services.

Because of the broad-based nature of current initiatives, organizations previously in competition with each other are required to collaborate productively.

Organizations are also redirecting their focus of accountability from a "community-based" to a "community-centered" status. The first emphasizes the physical location of programs in communities, collaboration among professionals, and the integration of professional services, but gives little accountability to community members. The second recognizes the importance of community participation and accountability and treats families and other community members as equal partners in social enterprises.

Beyond community-centered accountability, it is important for organizations to recognize affiliations for mutual assistance organized by community members themselves. Such affiliations are represented, for example, by the provision of kinship care and by peer-led social movements. When community members organize for mutual assistance, the role of professionals is to appreciate, perhaps to facilitate, these efforts, taking care not to deter the changes that affiliations can make for community well-being.

As such, social workers and other professionals must rethink how they understand and approach communities. The task is not easy; it requires major adjustments in professional mindset—from principles of practice to breadth of services provided, empowerment of natural support systems, styles of collaboration with families and other community members, accountability to communities for services rendered, and redefinition of professional roles and functions.

Community Building: Renewal, Well-Being, and Shared Responsibility provides examples of community building brought about by community members and professionals working in partnership. This book is intended as a resource for practitioners, students, educators, researchers, and policymakers in all fields of social work practice. The book makes a timely contribution to current dialogue and collaborative work on community renewal and shared responsibility, advancing social workers to the forefront of community practice in the 21st century.

Patricia L. Ewalt
Edith M. Freeman
Dennis L. Poole

Part I

COMPREHENSIVE COMMUNITY INITIATIVES

The Revitalization of Impoverished Communities

Patricia L. Ewalt

Over the past 50 years, people with low incomes have been increasingly concentrated and isolated in central cities characterized by deteriorated, unsafe housing. These neighborhoods lack access to basic resources such as transportation, employment, health care, public safety, or education that adequately prepare people for employment (Mulroy, 1995; Wilson, 1996).

Because of the compounding and interrelatedness of problems, it is clear that redeveloping impoverished communities requires a multifaceted approach that addresses the physical and economic conditions of neighborhoods as well as the social and cultural aspects. Philanthropic funders have concluded that sectional funding, for example, for housing rehabilitation or social services alone, may not hold as much promise as the funding of comprehensive community initiatives (Ford Foundation, 1994; Kubisch, Weiss, Schorr, & Connell, 1995; Pew Charitable Trusts, 1995; U.S. General Accounting Office [GAO], 1995).

According to Kubisch et al., comprehensive community initiatives (CCIs),

> contain several or all of the following elements and aim to achieve synergy among them: expansion and improvement of social services and supports, such as child care, youth development, and family support; health care, including mental health care; economic development; housing rehabilitation and/or construction; community planning and organizing; adult education; job training; school reform; and quality-of-life activities such as neighborhood security and recreation programs. (p. 1)

To this list should be added micro and macro enterprise and job development (GAO, 1995; Linder & Staff of Urban Strategies Council, 1996; Weil, 1996) within or outside the neighborhood (Kahn & Kamerman, 1996).

In addition to comprehensive strategies, it is posited that CCIs depend on, at the least, community partnership in development (Weil, 1996) or, as some suggest, community control of governance (Kubisch et al., 1995). In this approach, the earlier conceptualization of citizen participation is transformed into residents' partnership in or control of the change process (Flynn, Ray, & Rider, 1994). As expressed by Flynn et al. (1994), "Theorists have emphasized citizen participation as important in the development of local politics, yet participation by itself is not necessarily empowering. Further actions are required to convert mere participation into citizens' ability to influence public decisions" (p. 395).

As reported in the history of one CCI, the Dudley Street Neighborhood Initiative in the Roxbury area of Boston, residents demonstrated that they fully grasped the difference between participation and control and fully intended to exercise the latter: "The Dudley Street Initiative's commitment to community power was put to the test early by neighborhood residents refusing to confuse resident participation with resident control" (Medoff & Sklar, 1994, p. 256). Hence, comprehensive community initiatives intend to create environments that enable people to meet their basic needs and give people influence over how those environments will be created. Kahn and Kamerman (1996) aptly expressed the goal as to construct "'platforms and ladders,' not 'safety nets'" for disadvantaged people in the community (p. 15).

Research increasingly supports the concept of neighborhood effects, positive or negative, on child development (Coulton, 1996). This research builds on earlier formulations by Bronfenbrenner (1986) that explain how external environmental factors affect family functioning, which in turn affects human development. Thus, the family's interactions with schools, the workplace, the neighborhood, and the larger community are all deemed to affect the family and individuals within it.

The differential effects of neighborhoods on subgroups or the mechanisms through which effects occur are not yet well understood (Coulton, 1996; Mincy, 1994). Adequate evaluation of comprehensive community initiatives is also difficult to achieve (Kubisch et al., 1995). Nevertheless, the GAO (1995) reported to Congress that "community development experts—researchers, government officials, and practitioners—advocate a comprehensive approach to address the problems of distressed neighborhoods because such complex, interrelated problems are better addressed in tandem than individually" (p. 2). The experts who were interviewed advised that conditions in deteriorated communities could not be reversed except over extended periods and that results of interventions were difficult to demonstrate. Yet they felt that because of the new integrated strategies available, the work of change was both important and feasible.

Hence, social work is challenged to produce knowledgeable practitioners capable of contributing effectively to the comprehensive community-building initiatives of the future.

REFERENCES

Bronfenbrenner, U. (1986). Ecology of the family as a context for human development: Research perspectives. *Developmental Psychology, 22,* 723–742.

Coulton, C. J. (1996). Effects of neighborhoods on families and children: Implications for services. In A. J. Kahn & S. B. Kamerman (Eds.), *Children and their families in big cities: Strategies for service reform* (pp. 87–120). New York: Columbia University, Cross-National Studies Research Program.

Flynn, B. C., Ray, D. W., & Rider, M. S. (1994). Empowering communities: Action research through healthy cities. *Health Education Quarterly, 21,* 395–405.

Ford Foundation. (1994). *Current interests of the Ford Foundation, 1994 and 1995.* New York: Author.

Kahn, A. J., & Kamerman, S. B. (1996). Themes and viewpoints. In A. J. Kahn & S. B. Kamerman (Eds.), *Children and their families in big cities: Strategies for service reform* (pp. 1–29). New York: Columbia University, Cross-National Studies Research Program.

Kubisch, A. C., Weiss, C. H., Schorr, L. B., & Connell, J. P. (1995). Introduction. In J. P. Connell, A. C. Kubisch, L. B. Schorr, & C. H. Weiss (Eds.), *New approaches to evaluating community initiatives: Concepts, methods, and contexts.* Washington, DC: Aspen Institute.

Linder, W. J., & Staff of the Urban Strategies Council. (1996). Two community development initiatives: The New-Community Corporation and the Urban Strategies Council. In A. J. Kahn & S. B. Kamerman (Eds.), *Children and their families in big cities: Strategies for service reform* (pp. 138–150). New York: Columbia University, Cross-National Studies Research Program.

Medoff, P., & Sklar, H. (1994). *The fall and rise of an urban neighborhood.* Boston: South End Press.

Mincy, R. B. (1994). The underclass: Concept, controversy, and evidence. In S. H. Danziger, G. D. Sandefur, & D. H. Weinberg (Eds.), *Confronting poverty: Prescriptions for change* (pp. 109–146). Cambridge, MA: Harvard University Press.

Mulroy, E. A. (1995). *The new uprooted: Single mothers in urban life.* Westport, CT: Auburn House.

Pew Charitable Trusts. (1995). *1995 program guidelines.* Philadelphia: Author.

U.S. General Accounting Office. (1995, February). *Community development: Comprehensive approaches address multiple needs but are challenging to implement* (Publication No. GAO/RCED/HEHS-95-96). Washington, DC: U.S. Government Printing Office.

Weil, M. O. (1996). Community building: Building community practice. *Social Work, 41,* 481–499.

Wilson, W. J. (1996). *When work disappears: The new world of the urban poor.* New York: Alfred A. Knopf.

This chapter was originally published in the September 1997 issue of Social Work, vol. 42, pp. 413–414.

2 Countering Urban Disinvestment through Community-Building Initiatives

Arthur J. Naparstek and Dennis Dooley

Since 1933 housing and community development legislation has been directed at halting the physical deterioration of U.S. cities. Help has come from federally subsidized public housing, the Federal Housing Administration (FHA), urban renewal grants, Model Cities programs, revenue sharing, community development revenue sharing, and housing allowances. More recently, cities have received federal money through tax breaks and direct grants: Urban Development Action Grants of the 1970s, the enterprise zones of the 1980s, the empowerment zones of the 1990s, and the urban revitalization demonstration public housing grants of the 1990s.

This chapter reviews policy approaches to and legislation for community revitalization and discusses how early federal policies contributed to the segregation and isolation of poor neighborhoods. The chapter describes how new community-based programs and proposed federal initiatives are building on the accumulated expertise of the past 25 years. These initiatives pose challenges for research, policy, and community-level programs by creating policies and programs that transcend people-place dichotomies and recognizing the need for comprehensive community-building strategies.

URBAN DISINVESTMENT

Disinvestment is a series of progressive steps by which area lending institutions extricate themselves from neighborhoods they expect to deteriorate. Among the principal tactics is "redlining," thus termed because more blatant disinvestment practice involves drawing red lines around target neighborhoods on area maps. Redlining may consist of outright refusal to accept mortgage or home-improvement loan applications, or it may involve a number of more subtle actions: awarding mortgage loans on inordinately short terms with high down payment requirements, refusing to lend on properties older than a prescribed number of years, stalling on appraisals to discourage potential borrowers, underappraising, refusing to lend in amounts below a fixed minimum figure, and charging inordinately high closing costs. As a policy, disinvestment is defended on the grounds that investment in high-risk areas is equivalent to mismanagement of depositors' funds and is ultimately counterproductive, both for the depositor and for the lending institution.

In practice, however, redlining is less a protective action against unnecessary financial risk than a self-fulfilling prophecy of decline for specific neighborhoods.

First, the decision to redline is based on a subjective assessment of the likely effects of the race or ethnicity of potential buyers, the age of the housing stock, and the potential for financial loss in a given community. Second, the assessment of decline is often made before evidence of actual decline and without reference to such factors as residents' credit ratings, the current condition of the housing stock regardless of age, and the viability of the community as a whole (including the ability to attract new buyers and the solvency of its businesses) (Naparstek & Cincotta, 1976).

Consequently, redlining can undermine healthy communities. And because the immediate result of the decision to redline is the withdrawal of monies required to maintain that community's health, disinvestment ensures that decline will, in fact, occur. Local depositors living in a redlined area find that their savings, instead of being converted to mortgage and home improvement loans for local use, are directed to other, less risky areas, usually new suburban developments. Thus, the residents of redlined neighborhoods are doubly victimized, by the banks' ensuring their neighborhoods' gradual decline and by being deprived of the rightful use of their own savings. Bound inextricably to governing credit policies and to the fiscal well-being of urban centers, redlining has destructive long- and short-term consequences, both for inner-city residents and their communities (Galster, 1996; LaCouer-Little, 1996). Squires (1992) noted that racially discriminatory appraisal practices and redlining by lenders and property insurers have contributed to the decline of central cities, the rise of the suburbs, and the racial exclusivity of both.

NEIGHBORHOOD EVOLUTION THEORY

The National Commission on Neighborhoods (1979) noted that planners and policymakers in the public sector and investors, lenders, and other members of the private sector have generated a set of negative assertions about revitalizing older, inner-city neighborhoods.

- Older neighborhoods, either through natural forces or the competition of the marketplace, invariably decline and move toward blight as they filter into the hands of poorer residents.
- Change in the racial makeup of a neighborhood is a precursor to decline.
- Mixed land uses or the introduction of commercial or industrial uses into residential areas indicate and contribute to decline.

All three assertions stem from the same root and are related to issues of filtering, racial change, and diversity. They evolved from the federal response to poor neighborhoods during the Great Depression. In the mid-1930s FHA and the Home Owner Loan Corporation (HOLC) were created and given the job of developing sound and uniform housing policies. FHA and HOLC drew heavily on the human ecology model that was being developed at the University of Chicago.

When applied to neighborhoods, this model holds that groups of people "infiltrate" and "invade" territory held by others (Hoyt, 1939). Through a process of "competition" (that is, a war of survival), the group most suited to the environment takes over completely. Neighborhoods were seen as being subject to

the laws of nature and going through life cycles. This theory held that neighborhoods grow to a point of success, and then as the technology of the society develops and favors different locations, there is invasion and succession by lower-
income people (Hoyt, 1939).

Homer Hoyt, a professor of real estate at the University of Chicago, translated these theories into real estate terms. In a study commissioned and published by FHA in 1939, Hoyt developed the filtering, or trickle-down, model of
neighborhood life cycles. This theory was endorsed by FHA and became the
foundation of federal housing and urban development policies. Hoyt's theory
holds that as individual properties and neighborhoods age, they filter down
from higher-income groups to poorer people until they become slums.

Hoyt and colleague Frederick Babcock added to this theory of decline by suggesting that racial and ethnic change contributes to neighborhood decline. Babcock
(1932), in his early text on real estate, linked race to neighborhood decline:

> Most of the variations and differences between people are slight, and value
> declines are, as a result, gradual. But there is one difference in people, namely
> race, which can result in a very rapid decline; usually, such declines can be
> partially avoided by segregation, and this device has always been in common
> usage in the south where white and Negro populations have been separated.
> (p. 91)

The FHA employed Babcock and incorporated his model into its underwrit-
ing and real estate approval standards. The National Commission on Neighborhoods (1979) noted that these models became officially certified government
policy and the basis of the principles used by the major appraisal and under-
writing organizations. In 1965 the U.S. Department of Housing and Urban Development (HUD) was created and took over FHA. The impact of the
Hoyt-Babcock set of assumptions was apparent in a 1975 HUD publication, *The
Dynamics of Neighborhood Change*, which sets out five stages through which neighborhoods are presumed to pass. The publication describes the process of decay
in terms of five stages: (1) healthy, (2) incipient decline, (3) clearly declining,
(4) accelerated decline, and (5) abandoned. This orientation to a community has
served as the intellectual justification for redlining. Research findings collected
during the past 20 years document the impact of the Hoyt-Babcock perspective
on neighborhoods.

POLICY TOOLS TO COUNTER DISINVESTMENT

During the 1970s, community organizations throughout the country, largely
stimulated by National Peoples Action led by Gail Cincotta and the National
Center for Urban Ethnic Affairs led by Monsignor Geno Baroni, initiated action
that became the basis for the community reinvestment movement. The legislative framework for building the movement revolved around two legislative initiatives: the Home Mortgage Disclosure Act of 1975 (HMDA) (P.L. 94-200) and
the Community Reinvestment Act of 1977 (CRA) (P.L. 95-128). HMDA and CRA
offered community groups the legal tools to act against discriminatory lending
practices in neighborhoods throughout the country (Fishbein, 1994; Naparstek
& Cincotta, 1976; Squires, 1992).

Researchers concerned with discrimination and redlining have used the HMDA data to document disinvestment patterns in the inner city. Galster (1996) noted that the issue of discrimination directed toward mortgage applicants of color received a significant increase in attention during the 1990s: "A variety of evidence, including disparities observed in Home Mortgage Disclosure Act data, stories of blatant discrimination, a smattering of court cases, pilot studies using paired testers, and multivariate statistical analyses of lenders' loan application files, has combined to substantiate the view that discrimination in mortgage lending exists" (p. 33).

LaCouer-Little (1996) pointed out that the Boston Federal Reserve study undertaken in 1992 on the basis of 1990 HMDA data substantiated discriminatory lending. Denial rates for people of color were high; for example, black and Hispanic applicants had a 28 percent denial rate compared with slightly over 10 percent for white applicants. The authors of the Boston Federal Reserve study concluded the following:

> The results of this study indicate that race does play a role as lenders consider whether to deny or approve a mortgage loan application. The higher denial rate for minorities in Boston are accounted for, in large part, by their having higher loan-to-value ratios and weaker credit histories than whites. They are also more likely to be trying to purchase a two-to-four unit property rather than a single family home. Nevertheless, after taking account of such factors, a substantial gap remains. A black or Hispanic applicant in the Boston area is roughly 60 percent more likely to be denied a mortgage than a similarly situated white applicant." (p. 15)

The CRA has provided a tool to reverse or counter redlining. The act states that federally regulated financial institutions "have a continuing and affirmative obligation to help meet the credit needs of the local communities in which they are chartered consistent with safe and sound operation of such institutions" (p. 3).

Fishbein (1994) noted that the law is based on the view that although banks are privately capitalized, a federally insured lender is subject to a charter obligation to serve the banking needs of its local community. These public obligations form the quid pro quo for extensive government backing, such as federal deposit insurance and access to the Federal Reserve System's lender of last resort facility. The CRA gives the government power to impose sanctions on institutions with weak records. However, federal regulatory agencies have rarely initiated any action on the basis of a CRA evaluation. The power of CRA is that it permits third parties to file challenges to applications on the basis of poor CRA performance and that such challenges can and do delay consideration of all applications. Often community-based organizations with city government backing have mounted these challenges.

Delays in processing applications have proved to be quite costly for banks. Consequently, rather than engage in extended litigation regarding the merits of CRA challenges, lenders generally enter into negotiations with local governments or community groups. On a national level, reinvestment commitments totaling more than $20 billion have been negotiated in over 70 cities (Fishbein, 1994).

Fishbein (1994) suggested that CRA agreements have resulted in significant changes in the institutional behavior of lenders. For example, in Chicago, banks in the mid-1980s promised to lend $153 million to targeted neighborhoods, and in 1996 in Cleveland, more than $1.25 billion was targeted for neighborhood-based loans. In Boston a $400 million reinvestment commitment by the city's major banks was made in the mid-1980s; in Pittsburgh a $109 million commitment was negotiated; and in Detroit a $2.9 billion settlement came about as a result of the aggressive enforcement of a state community reinvestment act by the commissioner of the Michigan Financial Institutions Bureau. In California a series of statewide campaigns culminated in several reinvestment agreements including a 10-year, $8 billion commitment by that state's major banks.

Fishbein (1994) further pointed out that notwithstanding the success of many CRA challenges, community groups still complained about the lax enforcement of the law. Federal regulators have been accused of being too cozy with the institutions they supervise and indifferent about their enforcement responsibilities. Weak enforcement in turn hampers the efforts of local community groups to negotiate directly with lending institutions.

REVERSING DISINVESTMENT THROUGH COMMUNITY DEVELOPMENT CORPORATIONS

The majority of community development corporations (CDCs) have been formed since 1960, growing out of the War on Poverty, the civil rights movement, tenant organizing, and more recently the antiredlining movement (Vidal, 1992). CDCs, which have used the CRA as a tool to revitalize communities, are the instruments communities have created to insert themselves into the mainstream of economic and social services decision making (Mott, 1985).

Sullivan (1993) pointed out that community development is an antipoverty strategy that aims to revitalize poor neighborhoods rather than to disperse their residents. Sullivan's research on CDCs suggests that they use elements of the following strategies in bringing about social change in a neighborhood:
- changing the ethnic composition of the residents
- changing the attitudes of individual residents who are already there
- changing the way individuals relate to one another
- changing the way the neighborhood and its residents interact with powerful people and institutions outside the neighborhood.

The four strategies are generally applied by CDCs through housing development programs or commercial revitalization initiatives. CDCs will use selection and eviction to control the composition of the residents of their buildings. Through property management's enforcement of rules and provision or referral of social services, CDCs work with individuals and families to overcome problems and foster personal development. Through tenant and community organizing, CDCs influence the ways residents relate to one another, and through advocacy CDCs attempt to change the ways in which their neighborhood and residents are treated by powerful forces outside the neighborhoods. By using the tools that are available to counter disinvestment, CDCs have made significant progress attacking place-based issues related to new housing.

COMMUNITY-BUILDING STRATEGIES

During the 1970s and early 1980s, the CDCs focused on place-based strategies with special emphasis on housing and economic development (Kingsley, 1996). However, evaluations of CDC performance carried out in the mid-1980s and early 1990s suggest that although physical development is still a dominant program component, CDCs have begun to seek to influence community life along many dimensions—physical, social, economic, individual, institutional, and political (Leiterman & Stillman, 1993).

The National Congress of Community Economic Development (1991) reported that more than two-thirds of CDCs nationwide were active not only in physical, but also in social community development. Walker and Weinheimer (1996) concluded that CDCs have increased their capacity in areas beyond housing to include economic development, social services provision, and community-building initiatives. Stimulated by national and community foundations, community building through CDCs is reconciling the dichotomy between people-based and place-based strategies. Connell, Kubisch, Schorr, and Weiss (1995) elaborated on the integration of people-based and place-based strategies:

> While varied, they all have the goal of promoting positive change in individual, family and community circumstances in disadvantaged neighborhoods by improving physical, economic and social conditions. Most . . . aim to achieve synergy by expansion and improvement of social services and supports such as child care, youth development, and family support health care, including mental health care; economic development; housing rehabilitation and/or construction; community planning and organizing; school reform; and quality of life activities such as neighborhood security and recreation programs. (p. 1)

Linking place- and people-based strategies through community building has significant implications for social work, because it means improving the delivery and quality of human services, strengthening community organization, stimulating economic development, and in every possible way improving the quality of life of residents while affecting physical improvements. Over the years, numerous public and philanthropic initiatives have addressed such concerns as poverty, welfare, unemployment, inadequate education, housing, and crime. But past efforts have tended to consider these problems one at a time. People- and place-based strategies address the fact that the coexistence of problems within a neighborhood creates a mutually reinforcing process of decay that in turn limits the effectiveness of narrowly focused initiatives (Svirdoff, 1994).

Community building offers a different set of strategies when linked to urban disinvestment. A community-building approach looks at the whole picture, acknowledges the interconnectedness of people- and place-based strategies, and recommends a course of action in which solutions are tied together in such a way that they reinforce one another. The community-building approach calls for the design of specific mechanisms that will give neighborhood residents more control over changes and the ability to hold accountable the larger systems that ought to be serving them. CDCs can serve as the mechanisms that will link place-based strategies with people-based strategies through comprehensive approaches (Svirdoff, 1994).

The Cleveland Foundation Commission on Poverty's (Naparstek, 1992) review of the literature and its own related research found that effective community-building initiatives should be guided by the following principles:

- Strategies must be comprehensive and integrated.
- Strategies should be tailored to the individual neighborhood involved and be focused on an area of manageable size.
- Strategies should begin not merely with a neighborhood's needs but with an inventory of its assets.
- Strategies must involve residents and other local stakeholders in setting goals and priorities and shaping plans to address them.

Comprehensive Strategies

Because poverty is the result of interlocking problems that reinforce and complicate one another, a single cure is impossible. Any sensible plan, therefore, not only will take all these factors into consideration, but will build on and use those linkages to create new synergies.

The research of Coulton, Chow, and Chantos (1990), Wilson (1991), Connell et al. (1995), and Schorr (1988) suggested the need for comprehensive approaches.

> There was and continues to be a sense that we know a great deal about "what works" for at-risk populations and that if we could manage to concentrate and integrate resources and program knowledge in particular communities over a sustained period of time, we could demonstrate that positive outcomes are indeed within our reach. This call for cross-sector, cross-system reform has been further justified by recent social science research that has begun to identify the linkages and interconnectedness among the various strands of an individual's life and of the importance of family and neighborhood influences in determining individual level outcomes. (Connell et al., 1995, p. 3)

Solutions should be community specific as well as community building, building on the individual character and resources of that neighborhood and addressing its particular needs. The interdependence of residents and local institutions is key to any community-building effort.

Manageable-Size Targets

Targeting a specific geographic neighborhood offers the opportunity to identify community-based factors that can be singled out as critical to supporting families and individuals. Wilson (1991) and Naparstek, Biegel, and Spiro (1980) found that in many poor communities, informal support and networks that help people are not as effective as they could be. The best means of engaging residents in shaping community-building strategies is through targeting. Furthermore, different neighborhoods have different needs and meet them in different ways. Only by engaging people can the networks become energized.

Putnam (1993) and Case and Katz (1992) demonstrated through their research findings in a wide range of contexts that by strengthening neighborhood-based norms and networks, education outcomes improve, poverty is diminished, crime is inhibited, economic performance is boosted, and mortality rates are reduced. Conversely, deficiencies in community-based networks contribute to a wide range of social, economic, and political ills.

Inventory of Assets

A neighborhood's assets must include not only its material resources (everything from schools and bank branches to vacant storefronts and welfare checks), but also its human assets—such as life experiences, skills, and readiness to commit time and energy to a sustained effort. Any serious attempt to help people regain control of their lives must provide opportunities to invest and build on such assets (Kretzmann & McKnight, 1993).

There is empirical evidence that supports the efficacy of community-based assets. Naparstek et al. (1980) identified opportunity structures through neighborhood-based networks that supported individual and family life and reduced stress. Putnam's (1993) comparative study of communities in northern and southern Italy revealed that organizations such as guilds, religious fraternities, cooperatives, mutual-aid societies, and neighborhood associations are preconditions for local economic development.

Two kinds of existing community associations are suited to the job of building a neighborhood's assets and capacities. One is the multi-issue community organization built along evaluation lines. Community organizers understand the importance of association life to the well-being of neighborhoods. Another is the CDC.

Resident Involvement and Control

"Top-down" solutions imposed on communities tend to undermine the sorts of local initiatives that should be supported and encouraged. If the people affected are not engaged in the process, the work will go nowhere. Government's role is to change ways of proceeding through collaborative decision making. The movement toward devolution of program authority from federal to local (state and county) through block grants puts substantial pressure on local health, education, and social services agencies to meet residents' needs. The key to making this devolution process work is to engage the community through new forms of collaboration and partnerships (Naparstek & Dooley, 1997).

In effect, devolution is both a top-down and a bottom-up process. Experience has shown that applying only one approach to alleviating poverty is inadequate. An exclusively top-down strategy lacks significant input from residents and other stakeholders. On the other hand, approaches that are solely bottom up, although often effective for building support for single issues, are less likely to produce the comprehensive changes needed to address more complex realities. Successful strategies borrow effective aspects of involving residents and other stakeholders, such as strengthening the traditional sources of support in communities—families, churches, social clubs, and CDCs.

RECENT FEDERAL POLICIES

Two recent legislative initiatives passed by Congress support the four principles of community building by integrating place-based and people-based approaches. These groundbreaking initiatives offer great opportunities for social work practice in the areas of community organization, family development, and health, as well as economic development, housing, and job creation.

The Empowerment Zone Program, now funded at well over a billion dollars, responded to the call for reinvestment in the nation's distressed communities by creating 12 empowerment zones and 100 enterprise communities. This promising initiative was based on the recognition that the answers to a community's problem must be generated by that community and that any meaningful strategy for job growth and economic development must be comprehensive in nature and integrated in its implementation. A combination of tax incentives, investment grants, and other federal resources are made available to a local partnership in each community that has developed a comprehensive strategic plan for job growth and economic recovery and that coordinates economic, human, and physical development.

The 1993 Urban Revitalization Demonstration Project (HOPE VI) has thus far allocated $2.1 billion to a program to transform some of the nation's most distressed public housing developments into well-functioning, supportive communities that can help residents move toward sustainable independence. Inspired by the Cleveland Community-Building Initiative and its principles for community building, HOPE VI went beyond the traditional use of federal funds for "bricks-and-mortar" improvements to include people-based interventions.

The original legislation designated up to 20 percent of each award for community-building activities that promote and support the attainment of self-reliance and a new sense of responsibility for one's community. HOPE VI breaks new ground by linking individual outcomes such as increasing employment, overcoming substance dependency, and expanding the possibility of home ownership with community outcomes such as crime reduction and increased access to area resources and opportunities. Resident organizations design and coordinate a comprehensive strategy for their communities that offers residents opportunities for civic engagement and decision making in matters affecting their lives, the chance to define the values and behaviors acceptable to the community (for example, evictions, which are enforced by police and public housing authority), and access to a range of life opportunities (jobs, education, and housing options).

CONCLUSION

The implications for social work practice are significant. Each legislative initiative described offers a framework that links community building to social work practice in a form that requires competence in the processes of place-based and people-based strategies. Programs evolving from the Empowerment Zone and HOPE VI initiatives suggest the need for social work practitioners who are familiar with community theory and community organizations, who understand the process of physical and economic development, and who have core knowledge of social work values and commitment to grassroots participation. Rothman (1995) supported this pattern for social work practice as he noted that macro-oriented community intervention, with its emphasis on structural change, prevention, and social reform, and micro-oriented intervention, with its emphasis on personal renewal and political reform, are both relevant to HOPE VI and the Empowerment Zone policies. Finally, these bottom-up development

efforts reflect the emergence of a new form of empowerment based on old social work values.

REFERENCES

Babcock, B. (1932). *The valuation of real estate.* New York: McGraw-Hill.

Case, A., & Katz, S. (1992). *The company you keep: The effects of family and neighborhood on disadvantaged youth* (Working Paper No. 3705). Washington, DC: National Bureau of Economic
Research.

Community Reinvestment Act of 1977, P.L. 95-128, 91 Stat. 1147, 1148.

Connell, J., Kubisch, A., Schorr, L., & Weiss, C. (1995). *New approaches to evaluating community
initiatives: Concepts, methods, and contexts.* Washington, DC: Aspen Institute.

Coulton, C., Chow, J., & Chantos, P. (1990). *An analysis of poverty and related conditions in
Cleveland, Ohio neighborhoods over the past decade.* Cleveland: Case Western Reserve University, Mandel School of Applied Social Sciences, Center for Urban Poverty and Social Change.

Fishbein, A. (1994). *Community reinvestment.* Unpublished manuscript, Center for Community
Change, Washington, DC.

Galster, G. (1996). Comparing loan performance between races as a test for discrimination.
Cityscape: A Journal of Policy Development and Research, 2, 33–39.

Home Mortgage Disclosure Act of 1975, P.L. 94-200, 104 Stat. 2766.

Hoyt, H. (1939). *The structure and growth of residential neighborhoods in American cities.* Washington, DC: Federal Housing Administration.

Kingsley, T. (1996). *Community building: Coming of age.* Unpublished manuscript, Urban Institute, Washington, DC.

Kretzmann, J., & McKnight, J. (1993). *Building communities from the inside out: A path toward
finding and mobilizing a community's assets.* Evanston, IL: Northwestern University.

LaCouer-Little, M. (1996). *Estimation of demand and supply of mortgage credit from the Boston
Federal Reserve study of mortgage discrimination.* Unpublished manuscript, University of
Wisconsin-Madison, School of Business.

Leiterman, M., & Stillman, J. (1993). *Building community.* New York: Social Initiative Support
Corporation.

Mott, A. H. (1985, September). *The decades ahead for community organizations.* Paper presented at
the National Neighborhood Coalition, Washington, DC.

Naparstek, A. (1992). *Cleveland Community Building Initiative: Report and recommendations of the
Cleveland Foundation Commission on Poverty.* Cleveland: Cleveland Foundation, Commission
on Poverty.

Naparstek, A., Biegel, D., & Spiro, H. (1980). *Neighborhood networks for humane mental health care.*
New York: Plenum Press.

Naparstek, A., & Cincotta, G. (1976). *Urban disinvestment: New implications for community
organization research and public policy.* Washington, DC: National Center for Urban Ethnic
Affairs.

Naparstek , A., & Dooley, D. (1997). Community building: New strategies for community
development. In R. L. Richards (Ed.-in-Chief), *Encyclopedia of social work, 1997 suppl.* (19th
ed.). Washington, DC: NASW Press.

National Commission on Neighborhoods. (1979). *People building neighborhoods: Report to the
president and Congress.* Washington, DC: Author.

National Congress of Community Economic Development. (1991). *Changing the odds.* Washington, DC: Author.

Putnam, R. (1993). *Making democracy work: Civic traditions in modern Italy.* Princeton, NJ:
Princeton University Press.

Rothman, J. (1995). Approaches to community interventions. In J. R. Rothman, J. Erlich, & J.
Tropman (Eds.), *Strategies of community intervention* (pp. 3–26). Itasca, IL: F. E. Peacock.

Schorr, L. (1988). *Within our reach: Breaking the cycle of disadvantage.* New York: Doubleday.

Squires, G. (1992). *From redlining to reinvestment: Community response to urban disinvestment.*
Philadelphia: Temple University Press.

Sullivan, M. (1993). *More than housing: How community development corporations go about changing lives and neighborhoods.* New York: New School for Social Research, Graduate School of Management and Urban Policy, Community Development Research Center.

Svirdoff, M. (1994). The seeds of urban revival. *Public Interest, 114,* 82–103.

U.S. Department of Housing and Urban Development. (1975). *The dynamics of neighborhood change.* Washington, DC: U.S. Government Printing Office.

Vidal, A. (1992). *Rebuilding communities: A national study of urban community development corporations.* New York: New School for Social Research.

Walker, C., & Weinheimer, M. (1996). *The performance of community development systems: A report to the National Community Development Initiative.* Washington, DC: Urban Institute.

Wilson, W. J. (1991). Public policy research and the truly disadvantaged In P. Jencks (Ed.), *The urban underclass* (pp. 460–481). Washington, DC: Brookings Institution.

This chapter was originally published in the September 1997 issue of Social Work, *vol. 42, pp. 506–514.*

3 Implementing Comprehensive Community Development: Possibilities and Limitations

Robert J. Chaskin, Mark L. Joseph,
and Selma Chipenda-Dansokho

Over the past decade, private philanthropies have spearheaded a great deal of activity known in the field as "comprehensive, community-building initiatives" (for an overview of this field, see, for example, Eisen, 1992; Kubisch et al., in press; Stone, 1996). The public sector has also seen increasing activity of this type: The Empowerment Zone program, launched through federal legislation in 1993, is the most obvious example. These efforts, public and private, share a general approach to neighborhood development and the alleviation of the effects of poverty characterized by four crucial elements. First, they focus on geographically defined target areas, variously defined but almost always limited to a portion or portions of a city. Second, they provide support for a process of strategic planning based on a recognition of community assets and available resources as well as needs. Third, they insist on "community participation" in the governance, planning, and implementation of development activities at the local level. Finally, they focus on comprehensive development, including an attempt to integrate economic, physical, and human development activities.

This chapter focuses on the last element. We are particularly interested in exploring community-based attempts to interconnect development strategies for maximizing the effects of resources and extent of neighborhood change. The chapter outlines the rationale for comprehensive development and examines possible approaches to its realization, drawing briefly on the literature in an attempt to put the concept in historical and current practice perspectives. It then examines the attempt to operationalize the idea of comprehensive development in one effort, the Neighborhood and Family Initiative (NFI) sponsored by the Ford Foundation, which is currently being implemented in a neighborhood in each of four American cities. The analysis is based on data collected through ongoing fieldwork, including qualitative interviews and focus groups and observation of collaborative-sponsored meetings, events, and relevant neighborhood activities. It is also based on a review of site-produced materials, including administrative documents, results of local evaluation, correspondence, and minutes, as well as materials in the Ford Foundation archives. (For a more detailed analysis of the initiative's principles and approaches to collaborative planning and integrated development, see Chaskin, 1992; Chaskin & Joseph, 1995; Chaskin & Ogletree, 1993.)

RATIONALE FOR COMPREHENSIVE DEVELOPMENT

The interrelationship among a number of social problems, such as joblessness, lack of education, low income, poor housing, and inadequate health care, is broadly acknowledged and has provided much of the impetus for efforts to address multiple social needs by integrating strategies. This is especially true of efforts that seek to alleviate conditions of poverty, given that low-income families and individuals are more likely than middle-income families to encounter many of these problems concurrently. Levitan, Mangum, and Pines (1989), for example, suggested that although nearly 93 percent of middle-class families face one or fewer "obstacles to self-sufficiency," 81 percent of families in poverty face two or more such obstacles, and more than half face three or more.

The concurrence of such disadvantages and social ills can be seen beyond the family level, clustered in particular, definable neighborhoods. Such neighborhood-level interactions are especially clear among poor, inner-city neighborhoods with populations of color, leading to what Wilson (1987) termed "concentration effects." The recognition of this interaction of individual and family circumstances at the neighborhood level is one rationale for the current focus on community-based comprehensive development. The assumption is that because needs and circumstances are varied and interrelated at the neighborhood level, any effective attempt to address these needs must take into account the whole range of issues and circumstances and be framed in an equally comprehensive and integrated manner.

Historical Perspective

The belief in the need for a comprehensive approach to neighborhood development is not new. The roots of the idea can be traced back at least as far as the work of settlement houses of the late 19th century and the wide range of services they offered to residents of low-income neighborhoods (Halpern, 1991, 1995; Miller, 1981). Social policy in the 1960s saw a re-emergence of interest in the approach. In 1961 the Ford Foundation (1964) sponsored the Gray Areas projects explicitly to emphasize and promote institutional reform through the coordination of activities and a comprehensive view of needs. Informed in part by this effort, as well as by the thinking of such programs as Mobilization for Youth and the President's Council on Juvenile Delinquency, the Office of Economic Opportunity under the Johnson administration developed the Community Action and Model Cities programs to foster local identification of a broad set of neighborhood needs and the development of strategies to address them (Marris & Rein, 1982).

Around the same time, community development corporations (CDCs) began to establish themselves in urban areas across the country with a specific focus on comprehensive development (Ford Foundation, 1973). Although many CDCs have since narrowed their focus to housing and physical development, several have maintained an emphasis on comprehensive programs that provide social services and engage in economic and commercial development.

Current Programs

Currently, a growing number of foundation-funded, neighborhood-based initiatives are renewing the effort to develop a viable alternative to fragmented community-change strategies. Community revitalization efforts such as the Community Building in Partnership Initiative in Baltimore; the Dudley Street Neighborhood Initiative in Boston; the Comprehensive Community Building Initiative in New York; and the Neighborhood and Family Initiative in Detroit; Hartford, Connecticut; Memphis, Tennessee; and Milwaukee, have been put in place to find ways to address multiple neighborhood needs through comprehensive strategies.

OPERATIONALIZING COMPREHENSIVE DEVELOPMENT

In practice, most of the comprehensive development efforts have approached the issue primarily through one of several strategies, although the strategies are not necessarily mutually exclusive. They include social services integration, incremental expansion from one area of development (economic, physical, or social) into others, the parallel provision of activities in different areas, and the integration of strategies across the areas of economic, physical, and social development. It is this fourth strategy that the Ford Foundation set out to test with the NFI.

Integration of Social Services

Based on the perceived failings of a social services system characterized by fragmentation, a short-term focus, and unnecessary duplication of services (Bruner, 1991; Committee for Economic Development, 1991; Edelman & Radin, 1990; Gardner, 1989; Levitan et al., 1989; Schorr, 1988), both public and private efforts have sought integration of services in the interest of a more comprehensive approach. Efforts initiated by the federal government, for example, to promote social services integration include the Services Integration Targets of Opportunity projects, the Comprehensive Human Services Planning and Delivery System, Project SHARE, Title XX of the Social Security Act, and Head Start (Kusserow, 1991; U.S. General Accounting Office, 1992). Several community-based efforts have also focused on social services as a means of promoting comprehensive neighborhood change. For example, as part of the Gray Areas program, Community Progress, Inc., in New Haven, Connecticut, acted as a "catalyst and coordinator," developing and coordinating services that included skills-training programs, neighborhood employment centers, preschool education, legal services, and community nursing teams (Ford Foundation, ca. 1967; Marris & Rein, 1982). A contemporary example among comprehensive community-building initiatives is the Agenda for Children Tomorrow (ACT), which supports neighborhood-based service integration in New York City. ACT aims to develop and strengthen family-focused services for low-income families in such areas as health care, housing, child welfare, job training, and youth services (ACT, n.d.).

Building Incrementally toward Comprehensiveness

Another comprehensive approach is to begin within one area of activity—such as physical revitalization or business development—that is seen as a viable first step in a linear progression toward more comprehensive activities. This strategy is often used by CDCs. The development of new businesses or of the physical structures of the neighborhood serves to "improve the environment, create community amenities, develop locations for new businesses, and increase employment," and the profits produced by successful ventures can be reinvested in "socially beneficial projects such as day care centers, centers for the elderly, health centers," and the like (Berndt, 1977, p. 35). This incremental approach can also work the other way around. The National Temple Nonprofit Corporation in Philadelphia, for example, began in 1968 with a focus on community organization, advocacy, and social services provision and has since expanded to include other areas of development, including housing and business development (Vidal, Howitt, & Foster, 1986).

Parallel Provision of Activities

A third strategy advances the parallel provision of a wider range of social services alongside strategies geared toward physical and economic revitalization. For example, the Shorebank Corporation provides banking, real estate, and other services to support development in a southside Chicago neighborhood through four affiliated organizations. The central organization, South Shore Bank, is committed to providing credit to and reinvesting in the neighborhood. In addition, one for-profit subsidiary concerns itself with real estate rehabilitation, whereas another invests in small business enterprises in the neighborhood. Finally, a not-for-profit affiliate operates as a community organization. It advocates on behalf of residents threatened with displacement, provides job training and placement services, attracts philanthropic and government investment, and engages in housing development (Taub, 1988).

Another example, Chicanos por la Causa, a statewide CDC in Arizona, provides a wide range of social services, including housing counseling and home improvement support, child care, and health services; provides support for economic development through its own credit union and loan funds; and engages in substantial real estate development, including housing renovation and construction of commercial and residential properties (Erdmann, Gradin, & Zdenek, 1985).

Many of today's comprehensive community-building initiatives use this parallel provision strategy to promote a comprehensive agenda. For example, the Community Building in Partnership Initiative in Baltimore aims to "transform" the Sandtown–Winchester neighborhood through development efforts that include housing, education, health care, employment, human services, and commercial development. Projects in these areas include the construction and refurbishing of housing units; the opening of health clinics in elementary schools; and the establishment of a neighborhood-based job assessment, training, and placement center (Enterprise Foundation, 1995).

Integrating Development Strategies

A fourth strategy is to find ways to explicitly link activities across the areas of economic, physical, and social development. The three approaches to neighborhood development already discussed remain for the most part focused within discrete development areas; although a range of strategies may be pursued con-currently, they are not necessarily integrated. For example, there may be little or no connection between the provision of social services and the development of the commercial or physical infrastructure of the neighborhood. The rationale for integrating strategies is that the more various individual strategies can be integrated and used to build off one another, the more the overall implementa-tion strategy can fully exploit and respond to the inherent interconnections among neighborhood needs and circumstances. By linking efforts in different spheres of activity, resources can be used more effectively and various efforts can be harnessed to promote synergistic neighborhood change.

For example, in a neighborhood where unemployment is high and individu-als lack vocational training, a housing renovation project might seek to hire and train residents (perhaps by linking the renovation project to a local job training and employment initiative) rather than employing outside contractors, thus developing human capital resources within the neighborhood. Such an effort could perhaps be further linked to neighborhood home-ownership programs (for example, through sweat-equity provisions supporting current residents' opportunity to buy) and to the provision of other services (for example, a day care center could be opened in a renovated building). Integrating these various strains of activity would thus train and employ neighborhood residents, sup-port the creation of a small business enterprises, and provide easy access to needed services.

Similarly, a neighborhood clean-up project could be linked to the develop-ment of a recycling facility and the cultivation of a community garden. This process could provide training and income for residents at the levels of plan-ning, management, and implementation and could lead to the further develop-ment of a cooperative farmers' market (or some other outlet for neighborhood-grown produce) and the provision of recreational facilities for neighborhood children (in the form of renovated parks or play lots). Thus, physical improve-ment, economic opportunity, and social needs could be addressed through a set of consciously integrated projects.

Casa de Primavera, for example, a project of Chicanos por la Causa, is en-gaged in multifaceted planning combining the physical, social, and (to a limited extent) economic spheres. It provides 162 units of subsidized housing for eld-erly or disabled people and within the building supports services such as medi-cal care, recreational and educational programs, a theater, and a gift shop that generates income for residents (Erdmann et al., 1985). Bethel New Life, a CDC on the west side of Chicago, is another example. Bethel New Life runs service programs for senior citizens, a health center, a recycling center, and job place-ment centers; provides other counseling and social services; and retains a staff architect and construction crews (Pierce & Steinbach, 1987). Although the projects are not all explicitly integrated with one another, they are connected at certain points, such as the location of low-income housing units and a school in a Bethel-renovated building and the employment of local residents in various revitaliza-tion projects.

FORD FOUNDATION'S NFI

The Ford Foundation created the NFI, in part, to more definitively test the notion of integrating strategies as part of a comprehensive community development effort. In four target neighborhoods, each in a different city, "neighborhood collaboratives" were charged with designing and implementing comprehensive development strategies. The planning groups were directed to weave individual development strategies into a strategic whole, the elements of which would work together to foster synergistic, sustainable change (Chaskin, 1992).

The initiative was given a similar form in each of the four participant sites: Detroit; Hartford, Connecticut; Memphis, Tennessee; and Milwaukee. The NFI target neighborhoods range in population from 9,000 to 18,000 people. In the Detroit and Milwaukee neighborhoods, over 50 percent of the population is below the poverty level, whereas in the Hartford and Memphis neighborhoods, around 30 percent of the population is below the poverty level. The neighborhoods are predominantly African American; the Hartford and Milwaukee target neighborhoods have significant Latino populations (about 15 percent and 8 percent, respectively), and the Hartford target neighborhood also has a substantial West Indian population representing about 15 percent of the majority African American population (Chaskin, 1992).

In each city, a community foundation was chosen as the local fiscal agent and was charged with the identification of a target neighborhood, the hiring of a staff director, and the creation of a neighborhood collaborative. In turn, the collaboratives were charged with identifying neighborhood needs and their connections to one another and developing strategies to address these needs. The membership of each of the four collaboratives was structured to include residents of the target neighborhood; neighborhood business owners and professionals; and representatives from the city's public, private, and nonprofit sectors. The notion was that by bringing together a wide range of participants with different experiences, different fields of expertise, and different access to resources on "equal footing," the group could work toward more integrated development strategies.

COMPREHENSIVE DEVELOPMENT IN NFI

After six years of funding, the NFI collaboratives have, for the most part, succeeded in casting their nets wide and developing programs that address a broad range of issues: housing, jobs, education, community organizing, and health and social services. Although there is some similarity in the issues or program areas identified, the sites have differed in the types of intervention and strategic focuses chosen (Table 1). For example, although the Hartford collaborative sees its primary role as that of organizing the community for the identification of needs and the development of program priorities, the collaborative in Milwaukee has focused on the creation of new organizations and direct implementation of programs to provide livable wages to residents.

The NFI sites' strategic planning processes have resulted in the development of three approaches to integrating strategies. The first approach is based on the

Table 1

Areas of Program Development for the Neighborhood and Family Initiatives

Strategic Focus	Detroit: Strengthening Linkages	Hartford, CT: Community Organizing	Memphis, TN: Neighborhood Supports, Housing, and Leadership	Milwaukee: Livable Wages
Employment	X			X
Economic development	X	X	X	X
Housing	X	X	X	X
Social services	X	X		
Block clubs		X		
Education		X	X	
Physical revitalization	X			X
Leadership development			X	X
Youth development			X	X
Communication and neighborhood supports		X	X	

notion of finding opportunities for integration at the project level. Each project is the focus for integration and is meant to address in some way a combination of economic, physical, and social needs and circumstances. In Memphis, for example, the stated purpose of the Orange Mound Development Corporation (OMDC) is to carry out the collaborative's mission in providing housing, business development, and job training activities. OMDC's activities have included housing construction, neighborhood outreach activities, a community clean-up campaign, participation in a home-repair program and housing renovation project, and the organization of a first-time home-buyers' class.

Another approach attempts to link projects at a broader strategic level to build from or complement other projects. The stated strategic focus in Detroit, for example, is on "strengthening linkages" among organizations and institutions in the Lower Woodward Corridor and fostering greater connection between these organizations and residents of the neighborhood. Early in the strategic planning process, the collaborative and community foundation agreed that, given the number of community service agencies already present in the Lower Woodward Corridor, the most effective use of NFI resources would be to improve collaboration and communication among the existing service providers, rather than duplicating existing services. The intent was to ensure that a comprehensive set of services could be offered to the families living in the corridor.

A third approach sees integration as the product of planning guided by a strategic "lens." Strategies meant to address concerns in any given sphere of activity (economic, physical, or social) come together through their ultimate focus on a given overarching goal. The strategic focus of NFI in Milwaukee is the provision of "livable wages" for Harambee families through employment and economic development. Several of the collaborative's projects have been created with reference to this overarching theme, including the creation of a loan fund to promote neighborhood business development and expansion and the development of an industrial park to support the revival of small-scale manufacturing.

LIMITATIONS OF COMPREHENSIVE DEVELOPMENT

In spite of these approaches to integrating strategies, the collaboratives' programmatic activities are not, for the most part, explicitly linked to one another;
furthermore, the notion of comprehensive, integrated development is not the
primary impetus for project selection or program implementation. Over time,
the collaboratives, like earlier community change efforts, have focused much
more on the parallel provision of services and less on the integration of strategies. We have identified three reasons for this:

1. Understanding and reaching consensus on what comprehensive development means and how to implement it is very difficult and time consuming.
2. Operational barriers such as time, resources, and organizational structure
   inhibit their development of integrated programs.
3. Competing motivating factors that influence collaborative activity and decision making may interfere with integration of projects.

Understanding Concepts and Reaching Consensus

One clear reason for the limited realization of the concept of comprehensive
development was the difficulty that collaborative members and other NFI participants had in understanding and reaching consensus about its meaning. Although all participants grasped the strategy of fostering change in a variety of
areas of community life, there was little consensus as to how those changes could
be linked to one another to greater effect. Not only did collaborative members
have difficulty reaching agreement, but there was a sense that other key initiative participants—funders, technical assistance providers, and evaluators—held
different and competing notions of comprehensive development.

Furthermore, it was unclear to what extent the charge to be comprehensive
was meant to drive the planning and implementation process. Did it mean developing a fully articulated comprehensive plan for the neighborhood? Did it
mean developing strategies incrementally over time, linking them to one another where possible? Did it simply mean initiating a range of strategies and
hoping that their collective effect would be "comprehensive"? Unable to proceed very far in developing strategic plans that incorporated guidelines for program integration, the collaboratives focused instead on implementing a broad,
but parallel, set of activities.

Operational Barriers

Developing and implementing a comprehensive strategy not only is financially
expensive, but also is demanding in terms of the time needed for governance
activities—planning, decision making, assessment, problem-solving—and the
complicated nature of such activities. Given that the collaboratives' activities
are run by a small staff (in one case, a single staff member) and a committee of
volunteers from diverse backgrounds, time has proved to be a major constraint
on the development of programmatic strategies.

One of the collaboratives' earliest challenges was to develop an organizational structure that would promote comprehensive programming. All four

collaboratives developed several committees and task forces; each focused on a different strategic area of neighborhood development (for example, housing, employment, safety, and education). Although this structure successfully promoted the development of strategies across a range of areas, it did not promote the integration of those strategies. Despite the fact that each collaborative has some form of executive committee that oversees collaborative activities, these committees have spent most of their time focused on issues of administration and have had little opportunity to discuss possibilities for program integration.

Competing Motivating Factors

Particular opportunities for program development and implementation have arisen within each local context that have presented attractive possibilities for the collaboratives to pursue. These opportunities have often provided a stronger impetus and a clearer strategic rationale than the general charge to be "comprehensive." For example, in Detroit, the interest of a major local institution—the Detroit Medical Center—in focusing on neighborhood outreach and in developing an employment training and placement program provided the collaborative with a clear opportunity on which to build.

Similarly, the availability of an abandoned American Motors Corporation plant in Milwaukee and the willingness of a local company to help purchase this land for development made it possible to build an industrial park and played a major role in structuring collaborative deliberation and guiding strategic planning.

Additional Constraints

Related to the issue of opportunity, existing networks of associations, to some extent, guide the collaboratives' strategic decisions. In particular, the instrumental connections provided by certain NFI participants have provided both the knowledge of opportunities that could be built on and access to these opportunities. These connections have been vital to collaboratives' ability to plan and move beyond planning to implementation and have contributed to the tendency to let opportunity drive planning rather than broad, integrated strategizing.

Structures of control present another obstacle to collaboratives' ability to focus on plans for integrating development activities. For example, collaboratives are often under pressure to make programmatic strides within timelines dictated in large part by foundation-driven grant periods. This pressure has, to a large degree, superseded the importance of developing integrated strategies in favor of showing some progress on the ground. The lack of clarity about expected time frames in which to show change and the lack of certainty about long-term support contribute to this problem. Given the uncertainty about support, the collaboratives have often opted for discrete, short-term programs rather than more complex ventures requiring a longer-term commitment.

CONCLUSION

The field of community-based efforts that seek to catalyze comprehensive change will in all likelihood continue to grow. An overview of historical and current practice suggests that these efforts would benefit from further investigation of several key issues: What operational structure will best serve to promote comprehensive programming that exploits the interconnections among strategies? What forms of support staff, technical assistance, funding, and evaluation can help a community planning group fully develop and implement a comprehensive development strategy? How can these efforts make the most of existing opportunities for change while attempting to link individual strategies to build toward a more comprehensive, lasting impact? Although these questions are difficult to answer, it is in continuing to test new approaches to these issues that community-based efforts can fulfill their promise as instruments of neighborhood revitalization.

There are some conclusions that can be drawn, however, and early findings from our evaluation of the NFI seem to be supported to a large extent by the experiences of other comprehensive community initiatives (Kubisch et al., in press). First, although the charge to be comprehensive has facilitated the engagement of actors with varying interests in the strategic planning process, there is a need for greater clarity in defining what comprehensive development means in operational terms. This clarity might be achieved through open and ongoing communication among key initiative participants who can then determine goals and expectations and establish reasonable time frames (complete with the identification of measurable benchmarks) within which to achieve the goals. Key participants would have to negotiate and agree on basic operational issues, such as the range of activities needed, the ways these activities would be implemented, the duration of programmatic activity, how programs (or their effects) are to be linked to one another, the expected outcomes, length of time to produce the outcomes, and how outcomes can be measured.

Second, although the strategic plans provide a useful map of potential activities, competing motivating factors (such as arising opportunities and existing networks of associations) have provided and probably will continue to provide a stronger and clearer impetus for program development and implementation. Strengthening the ability of community-change efforts to identify and tap into such opportunities in a timely manner could increase their impact on the neighborhood. The challenge for comprehensive community development efforts is to seize these opportunities in the advancement of their own planning and implementation goals, rather than either becoming "stuck" at the level of taking advantage of discrete opportunities or ignoring them in the pursuit of a "complete" strategic plan on which to base implementation activities.

Finally, a recognition of the depth and persistence of problems affecting low-income neighborhoods and the structural and resource limitations of comprehensive community-building initiatives suggests a need for more responsive, long-term funder–grantee relationships as well as an increased ability to leverage additional resources and expertise. The charge to plan for comprehensive neighborhood development when core funding is limited to operational support and limited programmatic funds has caused some frustration among participants. Concrete technical assistance that provides information on working strategies and an active focus on building local capacity to apply such strategies (including sources of additional funding and guidance on how to obtain access to them) is critical in this regard. Perhaps most important, an adequate level of staffing is needed if initiatives are to be expected to clarify plans, pursue opportunities, and follow through on identified activities.

Although comprehensive development is not a new approach, and in spite of the fact that there are a growing number of comprehensive community-change efforts across the country, it remains unclear how to operationalize the concept most effectively. The charge to be comprehensive has provided important freedom from some constraints—the "permission" to construct the problem broadly and to seek solutions on the basis of local context and with an eye toward systemic change (Kubisch et al., in press). But without further specification, it is an idea that provides only limited operational utility. Its usefulness as a guide to action can be increased through the development of greater clarity of its meaning, components, and reasonable expectations—crafted through explicit negotiation and empirical trial on the ground—as well as through more targeted support to fund, guide, and make use of opportunity in the service of its realization.

REFERENCES

Agenda for Children Tomorrow. (n.d.). *ACT: Building on the strengths of families and neighborhoods.* New York: Author.

Berndt, H. E. (1977). *New rulers in the ghetto: The community development corporation and urban poverty.* Westport, CT: Greenwood Press.

Bruner, C. (1991). *Thinking collaboratively: Ten questions and answers to help policy makers improve children's services.* Washington, DC: Education and Human Services Consortium.

Chaskin, R. J. (1992). *The Ford Foundation's Neighborhood and Family Initiative: Toward a model of comprehensive, neighborhood-based development.* Chicago: University of Chicago, Chapin Hall Center for Children.

Chaskin, R. J., & Joseph, M. L. (1995). *The Ford Foundation's Neighborhood and Family Initiative: Moving toward implementation.* Chicago: University of Chicago, Chapin Hall Center for Children.

Chaskin, R. J., & Ogletree, R. (1993). *The Ford Foundation's Neighborhood and Family Initiative: Building collaboration.* Chicago: University of Chicago, Chapin Hall Center for Children.

Committee for Economic Development. (1991). *The unfinished agenda: A new vision for child development and education.* New York: Author.

Edelman, P. B., & Radin, B. A. (1990, November). *Effective services for children and families: What do we know and what do we do now as a consequence?* Paper presented at the Workshop on Effective Services for Young Children, Washington, DC.

Eisen, A. (1992, March). *A report on foundations' support for comprehensive neighborhood-based community-empowerment initiatives* (Report sponsored by East Bay Funders, the Ford Foundation, the New York Community Trust, the Piton Foundation, and the Riley Foundation). New York: New York Community Trust.

Enterprise Foundation. (1995). *Community building in partnership: Program summary.* Baltimore: Author.

Erdmann, R. J., Gradin, H., & Zdenek, R. O. (1985). *Community development corporation profile book.* Washington, DC: National Congress for Community Economic Development.

Ford Foundation. (1964). *Public affairs: Gray areas* (Program Report No. 002845). New York: Ford Foundation Archives.

Ford Foundation. (ca. 1967). *Uniting two Americas* (Program Report No. 001547). New York: Author.

Ford Foundation. (1973). *Community development corporations: A strategy for depressed urban and rural areas* (Ford Foundation Policy Paper). New York: Author.

Gardner, S. (1989, Fall). Failure by fragmentation. *California Tomorrow,* pp. 18–25.

Halpern, R. (1991). Supportive services for families in poverty: Historical perspectives, dilemmas of reform. *Social Service Review, 65,* 343–364.

Halpern, R. (1995). *Rebuilding the inner city: A history of neighborhood initiatives to address poverty in the United States.* New York: Columbia University Press.

Kubisch, A. C., Brown, P., Chaskin, R., Hirota, J., Joseph, M., Richman, H., & Roberts, M. (in press). *Voices from the field: Learning from comprehensive community initiatives.* Washington, DC: Aspen Institute.

Kusserow, R. P. (1991, January). *Services integration: A twenty-year perspective* (HHS Policy Paper OEI-01-91-00580). Washington, DC: U.S. Department of Health and Human Services, Office of Inspector General.

Levitan, S. A., Mangum, G. L., & Pines, M. W. (1989). *A proper inheritance: Investing in the self-sufficiency of poor families.* Washington, DC: George Washington University, Center for Social Policy Studies.

Marris, P., & Rein, M. (1982). *Dilemmas of social reform: Poverty and community action in the United States* (2nd ed.). Chicago: University of Chicago Press.

Miller, Z. L. (1981). The role and concept of neighborhood in American cities. In R. Fisher & P. Romanofsky (Eds.), *Community organization for urban social change: A historical perspective* (pp. 3–32). Westport, CT: Greenwood Press.

Pierce, N. R., & Steinbach, C. F. (1987). *Corrective capitalism: The rise of America's community development corporations.* New York: Ford Foundation.

Schorr, L. B. (1988). *Within our reach.* New York: Anchor Press.

Stone, R. (Ed.). (1996). *Core issues in comprehensive community-building initiatives.* Chicago: University of Chicago, Chapin Hall Center for Children.

Taub, R. P. (1988). *Community capitalism.* Boston: Harvard Business School Press.

U.S. General Accounting Office. (1992). *Integrating human services: Linking at-risk families with services more successful than system reform efforts* (Report to the Chairman, Subcommittee on Children, Family, Drugs and Alcoholism, Committee on Labor and Human Resources, U.S. Senate) (Publication No. GAO/ HRD-92-108). Washington, DC: U.S. Government Printing Office.

Vidal, A. C., Howitt, A. M., & Foster, K. P. (1986, June). *Stimulating community development: An assessment of the Local Initiative Support Corporation.* Cambridge, MA: Harvard University, John F. Kennedy School of Government, State, Local and Intergovernmental Center.

Wilson, W. J. (1987). *The truly disadvantaged.* Chicago: University of Chicago Press.

This chapter was originally published in the September 1997 issue of Social Work, *vol. 42, pp. 435–444.*

4 Youths and Communities: Toward Comprehensive Strategies for Youth Development

William H. Barton, Marie Watkins, and Roger Jarjoura

As the 21st century approaches, communities across the United States remain concerned, frustrated, occasionally fearful, and sometimes outraged by the behavior of some adolescents. Issues of teenage pregnancy, school dropout, substance abuse, juvenile delinquency, and violence persist despite various attempts to deal with them.

We believe that attacking problems of youths in isolation is ineffective because it ignores the considerable overlap among the causes and occurrences of youth problem behaviors. Research over the past few decades has clearly identified risk factors for these behaviors, many of which are implicated for several behaviors. Similarly, there are overlapping "protective factors" that can counter the risk factors. These risk and protective factors exist at several levels—individual, family, peer group, school, and community (Hawkins, Catalano, & Associates, 1992). Therefore, a prevention strategy that assesses a community's specific risks and assets at multiple levels is more likely to reduce problem behaviors than programs addressing the problem behaviors themselves.

This chapter presents a national profile of youth problems and a literature review that focuses on the causes of each of the problem areas and reviews what is known about preventive measures and the effectiveness of existing intervention strategies. Conclusions from this review encourage a paradigm shift in perspective away from a focus on correcting "deficits" in individual youths toward enhancing the potential for healthy youth development in all youths in the community.

Enactment of a youth development vision requires a communitywide collaborative effort among public officials, current service providers, primary institutions (such as churches, recreational facilities, libraries, and schools), and citizens (including youths themselves). In the past few years, several "comprehensive community initiatives" have begun across the country. This chapter discusses several of these. Although they have not existed long enough to amass conclusive evaluation results, their attempts to forge collaborative relationships can provide lessons for other communities.

STATUS OF YOUTHS

Poverty, child abuse and neglect, health risks such as teenage pregnancy and low-birthweight babies, juvenile crime, and homelessness conspire to erode the real and perceived quality of life of youths. Recent statistics from a variety of sources illustrate the amount and persistence of youth problems in this country. These indicators suggest that childhood poverty, the teenage unmarried birth rate, child abuse and neglect, and juvenile violent crime have increased during the past 20 years. The rate of high school dropouts has remained steady at about 10 percent. The prevalence of binge drinking and marijuana use, while declining slightly over the period, is still at an alarmingly high rate (Table 4.1) (Annie E. Casey Foundation, 1996; Children's Defense Fund, 1996; U.S. Department of Health and Human Services, 1996).

It is reasonable for communities to be concerned about these statistics. Why are the problems so persistent? What can be done?

Problem Areas

Teenage Pregnancy. Adolescents are at risk of pregnancy if they are sexually active and not using contraception (Dryfoos, 1990). The younger the youths are when they begin sexual activity, the less likely they are to use contraception, increasing the likelihood of teenage pregnancy (Dryfoos, 1990; Franklin, Grant, Corcoran, O'Dell, & Bultman, 1995). An early onset of sexual intercourse is more likely for black youths, especially young men, and those going through early

Table 4.1

National Indicators of Problems of Adolescents: 1975–1995

Indicator	Year				
	1975	1980	1985	1990	1995
Child poverty rate (% of children under age 18 living below the poverty level)[a]	17.1	18.3	20.7	20.6	21.2[d]
Adolescent unmarried birth rate (births per 1,000 unmarried females ages 15 to 19)[a]	23.9	27.6	31.4	42.5	44.5[e]
Reports of abuse or neglect (per 1,000 children)[a]	NA	18.0	31.0	41.0	43.0[e]
Juvenile violent crime arrest rate (ages 10 to 17, per 100,000 youths)[b]	NA	NA	305.0	429.0	506.0[e]
Percentage of adolescents who are high school dropouts (ages 16 to 19)[b]	NA	NA	11.0	10.0	9.0[e]
Percentage of 12th graders reporting binge drinking[c]	36.8	41.2	36.7	32.2	29.8
Percentage of 12th graders reporting marijuana use[c]	27.1	33.7	25.7	14.0	21.2

NOTE: NA = not available.

[a]Children's Defense Fund. (1996). *The state of America's children yearbook 1996.* Washington, DC: Author.

[b]Annie E. Casey Foundation. (1996). *Kids count data book: State profiles of child well-being, 1996.* Baltimore: Author.

[c]Data are from the Monitoring the Future surveys as reported in U.S. Department of Health and Human Services, Office of the Assistant Secretary for Planning and Evaluation. (1996). *Trends in the well-being of America's children and youth: 1996.* Washington, DC: Author. *Binge drinking* is defined as having had five or more drinks in a row within the preceding two weeks. *Marijuana use* is defined as having used marijuana within the past 30 days.

[d]Data are for 1994, the most recent available.

[e]Data are for 1993, the most recent available.

puberty. Lower-income adolescents are more likely to initiate sexual activity earlier, as are those whose parents have low levels of educational attainment.

Parents who communicate poorly with their adolescents or who are not supportive are more likely to have teenagers who engage in early sexual activity. Poor school performance and lower levels of involvement in school activities are also predictive of early sexual intercourse. Other problem behaviors, such as truancy and drug or alcohol use, are also predictive of early initiation of sexual behavior. Having peers who are sexually active at an early age is another predictor. Finally, youths living in poor communities of color are more likely to be sexually active at an early age (Dryfoos, 1990).

Teenage pregnancy prevention programs, although they have little effect on the sexual behavior of adolescents, have been shown to increase the use of contraceptives and, ultimately, to reduce pregnancy rates (Franklin et al., 1995). The most effective of these programs teach information on contraception and provide for the distribution of contraceptive devices. Programs administered within clinics are more effective than those run in nonclinic settings. Furthermore, clinic-based programs are more effective when run in the community rather than within the school setting (Franklin et al., 1995).

Miller, Card, Paikoff, and Peterson (1992) identified several principles that increase the effectiveness of teenage pregnancy prevention efforts:

- The goals and objectives of the program must be clear and specific.
- The program should serve the younger teenagers.
- The intensity of the program must be substantial in terms of both frequency and duration.
- The program must be comprehensive in scope. Teaching facts is not enough; an effective program also will teach decision-making and social skills and provide life options along with health services.
- The program needs to involve the parents and provide for peer support.

The best evidence suggests that "young people at high risk of early childbearing may need an array of comprehensive services, including alternative schools, preparation for employment, job placement, and case management" (Dryfoos, 1990, p. 194).

School Dropout. There are many early predictors of dropping out of school. Poor school performance and being held back in early grade levels both increase the likelihood of dropping out (Wehlage, Rutter, Smith, Lesko, & Fernandez, 1989). Family income and the quality of parental support have been shown to affect the decision to drop out (Dryfoos, 1990). Men and youths of color are more likely to drop out, as are youths growing up in poverty or on welfare. In addition, youths who drop out are likely to have family and friends who have also dropped out. Earlier evidence of problems is predictive of dropping out later in adolescence, including such factors as truancy, suspensions and expulsions from school, and delinquency. Early sexual intercourse is also associated with a higher likelihood of dropping out (Dryfoos, 1990; Wehlage et al., 1989).

Most of the dropout prevention programs have been administered within the school setting (Wehlage et al., 1989). Early intervention (that is, preschool) is critical, as is early identification of high-risk youths. Alternative school programs that stress individualized attention and instruction have been successful with certain types of youths. Building in vocational components that enhance the school-to-work experience has also been effective with certain types of youths. In this context, success can mean better school performance, higher educational attainment, higher graduation rates, and higher expectations about educational attainment by the youths (Dryfoos, 1990).

To work with troubled youths within the school setting effectively, counseling and support services must be available. Building in parental involvement and peer support is also important. Comprehensive initiatives involving schools, families, social services, health services, and community groups are essential for effectively preventing school dropouts.

Substance Abuse. Despite recent declines in the prevalence of adolescent substance abuse, the proportion of youths who use alcohol or drugs is still substantial (Johnston, O'Malley, & Bachman, 1994). Imposing tougher drug laws and more aggressive law enforcement has resulted in high rates of incarceration for drug dealers. Increased drug enforcement efforts may have helped reduce rates of substance abuse, but the persistence of the problem suggests they are not sufficient. Attempts to reduce the demand through treatment and prevention are also necessary. The most promising strategies involve prevention efforts aimed at reducing known risks and enhancing known buffers.

Risk factors for adolescent substance abuse exist at both the environmental and individual levels (Hawkins, Catalano, & Associates, 1992; Hawkins, Catalano, & Miller, 1992). These include economic and social deprivation, low neighborhood attachment and community disorganization, transitions and mobility, community norms, drug and alcohol availability, family history of alcoholism or drug use, poor family management practices, academic failure, low commitment to school, early antisocial behavior and aggressiveness, association with drug-using peers, favorable attitudes toward drug and alcohol use, and early first use of drugs. Protective factors, which have been shown to prevent delinquency and violence, include strong attachments to adults, school, positive peers, and the community (Hawkins, Catalano, & Associates, 1992).

Interventions aimed at changing youths' attitudes toward drugs and enhancing their social skills to make them more resistant to peer pressure have not achieved a sustained reduction in the use of drugs and alcohol (Hawkins, Catalano, & Associates, 1992). Multifaceted interventions that address the full range of risk and protective factors at the community level appear necessary. The "communities that care" (Hawkins, Catalano, & Associates, 1992) approach is one such community mobilization strategy that encompasses promising approaches at several levels: prenatal and infancy programs, early childhood education, parent training, school organization and management, instructional improvement in schools, drug and alcohol prevention curricula, community and school drug use policies, and media mobilization.

Juvenile Delinquency and Violence. Although the overall rates of juvenile crime may not be increasing, the rate of violent juvenile crime has risen sharply in the past few years (Snyder, 1994). Since 1988 the arrest rates of juveniles for serious violent crimes including aggravated assault, robbery, and murder have increased by 50 percent. Many attribute this rise to the increased availability of firearms (Howell, 1995).

A variety of studies have shown that the large majority of adolescents, perhaps as many as 80 percent, engage occasionally in some form of (usually minor) delinquent behavior. Only a relatively small proportion of juveniles (about 5 percent to 10 percent), however, account for the vast majority (60 percent to 80 percent) of the serious and violent crimes committed by juveniles (Elliott, 1994; Hamparian, Schuster, Dinitz, & Conrad, 1978; Shannon, 1991; Tracy, Wolfgang, & Figlio, 1990; Wolfgang, Figlio, & Sellin, 1972). Moreover, this small percentage of serious offenders also accounts for a great deal (about half) of all crimes committed by juveniles.

Recent reviews of existing research have identified a list of predictors of delinquent behavior. Factors that predict delinquent involvement include poverty, biological disabilities, poor parenting, difficult temperament, cognitive deficits, poor bonding to parents and school, poor peer relations, and school problems (Dryfoos, 1990; Tremblay & Craig, 1995). Combining results from recent large-scale longitudinal studies, we can identify predictors of chronic violent offending. Chronic violent offenders are more likely to be exposed at an early age to violence, have little attachment to their parents, be subject to poor monitoring of their behavior by parents, have little attachment to teachers, lack commitment to school, have higher numbers of delinquent peers, have favorable attitudes toward deviance, and reside in high-crime areas (Elliott, 1994; Thornberry, Huizinga, & Loeber, 1995).

Efforts at prevention of delinquency have sought to address one of three primary risk factors: socially disruptive behavior, cognitive deficits, and poor parenting. When delinquency is the outcome of interest, results of prevention experiments are more likely to be positive if interventions target more than one risk factor. Positive results are also more likely when the interventions are longer and when they target preadolescents (Tremblay & Craig, 1995). To effectively prevent serious forms of delinquency and violence, though, interventions must be comprehensive in addressing multiple risk factors and co-occurring problem behaviors (Thornberry et al., 1995).

Juvenile Justice System

A great deal of overlap exists in the etiology of the different problem behaviors considered here. Youths who engage in the most serious delinquent and violent behaviors tend to be "multiproblem" youths who are exposed to relatively more risk factors at multiple levels (family, peers, community) and fewer protective factors than their peers who do not engage in these behaviors. The Office of Juvenile Justice and Delinquency Prevention recently outlined a "Comprehensive Strategy for Serious, Violent, and Chronic Juvenile Offenders" (Howell, 1995). The strategy combines the "communities that care" prevention model of Hawkins and his colleagues (1992) with the juvenile justice recommendations of Howell, Krisberg, Hawkins, and Wilson (1995) from the National Council on Crime and Delinquency (see also the ecological–developmental perspective described by Fraser, 1996). The strategy consists of a continuum of services, from primary prevention programs (Hawkins, Catalano, & Associates, 1992) pursuing positive youth development goals for all young people to a graduated array of intermediate, community-based sanctions that would reserve the most costly and restrictive residential programs for offenders who persist in serious violent delinquency.

Bernard (1992) argued that the juvenile justice system cannot do much to reduce juvenile crime, because by the time the juvenile justice system intervenes, it may be too late to turn many young lives around. More important, because the juvenile justice system by itself can do little to alter the risk and protective factors that cause or prevent delinquency, only coordinated community efforts can promote healthy youth development.

YOUTH DEVELOPMENT PERSPECTIVE

Many researchers, youth advocates, and practitioners are urging communities to make a greater investment in youths by moving beyond programs and policies that merely respond to youth problems. In a major conceptual shift, they advocate replacing an emphasis on specific prevention, intervention, or treatment efforts with an emphasis on policies and programs that support and build competence to prepare youths for adulthood (Carnegie Council on Adolescent Development, 1992, 1995; Center for Youth Development and Policy Research, 1994; Pittman & Cahill, 1991). The underlying premise is that better long-term outcomes evolve from increasing developmental supports and opportunities available to young people. Pittman and Cahill (1991) advocated that "the operating assumption must shift from thinking that youth problems are the principal barrier to youth development and therefore the focus should be on problem prevention—to thinking that youth development serves as the most effective strategy for prevention of youth problems" (p. 15).

Although a single definition of youth development does not exist, critical components have been identified. These include a sense of
- safety and structure
- belonging and membership
- self-worth and an ability to contribute
- independence and control over one's life
- closeness and several good relationships
- competence and mastery.

Enhancing youths' competencies requires the development of adequate attitudes, skills, and behaviors in key areas, including health; personal and social skills; reasoning, knowledge, and creativity; vocational awareness; and citizenship (Carnegie Council on Adolescent Development, 1995; Pittman & Cahill, 1991).

Public/Private Ventures (1993) identified several important supports and opportunities for successful adolescence and, specifically, for the transition to economic self-sufficiency: adult support and guidance, work as a multipurpose tool, filling of critical gaps and facilitating transitions; continuity from early adolescence through early adulthood, and promotion of individual involvement and positive peer influence. These supports may be limited in resource-poor communities and can be influenced by social policy.

Adolescence

This broader, holistic framework of youth development draws from theory and research on adolescence (Carnegie Council on Adolescent Development, 1992, 1995; Center for Youth Development and Policy Research, 1994; Pittman & Cahill, 1991). Adolescence is a time of dramatic change in terms of physical growth, sexual development, cognitive abilities, and identity development, all in the social and interpersonal context of changing schools, developing peer relationships, dating, and part-time employment (Blos, 1962; Crain, 1985; Steinberg, 1985; Tanner, 1962). The quest for healthy youth development outcomes should be framed in light of these individual and social developmental processes. Accordingly, although youth development approaches may focus solely on individual youths or target a single aspect of their behavior, they should simultaneously pursue multiple strategies that encompass both the individual youths and their social context.

Healthy Outcome Indicators

The youth development framework is entirely compatible with what we know about the causes of and strategies for dealing with youth problems. The healthy outcomes described in the youth development literature are indicators of strong bonds between youths and families, neighborhoods, schools, and communities— precisely the factors demonstrated to provide effective protection from the risks of developing problem behaviors. Reviewing results from three longitudinal studies, Thornberry and colleagues (1995) identified a list of protective factors, including commitment to school, good school performance, higher levels of anticipated educational attainment, high levels of parental supervision, strong attachments to parents, associations with conventional peers, and association with peers who meet with parental approval. For youths classified as "high risk," the presence of multiple protective factors was associated with a much lower involvement in delinquency and violent offending.

These findings support recommendations of Dryfoos (1990) and Hawkins and colleagues (1992) that prevention efforts address multiple risks and protective factors. It is noteworthy that those concerned with addressing the manifest problems of youths and those advocating a reconceptualization in terms of enhancing youths' strengths both endorse multisystemic, multifaceted, communitywide strategies for optimizing youth development.

COMPREHENSIVE COMMUNITY INITIATIVES

Exhortations to pursue the goals of healthy youth development are helpful and necessary but insufficient to move whole communities systematically to change the ways they pursue these goals. Categorical funding and services for children have not achieved the desired outcomes. Poverty remains an important factor limiting the potential outcomes of youth development efforts. Poor parents are less able than other parents to prevent their children's exposure to harm and to promote positive health and developmental outcomes (Children's Defense Fund, 1990). The key role of poverty, the interconnectedness of the youth problems, and the holistic framework of adolescent development have led the Carnegie Council on Adolescent Development (1995) and others to propose "comprehensive community initiatives." Such initiatives can create opportunities for more responsive interventions for children and their families and open new possibilities for community building (Brown, 1993; Chaskin & Ogletree, 1993; Connell, Aber, & Walker, 1995; Hawkins, Catalano, & Associates, 1992; Merry, Berg, Baker, & Wynn, 1995; Rosewater, 1992; Wynn, Costello, Halpern, & Richman, 1994). The council also made strong recommendations for these pivotal institutions to maintain active, positive involvement in the lives of children as the institutions reconsider their roles in the preparation of youths for adulthood.

First, families need to re-engage with their adolescent children through greater parental involvement in school-time and after-school activities, for example. Family-friendly employment policies and child care tax credits can facilitate this. Second, developmentally appropriate schools for adolescents are necessary. Small-scale, safe schools that promote relationships with intellectually stimulating cooperative learning environments should be created. A third recommendation calls for the development of health-promotion strategies for young adolescents. Instilling knowledge, skills, and values is important to change behavior-related problems such as gun-related homicides, abuse of drugs, teenage pregnancy, and so on. Fourth, policies should seek to strengthen community ties with young adolescents. For instance, out-of-school leisure time needs to be safe and growth-promoting, and youth organizations need to reach beyond traditional services. Finally, because the media can impart healthy behavior messages, promoting the constructive potential of the media is important.

During the past five years, up to 50 comprehensive local initiatives have been established through funding from foundations and partnerships with local or state governments (Brown, 1993; Eisen, 1992; Rosewater, 1992). Such initiatives are based on a holistic, broad understanding of community infrastructures and their subsequent influence on the needs of children and families. These initiatives attempt to rebuild social and community infrastructures within distressed neighborhoods to support the developmental needs of children and families. Comprehensive initiatives recall the work of settlement houses and involve community-based, coordinated efforts to produce healthy youth development rather than the elimination of negative influences in communities (Stone, 1994).

Brown (1993) highlighted some key goals of comprehensive, neighborhood-based initiatives: economic opportunity and security, adequate physical development and infrastructure, safety and security, well-functioning institutions, and social capital. Neighborhood initiatives that offer promise for the development of potential assets in distressed neighborhoods can create opportunities for increased communication and social interaction, intergenerational relationships, and resident involvement in community-based organizations to address community issues. Examples of the range of strategies within these initiatives include promoting access to "one-stop shopping" for multiple services at settlement houses or schools, intensive case management to link families with community services, service redefinition to create roles for and partnerships between primary and specialized services, and major bureaucratic social services reform.

Children, Youth, and Families Initiative

Funded by the Chicago Community Trust, this project seeks to create a community-directed infrastructure to enhance the development of children and families and social responsibility for their well-being (Brown, 1993). To date there has been evidence of increases in innovative social services, collaborative service delivery, primary services and their linkages with specialized services, opportunities for staff and volunteer training, and creative new approaches for access to services.

Ford Foundation's Neighborhood and Family Initiative

Launched in 1990 to strengthen the infrastructure of distressed communities through a prescribed structure for comprehensive neighborhood development, the Neighborhood and Family Initiative lends support to local leadership and addresses social, economic, and physical needs of targeted neighborhoods through a model of grassroots, participatory community development (Merry et al., 1995).

Communities That Care

Communities That Care (Hawkins, Catalano, & Associates, 1992) is a blueprint for local community planning efforts aimed at reducing risks and enhancing protective factors for youths; it includes a detailed list of risk and resource indicators that local communities can use in the planning and monitoring of programs. Among the many appealing aspects of this approach are its careful grounding in the research literature on causes and correlates of youth problem behaviors and its attention to both youth-related programming and community development strategies.

The community development strategy involves the creation of a collaborative task group linking service providers, funders, and local citizens. The federal Office of Juvenile Justice and Delinquency Prevention has adopted this model, currently under way in several counties, as part of its Comprehensive Strategy (Howell, 1995).

New Futures

Beginning in 1988, the Annie E. Casey Foundation (1995) funded a multisite, comprehensive community-based strategy targeting at-risk youths. The foundation provided about $2 million per year to each of five cities for the duration of five years. Motivated by a need to do more to address the needs and problems of at-risk youths while working under scarce public resources, the foundation conceived New Futures as a way to reform the current systems rather than add new programs.

The goals of the New Futures initiatives are comprehensive. They include the realization of better outcomes for youths and the development of improved methods of measuring the well-being of children. In addition, these initiatives seek to restructure community decision making and cause an improvement in service delivery. Through these efforts New Futures programs strive to increase local awareness of the needs of at-risk children.

The foundation has identified four critical steps in carrying out comprehensive community initiatives:

1. Building constituencies politically committed to long-term efforts is important.
2. Detailed assessments of current conditions and the current state of services and resources are necessary.
3. Comprehensive initiatives must also allow for careful and detailed planning of strategically sequenced change.
4. Building the required management capacities to sustain the effort over time and through changes in leadership is necessary.

The New Futures initiatives have taught us many important lessons. First, the comprehensive reform process is very difficult. Service providers are more inclined to develop new programs than to build coalitions with other existing service providers. In addition, getting all the local service providers to agree on a common set of goals and expectations is difficult. Differences of race, ethnicity, and power further complicate communication problems. These barriers to working together effectively mean that the comprehensive reform process requires much time and patience.

A second lesson is that a great deal of time is required during the planning stages to build the necessary coalitions. The actual time demands of the participants exacerbate this.

A third lesson is that the community has to be "ready" for such an initiative to have a chance for success. To be ready, the community must have strong leadership that can build the necessary coalitions, set clear goals, and gather community support. In addition, there must be a "conviction that the existing systems are badly flawed and require fundamental change so that they create better opportunities for at-risk youth" (Annie E. Casey Foundation, 1995, p. 12). There should be a "lead agency" seen as an expert in providing information on the status of at-risk youths that can provide continual guidance to the intervention approach.

A fourth lesson is that to create long-term change in the approach to the needs of at-risk youths, the local community must take ownership for its success. To facilitate this, "the best initiative design will contain funds that are significant enough to get the initiative going, establish legitimacy, and keep the stakeholders on board" (Annie E. Casey Foundation, 1995, p. 18).

A fifth lesson is that although a well-developed plan is important in the initial stages of comprehensive reform, opportunities for reviewing and revising plans during the process are necessary. Sixth, there is clearly a need to "communicate effectively with external audiences" about the effects of the initiative, including information on interim outcomes that serve as markers of progress. Finally, in low-income communities, comprehensive initiatives will also need to be enhanced with strategies that build social capital and encourage economic development that targets the whole community.

CONCLUSION

Adolescence is a challenging period both for youths themselves and for those whom they affect, which is all of us. Problems of teenage pregnancy, school dropout, substance abuse, delinquency, and violence remain as prevalent today as ever. Although we will never discover a simple, quick fix to these problems, we have learned a great deal about them and about what does and does not work in attempts to address them. What does not seem to work is to focus solely on each problem after it becomes manifest. The phrase "it takes a village to raise a child" is becoming somewhat of a cliché these days, but it remains a profound truth. Our challenge is to define the "village" and engage all the villagers in pursuit of the common goals of healthy youth development. That is really what comprehensive community initiatives, such as those reviewed above, are all about.

None of the existing initiatives can or should be replicated in all its details. The state of the art is too new, too tentative, too untested. In any event, no amount of information from the experiences of other communities can replace the requirement that local people develop plans based on their own community's array of risks and resources. What we have learned from the state of the art are the following:

- There must be a unifying vision or perspective about youth development, the inseparability of the many problems of adolescents, and the inadequacy of focusing solely on problems to the exclusion of healthy outcomes.
- There must be a framework for developing a comprehensive community approach to promote healthy youth development.
- There are guidelines for the planning process and examples of promising programs from other communities that address risks and protective factors at various levels.

Communities seeking to adopt a comprehensive approach to youth development first need to promote that unifying vision through education of key community leaders. Then they need to conduct baseline assessments of current risks and resources; develop priorities for appropriate support, prevention, and intervention programs; select and implement those programs; and monitor their effectiveness against the baseline assessments. The comprehensive community approach is unlikely to succeed unless collaborative funding and service delivery schemes replace conventional categorical funding mechanisms and fragmented services. To implement comprehensive initiatives successfully, communities need a combination of vision, leadership, inclusiveness, long-term commitment of resources, systematic planning, action, responsiveness to evaluative information, and patience.

REFERENCES

Annie E. Casey Foundation. (1995). *The path of most resistance: Reflections on lessons learned from New Futures.* Baltimore: Author.

Annie E. Casey Foundation. (1996). *Kids count data book: State profiles of child well-being.* Baltimore: Author.

Bernard, T. (1992). *The cycle of juvenile justice.* New York: Oxford University Press.

Blos, P. (1962). *On adolescence: A psychoanalytic interpretation.* New York: Free Press.

Brown, P. (1993). *Comprehensive neighborhood-based initiatives: Implications for urban policy.* Chicago: University of Chicago, Chapin Hall Center for Children.

Carnegie Council on Adolescent Development. (1992). *A matter of time: Risk and opportunity in the nonschool hours.* New York: Carnegie Corporation of New York.

Carnegie Council on Adolescent Development. (1995). *Great transitions: Preparing adolescents for a new century.* New York: Carnegie Corporation of New York.

Center for Youth Development and Policy Research. (1994). *Enriching local planning for youth development: A mobilization agenda.* Washington, DC: Author.

Chaskin, R., & Ogletree, R. (1993). *The Ford Foundation's Neighborhood and Family Initiative (NFI)—Building collaboration: An interim report.* Chicago: University of Chicago, Chapin Hall Center for Children.

Children's Defense Fund. (1990). *Five million children: A statistical profile of our poorest young citizens.* Washington, DC: Author.

Children's Defense Fund. (1996). *The state of America's children yearbook 1996.* Washington, DC: Author.

Connell, J., Aber, J., & Walker, G. (1995). How do urban communities affect youth? Using social science research to inform the design and evaluation of comprehensive community initiatives. In J. Connell, A. Kubisch, L. Schorr, & C. Weiss (Eds.), *New approaches to evaluating community initiatives: Concepts, methods, and contexts* (pp. 93–125). Washington, DC: Aspen Institute.

Crain, W. C. (Ed.). (1985). *Theories of development: Concepts and application* (2nd ed.). Englewood Cliffs, NJ: Prentice Hall.

Dryfoos, J. G. (1990). *Adolescents at risk: Prevalence and prevention.* New York: Oxford University Press.

Eisen, A. (1992). *A report on foundations' support for comprehensive neighborhood-based community empowerment initiatives.* Unpublished manuscript.

Elliott, D. S. (1994). Serious violent offenders: Onset, developmental course, and termination—The American Society of Criminology 1993 presidential address. *Criminology, 32,* 1–21.

Franklin, C., Grant, D., Corcoran, J., O'Dell, P., & Bultman, L. (1995). *Effectiveness of prevention programs for adolescent pregnancy: A meta-analysis.* Austin: University of Texas at Austin, School of Social Work.

Fraser, M. W. (1996). Aggressive behavior in childhood and early adolescence: An ecological–developmental perspective on youth violence. *Social Work, 41,* 347–361.

Hamparian, D. M., Schuster, R., Dinitz, S., & Conrad, J. (1978). *The violent few: A study of dangerous juvenile offenders.* Lexington, MA: Lexington Books.

Hawkins, J. D., Catalano, R. F., & Associates. (1992). *Communities that care: Action for drug abuse prevention.* San Francisco: Jossey-Bass.

Hawkins, J. D., Catalano, R. F., & Miller, J. Y. (1992). Risk and protective factors for alcohol and other drug problems in adolescence and early adulthood: Implications for substance abuse prevention. *Psychological Bulletin, 112,* 64–105.

Howell, J. C. (Ed.). (1995). *Guide for implementing the comprehensive strategy for serious, violent, and chronic offenders.* Washington, DC: U.S. Department of Justice, Office of Juvenile Justice and Delinquency Prevention.

Howell, J. C., Krisberg, B., Hawkins, J. D., & Wilson, J. J. (Eds.). (1995). *Serious, violent, and chronic juvenile offenders: A sourcebook.* Thousand Oaks, CA: Sage Publications.

Johnston, L., O'Malley, P., & Bachman, J. (1994). *National survey results on drug use from the Monitoring the Future study 1975–1993.* Washington, DC: National Institute on Drug Abuse.

Merry, S., Berg, P., Baker, S., & Wynn, J. (1995). *The Children, Youth, and Families Initiative: Annual report.* Chicago: University of Chicago, Chapin Hall Center for Children.

Miller, B., Card, J., Paikoff, R., & Peterson, J. (Eds.). (1992). *Preventing adolescent pregnancy: Model programs and evaluations.* Newbury Park, CA: Sage Publications.

Pittman, K., & Cahill, M. (1991). *A new vision: Promoting youth development* (Commissioned Paper No. 3). Washington, DC: Academy for Educational Development, Center for Youth Development and Policy Research.

Public/Private Ventures. (1993). *Community change for youth development: Establishing long-term supports in communities for the growth and development of young people.* Philadelphia: Author.

Rosewater, A. (1992). *Comprehensive approaches for children and families: A philanthropic perspective.* Washington, DC: Grantsmakers for Children, Youth and Families.

Shannon, L. (1991). *Changing patterns in delinquency and crime: A longitudinal study in Racine.* Boulder, CO: Westview Press.

Snyder, H. (1994). *Are juveniles driving the violent crime trends?* (Fact Sheet No. 16). Washington, DC: U.S. Department of Justice, Office of Juvenile Justice and Delinquency Prevention.

Steinberg, L. (1985). *Adolescence.* New York: Alfred A. Knopf.

Stone, R. (1994). *Comprehensive community-building strategies: Issues and opportunities for learning.* Chicago: University of Chicago, Chapin Hall Center for Children.

Tanner, J. M. (1962). *Growth at adolescence* (2nd ed.). Oxford: Blackwell Scientific Publications.

Thornberry, T. P., Huizinga, D., & Loeber, R. (1995). The prevention of serious delinquency and violence: Implications from the program of research on the causes and correlates of delinquency. In J. C. Howell, B. Krisberg, J. D. Hawkins, & J. J. Wilson (Eds.), *Serious, violent, and chronic juvenile offenders: A sourcebook* (pp. 213–237). Thousand Oaks, CA: Sage Publications.

Tracy, P., Wolfgang, M., & Figlio, R. (1990). *Delinquency in two birth cohorts.* Washington, DC: U.S. Department of Justice, Office of Juvenile Justice and Delinquency Prevention.

Tremblay, R. E., & Craig, W. M. (1995). Developmental crime prevention. In M. Tonry & D. P. Farrington (Eds.), *Building a safer society: Strategic approaches to crime prevention* (pp. 151–236). Chicago: University of Chicago Press.

U.S. Department of Health and Human Resources, Office of the Assistant Secretary for Planning and Evaluation. (1996). *Trends in the well-being of America's children and youth: 1996.* Washington, DC: Author.

Wehlage, G., Rutter, R., Smith, G., Lesko, N., & Fernandez, R. (1989). *Reducing the risk: Schools as communities of support.* London: Falmer Press.

Wolfgang, M., Figlio, R., & Sellin, T. (1972). *Delinquency in a birth cohort.* Chicago: University of Chicago Press.

Wynn, J., Costello, J., Halpern, R., & Richman, H. (1994). *Children, families, and communities: A new approach to social services.* Chicago: University of Chicago, Chapin Hall Center for Children.

This chapter is adapted and updated from a paper presented at the Indianapolis Coalition for Human Services Planning Conference, March 1996, Greencastle, IN. The authors thank Roberta Greene for providing helpful comments on earlier drafts.

This chapter was originally published in the September 1997 issue of Social Work, *vol. 42, pp. 483–493.*

Part II

ECONOMIC REVITALIZATION AND COMMUNITY SELF-SUFFICIENCY

5 Asset Building as a Community Revitalization Strategy

Deborah Page-Adams and Michael Sherraden

Asset building, an emerging theme in community revitalization, sometimes is defined broadly to include all potential resources in a community—not only financial resources but also the talents and skills of individuals, organizational capacity, political connections, buildings and facilities, and so on (Kretzmann & McKnight, 1993). In this usage, the term "assets" may appear to mean "all good things" and is thus only a vague guide to social work practice. Moreover, from the standpoint of knowledge building, theoretical statements and empirical confirmation are elusive with such a wide-ranging concept.

Before Kretzmann and McKnight's (1993) proposal to build assets in community development, Sherraden (1988, 1990, 1991) suggested that households and communities develop not by income alone (the dominant theme of the welfare state), but also by savings and asset building. In this usage, the term "assets" is restricted to the concept of wealth, including both property and financial holdings. Sherraden's work includes propositions about the personal, social, economic, and community effects of asset holding that invite empirical tests.

As often happens, community development and policy initiatives based on asset building have advanced before the establishment of a sound knowledge base. Sherraden proposed a system of individual development accounts (IDAs)—matched savings for purposes such as education, home ownership, and small business development. As a result of this proposal, a number of IDA projects have emerged around the country (Edwards, 1997). Oliver and Shapiro (1995) have made a particularly strong case for asset building in revitalization of African American communities. Most states have raised asset limits in welfare reform; 15 states have set up IDAs or some other special savings program for the poor population, and seven states provide a progressive subsidy for these savings (Corporation for Enterprise Development, 1995). IDAs recently were adopted as a national project of AmeriCorps VISTA, in which volunteers will help create IDA programs in community development credit unions. The Personal Responsibility and Work Opportunity Reconciliation Act of 1996 (P.L. 104-193) allows states to use welfare block grants to match savings in IDAs and encourages the private sector to match savings as well. All such savings will be disregarded from asset limits in means-tested federal programs. Congressional bills for IDA demonstrations, such as the Assets for Independence Act (U.S. Senate, 1995), cosponsored by Sen. Dan Coats (R-IN) and Sen. Carol Moseley-Braun (D-IL), have bipartisan support. In the private sector, the largest funder of community development initiatives is the Ford Foundation, which has recently reorganized a division called "Asset Building and Community Development."

Studies that evaluate the implementation, performance, and effects of IDAs and other asset-based community revitalization initiatives will be critical to assessing the potential of domestic policy built in part on individual savings accounts. For example, the Center for Social Development at Washington University in St. Louis is undertaking a six-year evaluation of a multisite IDA demonstration funded by a consortium of foundations. In planning and implementing such studies, IDA evaluators can be guided in part by previous research on effects of asset holding. The key question is, Does asset holding have positive effects and, if so, for whom and under what circumstances? This chapter summarizes findings from studies that address effects of asset holding on personal well-being, economic security, civic behavior, women's status, and children's well-being.

EFFECTS OF ASSET BUILDING

The studies summarized in this chapter were chosen in a somewhat arbitrary manner and thus provide only an initial look at the effects of assets. Nonetheless, asset holding appears to have multiple positive effects, particularly for people who are economically vulnerable. Applied research is needed to confirm these outcomes in the context of community revitalization.

Personal Well-Being

Some studies suggest positive effects of assets on life satisfaction and self-efficacy and negative effects on depression and alcohol abuse (Finn, 1994; Page-Adams & Vosler, 1995; Rohe & Stegman, 1994a; Yadama & Sherraden, 1996) (Table 5.1). Assets appear to be associated with being self-directed, intellectually flexible, and future oriented (Kohn, Naoi, Schoenbach, Schooler, & Slomczynski, 1990; Yadama & Sherraden, 1996). In research on relationships among assets, age, and physical health, Robert and House (1996), controlling for the effects of education and income, found that assets were positively associated with health throughout adulthood and old age. The association was particularly strong for those ages 65 through 84.

However, the effect of assets on stress is not consistent from study to study, with some research suggesting a positive relationship between assets and stress for low-income families (Finn, 1994; Rocha, 1994). Stress is a conceptually problematic dependent variable because it can have both constructive and destructive features.

Economic Security

Research on the relationship between assets and economic security suggests positive outcomes for diverse groups (Table 5.2), whether security is measured objectively or subjectively. For example, assets help reduce welfare receipt among low-income people with small businesses and help reduce perceived economic strain among automobile workers stressed by a plant closing (Page-Adams & Vosler, 1995; Raheim & Alter, 1995). In a study of the effects of home ownership

Table 5.1
Effects of Asset Holding on Personal Well-Being

Study	Purpose	Sample	Description	Findings
Kohn, Naoi, Schoenbach, Schooler, & Slomoczynski (1990)	To test effects of ownership on the psychological well-being of men in three countries	Representative samples of men employed in civilian jobs in United States, Japan, and Poland	Class is conceptualized as ownership, control of means of production, and control of labor power	Ownership has significant positive effects on three of four measures of well-being
Robert & House (1996)	To explore relationships among assets, age, and physical health, with a focus on older adults	Stratified random sample of 3,617 adults from the Americans' Changing Lives Study	Explored health effects of assets for various age groups, controlling for education and income	Assets are positively associated with physical health, especially for adults ages 65 to 84
Rocha (1994)	To explore the role of saving and investment in explaining stress among two-parent families	1,500 randomly sampled women in two-parent families with dependent children from the National Survey of Families and Households	Assets modeled as mediating relationships among income, number of children, and stress	Stress increases as assets increase for working-poor families, controlling for income and children
Rohe & Stegman (1994a)	To test effects of home owning on three measures of well-being among low-income people	125 low-income homeowners and 101 Section 8 control group renters, 92% of whom were African Americans	Home owning effects tested controlling for income and education, among other variables	Home owning positively affects life satisfaction but not self-esteem or sense of control
Yadama & Sherraden (1996)	To test effects of assets on efficacy, horizons, prudence, effort, and connectedness	Data from 2,871 respondents from the Panel Study of Income Dynamics in 1972, controlling for attitudes and behaviors in 1968	Effects of assets (home value and amount of savings) tested, controlling for income	Savings but not home value had positive effects on efficacy, horizons, and prudence

Table 5.2

Effects of Asset Holding on Economic Security

Study	Purpose	Sample	Description	Findings
Krumm & Kelly (1989)	To test causal effects of home ownership and value of home on household savings	Secondary analysis of data from the 1976 Survey on Consumer Credit	Tested the causal effects of home ownership on savings, controlling for wages and education	Home owning positively affects savings, especially among those with high home values
Massey & Basem (1992)	To explore determinants of savings, remittances, and spending among Mexican immigrants	Randomly selected households in four Mexican communities; sample of 295 men	Tested effects of owning and of being from a community with many land or business owners	Saving and remitting higher among those from communities with many land and business owners
Page-Adams & Vosler (1995)	To test effects of home owning on stressed automobile workers, controlling for income and education	193 automobile workers in midwestern city in 1992; half laid off by plant closing	Economic strain was one of four outcomes, in addition to social and emotional well-being	Home owning related to lower economic strain, alcoholism, and depression
Raheim & Alter (1995)	To evaluate the first publicly funded U.S. microenterprise program for low-income people	Random sample of 120 participants in Self-Employment Investment Demonstration who started businesses (68% were single parents)	Six-year follow-up focused on economic well-being of participants and their businesses	Self-Employment Investment Demonstration businesses had high survival rates, created jobs, and reduced welfare receipt
Sherraden, Nair, Vasoo, Liang, & Sherraden (1995)	To assess effects of asset accumulation through Singapore's Central Provident Fund	Sample of 356 active fund members, representative of fund total population	Explored impact of asset accumulation on economic, social, and psychological well-being	Fund improves economic well-being, foremost through housing and health care

on household savings, Krumm and Kelly (1989) found that home owning had positive effects on savings, especially for families with high home values. Other studies found that perceived economic security helps explain the nearly universal desire for home ownership among British military families (Chandler, 1989) and that high rates of land and small business ownership in one's community of origin have positive effects on future economic security among Mexican immigrants (Massey & Basem, 1992). Asset accumulation in Singapore's Central Provident Fund has improved the economic well-being of fund members, especially in terms of housing and health care (Sherraden, Nair, Vasoo, Liang, & Sherraden, 1995).

Civic Behavior

Evidence on the relationship between assets and civic behavior is mixed (Table 5.3). Although some studies suggested positive effects of assets on recycling behavior and involvement in block associations, others found limited effects on civic involvement beyond the neighborhood level (Oskamp et al., 1991; Perkins, Florin, Rich, Wandersman, & Chavis, 1990; Rohe & Stegman, 1994b; Thompson, 1993). In research addressing home ownership and neighborhood reinvestment, Galster (1987) found that those who own and occupy homes are more likely than absentee owners to maintain and improve their residences. Controlling for other household and neighborhood characteristics, owner occupants made repairs more often and spent more money maintaining their homes than absentee owners. These positive home ownership effects were particularly strong for poor people. Galster noted that "expanding the number of homeowners appears to be by far the single most potent means of encouraging the upkeep of dwellings in a neighborhood" (p. 297).

If assets do have effects on home maintenance and other civic behavior, the effects may not be direct. One study found positive effects on home maintenance, work behavior, and community involvement but showed them occurring almost entirely through cognition or knowledge about asset accumulation strategies (Cheng, Page-Adams, & Sherraden, 1995).

Women's Status

For women, assets are associated with higher levels of social status in the home and community, increased contraceptive use, and improved material conditions of families (Noponen, 1992; Schuler & Hashemi, 1994) (Table 5.4). Several studies pointed to a relationship between asset holding and lower levels of marital violence (Levinson, 1989; Page-Adams, 1995; Petersen, 1980; Schuler & Hashemi, 1994). This relationship seems to hold whether assets are measured at the individual level or at the household level, suggesting that both individual and joint ownership of assets increase safety from marital violence. The consistent findings in this area are noteworthy because domestic violence research in the United States has focused on psychological rather than economic issues.

Children's Well-Being

Studies addressing the relationship between parental assets and children's well-being have found positive effects on self-esteem among adolescents

Table 5.3
Effects of Asset Holding on Civic Behavior

Study	Purpose	Sample	Description	Findings
Galster (1987)	To test effects of home ownership on time and money spent to repair and maintain home	Systematic random sample of 1,061 homes in 26 Wooster, Ohio, neighborhoods	Tested causal effect of home ownership on home maintenance efforts, controlling for income	Positive effects of home owning on home maintenance, especially for poor homeowners
Oskamp et al. (1991)	To investigate factors that encourage and discourage recycling in a suburban U.S. city	Survey of 221 randomly selected adults in city with new curbside recycling program	Tested associations among demographics, attitudes, conservation knowledge, and recycling	Strongest predictors of recycling were living in a single-family house and owning one's own home
Perkins, Florin, Rich, Wandersman, & Chavis (1990)	To explore demographic and social correlates of participation in block associations	Data from 48 blocks in New York City using observation, police records, and surveys	Tested association between home owning and civic involvement in block associations	Home ownership positively associated with civic involvement in block associations
Rohe & Stegman (1994b)	To test the effect of home owning, controlling for other variables, on civic involvement	125 low-income homeowners and 101 Section 8 control group renters	Studied neighboring and civic involvement before and 18 months after home purchase	Homeowners had significant increase in neighborhood and block association involvement
Thompson (1993)	To compare demographic and social characteristics of volunteers and the general population	Survey of rural New York county done as part of the 1990 census	Explored differences between two groups to inform volunteer recruitment efforts	Volunteers more likely to own their own small businesses but not their own homes

Table 5.4
Effects of Asset Holding on Women's Status

Study	Purpose	Sample	Description	Findings
Levinson (1989)	To test an economic model of wife abuse using data on small-scale and peasant societies	90 societies selected from the Human Relations Area Files–Probability Sample Files; data from ethnographic reports	Three of the four indicators of economic inequality were asset-based measures	Suggest that "male control of wealth and property is the basic cause of wife beating"
Noponen (1992)	To evaluate economic and social effects of microenterprise loans to poor women in India	Random sample of 300 women participants in a model loan program surveyed in 1980 and 1985	Explored effects of access to credit for both women and their families over a five-year period	Access to credit improved social status of women and material conditions of families
Page-Adams (1995)	To test effect of home ownership on marital violence, controlling for income and education	2,827 married women whose husbands also completed questionnaires for National Survey of Families and Households in 1987–88	Analysis was designed as one test of the theory of well-being based on assets	Controlling for income, home owning is negatively associated with violence
Petersen (1980)	To explore relationships between several measures of household socioeconomic status and wife abuse	Random statewide telephone survey of 602 married women living in Maryland in 1977–78	Measures included home ownership in addition to husband's income, education, and so forth	22% of women who rent, but only 2% of women who own, reported abuse
Schuler & Hashemi (1994)	To test effects of credit on contraception and empowerment among Bangladeshi women	1,305 women; two random samples of program members; two comparison group samples	Effects of access to credit and living in village served by credit program were tested	Credit programs increase family support, leading to empowerment, leading to contraception

(Whitbeck et al., 1991); on teenagers' staying in school, avoiding early pregnancy, and saving money (Green & White, 1997; Pritchard, Myers, & Cassidy, 1989); and on home owning among adult children (Henretta, 1984) (Table 5.5). Assets also appear to reduce vulnerability to poverty for children in white and African American female-headed households (Cheng, 1995). The evidence of positive effects of home ownership for children is particularly convincing, and many of these effects are largest for children from low-income families.

Research on parental asset holding and the educational attainment of children deserves special attention because of its theoretical and practical importance. Green and White's (1997) findings on the positive effects of parental home owning on staying in school are consistent with the work of Hill and Duncan (1987). Using Panel Study of Income Dynamics data and controlling for other social and economic resources, Hill and Duncan found no significant effects of parental asset income on the wage rates of adult children but found strong support that assets affect educational attainment. The effect of parental asset income on school completion for daughters appears to be especially positive.

> Higher schooling levels are observed for sons and daughters raised in families with asset income. However, significant effects are not observed for wage rates, nor are there significant effects of additional dollars of asset income on the education of sons. Families with asset income may be better able to set and attain goals for their children's education, quite apart from the total amount of savings they have available for that purpose. (pp. 64–65)

This interpretation is consistent with the propositions that assets work in part to enhance well-being by creating a future orientation and that positive effects may have more to do with asset holding than with the value of those assets (Sherraden, 1991). Hill and Duncan's findings also support the notion that the positive effects of assets may be particularly strong for girls and women (see also Sherraden, Page-Adams, & Yadama, 1995).

ASSET-BUILDING DEMONSTRATIONS AND RESEARCH

Evaluators of asset-building initiatives can benefit from previous theoretical and empirical work on asset effects.

Hypotheses about Effects

Hypotheses about the personal and social effects of assets can focus evaluation efforts. These propositions hold that assets provide greater household stability, create long-term thinking and planning, lead to greater care and effort in maintaining assets, lead to greater development of human capital, provide a foundation for risk taking, increase personal efficacy, increase social status and influence, increase community involvement and political participation, and enhance the welfare of children (Sherraden, 1991; Sherraden, Page-Adams, & Yadama, 1995). Evaluations that measure these hypothesized outcomes will help build the knowledge base. Because assets also appear to be positively associated with women's status in the home and community, researchers should pay attention to gender issues as well. At this stage hypotheses are crudely stated and are not organized into a larger theory. A great deal of theoretical specification lies ahead.

Table 5.5

Effects of Asset Holding on Children's Well-Being

Study	Purpose	Sample	Description	Findings
Cheng (1995)	To test effects of parents' socioeconomic status, education, and assets on poverty among adult daughters who have children	836 female heads of household from National Survey of Families and Households; 548 white and 288 black single women with dependent children	Tested effects of assets on adult daughters' socioeconomic status, controlling for parents' status and daughter's education	Assets have positive economic effects for female-headed families, controlling for education and parents' socioeconomic status
Green & White (1997)	To test whether children of homeowners were less likely to drop out, have children, and be arrested	Four large representative data sets—Panel Study of Income Dynamics, High School and Beyond Survey, 1980 census, and 1989 National Bureau of Economic Research-Boston Youth; teenagers ages 17 and 18	Effects of parental home owning tested, controlling for parents' income and education	Teenagers of homeowners were less likely than those of renters to drop out and to have children
Henretta (1984)	To test effects of parents' home owning and home value on same for adult children	Panel Study of Income Dynamics cases containing data on a sample member who was a child in an earlier wave (1968–79)	Effects of parental home owning and home value tested, controlling for parental income and gifts	Parents' home owning associated with same for adult children, controlling for income and gifts
Hill & Duncan (1987)	To test effects of parental income from various sources on children's attainment	854 Panel Study of Income Dynamics cases with income averaged for the years when the child was ages 14, 15, and 16	Tested effects of asset income on children's attainment, controlling for other resources	Parental income from assets positively affects education, but not wages, of adult children
Pritchard, Myers, & Cassidy (1989)	To explore individual and family factors associated with saving and spending patterns among teenagers	1,619 employed teenagers and their parents from the 1982 sophomore cohort of the High School and Beyond Survey	Family factors included parental saving behaviors and whether they had saved for college	Parents' saving patterns and saving for college associated with teenagers' saving patterns

Longitudinal Design

Evaluations that identify the effects of assets at two or more points in time will be particularly helpful. Longitudinal designs are necessary because of the causal nature of the theoretical statements underlying asset-based policy proposals.

Alternative Explanations

The best evaluation designs will address alternative explanations for findings that support the suggestion that assets have positive effects on well-being. There are two alternative explanations for such findings: (1) positive effects on well-being could result from income rather than assets, and (2) certain personal, family, or community characteristics could be causes, rather than consequences, of asset accumulation. In other words, evaluations should determine the effects of asset accumulation on well-being while controlling for the effects of income and should test for reciprocal relationships between asset accumulation and well-being. These are not mutually exclusive explanations; all can be true simultaneously and, in fact, are likely to be so (Sherraden, 1991; Yadama & Sherraden, 1996).

Personal Well-Being

Asset accumulation may have positive effects on some dimensions of personal well-being and negative effects on others. For example, home ownership appears to increase both stress and self-efficacy for low-income people.

Evaluations should include brief questions asking people to assess the effects of assets in their lives. Information gleaned from such questions does not always completely parallel correlations based on standardized measures. Although response bias may play a role in this kind of discrepancy, some standardized measures of personal and social well-being may not be adequate for tracking asset effects.

Economic Security

Evaluators should keep economic security at the center of investigations given the suggested positive economic effects of assets. It is important to include both objective and subjective measures. One key question to be answered is, Are people better off when they are accumulating assets? Measuring this on the basis of dollars in asset accounts and on how participants feel about their economic circumstances in light of those accounts will be central to understanding the economic effects of asset-building programs.

Civic Behavior

It is important to assess community involvement at several levels. Although several standardized measures have been used to assess community involvement in social research, many have focused on connections with voluntary associations. Evaluators will want to assess effects within the immediate neighborhood, perhaps even at the block level. This will be of particular importance in programs involving home ownership and microenterprise.

   In addition, basic economic knowledge and program knowledge about asset accumulation may help explain the relationship between asset accumulation and civic behavior. Researchers should assess participants' knowledge about building assets and other aspects of economic literacy.

Women's Status and Children's Well-Being

Sherraden, Page-Adams, and Yadama (1995) suggested that future studies of intrafamily asset distribution may be fruitful given gender and generational diversity within households. The best evaluations will gather information from various members of a household rather than from a single informant.

CONCLUSION

Asset building is a new way of thinking about antipoverty strategies; its emphasis on resources rather than problems has much in common with the strengths perspective in social work practice and policy development (Chapin, 1995; Saleebey, 1992). Antipoverty policy has historically discouraged—through asset limits in means-tested programs—asset accumulation among the poor population. Although asset-based community development is in the early stages of formation and little guidance exists about how to proceed in terms of models and implementation, the concept invites innovation, creativity, and adaptation to many populations and purposes.

   Under these conditions, experimentation is desirable and inevitable. A range of community-based models is preferable to cookie-cutter replication of a fixed design. However, evaluation is challenging and messy in such circumstances. It will be important to learn as much as possible from every demonstration and program, no matter how small. In the beginning, there will be an important role for studies of implementation and preliminary information on outcomes, whether accomplished through case studies, in-depth interviews, or focus groups (Sherraden et al., 1995). Control or comparison-group designs may be possible in some cases and should be pursued.

   Evaluations of asset-building initiatives should do more than count asset accumulation. Asset-based interventions are theoretically driven; there are hypotheses on economic, personal, and community effects. In this situation, no separation exists between "basic research" and "applied research." There is a long-standing debate in the social sciences about whether social inquiry should be basic or applied, oriented toward fundamental questions of human interaction or toward pressing issues of the day. When an intervention is carefully planned, with hypothesized effects, the distinction between basic and applied social science becomes minimal (see also Rossi, 1980).

   Along these lines, evaluators should be aware that their investigations of the effects of asset-building programs will likely affect a larger antipoverty discussion. The overwhelming majority of studies addressing poverty in the United States has focused exclusively on income distribution and welfare recipiency. Yet, the studies reviewed in this chapter suggest that assets have strong positive effects among economically vulnerable populations. More collaborative work between traditional poverty researchers and evaluators of asset-based community strategies would be highly desirable.

REFERENCES

Chandler, J. (1989). Marriage and the housing careers of naval wives. *Sociological Review, 37,* 253–276.

Chapin, R. K. (1995). Social policy development: The strengths perspective. *Social Work, 40,* 506–514.

Cheng, L. (1995, April). *Asset holding and intergenerational poverty vulnerability in female-headed families.* Paper presented at the Seventh International Conference of the Society for the Advancement of Socio-Economics, Washington, DC.

Cheng, L., Page-Adams, D., & Sherraden, M. (1995, April). *The role of cognition in mediating effects of asset accumulation.* Paper presented at the Seventh International Conference of the Society for the Advancement of Socio-Economics, Washington, DC.

Corporation for Enterprise Development. (1995). *State individual development accounts sourcebook.* San Francisco: Author.

Edwards, K. (1997). *Individual development accounts: Creative savings for families and communities.* St. Louis: Washington University, Center for Social Development.

Finn, C. M. (1994). *Empowerment in Habitat for Humanity housing: Individual and organizational dynamics.* Doctoral dissertation, Case Western Reserve University, Cleveland.

Galster, G. C. (1987). *Home ownership and neighborhood reinvestment.* Durham, NC: Duke University Press.

Green, R. K., & White, M. J. (1997). Measuring the benefits of home owning: Effects on children. *Journal of Urban Economics, 41,* 441–461.

Henretta, J. C. (1984). Parental status and child's home ownership. *American Sociological Review, 49,* 131–140.

Hill, M. S., & Duncan, G. J. (1987). Parental family income and the socioeconomic attainment of children. *Social Science Research, 16,* 39–73.

Kohn, M. L., Naoi, A., Schoenbach, C., Schooler, C., & Slomczynski, K. M. (1990). Position in the class structure and psychological functioning in the United States, Japan, and Poland. *American Journal of Sociology, 95,* 964–1008.

Kretzmann, J. P., & McKnight, J. L. (1993). *Building communities from the inside out: A path toward finding and mobilizing a community's assets.* Evanston, IL: Northwestern University, Center for Urban Affairs and Policy Research.

Krumm, R., & Kelly, A. (1989). Effects of home ownership on household savings. *Journal of Urban Economics, 26,* 281–294.

Levinson, D. (1989). *Family violence in cross-cultural perspective.* Newbury Park, CA: Sage Publications.

Massey, D. S., & Basem, L. C. (1992). Determinants of savings, remittances, and spending patterns among U.S. migrants in four Mexican communities. *Sociological Inquiry, 62,* 185–207.

Noponen, H. (1992). Loans to the working poor: A longitudinal study of credit, gender and the household economy. *International Journal of Urban and Regional Research, 16,* 234–251.

Oliver, M., & Shapiro, T. (1995). *Black wealth/white wealth: A new perspective on racial inequality.* New York: Routledge.

Oskamp, S., Harrington, M. J., Edwards, T. C., Sherwood, D. L., Okuda, S. M., & Swanson, D. C. (1991). Factors influencing household recycling behavior. *Environment and Behavior, 23,* 494–519.

Page-Adams, D. (1995). *Economic resources and marital violence.* Doctoral dissertation, Washington University, St. Louis.

Page-Adams, D., & Vosler, N. R. (1995, April). *Effects of home ownership on well-being among blue-collar workers.* Paper presented at the Seventh International Conference of the Society for the Advancement of Socio-Economics, Washington, DC.

Perkins, D. D., Florin, P., Rich, R. C., Wandersman, A., & Chavis, D. M. (1990). Participation and the social and physical environment of residential blocks: Crime and community context. *American Journal of Community Psychology, 18,* 83–115.

Personal Responsibility and Work Opportunity Reconciliation Act of 1996, P.L. 104-193, 110 Stat. 2105.

Petersen, R. (1980). Social class, social learning, and wife abuse. *Social Service Review, 54,* 390–406.

Pritchard, M. E., Myers, B. K., & Cassidy, D. J. (1989). Factors associated with adolescent saving and spending patterns. *Adolescence, 24,* 711–723.

Raheim, S., & Alter, C. F. (1995). *Self-employment investment demonstration final evaluation report.* Iowa City: University of Iowa, School of Social Work.

Robert, S., & House, J. S. (1996). SES differentials in health by age and alternative indicators of SES. *Journal of Aging and Health, 8,* 359–388.

Rocha, C. J. (1994). *Effects of poverty on working families: Comparing models of stress by race and class.* Doctoral dissertation, Washington University, St. Louis.

Rohe, W. M., & Stegman, M. A. (1994a). The effects of home ownership on the self-esteem, perceived control and life satisfaction of low-income people. *Journal of the American Planning Association, 60,* 173–184.

Rohe, W. M., & Stegman, M. A. (1994b). The impact of home ownership on the social and political involvement of low-income people. *Urban Affairs Quarterly, 30,* 152–172.

Rossi, P. (1980). Presidential address to the American Sociological Association. *American Sociological Review, 45,* 889–904.

Saleebey, D. (1992). *The strengths perspective in social work practice.* New York: Longman.

Schuler, S. R., & Hashemi, S. M. (1994). Credit programs, women's empowerment, and contraceptive use in rural Bangladesh. *Studies in Family Planning, 25,* 65–76.

Sherraden, M. (1988). Rethinking social welfare: Toward assets. *Social Policy, 18*(3), 37–43.

Sherraden, M. (1990). Stakeholding: Notes on a theory of welfare based on assets. *Social Service Review, 64,* 580–601.

Sherraden, M. (1991). *Assets and the poor: A new American welfare policy.* New York: M. E. Sharpe.

Sherraden, M., Nair, S., Vasoo, S., Liang, N. T., & Sherraden, M. S. (1995). Social policy based on assets: The impact of Singapore's Central Provident Fund. *Asian Journal of Political Science, 3*(2), 112–133.

Sherraden, M., Page-Adams, D., Emerson, S., Beverly, S., Scanlon, E., Cheng, L., Sherraden, M. S., & Edwards, K. (1995). *IDA evaluation handbook: A practical guide and tools for evaluation of pioneering IDA projects.* St. Louis: Washington University, Center for Social Development.

Sherraden, M., Page-Adams, D., & Yadama, G. (1995). Assets and the welfare state: Policies, proposals, politics, and research. *Research in Politics and Society, 5,* 241–268.

Thompson, A. M. III. (1993). Rural emergency medical volunteers and their communities: A demographic comparison. *Journal of Community Health, 18,* 379–392.

U.S. Senate. (1995). *S. 1212, Assets for Independence Act: A bill to create an individual development account demonstration.* Washington, DC: U.S. Government Printing Office.

Whitbeck, L. B., Simons, R. L., Conger, R. D., Lorenz, F. O., Huck, S., & Elder, G. H. Jr. (1991). Family economic hardship, parental support, and adolescent self-esteem. *Social Psychology Quarterly, 54,* 353–363.

Yadama, G. N., & Sherraden, M. (1996). Effects of assets on attitudes and behaviors: Advance test of a social policy proposal. *Social Work Research, 20,* 3–11.

An earlier version of this chapter was presented at the Seventh International Conference of the Society for the Advancement of Socio-Economics, April 1995, Washington, DC, and at the Annual Program Meeting of the Council on Social Work Education, February 1996, Washington, DC.

This chapter was originally published in the September 1997 issue of Social Work, *vol. 42, pp. 423–434.*

6 Effects of Assets on Attitudes and Behaviors: Advance Test of a Social Policy Proposal

Gautam N. Yadama and Michael Sherraden

In his 1994 welfare reform proposal, President Clinton included a number of measures to increase asset limits and create special savings accounts called "individual development accounts" (IDAs). These proposals, presented as legislation, were sponsored by Senators Daniel Moynihan (D-NY) and Edward Kennedy (D-MA), Representatives Sam Gibbons (D-FL) and Dick Gephardt (D-MO), and others. Other proposals for IDA demonstrations had already been introduced by Representatives Tony Hall (D-OH), Bill Emerson (R-MO), and Cardiss Collins (D-IL) and by Senator Bill Bradley (D-NJ). Almost every welfare reform proposal, Republican and Democrat, would raise asset limits to encourage saving. This bipartisan emphasis on asset building is a new and untested approach to antipoverty policy.

Assets are typically viewed as a storehouse for future consumption, but they may have important psychological and social effects as well. A fundamental theme in American culture suggests that wealth and property holding may have positive effects on personal well-being, social status, and citizen participation. This theme has deep historical roots and a long-lasting influence on public policy. It is an idea that was expounded by Thomas Jefferson; recorded in the observations of Alexis de Tocqueville; and later invoked as a rationale for such policies as the Homestead Act, government-backed home mortgage lending programs, employee stock ownership plans, and proposals for ownership of public housing. Related proposals in public policy regarding the idea of capital accounts, primarily for youths, have been suggested by Tobin (1968), Haveman (1988), and Sawhill (1989). These proposals are for a single lump-sum distribution, to be given to recipients late in adolescence, that might be thought of as a multipurpose voucher for health, welfare, and education choices. However, the intention of these proposals is to provide a fund for welfare consumption choices. Effects of asset holding, other than for consumption choices, have not been discussed by these authors.

Specification of the psychological and social effects of asset holding is not well developed. Typically, effects of asset holding have been presented as broad normative statements (for example, by Thomas Jefferson) or as sweeping narrative observations (for example, by Alexis de Tocqueville). To be sure, a number of eminent scholars, including Adam Smith, Karl Marx, Max Weber, Thorstein Veblen, and William James, have commented in various ways on the effects of property holding, but clear propositions have seldom been formulated. The discussion has been more in the realm of social philosophy than the social sciences. The study described in this chapter provides an empirical test of the effects of assets on attitudes and behaviors.

STUDIES OF ATTITUDES, BEHAVIORS, AND ECONOMIC STATUS

In related research, several studies have been undertaken to assess relationships among attitudes, behaviors, and subsequent changes in labor force participation and income. Duncan and Hill (1975) examined the extent to which attitudes such as efficacy, trust, aspiration and ambition, risk avoidance, connectedness, time horizon, and economizing behavior affect economic status. Their study examined the effect of attitudes, behaviors, and economic status over a five-year period between 1968 and 1972. These researchers concluded that the effects of attitudes and behaviors on economic status are negligible and that "despite the fact that some attitudes and behavior patterns had statistically significant effects on income change, they did not have powerful effects" (Duncan & Hill, 1975, p. 99). Andrisani (1977, 1981) studied the relationship between internal and external attitudes and labor market experience. On the basis of modest effects, he concluded that internal and external attitudes are systematically related to labor market experiences such as growth in average hourly earnings and occupational attainment. Duncan and Morgan (1981), on the other hand, concluded that attitudes are not important in explaining economic success.

In looking at this research overall, two features are evident. First, most of the studies focused on effects of attitudes and behavior on subsequent economic status rather than vice versa (although occasionally researchers have examined effects of income on social and psychological factors; see Duncan & Hill, 1975). Second, most of the measures of economic status are based on some measure of income or an income-to-needs ratio. There is little systematic research on assets and their possible relationships with attitudinal and behavioral variables.

STUDIES RELATING ASSETS WITH SOCIAL AND PSYCHOLOGICAL VARIABLES

There is a long history of cross-national research on correlates of property holding in anthropology and sociology (Rudman, 1992, provides an excellent review). Most of the work is ethnographic, although limited systematic studies have appeared in the past half-century. The unit of analysis in these studies is not at the individual or household level, and the work generally does not speak to attitudinal and behavioral variables. Much of this body of work has a marked ideological bias, either categorizing the harmful results or extolling the virtues of private property.

In modern sociology there is a large literature associating assets with social power (Domhoff, 1971; Kolko, 1962; Mills, 1956), but the focus is typically on the social power of the upper class, where assets are concentrated. There is little attempt to examine effects of asset holding among other population groups or to specify propositions that might be tested in heterogeneous populations. However, there are some noteworthy exceptions, in which the authors stated clear hypotheses and used empirical data. Kohn, Naoi, Schoenbach, Schooler, and

Slomczynski (1990) systematically tested psychological effects of asset holding, including self-directedness and intellectual flexibility, in Japan, Poland, and the United States, and Vosler and Page-Adams (1993) tested the relationship between property holding and depression among auto workers in the United States. In both of these studies, significant effects of asset holding were found after controlling for income and education.

As an additional step toward formulating this idea in terms that are accessible to systematic analysis, Sherraden (1990, 1991) developed propositions regarding attitudinal and behavioral effects of asset holding. The suggested effects include greater household stability, increased long-term thinking and planning, increased effort in maintaining and enhancing assets, increased human capital development, increased risk taking, greater personal efficacy and self-esteem, increased social status, increased community involvement, and increased political participation. These propositions are stated at a general level, but they invite systematic tests. Haveman (1992) suggested that Sherraden may have had "the signs on the relevant coefficients correct" (p. 1521) but that confirmatory evidence was lacking.

For obvious reasons, it is very desirable to test asset-based policy proposals in advance, using any available empirical data. However, because assets and their effects have not been a focus of previous theory and research, most data sets do not offer opportunities for such tests. Fortunately, between 1968 and 1972, and only in these years, the Panel Study of Income Dynamics (PSID) included a wide range of attitudes and behaviors. When combined with PSID asset measures of savings and house value, the opportunity exists—as far as we know the only opportunity—for a longitudinal test. In addition, we can simultaneously test for two major alternative explanations. The first alternative explanation is that attitudes and behaviors cause assets rather than vice versa. The second alternative explanation is that income, not assets, affects attitudes and behaviors. These different explanations are not mutually exclusive. It is likely that both income and assets affect attitudes and behaviors in similar directions, but to some extent independently, and the relationship between assets and attitudes and behaviors probably works both ways (Sherraden, 1991).

In this chapter, we take a step toward testing the general theoretical statement that assets have effects on certain attitudes and behaviors (usually thought of as positive). Taking into account the theoretical statement and the two alternative explanations, we tested for the effect of assets on attitudes and behaviors, the effect of attitudes and behaviors on assets, the effect of income on attitudes and behaviors, and the effect of attitudes and behaviors on income.

DATA AND PROCEDURES

A large proportion of the research on attitudes, behavior, and economic status is based on the PSID, an ongoing longitudinal survey of 5,000 families that began in 1968 and was conducted by the Survey Research Center at the University of Michigan (Hill, 1992). The study began with 4,802 households—1,872 low-income households were drawn from the Survey of Economic Opportunity and another 2,930 households were drawn from the national sampling frame of the

Survey Research Center (Hill, 1992). Heads of household from PSID were selected to study the relationship between assets and attitudes and behaviors. We
arrived at the final sample of 2,871 cases after filtering the data for accuracy and
for those who were heads of household in both 1968 and 1972. The mean age of
study participants was 43 years. Overall, 75 percent of the household heads
were men and 25 percent were women. Regarding race, 66 percent were white;
32 percent were black; and the remaining 2 percent were Puerto Rican, Mexican,
or other.

It is possible to use the PSID to explore effects of assets on attitudes and behaviors and vice versa. Specifically, we could examine the effects of assets on
prudence, efficacy, horizons, connectedness, and effort. However, the analysis
is constrained by certain limitations in the data set. As with Duncan and Hill
(1975), we restricted our analysis to a five-year period from 1968 to 1972 because data on attitudes and behaviors have not been collected after 1972. (More
reliable data on assets were gathered in 1984; however, because PSID data on
attitudes and behaviors precedes the more reliable data on assets, it is not possible to examine the effect of assets on attitudes and behaviors after 1972.)

The PSID data set also enabled us to examine simultaneously the two major
alternative explanations. Accordingly, we examined the effect of income while
testing for the effect of assets on attitudes and behaviors, and we also tested for
the second alternative explanation, that attitudes and behaviors affect assets
rather than vice versa. All the effects were simultaneously estimated as a path
model of directly observed variables using LISREL 8. A causal model with directly observed variables, such as the one tested here, is classified in LISREL as
submodel 2 (Jöreskog & Sörbom, 1989), a class of models in which the dependent and explanatory variables are directly observed.

Variables such as house value and income are directly observed and are used
as such in the path model. All of the attitude and behavior variables and the
savings variable are indices derived from other observed variables. Every index
used in this analysis was derived by the PSID staff from a combination of weight-
ing and aggregation of responses to specific sets of observed variables. The primary reason for using the PSID indices is that they have been used in previous
analyses (Andrisani, 1977; Duncan & Hill, 1975; Duncan & Morgan, 1981), enabling us to compare our results with the relevant research. Each index in the
present study is used as an observed variable. Computation of a measurement
model is not relevant because we used each of the indices as an observed variable; therefore, we use a path model instead of a structural equation model with
latent variables.

Unlike traditional path models, it is possible to simultaneously estimate all
effects in a path analysis model for directly observed variables using LISREL. In
the traditional path-analytic model, one obtains reduced-form equations first
and then solves for the structural parameters (Jöreskog & Sörbom, 1989), whereas
in LISREL, a path model is considered as a system of equations, and all structural
coefficients are estimated directly and the reduced form obtained as a byproduct
(Jöreskog & Sörbom, 1993). In causal models of directly observed variables, there
are no latent variables, only directly measured variables: ys and xs. Because there

are no latent constructs, a measurement model and the associated factor loadings (represented in λ–x and λ–y matrices) and correlations of measurement error (represented in θ–δ and θ–ε matrices) are not relevant and therefore not estimated. Matrices representing factor loadings are fixed to identity, and matrices of measurement error are fixed to zero (Bollen, 1989). Moreover, in this submodel, the covariance matrix of independent constructs is assumed to be an unconstrained free covariance matrix of x variables (Jöreskog & Sörbom, 1989).

We estimated the effect of assets in 1968 on all the attitudes and behaviors in 1972 while controlling for the effects of the respective attitudes and behaviors in 1968. Similarly, we estimated the effects of attitudes and behaviors in 1968 on assets in 1972 while controlling for time 1 effects of assets and income. Both sets of effects were tested simultaneously in the same model. In addition, we simultaneously estimated the effects of income in 1968 on attitudes and behaviors in 1972, and vice versa, in the same model.

Control Variables

Age, race, gender, education of the head of household, and a variable indicating the presence of young children in the family were used as control variables. Age was the reported age of the head of household, and education was the number of years of school completed by the head of household. Race (1 = white, 0 = person of color) and gender (1 = male, 0 = female) were ordinal variables that had been dummy coded. The question "How old is the youngest child under 18 in the family unit?" was used as a control for the presence of young children in the family. Values for this variable ranged between 1, indicating the presence of a child less than two years old, and 9, indicating the presence of no children under age 18. These control variables were of no theoretical or policy interest in the present discussion. Nonetheless, controls were used here to remove doubt about the independence of asset effects.

Variables of Theoretical and Policy Interest

The variables in this study were house value, savings, income, prudence, efficacy, horizons, connectedness, and effort. House value, savings, and income in 1968 were independent variables affecting attitudes and behaviors in 1972 after controlling for the effects of attitudes and behaviors in 1968. Attitudes and behaviors in 1968 were independent variables affecting assets and income in 1972 after controlling for the effects of assets and income in 1968. All of these effects were estimated while simultaneously controlling for the effects of the demographic variables identified earlier.

Attitude and behavior variables were prudence, efficacy, horizons, connectedness, and effort. Together, the five attitude and behavior variables were the closest approximations that PSID data provided to the hypothesized asset effects suggested by Sherraden (1990, 1991). Overall, these variables represented desirable personal and social attributes consistent with the aims of social policy. Horizons, connectedness, and effort were particularly relevant to the content of the current welfare reform debate. See Table 6.1 for descriptive statistics of all variables used in the analysis.

Table 6.1

Descriptive Statistics of Asset, Income, Attitude, and Behavior Variables Used in the Analysis

Variable	1968		1972	
	M	*SD*	*M*	*SD*
House value	9,110.49	12,590.57	11,699.55	14,165.68
Savings	2.73	1.72	2.66	1.74
Income	8,656.49	6,925.67	10,140.22	7,776.04
Prudence	4.69	1.27	3.68	1.16
Efficacy	3.38	1.68	3.01	1.54
Horizons	4.27	1.30	4.28	1.02
Connectedness	5.89	1.70	6.02	1.64
Effort	1.85	1.30	2.13	1.49

NOTE: See text for explanation of numerical values.

There were two attitude and behavior indices that were available in the PSID but not used in this analysis. The first, an aspiration–ambition index, was not used because it has resulted in counterintuitive effects in the past and because the measure may be flawed. Duncan and Hill (1975) found a negative effect of income on the aspiration–ambition index, which they suggested was the result of certain components of the index, such as planning for or doing something about a better job, which are components generally associated with unsatisfactory income. The second index, an economizing behavior index, was not used because we could not find any proposition in the literature that suggested a relationship between asset holding and economizing behavior. Duncan and Hill (1975) discussed other possible behavioral measures at length. All indexes were developed and previously used by the Survey Research Center of the University of Michigan. Prior use of the indexes added to their usefulness in the current analysis.

House Value. The house value measure was used as an indicator of asset holdings. For respondents who did not own a home, this variable indicated a value of zero, and for those who owned a home, the actual value of the home was reflected in this variable. Whether a person lived in a rental property at the time of the study and the amount of rent they paid were assessed separately from home ownership elsewhere in the survey. Appropriate accuracy codes were used to filter out inaccurate estimates of house value, and 1968 house values were adjusted to 1972 dollars.

Savings. Household savings was the other asset variable. The savings measure was the reserve funds index, which was a measure of savings undertaken by a family. A score of 5 indicated that the family had current savings of two or more months' income, and a score of 1 indicated that the family did not have any savings. The savings reserve index was computed by the PSID staff using three other specific variables. In the first question respondents were asked if they had savings in the form of checking or savings accounts or government bonds. The second question assessed the extent of savings as a proportion of income. A third variable used in the computation of the reserve funds index reflected the extent of savings in the past five years. For details on the particular variables and the computational method for the reserve funds index, see Survey Research Center (1972b, p. 261). The savings measure used in the savings reserve index was truncated. It did not differentiate those who had savings of only two months' income from those who had savings greater than two months' income. Although asset-based policy demonstrations were not limited to encouraging savings of only two months' income, we were limited by the available data on savings included in the PSID. The original reserve fund index variable was reversed to make signs consistent throughout.

Income. The income measure refers to total family money income. This includes labor market earnings, public and private income transfers, rent, and interest income for all members of the family. Income in 1968 was adjusted to 1972 dollars.

Prudence. The prudence index was a modified form of the risk avoidance index developed by the PSID staff. This index was constructed by summing the standardized responses to questions about auto insurance, medical insurance, and personal smoking habits. One other question that was used to compute the index dealt with personal savings. To avoid any measurement confounding between the risk avoidance index and one of the asset variables (savings and reserve index), we recomputed prudence by partialing out the contribution of the savings variable. Prudence was represented by a revised form of variables V397 (1968) and V2945 (1972) in our analysis. For details on the variable numbers and the specific questions used to compute this index, see Survey Research Center (1972a, p. 364) and Duncan and Hill (1975, p. 74). Risk avoidance was considered positive in this context because it "is not the potentially beneficial entrepreneurial risk but rather is undue or unnecessary risk, indicated by excessive cigarette smoking, failure to fasten seat belts, having inadequate medical insurance or savings or operating uninsured vehicles" (Duncan & Hill, 1975, p. 74). In our analysis, unlike the original risk avoidance index, the index for prudence did not incorporate the adequacy of savings as one of the proxy measures. In other words, the measure of prudence was the same as the risk avoidance index minus the reserve funds measure. We undertook this alteration in the risk avoidance index to avoid confounding variables, because one of our asset variables is the savings reserve index.

Efficacy. Efficacy was measured with the efficacy-planning index developed by PSID staff from responses to specific questions about feelings, expectations, and confidence about the future. The index was computed using five questions measuring a personal sense of effectiveness in carrying out plans and also a general future orientation of the respondent. Respondents were asked if they thought life would work out, if they generally got to carry out the plans they envisioned, and if they were future oriented or lived from day to day. In our path analysis we used the efficacy planning index for 1968 (V419) and 1972 (V2939) to assess the effect of assets while controlling for time 1 effects. For greater detail on the questions and the variables, see Survey Research Center (1972a, p. 367) and Duncan and Hill (1975, pp. 83–89). The index reflects a respondent's satisfaction with self and confidence about the future (Survey Research Center, 1972a).

Horizons. Horizons were measured with the horizon proxies index of PSID, which included responses to questions about moving to obtain a new job, having more children, and having educational goals for one's children. All asset effects on the horizons index were examined after controlling for the effects of prior horizons. The horizons index for 1968 is V391 and for 1972 is V2946. For greater detail see Survey Research Center (1972a, p. 364), and for prior application of the horizons index, see Ehrlich (1975, pp. 189–207).

Connectedness. The connectedness index determined the extent to which a head of household was in touch with sources of information and help. The index assessed whether a respondent was in contact with relatives and neighbors or was active in certain organizations. "Contact with relatives and neighbors belonging to organizations, and use of the media are hypothesized to enhance opportunities for information and its potential use" (Survey Research Center, 1972a, p. 363). This index was computed using nine specific variables that assessed attendance at organizations, use of the media, acquaintance with neighbors and relatives, and participation in any labor union (Duncan & Hill, 1975, p. 113; Survey Research Center, 1972a, p. 363). The connectedness index was represented by variables V393 (1968) and V2947 (1972). Both the horizon proxies index and the connectedness index have been termed "advantageous behaviors" in prior research (Duncan & Hill, 1975).

Effort. Effort was measured using the real earning acts index, which was composed of behaviors that resulted in nonmoney income or investment in human capital (Survey Research Center, 1972a, p. 364); effort has been termed a "coping behavior" by Duncan and Hill (1975). The index was constructed from responses to questions on the extent of home repair, car repair, home gardening, and other productive money-saving or human capital accumulation activities undertaken in one's spare time. The index was calculated from responses to four specific questions (see Duncan & Hill, 1975, pp. 94–96). The effort index was represented by variables V395 (1968) and V2943 (1972). In the current analysis, we did not distinguish between advantageous behaviors and coping behaviors (for a discussion of the content and construction of indexes used in this analysis, see Survey Research Center, 1972a, pp. 363–372, and 1972b, pp. 787–792).

RESULTS

The overall fit of the baseline structural equation model was adequate. The model had a goodness-of-fit index (GFI) of .96, adjusted goodness-of-fit index (AGFI) of .81, comparative fit index (CFI) of .94, and a relative fit index (RFI) of .74. Although the GFI indicates a very good fit, the chi-square measure of fit indicated a less than adequate fit [$\chi^2(48, N = 2,871) = 1,115.40, p = .00$]. Discrepancy among measures of fit can be easily explained. It is known that some measures of model fit—chi-square is foremost among them—are prone to sample size effects. As sample size becomes large, so does the chi-square statistic, leading one to falsely reject a model even if the model has an adequate fit (Yadama & Pandey, 1995). Because our analysis is based on a large sample size ($N = 2,871$), it is reasonable to expect large chi-square values. Therefore, we relied on other mea-sures of fit that are not as affected by sample size.

Our results indicate that several of the errors in equations (zs) predicting the dependent variables are correlated. Errors in equations predicting income and house value were allowed to correlate, and so were errors in equations predict-ing savings and horizons. The final model, with the loss of only two degrees of freedom, is a markedly improved model with excellent indicators of fit. The fit of our model improved on freeing these error terms [$\chi^2(46, N = 2,871) = 383.22, p = .00$, GFI = .99, AGFI = .93, CFI = .98, RFI = .91]. The root mean square residual for the final model is low (.021), and the root mean square error of approxima-tion is .051 (p value for test of close fit = .40), both indicating a good overall fit.

Table 6.2 reports the results of our analysis testing for the effects of income and assets on attitudes and behaviors and vice versa. Effects of each asset vari-able on the five attitude and behavior measures were assessed only after con-trolling for age, race, gender, education, age of youngest child, and the effect of the time 1 score of a given dependent variable. Coefficients for control variables are not reported here because they are not of analytical interest. (However, the effects of assets actually increased in the presence of control variables, whereas effects of income diminished.) As stated earlier, income is included in the analy-sis as an alternative explanation for attitudes and behaviors.

In this analysis we found a number of significant but modest effects (Table 6.2). Five of the 10 standardized coefficients relating the two asset variables and five attitude and behavior variables were significant, all in the expected direc-tion. As predicted, savings had a significant positive effect on prudence ($b = .20$, $p \leq .01$), efficacy ($b = .10, p \leq .01$), horizons ($b = .19, p \leq .01$), and connectedness ($b = .05, p \leq .05$). The other proxy asset variable, house value, had one significant effect on horizons ($b = .07, p \leq .01$). Effort was the only variable not related to either of the asset variables.

As alternative explanations, we turned first to the possibility that it is income rather than assets that affects attitudes and behaviors. Looking at standardized path coefficients (Table 6.2), two of the five effects of income on attitudes and behaviors were significant and positive: prudence ($b = .05, p \leq .05$) and horizons ($b = .05, p \leq .05$). Efficacy, connectedness, and effort were not significantly re-lated to income. Although there were some income effects, as anticipated, the income effects were overall not as prominent and strong as the savings effects (Table 6.2).

We considered next the possibility that attitudes and behaviors cause assets rather than vice versa. We estimated the effects of attitudes and behaviors on savings, house value, and income (Table 6.2). Four of the 10 effects relating to assets were significant: prudence had a significant positive effect on house value ($b = .05, p \leq .01$) but not on savings, efficacy had a significant positive effect on savings ($b = .05, p \leq .01$), connectedness had a significant positive effect on savings ($b = .04, p \leq .01$), and effort had a significant effect on house value ($b = .03, p \leq .05$). One relationship was significant in the opposite direction: effort had a significant negative effect on savings ($b = -.06, p \leq .01$). Overall, the effects of attitudes and behaviors on assets were in the predicted pattern, but quite modest.

Table 6.2

Standardized Path Coefficients for Changes in Attitudes, Behaviors, Assets, and Income at Time 1 (1968) on Attitudes, Behaviors, Assets, and Income at Time 2 (1972)

Variable	Prudence (1972)		Efficacy (1972)		Horizons (1972)		Connectedness (1972)		Effort (1972)		House Value (1972)		Savings (1972)		Income (1972)	
	b	t	b	t	b	t	b	t	b	t	b	t	b	t	b	t
Prudence (1968)	.37**	21.88	—		—		—		—		.05**	4.17	-.02	1.39	.04**	3.04
Efficacy (1968)	—		.35**	20.07	—		—		—		-.01	-.63	.05**	3.72	.03**	2.72
Horizons (1968)	—		—		.08**	4.43	—		—		.01	1.08	.02	1.00	.07**	5.26
Connectedness (1968)	—		—		—		.41**	23.70	—		-.02	-1.61	.04**	2.62	.01	.55
Effort (1968)	—		—		—		—		.33**	18.22	.03*	2.13	-.06**	-4.19	.00	-.17
House value (1968)	.04	1.75	.04	1.75	.07**	3.35	.03	1.35	.02	.71	.62**	40.48	.04*	2.07	.11**	7.60
Savings (1968)	.20**	10.17	.10**	4.72	.19**	9.13	.05*	2.32	-.01	-.49	.06**	4.09	.46**	24.75	-.02	-1.67
Income (1968)	.05*	2.09	.03	1.14	.05*	2.50	.00	.08	-.03	-1.28	.14**	9.24	.06**	2.97	.61**	40.32
R^2	.25**		.23**		.26**		.22**		.14**		.62**		.43**		.64**	

NOTES: All of the reported effects are after controlling for race, gender, age, education, and age of youngest child in the family unit. Estimates are computed using LISREL 8. $N = 2,871$.

SOURCE: Data are from Panel Study of Income Dynamics, heads of household in 1968 and 1972 (Survey Research Center, 1972a, 1972b).

$*p \leq .05. **p \leq .01.$

DISCUSSION

Although this test of asset effects is far from perfect, it does have two highly desirable features: it is longitudinal, and it simultaneously considers two alternative explanations. All of this occurs in a single statistical test. In this regard, the design of the analysis is as concise and elegant as one could hope. Seldom in social sciences research is there an opportunity for a simultaneous test of key competing theories. We are very fortunate indeed that a data set existed that made the test possible.

Results support some of the hypothesized effects. One of the asset variables—savings—has significant effects in the predicted direction on three of the attitude and behavioral variables. House value has a significant positive effect on prudence. Also, the savings and house value effects on attitudes and behaviors occur beyond the effects of income. In addition, because of the construction of the statistical tests across longitudinal data, savings at one point affect attitudes and behaviors at a second point. A similar conclusion can be drawn for the effect of house value on prudence.

In this study, savings stand out as being particularly important in possibly influencing attitudes and behaviors. These effects are consistent with Sherraden's (1991) broadly stated propositions that assets have a positive effect on expectations and confidence about the future; influence people to make specific plans with regard to work and family; induce more prudent and protective personal behaviors; and lead to more social connectedness with relatives, neighbors, and organizations. Clearly, much more work remains to be done in theoretically specifying and confirming these assets effects, but overall results suggest that the thinking is on the right track.

One of the dependent variables, effort, is unrelated to assets. The general proposition is that when people have assets, they put forth more effort in maintaining those and other assets. Although the home ownership and other literature largely supports this view, the current study does not. As an alternative proposition, perhaps when people have assets they tend to purchase services (home repair, car repair) and do not try as hard for human capital improvements (training for a new job, going back to school). This question is certainly fundamental to any consideration of asset-based social policy, and more studies are needed.

Looking at the first alternative explanation, the effects of income on attitudes and behaviors are not as strong as the effects of savings. This finding deserves considerable attention. Social policy in Western welfare states is dominated by the provision of income, either as "social insurance" or means-tested transfer. If savings provide equal or stronger effects on attitudes or behaviors—and at the same time, economic development of households—then perhaps more social policy should promote asset accumulation in this form.

In a test of the second alternative explanation—that attitudes and behaviors cause assets—we found that attitudes and behaviors do have some significant effects on asset accumulation. Thus, without overstating the strength of the findings, it appears that assets lead to more positive attitudes and behaviors, and the same attitudes and behaviors lead to more assets. This is perhaps an empirical glimpse of a "virtuous circle" in household development—assets lead to more positive attitudes and behaviors, which in turn lead to more assets, and so on.

Turning to research issues, these results, although not overwhelming, suggest that assets deserve as much attention as income in studies that relate economic status with psychological and social variables. Moreover, the traditional emphasis on studying economic status as an outcome of attitudes and behaviors should be expanded to include the reverse proposition: in this case, that assets positively affect certain attitudes and behaviors.

Considering the restricted five-year period used in this analysis, it is also possible that the observed effects could be different—either larger or nonexistent—over a longer period. Ideally, future longitudinal tests should incorporate a longer time frame (although absence of attitudinal and behavioral measures in the PSID since 1972 is a problem in this regard). Future studies should also include more robust measures of attitudes and behaviors. It would also be helpful if future research examined these questions through a variety of methods.

Regarding asset-based policy demonstrations, as of this writing Iowa has passed legislation for an individual development account demonstration over five years. Several small IDA projects are under way at local agencies around the country. Evaluation designs for most IDA experiments are to include social and psychological effects. President Clinton's proposal for an IDA demonstration also would require testing social and psychological effects. Given the results of this study, we conclude that the policy demonstrations are warranted.

REFERENCES

Andrisani, P. J. (1977). Internal–external attitudes, personal initiative, and the labor market experience of black and white men. *Journal of Human Resources, 12,* 308–328.

Andrisani, P. J. (1981). Internal–external attitudes, sense of efficacy, and labor market experience: A reply to Duncan and Morgan. *Journal of Human Resources, 16,* 658–666.

Bollen, K. A. (1989). *Structural equations with latent variables.* New York: John Wiley & Sons.

Domhoff, G. W. (1971). *The higher circles: The governing class in America.* New York: Vintage.

Duncan, G. J., & Hill, D. (1975). Attitudes, behavior, and economic outcomes: A structural equations approach. In G. J. Duncan & J. N. Morgan (Eds.), *Five thousand American families: Patterns of economic progress* (Vol. 3, pp. 61–113). Ann Arbor: University of Michigan, Institute for Social Research, Survey Research Center.

Duncan, G. J., & Morgan, J. N. (1981). Sense of efficacy and subsequent change in earnings—A replication. *Journal of Human Resources, 16,* 649–657.

Ehrlich, E. (1975). Involuntary disruptions of "life-cycle" plans. In G. J. Duncan & J. N. Morgan (Eds.), *Five thousand American families: Patterns of economic progress* (Vol. 3, pp. 189–219). Ann Arbor: University of Michigan, Institute for Social Research, Survey Research Center.

Haveman, R. H. (1988). *Starting even: An equal opportunity program to combat the nation's new poverty.* New York: Simon & Schuster.

Haveman, R. H. (1992). Review of M. Sherraden, *Assets and the Poor. Journal of Economic Literature, 30,* 1520–1521.

Hill, M. S. (1992). *The panel study of income dynamics: A user's guide.* Newbury Park, CA: Sage Publications.

Jöreskog, K., & Sörbom, D. (1989). *LISREL 7: User's reference guide.* Mooresville, IN: Scientific Software.

Jöreskog, K., & Sörbom, D. (1993). *LISREL 8: Structural equation modeling with the SIMPLIS command language.* Chicago: Scientific Software International.

Kohn, M., Naoi, A., Schoenbach, C., Schooler, C., & Slomczynski, K. (1990). Position in the class structure and psychological functioning in the United States, Japan, and Poland. *American Journal of Sociology, 95,* 964–1008.

Kolko, G. (1962). *Wealth and power in America.* New York: Praeger.

Mills, C. W. (1956). *The power elite.* New York: Oxford University Press.

Rudman, F. W. (1992). Cross-cultural correlates of the ownership of private property. *Social Science Research, 21*(1), 57–83.

Sawhill, I. V. (1989). The underclass: An overview. *Public Interest, 96,* 3–15.

Sherraden, M. (1990). Stakeholding: Notes toward a theory of welfare based on assets. *Social Service Review, 64,* 580–601.

Sherraden, M. (1991). *Assets and the poor: A new American welfare policy.* New York: M. E. Sharpe.

Survey Research Center. (1972a). *A Panel Study of Income Dynamics: Study design, procedures, available data, 1968–1972 interviewing years* (Vol. 1). Ann Arbor: University of Michigan, Institute for Social Research.

Survey Research Center. (1972b). *A Panel Study of Income Dynamics: Tape codes and indexes, 1968–1972 interviewing years* (Vol. 2). Ann Arbor: University of Michigan, Institute for Social Research.

Tobin, J. (1968). Raising the incomes of the poor. In K. Gordon (Ed.), *Agenda for the nation* (pp. 77–116). Washington, DC: Brookings Institution.

Vosler, N., & Page-Adams, D. (1993, February). *A study of economic resources and depression.* Paper presented at 39th Annual Program Meeting of the Council on Social Work Education, New York.

Yadama, G. N., & Pandey, S. (1995). Effect of sample size on goodness-of-fit indices in structural equation models. *Journal of Social Service Research, 20*(3–4), 49–70.

Analysis for this chapter was made possible by a faculty research grant of the George Warren Brown School of Social Work, Washington University, St. Louis. An earlier version of this chapter was presented at the Seventh International Conference of the Society for the Advancement of Socio-Economics, Washington, DC, April 1995. The authors thank David Gillespie, Deborah Page-Adams, Shanta Pandey, Robert Plotnick, and two anonymous reviewers for their helpful comments.

This chapter was originally published in the March 1996 issue of Social Work Research, *vol. 20, pp. 3–11.*

7 Problems and Prospects of Self-Employment as an Economic Independence Option for Welfare Recipients

Salome Raheim

As the welfare reform debate rages, it is important for social workers to participate fully in the debate by advocating programs and policies that will improve the material well-being of poor families. Social workers can provide effective leadership in changing social welfare policy only when they are informed about a wide range of policy and program options and their consequences. Self-employment development is among the policy options that merit attention.

Social policymakers have begun to explore self-employment development, also known as microenterprise, as a route off welfare, but the profession of social work has paid little attention to this economic independence option. With the passage of the Personal Responsibility and Work Opportunity Reconciliation Act of 1996 (P.L. 104-193), it is important for social workers to understand the benefits and the limits of self-employment development. With this knowledge, social workers can more effectively influence the shaping of welfare reform in the states.

SELF-EMPLOYMENT AND DISADVANTAGED GROUPS

Many people who are poor, unemployed, or socially marginal may pursue self-employment or informal sector activities because jobs are not available, not accessible, or not adequate in providing a living wage. For poor women, barriers such as the lack of child care and transportation, as well as little education and few job skills, further limit their employment opportunities (Hagen & Lurie, 1993; Miller, 1990). Although women must frequently deal with competing family and employment responsibilities, employment options for poor women rarely offer the ability to control their time to adequately handle the dual roles of parent and employee (Keeley, 1990; Raheim & Bolden, 1995).

For recent immigrant and refugee populations, other kinds of obstacles exist. Language and other cultural barriers may make mainstream employment inaccessible. Discrimination and labor market segregation often limit employment opportunities for immigrants and refugees, people of color, and women. For members of marginalized and oppressed groups, self-employment can provide a level of freedom and flexibility, as well as an option for earning a living wage, that the labor market may not provide (Keeley, 1990; Raheim & Bolden, 1995).

Unfortunately, the same factors that encourage members of marginalized groups to pursue self-employment may contribute to their economic marginalization as entrepreneurs (Brush, 1990; Keeley, 1990; Light, 1972). For some families, self-employment is their sole source of support. For others, income from informal sector activities is an important part of the family's total income package, which may include income from jobs or welfare benefits (Clark & Huston, 1993). A recent study by Spalter-Roth, Soto, and Zandniapour (1994) based on the 1984, 1986, 1987, and 1988 panels of the Survey of Income and Program Participation revealed that over 100,000 women were supporting their families through a combination of self-employment income and welfare benefits. In addition, almost 500,000 former welfare recipients were supporting themselves through self-employment.

BARRIERS TO SELF-EMPLOYMENT

Despite the number of low-income people engaged in self-employment activities, numerous barriers exist to starting and operating a viable business for people receiving public assistance. The primary obstacles are lack of business knowledge and skills, lack of access to capital and other resources, social welfare policy barriers, and psychosocial barriers.

Lack of Business Knowledge and Skills

The ability to start and operate a profitable business has been linked to business knowledge and skills, such as finance and marketing, as well as previous employment experience (Brush, 1990). When microentrepreneurs do not have the knowledge and skills needed to operate effectively and efficiently in the marketplace, their businesses may not generate sufficient income to support themselves and their families.

Microentrepreneurs from disadvantaged groups are less likely to have access to the information resources that would make such knowledge and skills available to them (Brush, 1990; Gould & Parzen, 1990; Keeley, 1990). Although business assistance is available through the U.S. Small Business Administration, this agency is not designed to assist individuals who do not have basic business knowledge (Office of Management and Budget, 1995).

Lack of Access to Capital and Other Resources

Lack of access to capital may be the biggest obstacle that people receiving public assistance encounter, limiting opportunities for business start-up and success. In the absence of supportive policies and programs, banks are reluctant to finance the business ventures of low-income people, who may have poor credit histories and no collateral. Furthermore, the size of the loans needed to finance many self-employment activities for low-income people is too small to be of interest to many banks. Without financing, starting a small business may be impossible. If start-up is possible, chronic undercapitalization may make a business vulnerable to failure or prolong the period needed to grow to a size that permits the business to be profitable (Brush, 1990; Drury, Walsh, & Strong, 1994).

Lack of capital also limits the types of businesses that can be created. Low-income entrepreneurs are often forced to establish labor-intensive businesses in the service sector rather than capital-intensive ventures such as wholesaling and manufacturing. If the service sector of the market becomes overcrowded (for example, more beauty salons or child care businesses than demand will support), prices are depressed, and microentrepreneurs must create sales volume to compensate for the low wages they receive for their services. Under these circumstances, it is a challenge for entrepreneurs to earn a living wage solely through their business income (Bates, 1993; Drury et al., 1994).

Although the primary consequence of undercapitalization and lack of access to business information, assistance, and networks may be low business income, an important secondary consequence is unavailability of health insurance. Many small businesses do not generate sufficient income to provide health and disability benefits for business owners and their employees. This lack of health coverage leaves these individuals without access to affordable health care and vulnerable to excessive health care costs in the event of a major illness. Unanticipated major medical expenses can easily bankrupt small business owners.

Social Welfare Policy Barriers

For microentrepreneurs who receive income support payments, there are unique problems. The policies of many income-support programs limit the income and assets recipients can have and remain eligible for benefits. For example, acquiring a business loan or equipment in excess of $1,000 would make a family ineligible for Aid to Families with Dependent Children (AFDC) (U.S. House of Representatives, 1994). Yet those same resources that have made the entrepreneur ineligible for benefits cannot be used to provide support for subsistence needs if the business is to have any possibility for survival and growth. For those receiving income support, pursuing self-employment to improve their material conditions can result in worsened financial circumstances.

Job Opportunity and Basic Skills Training (JOBS) programs in some states and localities do not recognize self-employment training as a legitimate type of basic skills training for AFDC recipients. Without the sanction of JOBS programs to pursue self-employment training, individuals are forced to enroll in other kinds of training to satisfy program requirements or risk losing benefits. Disregarding self-employment training as a legitimate form of self-sufficiency preparation limits both access to needed information resources and benefits that would help people pursue this option, such as child care and assistance with transportation. It also limits funding to self-employment development programs that serve low-income people.

Job Training Partnership Act (JTPA) (P.L. 97-300) policies create similar barriers. Self-employment was not included as a job option when JTPA policies were designed. Consequently, what are considered appropriate training, performance standards, and definitions of important program milestones, such as placement and successful termination of participants, are not well suited for self-employment development. Broadening the conceptualization of job preparation to include self-employment training and changing performance standards and other program definitions accordingly would remove some of the barriers created by current JTPA policy (Drury et al., 1994).

Restrictions on the use of program funds also minimize the JTPA's usefulness to low-income entrepreneurs. JTPA policy prohibits the use of program funds for capitalizing loan funds (Drury et al., 1994). This constraint eliminates a potential source of capital to start businesses for low-income entrepreneurs. Revising JTPA policy to permit the capitalization of loan funds would increase the sources of capital for participants attempting to create jobs for themselves through self-employment.

Psychosocial Barriers

In addition to structural obstacles to self-employment, the disempowering effects of poverty and being labeled "welfare dependent" often result in low self-esteem and lack of confidence for many people receiving public assistance (Alter, 1995). Consequently, many welfare recipients are unsure of their abilities to set and achieve goals. These factors can discourage pursuit of self-employment.

SELF-EMPLOYMENT DEVELOPMENT INITIATIVES

To lower the barriers to self-employment that welfare recipients and other disadvantaged groups face, self-employment development initiatives have been designed. Over the past 20 years, the merit of promoting self-employment or "informal sector" activities among poor people in developing countries has been recognized through U.S. Agency for International Development projects such as the PISCES, ARIES, and GEMINI (Ashe, 1985; Grindle, Mann, & Shipton, 1987) conducted in Africa, Asia, and Latin America, as well as through other studies conducted in various countries (Bromley & Gerry, 1979; Hart, 1973; International Labour Office, 1985; Mazumdar, 1976; Portes, Castells, & Benton, 1989; Thomas, 1992; World Bank, 1991). More recently, self-employment development has gained attention in industrialized countries. The United States, Great Britain, and France have each launched projects to encourage self-employment among disadvantaged groups (Balkin, 1989).

Self-Employment Investment Demonstration Program

In the United States, a variety of state and federal agencies have funded self-employment demonstrations, including the U.S. Department of Health and Human Services (1990, 1994), the U.S. Department of Housing and Urban Development (Aspen Systems Corporation, 1993), and the U.S. Department of Labor (Benus, Johnson, Wood, Grover, & Shen, 1995; Drury et al., 1994). Of particular significance to welfare recipients is the Self-Employment Investment Demonstration (SEID), a national demonstration project conducted in Iowa, Maryland, Michigan, Minnesota, and Mississippi.

SEID was designed to help people receiving public assistance start or expand small businesses by creating access to the knowledge, skills, and capital needed to start or continue economically viable self-employment activities and by removing social welfare policy barriers that hinder these efforts, including obtaining waivers to prevent reduction of participants' AFDC grants because of income and assets generated during their first year of business operation (Corporation for Enterprise Development, 1991; Guy, Doolittle, & Fink, 1991; Raheim & Alter, 1995).

The underlying philosophy of the SEID intervention model is that low-income people can learn to operate profitable businesses by building on skills and talents they already have (Clark & Huston, 1993). The model contains four basic elements: (1) group business training; (2) personal development workshops, including self-esteem training; (3) individual technical assistance; and (4) assistance with securing business financing.

Participants were recruited in cooperation with local welfare departments; some mailed program announcements with welfare checks. Participants self-selected into the program after attending informational meetings about the program and the demands of self-employment. SEID program operators provided training that culminated in participants writing their own business plans. After participants completed business plans, program staff helped them apply for loans from local banks or from the programs' revolving loan funds. Program staff provided individual technical assistance during training and after participants started their businesses (Corporation for Enterprise Development, 1991; for a detailed description of the intervention model, see Raheim, 1995).

Final evaluation of SEID included a cost analysis and a follow-up study with a random sample of 120 of the 408 participants who started businesses. Using telephone interviews, the study was designed to identify outcomes for participants who started businesses, including the nature and size of their businesses, changes in family circumstances, and changes in economic self-sufficiency (that is, ability to be self-supporting without AFDC) (Raheim & Alter, 1995). Process evaluation data were also collected through the midpoint of the demonstration (Corporation for Enterprise Development, 1991; Guy et al., 1991).

Self-Employment Learning Project

In addition to SEID and other microenterprise evaluations, valuable data on self-employment development with welfare recipients have been gathered through the Self-Employment Learning Project (SELP). SELP is a longitudinal study of seven U.S. microenterprise development organizations and the 405 entrepreneurs participating in their programs. All of these organizations target their services to economically disadvantaged communities, and three of them actively target welfare recipients to help them leave welfare through self-employment. To date, data are available from the first year of the five-year study (Clark & Kays, 1995).

LESSONS LEARNED FROM SELF-EMPLOYMENT DEVELOPMENT INITIATIVES

Findings from SEID (Corporation for Enterprise Development, 1991; Guy et al., 1991; Raheim & Alter, 1995), other microenterprise evaluations (Drury et al., 1994; Raheim & Yarbrough, 1995; Yarbrough, 1994), and SELP (Clark & Kays, 1995) provide important lessons about self-employment development with welfare recipients. Self-employment is a viable economic independence strategy for a small number of low-income and unemployed people. Of the 1,300 who enrolled in SEID, 408 started businesses during the demonstration. Fifty-two percent of the 120 business starters in the follow-up study left AFDC. Of the participants who continued to receive cash benefits, 32 percent were generating income from self-employment or jobs, and 22 percent no longer relied on AFDC as their primary source of income, demonstrating movement toward self-sufficiency (Raheim & Alter, 1995). Other research has shown that about 5 percent of people receiving welfare are likely to use self-employment as a way of improving their economic well-being (Spalter-Roth et al., 1994).

Self-employment development programs that provide a combination of business training, technical assistance, and assistance with obtaining financing have demonstrated success in facilitating the start and growth of small businesses among disadvantaged groups. Although women and people of color are underrepresented as business owners in the general population, both groups were well-represented among sample SEID and SELP business owners. Women were 82 percent of SEID and 78 percent of SELP entrepreneurs. People of color constituted 40 percent of SEID and 62 percent of SELP business owners (Clark & Kays, 1995; Corporation for Enterprise Development, 1991; Guy et al., 1991; Raheim & Alter, 1995).

Economic Benefits

Businesses begun through self-employment initiatives for low-income people have a higher survival rate than the national average. Seventy-nine percent of SEID businesses in the follow-up study were still operating and had been for 2.6 years on average (Raheim & Alter, 1995).

Self-employment programs for welfare recipients and other low-income people can increase access to capital through program loan funds and facilitation of relationships with commercial lending institutions. SEID programs loaned a total of $229,800 to businesses in the sample. The average loan amount was $5,605. Commercial banks loaned SEID businesses a total of $164,650, with an average amount of $9,685 (Raheim & Alter, 1995).

Businesses begun through self-employment initiatives for low-income people have economic development effects, creating jobs for people other than the owner. SEID businesses created 0.53 full- and part-time nonowner jobs per business (Raheim & Alter, 1995).

Self-employment development promotes asset accumulation. SEID business owners in the survey had a total of $1,261,182 in business assets and a total net worth of $584,032 (an average net worth of $4,867). In addition, these participants had accumulated a total of $1,048,541 (an average of $8,738) in personal assets subsequent to their enrollment in SEID (Raheim & Alter, 1995). A number of studies have shown that asset accumulation is positively related to family well-being (Cheng, 1995; Cheng, Page-Adams, & Sherraden, 1995; Green & White, 1994; Sherraden, 1991).

Social Benefits

Social development benefits (that is, increases in human capital) result from participation in self-employment development programs. SEID business owners in the follow-up study reported significant increases in their business knowledge and skills, their self-esteem, and their levels of confidence in their abilities to influence outcomes in their lives and their environment (Raheim & Alter, 1995).

Effects on Welfare

For individuals who voluntarily participate, self-employment programs may achieve better outcomes than traditional welfare-to-work strategies. In a state-level microenterprise program that followed SEID, participants spent significantly less time on welfare after enrollment than those in a matched comparison group of traditional welfare-to-work program participants (Raheim & Alter, in press). These findings do not suggest that self-employment development is a better intervention for all AFDC recipients. However, for those who would voluntarily enroll in such programs, self-employment may be a more effective intervention.

The cost of self-employment programs for welfare recipients is comparable to that of traditional welfare-to-work programs. Costs per participant in voluntary JOBS programs range from $2,019 to $17,981 (Gueron & Pauly, 1991). The average cost per SEID participant was $2,233, although the average cost per business start was $7,200. For self-employment programs, it is also appropriate to calculate cost per job created, which includes both business owners and the employees they hire. Estimates based on surviving SEID businesses in the follow-up study and their employees suggest that the average cost per job created was $5,435. When business owners are included in these calculations only if they are no longer supported by AFDC, the average costs rises to $6,969 (Raheim & Alter, 1995).

Many participants who complete self-employment programs but do not start their own businesses select other positive paths to economic self-sufficiency. Of those who had completed SEID by December 1990 but did not start a business, 34 percent selected other routes to self-sufficiency. Twenty-two percent acquired wage employment, and 12 percent pursued further education or training (Corporation for Enterprise Development, 1991).

A small percentage of welfare recipients who pursue self-employment may experience worsened economic conditions. Fewer than 10 percent of SEID business starters reported that their family income was worse than before enrolling in the program. In some cases, the new business placed a strain on household income. In others, participants incurred business debts (for example, loans) that they were unable to repay because of poor business performance or business failure. Individuals who pursue self-employment face greater financial risks than those who choose traditional welfare-to-work options.

POLICY CONSIDERATIONS

Self-selected participation appears to be a more effective and empowering strategy than attempts to target individuals based on beliefs about their potential for success. No correlations were found between business success and type of business (that is, service or retail) or a variety of participant characteristics, such as age, education, marital status, or number of children (Raheim & Alter, 1995).

Revising AFDC regulations to permit recipients to obtain income and asset waivers for one to two years during business start-up eliminated major obstacles to pursuing self-employment as a route off welfare. Most SEID business owners in the survey (79 percent) received waivers that prevented reduction of their AFDC grants because of their business income and assets during their first year of business operation. Sixty-nine percent of the participants with waivers said they could not have started their businesses without them (Raheim & Alter, 1995).

In addition to providing income security, waivers prevented the loss of other benefits while welfare recipients were in the early stages of starting a business. Medical assistance may be one of the most important benefits, protecting the family from potentially large financial losses due to health care costs.

ROLE OF SOCIAL WORKERS

Human services professionals can play an important role in enabling clients to pursue self-employment as a route off welfare. In a demonstration project that combined family development and self-employment training, family development specialists linked clients to business training resources and advocated with PROMISE JOBS for the inclusion of self-employment training as legitimate employment training. They also helped clients secure needed support services, such as child care, and address personal and family problems that could hinder successful business ownership (Raheim, 1995; Raheim & Yarbrough, 1995; Yarbrough, 1994). Currently, over 200 microenterprise development organizations exist that could support clients' self-employment efforts (Clark, Huston, & Meister, 1994).

DISCUSSION

The lessons learned from studies of microenterprise programs indicate that social welfare policy changes would increase the viability and availability of self-employment as a route off welfare. The two broad aims of such policy changes would be (1) to increase welfare recipients' access to business knowledge, skills, and capital and (2) to eliminate policies that discourage or prohibit them from pursuing self-employment. Unfortunately, the rhetoric of many welfare reform efforts frames the problem as a lack of individual responsibility rather than a lack of economic opportunity (for example, H.R. 4, the Personal Responsibility Act, vetoed by President Clinton).

In a conservative political climate, self-employment as a strategy for people to improve their material conditions is likely to find increasing support. When articulated in the context of individualist ideology, self-employment is consistent with the conservative agenda of making individuals solely responsible for their economic welfare. This ideological position asserts that the capitalist economy will provide the necessary opportunities for poor people to ensure their own economic well-being through individual effort, hard work, and ingenuity (Midgley, 1995).

However, this noninterventionist position does not recognize the need for government action to provide the resources that members of disadvantaged groups need to create economic opportunities for themselves. State block grant funding is a noninterventionist approach that could have devastating effects on the availability and viability of self-employment programs for welfare recipients.

Although some states have developed the necessary infrastructure and experience through federal demonstration projects to implement successful microenterprise programs for welfare recipients, others have not. Without federal funding and guidelines to encourage demonstration projects, some states may never develop the capacity to support self-employment as a route off welfare.

In contrast, some welfare reform proposals would strengthen microenterprise development for welfare recipients. President Clinton's Work and Responsibility Act (S. 2224, 1994) proposed the establishment of a minimum five-year microenterprise demonstration program to be jointly administered by the U.S. Department of Health and Human Services and the Small Business Administration. Local organizations would implement the demonstration programs, targeting AFDC and JOBS clients. A demonstration of this magnitude would have increased the resources available for self-employment development and increased states' capacities to support microenterprise development for welfare recipients.

Other supportive proposals have been aimed at eliminating existing policy obstacles. Both Representative Tony Hall's (D-OH) Microenterprise and Asset Development Act (H.R. 950, 1995) and Senator Tom Harkin's (D-IA) Welfare to Self-Sufficiency Act (S. 736, 1995) proposed to amend Title IV of the Social Security Act to eliminate barriers and disincentives to asset accumulation and self-employment income generation. These types of policy revisions, in concert with large-scale, federally funded self-employment demonstrations, such as the one President Clinton proposed, would significantly advance self-employment for welfare recipients.

CONCLUSION

Touting self-employment as an economic self-sufficiency or economic development strategy without including the supportive policies and programs needed to make this approach effective is a prescription for worsening the conditions of poor people. This development strategy alone will not result in the alleviation of poverty in the long run. Self-employment development cannot be implemented as a laissez-faire, individualist economic development policy and have any possibility of success.

A comprehensive approach to development is needed to address the needs of a region or a nation, and microenterprise development can play an important role in a comprehensive economic development plan. With an understanding of the problems and prospects of self-employment as a route out of poverty, social workers can advocate for welfare reform and economic development policies that will create greater economic opportunities for the populations they serve.

REFERENCES

Alter, C. (1995). *Family Development and Self-Sufficiency Program: Final report.* Iowa City, IA: Institute for Social and Economic Development.

Ashe, J. (1985). *The PISCES II experience: Local efforts in micro-enterprise development* (Vol. 1). Washington, DC: U.S. Agency for International Development.

Aspen Systems Corporation. (1993). *Creating economic lift: Jobs, training, and business opportunities in public and Indian housing.* Rockville, MD: U.S. Department of Housing and Urban
Development.

Balkin, S. (1989). *Self-employment for low-income people.* New York: Praeger.

Bates, T. (1993). *Banking on black enterprise.* Washington, DC: Joint Center for Political and
Economic Studies.

Benus, J. M., Johnson, T. R, Wood, M., Grover, N., & Shen, T. (1995). *Self-employment programs: A
new reemployment strategy: Final report on the UI Self-Employment Demonstration* (Unemployment Insurance Occasional Paper 95-4). Washington, DC: U.S. Department of Labor,
Employment and Training Administration, Unemployment Insurance Service.

Bromley, R., & Gerry, C. (Eds.). (1979). *Casual work and poverty in third world cities.* New York:
John Wiley & Sons.

Brush, C. G. (1990). Women and enterprise creation: Barriers and opportunities. In *Local
initiatives for job creation: Enterprising women* (pp. 37–55). Paris: Organization for Economic
Cooperation and Development.

Cheng, L. (1995, April). *Asset holding and intergenerational poverty vulnerability in female-headed
families.* Paper presented at the Seventh International Conference of the Society for the
Advancement of Socio-Economics, Washington, DC.

Cheng, L., Page-Adams, D., & Sherraden, M. (1995, April). *The role of cognition in mediating effects
of asset accumulation.* Paper presented at the Seventh International Conference of the Society
for the Advancement of Socio-Economics, Washington, DC.

Clark, P., & Huston, T. (1993). *Assisting the smallest business: Assisting microenterprise development
as a strategy for boosting poor communities* (Interim report). Washington, DC: Aspen Institute
for Humanistic Studies, Self-Employment Learning Project.

Clark, P., Huston, T., & Meister, B. (1994). *1994 directory of microenterprise programs.* Washington,
DC: Aspen Institute for Humanistic Studies, Self-Employment Learning Project.

Clark, P., & Kays, A. J. (1995). *Enabling entrepreneurship: Microenterprise development in the United
States* (Baseline year report of the Self-Employment Learning Project). Washington, DC:
Aspen Institute for Humanistic Studies, Self-Employment Learning Project.

Corporation for Enterprise Development. (1991). *Interim lessons from the Self-Employment
Investment Demonstration: Executive summary.* Washington, DC: Author.

Drury, D., Walsh, S., & Strong, M. (1994). *Evaluation of the EDWAA Job Creation Demonstration.*
Washington, DC: U.S. Department of Labor, Employment and Training Administration.

Gould, S. K., & Parzen, J. (1990). Recommendations, conclusions, and plans for action. In *Local
initiatives for job creation: Enterprising women* (pp. 85–99). Paris: Organization for Economic
Cooperation and Development.

Green, R. K., & White, M. J. (1994). *Measuring the benefits of homeowning: Effects on children.* Ann
Arbor: University of Michigan, Department of Economics.

Grindle, M. S., Mann, C. K., & Shipton, P. M. (1987). *ARIES (Assistance to Resource Institutions for
Enterprise Support): Capacity building for resource institutions for small and micro-enterprises—A
strategic overview paper* (Prepared by the Harvard Institute for International Development for
the Office of Rural and Institutional Development, Bureau for Science and Technology, and
Office of Private and Voluntary Cooperation, Bureau of Food for Peace and Voluntary
Assistance, U.S. Agency for International Development). Washington, DC: U.S. Agency for
International Development.

Gueron, J. M., & Pauly, E. (1991). *From welfare to work.* New York: Russell Sage Foundation.

Guy, C., Doolittle, F., & Fink, B. L. (1991). *Self-employment for welfare recipients: Implementation of
the SEID program.* New York: Manpower Demonstration Research Corporation.

Hagen, J. L., & Lurie, I. (1993). The Job Opportunities and Basic Skills training program and
child care: Initial state development. *Social Service Review, 67,* 199–216.

Hart, K. (1973). Informal income opportunities and urban employment in Ghana. *Journal of
Modern African Studies, 11*(1), 61–89.

International Labour Office. (1985). *Informal sector in Africa.* Geneva: Author.

Job Training Partnership Act, P.L. 97-300, 96 Stat. 1322 (1982).

Keeley, K. (1990). The role of intermediaries in strengthening women's business expansion activities. In *Local initiatives for job creation: Enterprising women* (pp. 75–84). Paris: Organization for Economic Cooperation and Development.

Light, I. (1972). *Ethnic enterprise in America: Business and welfare among Chinese, Japanese, and blacks.* Berkeley: University of California Press.

Mazumdar, D. (1976). The informal sector. *World Development, 4,* 665–679.

Microenterprise and Asset Development Act, H.R. 950, 104th Cong., 1st Sess. (1995).

Midgley, J. (1995). *Social development: The developmental perspective in social welfare.* London: Sage Publications.

Miller, D. C. (1990). *Women and social welfare: A feminist analysis.* New York: Praeger.

Office of Management and Budget. (1995). *Catalogue of federal assistance programs.* Washington, DC: U.S. Government Printing Office.

Personal Responsibility and Work Opportunity Reconciliation Act of 1996, P.L. 104-193.

Portes, A., Castells, M., & Benton, L. (Eds.). (1989). *The informal economy: Studies in advanced and less developed countries.* Baltimore: Johns Hopkins University Press.

Raheim, S. (1995). Self-employment training and family development: An integrated strategy for family empowerment. In K. Nelson & P. Adams (Eds.), *Reinventing human services* (pp. 127–143). Hawthorne, NY: Aldine de Gruyter.

Raheim, S., & Alter, C. F. (1995). *The Self-Employment Demonstration final evaluation report: Part 1. Participant survey.* Washington, DC: Corporation for Enterprise Development.

Raheim, S., & Alter, C. F. (in press). Self-employment as a social and economic development intervention for recipients of AFDC. *Journal of Community Practice.*

Raheim, S., & Bolden, J. (1995). Economic empowerment of low-income women through self-employment. *Affilia, 10,* 138–154.

Raheim, S., & Yarbrough, D. (1995). *Family/Self-Employment Training (FAST): Final evaluation report.* Washington, DC: U.S. Department of Health and Human Services, Administration for Children and Families, Office of Community Services.

Sherraden, M. (1991). *Assets for the poor: A new American welfare.* Armonk, NY: M. E. Sharpe.

Spalter-Roth, R., Soto, E., & Zandniapour, L. (1994). *Micro-enterprise and women: The viability of self-employment as a strategy for alleviating poverty.* Washington, DC: Institute for Women's Policy Research.

Thomas, R. (Ed.). (1992). *Education's role in national development plans: Ten country cases.* New York: Praeger.

U. S. Department of Health and Human Services, Administration for Children and Families, Office of Community Services. (1994). *Demonstration Partnership Program: Summaries and findings, FY 1990 Demonstration Partnership Program projects.* Washington, DC: U.S. Government Printing Office.

U. S. Department of Health and Human Services, Family Support Administration, Office of Community Services. (1990). *Demonstration Partnership Program: Summaries and findings, FY 1987 Demonstration Partnership Program projects.* Washington, DC: U.S. Government Printing Office.

U.S. House of Representatives, Committee on Ways and Means. (1994). *1994 green book.* Washington, DC: U.S. Government Printing Office.

Welfare to Self-Sufficiency Act, S. 736, 104th Cong., 1st Sess. (1995).

Work and Responsibility Act, S. 2224, 103rd Cong., 2nd Sess. (1994).

World Bank. (1991). *World development report 1991: The challenge of development.* New York: Oxford University Press.

Yarbrough, D. (1994). Process and outcomes of the Small Enterprise and Family Development Project. In U.S. Department of Health and Human Services, Administration for Children and Families, Office of Community Services (Ed.), *Demonstration Partnership Program: Summaries and findings FY 1993* (pp. 20–37). Washington, DC: U.S. Department of Health and Human Services.

This chapter was originally published in the January 1997 issue of Social Work, *vol. 42, pp. 44–53.*

8 Role of Latina-Owned Beauty Parlors in a Latino Community

Melvin Delgado

The United States is currently struggling with how to best address persistent poverty and the high rates of social problems associated with its existence in urban centers (Hoechstetter, 1996; Jennings, 1994). Moore and Pinderhughes (1993) characterized the debate on the underclass as "who is responsible for the condition of the poor—the individual or society? Is persistent poverty caused by behavioral pathology or the economic structure?" (p. xii). The answers to these questions have profound implications for the development of strategies to eliminate persistent poverty. Unfortunately, the debate has taken a deficit perspective toward communities (Saleebey, 1992, 1996) and has ignored community assets in the search for revitalization strategies (Kretzmann & McKnight, 1993; McKnight & Kretzmann, 1991).

A focus on community social problems has a long historical record in the United States (Halpern, 1995):

> The neighborhood has long been an important locus for efforts to address the causes and consequences of poverty in American society. Over the course of the past century neighborhood-based initiatives have been called on to reduce class conflict, counter feelings of anger and alienation, localize control of institutions, create jobs and reverse neighborhood decline, and address a variety of specific poverty-related problems. (p. 1)

Thus, the revitalization of neighborhoods presents many challenges for social work and other professions in helping to promote policies and services that address the needs of communities in a manner that meaningfully involves their populations in the decision-making process.

Much attention has been paid to the high-risk environment of inner-city children and their families (Kozol, 1995) and the need for government (local, state, and federal) and the private sector to collaborate to create positive change at the community level (Perez & Martinez, 1993). Any efforts to revitalize these communities must enhance local assets. This chapter examines the nature and extent of persistent poverty among one population of color—the Latino population. A case study of Latina-owned beauty parlors in a large New England city illustrates the multifaceted role Latino businesses can play in the social–economic network of the community. Implications for social work practice in Latino communities are presented.

LITERATURE REVIEW

Poverty

There are an estimated 22 million Latinos in the United States (Castex, 1994). The median income for Latino families is $23,884, compared to $39,239 for non-Latino white families (Institute for Puerto Rican Policy, 1993). All Latino groups have incomes below the national median (Holmes, 1996); Puerto Rican families have the lowest income of any group ($20,654), followed by Mexican families ($23,018). Cuban families have the highest median income of any Latino group ($30,095). Puerto Rican families have the highest percentage of people living below the poverty rate (39.4 percent), followed by Mexican families (29.5 percent), Central or South American families (24.6 percent), other Latino families (20.6 percent), and Cuban families (18.0 percent). These rates are in sharp contrast with the poverty rate of 9.4 percent for non-Latino white families (Institute for Puerto Rican Policy, 1993).

However, despite the high concentration of poverty among most Latino subgroups, they have not received sufficient national attention. Enchautegui (1994) identified five reasons for this inattention: (1) misperceived identity, (2) lack of widespread attention to the working-poor population, (3) geographical concentration, (4) lack of political participation, and (5) differences among Latino subgroups. The interplay among these factors has resulted in Latinos being considered "invisible" in national policy.

The literature on Latino poverty can be categorized into three schools of thought (Borges-Mendez, 1993; Enchautegui, 1994; Hurtado, 1995; Institute for Puerto Rican Policy, 1996; Melendez, 1993; Moore & Pinderhughes, 1993; Morales & Bonilla, 1993; Perez & Cruz, 1994; Perez & Martinez, 1993; Segura, 1992; Torres, 1995): (1) Poverty is the result of an interplay between immigrant status and rapid demographic changes (high rates of female-headed households and fertility); (2) Latinos are an "underclass" (low formal educational achievement and lack of or inconsistent employment history); and (3) a lack of market-attractive skills exclude Latinos from high-wage jobs. Morales and Bonilla (1993), in their analysis of the economic forces of the 1980s, raised serious concerns about the limited economic opportunities for Latinos and other people of color:

> White family incomes and net worth rose, even as these indicators fell among African Americans and Latinos. . . . The resources available to individuals narrowly defined their ability to improve and invest in communities, thereby reinforcing spatial demarcations in the spread of economic social inequality. . . . Members [Latinos] of this large and expanding segment of society are having to come to terms with the possibility that they may never reach parity with the average American without concerted efforts to change their circumstances that must involve the nation as a whole. (pp. 1–2)

Their summary of results from a series of studies on the economic status of Latinos noted "economic structuring has been critical in increasing poverty in Latino communities. But the emphasis is on the complexity of economic restructuring rather than on the construction of the manufacturing sector alone. . . . New Latino immigrants [can] help to revitalize and stabilize impoverished Latino communities" (p. xxxvii).

Melendez (1993) focused on the local level:

> Notwithstanding the difficulties involved in dissecting the causes of poverty
> for Latinos in Massachusetts, it is of foremost importance that. . .from a policy
> perspective, we need to know whether human-capital strategies or industrial
> policies are more likely to have a positive impact on the labor-market standing
> for Latinos, and whether social policies targeting support services for families
> will have a stronger impact than economic development or labor-market inter-
> ventions. (p. 25)

Osterman's (1989) profile of the poor population in Boston noted,

> Who is poor in Boston? . . . The short answer is that Boston poverty has de-
> creased since 1980; and that the substantial poverty which remains in 1989 is a
> phenomenon of women, single parents, families, minorities, and the disabled. .
> . . Further, by adding any of these factors together, poverty rates (percentage of
> a group that is poor) grow even higher. For instance, if you consider the group
> with the highest poverty rate in Boston—Hispanics—and the family structure
> with the highest poverty—single parents—you get a startling result: eight out
> of ten Hispanic single parents are poor. And nearly three-quarters of Hispanic
> children are growing up in poverty. (p. 9)

Ethnic Small Businesses

The social work profession has largely ignored the presence and role of small
businesses in the life of communities of color. This lack of attention may be the
result of an interplay among several factors: a general lack of attention given to
ethnic businesses in professional education; a pervasive feeling that ethnic businesses, like their white counterparts, are capitalistic in nature, and thus should
be avoided; and a lack of knowledge of how these establishments can work
with social workers to reach underserved groups. However, despite these views,
ethnic businesses can play critical roles in the life of a community (Halter, 1995).
Delgado (1996), in a study of Puerto Rican grocery stores and restaurants, identified eight key roles these institutions can play in the life of the community that
extend beyond the selling of food: (1) providing credit; (2) cashing checks (many
Latino communities do not have automatic teller machines); (3) providing community-related news and information; (4) providing information from the homeland; (5) counseling customers in distress; (6) providing information about and
referral to social services agencies; (7) assisting in filling out or interpreting government forms; and (8) providing cultural connectedness to the homeland
through the selling of videotapes, publications, and so forth.

The development of ethnic businesses necessitates the allocation of resources
beyond obtaining start-up capital. According to Waldinger, Aldrich, and Ward
(1990), owners of ethnic businesses confront at least seven major challenges in
establishing a business: (1) obtaining the information about establishing a business, (2) acquiring start-up and operational capital, (3) obtaining the skills and
knowledge to operate a business, (4) recruiting and supervising employees, (5)
relating to customers and suppliers, (6) surviving business competition, and (7)
withstanding political attacks. As a result, an ethnic business represents a ba-
rometer of the extent to which a community can or is willing to support "its

own." Thus, any neighborhood revitalization strategy must actively promote the development and support of small businesses (Halpern, 1995; Levitt, 1993; Melendez, 1993).

Latino Small Businesses

Latino small businesses can play an influential role in the community that goes beyond that usually associated with a commercial establishment (Sarason & Koberg, 1994). According to Levitt (1995), owners of Latino commercial establishments are motivated by more than economic motives; they are also motivated by a sense of "social responsibility" that translates into providing culturally appropriate help for those customers in need, including financial assistance, counseling or advice, and information on formal and informal resources for help. Consequently, Latino businesses can take on the role of nontraditional social services centers.

Delgado and Humm-Delgado (1982) identified a number of Latino merchant establishments in their analysis of Latino natural support systems and noted that these establishments were attractive to Latinos because they were owned, operated, staffed, and controlled by those in the community. Owners often lived in the community and fulfilled leadership roles. The authors, however, did not mention gender-based natural supports such as beauty parlors. These institutions, with few exceptions, cater to women and are an excellent source for outreach to Latinas. Delgado (in press b) referred to these institutions as "nontraditional settings."

Nontraditional settings are an indigenous source of support and are a place where individuals can gather to purchase a product or service or congregate for social purposes. These settings can facilitate conversation and the exchange of concerns and advice, minimizing the stigma for those seeking assistance. Exchange of advice and assistance is mutual; these settings are generally staffed by individuals who share the same ethnic, socioeconomic, and other key factors such as gender and religion as the patrons (maximizing psychological, geographical, and cultural access) and have a primary role that incorporates being a "helper."

Latina Beauty Parlors

The professional literature has not examined beauty parlors as economic settings and sources of support for Latinas and other women of color (Delgado, in press a). The popular press has reported on a number of beauty parlors where concerted efforts have been made to reach women in distress, with or without support from social services agencies. However, a systematic study of the role of and services provided by these establishments, their motivation for helping, characteristics of owners, and experiences in helping women with personal problems has not been reported in the popular press or the literature.

METHOD

Questions

This study asked the following questions to guide social services organizations in their quest to better serve the Latino community in the United States: Who are Latina beauty parlor owners and their customers? What are the operational characteristics of typical beauty parlors? What prompted the Latina owners to help customers? What kinds of social services are provided?

Procedure

In spring 1996, a small-scale survey of Latina beauty parlors was conducted in the city of Lawrence, Massachusetts. Lawrence is located about 35 miles north of Boston and has the highest concentration of Latinos in the state. The total population is about 72,000, of which 29,000 are Latino (41.6 percent). The Latino community is almost equally divided between Dominicans and Puerto Ricans (Gaston Institute, 1992, 1994).

This study built on an earlier one conducted in Holyoke and Lawrence (Delgado, in press a). The initial study involved four beauty parlors (two in each city) and six botanical shops (five of which were located in Lawrence). In that study, geographical sections in each city were selected, and all Latino-owned establishments (for profit and not for profit) were identified and interviewed. The Lawrence study reported in this chapter was done in a different geographical area of the city selected because of its high concentration of Latino-oriented establishments. A local Latino community-based agency (Centro Panamericano) cosponsored the research. This agency was selected because of its reputation in the community and previous collaboration with the author.

The study involved a two-stage process. The initial stage required locating and listing all of the beauty parlors within a geographical area. The second phase involved an interviewer (Latina staff member) visiting the establishments and conducting an in-person interview with the owners. The interviews lasted about 50 minutes.

Survey Instrument

The survey instrument consisted of four sections and 32 open-ended questions. Data were obtained on the following topics: development of a business and customer profile, identification of social services provided, identification of customer needs, and owner willingness to collaborate with agencies in delivery of services. Unfortunately, the instrument obtained only minimal information about such topics as financing the start of a business, revenue, and expenditures. (All of the beauty parlor owners received financial support for business development from their families.)

FINDINGS

Latina-owned beauty parlors attracted a client base that was far broader than just adult Latinas (Table 8.1). Surprisingly, all of the beauty parlors served men, with two establishments serving an equal number of men and women. All of the beauty parlors served a wide range of ages, reaching children, adults, and elderly people.

All but two of the beauty parlors had been in existence less than five years (Table 8.2). Hours of operation were fairly similar among the establishments. Days of operation only differed on whether or not the parlor was open on Mondays or Tuesdays, with most open six days per week.

Table 8.1

Characteristics of Clients of Latina-Owned Beauty Parlors

Beauty Parlor	Racial/Ethnic Composition (%)			Gender (%)		Age Range (Years)
	Latino	White	African American	Female	Male	
A	80	10	10	80	20	5–80
B	90	5	5	50	50	6–70
C	85	10	5	50	50	10–50
D	90	5	5	60	40	13–65
E	75	10	15	90	10	5–70
F	80	5	15	55	45	7–80
G	90	5	5	85	15	6–75

The beauty parlors fulfilled a multifaceted role in the community (Table 8.3). The Latina owners expressed willingness to involve themselves in leadership roles on social agency boards, advisory committees, task forces, and so forth. None of the owners, however, had ever been approached by local social services agencies to engage in collaborative projects. All of the owners indicated a willingness to collaborate with local human services agencies in an effort to help the community in a variety of social services areas, most notably alcoholism and family violence. The women, with few exceptions, recognized the impact of social problems on the customers and their families. Some of the beauty parlors, however, were willing to collaborate only in particular activities; only two were willing to collaborate in all activities mentioned in the survey.

Lazzari, Ford, and Haughey's (1996) research on Latinas identified as being leaders in the community found that these women possessed a belief in themselves, were willing to accept the responsibility that goes with leadership, and

Table 8.2

Beauty Parlor Organizational Characteristics

Beauty Parlor	Year Opened	Hours of Operation	Days of Operation
A	1994	7 hours Tuesday through Thursday 10 hours Friday and Saturday	Tuesday through Saturday
B	1986	8 hours Tuesday through Thursday 10 hours Friday and Saturday	Tuesday through Saturday
C	1989	8 hours Monday 9 hours Tuesday through Thursday 10 hours Friday and Saturday	Monday through Saturday
D	1991	8 hours Tuesday through Thursday 10.5 hours Friday and Saturday	Monday through Saturday
E	1995	9 hours	Monday through Saturday
F	1994	8 hours Monday through Thursday 11 hours Friday and Saturday	Monday through Saturday
G	1996	9 hours	Monday through Saturday

Table 8.3

Activities Provided by Latina-Owned Beauty Parlors and Social Services Collaborative Possibilities

Beauty Parlor	Willingness to Participate in Leadership Role	Approached by Social Agency to Collaborate	Willingness to Collaborate	Distribute Pamplets	Distribute Videotapes	Hold Lectures or Discussions	Provide Counseling or Advice	Provide Information or Referrals
A	Yes	No	Yes	Yes	No	Yes	Yes	No
B	Yes	No	Yes	Yes	No	No	No	No
C	Yes	No	Yes	Yes	No	Yes	Yes	Yes
D	Yes	No	Yes	Yes	No	No	Yes	No
E	Yes	No	Yes	Yes	Yes	Yes	Yes	Yes
F	Yes	No	Yes	Yes	No	No	No	No
G	Yes	No	Yes	Yes	Yes	Yes	Yes	Yes

viewed their work as a "duty" to the community: "Factors that supported and sustained the women in their extensive amount of community involvement included seeing the need, feeling personal satisfaction, receiving support from others, and having personal beliefs and characteristics" (p. 201). Quotes from this study's beauty parlor owners (translated from Spanish) touched on the factors identified by Lazzari et al.: "I cannot stand by and watch my community suffer," "A job well done entails not just making the customer more attractive physically but also emotionally," "Simply put, I could not have succeeded without the support of my family, friends, and customers," "Being a part of the community requires more than operating a business; it requires caring about what goes on beyond the walls of my beauty parlor."

DISCUSSION AND IMPLICATIONS FOR PRACTICE

This study highlights the important role Latina-owned beauty parlors can play in the community. The high number of beauty parlors established during a recession period in the state reflected a strong resiliency base within the community. These settings attracted a diverse client base, thus having the potential to reach a wide sector of the community. Community revitalization efforts, as a result, must incorporate these and other small businesses in their work.

Latino small businesses have a ready-built market that can be expected to continue to expand. This trend, in combination with increasing residential segregation, will increase the influence these institutions can wield in the community.

The results also highlight the need for policy development to encourage small business development. Waldinger, Aldrich, Bradford, et al. (1990) suggested that policies that encourage development of ethnic businesses must be twofold: "building an infrastructure that fosters small business development in general and enacting and enforcing systemic policies of equal economic opportunity for ethnic and racial minorities" (p. 197). These suggestions can take the form of social services organizations sponsoring workshops for small business development, contracting with small businesses for goods and services whenever possible, and facilitating the provision of consultation for owners. Latino small businesses can be organized into coalitions to increase their visibility, advocacy, purchase of supplies, and so forth. In turn, owners are an excellent community resource to be tapped for agency boards, advisory committees, task forces, and commissions.

Latino small businesses can provide access to services for disempowered groups in their role as urban sanctuaries (residents can patronize a business without fear of being rejected because of their ethnic or racial background), as providers of culture-specific items and services, and as providers of information related to the homeland. Their accessibility to the community (geographical, psychological, cultural, and logistical) makes these institutions excellent settings for collaboration with social services organizations (Delgado, 1995a, 1995b). Beauty parlors and other small businesses can help distribute public education information (in Spanish), make referrals, perform crisis intervention, help interpret correspondence for non-English-speaking clients, and fulfill other important roles. However, these establishments should not be expected to engage in all possible collaborative activities.

Although many of these establishments are willing to collaborate if asked, unfortunately, few have been provided with this opportunity. Approaching these establishments should be viewed developmentally. Collaboration will be labor intensive and require a great deal of patience and follow-through on the part of social services organizations (Delgado, 1994). Nevertheless, such efforts will prove rewarding for the profession, the initiating social service agency, and the Latino community (De La Rosa, 1988).

CONCLUSION

Neighborhood revitalization will be an elusive goal if indigenous assets are not a part of the strategy. Latinos, like other people of color, have endured tremendous hardships in the United States. Small businesses have historically played and continue to play an influential role within ethnic communities. This role extends far beyond the selling of a product or a service for profit.

Only now has the social work profession, probably more so than any other helping profession, taken a serious look at Latino businesses as a community resource. Latina-owned beauty parlors take on greater significance because they address the needs of an undervalued subgroup. The social needs of Latinas are addressed within a cultural context that both respects and appreciates their struggles in society. These settings have women providing services in an affirming and nonstigmatizing manner. However, for those business owners who are willing to help, endless possibilities exist for primary, secondary, and tertiary intervention projects.

REFERENCES

Borges-Mendez, R. (1993). The use of Latino immigrant labor in Massachusetts manufacturing: Evidence from Lowell, Lawrence, and Holyoke. In E. Melendez & M. Uriate (Eds.), *Latino poverty and economic development in Massachusetts* (pp. 104–124). Boston: University of Massachusetts, Mauricio Gaston Institute for Latino Community Development and Public Policy.

Castex, G. M. (1994). Providing services to Hispanic/Latino populations. *Social Work, 39,* 288–296.

De La Rosa, M. (1988). Natural support systems of Hispanic Americans: A key dimension of well-being. *Health & Social Work, 13,* 181–190.

Delgado, M. (1994). Hispanic natural support systems and the alcohol and drug abuse field: A developmental framework for collaboration. *Journal of Multicultural Social Work, 3,* 11–17.

Delgado, M. (1995a). Hispanic natural support systems and the AOD field: Issues and challenges. *Alcoholism Treatment Quarterly, 12,* 17–32.

Delgado, M. (1995b). Puerto Rican elders and natural support systems: Implications for human services. *Journal of Gerontological Social Work, 24,* 115–130.

Delgado, M. (1996). Puerto Rican food establishments as social service organizations: Results of an asset assessment. *Journal of Community Practice, 3,* 57–77.

Delgado, M. (in press a). Latina-owned businesses: Community resources for the prevention field. *Journal of Primary Prevention.*

Delgado, M. (in press b). *Social work practice in non-traditional urban settings.* New York: Oxford University Press.

Delgado, M., & Humm-Delgado, D. (1982). Natural support systems: Source of strength in Hispanic communities. *Social Work, 27,* 83–89.

Enchautegui, M. (1994). *Latino neighborhood and Latino neighborhood poverty.* Washington, DC: Urban Institute.

Gaston Institute. (1992). *Latinos in Lawrence.* Boston: University of Massachusetts.

Gaston Institute. (1994). *Latinos in Lawrence: Poverty, income, education, employment and housing.* Boston: University of Massachusetts.

Halpern R. (1995). *Rebuilding the inner city: A history of neighborhood initiatives to address poverty in the United States.* New York: Columbia University Press.

Halter, M. (Ed.). (1995). *New migrants in the marketplace: Boston's ethnic entrepreneurs.* Boston: University of Massachusetts Press.

Hoechstetter, S. (1996). Taking new directions to improve public policy [Editorial]. *Social Work, 41,* 343–346.

Holmes, S. A. (1996, October 13). For Hispanic poor, no silver lining. *New York Times,* p. E5.

Hurtado, A. (1995). Variations, combinations, and evolutions: Latino families in the United States. In R. E. Zambrana (Ed.), *Understanding Latino families: Scholarship, policy, and practice* (pp. 40–81). Thousand Oaks, CA: Sage Publications.

Institute for Puerto Rican Policy. (1993). *Puerto Ricans and other Latinos in the United States: March 1992* (Datanote). New York: Author.

Institute for Puerto Rican Policy. (1996). *The status of Puerto Rican children in the U.S.* (Datanote). New York: Author.

Jennings, J. (1994). *Understanding the nature of poverty in urban America.* Philadelphia: Temple University Press.

Kozol, J. (1995). *Amazing grace: The lives of children and the conscience of a nation.* New York: Crown.

Kretzmann, J. P., & McKnight, J. L. (1993). *Building communities from the inside out.* Evanston, IL: Northwestern University, Center for Urban and Policy Research.

Lazzari, M. M., Ford, H. R., & Haughey, K. J. (1996). Making a difference: Women of action in the community. *Social Work, 41,* 197–205.

Levitt, P. (1993). The social aspects of small-business development: The case of Puerto Rican and Dominican entrepreneurs in Boston. In E. Melendez & M. Uriate (Eds.), *Latino poverty and economic development in Massachusetts* (pp. 143–158). Boston: University of Massachusetts, Mauricio Gaston Institute for Latino Community Development and Public Policy.

Levitt, P. (1995). A todos les llamo primo (I call everyone cousin): The social basis for Latino businesses. In M. Halter (Ed.), *New immigrants in the marketplace: Boston's ethnic entrepreneurs* (pp. 120–140). Boston: University of Massachusetts Press.

McKnight, J. L., & Kreztmann, J. P. (1991). *Mapping community capacity.* Evanston, IL: Northwestern University, Center for Urban and Policy Research.

Melendez, E. (1993). Latino poverty and economic development in Massachusetts. In E. Melendez & M. Uriate (Eds.), *Latino poverty and economic development in Massachusetts* (pp. 15–27). Boston: University of Massachusetts, Mauricio Gaston Institute for Latino Community Development and Public Policy.

Moore, J., & Pinderhughes, R. (1993). Introduction. In J. Moore & R. Pinderhughes (Eds.), *In the barrios: Latinos and the underclass debate* (pp. xi–xxxix). New York: Russell Sage Foundation.

Morales, R., & Bonilla, F. (1993). Restructuring and the new inequality. In R. Morales & F. Bonilla (Eds.), *Latinos in a changing U.S. economy: Comparative perspectives on growing inequality* (pp. 1–27). Newbury Park, CA: Sage Publications.

Osterman, P. (1989). *In the midst of plenty: A profile of Boston and its poor.* Boston: Boston Foundation, Persistent Poverty Project.

Perez, S. M., & Cruz, S. (1994). *Speaking out loud: Conversations with young Puerto Rican men.* Washington, DC: National Council of La Raza.

Perez, S. M., & Martinez, D. (1993). *State of Hispanic America: Toward a Latino anti-poverty agenda.* Washington, DC: National Council of La Raza.

Saleebey, D. S. (Ed.). (1992). *The strengths perspective in social work practice.* New York: Longman.

Saleebey, D. S. (1996). The strengths perspective in social work practice: Extensions and cautions. *Social Work, 41,* 296–305.

Sarason, Y., & Koberg, C. (1994). Hispanic women small business owners. *Hispanic Journal of Behavioral Sciences, 16,* 355–360.

Segura, D. (1992). Walking on eggshells: Chicanas in the labor force. In S. B. Knouse, P. Rosenfeld, & A. L. Cubertson (Eds.), *Hispanics in the work force* (pp. 173–193). Newbury Park, CA: Sage Publications.

Torres, A. (1995). *Between melting pot and mosaic: African Americans and Puerto Ricans in the New York political economy.* Philadelphia: Temple University Press.

Waldinger, R., Aldrich, H., Bradford, W. D., Boissevain, W. D., Chen, G., Korte, H., Ward, R., & Wilson, P. (1990). Conclusions and policy implications. In R. Waldinger, H. Aldrich, & R. Ward (Eds.), *Ethnic entrepreneurs: Immigrant business in industrial societies* (pp. 177–197). Newbury Park, CA: Sage Publications.

Waldinger, R., Aldrich, H., & Ward, R. (1990). Opportunities, group characteristics, and strategies. In R. Waldinger, H. Aldrich, & R. Ward (Eds.), *Ethnic entrepreneurs: Immigrant business in industrial societies* (pp. 13–48). Newbury Park, CA: Sage Publications.

This chapter was originally published in the September 1997 issue of Social Work, *vol. 42, pp. 445–453.*

Part III

COMMUNITY ACTION
THROUGH COLLABORATIONS

9 Nonprofit Organizations and Innovation: A Model of Neighborhood-Based Collaboration to Prevent Child Maltreatment

Elizabeth A. Mulroy and Sharon Shay

Federal policymakers are limiting public investment in community development to specific geographic neighborhoods and are seeking innovative, locally derived solutions. President Bill Clinton's national urban policy report, *Empowerment: A New Covenant with America's Communities*, articulates an approach to link poor families in distressed communities to opportunities in the wider metropolitan region. One principle on which the strategy is based is "locally driven, emphasizing solutions that are locally crafted and implemented by entrepreneurial public entities, private actors, and the growing network of community-based organizations" (U.S. Department of Housing and Urban Development, 1995, p. 2).

However, shifting forces in the political economy have changed sector relations in profound ways, and these changes affect the organizational behavior of local actors. To achieve the goal of community strengthening through local cooperation, social work practitioners must understand how to implement an interorganizational collaboration in a low-opportunity, urban neighborhood during a time of scarce resources.

Public authorities contract with nonprofit organizations (NPOs) in part because they anticipate that NPOs will produce innovative solutions to vexing social problems. However, until very recently scholars in social welfare have generally ignored how the voluntary sector has responded to this challenge, preferring instead to study the welfare state (Ostrander, 1987; Perri 6, 1993). This chapter presents a theoretical and conceptual framework for understanding how NPOs have used collaboration to achieve neighborhood development goals. An example is given of a study of the prevention of child maltreatment. Implications for social policy, social work practice, and social work research are discussed.

LITERATURE REVIEW

Entrepreneurial Leadership and Innovation

In a rapidly changing world, a dynamic brand of human services management is required that not only keeps pace with change, but stays ahead of it (Edwards, Cooke, & Reid, 1996). Young (1991) suggested that this brand of leadership is "entrepreneurial." *Entrepreneurial leadership* is a process of putting new ideas into practice—of bringing together and catalyzing people, financial resources, organizational arrangements, and technologies—necessary to implement a new concept. "The entrepreneurial leader takes an idea, or an 'invention,' off the drawing board and into practice, thereby achieving innovation" (p. 62).

Although assumptions exist that a new practice method should be implemented typically from an "expert" passing on information or instructions or that a new policy should be implemented with top-down knowledge emanating from the apex of the organization (Smale, 1993), entrepreneurial leadership and innovation are not found solely in executive management. For example, in the United Kingdom innovations are transferred through partnerships in which participants create and share information—where communication is a two-way process of convergence and not a one-way linear act (Rogers cited in Smale, 1993).

Partnerships in community-based practice can include a wide range of residents and representatives from local organizations who come together in shared decision making based on a recognition of who can offer what to the resolution of a social problem. Part of the innovation is the professional shift from working with client-centered "patients" to working in partnership with local residents and organizations to solve social problems in which "clients" are a part (Smale, 1993).

Theories of Innovation

Theorist Perri 6 (1993) contended that *innovation* is the introduction of changes in the production of goods and services—an overall sequence of change over time represented as invention → innovation → diffusion. "*Invention* is the discovery of new knowledge or the development of new information: a concept, a theory, or a hypothesis" (p. 398). Invention has its own sequence: pure research → applied research → model development. *Innovation* is the application of that new knowledge to the production of goods and services, which involves recognizing both production and marketing possibilities. *Diffusion* is the adoption of that innovation by other producers of similar goods and services. There are three types of innovation: (1) *product innovation* introduces new goods or services, (2) *process innovation* introduces new ways to produce goods or services, and (3) *organizational innovation* introduces restructuring within an agency or externally to allow a merger or collaboration with other organizations. "Innovating nonprofit organizations may be responding to a wide variety of variables and incentives. They may be maximizing subsidies from funders that use innovation policies (see Kramer, 1981), or they may be maximizing their budgets (see Niskanen, 1971) or their output (see Schiff & Weisbrod, 1991)" (p. 404).

New Systems of Care

Policymakers are charging local actors with the design of new systems of care. Examples of innovative service integration and continua of care have been developed in both the public and nonprofit sectors (Alter, 1990; Glisson & James, 1992; Gulati & Guest, 1990; Hadley, 1993; Wallis, 1994). An innovative system of care as conceived by Richman, Brown, and Venkatesh (1996) would achieve coherence and legitimacy by offering both breadth and depth; *breadth* refers to universally provided services that do not exclude or stigmatize anyone, and *depth* is achieved by tiering services, using diverse agency types to target populations at risk, such as youth offenders, teenage mothers, or low-birthweight infants.

Coulton (1996) cautioned that in designing new systems to support children and families who live in concentrated poverty, it is imperative to plan for both families and communities. Delgado (1996), Becerra and Iglehart (1995), and Gutierrez (1992) pointed out that the field of human services is slowly shifting its approach to undervalued communities through the use of a community assets and strengths perspective. However, Halpern (1993) contended that there are limitations to a neighborhood initiative approach: "[the] neighborhood initiative has to be supported in the context of an understanding that poor, isolated neighborhoods cannot be transformed, nor the life chances of their residents significantly improved, by focusing reform just within the neighborhood itself" (p. 132).

Uneven Local Capacity

The capacity of a community-based NPO to serve as a community builder is affected by an organization's geographic location and by conditions in its external environment. For example, community development is facilitated where there is community social organization—that is, where there are "patterns and functions of formal and informal networks, institutions, and organizations in a locale" (Coulton, 1996, p. 98). Yet there is national geographic unevenness in local capacity to deliver social services, because the nonprofit sector is differentially developed. In a six-city study, Wolch (1990) found local variations based on the basic characteristics of urban economies; government and charity; and the behavioral responses of local market, state, charitable, and voluntary institutions to contextual changes imposed from the outside. The outcome of these interactions and interdependencies provoked uneven patterns of development into voluntary-sector-rich and voluntary-sector-poor locales.

INNOVATION IN THE PREVENTION OF CHILD MALTREATMENT

Background

Selected NPOs received a federal demonstration grant to develop a model to prevent child abuse and neglect in a low-income neighborhood of a city in the Northeast. The funders expected innovation in the project that would redirect child maltreatment services from large-scale public bureaucracies under scrutiny for failing to adequately protect children to community-based, prevention-oriented approaches (Advisory Board on Child Abuse and Neglect, 1991). The project developed a complex neighborhood service network of complementary programs that are described elsewhere (Mulroy, 1997).

The example considered here was institutionalized into its target neighborhood during the five-year grant period, and an adapted model was replicated in two other poverty neighborhoods. All sites continue to serve their respective constituencies two years after the demonstration project ended.

The Invention: Ecological Theory

The sponsoring agency had a mission and purpose theoretically grounded in the ecological approach to the prevention of child abuse and neglect. The etiology of child maltreatment involves a multiplicity of factors that combine to create role malfunction and pathological adaptation by caregiver and child (Belsky, 1980). Risk factors are manifold; some are attributes of the child or parent, and others point to the broader family context or the social–cultural environment. Although many aspects of parents and families have been studied, most could be placed in a model that associates child maltreatment with family stress, particularly among young or single parents living in impoverished conditions and in contexts that do not provide adequate social support and guidance from other adults (National Committee for Injury Prevention & Control, 1989; Sack, Mason, & Higgins, 1985; Schloesser, Pierpont, & Poertner, 1992). The ecological model advanced by Bronfenbrenner (1979) and adapted as a framework to study child maltreatment (Belsky, 1980; Garbarino & Kostelny, 1992; Garbarino & Sherman, 1980) encompasses these multiple levels of risk. Project sponsors also were influenced by studies that identified a systemic institutional failure in the fragmented public child welfare system—studies that called for preventive services delivered comprehensively by a team of professionals who work as a single unit (Helfer, 1987; Newberger & Newberger, 1982).

The Innovation: Multifocused Practice

The project's mission and purpose were based on empirical evidence that community-level interventions can be the most appropriate way to ameliorate child maltreatment in situations of urban poverty and social decay. An urban community where risk factors for child maltreatment were clustered was selected as the targeted geographic area. The project attempted to enhance protective risk factors and modify the influences that place children at risk.

A model was developed that focused on families and communities simultaneously (Coulton, 1996; Shay, 1995). A prevention model was developed for each ecological level surrounding families, a modification of Bronfenbrenner's ecological framework for child development (Figure 9.1). Using nested concentric circles, Bronfenbrenner defined levels of influence that affect individuals. The immediate and most powerful setting, the family, is embedded in and interacts with institutional systems such as a neighborhood, school, workplace, or church. These institutions are, in turn, contained in a broader cultural context that limits and shapes what occurs in the inner circles. Ecological theory assumes a progressive mutual adaptation of organism and environment and recognizes the interdependence of systems and the importance of social context.

Next, community-level change strategies were articulated. The inner circle surrounding families includes informal support from natural helping networks of friends and neighbors brought together through family cooperatives—centers for support and exchange for neighborhood families. The middle circle

Figure 9.1

Conceptual Framework of Neighborhood-Based Child Abuse Prevention

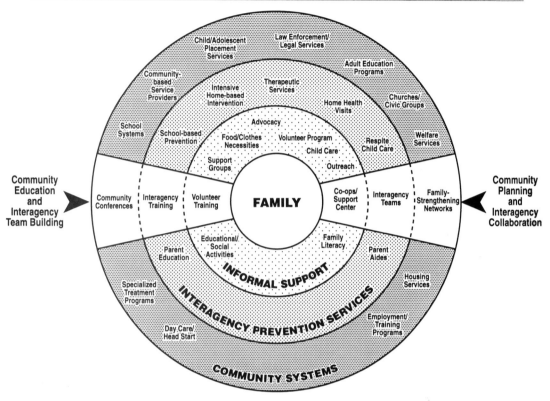

Source: Shay, S. (1995). *Building the twenty-first century ark: The CARES Model for comprehensive family support* (Final report to the National Center on Child Abuse and Neglect, Grant No. 90-CA-1417). Washington, DC: U.S. Government Printing Office.

represents interagency prevention services—the project's more formally organized programs that proactively target families in situations or events that increase risk to children. The outer circle represents community systems outside the project's service network with which resident consumers interact, such as law enforcement, public schools, and welfare services.

Finally, model development was influenced by a transformational shift in project leadership that resulted in an identification with low-income residents as partners rather than as clients. Many residents were involved with the public child welfare system as clients or foster parents. A commitment to empowerment (Solomon, 1976) and to a community asset approach (Delgado, 1996; Kretzmann & McKnight, 1993; Shiffman & Motley, 1990) followed. This paradigm shift in professional orientation was compatible with ecological theory, and its application is reflected in the overlay of community education, planning, and collaboration as a means of achieving empowerment goals in every concentric circle in the model. Thus, the preventive intervention had a multipronged strategy: collaboration, advocacy, resource development, education, and services (CARES—the project's name, identity, and purpose).

The overlays depict two streams of actions. First, community planning was intended to link the network across systems to coordinate and thereby strengthen the formal and informal support programs in the project's own network and also to integrate it into the existing and emerging citywide health and family support consortia and coalitions. Second, the education overlay was intended to disseminate knowledge of the CARES model to involved residents through participation; to program staff through cross-training; and to the health and human services community and the general public through annual communitywide conferences, reports, and media stories.

This framework depicts several basic assumptions that underlie the project. Strengthening families and neighborhoods is a long-term goal, and multisector cooperation is needed. Parents' capacity to nurture their children is enhanced by reducing their social isolation and strengthening informal and formal family support systems. Vertical dimensions (that is, external economic, political, and social linkages) and horizontal dimensions (that is, local groups and resources) exist that influence service access and implementation; complex interactions exist among diverse institutional entities.

System Components

A new system of care emerged that had three components: (1) a steering committee of seven partner agency executive directors and resident members, (2) a network of service programs, and (3) an administrative infrastructure that included the project director and a small staff (Figure 9.2). This configuration depicts multiple nodes of collaborative action and a nonhierarchical structure (Alter & Hage, 1993) in which all participants have equal status.

In addition, the collaboration was facilitated by the interpersonal skills of agency executive directors, project director and staff, and team-oriented frontline practitioners. All exhibited skills in shifting roles and flexibly adapting to the different tasks required as the model evolved. Committee members were sensitive to timing—when one should assume a lead role or a supporting role— which maximized use of their respective management talents with minimum ego involvement.

Steering Committee. The steering committee addressed matters of governance, membership, and policy. Members included a small, nonprofit statewide child advocacy agency that was a chapter of the National Committee for the Prevention of Child Abuse; the central office of a community-based federation of settlement houses in the target area; a neighborhood settlement house and host site for program operations; a neighborhood health center; a large, traditional family services organization with a metropolitan focus and downtown headquarters; a community-based settlement house selected as the network's first replication site; a community-based settlement house selected as the second replication site; and five highly involved consumer members.

Perri 6 (1993) posited that when interorganizational collaboration is sought, agencies must engage in organizational innovation. This innovation requires a

Figure 9.2

Interorganizational Collaboration to Prevent Child Abuse: A Neighborhood Network

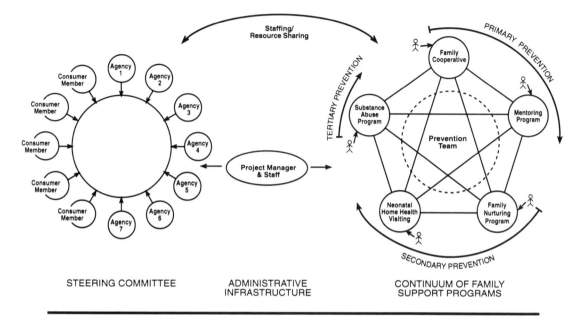

STEERING COMMITTEE   ADMINISTRATIVE INFRASTRUCTURE   CONTINUUM OF FAMILY SUPPORT PROGRAMS

readjustment of an agency's external boundaries—that is, the way it relates to other organizations. Each agency on the steering committee adjusted its own external organizational relationships to participate in the project. For example, the sponsoring agency narrowed its external relations from a statewide scope to one bounded geographic area in the state's largest city. The federation, the co-sponsoring entity, adjusted its external relations by agreeing to share turf with two non-community-based agencies. As the physical site of three of the network's programs, the host site settlement house shared space, resources, identity, and power. The large family services organization narrowed its external relations to the geographic target area. This external organizational innovation facilitated new structural relationships among participating agencies that resulted in a collaborative forum. All agencies were intended equal partners regardless of size, budget, service technology, location, professional status, or role.

Member agencies had clear roles, but not all agencies provided services. The service agencies generated funded positions for specific programs, and some had multiple funding streams. This set-up leveraged each agency's investment because it could share resources and in effect "own" the whole program without having total financial obligation for it. A different agency served as fiscal agent for each program to streamline monitoring and reporting functions for complex financial arrangements, and the sponsoring agency served as fiscal agent for the project itself.

Service Network. Figure 9.2 depicts the service programs as a continuum of primary-, secondary-, and tertiary-level preventive interventions linked in an integrated network. The network received its breadth from the primary, informal family support programs of the family cooperative and the mentoring program, which were advocated by resident consumers who sought nonstigmatizing resources available to all. The network received its depth from the secondary, more formalized home health visiting program for pregnant women and their newborns and the family nurturing program, and from the tertiary and intensive home-based substance abuse program.

Each program was staffed by an interdisciplinary, interagency team of professionals and paraprofessionals who worked cooperatively to implement goals. These frontline workers served as family advocates for residents with systems external to the project's service network. Service coordination and integration were facilitated by an interprogram prevention team of representatives from each network program. The model affirms as realistic the proposal by Richman et al. (1996) that responsive service systems should possess both breadth and depth through the participation of multiple agency types.

Administrative Infrastructure. A full-time project director and staff engaged in organization building to empower all network participants. They developed and maintained an overarching organizational structure, served as the communications center, monitored project implementation, and designed and coordinated the community planning and educational aspects of the preventive intervention. Project management reached out laterally to build, coordinate, and broker relationships and to balance power on the steering committee and in the service network. The project manager and staff articulated the vision of what participants wanted the project to achieve and the consensus about the model as it evolved and disseminated the theory and philosophy of the innovation to multiple and diverse audiences.

Planned Diffusion

Project leadership planned for knowledge diffusion by adding to the steering committee the two executive directors of the agencies responsible for replicating the network in the project's final phase of institutionalization. Participation in governance, long-term planning, and decision making during the network's implementation phase prepared them with knowledge of the innovation and entrepreneurial skills needed to adapt the innovation in their respective neighborhoods.

DISCUSSION

These processes support Perri 6's (1993) theory of innovation as a sequence of change over time from invention to innovation to diffusion. Characteristics of entrepreneurial leadership (Young, 1991) were key to interpreting the invention to a wide audience and to bringing together and catalyzing people, financial resources, organizational arrangements, and technologies that permitted implementation and diffusion of the new concept. The ecological framework resulted in application of a multifocused practice that considered families and communities simultaneously, an approach that has implications for social policy, social work practice, and social work research.

Implications for Social Policy

Funding. Public funding for the CARES administrative infrastructure, which was central to organizational development and local capacity building in the original model and funded by the demonstration grant, disappeared with the federal grant. Most subsequent funding streams excluded administrative costs. Yet diffusion of a successful innovation requires a commitment to longer-term flexible funding. Otherwise, local-serving organizations cannot institutionalize successful programs, and low-opportunity neighborhoods continue to be repositories of repeated demonstration grants that alone are unlikely to achieve long-term outcomes.

Implications for Social Work Practice

Innovation Knowledge. Community-based interorganizational collaboration requires human services practitioners to work across multiple systems simultaneously, yet most are not trained conceptually or substantively to do this. First, practitioners must know the invention and innovation. For Project CARES, sponsors framed the issue of child maltreatment broadly and comprehensively. Knowledge of ecological theories situated the intervention compatibly in the community context, with a multifocused practice on families and communities (Coulton, 1996). Values implicit in the empowerment approach guided the evolution of a new care system that included a breadth and depth appropriate to resident needs and expressed desires as well as partner agencies' capacity to provide.

Second, interorganizational collaboration occurs at both the managerial and operations levels and involves entrepreneurial skills of risk taking and strategic judgment (Young, 1991). The CARES project was initiated at the management level and sustained when managers knew how frontline successes benefited their respective agencies. The lateral flow of information among the steering committee, project management, and frontline programs helped to transfer the innovation in a two-way process of communication.

Teamwork. A critical dimension of collaboration is teamwork and its need for cooperative behavior. In this case, practitioners learned about team development and acquired skills in consensus decision making, shared leadership, and giving and receiving feedback.

Community Assets. New systems of care need to formulate an ecological perspective that includes assessment and utilization of local community assets (Delgado, 1996). Local participants in the CARES collaboration were highly flexible in responding to their external environments and adaptable in coping with complex needs and circumstances of residents. Moreover, the area was a voluntary-sector-rich locale, confirming Wolch's (1990) findings that benefits accrue when resources are targeted to an area with local institutional capacity for flexibility and innovation.

This finding has implications for the trend by government to decentralize and privatize formerly public social services. For example, some states are soliciting for-profit and nonprofit contractors to develop "first-to-work" training programs for welfare recipients in targeted areas to implement the recently passed Temporary Assistance to Needy Families Block Grant. Practitioners involved in such initiatives need to assess and use existing local institutions in the targeted geographic area and cooperate with colleagues employed there to build on family and community development initiatives already under way.

Implications for Social Work Research

Community-Oriented Research. The evaluation of complex community-based interventions involving interorganizational collaboration requires sustained field observation and multiple methods of applied, community-oriented research. O'Connor (1995) and Weiss (1995) argued that the evaluation of complex neighborhood initiatives requires methods that are both quantitative and qualitative, contextual and theory based. A theory-based evaluation of Project CARES, for example, would identify theories of change, that is, the evaluation would detail all theories, identifying all assumptions built into the program. Data collection and analysis would track the unfolding of assumptions. "Tracking the microstages of effects as they evolve makes it more plausible that the results are due to program activities and not to outside events or artifacts of the evaluation, and that the results generalize to other programs of the same type" (Weiss, 1995, pp. 72–73).

Organizations involved in creating innovations seek usable knowledge to assess interim outcomes. Empowerment evaluation (Fetterman, Kaftarian, & Wandersman, 1996) and utilization-focused evaluation (Quinn Patton, 1997) show promise, with their focus on organizational learning, alternative ways of knowing, and utility for serving multiple audiences.

Effects of Privatization. More research is needed that examines the contracting relationship between government and NPOs that has heightened concern about nonprofit autonomy (Ostrander, 1987; Smith & Lipsky, 1993; Wolch, 1990). Most service NPOs rely on government support for more than half of their revenues (Smith & Lipsky, 1993). This dependency is a potential problem for neighborhood-based initiatives in which the locus of management decisions should rest at the community level. Wolch (1990) suggested that community-based agencies may not be able to remain autonomous when targets of change are likely public agencies that are also existing or potential funders. Fiscal resource dependencies that push NPOs toward entrepreneurial behavior and collaboration may create conditions under which competition undermines cooperative behavior (Alter & Hage, 1993; Mulroy, 1997). Further research is needed to help untangle these perplexing issues.

REFERENCES

Advisory Board on Child Abuse and Neglect. (1991). *Creating caring communities: Blueprint for an effective federal policy on child abuse and neglect* (Second Report). Washington, DC: U.S. Department of Health and Human Services.

Alter, C. (1990). An exploratory study of conflict and coordination in interorganizational service delivery systems. *Academy of Management Journal, 33*, 478–501.

Alter, C., & Hage, J. (1993). *Organizations working together.* Newbury Park, CA: Sage Publications.

Becerra, R. M., & Iglehart, A. P. (1995). *Social services and the ethnic community.* Boston: Allyn & Bacon.

Belsky, J. (1980). Child maltreatment: An ecological integration. *American Psychologist, 35,* 320–335.

Bronfenbrenner, U. (1979). *The ecology of human development.* Cambridge, MA: Harvard University Press.

Coulton, C. (1996). Effects of neighborhood on families and children: Implications for services. In A. Kahn & S. Kamerman (Eds.), *Children and their families in big cities* (pp. 87–110). New York: Columbia University, Cross-National Studies Research Program.

Delgado, M. (1996). Community asset assessments by Latino youths. *Social Work in Education, 18,* 169–178.

Edwards, R. L., Cooke, P., & Reid, P. N. (1996). Social work management in an era of diminishing federal responsibility. *Social Work, 41,* 468–480.

Fetterman, D., Kaftarian, S., & Wandersman, A. (1996). *Empowerment evaluation.* Thousand Oaks, CA: Sage Publications.

Garbarino, J., & Kostelny, K. (1992). Child maltreatment as a community problem. *Child Abuse and Neglect, 16,* 455–464.

Garbarino, J., & Sherman, D. (1980). High-risk neighborhoods and high-risk families: The human ecology of child maltreatment. *Child Development, 51,* 188–198.

Glisson, C., & James, L. (1992). The interorganizational coordination of services to children in state custody. *Administration in Social Work, 16*(3/4), 65–80.

Gulati, P., & Guest, G. (1990). The community-centered model: A garden variety approach or a radical transformation of community practice? *Social Work, 35,* 63–68.

Gutierrez, L. M. (1992). Empowering ethnic minorities in the twenty-first century: The role of human service organizations. In Y. Hasenfeld (Ed.), *Human services as complex organizations* (pp. 330–338). Newbury Park, CA: Sage Publications.

Hadley, R. (1993). Decentralization, integration, and the search for responsive human services. In E. E. Martinez-Brawley & S. M. Delevan (Eds.), *Transferring technology in the personal social services* (pp. 31–49). Washington, DC: NASW Press.

Halpern, R. (1993). Neighborhood-based initiative to address poverty: Lessons from experience. *Journal of Sociology and Social Welfare, 20,* 111–135.

Helfer, R. (1987). Commentary: Back to the future. *Child Abuse and Neglect, 11,* 13–14.

Kramer, R. (1981). *Voluntary agencies in the welfare state.* Berkeley: University of California Press.

Kretzmann, J., & McKnight, J. (1993). *Building communities from the inside out.* Evanston, IL: Northwestern University, Center for Urban Affairs and Policy Research, Neighborhood Innovations Network.

Mulroy, E. (1997). Building a neighborhood network: Interorganizational collaboration to prevent child abuse and neglect. *Social Work, 42,* 255–264.

National Committee for Injury Prevention & Control. (1989). Child abuse. *Injury Prevention: Meeting the Challenge* [Suppl. *American Journal of Preventive Medicine*], *5,* 213–222.

Newberger, C., & Newberger, E. (1982). Prevention of child abuse: Theory, myth, and practice. *Journal of Preventive Psychiatry, 1,* 443–451.

Niskanen, W. A. (1971). *Bureaucracy and representative government.* Chicago: Aldine-Atherton.

O'Connor, A. (1995). Evaluating comprehensive initiatives: A view from history. In J. P. O'Connell, A. C. Kubisch, L. B. Schorr, & C. H. Weiss (Eds.), *New approaches to evaluating community initiatives* (pp. 23–63). Washington, DC: Aspen Institute.

Ostrander, S. (1987). Elite domination in private social agencies. In W. Domhoff & W. Dye (Eds.), *Power elites and organizations* (pp. 85–102). Thousand Oaks, CA: Sage Publications.

Perri 6. (1993). Innovation by nonprofit organizations: Policy and research issues. *Nonprofit Management and Leadership, 3,* 397–414.

Quinn Patton, M. (1997). *Utilization-focused evaluation: The new century text* (3rd ed.). Thousand Oaks, CA: Sage Publications.

Richman, H., Brown, P., & Venkatesh, S. (1996). The community base for new service delivery strategies. In A. Kahn & S. Kamerman (Eds.), *Children and their families in big cities* (pp. 151–162). New York: Columbia University, Cross-National Studies Research Program.

Sack, W. H., Mason, R., & Higgins, J. (1985). The single-parent family and abusive child punishment. *American Journal of Orthopsychiatry, 55,* 252–259.

Schiff, J., & Weisbrod, B. (1991). Competition between for-profit and nonprofit organizations in commercial markets. *Annals of Public and Cooperative Economics, 62,* 619–640.

Schloesser, P., Pierpont, J., & Poertner, J. (1992). Active surveillance of child abuse fatalities. *Child Abuse and Neglect, 16,* 3–10.

Shay, S. (1995). *Building the twenty-first century ark: The CARES Model for comprehensive family support* (Final report to the National Center on Child Abuse and Neglect, Grant No. 90-CA-1417). Washington, DC: U.S. Government Printing Office.

Shiffman, R., & Motley, S. (1990). *Comprehensive and integrative planning for community development.* New York: Community Development Research Center, New School for Social Research.

Smale, G. G. (1993). The nature of innovation and community-based practice. In E. E. Martinez-Brawley & S. M. Delevan (Eds.), *Transferring technology in the personal social services* (pp. 14–26). Washington, DC: NASW Press.

Smith, S., & Lipsky, M. (1993). *Nonprofits for hire: The welfare state in the age of contracting.* Cambridge, MA: Harvard University Press.

Solomon, B. B. (1976). *Black empowerment: Social work in oppressed communities.* New York: Columbia University Press.

U.S. Department of Housing and Urban Development, Office of Policy Development and Research. (1995, October). *Recent research results.* Washington, DC: Author.

Wallis, A. (1994, October). *Value barriers to coordination in human service networks.* Paper presented at a meeting of the Association for Research on Nonprofit Organizations and Voluntary Action, Berkeley, CA.

Weiss, C. (1995). Nothing as practical as good theory: Exploring theory-based evaluation for comprehensive community initiatives for children and families. In J. Connell, A. Kubisch, L. Schorr, & C. Weiss (Eds.), *New approaches to evaluating community initiatives* (pp. 65–92). Washington, DC: Aspen Institute.

Wolch, J. (1990). *The shadow state.* New York: Foundation Center.

Young, D. R. (1991). Providing entrepreneurial leadership. In R. L. Edwards & J. A. Yankey (Eds.), *Skills for effective human services management* (pp. 62–75). Washington, DC: NASW Press.

Research for this chapter was supported by the Nonprofit Sector Research Fund, Aspen Institute, Grant No. 92-NSRF-23.

This chapter was originally published in the September 1997 issue of Social Work, *vol. 42, pp. 515–524.*

10 Strengthening Neighborhoods by Developing Community Networks

John D. Morrison, Joy Howard, Casey Johnson,
Francisco J. Navarro, Beth Plachetka, and Tony Bell

Many urban neighborhoods are in trouble, as are the youths and families who reside in them. Most vulnerable are neighborhoods affected by high levels of poverty and racial segregation (Massey & Denton, 1993). Changes in employment patterns such as the decline in manufacturing jobs, increasing suburbanization, globalization of jobs, and racial discrimination in hiring have undermined already frail economies (Wilson, 1996). The result has been the unraveling of social ties and community life.

Many lament the perceived loss of a sense of community in local neighborhoods. This loss is often characterized by too little communication and too much isolation (Kotlowitz, 1991). Striking is the continuing decrease in interaction among families, which works against community building and mutual problem solving. In addition, the poorest urban communities have become isolated (Wilson, 1996); although many impoverished neighborhoods are located near more affluent areas, the people in the poor communities may be socially isolated from the larger mainstream society. Further, these neighborhoods may have low levels of social control over their immediate environment, including the influences that adversely affect their children.

Frequently, families and children receive limited support in coping with the stress of everyday life in a modern, complex society. Consequently, neighborhoods and sometimes families are disorganized and unable to deal with the issues they face. This disorganization has a deleterious affect on young people. Often youths experience what Lerner (1995) called "rotten outcomes," in which children's potential is not realized. Moreover, these weak community structures overshadow opportunities for the optimum development of youths, thus facilitating the survival of gangs and the presence of drug abuse, early pregnancy, and school failure. Spergel (1995) believed that "social disorganization" allows gang activity to thrive and that community mobilization is important to reducing the conditions that allow gangs to develop.

Social organization—"the sharing of behavior and outlook in a community," which depends on "the group's isolation from the broader society [and] the material assets and resources they control" (Wilson, 1996, p. 66)—also affects the role of culture.

> Neighborhoods that feature higher levels of social organization—that is, neighborhoods that integrate adults by means of an extensive set of obligations,

> expectations, and social networks—are in a better position to control and super-
> vise the activities and behavior of children. Youngsters know they will be held
> accountable for their individual and group action; at the same time, they know
> they can rely on neighborhood adults for support and guidance. (pp. 61–62)

Similarly, Ianni (1989) discussed the importance of clear community standards, expectations, and structure in supporting children. Coleman and Hoffer (1987) argued that social capital (relationship and organizational skills) is as important as human capital (education and job skills). All suggested the importance of clear expectations, caring and support, and opportunities for participation in fostering youth development (Benard, 1992).

Services often are too poorly designed to meet the needs of youths and families from low-income, multicultural communities (Specht & Courtney, 1994) and do too little to contribute to building an overall neighborhood structure. Services and funding are fragmented, which minimizes efforts to build supports. Few incentives are in place that would reduce this fragmentation and encourage co-ordination. Community members or recipients of services may not be valued or involved in planning processes, which are often centralized and expert driven. As a consequence, existing service arrangements have not always fostered com-munity development or empowerment. Specialization, narrowly focused fund-ing streams, and agency competition for scarce resources have meant that tradi-tional services are not always assessable, affordable, appropriate, or comprehensive. There also has been an overemphasis on individual remediation and treatment and an underemphasis on prevention and development.

Needed is rebuilding neighborhoods in a way that will enable communities to be more supportive of families and youths. Kotlowitz (1996) and Wilson (1996) believed that a large-scale jobs program is needed to rebuild the economic and social fabric. Although this program may not be feasible in today's political cli-mate, people do need to be connected. This connectedness should be encour-aged and promoted so that the individual "silence" and isolation that tolerate and sustain neighborhood problems and sabotage mobilization efforts are cur-tailed. While rebuilding community structures, families can be supported and "rebuilt" as well (Kotlowitz, 1996).

The George Williams College at Aurora University School of Social Work (AUSSW), Illinois, is demonstrating a collaborative approach that deals with these issues. Through the efforts of the AUSSW, the City of Aurora, the Aurora Police Department, local social services agencies, the clergy, the Aurora East Side Public School District, and funding entities, work is under way to develop, establish, and implement a strategy for building a healthy community for youths and families. This chapter describes these efforts and discusses implications for social work education and practice.

NEIGHBORHOODS IN PARTNERSHIP

Setting

The City of Aurora, located about 40 miles from Chicago, is experiencing the rapid growth of new housing at the edge of the Chicago metropolitan area. The city has a population of about 110,000; more than one-third (35 percent) are African American or Latino (U.S. Bureau of the Census, 1994).

Aurora is a 19th-century industrial river city with strong differences between the east and west neighborhoods. Many problems are focused on the east side. Gang activity is prevalent, as evidenced by the increasing number of homicides. In 1994 there were 15 homicides; 12 were gang related. In 1995 there were 25 homicides; 12 were gang related. Of those slain, nine were younger than age 20 (Dardick, 1996).

Process

During the past decade, AUSSW has collaborated with the City of Aurora on a number of joint-needs assessment projects. Recent discussions between faculty and members of the Aurora City Council and police officials led to an agreement in which the Aurora Police Department would pay for a part-time MSW-level supervisor hired by the AUSSW to supervise a number of interns engaged in neighborhood development and community-policing efforts. This supervisor receives consultation from an AUSSW faculty member. The project was named Neighborhoods in Partnership (NIP) by the student interns.

Activities

Community–Middle School Consortium. Perhaps the most ambitious activity has been the development of a consortium of agencies around an Aurora middle school in the east side designed to meet the needs of students, parents, and the community at large. Traditionally, schools in Aurora's east side have had difficulty dealing with increasing problems of gangs, drugs, and child abuse. Cultural and language differences also affect the quality and quantity of learning each student receives. One middle school has been a focus of the AUSSW interns' efforts; during the 1995 school year, at least 256 students of the school's population of about 550 were suspended for a total of 868 days. Many at-risk students were not eligible for any type of special education services. High school graduation rates were projected at only 36 percent.

Before the development of the consortium, a few community social services agencies provided a limited number of services at the school during school hours, after school, on weekends, and during summer vacations. Included were limited youth development services (for example, recreation services), parent support, and counseling. However, even with existing interventions, school personnel realized they could not meet the challenges of the student population alone. The principal requested assistance from the City of Aurora and AUSSW. Work began in developing a partnership between the school and community social services agencies. One social work intern was responsible for much of the evolution of the consortium of agencies.

Hooper-Briar and Lawson (1994) discussed how schools must become more nurturing and ready to meet the developmental, learning, and health needs of all children and their families. Health and human services professionals must become more attuned to promoting healthy development and preventing crises in children and their families. They described a "partner school"—a partnership established among school, university, and family, with children and families at the center. Efforts at the Aurora middle school were focused on the development of a "partner school." Multiple community social services agencies were incorporated into the partnership; their services were coordinated mostly by one agency.

Since the inception of the partner school project, many promising outcomes have occurred. First, 12 community-based social services agencies are providing programs at the school. Services to students and families are provided through home visits, onsite school appointments during and after school, or visits to the agencies. The educational component provides tutoring, homework clubs, and parent support to parents and children from nearly 50 families within the school. Several students receive support with food and clothing, and 236 students have participated in anger management groups. Finally, 46 individuals have been referred for mental health treatment.

In addition to being accessible, the services are free. To provide these services at no cost, the community, the social services agencies, and the school worked together, raising about $35,000 for the first year of operation. Funding entities restructured their allotments, the City of Aurora provided financial backing, and the school and district applied for several grants.

During summer 1996, 144 parents were surveyed to determine their interest in having additional social services programs at the school. This survey was conducted in English and Spanish primarily by parents with assistance from City of Aurora personnel. The results were positive as noted by the development of a family resource center, a parent advisory board, and a parent volunteer network.

Lerner (1995) and Schorr (1988) discussed attributes of effective programs, including dealing with children as part of a family and with families as part of a neighborhood, comprehensiveness and responsiveness, and flexibility and the ability to transcend agency and professional barriers. The partner school program has shown positive outcomes because of the interdisciplinary effort among teachers, social workers, agency staff, community members, and others. The services surrounded the students and their families instead of being provided at a distance. While emphasizing long-term change and development, staff built trusting relationships with the youths and their families.

Community Policing and Community Organizing. In 1989 the Aurora Police Department determined that a grassroots approach to policing would earn more positive results in the reduction of crime; *community policing*—the formation of a partnership between the department and the community at large—became a pivotal component of daily activities. Officers work at local schools and park districts and are accessible and active members in community and neighborhood groups. Many volunteer as sports coaches, mentors, and role models.

AUSSW interns worked with the department to further the development of community policing. Teams of an intern and police officer surveyed door-to-door a number of residential blocks that had crime and gang problems to determine resident perceptions, cohesion, and demographics. Once the survey was completed and the data compiled, a block profile was presented to the department that contained recommendations from the interns for future interventions and activities.

The majority of the residents were Latino and spoke Spanish as their primary language. Many felt isolated because of cultural and language barriers. There was a lack of cohesion among neighbors and limited neighborhood organization. Few residents were acquainted with each other and also felt that they had limited access to resources. Gang activity and crime were perceived as ever-present dangers. In response, block associations and Neighborhood Watch programs were developed in areas of heavy gang activity. Organizing was initiated by teams of a social work intern and a community-policing officer. The groups used a local school for meetings and held a year-end neighborhood festival staged by residents with consultation from the interns. An intern and the police department developed a series of cultural sensitivity seminars for the neighborhood groups and police personnel.

A year later a follow-up survey was conducted by the interns on the same blocks to determine resident perception of change. Residents stated that they felt more unified with their neighbors because of the block-party activities. The majority participated in the Neighborhood Watch program and knew their block captains. They felt there was more of a police presence in their area. All felt that their community was a safer place to live.

In addition to the resident survey, interviews were conducted by an intern with the police officers at the administrative and patrol levels to determine if the strategies and interventions positively or negatively affected the community. Of the officers interviewed, all felt that community policing made a positive difference, particularly in the areas targeted for intense intervention. Calls for needed police service were drastically reduced in the targeted areas. Further, members of the department felt that the addition of the social worker supervisor and MSW interns on staff added a viable resource for the officers and residents. According to one officer, "Social work goes hand in hand with the new concept of community-oriented policing."

Parent Involvement. University interns from social work, teacher education, recreation administration, and physical education began a series of programs that provided before-school, after-school, and noon-time activities for students in an elementary school located in a multicultural, low-income neighborhood on the city's east side. The school had about 800 students in grades K through 5. The university and school faculty examined ways to increase the school's overall parent participation level in the school.

In previous years the school planned one "family night" activity per year. Participation by parents and children was low. Under the supervision of an AUSSW professor, interns worked to develop new family nights. On several nights family members had fun together playing noncompetitive, cooperative games. Up to 600 people participated in these activities, a significant number for a school that once had only a few parents involved.

Throughout the year parents and faculty were asked to complete surveys to assess changes since the program began. In the parent questionnaire, of the 73 surveyed, 32 stated that they did not participate in school programs before the reorganized family night activities. Forty-one stated that they attended school-supported activities. School faculty completed two surveys. One evaluated the

impact of parental participation in the classroom since the project began; respondents noted that parental participation had a positive affect. All respondents stated that parents were working as volunteers in the classroom. The other
survey of fifth-grade teachers evaluated the influence of the intervention on
student attendance. In all the fifth-grade classes, student attendance improved
by nearly 90 percent.

In a third elementary school, AUSSW interns and parents established several
parent committees to work with school faculty to develop strategies to better
meet the needs of students and their families. Parent support groups and general equivalency diploma classes were developed.

DISCUSSION

Readiness for Change

Several factors contributed to the first year of favorable outcomes. First, the
Aurora community has all the components of a larger urban community but not
the political and structural complexity and population density. Further, the climate was right for change, as evidenced by the police department's earlier adoption of community policing. Aurora was also the first city in Illinois to establish
an antigang education program in the schools (Gregory & Barnum, 1996). Moreover, a local task force was established to examine gang violence, and a five-
year longitudinal study was authorized by the governor's office to study murder trends in the city (Dardick, 1996).

According to Monkman (1991), the climate of an organization (or community) directly affects the productivity of that organization, and the organization's
climate is often a target for change. Individuals from the local government, the
schools, the community, and AUSSW determined that working together to develop and utilize existing resources to solve the city's problems would yield
higher benefits than prior efforts. Coordinating services and communicating
can better meet the needs of children and their families and stretch the ever-
shrinking funding dollar.

There is a high correlation among many of the most troublesome urban problems such as poverty, poor educational outcomes, and early pregnancy, and a
single solution will not affect all of them. Likewise, a particular intervention
may have an effect on more than one problem. Needed is a package of services
in each community aimed at changing the developmental system in which people
are embedded rather than changing individuals (Dryfoos cited in Lerner, 1995).
Most important, interdisciplinary work should be emphasized; teachers, social
workers, recreation workers, and police officers should be expected to coordinate. Bottom-up rather than top-down planning should be emphasized.

Community Networks

An innovative approach to social work is required for treating long-standing
problems. Work was done at the mezzo (neighborhood and identified blocks)
and macro (the larger school community and the East Side School District) practice levels. The process was enhanced by the use of "new" social work theoretical

perspectives such as the ecological and holistic approaches, the strengths perspective (Saleebey, 1992) or assets-based development (McKnight, 1995), the empowerment approach (Lee, 1994), and a generalist model. These approaches tend to be broader and more social and cultural than past models and can provide a necessary balance to psychological approaches. Social work has only begun to realize the full potential of these perspectives; too often social workers have developed only contextualized casework practice.

Building on existing neighborhood assets and entities will maximize community organization and potential support for families and youths. A coordinated development–empowerment process of network building should include concurrent work with neighborhood-based public and human services (local government, police, schools, and youth development agencies) and resident groups and local institutions (churches, block associations, youth groups), with close communication between the two segments of the neighborhood.

Efforts can be most effective when focused on a neighborhood of limited size. In an urban setting this area might be no larger than that served by a school. Limits help recapture the neighborhood focus of the settlement house movement in a way that creates "urban support villages" (Lawson & Hooper-Briar, 1994) similar to Chestang's (1976) concept of the "nurturing environment."

Effects of Organization

Community development can help overcome disorganization and fragmentation of services and funding sources. The approach suggested in this chapter starts with a comprehensive, generalist process that builds networks and communication at the neighborhood level rather than focusing on individual client treatment. The approach assumes that considerable resources already exist in a neighborhood and, if better coordinated, these resources can make a difference in opportunities available to the community. Mobilization is enhanced when entities such as public schools and police become part of the network. A local university can provide important resources, particularly if the university is committed to community service, applied programs, and interdisciplinary approaches (Harkavy & Pickett, 1994; Lawson & Hooper-Briar, 1994).

Recent developments in neighborhood-based non–social work services—for example, the community schools movement, community-based policing, and a resurgence of community centers and positive youth development and family support (Costello & Ogletree, 1993; Lerner 1995)—offer new opportunities for collaboration among all human services providers. Many communities have "community schools," "full-service schools," or settlement houses located in schools to better serve the needs of residents (Dryfoos, 1994; Hendrickson & Omer, 1995; Lewis, 1995; Litzelfelner, 1996). Many police departments have embraced community policing; in addition, police can provide a sense of urgency in confronting local problems (Thurman, 1995). Neighborhood and tenant associations, parent groups, and youths themselves can be involved in guiding and implementing youth development activities.

Although young people need and want meaningful roles in society, they often are not involved in their communities, perhaps because few opportunities

allow such experiences. Checkoway, Finn, and Pothukuchi (1995) discussed involvement of youths in a neighborhood-based research project, and many examples exist where youth services agencies use youth volunteers who not only
provide valuable service but are also positive role models for younger youths.
In our model youths were not directly involved in the partnership's implementation; however, they are stakeholders in the overall process and are represented
in the youth agencies involved in the effort.

IMPLICATIONS FOR EDUCATION AND PRACTICE

All human services professionals should be trained to collaborate with professionals from other disciplines. AUSSW has developed a noncredit interdisciplinary seminar for students that will continue as the university's community involvement develops and expands. An elective course in community-based
prevention and development is offered to students across all human services
disciplines. Insights from the demonstration efforts are being used to modify
existing courses.

Greater balance between prevention–development and remediation is called
for in class and field education. Primary prevention and promoting resiliency
and increasing the competence of youths are typically accomplished through
community efforts that are sensitive to normal developmental needs (Benard,
1992; Simeonsson, 1994). Moreover, universities need to consider being partners in promoting community involvement and interdisciplinary work.

Differentiation in traditional social work roles of case worker, group worker,
and community organizer are not functional for the holistic model suggested in
this article. Rather, social workers should be equipped to handle all these roles.
True generalist practitioners are needed who possess a holistic approach that
emphasizes the environment as well as the person in environment. Field experiences should place students in a neighborhood network rather than in a single
agency so that students can experience the context of services as well perform a
variety of social work roles. Such placements might offer enough variety to be
used for more than one year.

Most important, social work must increase its recognition of the importance
of community influences in fostering a healthy environment for children and
families. Practice in neighborhoods and communities should be based on the
new social work perspectives and should focus on changing the culture of what
is seen as valued, possible, and appropriate in these communities, which in turn
will modify the opportunity systems for children and families. Accepting the
contextual environment and building on the strengths and abilities of these networks will endow each participant with the "power" to bring about change in
recognition that it does "take a whole village to raise a child."

REFERENCES

Benard, B. (1992). Fostering resiliency in kids: Preventative factors in the family, school and
    community. *Prevention Forum, 12*(3), 1–15.
Checkoway, B., Finn, J., & Pothukuchi, K. (1995). Young people as community resources: New
    forms of participation. In P. Adams & K. Nelson (Eds.), *Reinventing human services: Commu-
    nity- and family-centered practice* (pp. 189–202). New York: Aldine de Gruyter.

Chestang, L. (1976). Environmental influences on social functioning: The black experience. In P.S.J. Cafferty & L. Chestang (Eds.), *The diverse society: Implications for social policy* (pp. 59–74). Silver Spring, MD: National Association of Social Workers.

Coleman, J. S., & Hoffer, T. (1987). *Public and private high schools: The impact of community.* New York: Basic Books.

Costello, J., & Ogletree, R. (1993). *Creating a consortium for the education and training of children's services workers: The need and possible approaches.* Chicago: University of Chicago, Chapin Hall Services for Children.

Dardick, H. (1996, January 2). Kane ends year with record 33 murders. *Chicago Tribune, DuPage Sports, Final Edition,* p. 1.

Dryfoos, J. G. (1994). *Full-service schools: Revolution in health and social services and families.* San Francisco: Jossey-Bass.

Gregory, T., & Barnum, A. (1996, November 12). Aurora still has miles to go in war on gangs: Boy's death linked to city's festering problem. *Chicago Tribune, Metro Southwest Edition,* p. 4.

Harkavy, I., & Pickett, J. (1994). Lessons from Hull House for the contemporary urban university. *Social Service Review, 68,* 299–321.

Hendrickson, J. M., & Omer, D. (1995). School-based comprehensive services. In P. Adams & K. Nelson (Eds.), *Reinventing human services: Community- and family-centered practice* (pp. 145–162). New York: Aldine de Gruyter.

Hooper-Briar, K., & Lawson, H. A. (1994). *Serving children, youth and families through interdisciplinary collaboration and service integration: A framework for action.* Oxford, OH: Danforth Foundation and Institute for Educational Renewal at Miami University.

Ianni, F. A. (1989). *The search for structure: A report on American youth today.* New York: Free Press.

Kotlowitz, A. (1991). *There are no children here: The story of two boys growing up in the other America.* New York: Doubleday.

Kotlowitz, A. (1996). *Lecture.* Oak Park Public Library, Oak Park, IL.

Lawson, H. A., & Hooper-Briar, K. (1994). *Expanding partnerships: Involving colleges in interprofessional collaboration and service integration.* Oxford, OH: Danforth Foundation and Institute for Educational Renewal at Miami University.

Lee, J.A.B. (1994). *The empowerment approach to social work practice.* New York: Columbia University Press.

Lerner, R. M. (1995). *America's youth in crisis: Challenges and options for programs and policies.* Thousand Oaks, CA: Sage Publications.

Lewis, M. (1995). Linking schools with family and community services. In P. Adams & K. Nelson (Eds.), *Reinventing human services: Community- and family-centered practice* (pp. 163–173). New York: Aldine de Gruyter.

Litzelfelner, P. (1996). Neighborhood schools: Environmental strengths—Social niches. *School Social Work Journal, 20*(2), 1–10.

Massey, D. S., & Denton, N. A. (1993). *American apartheid: Segregation and the making of the underclass.* Cambridge, MA: Harvard University Press.

McKnight, J. (1995). *The careless society: Community and its counterfeits.* New York: Basic Books.

Monkman, M. M. (1991). The characteristic focus of the social worker in the public schools. In R. Constable & S. McDonald (Eds.), *School social work* (pp. 30–49). Chicago: Lyceum Books.

Saleebey, D. (1992). *The strengths perspective in social work practice.* New York: Longman.

Schorr, L. (1988). *Within our reach: Breaking the cycle of disadvantage.* New York: Doubleday.

Simeonsson, R. J. (1994). *Risk, resilience and prevention: Promoting the well-being of children.* Baltimore: Paul H. Brookes.

Specht, H., & Courtney, M. (1994). *Unfaithful angels: How social work has abandoned its mission.* New York: Free Press.

Spergel, I. (1995). *The youth gang problem.* New York: Oxford University Press.

Thurman, Q. C. (1995). Community policing: The police as a community resource. In P. Adams & K. Nelson (Eds.), *Reinventing human services: Community- and family-centered practice* (pp. 175–187). New York: Aldine de Gruyter.

U.S. Bureau of the Census. (1994). *Census of the population: County and city data book.* Washington, DC: U.S. Government Printing Office.

Wilson, W. J. (1996). *When work disappears: The world of the new urban poor.* New York: Alfred A. Knopf.

Some of the material for this chapter was developed for a research project required for the MSW degree, which was supervised by Dr. Morrison.

This chapter was originally published in the September 1997 issue of Social Work, vol. 42, pp. 527–534.

Assessing the Impact of Community Violence on Children and Youths

Neil B. Guterman and Mark Cameron

"The spot where Quentin Carter died on Monday had been turned into a small shrine, where 13 votive candles burned to mark the 13th birthday Quentin did not live to celebrate. Quentin's aunt, Sharon Ellis, said the boy's mother, Wanda, could do little but cry and clutch one of Quentin's basketball shirts. His six younger siblings, she said, keep asking, 'Does this mean Junior's not coming back?'"

—(Goldberg, 1995)

Community violence experiences are all too common among young people, particularly for those living in America's urban centers. Recent studies indicate that 80 percent to 90 percent of children living in urban settings are direct victims of or witnesses to significant acts of violence in their neighborhoods, schools, or communities (Fitzpatrick & Boldizar, 1993; Jenkins & Bell, 1997; Osofsky, Wewers, Hamn, & Fick, 1993; Richters & Martinez, 1993). Fatal violence from handguns alone has claimed the lives of more American children and youths over the past decade and a half than the total number of American soldiers killed in the Vietnam War (Metzenbaum, 1994). Especially profoundly affected are African American youths, who have a fourfold greater risk of being murdered than white children (Snyder & Sickmund, 1995). The problem of community violence in the United States, however, clearly transcends ethnic, class, or geographic lines. Findings by Campbell and Schwarz (1996) and Gladstein, Slater Rusonis, and Heald (1992), for example, show that although inner-city youths may report somewhat higher rates of exposure to community violence, the large majority of upper-middle-class and suburban youths also report substantial direct experiences with violence in their communities.

Despite a recent decline in the violent crime rates for both adults and youths (Butterfield, 1996), unless significant steps are taken, exposure to community violence among young people will remain a serious problem. Between 1984 and 1993 the number of handgun murders against children and youths rose by 500 percent (Snyder & Sickmund, 1995) before slightly decreasing in 1994 and 1995. Because a large proportion of violence perpetrated against youths is by other youths (Snyder & Sickmund, 1995), demographic changes suggest an upward trend in the absolute numbers of children and youths encountering community violence. For example, over the next decade the number of 15- to 19-year-olds will increase by 21 percent, and the rates are even higher for children of color: 24 percent for African American teenagers and 47 percent for Latino teenagers (Gest

& Friedman, 1994). On the basis of such data, the U.S. Department of Justice projected that the rate of juvenile violent crime arrests will double between 1992 and 2010 (Snyder & Sickmund, 1995).

Like survivors of family violence, young survivors of community violence frequently suffer serious psychosocial consequences including posttraumatic stress disorder (PTSD) (Fitzpatrick & Boldizar, 1993; Garbarino, Kostelny, & Dubrow, 1992; Horowitz, Weine, & Jekel, 1995), increased depression (Freeman, Mokros, & Poznanski, 1993), cognitive and academic delays (Osofsky et al., 1993; Shakoor & Chalmers, 1991), and increased aggression (DuRant, Pendergrast, & Cadenhead, 1994; Schwab-Stone et al., 1995). At the same time, early epidemiological studies of children and youths suggested that violence experiences are far more common outside the home than inside (Fitzpatrick & Boldizar, 1993; Osofsky et al., 1993; Richters & Martinez, 1993). As one indicator, of the 12 children and youths (age 19 or younger) murdered on average each day in the United States in 1993, nine were murdered by perpetrators from outside the home (Federal Bureau of Investigation, 1994; U.S. Department of Health and Human Services, 1995). Given the widespread devastation that community violence visits on children and families and social workers' historic commitment to addressing the problem of violence within the family, it is imperative that the social work profession place the problem of community violence and its impact on children and youths in the forefront of its concerns.

Social work professionals are especially well positioned to handle this charge. Numerous settings employing social workers serve young clients at high risk for exposure to community violence, including hospitals, schools, child welfare agencies, community centers, and clinics. Further, the profession's epistemological emphasis on contextual understandings of client problems bestows on workers a perspective that highlights the role of community-based experiences in the presenting concerns of clients. It therefore remains perplexing that so little attention is devoted to the problem of community violence in social work practice with young clients (Campbell & Schwarz, 1996; Freeman, Schaffer, & Smith, 1996). Regardless of the reasons for such oversight, social workers still require knowledge to help them understand community violence and its role in the presenting concerns of their young clients.

This chapter examines the knowledge base on exposure to community violence among young people and offers an assessment framework with which social workers can begin to conceptualize the role that community violence plays in the lives of their young clients. This framework has been derived from the authors' empirical study of community violence exposure among children served in child welfare settings (Guterman & Cameron, 1996).

COMMUNITY VIOLENCE IN YOUNG PEOPLE'S LIVES

Community violence may be conceived of as acts of commission that cause physical or psychological harm deriving from outside the family—in neighborhoods, schools, or other local settings in which children and youths typically socialize (Cooley, Turner, & Beidel, 1995; Dubrow & Garbarino, 1989; Fitzpatrick & Boldizar, 1993; Pynoos & Eth, 1985; Richters, 1993). Although some children may be exposed to only one or several discrete acts of violence, others experience community violence as a chronic feature of life. In either case children's encounters with violence may take many forms. A child who is beaten or attacked with a weapon is a victim of community violence, as is the child who is threatened or chased on the way home from school. The child who observes someone holding another at gunpoint or knifepoint with the intention to do harm is a witness to violence. Children who are coerced to join with their friends in a robbery or rape are accomplices in violent acts. Although the roles of victim, witness, accomplice, and perpetrator may involve different experiences, each is likely to hold detrimental psychosocial consequences for the young people involved.

Specific experiences with violent incidents most often are embedded in broader community and social contexts. An impoverished physical environment characterized by abandoned buildings, empty lots, or deteriorated streets may provide a backdrop for violence. The manifestations of racism such as suspicion by neighbors or shopkeepers, hypervigilance of police and security guards, or exclusionary policies of landlords contribute to an awareness of mistrust and danger in one's community. The presence of organized crime or corruption in local institutions may lead to the eruption of violent altercations in the neighborhood. Indeed, young clients and their families encounter violence in many forms on multiple levels: as interpersonal events, as attitudes and experiences conveyed by other community members, and as institutional realities that shape life circumstances (Horowitz et al., 1995; Van Soest & Bryant, 1995).

From interviews about their community violence experiences (Guterman & Cameron, 1996), children in child welfare services settings often depict a banal sense of danger and lonely struggles to survive.

Jessica

Jessica, age 14, was repeatedly harassed by an older boy at school until she decided to challenge him. The boy threw her into the street, where she was almost hit by an oncoming car. The assistant principal at her school suspended Jessica for three days for fighting. When Jessica talked to her mother about what happened she was told to "stop getting into fights." Jessica became depressed because she felt that no one helped her and no one would want to be her friend having been labeled a "troublemaker." Out of resignation and fear of retribution by a neighborhood gang, Jessica stopped talking to anyone about these experiences.

Quinn

Quinn, age 16, knew a number of drug dealers in his neighborhood, their confederates, and people from whom he could purchase a gun. He revealed that some of his friends were recently arrested for murder. He stated that he had been threatened a number of times, but he adopted a nonchalant attitude about it: "A knife doesn't scare me. I will heal. A gun? . . . I've been threatened once or twice with a gun. . . . If you kill me, somebody's gonna kill half your family." Quinn stated that he did not speak with others much about his experiences. Discussions with his mother about witnessing violence elicited practical advice from her: "First thing she asks me is where was I, mind your own business, go home. . . ." Quinn said he does not talk to his social worker about these experiences in his neighborhood; he explained, "It's not important."

Victor

Victor, age 12, spent his childhood in a small, rural town. He stated that he used to try to protect smaller and younger children who were harassed by others until one day an older youth pulled a gun on him. Victor "froze" and started shaking uncontrollably. He had a nightmare about the incident that night, and the dream occasionally returns. He stated that this was the first time he had spoken to anyone about what had happened. Victor also was assaulted while riding his bicycle through a wooded park and had witnessed other violent acts that he refused to discuss. He stated that he gave up trying to help others, and now he walked away from fights. Victor explained that violence was a common occurrence in his hometown: "Where I live, it's never a boring day."

PSYCHOSOCIAL SEQUELAE FOR YOUNG PEOPLE EXPOSED TO COMMUNITY VIOLENCE

As the stories of Jessica, Quinn, and Victor suggest, experiences with community violence can leave a deep impression on young people. In reviewing work on the consequences of exposure to community violence in children, Garbarino et al. (1992) noted that the psychosocial profile of exposed children and youths may be strikingly similar to that of young survivors of war or other acute trauma. For example, symptom profiles consistent with PTSD often have been reported in young people of a wide range of ages (Fitzpatrick & Boldizar, 1993; Horowitz et al., 1995; Martinez & Richters, 1993).

Observed sequelae, however, may be mediated by a host of psychosocial factors (Berman, Kurtines, Silverman, & Serafini, 1996; Horowitz et al., 1995) and may vary with the young person's developmental stage. For example, preschool children who have witnessed violence outside the home appeared to develop passive and regressive symptoms such as thumb-sucking, loss of bowel and bladder control, crying, decreased verbalizations, irritability, sleep difficulties, and insecure attachment to a parent or caregiver (Peterson, Luborsky, & Seligman, 1983).

As children age, more overt symptoms associated with PTSD may become evident. Psychic numbing, for example, may be readily apparent in some school-age children. Used to cope with overwhelming feelings associated with trauma, psychic numbing may impair functioning in a number of psychosocial domains. Children may not be able to recall aspects of trauma in its aftermath, and memory in general may be diminished. Cognitive difficulties may develop, and children may become unable to sustain concentration, impairing their academic performance (Osofsky et al., 1993). Children may exhibit their emotional distress in school through disruptive or aggressive behavior or in play by re-enacting violent incidents or acting out rescue fantasies (Terr, 1979). Interest in activities that may trigger memories or feelings associated with violent experiences may be diminished. Likewise, intimacy with others may be curtailed to maintain a detached avoidance of feelings (Pynoos & Eth, 1985).

School-age victims or witnesses to community violence also may experience a constellation of depressive symptoms, including dysphoric affect, persistent feelings of guilt, lowered self-esteem, and worries about injury and death. Loss and grief reactions typically accompany violence exposure and may be unusually pronounced if a young client loses a close friend or family member to violence (Freeman et al., 1996; Osofsky et al., 1993; Pynoos & Eth, 1985; Pynoos & Nader, 1988). Although school-age children involved in violence frequently suffer from depression, preliminary evidence does not suggest a heightened risk for suicidality in this age group (Freeman et al., 1993). Instead, children more likely may erect a tough façade as a means of coping with the hurt and loss suffered when friends or family are injured or killed. A more generalized habituation to violence may appear as a nonchalant attitude toward such stressful experiences. As Wilson (1991) noted, "in these neighborhoods [troubled with violence] . . . , youngsters are more likely to see violence as a way of life" (p. xii).

Adolescents who have experienced community violence may exhibit fatalistic behaviors and thoughts, frequently convinced that they are likely to die at a young age as have other friends or family members (DuRant, Cadenhead, Pendergrast, Slavens, & Linder, 1994; van der Kolk, 1987). This sense of "futurelessness" may be apparent, for example, in dangerous play and thrill seeking or when chronically exposed adolescents are asked to consider their life goals (Kotlowitz, 1991; Schwab-Stone et al., 1995). An associated resignation or hopelessness may, in part, explain the higher rates of suicide observed for teenagers involved in violence (Rathus, Wetzler, & Asnis, 1995). Adolescents attempting to cope with a persistent fear of harm may seek to alleviate their anxiety by identifying with and joining aggressive individuals in the neighborhood, acquiring weapons, and carrying out even further violence (DuRant, Cadenhead, et al., 1994; Prothrow-Stith, 1991; Schwab-Stone et al., 1995). The remorseless acts of aggression and retribution associated with gang violence may, in part, be the result of the "truncated" moral development of children growing up in persistently dangerous neighborhoods (Fields, 1987). This damaged sense of morality may be exacerbated if children and youths do not have opportunities to discuss their moral dilemmas with trusted adults (Garbarino et al., 1992).

Underlying the suffering and psychosocial sequelae of children experiencing community violence may be an undeveloped or damaged sense of basic security in the world. "What has been destroyed for children traumatized by community violence is the idea of home, school, and community as a safe place. The traditional bastions of safety have been destroyed by external violence, which dictates every aspect of children's lives. Danger replaces safety as the organizing principle" (Garbarino et al., 1992, p. 83).

ASSESSMENT FRAMEWORK FOR YOUNG PEOPLE EXPOSED TO COMMUNITY VIOLENCE

Social workers must carefully consider the differential impact of community violence on their young clients so that they may effectively plan and implement appropriate ameliorative, protective, and preventive interventions. Based on a study of exposure to community violence among a sample of children in child welfare settings (Guterman & Cameron, 1996), we developed a framework by which social workers can assess the role of community violence in young clients' concerns as a part of routine assessment of other client concerns.

Methods

Seeking to develop an empirically grounded and useful assessment framework for practice, we used a "design and development" methodology (Rothman & Thomas, 1994). The aim of this methodology is to evolve effective helping technologies (rather than the development of empirical knowledge per se) through steps that ensure their systematic "design" and subsequent "development" in the field. This assessment framework has been produced according to the following design and development procedures: problem analysis, synthesis of available information, design of a prototype helping technology, and pilot testing in the field.

Initiation of these activities supported Richters' (1993) assertion that "the professionals most familiar with the phenomenon and the populations most affected tend not to have the training, [or] skills" (p. 4). We found, for example, little attention to children's exposure to community violence within the professional social work literature and no guidelines for assessment or intervention. Given this, we launched design and development activities, seeking to establish assessment guidelines within a larger ongoing study examining the psychosocial profile of young people in residential treatment and their exposure to community violence (Guterman & Cameron, 1996). We conducted a state-of-the-art review, culling information from a variety of sources, including academic and professional publications (via searches through MEDLINE, PsychInfo, and *Social Work Abstracts*), journalistic sources, consultations with experienced professionals in the field, and direct interviews with young people about their experiences with community violence. An analysis of these information sources served to fashion the boundaries and domains of the assessment framework. Because little was known about the process of assessing for community violence exposure among young people, we sought guidance and adapted from assessment procedures developed for similar life experiences, for example, drawing from the field of child maltreatment (Faller, 1990; Holder & Corey, 1986).

On the basis of these information sources, we constructed a prototype design of the assessment framework and tested it with feedback from selected experts in the field. After revisions were made we pilot tested elements of the prototype framework in the field through a limited number of intensive qualitative interviews with young people. Field notes from these interviews and information gathered from separate structured interviews using an adapted version of the Survey of Exposure to Community Violence for children and youths (Richters & Martinez, 1993) informed successive revisions of the model. Young people participating in both intensive qualitative interviews and interviews using the Survey of Exposure to Community Violence lived in three residential treatment sites serving a major northeastern city and its suburban and rural surroundings (Guterman & Cameron, 1996). These included boys and girls from urban and rural settings, representing a variety of ethnic backgrounds (African American, Latino, and white). Ages ranged from 12 to 18 years.

Assessment Framework

Figure 11.1 depicts the resulting integrative framework for conceptualizing and assessing community violence exposure through four major interrelated domains:

1. Identification of the young person's involvement in community violence and characterization of the nature of the involvement
2. Sequelae assessment to determine the impact of community violence on the young person
3. Lethality assessment to determine the degree to which the young person is in imminent or ongoing danger
4. Ecological assessment to best understand the presence of risks and protective factors shaping outcomes in the client's life.

This framework and its four domains (dubbed ISLE) can provide a heuristic device with which social workers can begin to map the role of exposure to community violence in their young clients' lives, thereby stimulating consideration of interventive pathways. Figure 1 highlights that information gathered in routine assessment can provide a trigger for the social worker to enter into a more

Figure 11.1

Assessing Children's Exposure to Community Violence: The ISLE Domains

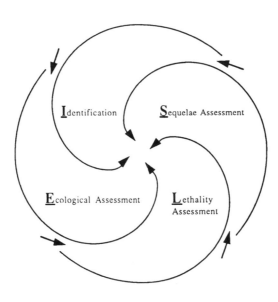

systematic assessment process considering each of the ISLE domains with respect to exposure to community violence. Once this process is entered, information gathered will open further segues for proceeding through other major assessment domains. For example, the social worker routinely mapping young clients' psychosocial sequelae can, if representational of community violence sequelae, assess the degree to which the sequelae can be identified as deriving from such experiences or elsewhere. If community violence experiences are confirmed, the social worker can unearth factual details of community violence experiences and consider if the young client presently faces lethal dangers. Similarly, the social worker mapping a client's developmental history may uncover factual information that identifies community violence experiences and then explore for the presence of likely psychosocial sequelae and ongoing lethality risks. Via either pathway the social worker can examine ecologically based risk and protective factors and intervention options.

Identification. Identification of exposure to violence includes uncovering key factual threads that can assist in understanding the violent consequences and meaning of the events for the young person. These include who the victims, witnesses, perpetrators, and accomplices were and the client's ties to these people; the chain of events leading up to the actual violent events themselves; the role the client played in the events; the frequency and recency of the exposure, which may assist in determining the degree to which the consequences of the events to the client are malleable or entrenched; the location of the events; and the client's behavioral, affective, and cognitive coping responses to the events, including his or her sense of responsibility and control with regard to the incidents.

Fact gathering can be done via multiple sources, including direct interviews with the young client, family members, and significant people in the young person's community including school personnel and neighbors. It is important to uncover information about community violence sensitively and in a timely fashion and to recognize that such knowledge can be difficult to uncover. For example, parents and significant others tend to underreport a child's exposure to violence, perhaps because of their own unawareness or as a means of coping by suppressing the painful acknowledgment of the child's exposure (Richters & Martinez, 1993). Therefore, direct assessment with the young client is essential in establishing the nature and extent of any exposure. At the same time direct exploration with a young client presents unique challenges, because such experiences are often highly emotionally charged and so traumatic that the client's sense of safety may become overwhelmed. Fears of reprisal or feelings of betrayal may arise, and the young person may believe that the events must remain a secret. As such, workers must balance garnering the client's assent to elicit information and actively probing to uncover hidden material. Furthermore, workers must take care to communicate confidentiality protections and their limitations in an age-appropriate fashion. It is possible that even in cases in which the young client divulges information about an experience, she or he may describe the experience with blunted or inappropriate affect as a result of psychic numbing or with a braggadocio that exaggerates and covers up the actual experience. Workers must not be misled or confused as to the depth or seriousness of the young person's reaction to the trauma.

Sequelae Assessment. Ascertaining a young client's psychosocial sequelae may indicate a client's experience with community violence before it is disclosed by the client or becomes otherwise known. Assessment for the typical sequelae found at varying developmental stages will assist in developmentally appropriate treatment planning. Social workers must take care to separate other possible influences in the psychosocial sequelae, such as the presence of family violence, sexual abuse, or traumatic losses.

Lethality Assessment. Because safety is of paramount importance, social workers must carefully assess for imminent or ongoing lethality concerns and be prepared to enter a crisis intervention mode if necessary. Assessment of lethality includes developing an understanding of the likelihood of harm reaching the young client in the near future. Specific areas of assessment include the young person's role and relationships with key players in the violent events; his or her contacts with potential future perpetrators; the degree of inclination expressed by him or her toward involvement in potentially dangerous situations; and possible suicidal ideation, particularly for older youths. In addition, workers must consider the presence or accessibility of weapons for the client and key others. Many youths can easily and clandestinely acquire a weapon within hours (Schubiner, Scott, & Tzelepis, 1993). If the young client appears to identify with an aggressor, seeks control through violence (Bell & Jenkins 1993), or exhibits reckless or re-enactment behavior, workers must carefully weigh the possibility that the client's own behavior will heighten lethality risk as well. Regardless of the source of likely future violence, workers must be familiar with state and agency policies on confidentiality limits and be prepared to violate confidentiality if required.

Ecological Assessment. Ecologically based factors can play a role in the amelioration or exacerbation of symptomatologies and can offer protective options for young clients at ongoing risk of exposure. Exploring the young person's developmental stage, resilience, and "perceptual set," or the perceptive lens by which events are filtered, will help in understanding the meaning of the violence for the child and the chosen coping responses. For example, religious or political beliefs have been found to play an important buffering role with violence-related trauma (Garbarino, Kostelny, & Dubrow, 1991).

Also important are the young person's primary relationships with parents, siblings, extended family, teachers, and peers. Assessment of the immediate support network of the young person can yield key information about the risk for and protection from future exposure, the response and adjustment to recent exposure, and possible direct targets of intervention to shore up the client's immediate support network (Berman et al., 1996; Campbell & Schwarz, 1996; Freeman et al., 1996). Assessment also should include an examination of other stressors the client faces, particularly those that can synergistically heighten the impact of exposure to community violence. These can include previous exposure to violence in the community, violence in the family, experiences with earlier losses or deaths, and the presence of substance abuse in the microsystem.

Assessing the role of parents or primary caregivers in the client's life is particularly important. Exposure to violence challenges a basic sense of security and safety. At the same time, young people's (especially younger children's) primary attachments to caregivers can promote security in interpersonal relationships and can buffer the effects of stress. However, parents who themselves are overwhelmed, isolated, depressed, or experiencing the effects of community violence can have greater difficulties engaging in attachment and comforting behaviors with their children (Dodge, Petit, & Bates, 1994). Clearly young people exposed to community violence who also have problematic relationships with primary caregivers face multiple stressors and may feel they have nowhere to turn.

Considering broader community factors can help determine longer-term possibilities for protection from violence and prognosis for the future. For example, an assessment of institutions such as police, neighborhood organizations, schools, and religious organizations can identify avenues for preventing violence, protecting children, and helping them cope in the aftermath of violence. An assessment of the physical condition of neighborhood buildings will provide clues as to the operability of ongoing illicit activity or the risk of encountering violence in abandoned or isolated places. Neighborhoods characterized by social and economic impoverishment hold substantial additional risks for families rearing children and, as such, can place young clients in a "double jeopardy" of violence and exposure to poverty.

Finally, although social workers providing direct support to young people and their families may have fewer opportunities to seek structural and community changes as explicit goals of clinical intervention, assessment of macro-level factors places in context the broader social forces that may have shaped clients' exposure to violence. Social workers should consider the consequences of community blight or revitalization, investment or divestment in the community, and cultural messages conveyed through mass media about the romance or reality of violence as a solution to problems (Friedlander, 1993; Prothrow-Stith, 1991).

DISCUSSION AND CONCLUSION

Allied human services professions such as medicine, psychiatry, and psychology recently have devoted significant attention to addressing the problem of community violence in young people's lives (see special issues of the *American Journal of Orthopsychiatry*, 1996; *Journal of the American Academy of Child and Adolescent Psychiatry*, 1995; *Journal of the American Medical Association*, 1995; and *Psychiatry*, 1993; and also American Psychological Association, 1993; Bell & Jenkins, 1993; Eron, Gentry, & Schlegel, 1994; Freeman et al., 1993; Garbarino et al., 1992; Pynoos et al., 1987; Schubiner et al., 1993). Why the social work profession has not devoted substantial attention to the problem of community violence is unclear. It may be that, as Van Soest and Bryant (1995) suggested, social work is operating under an "inadequate understanding" of the broader institutional sources of violence, thereby dismissing the problem of community violence as an exclusively inner-city issue and not worthy of sustained professional commitment. Nonetheless, attention is necessary not only to assessing the young victims of violence, but also to addressing institutional and interpersonal influences that allow such behaviors to persist. Assessing community violence exposure in young clients' lives after the fact is merely a starting point for workers struggling to help beleaguered young people and their families.

Effective practice approaches are sorely needed to address the multilevel challenges for young people and their families at risk of exposure to community violence. Community building, mediation, and advocacy efforts ultimately may be best suited for the complex and profound challenges that community violence presents to clients and professionals. Workers must use a holistic perspective and work skillfully not only with young people but also with their families, schools, neighborhoods, and community organizations. Efforts to dissolve the walls of isolation that surround many of the most troubled families and communities can reduce the likelihood that young people will continue to face violence in their everyday lives. Social work practitioners have the potential to significantly reduce community violence and its resulting fear and trauma. The social work profession maintains a historic commitment to this task. It remains incumbent on social workers to articulate and enact an effective response.

REFERENCES

American Journal of Orthopsychiatry. (1996). Special Section, *66,* 320–389.

American Psychological Association. (1993). *Violence and youth: Psychology's response, volume I: Summary report of the American Psychological Association Commission on Violence and Youth.* Washington, DC: Author, Public Interest Directorate.

Bell, C. C., & Jenkins, E. J. (1993). Community violence and children on Chicago's southside. *Psychiatry, 56,* 46–54.

Berman, S. L., Kurtines, W. M., Silverman, W. K., & Serafini, L. T. (1996). The impact of exposure to crime and violence on urban youth. *American Journal of Orthopsychiatry, 66,* 329–336.

Butterfield, F. (1996, August 9). After a decade, juvenile crime begins to drop. *New York Times,* p. A1.

Campbell, C., & Schwarz, D. F. (1996). Prevalence and impact of exposure to interpersonal violence among suburban and urban middle school students. *Pediatrics, 98,* 396–402.

Cooley, M. R., Turner, S. M., & Beidel, D. C. (1995). Assessing community violence: The children's report of exposure to violence. *Journal of the American Academy of Child and Adolescent Psychiatry, 34,* 201–208.

Dodge, K. A., Petit, G. S., & Bates, J. E. (1994). Socialization mediators of the relation between socioeconomic status and child conduct problems. *Child Development, 65,* 649–665.

Dubrow, N. F., & Garbarino, J. (1989). Living in the war zone: Mothers and young children in a public housing development. *Child Welfare, 68,* 3–20.

DuRant, R. H., Cadenhead, C., Pendergrast, R. A., Slavens, G., & Linder, C. W. (1994). Factors associated with the use of violence among urban black adolescents. *American Journal of Public Health, 84*(4), 612–617.

DuRant, R. H., Pendergrast, R. A., & Cadenhead, C. (1994). Exposure to violence and victimization and fighting behavior by urban black adolescents. *Journal of Adolescent Health, 15,* 311–318.

Eron, L. D., Gentry, J. H., & Schlegel, P. (1994). *Reason to hope: A psychosocial perspective on violence and youth.* Washington, DC: American Psychological Association.

Faller, K. C. (1990). *Understanding child sexual maltreatment.* Newbury Park, CA: Sage Publications.

Federal Bureau of Investigation. (1994). *Crime in the United States, 1993.* Washington, DC: U.S. Government Printing Office.

Fields, R. (1987, October). *Terrorized into terrorist: Sequelae of PTSD in young victims.* Paper presented at the meeting of the Society for Traumatic Stress Studies, New York.

Fitzpatrick, K. M., & Boldizar, J. P. (1993). The prevalence and consequences of exposure to violence among African-American youth. *Journal of the American Academy of Child and Adolescent Psychiatry, 32,* 424–430.

Freeman, L. N., Mokros, H., & Poznanski, E. O. (1993). Violent events reported by normal urban school-aged children: Characteristics and depression correlates. *Journal of the American Academy of Child and Adolescent Psychiatry, 32,* 419–423.

Freeman, L. N., Schaffer, D., & Smith, H. (1996). Neglected victims of homicide: The needs of young siblings of murder victims. *American Journal of Orthopsychiatry, 66,* 337–345.

Friedlander, B. Z. (1993). Community violence, children's development, and mass media: In pursuit of new insights, new goals, and new strategies. *Psychiatry, 56,* 66–81.

Garbarino, J., Kostelny, K., & Dubrow, N. (1991). *No place to be a child: Growing up in a war zone.* Lexington, MA: Lexington Books.

Garbarino, J., Kostelny, K., & Dubrow, N. (1992). *Children in dangerous environments: Coping with the consequences of community violence.* San Francisco: Jossey-Bass.

Gest, T., & Friedman, D. (1994). The new crime wave. *U.S. News and World Report, 117*(9), 26–28.

Gladstein, J., Slater Rusonis, E. J., & Heald, F. P. (1992). A comparison of inner-city and upper-middle class youths' exposure to violence. *Journal of Adolescent Health, 13,* 275–280.

Goldberg, C. (1995, July 20). Boy dies in a rage of bullets, and a 16-year-old is held. *New York Times,* pp. B1, B3.

Guterman, N. B., & Cameron, M. (1996, June). *Assessing children's exposure to community violence in child maltreatment service settings.* Paper presented at the Fourth National Colloquium of the American Professional Society on the Abuse of Children, Chicago.

Holder, W. M., & Corey, M. (1986). *Child protective services risk management: A decision-making handbook.* Charlotte, NC: ACTION for Child Protection.

Horowitz, K., Weine, S., & Jekel, J. (1995). PTSD symptoms in urban adolescent girls: Compounded community trauma. *Journal of the American Academy of Child and Adolescent Psychiatry, 34,* 1353–1361.

Jenkins, E. J., & Bell, C. C. (1997). Exposure and response to community violence among children and adolescents. In J. D. Osofsky (Ed.), *Children in a violent society* (pp. 9–31). New York: Guilford Press.

Journal of the American Academy of Child and Adolescent Psychiatry. (1995). Special Section, *34,* 1343–1380.

Journal of the American Medical Association. (1995). Special Issue, *273,* 1727–1806.

Kotlowitz, A. (1991). *There are no children here: The story of two boys growing up in the other America.* New York: Anchor Books.

Martinez, P., & Richters, J. E. (1993). The NIMH community violence project: II. Children's distress symptoms associated with violence exposure. *Psychiatry, 56,* 22–35.

Metzenbaum, H. M. (1994, March 1). Statements on introduced bills and joint resolutions. In *Congressional record* (Daily ed., pp. S2169–S2183). Washington, DC: U.S. Government Printing Office.

Osofsky, J. D., Wewers, S., Hamn, D. M., & Fick, A. C. (1993). Chronic community violence: What is happening to our children? *Psychiatry, 56,* 36–45.

Peterson, C., Luborsky, L., & Seligman, L. (1983). Attributions and depressive mood shifts: A case study using the symptom–context method. *Journal of Abnormal Psychology, 92,* 96–103.

Prothrow-Stith, D. (1991). *Deadly consequences.* New York: HarperCollins.

Psychiatry. (1993). Papers presented at the National Conference on Community Violence and Children's Development: Research and Clinical Implications, *56,* 1–136.

Pynoos, R. S., & Eth, S. (1985). Children traumatized by witnessing acts of personal violence: Homicide, rape, and suicidal behavior. In S. Eth & R. S. Pynoos (Eds.), *Post-traumatic stress disorder in children* (pp. 17–43). Washington, DC: American Psychiatric Press.

Pynoos, R. S., Frederick, C., Nader, K., Arroyo, W., Steinberg, A., Spencer, E., Nunez, F., & Fairbanks, L. (1987). Life threat and posttraumatic stress in school-age children. *Archives of General Psychiatry, 44,* 1057–1063.

Pynoos, R. S., & Nader, K. (1988). Psychological first aid and treatment approach to children exposed to community violence: Research implications. *Journal of Traumatic Stress Studies, 1*, 445–473.

Rathus, J., Wetzler, S., & Asnis, G. (1995, June 14). Posttraumatic stress disorder and exposure to violence in adolescents [Letter to the editor]. *JAMA, 273*, 1734.

Richters, J. E. (1993). Community violence and children's development: Toward a research agenda for the 1990's. *Psychiatry, 56*, 3–6.

Richters, J. E., & Martinez, P. (1993). The NIMH Community Violence Project: I. Children as victims of and witnesses to violence. *Psychiatry, 56*, 7–21.

Rothman, J., & Thomas, E. J. (Eds.). (1994). *Intervention research: Design and development for human service.* New York: Haworth Press.

Schubiner, H., Scott, R., & Tzelepis, A. (1993). Exposure to violence among inner-city youth. *Journal of Adolescent Health, 14*, 214–219.

Schwab-Stone, M. E., Ayers, T. S., Kasprow, W., Voyce, C., Barone, C., Shriver, T., & Weissberg, R. P. (1995). No safe haven: A study of violence exposure in an urban community. *Journal of the American Academy of Child and Adolescent Psychiatry, 34*, 1343–1352.

Shakoor, B. H., & Chalmers, D. (1991). Covictimization of African-American children who witness violence and the theoretical implications of its effects on their cognitive, emotional, and behavioral development. *Journal of the National Medical Association, 83*, 233–238.

Snyder, H. N., & Sickmund, M. (1995). *Juvenile offenders and victims: A national report.* Washington, DC: Office of Juvenile Justice and Delinquency Prevention.

Terr, L. (1979). Children of Chowchilla: A study of psychic trauma. *Psychoanalytic Study of the Child, 34*, 547–623.

U.S. Department of Health and Human Services, National Center on Child Abuse and Neglect. (1995). *Child maltreatment 1993: Reports from the states to the National Center on Child Abuse and Neglect.* Washington, DC: U.S. Government Printing Office.

Van der Kolk, B. A. (1987). *Psychological trauma.* Washington, DC: American Psychiatric Press.

Van Soest, D., & Bryant, S. (1995). Violence reconceptualized for social work: The urban dilemma. *Social Work, 40*, 549–557.

Wilson, W. J. (1991). Foreword. In D. Prothrow-Stith (Ed.), *Deadly consequences* (pp. xi–xii). New York: HarperCollins.

This research was an outgrowth of activities of the Odyssey Project, a national study of children in residential treatment, group homes, and therapeutic foster care, coordinated by the Child Welfare League of America. It was conducted under the auspices of the Center for the Study of Social Work Practice, a joint program of the Jewish Board of Family and Children's Services and the Columbia University School of Social Work. The authors thank Karen Staller, Terry Wolfer, and Piero di Porzio for their assistance on earlier drafts of this chapter.

This chapter was originally published in the September 1997 issue of Social Work, *vol. 42, pp. 495–505.*

12   The Little Village Project: A Community Approach to the Gang Problem

Irving A. Spergel and Susan F. Grossman

Community organization and direct services are not easily combined in the modern lexicon of social work methods. The current rhetoric distinguishing community and personal empowerment from various treatment modalities, however defined, may be insufficient for planning and dealing with the complex problems of troubled and troublesome people in fragmented, impoverished, and segregated communities (Mondros & Wilson, 1994). An older tradition of service delivery, interagency coordination, and social reform may need to be reinvigorated in more interactive and creative ways (Brager, Specht, & Torczyner, 1987; Ross, 1967). The complex present-day problems of juvenile delinquency and street gang crime may be a means to develop and test new service delivery, interagency coordination, and institutional reform strategies.

Youth gang crime and delinquency are major social problems that are no longer confined to inner-city areas. Both are now present in small as well as medium-size cities, suburban areas, and rural areas (Curry, Ball, & Decker, 1995; Klein, 1995a; Miller, in press; Spergel, 1995). However, there is no "hard" evidence that any specific social services or a suppression strategy has by itself contributed to the prevention or reduction of gang crime—either gang violence or gang-related drug dealing. Claims by various social intervention projects (for example, Goldstein, Glick, Carthon, & Blancero, 1994) or police departments about effective reduction of the problems have not been supported by good evidence. Gang crime fluctuates, is often seasonal and cyclical, and is more serious at some times and less so in others (Illinois Criminal Justice Information Authority, 1996; Klein, 1995b). Nevertheless, the trend for gang crime, especially gang violence, has been upward in scope and severity at least since the mid-1980s.

Traditional outreach, youth work, and gang work have emphasized direct counseling, crisis intervention, mediation, or mentoring and most recently has targeted younger at-risk youths. Group work interest in the youth gang problem has a long history (Puffer, 1912; Spergel, 1995; Thrasher, 1927). Street gang work flourished in the late 1940s through the early 1960s but declined until the early 1990s. Currently, youth gang work is experiencing a rebirth within a broader, more collaborative interagency and community framework in a variety of contexts: schools, inner-city neighborhoods, American Indian reservations, residential centers, and prisons.

Evaluation of a series of single-dimensional social outreach programs in the 1960s and 1970s suggested little positive impact of these efforts alone. Miller

(1962) in Boston and Gold and Mattick (1974) in Chicago reported no positive changes resulting from the programs they assessed; Klein (1968), in his evaluation of a Los Angeles County probation project, reported negative effects. Spergel, Castellano, Pleas, and Brown (1969) and Spergel (1995), in their evaluations of the Woodlawn Organization's Youth Manpower Project in Chicago, stated that the project assisted in the development of two major criminal gang structures—the Blackstone Rangers, later the Black P. Stone Nation and more recently the El Rukns, and the Devil's Disciples, later the Black Gangster Disciples, currently the largest gang in Illinois. Fragmentation of program and policy, lack of cooperation, and conflict among social and criminal justice agencies and local and national community organizations may have indirectly contributed to the failure of many gang control and prevention efforts.

Police interest in street gangs in their current serious criminal form evolved in the 1960s in Chicago and Los Angeles. Police responses, characterized by the creation of specialized gang units and a suppression or attack strategy, coincided with the weakening or demise of the social intervention approach. A suppression strategy by law enforcement came to be associated with increased arrests, improved prosecution, and longer sentences, but there was no consistent evidence of improved community control or a decline in the problem (Howell, 1996). Currently, suppression is the dominant approach in various social contexts: the local community, schools, public housing projects, or prison.

An effective approach to youth gang problems was developed in Philadelphia during the early 1970s. A Crisis Intervention Network (CIN) project involved a youth agency collaborating citywide with school personnel, police officers, adult probation officers, and a network of block clubs or small neighborhood resident groups. A sharp reduction of gang homicides followed and was associated with the project throughout the 1970s. However, an evaluation of this project was not conducted. Moreover, during this period a gang drug economy arose and may have mitigated the violence aspect of the gang problem. Further, some questions were raised about a change in police recording practices, which may have been related to changing homicide rates (Klein, Maxson, & Miller, 1995; Spergel, 1995).

The Little Village Gang Violence Reduction Project in Chicago represents an interorganizational and community approach to the youth gang problem in its most violent form. This approach is characterized by a team of community youth workers, probation officers, tactical police officers, and a community organization carrying out interrelated strategies involving social intervention, social opportunities provision, social control, and gang suppression within a framework of community activism. Applying the model in the community has reduced the problem of gang violence in Little Village in comparison to control areas in Little Village and elsewhere in Chicago over a four-year demonstration period (Spergel & Grossman, 1996). A principal factor in the reduction of gang violence has been the close collaboration of community youth workers, many who are themselves former gang members, and police officers, as well as probation officers and representatives of local organizations and residents through targeting hard-core gang youths (that is, those who possess guns, are repeat offenders, and are influentials in gang crime), particularly those who are in their middle to late teenage years or early 20s. The process of collaboration of workers from disparate agencies is of special interest in this discussion.

LITTLE VILLAGE PROJECT MODEL

The Little Village Gang Violence Reduction Project is a variation and further elaboration of the Philadelphia CIN Project. The Little Village Project also is based on a research and development process conducted between 1987 and 1991. The project is currently related to a follow-up national comprehensive, communitywide approach to gang prevention, intervention, and suppression being tested in 10 other cities. Funding for these initiatives has come mainly from the Bureau of Justice Assistance and the Office of Juvenile Justice and Delinquency Prevention (OJJDP) of the U.S. Department of Justice. The elements of the approach, as indicated above, consist of the following interrelated strategies (Spergel et al., 1994): community mobilization, opportunities provision, social intervention, suppression, organizational change and development, and targeting.

Community Mobilization

Community mobilization is the involvement of local citizens and organizations, including local residents and groups, youth agencies, police and probation officers, and former gang youths, in a common enterprise. Not only community and agency leaders but also street-level staff must be coordinated into a team. This integration is particularly important in communities with a chronic gang problem that are disorganized or seriously fragmented in their approach to that problem and where high levels of gang activity, especially violence, are present.

Opportunities Provision

This opportunities provision is based on the premise that relevant opportunities, such as more and better jobs, special education programs, and training programs, are critical to meeting the needs of low-income youths at particular points in their developmental cycles. For example, training and job opportunities should be accessible to older gang youths who, for a variety of reasons such as maturation and pressures to raise a family, may be ready to leave the gang. Remedial educational programs and alternative schools as well as work on family support structures may be required for younger youths at risk of becoming gang members.

Social Intervention

Social intervention refers to outreach to gang youths in the streets or in problematic social contexts and is based on the assumption that many youths are not able to use available opportunities to become adequately connected to legitimate social institutions. The primary purpose of the social intervener is to mainstream alienated youths. Social intervention must be ecological in nature, dealing appropriately with the individual, the gang structure, and the environmental resources in an interactive and interdependent way. The various modalities of social intervention—crisis counseling; individual and family counseling; and referral for services and resources such as drug treatment, jobs, training, educational programs, and some recreation—must be related not only to case management, advocacy, and coordination of agency programs, but also to resource development in particular social and physical contexts.

Suppression

Suppression for purposes of gang control requires the application of a variety of informal as well as formal controls on the behavior of individual youths and the structure and process of their gangs. Not only supervision and surveillance, arrest, probation, and imprisonment, but also positive communication with youths, information sharing with other agency service and control providers, and joint decision making among agency and community group representatives are essential elements of social control. Suppression also must be viewed as an integral component related to the other strategies described here.

Organizational Change and Development

Units of workers within and across key organizations must collaborate through a closely knit structure that develops a common set of objectives for reducing and preventing gang crime and mainstreaming gang youths or those at risk. The team must develop effective procedures to achieve these objectives. Mutual trust, interdependence, and high levels of morale need to evolve from a carefully supported and nurtured process of organizational change and development at the administrative level as well.

Targeting

A team of workers from different disciplines must be established to target specific youths, gangs, and social contexts who or which induce crime situations. Consensus must be achieved about who and what should be targeted in a particular community. Limited resources must be combined and focused on certain aspects of the problem. Essential to targeting is clarity and consistency of definition about who is a gang youth, what is a gang, and what is a gang incident. Only a relatively small number of youths in particular gangs are likely to be highly at risk or chronic gang offenders. The target youths often are from troubled or dysfunctional families and are located in certain neighborhoods, hangouts, schools, parks, streets, stores, or school buses (Spergel et al., 1994).

LITTLE VILLAGE AND THE GANG PROBLEM

The Little Village community was selected as a test of this strategic model. Criteria for selection were that the community had a serious problem of gang violence and preferably only a moderate drug problem, a more complex problem when interrelated with gang violence. There had to be sufficient institutional and community strengths to produce a significant and measurable program effect. The ages of the youths to be targeted, initially 17 to 24 years, were determined on the basis of the requirements of a Federal Urban Violence Reduction block grant, mandating that the age group responsible for most of the serious gang violence be targeted.

Until the 1970s Little Village, or La Villita, was a community of aging Central Europeans residing in small bungalows and apartment buildings. In 1992 Little Village had a population of 80,000, of which more than 90 percent were Mexican and Mexican American. It is a low-income area but does not have much public housing and is not one of the poorest communities in Chicago. Currently in the community is a wide array of small businesses and educational, medical, social, cultural, and religious institutions. A sizable number of factories are in the area, which provide jobs for the local population. The community, southwest of Chicago's central business district, consists of six beats of the 10th District of the Chicago Police Department. These beats became the boundaries for program implementation and evaluation purposes.

Gang violence in Little Village involved chronic, serious turf fighting mainly between two gangs: the Latin Kings and the Two Six. Many members of the two gangs had known each other for years, had attended the same elementary schools, and were occasionally from the same immediate or extended families. Each gang comprised about 10 to 15 sections identified by the names of particular neighboring streets or aggregations of such streets. The Latin Kings were the older, more established gang that lived in the eastern section in somewhat poorer three-story apartment housing. The Two Six comprised younger youths and lived in the western section in better bungalow-type housing with somewhat larger families.

The two gangs accounted for about 70 percent of the serious gang violence (gang homicides, batteries with firearms, and assaults with firearms) in Little Village. Furthermore, older gang youths, ages 17 to 24 and mainly male, accounted for about 75 percent of the serious gang violence in the target area. The Latin Kings were the more violent and criminal group; the Two Six engaged in more property crime. About 90 percent of the youths initially contacted ($n = 108$) by the project were already known to the Cook County Adult Criminal Court.

GANG VIOLENCE REDUCTION PROJECT

The goal was the absolute or relative reduction of serious violence among gang youths served in the project, compared to similar nonserved or noncontacted gang youths in the area or across similar gang areas over time. About 200 hardcore youths in the two gangs were targeted over the four-year project period. The mechanism for achievement of the goal was a team of workers consisting of a unit of police officers, including two full-time tactical officers, a part-time neighborhood relations sergeant, and a part-time clerical officer; a unit of three full-time Cook County Criminal Court adult probation officers, including a supervisor (and more recently one juvenile court intensive probation supervisor liaison); and a unit of community youth workers, including a full-time supervisor and two full-time and two part-time workers located at the School of Social Service Administration (SSA), University of Chicago, under the general direction of the senior author, who also acted as a coordinator of the overall project. Also closely related to the project team was the director of the Neighbors Against Gang Violence (NAGV), an independent local organization formed with the aid of the project coordinator and his assistant. NAGV comprised representatives of three Catholic churches, a Protestant church, a jobs agency, two boys and girls clubs, a major local youth agency, the local alderman's office, a large Latino community organization, and several local residents.

Each project unit carried out its organizational mission and simultaneously targeted hard-core gang youths in a collaborative fashion. Initial contacts were generally made by community youth workers, who were based on the streets. The targeted gang youths also were known to other units of the project through arrest, probation, family work, recreation, and religious contacts. One marked distinction from the original design of the project was that NAGV workers, although expected to encourage the development of local services and provide an interagency coordination function, instead performed mainly family services and recreational functions, focusing on younger male siblings in the families of the targeted youths. Early in the development of NAGV, several communitywide neighborhood meetings were held, although there was limited follow-up of concerns expressed by neighborhood residents and insufficient involvement by nonproject local organizations in the work of the Gang Violence Reduction Project. The project did not attempt and was not able to address general problems of interagency fragmentation and community development.

Over time, a high degree of interrelatedness and consistency of objectives and field operations developed among project workers. The tactical officers were on the streets at least four nights a week from 4:30 PM to midnight and later. Occasionally they were in court in the mornings or on special assignment. The community youth workers worked similar late afternoon and night hours but on a staggered basis so that all nights and days of the week were covered. In addition to street contacts, much of the community youth workers' time was taken up with job placement, school referrals and transfers, and occasional court appearances.

The probation officers were on duty two or three nights per week. Their caseloads were more inclusive of different types of gang offenders, particularly drug dealers or those convicted of drug offenses, than those of the police and community youth workers and included gang youths who were not from the immediate Little Village area. The NAGV workers, particularly the director who was the organization's only full-time worker, seemed to be available almost all of the time. The team members, including NAGV, met at least once every two weeks for general reporting, project development, and special targeting of youths who were recently most actively involved in violent activities. The group also met periodically for case management purposes, that is, to exchange information and plan treatment and contacts for youths in the program. These case management sessions lasted up to two hours and were conducted over a two-month period two or three times per year. More than 200 youths were assessed as to progress and treatment planning over each series of case management meetings.

The project workers regularly met for formal meetings at the probation office in the Little Village community. Sometimes meetings were held at the 10th District police station, although such meetings were not always comfortable for community youth workers, several of whom as former gang members were well known to some nonproject police officers. Meetings were also held at the SSA. Occasionally the district police commander, liaison officers of the police department's Research and Development Division, and the deputy chief of probation as well as the associate director of the Illinois Criminal Justice Information Authority (the State Planning Agency) attended project meetings. Each component unit also had separate weekly meetings in its own agency setting. Each unit continued to report to its administration and abide by its overall departmental regulations. Nevertheless, mechanisms were devised to facilitate almost daily communication and interaction. All of the workers had beepers, and police officers and probation workers had agency radios. Several police officers and community youth workers had cellular telephones. All of the police officers, community youth workers, and probation officers had access to and generally used protective vests. They also used their own or agency vehicles and regularly observed, but did not necessarily interact with, each other openly in the community.

PROJECT WORKER RELATIONSHIPS

Community Youth Workers and Police Officers

The most unusual and innovative relationships that developed were those between the police tactical officers and the community youth workers. The two tactical officers were in their late 20s and early 30s, originally with limited experience in dealing with gangs. Only one was of part-Mexican ancestry. The two officers had some college credit. All of the community youth workers were in their 20s, Mexican American, and from the target neighborhood. They were either former gang influentials or had grown up in the company of gang members. The community youth work supervisor and one of the senior community youth workers were college graduates; one community youth worker had a year of junior college, and two others were completing general equivalency diploma (GED) or evening high school classes. One had spent eight years in prison for a gang homicide; two had police records but had not served time in prison. Whereas the two tactical officers had been with the project since its inception four years earlier, the community youth workers had been on board for shorter, varying periods. During the first two years of the project, a half dozen community youth workers had to be replaced, mainly for reasons related to deficiencies in job performance. A few of the community youth workers were arrested for a variety of crimes off the job, such as stalking, traffic offenses, and probation violation.

Police and community youth workers shared a deep commitment to the project's goals and objectives. Police continued to be identified with their police peers in the tactical units but did not focus on making a certain number of arrests per day. The community youth workers functioned as youth workers but also were closely identified with the legitimate aspirations and interests of youths in the gangs from which they had originated. They were deeply concerned about gang violence and were prepared to reduce it by nearly any means possible.

Each of the workers, especially the police officers and community youth workers, sought information that would contribute to the project mission and shared such information with each other formally and informally. It was easier for probation officers and the neighborhood organizers to share information and collaborate with other staff; they were not at opposite ends of the ideological pole. The community youth workers and police officers were embedded in networks of relationships and situations that made teamwork problematic at first. The officers had to learn to communicate with gang youths in a manner that demonstrated genuine concern for the welfare of the youths and their families; they had to be as much concerned with prevention as with arrest. They learned to understand the youths. The officers referred the youths to community youth workers for jobs and school programs and collaborated with them but were careful not to be seen as too closely affiliated to avoid threatening the relationships of the workers with the gang members.

At first the project's police officers were regarded as "kiddy cops" by their peer officers. When the officers first began to talk to gang youths, they were regarded as gang members themselves by local residents, who sometimes reported their activities to the police. Project officers moved about in their unmarked cars, getting to know gang sections. They were soon able to identify the various gang structures, leaders, and hard-core youths to be targeted. The officers were instrumental in solving a high percentage of aggravated batteries and homicides in and out of the area in which local gang youths were involved. The other district tactical officers eventually came to depend on the project officers for critical information and advice about gang problems. County police and agents of the Federal Bureau of Investigation also found their information and contacts valuable. The district's police tactical teams began to use a similar approach as that of the project police, learning to better communicate with gang youths and in the process to more effectively carry out their law enforcement functions.

The community youth workers were embedded in a network of gang relationships although they were no longer engaged in fighting or in criminal behavior. The workers not only had to develop new quasi-professional skills related to referrals of gang youths to agency services or job placement, but they also had to learn to collaborate with police and probation officers in such a way that gang conflict was prevented or at least controlled. To the extent possible, the workers assisted the police to avoid arrest of the wrong youths and helped gang youths avoid probation violations by getting them to report to their probation officers on time. The workers learned to trust the project police officers and provided them with many leads to solve gang crime incidents.

The community youth workers were able to maintain the respect of gang youths while continuing to influence them through advice, counseling, job placement and school referrals, and encouragement to become more closely aligned with legitimate institutions and practices. Gang members eventually came to understand and accept not only the community youth workers' helping role but also their relationship with police and probation officers. This understanding helped gang youths avoid harassment from the police and incarceration and made life more tolerable in the community. Gang youths were helped to better distinguish "good" and "bad" cops and were advised on how to handle the latter in a "better way." They respected the new role of the community youth workers in protecting the resident bystanders as well as themselves from gang shootings.

Other Project Personnel

All of the project workers were enmeshed in a variety of interdependent project relationships. Probation staff sought the assistance of community youth workers in getting probationers to show up for regular contacts, to obtain jobs, and to return to school. The NAGV workers assisted community youth workers with supplementary information about gang youths, contacts with family, and services for training and jobs. The NAGV workers were quick to alert project workers to new graffiti, shootings, and community situations that could lead to further intergang conflict. This information was shared with both police officers and community youth workers.

A much closer relationship between the police and probation officers was established. The police officers now shared information about a gang case with probation officers within a matter of minutes, rather than weeks and having to wait for information to filter through agency channels. Police officers, probation officers, and community youth workers together supervised gang youths at graffiti "paint outs"; youths who put up the graffiti now expunged it. Project workers together were involved in softball games with gang members from the warring groups without mishap, although the games were played outside the neighborhood. Police and probation officers and community youth workers participated together with various factions of gang youths in group counseling sessions at the SSA. These sessions, however, did not progress to the point that members of the opposing gangs were present in the same session. At the same time, members of the two gangs occasionally participated with each other in basketball games and more general training workshops on the border between, or outside, the two gang territories. They also participated together in local citizen group meetings sponsored by the various project units.

The close relationships of police officers, community youth workers, probation officers, and NAGV workers with each other in working with hard-core gang youths contributed to project staff cohesion and high morale. All of the workers were highly visible to each other in the community, contributing to a high level of accountability and quality job performance. For example, the community youth workers could not "goof off" or engage in nonconstructive behavior (for example, drinking beer) with the gang youths in the streets or not show up for scheduled interagency meetings. The police officers maintained a high level of professional activity and came to be well respected by the gang youths, the community youth workers, and neighborhood residents.

INTEGRATION OF RESEARCH AND DEMONSTRATION

A key aspect of the project was the integration of program operations and evaluation. The SSA research team was the sole evaluator; although the team worked closely with the community youth workers, it was separate from them. The evaluators regularly disseminated information about the content, nature, and scope of the gang problem and progress of the project. They obtained aggregate crime data from the Crime Analysis Section of the Chicago Police Department and the Early Warning System of the Illinois Criminal Justice Information Authority. The evaluation team identified certain gangs, streets, age groups, and shifts in crime patterns that were useful to the program team. For example, information that more juveniles ages 14 to 16 were becoming involved in serious gang crime was the basis for lowering the age of the youths to be targeted. Information that most gang crimes were occurring between 6:00 PM and midnight and that female gang members were not substantially involved in serious gang violence aided the project's focus.

The evaluators performed a variety of tasks essential to measuring project impact and outcome. Community surveys of residents ($N = 200$) and local community organizations or agency representatives ($N = 100$) at two time periods on their perceptions about the nature and scope of the gang problem in Little Village and the comparison community—Pilsen—were useful in assessing changing levels of gang crime and the effects of policing with respect to these levels. Data from interviews of three cohorts of youths ($n = 194$) entering the program, as well as police data, court data, and detention data, were critical in determining the effectiveness of the project. Police data on the nontargeted youths arrested along with members of the target gangs at program entry were useful in the construction of control groups. Also critical were tracking data. Each project worker was surveyed as to what services and activities were provided and what progress was made by program youths. The extent of coordination among project workers was also determined. The aggregate results of each periodic evaluation were given to program personnel at intervals varying from three months to one year. These analyses provided preliminary but important estimates about the differential effects and effectiveness of the project.

Community youth workers were essential to the evaluators in locating and relocating targeted youths for yearly research interviews. The youth workers assisted in obtaining consent from the youths and their parents for interviews. They corrected information about youths' names and addresses (gang youths had street names and often used aliases). The meaning of the grouped data also was more clearly established with the aid of interpretations from community youth workers, police officers, and other project workers. However, names or identifying information about gang youths was not shared by researchers with program personnel or anyone else. Confidentiality and protection of data were strictly observed.

RESULTS

Process

Although only preliminary data are available on the effectiveness of the Gang Violence Reduction Project, the results appear to be consistently positive. Analysis of data for the 125 targeted youths, mainly cohort I and cohort II over three

years, on whom there is program information thus far, indicates that almost all
(98.4 percent) had contact with community youth workers, and a large proportion (36.8 percent) were contacted and sometimes arrested by project police.
Smaller percentages were contacted or served by probation officers (10.4 percent) and NAGV (14.4 percent). Almost half (45.6 percent) of the targeted youths
received contacts or services from more than one group of project workers, primarily police officers and community youth workers. The majority received some
kind of informal counseling or support from project personnel (95.2 percent).
Family contacts were made for almost two-thirds (64.0 percent) of the targeted
individuals served. Similarly, about two-thirds (65.6 percent) of the gang youths
were involved in some type of athletic activity (basketball nights, baseball games)
with project staff. Assistance or job-related referrals were made for nearly two-
thirds (64.0 percent), and slightly more than half (53.6 percent) received assistance or referral related to a school problem. Finally, police and probation personnel reported that they had engaged in suppression activities for 31.2 percent
of the 125 youths.

The impact of the project (as well as youth maturation) on school and job
attainment appears to be striking. The proportion of individuals in cohorts I
and II who graduated from high school or received GED certificates rose from
25.3 percent at the first baseline interview to 51.6 percent at the third annual
interview. Similarly, the proportion of individuals in cohorts I and II who were
currently employed increased from 30.8 percent at the first interview to 76.0
percent at the third interview. The increase was smaller for the Latin Kings, but
employment for members of this gang was more steady over the three years of
project service (Spergel & Grossman, 1996).

Outcome

Arrests for a three-year preprogram interval for targeted youths were compared
to a three-year program period for control youths (Grossman et al., 1996). The
program youths experienced a relative reduction in gang crime, especially gang
violence, compared to the two groups of control youths (that is, nontargeted
gang youths receiving some services but not receiving coordinated intensive
service or contacts and nontargeted or nonserved contacted youths from the
same gangs who were arrested for the same incidents in the first program year).
Crime patterns of program youths were compared not only with those of other
similar groups but with themselves in the preprogram period, controlling for
age in a modified cohort analysis (Grossman, Spergel, & Jacob, 1997).

Table 12.1 presents the results of a multivariate analysis using, as an outcome
measure, police data on arrests for violent crime—which included homicide,
aggravated battery, battery, aggravated assault, assault, armed robbery, and robbery—in the three-year project period for program and comparison group youths.
The two comparison groups were generated from police arrest data about individuals arrested along with the project youths from cohort I. The first of these
groups included individuals who were not known to project staff (*n* = 85). The
second group consisted of individuals who had had limited contacts or services
from the project team even though they were never directly targeted for service

Table 12.1

Model Predicting Arrests for Violent Crime in the Three-Year Project Period

Variable	ß	t	p > t
Intercept	1.173179	2.891	0.0043*
Individual is younger than 19	−0.103985	−0.569	0.5700
Individual is a Two Six member vs. a Latin Kings member	0.080611	0.596	0.5516
Arrests for violent crime in the three years before the project	0.201759	3.190	0.0016*
Individual is a project youth vs. a control group youth	0.158240	0.838	0.4027
Individual is control group youth who received services or was known to project staff vs. not receiving services or being a project youth	−0.341323	−1.876	0.0620
Individual is age 19 or older and a project youth vs. all others	−0.599957	−2.241	0.0261*

NOTES: Arrests for homicide, aggravated battery, battery, aggravated assault, assault, armed robbery, and robbery based on Chicago Policy Department classification. Overall adjusted R^2 for the model = .0790, $N = 216$, $df = 6$.

*The coefficient is statistically significant in the model.

or contacts ($n = 42$). Variables controlling for the influence of age, gang affiliation, prior criminal history, targeted versus comparison group status, and "contact" nontargeted comparison group status were included in the model, as was an interaction term controlling for both age and project service. Together these variables accounted for about 8 percent of the variance in arrests for violent crime in the three-year project period. The strongest predictor of outcomes was prior history; those who had been arrested for more violent crimes in the three-year preproject phase were more likely to be arrested for such offenses in the project period. Still, taking prior history into account, the project had a significant effect in reducing violent criminal activity, particularly for youths who were older when the project began. Those who were 19 or older did better over time and had fewer arrests when they received project services and contacts compared to project cases who were younger or to individuals from both comparison groups regardless of age. Similar analysis using the same variables for the combined first and second cohorts of project youths and control group cases revealed the same results for the interaction of age and service or contact variables (beta = 0.556392, $t = 2.418$, $p = .0163$, $N = 270$). None of the other variables, with the exception of prior arrests for violent crime, attained statistical significance in the equation.

However, looking at police arrest data in the third program year only, the younger age group did better during the program years than the older group. They did not do as well in the comparison of the three-year program versus three-year preprogram periods. Age or maturation and program effects interacted to produce different position results for these older youths.

Table 12.2 discusses self-reported crime data for youths from cohort I receiving coordinated services versus those who had contact with only community youth workers. The coordinated service group included youths who were served by community youth workers and police officers; police officers and NAGV; community youth workers and probation officers; community youth workers, police

Table 12.2

Self-Reported Crimes for Individuals Receiving Coordinated Services versus Those Having Contact with Only Community Youth Workers, Comparing First Program Year and Third Program Year (First Cohort)

| | Self-Reported Total Crimes | | | | | | Violent Crimes[a] | | | | | |
| | At Baseline | | At Third Interview | | Difference | | At Baseline | | At Third Interview | | Difference | |
Group	M	N	M	N	M	N	M	N	M	N	M	N
Coordinated services	76.6*	28	11.1	28	−65.5†††	28	46.6*	27	8.3	27	−38.3††	27
Community youth workers only	37.5	25	6.1	25	−31.4††	25	20.5	26	3.5	26	−17.0†	26
Total	58.2	53	8.7	53	−49.5†††	53	33.8	53	5.9	53	−27.9†††	53

| | Average Property Crimes[b] | | | | | | Average Days Selling Drugs | | | | | |
| | At Baseline | | At Third Interview | | Difference | | At Baseline | | At Third Interview | | Difference | |
Group	M	N	M	N	M	N	M	N	M	N	M	N
Coordinated services	29.8	28	2.6	28	−27.2††	28	154.7	27	69.3	27	−85.4	27
Community youth workers only	15.7	26	2.4	26	−13.3††	26	91.7	28	75.4	28	−16.3	28
Total	23.0	54	2.5	54	−20.5†††	54	122.6	55	72.4	55	−50.2	55

NOTES: For differences within groups between time periods: †$p \leq .05$, ††$p \leq .01$, †††$p \leq .001$. For differences between groups within time periods: *$p \leq .05$.
[a]Includes robbery with and without a weapon, threats with and without a weapon, gang intimidation, battery with and without a weapon, homicide, and drive-by shootings.
[b]Includes writing gang and nongang graffiti, destroying property worth $300 or less, entering or breaking into a building to commit a theft, stealing a car for joy riding, and breaking into a car and stealing parts.

officers, and probation officers; community youth workers, police officers, and NAGV; or all four types of project team members. Three individuals were served by community youth workers and NAGV; however, they were not included in the coordinated service group because they were receiving the same type of services (that is, variations of social intervention). Therefore, these three youths were excluded from the analysis, as were seven others who were interviewed but apparently received no services.

The coordinated services group had a significantly higher average number of reported total crime at the baseline interview compared to the noncoordinated group. Significant differences also existed at baseline in relation specifically to violent crimes; the coordinated services contact youths reported slightly more than twice the number of violent crimes on average compared to those receiving services from community youth workers only. This is consistent with the key objective of the project to target the most violent and criminal youths in the gangs; however, at the time of the third interview, a different picture emerged. The coordinated services contact group had averages similar to those in the noncoordinated group for all crimes as well as for violent and property crimes. The coordinated group had a slightly lower average number of reported days selling drugs and greater decreases over time in the number of reported crimes. Their average decrease between the first and third interviews for days selling drugs was slightly more than five times greater than those in the noncoordinated group; their declines were up to twice as great in the other categories of crime.

The results of the analysis of official police arrest data are similar to the outcomes for self-reported crimes (Table 12.3). In the first project year (October 1992 to September 1993), the coordinated services group had higher average numbers of arrests in all categories examined, with the exception of arrests for drug-related crimes (Table 12.4), which were identical for both groups. However, in the third project year (October 1994 to September 1995), differences between the groups were much smaller. In addition, in all categories in which declines occurred over time, the declines were greater for the coordinated services group. Further, the coordinated group had declines in both the Gang Violence Reduction Project (GVRP) and "Hotspots" violence indexes (see Table 12.3 for list of crimes), whereas the community youth workers only group experienced increases in both these categories. The coordinated services group also underwent statistically significant declines in arrests for property-related crimes, whereas the noncoordinated group experienced no change.

The one category in which outcomes differed relative to self-reported crime was with respect to drug-related arrests for possession as well as for manufacture and delivery (Table 12.4). However, the number of arrests in this category was small. There was no evidence of increase in the most serious drug-related crimes of manufacture and delivery; most of the arrests related more to drug use or possession.

An additional analysis of first- versus third-year program periods, especially for the first cohort, controlling for respondent's age indicated similar patterns; the coordinated services–contact group generally experienced either greater declines or had lower averages of reported criminal activity in the third year,

Table 12.3

Police Arrest Data for Individuals Receiving Coordinated Services versus Those Having Contact with Community Youth Workers Only: First Project Year versus Third Project Year

	Average No. All Arrests			Average No. of Arrests for GVRP Index Offenses[a]		
Group	First Project Year	Third Project Year	Difference	First Project Year	Third Project Year	Difference
Coordinated services (n = 31)	1.39**	0.65	−0.74††	0.26	0.19	−0.07
Community youth workers only (n = 31)	0.61	0.48	−0.13	0.10	0.16	+0.06
Total (n = 62)	1.00	0.56	−0.44†	0.18	0.18	0.00

	Average No. of Arrests for Hotspots Violence Offenses[b]			Average No. of Arrests for Property-Related Offenses[c]		
Group	First Project Year	Third Project Year	Difference	First Project Year	Third Project Year	Difference
Coordinated services (n = 31)	0.16*	0.13	−0.03	0.61*	0.06	−0.55**††
Community youth workers only (n = 31)	0.00	0.10	+0.10	0.16	0.16	0.00
Total (n = 62)	0.08	0.11	+0.03	0.39	0.11	−0.28†

NOTES: For differences between groups within time periods: $*p \leq .05$, $**p \leq .01$. For differences within groups between time periods: $†p \leq .05$, $††p \leq .01$.
[a]Includes robbery with and without a weapon, assault, aggravated assault, battery, aggravated battery, and murder; GVRP = Gang Violence Reduction Project.
[b]Includes aggravated battery, aggravated assault, and murder.
[c]Includes all arrests related to burglaries, thefts, motor vehicle damage and criminal trespass of motor vehicles, damage to property including graffiti, and trespass-related charges.

Table 12.4

Adult Police Arrest Data for Individuals Receiving Coordinated Services versus Those Having Contact with Community Youth Workers Only: First Project Year versus Third Project Year

	Average No. of Drug-Related Arrests[a]		
Group	First Year	Third Year	Difference
Coordinated services (n = 31)	0.06	0.16	+0.10
Community youth workers only (n = 31)	0.06	0.10	+0.04
Total (n = 62)	0.06	0.13	+0.07

[a]Includes possession of marijuana, possession of a controlled substance, and distribution or delivery of a controlled substance.

using self-report data, regardless of age. When official police data were used, differences between the youth workers only and coordinated groups were still present. However, differences between the two types of services–contact groups were greater among those who were younger. Again, the coordinated group had larger declines in arrests on average for younger and older program youths over time. Further analysis will focus on clarifying the aspects of the program and other characteristics of individuals—who seemed to have experienced greater decreases in criminal activity over time—under different conditions.

Aggregate crime data about the most serious gang-motivated violent incidents also indicated positive change. Little Village had the lowest increase in gang violence compared to six similar mainly Hispanic areas in Chicago with similar attributes and high levels of gang violence when a four-year program period was compared to an equivalent four-year preprogram interval (Grossman et al., 1996). The level of serious gang violence for the members of the Latin Kings and Two Six gangs generally (including those targeted and not targeted) was also lower or in some cases declined compared to other nontargeted or nonserved Latino or black gangs in the same police district for the same four-year program period compared to the four-year preprogram period.

Comparing Little Village and Pilsen at the beginning of the project and two years later indicated a greater statistically significant reduction in the perceived level of gang violence and gang property crime among residents (N = 200) and groups and organizations (N = 100) in Little Village. Further, Little Village residents viewed the police as more effective than Pilsen residents viewed them in addressing the gang problem in their community (Spergel & Grossman, 1996).

CONCLUSION

The Gang Violence Reduction Project was expected to target a significant number of hard-core and some peripheral gang members. Not only individual, but areawide rates of gang violence were to be lowered, relatively and absolutely, after a reasonable period. Furthermore, the perceptions of Little Village residents about rates of gang crime were expected to be lower compared to those of residents of Pilsen, an almost identical community nearby without the program.

The Gang Violence Reduction Project is a pioneering, cross-disciplinary, community-based effort to control and prevent serious gang crime, especially gang violence. Evidence of success was achieved based on realistic strategies generated within a theoretical framework consistent with social work values as well as theories from other disciplines, particularly social disorganization, opportunity, and anomie. The project idea is now being accepted as a possible extension of community policing. Integration of tactical police and adult probation efforts is planned. It is not clear, however, whether and how the community youth work component will be adapted.

Project ideas continue to be the basis for the development of two major programs from the OJJDP to prevent and control the gang problem in other large and medium-size cities of the United States: the OJJDP Comprehensive Communitywide Approach to Gang Prevention, Intervention, and Suppression Program and the Safe Futures Program. Of special interest to the office is further testing of the effectiveness of the combination of the community youth workers' and police officers' roles as part of a community-based approach in the reduction of the gang problem.

The Gang Violence Reduction Project may contribute to social work theory through its invigoration or further elaboration of the values of coordination as a key framework for the development of community organization practice. Community organization practice is not simplistically an issue of gaining power for those population groups who are disenfranchised. Practice should be based on realistic assumptions that social organization, community, and political systems often are complex, fragmented, and disassociated and can affect youths differently at different stages of development. Social workers can better address social problems through improved integration across organizational and community relationships. Methods of community organization, interagency coordination, and institutional change can be integrated through interrelated but complementary organizational and service delivery practices. Furthermore, much of community organization practice must consider an individual outcome as well as organizational change. Analysis of and prescriptions for social problems must not be based on ideology or notions in the abstract but related to specific facts and concerns by clients themselves, including gang youths and residents in particular communities.

The response to social problems such as gang violence is often stereotypic or opportunistic for organizational development or political purposes. Nevertheless, the problem of inadequate agency or community response can be overcome through a local and broader community interactive and collaborative process with appropriate incentives and constraints as well as good leadership (Spergel, 1995). No single agency, community group, discipline, or approach alone is sufficient to successfully address a complex problem such as gang crime.

REFERENCES

Brager, G., Specht, H., & Torczyner, J. L. (1987). *Community organizing* (2nd ed.). New York: Columbia University Press.

Curry, G. D., Ball, R. A., & Decker, S. H. (1995). *Developing national estimates of gang-related crime.* (Report to the National Institute of Justice). St. Louis: University of Missouri, Department of Criminology and Criminal Justice.

Gold, M., & Mattick, H. W. (1974). *Experiment in the streets: The Chicago youth development project.* Ann Arbor: University of Michigan, Institute for Social Research.

Goldstein, A. P., Glick, B., Carthon, W., & Blancero, D. (1994). *The prosocial gang.* Thousand Oaks, CA: Sage Publications.

Grossman, S. F., Lyndes, K., Barrios, E., Littleton, A., Jacob, A., & Spergel, I. (1996). *The Little Village Gang Violence Reduction Project evaluation progress report.* Chicago: University of Chicago, School of Social Service Administration.

Grossman, S. F., Spergel, I. A., & Jacob, A. (1997). *Use of the Modified Cohort Design Analysis.* Chicago: University of Chicago, School of Social Service Administration.

Howell, J. C. (1996). *Review of youth programs.* Washington, DC: U.S. Department of Justice, Office of Juvenile Justice and Delinquency Prevention, National Youth Gang Center.

Illinois Criminal Justice Information Authority. (1996, August). *Street gangs and crime* [Research Bulletin]. Chicago: Author.

Klein, M. W. (1968). *From association to guilt: The group guidance project in juvenile gang intervention.* Los Angeles: University of Southern California, Youth Studies Center, & Los Angeles County Probation Department.

Klein, M. W. (1995a). *The American street gang.* New York: Oxford University Press.

Klein, M. W. (1995b). *Street gang cycles.* In J. Q. Wilson & J. Petersilia (Eds.), *Crime* (pp. 217–236). San Francisco: Institute for Contemporary Studies.

Klein, M. W., Maxson, C. L., & Miller, J. (1995). *The modern gang reader.* Los Angeles: Roxbury Press.

Miller, W. B. (1962). The impact of a "total community" delinquency control project. *Social Problems, 19,* 168–191.

Miller, W. B. (in press). *The growth of youth gang problems in the United States: 1970–1995.* Washington, DC: U.S. Department of Justice, Office of Juvenile Justice and Delinquency Prevention, National Youth Gang Center.

Mondros, J. B., & Wilson, S. (1994). *Organizing for power and environment.* New York: Columbia University Press.

Puffer, J. A. (1912). *The boy and his gang.* Boston: Houghton Mifflin.

Ross, M. G. (1967). *Community organization, theory and principles* (2nd ed.). New York: Harper & Row.

Spergel, I. A. (1995). *The youth gang problem: A community approach.* New York: Oxford University Press.

Spergel, I. A., Castellano, T., Pleas, J., & Brown, P. (1969, February). *Evaluation of the youth manpower demonstration of the Woodlawn Organization* (Submitted to the Office of Economic Opportunity). Chicago: University of Chicago, School of Social Service Administration.

Spergel, I. A., Chance, R., Ehrensaft, K., Regulus, T., Kane, C., Laseter, K., Alexander, A., & Oh, S. (1994, October). *Gang suppression and intervention: Community models* [Research summary]. Washington, DC: U.S. Department of Justice, Office of Juvenile Justice and Delinquency Prevention.

Spergel, I. A., & Grossman, S. F. (1996). *Evaluation of a gang violence reduction project: A comprehensive and integrated approach.* Chicago: University of Chicago, School of Social Service Administration.

Thrasher, F. M. (1927). *The gang.* Chicago: University of Chicago Press.

The Chicago Police Department (Agency Award No. D50401) and the Illinois Criminal Justice Information Authority (Agency Award No. 11866-01-02) funded the program and the research. All views and conclusions expressed in this chapter are those of the authors and do not necessarily represent those of the above agencies. Laura Anderson, Louis Arata, Javier Avila, Elisa Barrios, Lisa DeVivo, Ayad Jacob, Joshua Levy, Annot

Littleton, Kathryn Lyndes, Rolando Sosa, and Kwai Ming Wa assisted with community gang problem assessment, project planning, data collection, access to youths, and data analysis.

This chapter was originally published in the September 1997 issue of Social Work, vol. 42, pp. 456–470.

Part IV

COMMUNITY ACTION
THROUGH AFFILIATIONS

13 Elizabeth Ross Haynes: An African American Reformer of Womanist Consciousness, 1908–1940

Iris Carlton-LaNey

As a pioneer social worker, author, politician, "race woman," and community activist, Elizabeth Ross Haynes constantly advocated and agitated for the rights of African Americans and for the rights of women. In 1937 she challenged her contemporaries with the following question:

> If Frances Perkins (the Honorable Frances Perkins), secretary of labor, can fill one of the most difficult posts in the Cabinet of the President of these United States—and this she had done superbly despite any criticisms—is not the time ripe for women, black and white, to extend and enlarge the opportunity fought for by Susan B. Anthony and Sojourner Truth, especially since the latter could neither read nor write? (Haynes, n.d.)

Haynes offered herself as a role model. She involved herself in researching, writing, and speaking about women's labor issues, women's spiritual and Christian growth, women's roles in the political arena, and women's use of all their talents and skills and did these to such an extent that she can be described as a pioneer in the women's movement of the Progressive Era and beyond.

Like most African American women of her time, however, Haynes has been virtually ignored in the study of women's contributions to social welfare history and to the development of social welfare institutions for African Americans and for the larger community. This invisibility of African American women in history leaves gaps in social workers' cognition, distorting the knowledge base. As Brown (1989) noted, an even greater problem is that because of the exclusion of African American women like Haynes, the "concepts, perspectives, methods, and pedagogues of women's history and women's studies have been developed without consideration of the experiences of black women" (p. 610). Furthermore, recent efforts to uncover African American women's history occurred parallel to the development of feminist theory. The consequence of this timing is that African American women's history is often couched inside the feminist perspective, which, according to Brown, was designed to omit the experiences of women of color. African American women generally have held marginal positions in the feminist movement. The misperception is that African American women deal either with women's issues or with race issues, and then sequentially, not simultaneously. White women have complained that they did not want to dissipate their energies dealing with issues of race, because their time could be better spent addressing issues of importance to all women (Giddings, 1984; Smith, 1985). For them, the primacy of female oppression denies the structured inequalities of race. On the other hand, McDougald (1925) stated that the African American woman's "feminist efforts are directed chiefly toward the realization of the equality of the races, the sex struggle assuming a subordinate place" (p. 691).

Some writers (Palmer, 1983; Terborg-Penn, 1983) have argued that the term "feminism" is partly responsible for the exclusion that African American women feel, because "feminism" puts a priority on gender, not race. To deal with the problem of terminology, author Alice Walker (1983) and others (Hine, 1996; Ogunyemi, 1985) have used the words "womanist" and "womanism" to describe the African American female experience. Walker defined *womanist* as a consciousness that incorporates racial, cultural, sexual, national, economic, and political considerations for all people. Hine believed that *womanism* speaks to a double legacy of oppression and a resistance movement among African American women. The term may be uncomfortable for some, but its ideals are descriptive of the life careers of many African American pioneer social welfare leaders of the Progressive Era. Leaders such as Ida B. Wells-Barnett, Janie Porter Barrett, and Birdye Henrietta Haynes knew that their oppressed positions in society resulted from both gender and race and that their struggle must include both, because they were not fragmented individuals but whole and holistic in consciousness and purpose.

This chapter focuses on Haynes's work in the interest of African American social welfare. With race and gender consciousness as the foundation of her social welfare activism, Haynes worked with African American women through the Young Women's Christian Association (YWCA) and the U.S. Department of Labor's Women in Industry Service (WIS). Her role as an elected leader in Harlem's 21st Assembly District is also discussed as one of several mechanisms for planned change on the community level.

"WOMANIST RACE WORKER"

Throughout her life, Haynes, affectionately known as "Rossie," articulated a womanist consciousness. It is unlikely that Haynes would have considered herself a feminist. She may well have been affronted by such a label, because her life's work incorporated the numerous issues of race, gender, culture, economics, and politics. Born in Mount Willing, Lowndes County, Alabama, in 1883, Haynes was the only child of Henry and Mary Ross. Lowndes County was one of the poorest areas in Alabama, where African Americans far outnumbered white people. The Ross family amassed some wealth through the purchase of land, which eventually grew to become a 1,500-acre plantation, giving them the luxury of educating their daughter at a level well beyond that of most African Americans of their time (Bogin, 1980; Lasch-Quinn, 1993). Haynes attended the State Normal School in Montgomery and later won a scholarship to Fisk University, where she was awarded an AB degree in 1903. She taught school in Alabama and Texas for several years after graduation, and during the summers of 1905 and 1907 she attended summer school at the University of Chicago.

In 1908 Haynes was invited to work with "colored students" for the Student Department of the National Board of the YWCA. She traveled to college campuses and cities where branches of the YWCA were established for African Americans. Although Haynes resigned from paid employment with the YWCA in 1910 when she married George Edmund Haynes, cofounder and first executive director of the National Urban League, her work with this organization continued for many years thereafter (Bogin, 1980). Her concern for women's equity and economic well-being was just beginning.

Labeling Haynes is a challenge, because the scope of her work is so broad and varied. McDougald (1925) described the following four groups into which African American women were divided during the 1920s, based on their work and activities:

> First, comes a very small leisure group—the wives and daughters of men who are in business, in the professions, and in a few well-paid personal service occupations. Second, a most active and progressive group, the women in business and the professions. Third, the many women in the trades and industry. Fourth, a group weighty in numbers struggling on in domestic service, with an even less fortunate fringe of casual workers, fluctuating with the economic temper of the times. (p. 689)

Haynes defies McDougald's categorization. Although she had a fairly privileged childhood and later gave up paid employment on her marriage, she did not while away her time in search of other black families who could boast of the same achievement and leisure. In her world privilege carried an obligation to those less fortunate; she became a professional volunteer using her knowledge, expertise, and social and political power for planned change on behalf of African Americans.

Haynes can be described as a "race woman" with a womanist consciousness. The work in which she engaged can best be described, in the vocabulary of her time, as "race work." In contemporary terms, "community work" best identifies her work. For Haynes, this work involved community advocacy coupled with the constant struggle for social justice, race uplift, and gender equity. It included a pride in self, a collective consciousness, and the dynamics of multiple commitments which, according to Higginbotham (1992), resisted white hegemonic discourses. Gilkes (1988, pp. 67–68) used the phrase "lots of small pieces" to describe the "web of affiliations" in which African American women engaged to be effective community advocates. This wide variety of involvement with numerous organizations, whose aims included interracial cooperation, political empowerment, economic advancement, education, cultural enhancement, and community endurance, illustrates the complexity and multiplicity of women's activities. "Lots of small pieces" is a fitting phrase to describe Haynes's "womanist race work."

PREPARING GIRLS FOR WOMANHOOD THROUGH THE YWCA

Haynes began her social work career as the first African American national board staff member with the Student Department of the YWCA. Working among college students for more than two years, Haynes traveled extensively throughout the country encouraging, supporting, and modeling expected behavior for African American college women. Her work also included supervisory responsibilities in cities where African American YWCAs had been established.

With a genuine concern for the students' quality of life, Haynes wrote to the national office that "to get a fair and true idea of the girls themselves, the ones in whom we are most deeply interested, it is very necessary to see them in and through their conditions and surroundings to know what they think and what they do." She indicated that "the girls' rooms [on the college campuses], though plainly and poorly furnished, are well kept, are improved by artistic touches here and there, and the girls themselves for the most part are quite tidy in their dress." Haynes further noted with some trepidation that "many work from the early morning hours steadily with just a few minutes between for meals until night and then attend night school. Most of them are able to get work in the schools, but it is necessary for some who support themselves entirely to live out in private families and do the cooking or the laundry work, or the general house work." Haynes felt that in general the students were "cheerful and determined to push ahead, [but] occasionally an almost discouraged girl has made her way to my room seeking advice, information, and more than all a word of encouragement" (Ross, 1909). Haynes had tremendous respect for these young women and saw in them the irrepressible spirit that characterized her own life.

Haynes was realistic and positive in her reports. She also was observant, with a particular eye for the student who showed unusual promise. On visiting Paine College, which Haynes described as "one of the strongest Associations on the field," she found that the young president of the association was "worthy of being kept in mind as a possible Association worker somewhere" (Ross, 1909).

Haynes was proud of her work with the YWCA and noted that after one year as "special worker," the "colored student associations" had increased in number from only 17 in 1909 to 50 by 1910, and that seven associations were subscribers to the *Association Monthly*, the literary organ of the YWCA, whereas only three had subscribed the previous year. She also noted the extent to which the students and the teachers at the various schools had contributed money to the national board in support of the secretary's work and of the conferences sponsored in support of African American YWCAs (Ross, 1910).

Although Haynes acknowledged that the amount contributed was minimal, she felt that "it is a sign of wonderful progress along several lines and especially in self-help" (Ross, 1910). Self-help efforts have a distinguished tradition in the African American community and are recognized as mechanisms for counteracting adverse societal forces and social policies (Hill et al., 1993; Peebles-Wilkins & Francis, 1990). Furthermore, self-help has formed the foundation of social welfare for African Americans. In Haynes's assessment, self-help was a major strength of the African American college YWCA and indicated the students' commitment to participate in determining their life's courses.

When she resigned from the YWCA, Haynes recommended that Cecelia Holloway, a Fisk University graduate, succeed her as "special worker." Her recommendation was accepted, and Haynes worked with Holloway, participating in her training for several months. Such mentoring and training were common among African American women and served to broaden and strengthen the sociopolitical network within which Haynes thrived. Haynes rejoined the YWCA in 1922, when she was named to the newly created Council on Colored Work. In 1924 she became the first African American member of the association's national board, remaining in the post for 10 years.

AFRICAN AMERICAN WOMEN'S WORK

In 1918, when George Edmund Haynes accepted the position of director of Negro economics for the U.S. Department of Labor, Haynes accompanied her husband to Washington, DC, and busied herself with issues of women in industry. In 1919 she became a dollar-a-year worker for the Department's WIS (after World War I, this section became the Women's Bureau). Mary Van Kleeck was the director of WIS; Haynes and Helen Irvin, a Howard University graduate, were appointed to serve as special aides to Van Kleeck (Neverdon-Morton, 1989). *New York City Tribune* reporter Hannah Mitchell found the two women fascinating, but something of an enigma. Mitchell (1919) described in great detail the two women's light skin color, gentle manner, immaculate clothing, physical stature, and diction. Mitchell also spoke of their expertise in the area of women in industry service. But, almost as if to rationalize her praise of the two women, to justify their worthiness, and to account for her own comfort in their presence, the reporter wrote that when Irvin spoke, "she has the charm of not appearing to possess consciousness of race," and "the listener loses race consciousness himself" (p. 7). With a low-key, analytical, and dramatic speaking style (Giddings, 1984), Haynes also may have appeared to be dispassionate (it is more likely, however, that her style was a carefully developed mechanism used to persuade and to put the listener at ease). Furthermore, in describing Haynes's speaking voice as "beautifully modulated" and her diction as "perfect," Mitchell seemed to have felt that these significant attributes were rare among African Americans.

Van Kleeck relied heavily on Haynes and Irvin's expert advice regarding issues of African American women in industry. Haynes believed that many of the problems that African American women faced in industry were the results of inadequate training and preparation, and she was a strong advocate for job training as a prerequisite to economic self-sufficiency. Haynes and Irvin's investigations found conditions very good in two large mail-order houses (presumably Montgomery Ward and Sears and Roebuck) in Chicago. These mail-order houses had certain educational requirements and provided training to new employees. Haynes believed that complaints of absenteeism in some Chicago industries could be accounted for because the young women lived great distances from the factories and did not have access to transportation. Haynes did not blame these young women for their conditions and work habits. Rather, she felt that the women had responded to a national labor crisis in time of war and that "the country should have a sense of duty to them and help them procure the training which they needed" (Mitchell, 1919, p. 7). Haynes also believed that access services such as transportation were essential.

Of economic necessity, African American women had participated in the labor market at a rate much higher than their white counterparts and yet were given limited choices about the types of work in which they engaged (Dill, 1983).

Haynes praised "Negro girls" for their willingness "to take up hard and heavy work," or the "dirty work" of industry (Mitchell, 1919, p. 7). She also noted that white girls were unwilling to do these jobs and had refused them in the past. Haynes concluded that "Negro women . . . have one advantage over white women as a class. They have the habit of work. . . . There are few Negro women in the world who do not do their share, and sometimes more, in the support of their families" (Mitchell, 1919, p. 7). Involvement in the labor market served women in a number of ways. It helped to reduce economic dependence, but it also gave African American women a distinctive set of experiences that provided a different view of their material reality. Furthermore, the world of work provided the women an opportunity to identify with a self-sufficient and powerful group, distinct from their families (Collins, 1989).

Haynes also served as domestic service employment secretary of the U.S. Employment Service in Washington, DC, from January 1920 to May 1922. In 1922 she became the examiner. While in that post, she wrote of the conditions of African American women in labor in an article entitled, "Two Million Negro Women at Work." In that article, Haynes identified (1) domestic and personal service, (2) agriculture and manufacturing, and (3) mechanical industries as the three occupations in which the majority of women were engaged. Haynes found that after the war some women had lost their jobs to returning soldiers and declining labor needs. Companies no longer paid the minimum wage but expanded the duties of workers. Haynes (1922) also noted that with the increasing number of white women available for work, "Negro women were to a very large extent displaced" (p. 64). She also found that "as soon as some of the laundries [in Washington, DC] began to fear that they would be forced to pay the minimum wage they began to ask the employment bureaus about the possibility of obtaining white girls" (p. 65). According to Haynes, these employers were "perfectly satisfied with Negro women" (p. 65) as long as they were not required to pay them a minimum wage.

Haynes's research further revealed that among domestic servants, "the bond between mistress and maid . . . is not sufficiently strong for the mistress to learn her maid's surname or her address" (Haynes, 1922, p. 66). In fact, a pattern of exploitation was the norm for domestic workers in both the North and the South, and social distance was the rule. Mistrust and disrespect seemed to form the basis of their relationship, a recapitulation of the mistress–slave relationship. According to Jones (1985), white women justified the low wages they paid their African American servants by arguing that the servants were thieves who took both food and clothing at will. Feeling the weight of disdain and oppression, some African American domestic servants considered "toting" as their right, "a hard earned form of 'pay' for a distasteful job" (Jones, 1985, p. 132). Haynes (1922) noted that neither the domestic servant nor her white mistress "seemed personally interested in the other" and that in "too many cases the feelings of each borders on real dislike for the other." Haynes concluded that "neither has for the other that priceless possession—confidence" (p. 66).

Like many in the African American intelligentsia, Haynes (1922) advocated for "standardization of domestic service" and for "domestic-training schools in connection with public employment agencies" (pp. 66–67). On the other hand, women employed in these areas sought only to escape from what they perceived to be the most degrading of all women's work. The African American factory workers promised never to return to domestic work. Haynes's research showed that with economic shifts, scarcity of jobs, and racial discrimination, these women would easily be displaced, forcing them to return to domestic service. She understood the reality of limited opportunities available to those who lacked marketable skills. More trenchantly, middle-class African American women knew that even when they were well-educated, opportunities for employment commensurate with their training often eluded them because of the hatred and resentment of racism. Haynes emphasized the need for African American women to struggle constantly against restricted job opportunities in search of "economic independence."

In 1923, while pursuing an MA in political science at Columbia University, Haynes wrote an outstanding thesis analyzing domestic working women, entitled "Negroes in Domestic Service in the United States." In this study, she examined numerous issues including demographic data, turnover rates, training and efficiency, and wages. Haynes was holistic in her approach and to that end surveyed the living conditions, health, social life, and organizational affiliations of domestic workers. She found that the church played a significant role in their lives, as did secret orders (for example, the Eastern Star). Younger domestic workers spent leisure time in dance halls and billiard rooms. Haynes (1923) lamented that the meager social options open to younger domestic workers largely were the result of "social stigma attached to domestic service," which barred them from "many of the entertainments of real value and benefit" (p. 442).

THE "LADY POLITICIAN"

After moving to New York, Haynes worked with her husband while he served as Secretary of the Department of Race Relations of the Federal Council of the Churches of Christ in America, from 1922 to 1946. During this time she also became very involved in the politics of the Harlem community and was elected coleader of the 21st Assembly District in 1935. Haynes was committed to the political process and believed that the time was right for women to seek leadership positions in the political arena (Haynes, n.d.).

As coleader of the 21st district, Haynes worked for two years with a man whom she grew to distrust and with whom she ultimately severed ties. Herbert L. Bruce, a Harlem restaurateur born in Barbados and educated in New York, became the first African American member of the executive committee of Tammany Hall with his election in 1935 as the leader of the 21st district. Haynes served as Bruce's "lady coleader" for two years. Bruce was a well-respected community and business leader in Harlem (Lewinson, 1974; McKay, 1940). During the two years that Haynes worked with Bruce, however, she grew to disrespect him. She believed that he exercised poor judgment in his support of one of New York's elder senators who, as Haynes noted, "in all his years in the United States Senate, never lifted his voice in behalf of the Anti-Lynching Bill, voted to cut off Relief from the poor and [voted] to block the pure Food and Drug Act"

(Haynes, 1937). She further criticized Bruce for being a pawn under Al Smith's control, noting that while Smith was New York's governor, he "refused to sign a bill for a Judicial District wherein two Negro magistrates might be elected, saying he could not see two Negro men dressed up in black robes sitting on a judicial bench questioning white women." Haynes (1937) also believed that Bruce's "stubborn intolerance of people whose opinions are different from his, [stood] between him and any great good to the people." Furthermore, she believed that Bruce was mean-spirited and insincere. As an elected official, she felt he had "become too important to treat his electorate courteously, fairly and squarely," ultimately failing to provide genuine service to the people of Harlem. Finally, in 1937, she dissolved her political relationship with Bruce and ran unsuccessfully with Alderman Eustace V. Dench for coleadership of the 21st district.

Haynes (1937) believed that "Negro leadership, which is to serve the people, must be of such sterling character that it could not and would not stoop to any attempt to humiliate or frustrate every effort of any woman, black or white, whose reputation and character are unassailable and whose ability and cooperative spirit have been tried and proven." Haynes obviously felt that Bruce devalued her because of her gender. She proclaimed that as coleader of the 21st district, she had "worked day and night for the people" because of her genuine interest and appreciation of their confidence. Yet she felt that her efforts were taken for granted. She intimated that her former captain, like other male leaders, took credit for the hard work that female coleaders had done. Haynes believed that the time was right "for women . . . to step forward as aspirants, bargainers, and if necessary, contenders for the choicest official plums" (Haynes, n.d.). Weary of women staying in their traditional roles as helpmates, Haynes encouraged women to abandon the "hang over training to shove [men] forward instead of ourselves." She further acknowledged that "[women's] petty jealousness of one another are such mill stones about our necks." Always mindful of women's need to mobilize and have a voice in the politics that affect their lives, Haynes (n.d.) said "I have no fears in urging the women of the country, irrespective of race, to awake, register, vote, work and enlarge the fight for equality of opportunity in jobs, in office for women." Haynes clearly had no patience with leaders who were deceitful and who lacked commitment, and she was not reticent about expressing her opinion. In fact, she (1937) stated that her truthful assertions held "malice toward none, and justice for all." Haynes believed that candor and honesty were important qualities, and although she clearly held the honest person in high regard, she also understood that stating certain truths could be unpopular.

OUTREACH AND ORGANIZING WITH "LOTS OF SMALL PIECES"

Haynes was determined to serve wherever need existed and spent some of her vacation time in Alabama tutoring children in her community for several hours each afternoon. As she offered services to poor people, Haynes documented social problems as she saw them. Speaking out on the evils of the system was a hallmark of Haynes's style. On a visit to her home in Alabama, Haynes (Ross, 1910) noted that the

> three greatest immediate evils in the country life of that section of Alabama are the following: very poor school teachers, most incompetent ministers and most unworthy lawmakers and executors, who encouraged crime by permitting men of some means to buy off criminals for a few dollars, provided the criminals are spoken of as good work hands and are willing to enter a contract and that crimes are committed against other Negroes.

Haynes concluded this reflection of Lowndes County's social problems by citing "the very, very early marriage of so many children" as an evil certain to ensure a life of poverty and want. Acknowledging the desperate social, economic, and political conditions in her community, Haynes made monetary contributions to support African American social welfare. Alabama's Calhoun School benefited from Haynes's benevolence (Jones, 1936). The school's mission—to attack the social conditions diminishing the quality of life for Lowndes County residents—was a goal that Haynes shared. Furthermore, the school represented a grand self-help effort (Lasch-Quinn, 1993), a feature Haynes praised as essential for any successful race work.

Although Haynes engaged in solitary social action, she understood the importance of group efforts. To both surround herself with women who shared her vision of progressive African American womanhood and encourage and influence the lives of younger women, Haynes became a member of the Alpha Kappa Alpha (AKA) sorority in 1923 and a charter member of the Tau Omega graduate chapter in 1925. Through these organizations and others with which she was affiliated, Haynes continued to nurture and strengthen her relationships with other African American women. (This group of college-educated African American women also formed another network through which Haynes could work on behalf of women and girls.) Haynes believed that part of the sorority's purpose was "to build more stately mansions for womanhood" ("Proclamation," 1953) through social welfare programs, race work, and educational opportunities. By 1925 the AKA sorority's national agenda included programs that increased race consciousness and that fostered "aesthetic development of the public" as well as "increased community involvement" (McNealey, 1993, p. 24). In harmony with the national mandate, the New York chapter of the sorority conducted annual literary contests for high school girls in New York and New Jersey. The sorority and its members were prominent enough in the area that literary giants such as Langston Hughes and Countee Cullen, two of the Harlem Renaissance's greatest poets, served as judges for the literary contest at Haynes's request (Haynes, 1926).

Haynes also was a member of the National Association of Colored Women (NACW) and served as chair of the Industry and Housing Department of that organization. Her "web of affiliations" also included the Harlem Branch of the YWCA, the Mary F. Waring Club, the Dorrence Brooks Ladies' Auxiliary No. 528 of the Veterans of Foreign Wars, the New York Fisk University Club, and the Advisory Committee of Harlem Works Progress Administration (WPA) Theatrical Project. She also served as superintendent of the Junior Department of Abyssinian Baptist Church and as secretary of the board of managers of the Adam Clayton Powell Home for the Aged.

In 1937 New York Governor Herbert H. Lehman appointed Haynes to serve on the Temporary Commission on the Conditions of the Urban Colored Population. The commission was designed to study the economic and social conditions of urban African Americans in the state. Haynes was well-prepared for this charge, having committed much of her career to the study and eradication of social problems affecting African Americans. She was also appointed by Mayor Fiorello La Guardia to serve on the New York City Planning Commission. She was a member of the National Advisory Committee on Women's Participation in the 1939 New York World's Fair. Through her efforts the AKA sorority hosted a luncheon given at the Women's National Advisory Building of the World's Fair, an activity described by sorority members as "one of the most brilliant events of our history" ("Proclamation," 1953).

In addition, Haynes was recognized as a writer of stature. A Los Angeles YWCA girl's group voted to name their club the "Elizabeth Ross Haynes Club" in honor of Haynes's work with the YWCA and her literary contributions. Greater and more public recognition of Haynes's literary prowess came with her acceptance of an invitation to become an honorary member of the International Mark Twain Society. This award was an indication of public recognition of her contributions to literature ("Historical Statement," n.d.). Committed to an accurate historical record of African American people, Haynes wrote two books: *Unsung Heroes* (1921) was written, according to Haynes, to tell of the "victories in spite of the hardships and struggles of Negroes whom the world failed to sing about," and *The Black Boy of Atlanta* (1952) tells the story of Major Richard Robert Wright, a community leader, educator, and banker.

IMPLICATIONS FOR SOCIAL WORK PRACTICE

Haynes had a clear understanding that race problems and gender concerns were intertwined, and her work was based on the interconnection between the two. Haynes's work epitomized the elements of feminist organizing as described in contemporary America. Gutierrez and Lewis (1995) indicated that the goal of feminist organizing is to eliminate permanent power hierarchies among all people that can prevent the realization of human potential. They identified six factors that are common to feminist organizing: (1) using a gender lens to analyze the causes and solutions of community problems; (2) attending to the process of practice in an effort to create organizations based on feminist principles; (3) empowering through consciousness-raising; (4) assuming that the personal is political, with organizing therefore taking a grassroots, bottom-up approach; (5) bridging differences among women based on factors like race, class, physical ability, and sexual orientation, with the guiding principle that diversity is strength; and (6) organizing holistically. A discussion of Haynes's work based on these principles follows.

Gender Lens

Haynes recognized that her gender gave her a unique perspective. She was a member of a community of African American women through her sorority, the NACW, and the "colored" branches of the YWCA. Haynes lived and worked near the women and girls she tried to help. She understood their problems, shared their discomfort in race and gender isolation, and rejoiced in their triumphs (Carlton-LaNey, 1996).

Process of Practice

The NACW, one of the many organizations to which Haynes belonged, adhered to the motto "lifting as they climb." This motto suggests that the women's group work affected the conditions of all African American women and simultaneously helped the empowerment process for the race. It also suggests a collective identity and voice in an environment that was nurturing and supportive.

Consciousness-Raising

Through various group activities, Haynes engaged in consciousness-raising. The consummate teacher, she took every available opportunity to expose, educate, and enlighten girls and women to their strengths and potential for personal and system change. These opportunities included holding private, small-group tutorials on her back porch in Alabama, establishing literary contests for high schools in New York and New Jersey, and participating on speaker's bureaus for national organizations. Through these efforts, women were able to see the relationship between personal problems and political issues (Gutierrez & Lewis, 1995).

Grassroots Organizing

Haynes involved herself in service delivery at various points along a continuum. She held elected public office in New York City, served the state and city at the request of the governor and mayor, served on the national board of the YWCA, and served on the board of a local church-affiliated home for elderly people. The creation of services such as the Adam Clayton Powell Home for the Aged and many others were examples of service delivery to meet the needs of African Americans where the white system would not. Providing direct services to girls and women via women's groups like the NACW and the AKA sorority also were significant to Haynes's work as an organizer. One of the most outstanding projects of the sorority was the delivery of alternative health care services to African American sharecroppers in Holms County, Mississippi, during the summers from 1935 to 1942 by the Mississippi Health Project (Gordon, 1991). Haynes's organizing work and that of the myriad organizations with which she was affiliated reflect the issues and problems confronting women and African Americans daily.

Strength through Diversity

During the early 1900s, the Harlem community where Haynes lived was extremely diverse, consisting of African American migrants from the rural South, people from the West Indies, the subculture of extraordinarily talented Harlem Renaissance artists, poor, low-skilled laborers, and wealthy professionals and entrepreneurs. There were individuals who spoke of America with passion and patriotism and those who longed for the land of their ancestry through the Marcus Garvey Pan-African Movement. Within that community, Haynes was a member of an elite group. Her middle-class status set her apart from most other women of her time. Sometimes criticized as "a set of butterflies on dress parade" (DuBois, 1909, p. 88), Haynes and women like her put petty criticisms to rest through their dedication and commitment, through their recognition that diversity is strength, and through their identification with the lifestyles of the people they served (Carlton-LaNey, 1989).

Holistic Organizing

Haynes's career is an example of holistic organizing. Her keen insights and ability to identify needs from the minuscule and personal to the organizational and systemic provided numerous avenues for intervention. Her ability to operate within a holistic framework encouraged her to use the emotional, intellectual, spiritual, and artistic as avenues for creating group identity and solidarity among women and African Americans.

CONCLUSION

Elizabeth Ross Haynes died in 1953 in New York City at the age of 70. She left a legacy of activism, agitation for change, and effective race work. Her commitment to race work and the economic independence of all women regardless of color set a high standard for others to follow. Haynes's approach to dealing with race and gender oppression was to first prepare herself by gaining the necessary knowledge, skill, and expertise. As she matured personally and professionally, she used her web of affiliations to enhance her political powers, to provide skilled leadership, to model attainable goals for women, to organize communities, and to attack social problems at various levels along the causal chain. The social work profession has yet to recognize the pioneering efforts of Haynes, but it is not too late for social workers to learn from her life's work as a scholar, elected leader, social worker, and womanist.

REFERENCES

Bogin, R. (1980). Elizabeth Ross Haynes. In B. Sicherman, C. H. Green, I. Kantrov, & H. Walker (Eds.), *Notable American women: The modern period* (pp.324–325). Cambridge, MA: Belknap Press of Harvard University Press.
Brown, E. B. (1989). Womanist consciousness: Maggie Lena Walker and the independent order of Saint Luke. *Signs, 14,* 610–631.
Carlton-LaNey, I. (1989). Old folks' homes for blacks during the Progressive Era. *Journal of Sociology and Social Welfare, 26,* 43–60.
Carlton-LaNey, I. (1996). George and Birdye Haynes' legacy to community practice. In I. Carlton-LaNey & N. Burwell (Eds.), *African American community practice models historical and contemporary responses* (pp. 27–48). Binghamton, NY: Haworth Press.
Collins, P. (1989). The social construction of black feminist thought. *Signs, 14,* 745–773.
Dill, B. (1983). Race, class, and gender: All-inclusive sisterhood. *Feminist Studies, 9,* 129–150.
DuBois, W.E.B. (1909). *Efforts for social betterment among Negro Americans.* Atlanta: Atlanta University Press.
Giddings, P. (1984). *When and where I enter: The impact of black women on race and sex in America.* New York: Bantam Books.
Gilkes, C. T. (1988). Building in many places: Multiple commitments and ideologies in black women's community work. In A. Bookman & S. Margin (Eds.), *Women and the politics of empowerment* (pp. 53–76). Philadelphia: Temple University Press.

Gordon, L. (1991). Black and white visions of welfare: Women's welfare activism, 1890–1945. *Journal of American History, 78*, 559–590.

Gutierrez, L., & Lewis, E. (1995). A feminist perspective on organizing with women of color. In F. G. Rivera & J. L. Erlich (Eds.), *Community organizing in a diverse society* (pp. 95–112). Boston: Allyn & Bacon.

Haynes, E. R. (1922). Two million Negro women at work. *Southern Workman, 51*, 64–72.

Haynes, E. R. (1923). Negroes in domestic service in the United States. *Journal of Negro History, 8*, 384–442.

Haynes, E. R. (1926, April 20). Letter to Langston Hughes. New Haven, CT: Yale University, James Weldon Johnson Memorial Collection.

Haynes, E. R. (1937, September 11). Open letter to voters. New Haven, CT: Yale University, James Weldon Johnson Memorial Collection.

Haynes, E. R. (n.d.). *Women aspire for political plums.* New Haven, CT: Yale University, James Weldon Johnson Memorial Collection.

Higginbotham, E. B. (1992). African-American women's history and the metalanguage of race. *Signs, 17*, 251–274.

Hill, R. B., Billingsley, A., Engram, E., Malson, M. R., Rubin, R. H., Stack, C. B., Stewart, J. B., & Teele, J.E. (1993). *Research on the African-American family.* Westport, CT: Auburn House.

Hine, D. C. (1996). *Speak truth to power.* New York: Carlson.

Historical Statement of the International Mark Twain Society. (n.d.). New Haven, CT: Yale University, James Weldon Johnson Memorial Collection.

Jones, E. K. (1936, May 7). Letter to Elizabeth Ross Haynes. New Haven, CT: Yale University, James Weldon Johnson Memorial Collection.

Jones, J. (1985). *Labor of love, labor of sorrow.* New York: Vintage Books.

Lasch-Quinn, E. (1993). *Black neighbors race and limits of reform in the American settlement house movement, 1890–1945.* Chapel Hill: University of North Carolina Press.

Lewinson, E. R. (1974). *Black politics in New York City.* New York: Twayne.

McDougald, E. J. (1925). The double task. *Survey Graphics, 53*, 687–691.

McKay, C. (1940). *Harlem: Negro metropolis.* New York: E. P. Dutton.

McNealey, E. G. (1993). Alpha Kappa Alpha sorority. In D. Hine, E. Brown, & R. Terborg-Penn (Eds.), *Black women in America: An historical encyclopedia* (pp. 23–25). Bloomington: Indiana University Press.

Mitchell, H. (1919, March 23). Colored women represent their race in state and nation. *New York City Tribune*, p. 7.

Neverdon-Morton, C. (1989). *Afro-American women of the South and the advancement of the race, 1895–1925.* Knoxville: University of Tennessee Press.

Ogunyemi, C. (1985). Womanism: The dynamics of the contemporary black female novel in English. *Signs, 11*, 63–80.

Palmer, P. M. (1983). White women/black women: The dualism of female identity and experience in the United States. *Feminist Studies, 9*, 151–170.

Peebles-Wilkins, W., & Francis, A. (1990). Two outstanding black women in social welfare history: Mary Church Terrell and Ida B. Wells-Barnett. *Affilia, 5*, 87–100.

Proclamation. (1953, October). New Haven, CT: Yale University, James Weldon Johnson Memorial Collection.

Ross, E. (1909, March 31). *Special worker report to the YWCA.* New York: Archives of the National Board of the YWCA.

Ross, E. (1910, May 25). *Special worker report to the YWCA.* New York: Archives of the National Board of the YWCA.

Smith, B. (1985). Some home truths on the contemporary black feminist movement. *Journal of Black Studies and Research, 16*, 4–13.

Terborg-Penn, R. (1983). Discontented black feminists: Preludes and postscript to the passage of the nineteenth amendment. In L. Scharf & J. M. Jensen (Eds.), *Decades of discontent: The woman's movement, 1920–1940* (pp. 261–278). Westport, CT: Greenwood Press.

Walker, A. (1983). *In search of our mothers' gardens: Womanist prose.* New York: Harcourt, Brace.

The author thanks Sandra Carlton Alexander at North Carolina A&T State University, Yolanda Burwell at East Carolina University School of Social Work, and Maeda Galinsky at the University of North Carolina at Chapel Hill School of Social Work for their helpful comments on early drafts of this chapter. Research was supported in part by the University of North Carolina at Chapel Hill School of Social Work Jane Pfouts Research Grant. An earlier version of this chapter was presented at the Annual Program Meeting of the Council on Social Work Education, March 1995, San Diego. Manuscript collections containing documents by or about Elizabeth Ross Haynes include the Schomburg Center for Research in Black Culture, New York; the Archives of the National Board of the YWCA, New York; the James Weldon Johnson Memorial Collection, Yale University, New Haven, CT; the Moorland-Spingarn Research Center, Howard University, Washington, DC; and the George Edmund Haynes Papers, Fisk University, Nashville, TN.

This chapter was originally published in the November 1997 issue of Social Work, *vol. 42, pp. 573–583.*

14 Making a Difference: Women of Action in the Community

Marceline M. Lazzari, Holly R. Ford, and Kelly J. Haughey

This chapter presents findings from a qualitative study of Hispanic women who were active in their communities, that is, who were "making a difference." (The U.S. government identifier "Hispanic" encompasses the peoples of more than 25 countries. This chapter uses interchangeably the women's own ethnic identifiers.) There are numerous reasons for social workers to consider the contributions of these women. Because Hispanic people are the fastest growing ethnic group in the United States (Schick & Schick, 1991), social workers should increase cultural competency with this population whenever possible. Also, becoming more knowledgeable about gender and ethnic aspects of diversity supports the profession's efforts to eliminate discrimination, oppression, and injustice.

Because of the exploratory nature of the study, the findings generate a range of questions for social work practitioners and educators. Issues include bias in the literature, the lack of relevant developmental theories about Hispanic women, the significance of mentorship and relationship, acknowledging Hispanic women as generalist practitioners, and the possible negative effects of professionalism. All of the issues point to areas for further research and are challenges for the social work profession.

LITERATURE REVIEW

The social sciences and popular literature on Hispanic women, families, and culture is fragmented, disconnected, and not easily accessible. Much of the early writings of the 1970s characterized Hispanic men as macho and Hispanic women as passive and subservient (Melville, 1980). However, beginning in the 1980s, these stereotypes, especially the roles of women, were challenged (Andrade, 1982; Baca Zinn, 1980; Gonzalez, 1982; Melville, 1980; Vasquez-Nuttall, Romero-Garcia, & De Leon, 1987). According to Andrade (1982),

> there is a complex interaction of social class, race, sex, and regional history involved in the development of Hispanic family roles. Failure to acknowledge the interactive force of each variable . . . will lead to an overly simplistic or generalized portrayal of the role, influence, and behavior of Hispanic women within their families and communities. (p. 97)

A common factor in Hispanic/Chicana/Mexican American women's roles in family, employment, higher education, civic involvement, and leadership is the

centrality of relationships. This relational emphasis coincides with self-in-relation theory, which links relationships with the empowerment process (Gilligan,
1982; Miller, 1986, 1991; Surrey 1991a, 1991b). Proponents of this developmental
theory have contended that at least for women, "the self is organized and developed in the context of important relationships" (Surrey, 1991b, p. 52). Although
the significance of relationships for women is still at times pathologized, its
meaning is increasingly being understood and valued. Relationships are a source
of power and effectiveness: "Because this kind of power transfers effectively to
movement and action across many relationships, individual activity experienced
in a context of shared activity can feel very powerful and sustainable" (Surrey,
1987, p. 9).

A relational connection documented in the literature is the significance of
role models and mentors. The support and encouragement of teachers and counselors as well as family was cited as a contributor to the success of Mexican
American women in higher education and in their professions (Aguilar &
Williams, 1993; Avery, 1981; Bauman, 1983; Cardoza, 1991; Frase-Blunt, 1991;
Gandara, 1982; Mackowski, 1991; Salas Rojas, 1992; Sellers, 1987; Vasquez, 1982).
Family can include not only immediate and extended members, but also people
in kinship networks, the neighborhood, the geographic community (Avery, 1981),
and the Hispanic community at large (Melville, 1980; Pardo, 1990).

Using these types of tools, Hispanic women have been active in social change
in many areas, ranging from labor force movements to the Chicana Feminist
Movement (Amott & Matthaei, 1991a, 1991b; Bonilla-Santiago, 1991; Castro, 1986;
Garcia, 1990; Gonzales, 1980; Raines, 1988; Rose, 1990; Ruiz, 1985). Working toward the betterment of the community is reflected in the types of jobs that many
Mexican American women pursue (Frase-Blunt, 1991; Spitzer, 1993). Hispanic
women have a high participation rate in human services fields (Mackowski,
1991) and often emphasize careers or professions that involve work with ethnically diverse populations (Avery, 1981). To date, however, no research studies
have documented Hispanic/Chicana/Mexican American women's contributions
to the community.

METHOD

Research Questions

On the basis of the gaps in the literature and on our interest in Hispanic women's
community involvement, we asked the following research questions: How do
Hispanic women identify themselves as being active in the community? What
factors do Hispanic women identify that have influenced them to become active
in the community? What factors do Hispanic women identify that sustain and
support them in remaining active in the community?

Data Collection

We used the grounded theory approach (Glaser & Strauss, 1967; Strauss & Corbin,
1990) to collect the data. We chose a qualitative approach to reflect the richness
and meaning of responses as intended by the participants.

Twenty-one women active (that is, involved in a human services capacity and seen by others as being active) in a variety of Colorado Front-Range communities (rural, urban, and transitional) were chosen to participate in the study. Those women initially selected helped expand the sample by offering the names of other women who fit the profile. Selection was based on the frequency with which the names were mentioned by the women, potential participants' availability, and time (those identified later were given less consideration because of the study's time constraints).

Women were first sent a letter of introduction and explanation. After agreeing to participate, in-depth, semistructured interviews were done from January through April 1994. At the beginning of the interviews, previously mailed demographic questionnaires were collected from the women and reviewed. Using identical interview schedules, two interviewers each conducted about half of the interviews. All interviews were audiotaped and fully transcribed.

Data Analysis

Data analysis was accomplished using grounded theory procedures (Strauss & Corbin, 1990). General themes and categories were determined by comparing the empirical data with the conceptual categories until theoretical saturation was achieved. The central theme emerged in the beginning stages of data analysis. "Making a difference" occurred frequently and provided meaning to all the other categories, properties, conditions, and consequences of being active in the community.

To strengthen reliability, the three members of the research team coded all interviews. This triangulation of interpreters was critical, especially as the conceptualization of themes and categories became increasingly abstract. The inclusion of the entire team also provided a variety of viewpoints and reduced the possibility of selective perception and researcher bias.

Study Limitations

The small, nonrandom sample limits the generalizability of the study's findings. A possibility of bias exists due to self-selection of participants and perceptual differences among interviewers. Another limitation is in the self-reporting of events or situations from years past. However, this impact was reduced, because it was the women's perception of past experiences and not the experiences themselves that influenced their community involvement. Possible cultural differences between interviewers and participants must be considered.

FINDINGS

Participants

Of the 21 women interviewed, 12 described themselves as Chicana, eight as Hispanic, eight as Mexican American, and four as Latina (many of the women used multiple terms). Other identifiers included Spanish American, Mexicana, Mexican, Mestiza, and Peruvian. (For further discussion of the importance of ethnic self-identification, see Castex, 1994.) Nineteen were bilingual in English and Spanish; those who were not bilingual acknowledged a desire or intent to learn Spanish. Fourteen were born and raised in Colorado, five were born and raised in other states in the Southwest, and two were born outside of the United States.

Two women were in their twenties, five in their thirties, 10 in their forties, and four in their fifties. All of the women in the sample had either a high school or general equivalency diploma; nine had bachelor's degrees, and two had master's degrees. All women were employed or doing volunteer work in human services fields such as education; health care; local government and law enforcement; county social services; grassroots community organizations; and services for senior citizens, people with disabilities, and people who abuse substances.

Making a Difference

Making a difference was shown in the various ways in which the women were involved in community:

> [Being involved is] about making a difference in the community and getting things done.
>
> *   *   *
>
> Whatever I do, it will always be in a place that makes some meaningful difference for the folks who are really on the losing end.
>
> *   *   *
>
> To see that I am making a difference, even if it's a small difference, even if it's just that somebody felt good for five minutes, . . . feels good to me.
>
> *   *   *
>
> That is why I keep doing my piece and, hopefully, it will make a difference. . . . If something that I have done has made the difference in somebody's life, then it will have been worth it.

Activities and Service Populations. Community involvement activities included promoting changes to improve circumstances for people; creating, providing, and maintaining tangible human services; developing and sustaining individual and collective approaches to assuming responsibility for the well-being of self and community; promoting ethnic appreciation within one's own culture and among other cultures; and continuing change efforts. Each category affects the others. For example, by promoting changes to improve circumstances for people, one might create tangible human services. These services might involve promoting ethnic appreciation, which is a way to improve circumstances for people. This dynamic character extends to the interconnected system levels in which the women worked, including individuals, families, communities, institutions, and society:

> You can't have healthy communities unless you have healthy individuals, which make up healthy families. So I believe that my work directly impacts the community.
>
> *   *   *
>
> Change . . . doesn't mean tinkering. It means really creating opportunities, opening opportunities, trying new and different ways of behaving and acting, not just as individuals or even in terms of community, but institutionally.

Ways and Means. The women made a difference through paid employment and volunteer work. Some women juggled the responsibilities of numerous jobs, activities, and boards in which they participated. Other women illustrated their involvement more as an integration of their own sense of purpose and identity connected to their job or volunteer efforts:

> A lot of involvement [is] not only in connection with the job, but also away from the job as a volunteer . . . as a person, as a woman, as a mother, as a friend, as a neighbor.
>
> *   *   *
>
> [Speaking Spanish and working with the Hispanic population] are just two bottom liners for me. . . . I really need [those components]. The fact that I am bilingual, I find that very healing. It's a part of my identity, of who I am.

As the women described their numerous paid and volunteer activities, many expressed the challenge of trying to limit their involvement and of having to make conscious choices:

> I have found that I need to concentrate on those [issues for which] I can make some change. . . . It's really frustrating, . . . and I think a lot of Hispanic women get into [the] position [of] trying to do too much and, . . . feeling a real responsibility . . . that we need to help. If we don't do it, who's gonna do it, . . . but I think we also need to come to the realization that we can only do so much.

At the same time, however, many struggled with feeling that they were not as active as they should be:

> I'm not as active as I'd like to be . . . just because [of] work and a family and things like that and trying to juggle everything.
>
> *   *   *
>
> I may not be out in the community, but I am doing a lot of things behind the scenes to make sure that services to the Hispanic community are happening.

Strategies and Personal Qualities. The women used a range of strategies to make a difference, including performing tasks for others (for example, teaching, translating, connecting with resources), performing tasks for oneself to serve others (for example, becoming certified in domestic violence counseling, developing leadership skills, learning Spanish), and performing tasks with others to help others (for example, networking, grassroots organizing, participating in decision making). In addition, the women identified personal qualities that enhanced their efforts, both interpersonal (for example, being caring, nonjudgmental, and humble, as well as taking initiative and being bilingual) and relational (for example, being inclusive and trustworthy, validating feelings and struggles, and experiencing emotions with others).

Community Conditions. The women explained that they were making a difference in community because of societal oppression (racism, sexism, discrimination), the lack of acknowledgment and appreciation of diversity (as evidenced by inadequate resources for diverse groups of people, lack of diverse representation in visible and powerful positions and institutions, and inaccurate or incomplete history), and professionalism (moving away from communities, losing touch with the people).

> We live in . . . an oppressive system; it is a materialistic system based on consumerism, based on money, which is power, based on control, and based on exploitation of people . . . being predominantly people of color, the poor, and women.

Consequences of Actions. The myriad ways in which the women were active in community provided an avenue for giving back to the community and instilling in others the responsibility to be active. Giving back to the community was important for reasons such as being more fortunate than others, having had someone reach out to them, and feeling an obligation as a member of a particular ethnic group. By instilling in others the responsibility to be active in the community, the change efforts can move to the next generation:

> Hopefully, . . . I will be a good role model for [my own children] so they will eventually also give back to the community.
>
> *   *   *
>
> Now we're struggling at the preschool and elementary levels to teach kids to give back to their community. The kids [are] learning about . . . how they can give back to community, . . . whether it's a third grader reading to a preschooler, or whatever it is that they do.
>
> *   *   *
>
> [This] student group has worked to unify, to move forward, and to help students remember that you need to go back to your community once you graduate . . . [and] help someone else . . . [and] give back.

Influences That Led to Community Involvement

The influences that led the women to community involvement included experiences, important people, and interpersonal qualities.

Experiences. Types of experiences included those that were observed (for example, seeing injustice, watching others take initiative, and recognizing efforts that made a difference), those that were personally lived (for example, being encouraged to attend college, having confidence expressed by an employer, being on welfare, being denied access to higher-level classes in school), and those of participation (for example, joining in social action activities of the church, being a part of the Chicano Movement or Brown Berets, attending college).

Important People. For many of the women, family members were influential. Mothers, for example, were important role models by actualizing community involvement, helping others, and instilling a sense of self-confidence and self-value. Other family members mentioned as being significant were supportive husbands, a loving grandfather, and a "tough-love" father. Many mentioned the entire family as being an influence. The women also identified many Hispanic and non-Hispanic nonfamily members as being influential:

> I guess it comes from . . . the growing up, the helping people, you know, when you are young and your parents helped people.
>
> *   *   *
>
> They did it because they . . . cared. . . . You instill in people that they are very capable, . . . you show them, and you tell them, . . . just holding them by the hand or pushing them. But always encouraging them. And I had those people in my life. . . . You've got to give back when others have put into you.

Interpersonal Qualities. The women described interpersonal qualities as having a gift of being able to help people, having a God-given responsibility, and being independent and assertive:

> I have a drive, a drive that keeps telling me that I need to be out there to make a difference and to teach others to make a difference in the world.

Factors That Support and Sustain Community Involvement

Factors that supported and sustained the women in their extensive amount of community involvement included seeing the need, feeling personal satisfaction, receiving support from others, and having personal beliefs and characteristics.

Seeing the Need. The necessity to continue the change efforts to ameliorate and hopefully to eliminate oppressive conditions was prevalent:

> I see a big, big need. . . . I see a lot of kids that are really losing who they are, and so [there is] all this turmoil and then hate. It just seems to me [that] they're going through so many more struggles than I . . . did. . . . I guess that [is what] keeps me really involved.
>
> *   *   *
>
> Some things haven't changed, and some things haven't changed enough.

Feeling Personal Satisfaction. Personal satisfaction of seeing efforts make a difference included bringing joy to others, feeling appreciated, and gaining internal rewards:

> I think [of] the changes that I've seen . . . people are more open, discrimination is not as bad. . . . What a different life my two grandchildren are having in school. . . . So, I see those changes, and that makes me happy.

Receiving Support from Others. Supportive people, including family members, friends, and other women, were significant in sustaining the women in their community efforts, whether they acknowledged and encouraged the women's actions, valued the women's opinion, or mentored the women.

Having Personal Beliefs and Characteristics. Personal beliefs and characteristics that helped the women maintain their endeavors included having a strong sense of obligation and responsibility; being part of living in a community; and being a part of religion, faith, and spirituality.

DISCUSSION AND IMPLICATIONS

Several significant implications emerge to inform social work education, knowledge, ethics, and practice.

Bias in the Literature

Earlier investigations of Hispanic people lacked sensitivity to cultural, ethnic, and gender differences and perpetuated stereotypes. This study adds to the growing body of knowledge that refutes the stereotypic characterization of Hispanic/Chicana/Mexican American women. The women in this study represented skilled, dynamic, committed, and involved individuals whose efforts touched individuals, various groups, institutions, and communities.

Relevance of Theory

Women of all ethnic groups have been constrained by theories based on traditional white-male models of development (Erikson, 1963; Freud, 1933; Maslow, 1968) that emphasize separation of self from mother, family, and significant adults as the most important step toward individuation and growth. Self-in-relation theory, which addresses the differences in how men and women are socialized by examining women's development (Gilligan, 1982; Miller, 1986, 1991; Surrey, 1991a, 1991b), contends that for women the self develops and is organized by experiencing important relationships. To date this theory has been explored predominantly with white middle-class women. The results of this study concur with some of the primary components of the theory and extend its theory base. For the women in this study, relationships motivated and positively contributed to the experience of being active in community.

Although the focus of this study was not on the empowerment process, the women's actions reflected empowerment as it was discussed by Surrey (1987), Miller (1982), Kieffer (1984), and Gutiérrez (1990). The women exemplified the citizen participation that Kieffer (1984) described as "empowering transformation," which continues through community involvement. Further research is necessary, however, to document the nature of women's relational connection to individuals, family, extended family, community, and people of diverse cultures.

Significance of Mentorship and Relationships

All but one of the women attributed their success and commitment to community involvement to the encouragement of mentors. The caring men and women of Anglo descent as well as of other ethnic backgrounds in these women's lives included family members, friends, colleagues, and employers. Such information is important for both social work educators and practitioners to consider because for these women neither gender nor ethnicity presented barriers to effective mentorship.

This is not to minimize the importance of same-ethnicity role models for young Chicanas. One women clarified this point: "The idea of having a role model is [that] it's someone like me that I can identify with. They could do it, so I can do it." The women in this study recognized the lack of ethnic role models in their communities and cited this as one goal for their community involvement.

Hispanic Women as Generalist Practitioners

The women in this study serve as role models not only for young Hispanic women and men, but also for social work professionals. Their knowledge and skills are vast, yet their contributions go largely unrecognized. Although many of the women had the equivalent of a high school diploma, they were actively engaged in the roles of generalist social work practice, including educator, advocate, mediator, counselor, grassroots organizer, consultant, social conscience, liaison, case manager, facilitator, and director.

Much of what is illustrated daily by the women in this study is discussed in the Council on Social Work Education (1992a, 1992b) Curriculum Policy Statements for master's and bachelor's degree programs. The statements require that a number of infusion components (for example, social work values and ethics, diversity, social and economic justice, and populations at risk) accompany the more traditional foundation elements (for example, human behavior and the social environment, policy, practice, research, and field practicum). The infusion areas directly address the activities of making a difference as defined by the women in this study. Although none were formally educated in social work, the women breathed life into the principles that social work educators attempt to teach. A challenge for educators at the university level lies in how to instill passion and a sense of conviction in students seeking professional credentials and sanction. Stories of women such as those in this study present a unique opportunity for academicians. A second challenge lies in enlightening textbook authors, editors, and publishers of the legitimacy and value of bringing examples such as these into social work texts as one way to affirm the profession's historical roots.

Professionalism as a Barrier

Professionalism as defined by the women in the study involves a separation of the professional self from the lives of one's clients. These women attempted to avoid the pitfalls of distancing by exceeding what some view as professional boundaries. For example, one woman noted that when a young girl became homeless because of her mother's drug addiction, "she lived with me for six months until her mother got her act together." The women also saw education as a lifelong process: "Everybody has something to teach us . . . even a stinky homeless person." The women did not allow oppressed people to become the oppressors in the work environment by "building in from the very foundation consensus, conflict resolution, good communication, shared responsibilities, not setting up one leader but creating many leaders. . . . What we don't want to do is create an elite." In addition, the women maintained a commitment to remain in positions of direct service in the community: "I made a conscious choice to not accept jobs that would take me away from the front line, because the leadership is more important at the front line. All too often leaders at the community level [are] snatch[ed] up and put in a higher level of society . . . [where they] become somewhat ineffective." This is often done at a personal cost to the individual who chooses jobs at lower pay and less status that offer limited professional acknowledgement and advancement.

SOCIAL WORK'S CHALLENGE AND FUTURE

One cannot assume that all social workers will have a given level of commitment. However, all social workers in all arenas of practice must adhere to the expectations of ethical responsibility stated in the *NASW Code of Ethics* (NASW, 1996). Of particular relevance to this study are the areas related to professional knowledge development and promoting the general welfare of society. The findings provide new knowledge about Hispanic/Chicana/Mexican American women that can inform social work education and practice.

In an era of increased and, at times, conflicting pressures on the profession, it is critical that social workers both individually and collectively continue to reflect on personal and professional choices. One challenge is to constantly examine the ramifications of the drive to be "professional." To what extent might social workers lose the commitment demonstrated by the women of this study? To what extent might social workers remove themselves from working with and for others? To what extent might social workers lose their effectiveness?

Exploring the contributions of this group of women offers an opportunity to revisit social work's mission of promoting social change. Given the challenges that social workers face on a daily basis, it is sometimes difficult, if not impossible, to think about the broader picture. It is critical that social workers search for avenues that will facilitate working together with the women in this study and with others like them to alter the conditions that have motivated social change. By sharing collaborative efforts, social workers will also be in a better position to learn from and with one another and thus to strengthen future efforts to "make a difference" in the world.

REFERENCES

Aguilar, M. A., & Williams, L. P. (1993). Factors contributing to the achievements of minority women. *Affilia, 8,* 410–424.

Amott, T. L., & Matthaei, J. A. (1991a). The soul of Tierra Madre. In *Race, gender and work: A multicultural economic history of women in the United States* (pp. 63–93). Boston: South End Press.

Amott, T. L., & Matthaei, J. A. (1991b). Yo misma fui mi ruta (I was my own path). In *Race, gender and work: A multicultural economic history of women in the United States* (pp. 257–287). Boston: South End Press.

Andrade, S. J. (1982). Family roles of Hispanic women: Stereotypes, empirical findings, and implications for research. In R. E. Zambrana (Ed.), *Work, family and health: Latina women in transition* (pp. 95–106). Bronx, NY: Fordham University, Hispanic Research Center.

Avery, D. M. (1981). *Critical events shaping the Hispanic woman's identity.* Washington, DC: Women's Educational Equity Act Program.

Baca Zinn, M. (1980). Employment and education of Mexican American women: The interplay of modernity and ethnicity in eight families. *Harvard Educational Review, 50,* 47–61.

Bauman, R. (1983, December). *A study of Mexican American women's perceptions of factors that influence academic and professional goal attainment.* Unpublished doctoral dissertation, University of Houston, Department of Education.

Bonilla-Santiago, G. (1991). Hispanic women breaking new ground through leadership. *Latino Studies Journal, 2,* 19–37.

Cardoza, D. (1991). College attendance and persistence among Hispanic women: An examination of some contributing factors. *Sex Roles, 24,* 133–146.

Castex, G. M. (1994). Providing services to Hispanic/Latino populations: Profiles in diversity. *Social Work, 39,* 288–296.

Castro, M. G. (1986). Migrant women: Issues in organization and solidarity. *Migration World Magazine, 14,* 15–19.

Council on Social Work Education. (1992a, July 19). *Curriculum policy statement for baccalaureate-degree programs in social work education.* Alexandria, VA: Author.

Council on Social Work Education. (1992b, July 19). *Curriculum policy statement for master's-degree programs in social work education.* Alexandria, VA: Author.

Erikson, E. H. (1963). *Childhood and society* (2nd ed.). New York: W. W. Norton.

Frase-Blunt, M. (1991). Soldaderas: Hispanic women face the '90s. *Hispanic Business, 12,* 14, 16, 18.

Freud, S. (1933). *New introductory lectures on psychoanalysis.* New York: W. W. Norton.

Gandara, P. (1982). Passing through the eye of the needle: High-achieving Chicanas. *Hispanic Journal of Behavioral Sciences, 4,* 167–179.

Garcia, A. M. (1990). The development of Chicana feminist discourse, 1970–1980. In E. C. Dubois & V. L. Ruiz (Eds.), *Unequal sisters: A multi-cultural reader in U.S. women's history* (pp. 418–431). New York: Routledge.

Gilligan, C. (1982). *In a different voice.* Cambridge, MA: Harvard University Press.

Glaser, B. G., & Strauss, A. L. (1967). *The discovery of grounded theory.* New York: Aldine de Gruyter.

Gonzales, S. (1980). Toward a feminist pedagogy for Chicana self-actualization. *Frontiers, 5*(2), 48–51.

Gonzalez, A. (1982). Sex roles of the traditional Mexican family: A comparison of Chicano and Anglo students' attitudes. *Journal of Cross-Cultural Psychology, 13,* 330–339.

Gutiérrez, L. M. (1990). Working with women of color: An empowerment perspective. *Social Work, 35,* 149–153.

Kieffer, C. (1984). Citizen empowerment: A developmental perspective. In J. Rappaport, C. Swift, & R. Hess (Eds.), *Studies in empowerment: Toward understanding and action* (pp. 9–36). New York: Haworth Press.

Mackowski, J. M. (1991). Where's the fast track? Women executives tell how they built successful careers. *Hispanic Business, 13,* 26–28.

Maslow, A. H. (1968). *Toward a psychology of being* (2nd ed.). Princeton, NJ: Van Nostrand Reinhold.

Melville, M. B. (1980). *Twice a minority: Mexican American women.* St. Louis: C. V. Mosby.

Miller, J. B. (1982). *Women and power* (Work in Progress No. 82-001). Wellesley, MA: Stone Center for Development Services and Studies.

Miller, J. B. (1986). *Toward a new psychology of women* (2nd ed.). Boston: Beacon Press.

Miller, J. B. (1991). The development of women's sense of self. In J. V. Jordan, A. G. Kaplan, J. B. Miller, I. P. Stiver, & J. L. Surrey (Eds.), *Women's growth in connection* (pp. 11–26). New York: Guilford Press.

National Association of Social Workers. (1996). *NASW code of ethics.* Washington, DC: Author.

Pardo, M. (1990). Mexican American women grassroots community activists: "Mothers of East Los Angeles." *Frontiers, 9*(1), 1–6.

Raines, R. T. (1988). The Mexican American woman and work: Intergenerational perspectives of comparative ethnic groups. In *Mexicanas at work in the United States* (Mexican American Studies Monograph No. 5, pp. 33–46). Houston, TX: University of Houston, Mexican American Studies Program.

Rose, M. (1990). Traditional and nontraditional patterns of female activism in the United Farm Workers of America, 1962 to 1980. *Frontiers, 11*(1), 26–31.

Ruiz, V. L. (1985, Summer). Obreras y madres: Labor activism among Mexican women and its impact on the family. *Renato Rosaldo Lecture Series Monograph, 1,* 19–38.

Salas Rojas, A. (1992). Hispanic women in higher education. *Hispanic Outlook in Higher Education, 2*(5), 6–8.

Schick, F. L., & Schick, R. (1991). *Statistical handbook on U.S. Hispanics.* Phoenix, AZ: Oryx Press.

Sellers, J. M. (1987). Challenging the myth of the traditional woman. *Hispanic Business, 9,* 15–16, 48.

Spitzer, J. (1993). Interview: Maria Guarjardo. *Colorado Woman News, 7*(4), 17–18.

Strauss, A., & Corbin, J. (1990). *Basics of qualitative research: Grounded theory procedures and techniques.* Newbury Park, CA: Sage Publications.

Surrey, J. L. (1987). *Relationship and empowerment* (Work in Progress No. 30). Wellesley, MA: Stone Center for Development Services and Studies.

Surrey, J. L. (1991a). The relational self in women: Clinical implications. In J. V. Jordan, A. G. Kaplan, J. B. Miller, I. P. Stiver, & J. L. Surrey (Eds.), *Women's growth in connection* (pp. 35–43). New York: Guilford Press.

Surrey, J. L. (1991b). The "self-in-relation": A theory of women's development. In J. V. Jordan, A. G. Kaplan, J. B. Miller, I. P. Stiver, & J. L. Surrey (Eds.), *Women's growth in connection* (pp. 51–66). New York: Guilford Press.

Vasquez, M.J.T. (1982). Confronting barriers to the participation of Mexican American women in higher education. *Hispanic Journal of Behavioral Sciences, 4*, 147–165.

Vasquez-Nuttall, E., Romero-Garcia, I., & De Leon, B. (1987). Sex roles and perceptions of femininity and masculinity of Hispanic women: A review of the literature. *Psychology of Women Quarterly, 11*, 409–425.

This chapter was originally published in the March 1996 issue of Social Work, *vol. 41, pp. 197–205.*

15 The Politics of the Indian Child Welfare Act

Lou Matheson

In the past, state courts, social agencies, and religious organizations were free to remove American Indian children from their homes at will. Now, under the Indian Child Welfare Act of 1978 (ICWA) (P.L. 95-6087), state systems are designated supportive and cooperative roles with restricted decision-making power (Bureau of Indian Affairs [BIA], 1979). However, because most people who work within the system are not acquainted with the federal law or Indian history, they often remain under the impression that their local or institutional authority gives them autonomy in decisions regarding Indian families. This chapter describes the history and provisions of the ICWA and uses a composite case study to illustrate the issues involved.

CASE STUDY

A case involving the removal of three American Indian children from their family is being reviewed by a panel of 15 professionals with expertise in child and family matters, child abuse and neglect, child protection laws, and effective treatment for dysfunctional families. Only two members of the group are American Indian; one is a social worker, and the other is a member of the Local Indian Child Welfare Committee (LICWAC), a group of American Indians who advise social workers in state and private agencies in cases involving the removal of Indian children from their families.

The primary caseworker, who has not notified the tribe that the children are at risk for removal from their home, observes that the parents have not followed through with substance abuse treatment and anger management plans, although the father reported that he has been sober for six months following completion of an alcohol treatment program and that he regularly attends Alcoholics Anonymous meetings. The caseworker adds that a non-Indian family is willing to take all three children and may even consider adopting them. Two of the three children have already been placed in a non-Indian home. The third child, an infant, is with an Indian family.

The therapist who initially tested the children found them mute, unable to relate, and unable to complete simple tasks. One child is hyperactive and has symptoms of fetal alcohol syndrome. The therapist affirms that the children are thriving in their placement and appear to be bonding with the foster parents. Because the biological parents came to therapy only once, she suggests that the parents are not really interested in having their children returned to them. This impression could lay the groundwork for permanent separation.

Several people at the meeting concur with the American Indian representatives, who state that Indian children may respond as described when they feel threatened. Few understand, however, when the possibility is raised that neither the testing nor the treatment included cultural considerations. Rather, they become defensive and attempt to discredit the concept of cultural congruence. As the discussion becomes more hostile, several people complain of the constraints imposed by the ICWA and the political aspects in Indian cases. They declare that their "only interest is in the welfare of the children." One participant even suggests that the act should be ignored in this case, and another questions if Indians value their culture more than their children. The conflicts that permeate this meeting stem from the fact that with the exception of the attorney, the non-Indian participants have virtually no understanding of the ICWA.

INDIAN CHILD WELFARE ACT OF 1978

History

The Indian Child Welfare Act of 1978 became a federal law after 15 years of political struggle by American Indian leaders throughout the nation. By passing the law Congress hoped to prevent the continuing abuses of power by state agencies, the courts, and various church groups in the disruption of Indian families by enacting procedures for the removal and foster placement of Indian children and defining the roles and responsibilities of authority. American Indians hoped that the law would protect Indian families, communities, and tribes against further disintegration of their traditional systems.

Past legislation took a paternalistic position regarding American Indian tribes and communities. Supreme Court Justice Thurgood Marshall stated that the relationship between American Indians and the United States "is perhaps unlike that of any other two people in existence . . . marked by peculiar and cardinal distinctions which exist nowhere else" (cited in Dorsay, 1984, p. 21). In a 1976 case before the Supreme Court, the question of tribal tradition was answered by acknowledging that tribal sovereignty is limited only to the extent "specifically expressed by Congress" (Dorsay, 1984).

Federal policy governing American Indian affairs in the past involved kidnapping, forced religious conversions, and education by brutality. During congressional hearings on the ICWA, many Indian people described the abuses inflicted on them. One witness told how a social worker came to her family's home and removed a cousin living with them; no one understood why (Westermeyer, 1974). One woman related to this author that she and another child were forcibly taken into a bus while they were playing on the banks of a river near their home. They spent three years in a school; their parents believed they had drowned. Another unmarried woman having her first baby was told by a church representative that if she loved her baby she would let a white family adopt it. While in foster care one woman was never given a pair of socks, even in the winter.

Before enactment of the ICWA, many American Indian children were placed in foster care or institutions. Between 1969 and 1974 at least 35 percent of Indian children were placed in alternative care. In 16 states in 1969, 85 percent of the Indian children were placed with non-Indian families (Plantz, Hubbell, Barrett, & Dobrec, 1989). For the period 1971–72, 34,538 Indian children lived in institutional facilities, and more than 68 percent of them lived in schools administered by the BIA (Byler, 1977).

Child Placement and Culture

While advising attorney Craig Dorsay in the matter of the placement of an Indian child, Dr. Samuel Roll (personal communication from S. Roll, Arizona State University, Tempe, to C. Dorsay, Portland, OR, October 27, 1986) stated,

> Cross-racial adoptions (often) and cross-racial Indian adoptions (almost always) have a high likelihood of producing severe identity crisis in Indian children as those children become adolescents. The children thus raised are at more serious risk for depression, suicide, anti-social behavior, severe identity crisis, etc. In addition to the problems within the Indian child raised in non-Indian homes, there are also problems of social interaction (prejudice) which make the risk of psychological difficulties (isolation and displacement) in the Indian child even higher.

Social scientists (for example, Fischler, 1980; Guerrero, 1979) have agreed that the suicide rate among Indian youths, twice the national average, can be directly related to having been raised outside of their own cultural system. In one shelter for homeless youths, 35 percent were American Indian, about 75 percent of whom had been raised in non-Indian homes (personal communication with administrative staff of Crosswalk, Spokane, WA, October 1994).

IMPLEMENTING THE ICWA

The ICWA provides clear directions for child and family professionals who find cause to remove American Indian children from their biological parents' homes. A worker's first obligation is to verify the ethnic and tribal identity of the family. The second is to allow the tribe the opportunity to take jurisdiction over the case. If the tribe rejects jurisdiction, the caseworker must first attempt to place the child with a suitable family member. If none can be located who will accept the responsibility, the worker must seek placement with another family from the same tribe. If none is willing to take the child, the worker seeks placement with any Indian family that qualifies as foster parents. As a last resort, the worker may place the child in a non-Indian home (BIA, 1979; Washington State, 1987). Although the ICWA stresses keeping Indian families intact and refers to the disintegration of the extended family, the act does not refer specifically to siblings, even though in most cases children can be a support for each other. In the initial part of the process, the case must be presented to a LICWAC for input (American Indian Lawyer Training Program, 1979).

Every policy enactment or change regarding American Indian tribes and their people must travel the federal political process. To initiate congressional action, receive funding for social and health services, or alter procedures, Indian tribes must appeal to the federal government through the BIA, which was established to govern the tribes and is responsible for funding ICWA programs and providing training on and off reservations. The competition for funding in this political arena places Indian tribes at odds with each other and with other non-Indian groups.

Tribal and urban Indian programs are responsible for training and monitoring adherence to the mandates of the ICWA, which often leads to political conflicts and power struggles among Indians themselves, as well as with state and other agencies. Unfortunately, the quarrels around political issues and bids for power often have a deleterious effect on family relations, pitting relatives against each other. In child placement cases, those in the legal system occasionally use the observation of dissension to hold an Indian child in an inappropriate placement rather than adhering to the word or intent of the ICWA.

The ICWA addresses the issue of culture in several places. One quote from a Supreme Court decision states, "there can be no greater threat to essential tribal relations and no greater infringement on the right of the . . . tribes to govern themselves than to interfere with tribal control over custody of their children" (U.S. House of Representatives, 1978, p. 342). Others have expressed the opinion that to deprive children of their culture is a form of child abuse and even a genocidal act (Goodluck, 1988; Guerrero, 1979).

However, the issue of cultural relevance, congruence, or competence is not specified in the ICWA (Fischler, 1980). Some service providers continue to believe that they do not need to consider cultural aspects to work effectively with American Indians. But the spirit of the legislation requires that professionals possess knowledge and understanding of different cultural mores in relationship and communication patterns, living standards, and childrearing practices. Even problems of alcoholism, antisocial and other behavioral problems, and inadequate parenting need to be seen in their cultural and historical context (Blanchard & Barsh, 1980; Cross, 1986).

CONCLUSION

In the case study, which is an amalgam of several actual cases, inefficiency and angry feelings could have been avoided if the ICWA had been honored and adhered to. The children would have been properly placed, and the parents and their children may have received treatment and necessary services provided by Indian or culturally knowledgeable providers. The courts would have respected tribal authority, and the views of more than two Indian people would have been invited.

Plantz et al. (1989) reported encouraging figures about child placement since the passage of the ICWA. For example, American Indian parents are notified more often when their children are at risk of removal, from nearly 0 percent of the time in the years before 1978 to 65 percent to 70 percent of the time. Tribes are now notified up to 80 percent of the time, and Indian children who are removed are placed with relatives 47 percent of the time.

For conscientious service providers to American Indian families, possibly the most valuable knowledge to acquire is a thorough understanding of the ICWA.

The time misdirected in political maneuvering and avoiding the legal process will be diminished significantly when professional relationships are enhanced by mutual respect.

REFERENCES

American Indian Lawyer Training Program. (1979). *A law for our children.* Oakland, CA: Author.

Blanchard, E. L., & Barsh, R. L. (1980). What is best for tribal children? A response to Fischler. *Social Work, 25,* 350–357.

Bureau of Indian Affairs. (1979, November 26). Guidelines for state courts: Indian child custody proceedings. *Federal Register, 44,* 67586.

Byler, W. (1977). *The destruction of American Indian families.* New York: Association on American Indian Affairs.

Cross, T. (1986). Drawing cultural traditions in Indian child welfare practice. *Social Casework, 67,* 283–289.

Dorsay, C. J. (1984). *The Indian Child Welfare Act and laws affecting Indian children.* Boulder, CO: Native American Rights Fund.

Fischler, R. S. (1980). Protecting American Indian children. *Social Work, 25,* 341–349.

Goodluck, C. (1988). *Mental health issues of Native American transracial adoptions.* Unpublished manuscript.

Guerrero, M. P. (1979). Indian Child Welfare Act of 1978: A response to the threat to Indian culture caused by foster and adoptive placements of Indian children. *American Indian Law Review, 7,* 51–77.

Indian Child Welfare Act of 1978, P.L. 95-608, 92 Stat. 3069.

Plantz, M., Hubbell, T., Barrett, B., & Dobrec, A. (1989). Indian child welfare: A status report. *Children Today, 18*(1), 24–29.

U.S. House of Representatives. (1978). *Legislative history of the Indian Child Welfare Act of 1978* (House Report No. 95-1386). Washington, DC: U.S. Government Printing Office.

Washington State, Division of Child and Family Services. (1987). *An overview of the Indian Child Welfare Act of 1978.* Olympia: Author.

Westermeyer, J. (1974). *Testimony on the Indian Child Welfare Program presented before the Subcommittee on Indian Affairs, U.S. Senate, 93rd Congress, 2nd Session.* Washington, DC: U.S. Government Printing Office.

This chapter was originally published in the March 1996 issue of Social Work, *vol. 41, pp. 232–235.*

16 Kinship Care: The African American Response to Family Preservation

Maria Scannapieco and Sondra Jackson

African American children are entering out-of-home care in record numbers (American Public Welfare Association, 1990; Edelman, 1993; National Commission on Family Foster Care, 1991). In spite of the many family preservation efforts since the passage of the Adoption Assistance and Child Welfare Act of 1980 (P.L. 96-272), the population of children in foster care increased 45 percent between 1985 and 1991 (Edelman, 1993), and the percentage of children of color in substitute care steadily increased (Everett, Chipungu, & Leashore, 1991). This increase has been attributed to multiple factors, including increases in drug and alcohol use, teenage parenting, poverty, crime, and violence.

The African American community is responding to this critical threat to the preservation of the family in a resilient manner. This adaptive response is the increased use of informal and formal kinship care. This chapter discusses formal and informal kinship care as the African American response to family endangerment from both a historical and current perspective.

RESILIENCE DEFINED

Resilience has been most often defined as an individual's ability to overcome adversities and adapt successfully to varying situations (Garmezy, 1981; Masten, Best, & Garmezy, 1991; Rutter, 1990). Recently, the concept of resilience has been used to describe families (McCubbin & McCubbin, 1988; Werner, 1991) and schools and communities (Wang, Haertel, & Walberg, 1992). The concept of resilience has been refined through research in developmental psychopathology (Garmezy, 1985, 1991; Masten et al., 1991; Rutter, 1979, 1990). Contrary to the focus of risk research, which studies the psychopathology of the individual, research in resilience focuses on the psychologically healthy person (Garmezy, 1981).

Werner (1984) defined resilience as the "ability to recover from or adjust easily to misfortune or sustained life stress" (p. 68). Masten et al. (1991) defined resilience as the "capacity for or outcome of successful adaptation despite challenging or threatening circumstances" (p. 425). Others have similarly defined resilience (Musick, Stott, Spencer, Goldman, & Cohler, 1987; Rutter, 1990). All the definitions of resilience have a similar thread: the overcoming of some risk factor resulting in positive adaptation.

This chapter uses the concept of resilience as a framework for organizing and understanding the African American community's ability to overcome the disintegration of the family at a time of multiple environmental stressors. The African American family's protective factors and strengths are incorporated into the framework in examining the process of kinship care as a means of adaptation to halting the further decay of the family.

KINSHIP CARE

The phrase "kinship care" was inspired by the work of Stack (1974), who documented the importance of extended kinship networks in the African American community. The term "kin" often includes any relative by blood or marriage or any person with close nonfamily ties to another (Takas, 1993). Billingsley (1992) referred to this latter category as relationships of appropriation, that is, "unions without blood ties or marital ties. People can become part of a family unit or, indeed, form a family unit simply by deciding to live and act toward each other as family" (p. 31). Other authors prefer the terms "kinship caregivers" for those who provide private care and "kinship foster parents" for those whose care falls within the formal child welfare system (Berrick, Barth, & Needell, 1994). This chapter uses "kinship care" in the broadest sense.

HISTORICAL RESPONSE OF AFRICAN AMERICAN FAMILIES TO SEPARATION AND LOSS

It is important to examine the strength of the kinship bond as evidenced in African American history and to correct and balance some of the deficits-based interpretations of history.

The primary family unit in West Africa at the time of slavery in the United States was the extended family, which incorporated the entire community. Children belonged to, and were the responsibility of, the collective community (Martin & Martin, 1983). Yusane (1990) noted, in a discussion of cultural elements of West Africa, that "kinship relations were the foundation of social organization" and that the "extended family system is based on interdependent functions" (p. 54) that also serve as protection from calamities. African children were valued and viewed as an investment in the future.

Africans saw children as a part of their immortality, and there were no "illegitimate" children. All children were the shared concern of the community, and children were expected to care for their parents when the parents got old (respect for elders in the family and community continues as an African tradition). These and many other elements of African family life prevailed in the United States, in however modified a form, and account for the resilience of the family during slavery (Yusane, 1990). Gutman (1976) hypothesized that family kinship patterns associated with the societies of West Africa existed among those enslaved in the United States. People frequently quote the African proverb, "It takes a whole village to raise a child."

In the United States, the development of the extended family can be traced from the time of slavery. The enslavement of Africans for low-cost labor led to the disorganization of the family and created a situation in which children were often separated from biological parents (Dodson, 1983).

Pre–Civil War Era

As a result of the slave trade, relatives and nonrelatives on the slave-holding plantations were automatically given the responsibility for nurturing and supporting children separated from their parents. Although the slave trade and the enslavement experience initially destroyed traditional kinship family patterns, the newly enslaved Africans invested nonkin with symbolic kin status, establishing fictive kin relations. The development of inter- and intragenerational links among slave families was accompanied by obligation and mutual support and assistance (Everett et al., 1991).

Reconstruction Period

After the Civil War and emancipation, people reportedly searched to reclaim family members, thereby redefining the extended family (Billingsley, 1992). The period of Reconstruction, from about 1877 to the early 1900s, saw families helping families support and understand the new "freedom" and further highlighted the strength of the kinship bond (Billingsley, 1992). Following World War I, large numbers of African American people migrated to the North from the South. Kinship families shared living arrangements as a means of support until they were able to make it on their own. Children were often left in the South with grandparents and other relatives until their parents could arrange to bring them "up North" to live (Billingsley, 1992).

World War II

World War II created a tremendous influx of people into the urban areas. Stresses caused by urban living were apparent to many families as they attempted to live apart from the extended family system. Isolation and despair presented new problems for African Americans in large cities. Because of the lack of housing for black people as they moved into previously white immigrant areas of the cities, families were forced to live together in "rooming houses" and were often evicted for overcrowding apartments (Martin & Martin, 1983). Life in the big cities was extremely complicated and not always better than life in the South for some family members. Brothers and sisters would live together, share expenses, and send money to their parents and relatives in the South (Dodson, 1983).

Civil Rights Years

Between the Supreme Court's 1954 ruling that segregated schools were unconstitutional and Congress's approval of the 1965 Voting Rights Act (P.L. 89-110), the role of the extended family again changed. African American families in the North were experiencing a heightened degree of economic success resulting from stable factory employment and an increase in the number of African American professionals and entertainers (Billingsley, 1992). Children were sent "home" to the South for summer vacations to get to know extended family members and to get away from the crime in the cities. Sometimes they were sent to live with relatives because they were getting "mixed up" with gangs, and parents were concerned about their getting in trouble with the legal system. Sometimes children were sent from the South to the North to live with relatives for better schooling and to get away from the race riots, sit-ins, and civil disobedience actions.

Although the degree of connectedness and involvement with extended families varied, most African American families were not emotionally cut off, even when separated geographically.

1970s and 1980s

In the 1970s and 1980s, Puckrein (1984) reported that "millions of black Americans enjoyed a level of education, political participation and material well-being that approached that of the majority whites" (p. 4). The middle-class nuclear African American family—a single-family household with a mother, father, and children—often moved to the suburbs, leaving single mothers with children behind in the city, thus contributing to the creation of the urban underclass (Billingsley, 1992). Older parents and other relatives who were not part of this African American middle class were left to survive in the cities, where drugs and crime corrupted whole communities.

CURRENT CHALLENGES FOR THE AFRICAN AMERICAN FAMILY

The African American family has always been confronted with disparate challenges over the centuries, but the psychological, developmental, economic, physical, and social barriers facing families today are staggering. African Americans in the 1990s "face one of the worst crises since slavery and the black community must take the lead in doing something about it" (Edelman, 1993, p. 5). One response to this call for responsibility in the African American community is kinship care. Extended families are taking over the care of children who would otherwise be placed in out-of-home care. The African American family is overcoming incredible odds to maintain the stability of the family, confronting obstacles that far exceed the challenges of the past.

Poverty

African Americans made up 12.1 percent of the total population in 1990, but a disproportionate percentage of African Americans lived in poverty; 46 percent of all African American children and 32 percent of all African American families lived in poverty (U.S. Bureau of the Census, 1992). The infant mortality rate for African American children was 18 per 1,000 in 1990, compared with 7.6 per 1,000 for white children (U.S. Department of Health and Human Services, 1992). This mortality rate may result in part from the high rate of teenage pregnancy among African Americans: 116.2 live births per 1,000 African American women compared to 42.5 for white women (Child Trends, Inc., 1993).

AIDS

As of March 1993, 5,647 children and youths in the United States under the age of 20 were diagnosed with AIDS. African American children were 51.5 percent of these children. Thousands of other children are affected by relatives with this disease. Michaels and Levine (1992) have estimated that by the start of the 21st century, between 80,000 and 125,000 children will have lost their mothers to AIDS since the epidemic began.

Child Abuse and Neglect

There has been a steep rise in child abuse and neglect reports—a 147 percent increase during the past 15 years and 40 percent during the past five years. Of the 817,457 children abused or neglected in 1991, 26.7 percent were African American (Edelman, 1993; National Center on Child Abuse and Neglect, 1992). Partly as a result of this rise in abuse and neglect cases, between 1985 and 1991 the population of children in foster care rose 45 percent, with projections that the total would exceed 840,000 by 1995 (American Public Welfare Association, 1990; Edelman, 1993; National Commission on Family Foster Care, 1991).

Reductions in Services

Because of the cutbacks in social programs throughout the 1980s, African American families are facing decreased community supports to combat their economic and social difficulties (National Urban League, 1992). As a result, African Americans are being referred to clinics, hospitals, and mental health centers in record numbers, and their children are overrepresented in the child welfare system (Stevenson, Cheung, & Leung, 1992).

CURRENT RESPONSE OF AFRICAN AMERICAN FAMILIES TO SEPARATION AND LOSS

"The struggle to create a family system that can withstand the stress of the victim system has spawned a variety of family forms other than the traditional nuclear family" (Pinderhughes, 1982, p. 92). Although nuclear families do exist, generally they are found within the extended family culture (Boyd-Franklin, 1989). The extended family functions as a survival mechanism for a people who have been deprived of adequate resources. It provides tangible help such as "material support, income, child care, and assistance in household tasks," as well as nontangible support such as "expressive interaction, emotional support, counseling, instruction, and social regulation" (Wilson, 1989, p. 380).

Increasing numbers of children in care and the declining pool of traditional foster families are two of the forces that have led to a growing number and proportion of children in kinship care. Recent estimates suggest that 400,000 children are in kinship care arrangements in the child welfare system and that the total will exceed one-half million by 1995 (Center for the Study of Social Policy, 1990). Children in kinship care are predominantly African American (Berrick et al., 1994; Dubowitz, 1990; Iglehart, 1994; Task Force on Permanency Planning for Foster Children, 1990), and a larger proportion of African American children are in kinship care than in traditional foster care (Berrick et al., 1994; Iglehart, 1994).

Urban centers, many of which have predominantly African American populations, have seen the largest increase in kinship care placements. The number of children in formal kinship care in New York City increased from 151 in 1985 to 14,000 in 1989 (Thornton, 1991), and a more recent count shows a total of 23,591 in 1991 (Takas, 1993). In Philadelphia, which began making kinship placements only a few years earlier, relatives' homes provided 67 percent of total foster care homes by 1992 (Takas, 1992).

In addition, many children who live with relatives are not included in studies of the foster care system. For example, one study reported that the proportion of African American children in "informal adoptions" had increased in recent years, from 13.3 percent living with extended family members in 1970 to 16.5 percent in 1989 (Billingsley, 1992, p. 30). In 1990 as many as 1.3 million African American children lived with relatives in homes where neither parent was present (National Commission on Family Foster Care, 1991). Among these were three-quarters of a million children receiving Aid to Families with Dependent Children, 10 percent of the total AFDC rolls (National Commission on Family Foster Care, 1991).

PRACTICE AND POLICY IMPLICATIONS FOR KINSHIP CARE

Decision makers must come to terms with the impact of placement with relatives on the child welfare system. Because children in kinship care are predominantly African American (Berrick et al., 1994; Dubowitz, 1990; Iglehart, 1994; Task Force on Permanency Planning for Foster Children, 1990), a culturally based perspective is needed to grasp the intricacies and nuances of this increasing child welfare system of care (Scannapieco & Hegar, 1995). As policymakers attempt to confront kinship care as a child placement option, there arises a need to "affirm a black family kinship system that was historically strong, intact, resilient and adaptive" (Logan, Freeman, & McRoy, 1990, p. 71).

Social work practice within kinship care programs must recognize the resilient nature of the African American family and work with the "kinship triad," made up of the children, the biological parents, and the caregiver relatives. A system of services should be directed at this union of three to ensure a permanent living arrangement for the children.

In recognition of the kinship triad, social workers supervising the placement and working with the family should include all family members in their planning. It is important to acknowledge the importance of the extended family by including them in the development of the case plan. In the African American family, the relative caregiver often is the grandmother, who relies on her children and others to assist in the caregiving. Therefore, it is essential that all possible caregivers be involved in the service planning and decision-making process in case they need to take over as the part-time or full-time caregiver. The social worker must keep in mind that the caregiver relative does not consider himself or herself a foster parent in the traditional sense. The caregiver relative is responding to the needs of the family, not the needs of the child welfare system. His or her decision is preserving the African American family. As attempts are made to formalize this rich tradition, practitioners and policymakers should understand the value of relatives as a resource for African American children and examine the cultural issues that must be the foundation for the development of programs and policies.

CONCLUSION

As the child welfare system struggles to understand kinship care—a resilient, natural system of child rearing—the lack of policy formation and program development indicates that there is still limited recognition of the intrinsic value of supporting and empowering families to care for their own. Even though the need for kinship care is growing at an alarming rate, policymakers continue to question the cultural and familial strengths within the extended family systems of children who are in need of government intervention.

Current family and child welfare administrators and practitioners must confront their own inability to understand a cultural tradition that is contrary to Eurocentric family values. The value of extended families as the primary family unit in the African American culture is different, not necessarily better or worse, than the Eurocentric concept of the nuclear family. Practitioners must speak out and not accept policies and practices that polarize and destroy the cultural and familial strength that has contributed to the resiliency of the African American family. It is the responsibility of all providers to ensure that the system is sufficiently competent and skilled to respond to the unique needs of the kinship triad.

REFERENCES

Adoption Assistance and Child Welfare Act of 1980, P.L. 96-272, 94 Stat. 500.
American Public Welfare Association. (1990). *Characteristics of children in substitute and adoptive care: A status summary of the VCIS national child welfare data base.* Washington, DC: Author.
Berrick, J. D., Barth, R. P., & Needell, B. (1994). A comparison of kinship foster homes and foster family homes: Implications for kinship foster care as family preservation. *Children and Youth Services Review, 16*(1/2), 33–64.
Billingsley, A. (1992). *Climbing Jacob's ladder.* New York: Simon & Schuster.
Boyd-Franklin, N. (1989). *Black families in therapy.* New York: Guilford Press.
Brown v. Board of Education, 347 U.S. 483 (1954).
Center for the Study of Social Policy. (1990). *The crisis in foster care.* Washington, DC: Family Impact Seminar.
Child Trends, Inc. (1993). *Facts at a glance.* Washington, DC: Author.
Dodson, J. E. (Ed.). (1983). *Strengths of black families—An Afrocentric educational manual: Toward a non-deficit perspective in services to families and children.* Nashville: University of Tennessee, School of Social Work.
Dubowitz, H. (1990). *The physical and mental health and educational status of children placed with relatives: Final report.* Unpublished manuscript, University of Maryland Medical School, Baltimore.
Edelman, M. W. (1993). *Progress and peril: Black children in America.* Washington, DC: Children's Defense Fund.
Everett, J. E, Chipungu, S. S., & Leashore, B. R. (Eds.). (1991). *Child welfare: An Africentric perspective.* New Brunswick, NJ: Rutgers University Press.
Garmezy, N. (1981). Children under stress: Perspectives on antecedents and correlates of vulnerability and resistance to psychopathology. In A. I. Robbin, J. Aronoff, A. M. Barclay, & R. A. Zucker (Eds.), *Further explorations in personality* (pp. 196–269). New York: John Wiley & Sons.
Garmezy, N. (1985). Stress resistant children: The search for protective factors. In J. Stevenson (Ed.), *Recent research in developmental psychopathology* (pp. 126–146). Oxford, England: Pergamon Press.
Garmezy, N. (1991). Resiliency and vulnerability to adverse developmental outcomes associated with poverty. *American Behavioral Scientist, 34,* 416–430.
Gutman, H. G. (1976). *The black family in slavery and freedom, 1750–1925.* New York: Vintage Books.
Iglehart, A. P. (1994). Kinship foster care: Placement, service, and outcome issues. *Children and Youth Services Review, 16*(1/2), 107–122.

Logan, S.M.L., Freeman, E. M., & McRoy, R. G. (1990). *Social work practice with black families.* New York: Longman.

Martin, E. P., & Martin, M. (1983). The black extended family. In J. E. Dodson (Ed.), *Strengths of black families—An Afrocentric education manual: Toward a non-deficit perspective in services to families and children* (pp. 160–167). Nashville: University of Tennessee, School of Social Work.

Masten, A. S., Best, K. M., & Garmezy, N. (1991). Resilience and development: Contributions from the study of children who overcome adversity. *Development and Psychopathology, 2,* 425–444.

McCubbin, H. I., & McCubbin, M. A. (1988). Typologies of resilient families: Emerging roles of social class and ethnicity. *Family Relations, 37,* 247–254.

Michaels, D., & Levine, C. (1992). Estimates of the number of motherless youth orphaned by AIDS in the United States. *Journal of the American Medical Association, 268,* 3456.

Musick, J. S., Stott, F. M., Spencer, K. K., Goldman, J., & Cohler, B. J. (1987). Maternal factors related to vulnerability and resiliency in young children at risk. In E. J. Anthony & B. J. Cohler (Eds.), *The invulnerable child* (pp. 229–252). New York: Guilford Press.

National Center on Child Abuse and Neglect. (1992). *National child abuse and neglect data system: Working Paper 2, 1991 summary data component.* Washington, DC: U.S. Government Printing Office.

National Commission on Family Foster Care. (1991). *A blueprint for fostering infants, children and youth in the 1990s.* Washington, DC: Child Welfare League of America.

National Urban League. (1992). *The state of black America.* New York: Author.

Pinderhughes, E. B. (1982). Family functioning of Afro-Americans. *Social Work, 27,* 91–96.

Puckrein, G. (1984). America's black middle class: A progress report. *Wilson Quarterly Report, 3,* 3–4.

Rutter, M. (1979). Protective factors in children's responses to stress and disadvantage. In M. W. Kent & J. E. Rolf (Eds.), *Social competence in children: Primary prevention of psychopathology* (Vol. 3, pp. 49–74). Hanover, NH: University Press of New England.

Rutter, M. (1990). Psychosocial resilience and protective mechanism. In J. Rolf, A. S. Masten, D. Cicchetti, K. H. Nuechterlein, & S. Weintraub (Eds.), *Risk and protective factors in the development of psychopathology* (pp. 181–214). New York: Cambridge University Press.

Scannapieco, M., & Hegar, R. L. (1995). Kinship care: Two case management models. *Child & Adolescent Social Work, 12,* 147–156.

Stack, C. (1974). *All our kin: Strategies for survival in a black community.* New York: Harper & Row.

Stevenson, K. M., Cheung, K. M., & Leung, P. (1992). A new approach to training child protective services workers for ethnically sensitive practice. *Child Welfare, 71,* 291–304.

Takas, M. (1992). Kinship care: Developing a safe and effective framework for protective placements of children with relatives. *Children's Legal Rights Journal, 13*(2), 12–19.

Takas, M. (1993). *Kinship care and family preservation: A guide for states in legal and policy development.* Unpublished manuscript.

Task Force on Permanency Planning for Foster Children, Inc. (1990). *Kinship foster care: The double-edged dilemma.* Rochester, NY: Author.

Thornton, J. L. (1991). Permanency planning for children in kinship foster homes. *Child Welfare, 70,* 593–601.

U.S. Bureau of the Census. (1992). *1990 census report.* Washington, DC: U.S. Government Printing Office.

U.S. Department of Health and Human Services, National Center for Health Statistics. (1992). *Monthly vital statistics report: Advance report of final mortality statistics, 1990.* Washington, DC: Author.

Voting Rights Act of 1965, P.L. 89-110, 42 U.S.C.A. § 197.

Wang, M. C., Haertel, G. D., & Walberg, H. J. (1992, November). *Education resilience in inner cities.* Paper presented at the Invitational Conference on Resilience, Temple University, Philadelphia.

Werner, E. E. (1984, November). Research in review: Resilient children. *Young Children,* pp. 68–72.

Werner, E. E. (1991, July). *Vulnerability and resiliency in children and families: Focus on children with disabilities.* Paper presented at the annual conference of the Center for Children at Risk, Johns Hopkins University, Baltimore.

Wilson, M. N. (1989). Child development in the context of the black extended family. *American Psychologist, 44,* 380–383.

Yusane, A. Y. (1990). Cultural, political, and economic universals in West Africa in synthesis. In M. K. Asante & K. W. Asante (Eds.), *African culture: The rhythms of unity* (pp. 39–70). Trenton, NJ: Africa World Press.

This chapter was originally published in the March 1996 issue of Social Work, *vol. 41, pp. 190–196.*

17 Inner-City Youths Helping Children: After-School Programs to Promote Bonding and Reduce Risk

Julie O'Donnell, Elizabeth A. Michalak, and Ellen B. Ames

More than one-fifth of our nation's children live in poverty (Sawhill, 1992). Many live in the inner cities, where they are confronted daily with crime, violence at home and on the streets, substance abuse, inadequate schools and health care, lack of adult supervision, and child abuse and neglect (Schorr, 1988; Task Force on Youth Development and Community Programs, 1992). Children who grow up in poverty-ridden neighborhoods are at increased risk of problem behaviors such as juvenile delinquency, school failure and dropout, teenage pregnancy, and substance abuse (O'Donnell, Hawkins, Catalano, Abbott, & Day, 1995).

In addition to poverty, a number of other risk factors also appear to increase the likelihood that children will engage in these adolescent problem behaviors (Hawkins, Catalano, & Miller, 1992). Community risk factors include low neighborhood attachment and community disorganization and extreme economic deprivation. Early and persistent antisocial behavior, academic failure in elementary school, and lack of commitment to school are school risk factors. Individual and peer risk factors include friends who engage in problem behaviors and favorable attitudes toward problem behaviors (Hawkins & Catalano, 1992; Hawkins et al., 1992).

The cumulative effect of these risk factors, often present in inner-city neighborhoods, increases the risk for children and youths living there. Effective prevention programs must therefore intervene on multiple levels and specifically target identified risk factors (O'Donnell et al., 1995; Schorr, 1988) and involve collaboration among youths, families, schools, and community agencies.

SOCIAL DEVELOPMENT MODEL

The social development model (SDM) is an approach to preventing antisocial and health-compromising behaviors, which incorporates an understanding of the risk factors leading to problems in adolescence and the protective factors leading to healthy development (Hawkins & Catalano, 1992). This research-supported model emphasizes bonding as a key protective factor in children's resistance to problem behaviors. *Bonding* is a sense of belonging and contributing to family, school, peers, or the community. The components of bonding are *attachment*, defined as positive relationships with others, and *commitment*, defined as an investment in the future.

Bonding

The SDM hypothesizes that an individual's level of bonding is determined by the amount of opportunity available to an individual for involvement in a social unit, the skills which the individual applies in participating in the social unit, and the reinforcements provided by the unit for the individual's behavior (O'Donnell et al., 1995). When these socializing processes are consistent, a social bond develops between the individual and the socializing unit.

Programs that maximize these conditions should promote successful experiences, enhance bonding and, as a consequence, reduce problem behaviors. For example, an after-school program attempting to enhance bonding between children and peer mentors would provide children with opportunities for active involvement in the program, experiences that lead to skills for successful participation in activities, and consistent reinforcement from their youth mentors for productive involvement in program activities.

Prosocial Norms

Once children feel bonded to a social unit, they want to live according to its standards and norms. Clear behavioral guidelines are necessary so children know what is and is not acceptable for people their age (Hawkins & Catalano, 1992). Attitudes against problem behaviors are strengthened by promoting children's bonds and commitment to their various social groups (prosocial peers, families, schools, community) and by developing beliefs about what is healthy and ethical behavior (Hawkins et al., 1992). Children who are bonded to units with clear norms against problem behaviors are less likely to become involved in these behaviors, because involvement may threaten valued relationships (Hawkins & Catalano, 1992). Thus, it is important that youths working with children verbalize and model clear norms against involvement in problem behavior.

Peer Influence

Empirical evidence suggests that involvement with delinquent peers is a powerful predictor of delinquent behavior across ethnicities (Chavez, Oetting, & Swaim, 1994; Elliott, Huizinga, & Ageton, 1985; Mason, Cauce, Gonzales, & Hiraga, 1994). Although strong bonds to family and school can help youths avoid problem behavior, the influence of peers is often more important in determining involvement in or avoidance of problem behavior (Elliott et al., 1985; Mason et al., 1994).

The SDM recognizes the importance of peers in influencing antisocial behavior. Opportunities for interaction with antisocial others and for involvement in problem behaviors, interactions with others involved in problem behaviors, and perceived reinforcements for problem behaviors increase the likelihood of such behaviors (O'Donnell et al., 1995). Prevention programs designed to reduce risk should include a mixture of prosocial children as well as children experiencing some difficulty, so that positive peer relationships develop and prosocial norms take precedence over norms promoting involvement in problem behavior.

PEERS AS MENTORS AND ROLE MODELS

Providing children with opportunities for successful and rewarding interaction with prosocial peers and older youths may be an effective intervention and prevention strategy. Youths who model prosocial behaviors often have greater credibility with their peers than adults (Jason & Rhodes, 1989). Peers have successfully promoted improved social skills in children and youths with behavior disorders (Mathur & Rutherford, 1991). Prevention programs using peers were found more effective than any other approach in reducing substance use (Conrad & Hedin, 1991). School programs using peers trained to mediate conflict have also been successful in improving student behavior and reducing discipline problems (Lane & McWhirter, 1992). Elementary school children participating in programs led by former gang members were less likely to join gangs later than a control group of nonparticipants (Jason & Rhodes, 1989). Programs in which youths help youths may benefit both the helpers and recipients. When trained middle school students have tutored elementary school students, achievement test scores of both have increased (McLaughlin & Vacha, 1992). However, mentors need training to develop skills to tutor (Thomas & Jason, 1989).

Using adolescents from the same community and culture as the children they are mentoring may be particularly effective. Low-income teenage mentors paired with young, disadvantaged inner-city children have formed strong interpersonal bonds (Wright & Borland, 1992). These mentors can help high-risk youths of color bridge the gap between "street-smart" communication and effective communication in the majority culture. They can teach coping skills that give rise to competence (Blechman, 1992).

Community service can help youths feel connected to their community and promote problem-solving ability, social responsibility, and social competence (Conrad & Hedin, 1991). Middle and high school students performing volunteer work in their communities have shown significantly reduced problem behaviors (Allen, Kuperminc, Philliber, & Herre, 1994). Participation in the planning and implementation of prevention programs helps youths feel ownership of and commitment to the program (Jason & Rhodes, 1989).

The Task Force on Youth Development and Community Programs (1992) concluded that the hours after school pose considerable risk to low-income children and adolescents for getting involved in dangerous or illegal activities. However, these nonschool hours afford communities opportunities to make a difference in the lives of youths by providing activities to promote their successful development (Task Force on Youth Development and Community Programs, 1992). It is possible that using inner-city adolescents and young adults as mentors to children in after-school programs may promote bonding, result in the successful development of each group, and reduce their involvement in problem behaviors.

THE COLLABORATIVE AFTERSCHOOL PREVENTION PROGRAM

The Collaborative Afterschool Prevention Program was designed to reduce involvement in adolescent problem behaviors among low-income children and youths of color by targeting specific risk factors while increasing the protective factors of bonding and shared prosocial norms. This program used inner-city teenagers and young adults as leaders in an after-school program for elementary and middle school children from the same community. The youths had an active voice in program planning and the children and their mentors were given opportunities to contribute positively to their communities.

Participant Characteristics

The children and mentors lived in a community fraught with risk factors. Their neighborhoods were disorganized, violent, and transient, with high numbers of homeless people, gang members, and drug dealers. The rates of juvenile arrests, teenage pregnancies, child abuse reports, and school dropout were high. Children enrolled in second through eighth grade at four different schools were eligible for the program.

Of the 584 children enrolled in the program for at least three months over a two-year period, approximately 60 percent were Latino, 24 percent African American, 6 percent Asian American, 5 percent European American, 3 percent Native American, and 3 percent multiethnic. Sixty percent were boys, and 40 percent were girls. Fifty-eight percent of the parents reported yearly incomes of less than $10,000, 23 percent reported incomes between $10,000 and $15,000, and 19 percent reported incomes higher than $15,000.

Of the 54 mentors employed over the first two years of the project, 78 percent were young men, and 22 percent were young women. Forty-six percent were African American, 43 percent Latino, 5 percent Asian American, 4 percent European American, and 2 percent Native American. Ages ranged from 15 to 25.

Program Description

The Collaborative Afterschool Program was a partnership among the YMCA, three elementary schools and one middle school, the department of social work at an urban university, a church, a child guidance center, an art museum, and the county probation department. Representatives from these agencies joined community residents to design a collaborative prevention program for neighborhood children. Neighborhood teenagers and young adults were paid mentors and program facilitators in the after-school component. A governing committee composed of agency representatives, community members, and mentors met monthly to review program performance, resolve problems, celebrate successes, and refine the program.

All organizational partners provided direct services to support and enhance the after-school mentoring program. The YMCA hired the program director and mentors, provided weekly mentor training, daily program supervision, and space. Each school site donated program space and equipment, recruited children, and consulted with mentors about the children. Local high schools recruited the youth mentors and awarded academic credit for employment. The department of social work evaluated the program.

The church coordinated tutoring activities and "Family Nights," which brought children, families, and mentors together socially. The art museum ran a self-awareness art program, designed to help children express their feelings at each school, and hosted a Family Night exhibition of the art work at the museum. The probation department provided individual and family counseling to delinquency-prone youths. The child guidance center provided a project social worker who worked with children, mentors, and their families. Each organization also provided extensive training to the mentors.

The after-school program was run simultaneously at the four school sites three days a week for two hours a day. Each mentor was assigned a group of no more than seven children. Children were carefully placed so that those displaying more acting out behaviors were spread equally across the groups. The assignment process was necessary to reduce interaction with peers involved in problem behaviors and increase the likelihood that group norms would be prosocial. Each school had a college-age site director who supervised the mentors.

Services for Children

Highly structured small group activities, led by the mentors, provided opportunities and rewards for positive interaction, thus promoting bonding to prosocial others. Mentors established relationships with children and encouraged them to express their feelings. Various activities, including sports, arts, games, community projects, and field trips, helped children develop physical, social, and expressive skills. The mentors provided homework assistance at each session to increase children's academic skills. This component targeted the risk factors of early academic failure and lack of commitment to school. Children's social skills were developed using positive discipline and role modeling. The mentors set clear behavioral expectations, rewarded positive behavior, and modeled appropriate problem-solving and conflict resolution skills.

The program stressed social skills development, so children could take advantage of their involvement in the program. This component targeted early and persistent problem behavior and helped the children develop skills to interact successfully within their groups. Children with serious behavior problems were referred to the social worker for individual and family counseling.

Services for Mentors

In addition to providing the youths with an employment opportunity, the program helped them develop skills and rewarded positive performance. Care was taken to maximize these conditions so that they would become bonded to professionals from the collaborative agencies and each other. Staff and community professionals trained, supported, and encouraged youths to work hard at school and to think about attending college. Communication skills and prosocial norms were developed through retreats, weekly staff meetings, and frequent group social activities. The social worker and probation officer provided services to youths experiencing personal problems and to their families. Volunteer projects designed to improve their communities helped to develop community bonding. The services targeted the risk factors of interaction with problem peers, norms favorable to problem behaviors, alienation, lack of commitment to school, and low neighborhood attachment.

Training of Mentors

Prospective mentors were interviewed and carefully screened by two collaborative members who asked a series of standardized questions. The youths who
passed the interview attended five days of unpaid training, including a three-
day retreat in the mountains before being formally hired. The youths needed a
broad range of training to develop the skills needed to be successful group mentors. The first two days of training included sessions on assertive, preventive,
and proactive discipline; effective communication; anger de-escalation; child
development; child abuse reporting; prejudice awareness; cultural sensitivity;
gang involvement; and school site rules.

Although sessions at the three-day mountain retreat targeted active listening,
nonverbal communication, and leadership skills, the primary purpose was to
develop bonding among the mentors while training them to develop positive
relationships with children. Extensive time was devoted to the SDM and the
positive effect that mentors might have on children. These experiences helped a
group of diverse youths to identify themselves as all working toward an important goal—helping children.

Weekly training addressed anger management, leadership styles, responsibility, problem solving, cardiopulmonary resuscitation and first aid, conflict resolution, group dynamics, higher education, career choices, multicultural tolerance, assertiveness, and computer literacy. Each week mentors identified and
solved challenging situations concerning children and the program. They shared
positive experiences and learned from their mistakes in a supportive environment. The mentors also learned to resolve their own interpersonal conflicts. They
were then able to generalize these conflict resolution skills to deal effectively
with conflicts within their groups. The mentors were rewarded with frequent
celebrations at staff meetings and with trips.

The importance of establishing clear norms for behavior through consistent
training among the mentors became clear almost immediately. An incident early
in the program also reinforced the need for close supervision and training of
these young mentors. A third grader found a starter pistol and used it to intimi-
date other children in school restrooms throughout the day. During the after-
school program, he tried to give the pistol to his mentor but was told to put it
away or he would get into trouble and kicked out of school. He then gave the
pistol to the school-site director who put it in his gym bag and took it home on
the bus. The program director confiscated the pistol the next day after the principal called about gun rumors she had heard. This experience illustrated the
need to train mentors to respond to crises in a manner consistent with school
and program policies rather than teenage neighborhood norms. It also highlighted the importance of helping mentors make the transition from student to
authority figure by clarifying their roles and responsibilities.

Mentors' Involvement in the Community

The mentors were invited to join community improvement projects unrelated
to their jobs. Many mentors volunteered as basketball and soccer coaches in
YMCA leagues, as well as counselors at winter and summer camp. Together

with U.S. Navy volunteers, mentors built indoor soccer walls. The mentors participated in citywide cleanup days and joined with local groups to build or repair homes for low-income residents. They also volunteered for the annual YMCA fundraising campaign, raising $3,500 the first year and nearly $6,000 the second year. Participating youths were rewarded with a fishing trip by the YMCA Board of Managers. Mentors solicited donations from local businesses to build a yearly haunted house at the YMCA to give neighborhood children a safe and fun place to go on Halloween. The youths reported that these activities made them feel they were making an important contribution to their community.

Mentor Contributions to Program Development and Modification

The collaborative's governing body was committed to incorporating feedback from the mentors to improve and modify the program. The research team designed a survey to elicit the mentors' perceptions of how the program might be improved and the effects of the programs on children and themselves. The mentors were interviewed yearly by trained research assistants from the university if they consented to participate. Interviews, for which mentors were paid, lasted approximately an hour. Forty-six (86 percent) of the 54 mentors employed during the first two years of the project were interviewed.

One strength of the after-school program was that it evolved over time, largely in response to mentor feedback. During the first year, homework assistance for children was available at the church on afternoons when the program did not operate, but few participants used it. Some youths reported helping children informally with their homework, yet this aid was unorganized and left others in the group unsupervised. Year one interviews with mentors suggested that the program needed more structure so routines could be established, expectations set, and free time (when children might get into trouble) reduced. Mentors were also concerned that many of the children were failing academically.

The program was modified so that mentors tutored all children in their groups for 30 minutes daily. Church employees and volunteer teachers trained mentors to tutor and supervised the process. Mentors also said children needed exposure to other educational experiences. Field trips to public libraries, universities, zoos, art and history museums, and the oceanography institute were added in year two.

Although the collaborative committee was aware of ethnic divisions in the neighborhood, interviews with mentors brought racial concerns to the forefront and highlighted the need to develop tolerance and respect among the various ethnic groups. As one mentor said, "Having different ethnic group leaders is important because, when kids see different ethnic group leaders getting along, this helps them in turn to get along. It helps kids cooperate with each other across racial groups." Clearly, having mentors of mixed ethnicities was important in this community.

For some mentors, this job was their first experience in making friends with people outside their own ethnic groups. Although the modeling of cross-racial friendships was seen as positive, mentors suggested that the program needed a more organized approach to dealing with diversity. In response to these concerns, all mentors participated in cultural tolerance training to explore their own prejudices. Celebrations of cultural diversity, such as Cinco de Mayo and Black History Month, were incorporated into the program. A group to deal with racial tensions among children at the middle school and mentors was formed and met during school hours.

Another important program change in year two was to extend child guidance and probation support services to the mentors. Because the mentors lived in the neighborhood, they also experienced many of the same difficulties as the children. As the mentors felt bonded, they began to share their own personal difficulties with professional staff. Many struggled with homelessness, racism and prejudice, violence, gangs, teenage pregnancy, homophobia, sexual and physical abuse, school failure, deaths of friends and family, and substance abuse. When personal or school problems interfered with job performance, the collaborative provided support services rather than firing the mentor. For example, after drinking on a staff retreat, a mentor and his grandmother received services from the project social worker. The social worker also helped one mentor find housing after he was evicted from his foster home. If mentors' problems posed a threat to children after program assistance, they were referred to other services and dismissed.

Mentor Perceptions of Program Effects on Children

Interviews with 46 mentors were completed. Forty-five (98 percent) thought the program was helpful to children. As we hoped, the mentors said the program provided children with opportunities, skills, and rewards (Table 17.1). The most frequent benefit mentors noted was that the program provided children with a safe place to be after school. One mentor said, "It gives them another place to be children. Out in the streets they can't be children; they have to be part of the hood. They know how to load a gun before they know how to tie their shoes."

Mentors also said program participation improved children's social skills. Comments included: "Helps them make friends" and "I helped a kid learn to control his anger instead of getting into fights." Mentors reported that the program "teaches them study habits and gives them time to do their homework"

Table 17.1

Mentors' Perceptions of How the Afterschool Collaborative Program Helped Children (N = 45)

Perception	n	%
Safe place to go/keeps off streets	35	43.7
Builds trusting relationships	11	13.7
Teaches skills and values	11	13.7
Provides positive role models	7	8.7
Helps them forget problems	5	6.2
Builds self-worth	4	5.0
Helps with homework	4	5.0
Child care	2	2.5
Helps racial relations	1	1.2

NOTE: One mentor did not report that the program helped the children.

and "If they want to survive they have to start with homework, then a job. It's one of the most important parts."

Mentors also indicated that the children became bonded to them: "I got a hard-to-talk kid to open up and discuss the murder of his brother and friend." "They have at least one person that they can talk to when they really need it, and they know that person will be there for them." "They cling to us and like being with us. . . . Hear your name being called all the time."

Mentor Perceptions of Program Effects on Themselves

Almost 80 percent of the 46 mentors completing interviews spent time at the YMCA outside of work. On average, mentors spent eight additional hours at the YMCA suggesting that it became an important social unit for them.

Behavior and Attitude Change. Most of the 46 mentors (89 percent) said their attitudes and behavior had changed because of program employment. Comments about behavior changes included "[I am a] more conscious person regarding what I say, how I act. I used to hang out but now I need to be responsible and practice what I preach. I don't procrastinate with my homework" and "I used to fight a lot but now I fight less and help others to fight less." Comments about attitudinal changes included "I think about kids more—they're our future, if we don't take care of them, we don't have a future" and "We can make a difference in children's lives. Before I thought if a kid grew up in a certain hood, he was doomed to stay there. Now I see if we encourage and support the kids, they have a good chance of getting out."

Skills and Goal Development. Most mentors said they had learned new skills (96 percent, $n = 44$) and established new goals (67 percent, $n = 31$) while in the program. Mentors said, "I learned to take initiative, be persistent and responsible" and "I'm not shy like I used to be. I speak my mind and communicate to people in a more positive way." Goals also changed: "Before I just wanted to be a football player, now I want to be a psychologist so I can solve people's problems" and "I understand the importance of an education. Seeing those kids and families really opens your eyes to what you want to do in life. It pushes you a little harder to do better." More than 50 percent of the mentors' grades had improved and all of the graduating mentors went on to college after year one.

IMPLICATIONS FOR SOCIAL WORK

Anecdotal data from mentors provides some support for using inner-city adolescents and young adults as mentors in after-school programs for elementary and middle school children. Most of the mentors reported that they and the children benefited from program involvement. Feedback from the mentors also indicated that the program gave children and their mentors opportunities, skills, and rewards for involvement with prosocial peers, mentors, and the community. As predicted from the SDM, some children and mentors became bonded to these prosocial units and began to internalize their standards for prosocial behavior. These protective factors should reduce problem behaviors. The SDM appears to provide a viable framework for mentoring programs.

Experiences with this program suggest several guidelines for developing similar efforts. First, even the most successful inner-city adolescents can use support services to help them deal with the poverty, violence, and discrimination they face daily. Second, youths chosen to mentor children should be carefully screened and provided with ongoing training and supervision. Roles and program rules must be clearly established and frequently reinforced. Leadership, conflict resolution, behavior management, tutoring, and related skills must be developed for youths to be successful mentors. Third, prevention programs using youth mentors should be highly structured and include a mix of prosocial children as well as those who are more actively acting out. Fourth, programs in ethnically diverse areas must openly address issues of racial intolerance and model cultural sensitivity. Fifth, adolescents are experts in what children and youths need. Program planners should actively seek their opinions and implement their ideas. Finally, professionals need to be firmly committed to using youths as mentors and providing them with the necessary support.

Although more rigorous studies are needed, this project suggests that inner-city youth mentoring programs may promote social competence and bonding among children and adolescent mentors. Communities will benefit by including youths in their prevention efforts.

REFERENCES

Allen, J., Kuperminc, G., Philliber, S., & Herre, K. (1994). Programmatic prevention of adolescent problem behaviors: The role of autonomy, relatedness and volunteer service in the Teen Outreach Program. *American Journal of Community Psychology, 22*, 617–638.

Blechman, E. A. (1992). Mentors for high-risk minority youth: From effective communication to bicultural competence. *Journal of Clinical Child Psychology, 21*, 160–169.

Chavez, E. L., Oetting, E. R., & Swaim, R. C. (1994). Dropout and delinquency: Mexican-American and Caucasian non-Hispanic youth. *Journal of Clinical Child Psychology, 23*, 47–55.

Conrad, D., & Hedin, D. (1991). School-based community service: What we know from research and theory. *Phi Delta Kappan, 72*, 743–749.

Elliott, D., Huizinga, D., & Ageton, S. (1985). *Explaining delinquency and drug use.* Beverly Hills, CA: Sage Publications.

Hawkins, J. D., & Catalano, R. F. (1992). *Communities that care.* San Francisco: Jossey-Bass.

Hawkins, J. D., Catalano, R. F., & Miller, J. Y. (1992). Risk and protective factors for alcohol and other drug problems in adolescence and early adulthood: Implications for substance abuse prevention. *Psychological Bulletin, 112*, 64–105.

Jason, L. A., & Rhodes, J. E. (1989). Children helping children: Implications for prevention. *Journal of Primary Prevention, 9*(4), 203–212.

Lane, P. S., & McWhirter, J. (1992). A peer mediation model: Resolution for elementary and middle school children. *Elementary School Guidance and Counseling, 27*(1), 15–23.

Mason, C., Cauce, A., Gonzales, N., & Hiraga, Y. (1994). Adolescent problem behavior: The effect of peers and the moderating role of father absence and the mother-child relationship. *American Journal of Community Psychology, 22*, 723–743.

Mathur, S. R., & Rutherford, R. B. (1991). Peer-mediated interventions promoting social skills of children and youth with behavior disorders. *Education and Treatment of Children, 14*, 227–242.

McLaughlin, T. F., & Vacha, E. F. (1992). School programs for at-risk children and youth: A review. *Education and Treatment of Children, 15*, 255–267.

O'Donnell, J., Hawkins, J. D., Catalano, R. F., Abbott, R. D., & Day, L. E. (1995). Preventing school failure, drug use, and delinquency among low-income children: Long-term intervention in elementary schools. *American Journal of Orthopsychiatry, 65*, 87–100.

Sawhill, I. V. (1992, September). Poverty in the U.S.: Trends, sources, and policy implications. *Social Insurance Update No. 25*, pp. P-1–P-4.

Schorr, L. (1988). *Within our reach: Breaking the cycle of disadvantage.* New York: Doubleday.

Task Force on Youth Development and Community Programs. (1992). *A matter of time: Risk and opportunity in the non-school hours.* New York: Carnegie Corporation.

Thomas, N., & Jason, L. A. (1989). A preliminary study on improving tutoring skills among black inner-city children. *Journal of Black Psychology, 15,* 163–172.

Wright, L., & Borland, J. H. (1992). A special friend: Adolescent mentors for young, economically disadvantaged, potentially gifted students. *Roeper Review, 14*(3), 124–129.

The project and research were funded by grants from the James Irvine Foundation.

This chapter was originally published in the October 1997 issue of Social Work in Education, *vol. 19, pp. 231–241.*

18 Community Asset Assessments by Latino Youths

Melvin Delgado

The social work profession is at a critical juncture as it approaches the 21st century because of its historical reliance on a paradigm of scarcity, which has severely restricted meaningful dialogue and engagement with undervalued communities (Saleebey, 1992). A paradigm of scarcity is predicated on outside resources as the only answer to a community's needs. A paradigm of scarcity applied to Latino youths and communities takes any one, or a combination, of the following approaches: Youths do not possess the capabilities or resources to help themselves or their community; the problems youths face are generally the result of their own inadequacies, culture, or failure to acculturate; and only "adults," "experts," and "formal organizations" can possibly help youths and their communities (Heath & McLaughlin, 1993; McLaughlin, 1993).

The profession's shift from a scarcity to a strengths (empowerment and assets) paradigm requires a different strategy for service provision. This shift must incorporate principles of empowerment. It presents a new set of rewards and challenges for the profession, organizations, and communities. It not only fosters participation of the community, but also relies on and actively solicits it (Holmes, 1992).

This chapter describes a community asset assessment of the Puerto Rican community in Holyoke, Massachusetts. It focuses on the factors that facilitate or hinder community asset assessments using youths as interviewers. Implications for school and human services agency involvement of Latino youths in asset research are also discussed.

REVIEW OF THE LITERATURE

Research on Latino communities has ranged from conventional needs assessments (Delgado, 1981; Humm-Delgado & Delgado, 1986) to empirical studies with minimal concern for service delivery (Becerra & Zambrana, 1985; Marin & Marin, 1991; Rogler & Cooney, 1984). However, this literature has not reflected recent developments on Latino community strengths and empowerment (De La Rosa, 1988; Delgado, 1995; Delgado & Rosati, in press; Gutierrez, Ortega, & Suarez, 1990).

Youths have been the subject of increased attention in academic and policy-making circles; however, most of this attention has focused on youths as a group "at risk" and not as a resource (Dryfoos, 1990; McWhirter, McWhirter, McWhirter, & McWhirter, 1993; National Research Council, 1993; Urban Institute, 1993). Youths have generally not been allowed to play leadership roles in Latino communities. Culturally, youths are supposed to follow the lead set by adults and not question their authority and wisdom (Aguirre-Molina & Parra, 1995). Thus, viewing youths as current or future leaders has rarely been a perspective of the community.

Community Assets and the Strengths Perspective

The field of human services has slowly shifted its approach to undervalued communities (Becerra & Iglehart, 1995; Gutierrez, 1992). Proponents of the strengths-based approach, most notably Kretzmann and McKnight (1993), McKnight (1995), and Saleebey (1992), have stressed that community-based interventions (programmatic or research) must have four key elements to be successful: (1) an in-depth understanding of how a community defines itself and conceptualizes its needs and resources, (2) an active and meaningful role in the undertaking for all sectors, (3) interventions that facilitate and encourage participation, and (4) interventions that develop a community's capability to help itself. Asset studies incorporate all of these elements.

Sullivan's (1992) comments on the use of a strengths perspective in social work are also applicable to asset studies:

> A strengths perspective of social work practice offers an alternative conception of the environment. This perspective promotes matching the inherent strengths of individuals with naturally occurring resources in the social environment. . . . Recognizing, recruiting, and using these strengths can help maximize the potential of our clients and our community. In addition, when the environment is viewed as a source of opportunities for clients, rather than an ecology of obstacles, the sheer number of helping resources we perceive expands dramatically. (pp. 148–149)

Latino community assets have generally been conceptualized as natural support systems (De La Rosa, 1988; Delgado, 1994, 1995; Delgado & Humm-Delgado, 1982). These support systems generally fall into four categories: (1) family, friends, and close neighbors; (2) religion; (3) folk healers; and (4) commercial establishments and social clubs (Delgado, in press a, in press b).

Empowerment

The concept of empowerment has been widely accepted within the profession since it first appeared in the literature (Solomon, 1976). Lee (1994) identified three critical but interrelated components to empowerment that lend themselves to a community asset paradigm involving youths as interviewers: (1) development of self-esteem, (2) increased knowledge and skills, and (3) cultivation of indigenous resources. Holmes (1992) reinforced the relevance of empowerment to social work when he said, "Empowerment requires new thinking about old problems. Empowerment invites us to see the world differently as it abandons the limits and distortions of the pathology model and focuses on human strengths and abilities as the proper starting point for social work practice" (p. 158). Youth participation in decisions affecting the community, particularly those that influence how a "problem" is defined and "solved," represents an important dimension of empowerment (Marti-Costa & Serrano-Garcia, 1987).

Latino Youths as Field Interviewers

Efforts to place youths in leadership roles in conducting asset assessments open up critical opportunities for future generations. However, initial efforts casting youths as leaders may result in resistance from adults in the community. Delgado (1981), in an analysis of case studies (needs assessments) involving Latino adolescents as interviewers, identified helping and hindering factors. The five helping factors were (1) community participation—involvement of an undervalued group, (2) community entry—familiarity with culture and language, (3) resource pool of interviewers—availability of a sizable number of individuals who were unemployed or underemployed, (4) interviewer knowledge of community—geographic familiarity and high comfort level, and (5) cost—less expense involved in using youths than adults.

However, the use of Latino adolescents as interviewers was not without hindrances. Delgado (1981) identified six hindering factors: (1) restrictions on questions asked (youths could not inquire about sensitive topics), (2) confidentiality of data and possible bias (adults were concerned about youths sharing information with others), (3) training demands (most youths had limited employment experience), (4) increased level of supervision and field support (lack of interviewing experience required closer supervision and support compared with adults), (5) restrictions on scheduling interviews (youths were not available at night, on holidays, or on weekends), and (6) limitations on referrals to agencies (youths lacked ability to diagnose and knowledge of social services system).

DESCRIPTION OF PROJECT

Site

The city of Holyoke, Massachusetts, is situated approximately 100 miles west of Boston. In 1990 it had a population of approximately 44,000, of whom 12,700 were Latino; Puerto Ricans were the largest Latino subgroup (93.5 percent) (Gaston Institute, 1992). The Latino community had a median age of 18, with 46 percent under the age of 16; the community also had the largest proportion of people with incomes below the poverty rate—59.1 percent—more than four times the rate of the white population (Gaston Institute, 1994). This community, as a result, suffered all of the ills associated with high rates of economic poverty.

Sponsoring Organization

New Bridges (Nuevo Puente) was the sponsoring organization of the community asset assessment. New Bridges was created through a high-risk youth demonstration grant from the Center on Substance Abuse Prevention. Through the asset assessment, New Bridges sought to identify and enlist indigenous ("natural") resources for participation in substance abuse prevention activities.

Staff

Youths hired to work as interviewers were part of a larger cohort who participated in cultural and educational activities; learned about the effect of substance abuse on individuals, families, and communities; and undertook leadership training to carry out school and community education on alcohol, tobacco, and other drugs. The interviewers were six girls and four boys ages 13 to 15. They were paid $100 for their participation (six hours per week for four weeks). Youths conducted interviews in pairs or groups of three to provide mutual support. They were supervised by two adult staff members.

Goals

The asset assessment focused on a 40-block area with a high concentration of Latino commercial establishments and residents. It sought to locate all Puerto Rican or Latino natural support establishments (no effort was made to locate folk healers), provide youths with an appreciation of community strengths, raise school and human services agency awareness of community assets, and develop an assets directory (Delgado, in press a). The assessment sought data on type of establishment (commercial, religious, social, and so forth), its location, year opened, name of key contact person, days and hours of operation, listing of social services provided (for example, counseling, information and referral, credit), and willingness to collaborate with schools and agencies on community projects.

A total of 37 establishments were located, and 25 participated in the assessment: seven grocery stores, five clothing stores, four restaurants, two beauty parlors, two furniture stores, one radio station, one repair shop, one record store, one gift and party supply store, and one botanical shop. Four establishments refused to participate, and it was not possible for the youths to assess the eight Pentecostal churches because they conducted services during late evening hours (Delgado, in press a).

Phases

The assessment consisted of two phases. Phase 1 involved identifying all of the establishments. Phase 2 consisted of the actual interviews, which varied in time but generally lasted no more than 30 minutes.

Training and Field Support

Interviewers received six hours of training in asset assessment. However, the youths had received 70 hours of training earlier on cultural heritage, leadership skills, and drug refusal skills. A debriefing session was held at the end of each workday as a means of providing support, obtaining a better understanding of the data, problem solving, and resolving issues or problems encountered in the field.

LESSONS FROM THE FIELD

Asset assessments, like any other form of research, provide rewarding and challenging experiences (Delgado, 1981). Because the study focused on assets instead of needs and natural support organizations instead of individuals, a unique set of facilitating and hindering factors emerged. Any school or agency undertaking an asset assessment cannot help but benefit from the experience.

Facilitating Factors

Facilitating factors fell into five categories: (1) identification of indigenous resources, (2) development of community goodwill, (3) community capacity development, (4) leadership development, and (5) establishment of collaborative activities.

Identification of Indigenous Resources. Needs assessments focus on needs and resources (the latter are "formal"), and asset assessments focus on indigenous resources and how they can be used to meet local needs. The Holyoke study identified a rich network of indigenous resources (Delgado, in press a):

> Eighteen institutions stated that people were welcome to come in and converse and not have to purchase goods or services in order to do so. Six institutions provided information on social services and made appropriate referrals to social service agencies. Several establishments ($n = 4$) indicated that they provided crisis counseling, food . . . ($n = 4$), loans ($n = 3$), and credit ($n = 6$) as needed. One institution (botanical shop) indicated a willingness to take care of children in . . . a crisis. . . . The survey revealed an extensive array of . . . services being provided by these systems.

Development of Community Goodwill. Asset studies provide an excellent opportunity for organizations to develop community goodwill. However, youths may not be welcomed by all sectors of a Latino community. Once the initial distrust is addressed, the community should start to view an organization sponsoring the assessment in a favorable light. This can result in natural support establishments cosponsoring community events (for example, health fairs) or donating funds, food, and space.

There are endless possibilities for involving youths, natural support establishments, schools, and social services agencies. For example, the youths in the project wanted to raise money to pay for a trip. They decided on a car wash. However, unlike conventional car washes, where cars are charged a certain amount of money, the youths decided to ask Latino businesses to sponsor each car they washed (amounts ranged from 5 cents to 25 cents per car). These establishments, in turn, would be given recognition by having their names listed on a billboard displayed at the car wash.

Twenty-eight establishments agreed to sponsor the activity. Donations from washed cars were solicited but not required. The youths also decided to make a videotape of the activity to share with other youth agencies and to help other organizations generate funds.

The car wash raised $575. The funds, although important, were not as important as how the event was planned and the community involved. The car wash demonstrated that youths, if provided with the opportunity, can be concerned and contributing members of a community rather than a major source of embarrassment (subject of news stories emphasizing negative incidents) and fear (gangs).

Community Capacity Development. The investment of resources in preparing youths as interviewers also serves to develop the community's capacity to help itself. Youths not only have a "job" that pays them money, but also develop knowledge and skills that can be transferred to other arenas.

Leadership Development. Asset assessments identify not only service-focused resources, but also current and potential leaders (adults as well as youths). As a consequence of participation in the Holyoke study, three youths took a more active role in leading the team; these same youngsters went on to volunteer in other agencies and play leadership roles in their schools. It is unrealistic to assume that every youth who participates will take on a leadership role. Nevertheless, the core of an asset assessment (focus on strengths, resilience, and coping) is a natural context for developing leadership skills.

Establishment of Collaborative Activities. Latino natural support establishments are not perfect institutions—many have active campaigns of competition with each other for customers or converts. Delgado and Rosati (in press) found that very few Pentecostal churches collaborated with each other, even when located on the same city block.

Nevertheless, natural support establishments do not compete with human services organizations for funds or clients. Thus, an asset assessment opens up opportunities for collaborative activities without the worry of competition; in Holyoke, 20 establishments indicated a willingness to do so (Delgado, 1994, 1995).

Hindering Factors

Asset assessments are not without challenges, especially when the interviewers are adolescents. Hindering factors fell into seven categories: (1) logistical considerations; (2) scheduling; (3) interviewer bias against certain support systems; (4) lack of familiarity and comfort with the process; (5) interviewee bias against youths, schools, and social services organizations; (6) youths' beliefs; and (7) supervision and field support.

Logistical Considerations. Numerous logistical factors must be taken into consideration when undertaking an asset assessment in Latino communities. First, assessments must be undertaken in person; the use of telephones (which are often unavailable) or mailed questionnaires is not possible. Personal contact is grounded in Latino cultural values. There is no acceptable substitute, particularly if the organization conducting the study is unknown among natural support establishments (Humm-Delgado & Delgado, 1986).

Unlike needs assessments, which may use a directory of social services organizations, asset studies do not have such resources. It is necessary to go block by block to identify establishments, a time-consuming activity. The use of field interviewers, regardless of age, is also expensive.

Finally, it is necessary to inform parents of the participating youths about the study. The unconventional nature of an asset assessment, combined with the age of the interviewers, requires close and clear communication with parents. The Holyoke team held personal conversations with parents. Two youths' parents refused to allow their children to participate in this assessment process because they were concerned about safety. Informing parents also helps increase a community's consciousness about its assets.

Scheduling. Asset studies should avoid holiday periods, when establishments do their greatest volume of business. The Holyoke study took place during the

Christmas season, and several establishments refused to participate or required multiple rescheduling. In addition, it is advisable to conduct studies during nonwinter months in states where snow is a possibility, thus avoiding cancellation of appointments.

An asset assessment of Latino natural support establishments requires flexibility in the scheduling of appointments. Although many of these institutions operate six or seven days per week and have extensive hours, there are certain times when interviews are not possible, often in the late afternoon and early evening.

Delgado and Rosati (in press) reported that interviews for a study of Pentecostal churches in Holyoke occurred during late evening hours (after 10:00 P.M.) after religious services were completed. An adult conducted the interviews because an initial effort at involving youths was unsuccessful. In Holyoke, youths generally conducted interviews after school (3:00 P.M. to 5:30 P.M.), which also was a busy time for many establishments. The use of adults allowed interviews to take place later.

Interviewer Bias against Certain Support Systems. None of the youths were willing to interview folk healers because of beliefs that spells or hexes could result from their contact. Consequently, this vital source of natural support was not included in the assessment. All but two of the interviewers refused to interview a botanical shop owner because of similar concerns. The two willing youths knew the owner because their families patronized the establishment. Botanical shops sell herbs and healing paraphernalia, give consultations about spiritual problems, and often work closely with local folk healers.

Lack of Familiarity and Comfort with the Process. The lack of direct contact between natural support organizations, schools, and social services agencies makes any form of assessment difficult. Natural support organizations' lack of experience with surveys resulted in heightened fears about the assessment process. The focus on assets provided the following challenges:

1. Interviewees, not accustomed to answering survey questions, were even less accustomed to answering asset-related questions.
2. Confidentiality is difficult to maintain when questions are asked in crowded settings lacking privacy.
3. Adults often expressed concern that the youths really wanted information on income and annual business volume, which would then be used by their competitors or by taxing authorities to audit the establishment.
4. Adults expressed doubt about how their information could possibly help the community.

Interviewee Bias against Youths, Schools, and Social Services Organizations. Using youths (a group not usually in positions of authority within the community) further compounds a difficult assessment process. The youths were tested by adult interviewees. They were also questioned about the process, what would happen to the data once collected, and how they could bring about change when adults have not been successful.

Furthermore, Latino adults rarely view youths as leaders, opinion makers, or stakeholders and may show a lack of respect toward youths. The following statement was made by an adult who refused to participate in the study: "If this study is so important, why are they sending kids to do the job of an adult?" Youths, as a result, need to be prepared for this response through the use of "preconceived" responses, that is, responses that have been rehearsed to get a particular point across without appearing defensive or hostile.

Natural support establishments rarely interact with schools or human services agencies. In fact, many of these institutions are approached by residents to help them redress injustices caused by schools and agencies. This lack of familiarity with such institutions is a barrier to the development of trust between the interviewee and interviewer (Delgado, 1995).

Youths' Beliefs. To participate in asset assessments, youths must believe in the innate strengths and self-worth of individuals and communities. The Holyoke experience revealed the power of a deficit model. As part of their training, youths were asked to identify the needs, problems, and issues of the Puerto Rican community; they had no difficulty doing so. However, when asked to list community strengths, they could not list a single one.

The youths had developed a very strong and positive sense of self and cultural pride through previous training on Puerto Rican history, customs, music, and art. However, this sense of pride had not translated to the broader Latino community: The youths could identify personal and familial strengths but could not identify community strengths. As a result, much of the training on asset assessment focused on the definition and recognition of a community asset or strength, not on interviewing and data-recording techniques.

Supervision and Field Support. Youths require greater supervision and support than adults. The Holyoke study raised concerns about possible violence toward youths. An altercation erupted between two interviewers and members of a local gang. The interviewers entered the gang's "turf" to conduct an interview, which precipitated a fight involving several gang members. Fortunately, the interviewers did not suffer severe physical harm. However, project staff stopped the study and held a "talk session" to discuss the incident and possible nonviolent alternatives. This incident turned into an educational lesson. The use of adult interviewers would have minimized such incidents in the field.

IMPLICATIONS FOR SCHOOL SOCIAL WORK PRACTICE

Although the study discussed in this chapter was initiated by a community agency, there are important implications for schools. The following recommendations vary in labor intensity and the degree to which schools might be able to shift in paradigm from deficits to assets:

- School social workers can develop asset studies in schools or communities. A school-focused assessment can enlist youths in identifying potential student leaders, candidates for peer education programs, and possible projects involving natural support systems.
- Natural support establishments can be identified and enlisted to work closely with schools and students. A community asset assessment can be the foundation for enlisting the support of churches, grocery stores, restaurants, and other establishments for after-school activities and field trips.

- Schools can invite owners of natural support establishments to tell students the stories of how they started their businesses. Speakers from the community are very often excellent role models whom students can relate to in light of their own experiences.
- Students can undertake assessments for extra credit or as part of a community project. The skills and knowledge learned in the planning of a study can translate to other areas of their curriculums and influence career planning. Youths may select a career in social work or other human services field because of participation in such projects.
- Students can learn to use videotapes in documenting their experiences; these videos, in turn, can be shared with other schools or community agencies as a community service.
- Schools may undertake assessments in collaboration with other social services agencies. Collaboration with human services organizations and natural support establishments can minimize barriers between the school and the community. Opening up communication lines between parents and community leaders can encourage parents to participate in school events and thus reinforce their children's interest in education.
- The information gathered through an assessment can educate teachers and school personnel about a community's strengths and support networks. School personnel rarely venture into a community to discover for themselves where students live. If they depend on information presented in the local media, they can develop a deficit perspective on the community, which can translate into low expectations of student performance.
- An understanding and appreciation of assets can facilitate development of assignments that incorporate cultural strengths. A social studies teacher, for example, might assign a student to interview an elder member of his or her family or community about life in his or her place of origin as part of a lesson on ethnic origins.
- School social workers are in the best position to initiate asset assessments because of their understanding and appreciation of community. They can facilitate the development of bridges among schools, human services agencies, and indigenous institutions. An asset assessment can also provide linkages between the worker and other individuals with similar interests, thus developing important partnerships and reducing the isolation social workers often experience in urban school settings.

CONCLUSION

The use of Latino adolescents in community asset assessments offers much promise for the field of school social work. Although labor intensive, asset assessments are an excellent vehicle for involving a community and developing its capacity for self-determination. Organizations wishing to use an asset assessment to reach undervalued communities must understand that the means are just as important, if not more so, as the ends. The investment of time, resources, and energy in a process that will prove very rewarding and very frustrating is essential. The success of an asset assessment is possible only when all sectors own the process and, therefore, the results.

REFERENCES

Aguirre-Molina, M., & Parra, P. A. (1995). Latino youth and families as active participants in planning change: A community–university partnership. In R. F. Zambrana (Ed.), *Understanding Latino families: Scholarship, policy, and practice* (pp. 130–153). Thousand Oaks, CA: Sage Publications.

Becerra, R. M., & Iglehart, A. P. (Eds.). (1995). *Social services and the ethnic community.* Boston: Allyn & Bacon.

Becerra, R. M., & Zambrana, R. E. (1985). Methodological approaches to research on Hispanics. *Social Work, 30,* 42–49.

De La Rosa, M. (1988). Natural support systems of Puerto Ricans: A key dimension of well-being. *Health & Social Work, 13,* 181–190.

Delgado, M. (1981). Using Hispanic adolescents to assess community needs. *Social Casework, 62,* 607–613.

Delgado, M. (1994). Hispanic natural support systems and the AODA field: A developmental framework for collaboration. *Journal of Multicultural Social Work, 3,* 11–37.

Delgado, M. (1995). Hispanic natural support systems and alcohol and other drug services: Challenges and rewards for practice. *Alcoholism Treatment Quarterly, 12,* 17–31.

Delgado, M. (in press a). Community asset assessment and substance abuse prevention: A case study involving the Puerto Rican community. *Journal of Child and Adolescent Substance Abuse.*

Delgado, M. (in press b). Puerto Rican food establishments as social service organizations: Results of an asset assessment. *Journal of Community Practice.*

Delgado, M., & Humm-Delgado, D. (1982). Natural support systems: A source of strength in Hispanic communities. *Social Work, 27,* 83–89.

Delgado, M., & Rosati, M. (in press). Religion, asset assessment and AOD: A case study of a Puerto Rican community in Massachusetts. *Journal of Health and Social Policy.*

Dryfoos, J. G. (1990). *Adolescents at risk.* New York: Oxford University Press.

Gaston Institute. (1992). *Latinos in Holyoke.* Boston: University of Massachusetts.

Gaston Institute. (1994). *Latinos in Holyoke: Poverty, income, education, employment, and housing.* Boston: University of Massachusetts.

Gutierrez, L. M. (1992). Empowering ethnic minorities in the twenty-first century: The role of human service organizations. In Y. Hasenfeld (Ed.), *Human services as complex organizations* (pp. 320–338). Newbury Park, CA: Sage Publications.

Gutierrez, L. M., Ortega, R. M., & Suarez, Z. (1990). Self-help and the Latino community: The importance of groups. In T. J. Powell (Ed.), *Working with self-help* (pp. 218–236). Silver Spring, MD: NASW Press.

Heath, S. B., & McLaughlin, M. W. (1993). Building identities for inner-city youth. In S. B. Heath & M. W. McLaughlin (Eds.), *Identity and inner-city youth: Beyond ethnicity and gender* (pp. 13–35). New York: Teachers College Press.

Holmes, G. E. (1992). Social work research and the empowerment paradigm. In D. S. Saleebey (Ed.), *The strengths perspective in social work practice* (pp. 158–168). New York: Longman.

Humm-Delgado, D., & Delgado, M. (1986). Gaining community entree to assess service needs of Hispanics. *Social Casework, 67,* 84–89.

Kretzmann, J. P., & McKnight, J. L. (1993). *Building communities from the inside out: A path toward finding and mobilizing a community's assets.* Evanston, IL: Northwestern University, Center for Urban Affairs and Policy Research.

Lee, J. B. (1994). *The empowerment approach to social work practice.* New York: Columbia University Press.

Marin, G., & Marin, B. O. (1991). *Research with Hispanic populations.* Newbury Park, CA: Sage Publications.

Marti-Costa, S., & Serrano-Garcia, I. (1987). Needs assessment and community development: An ideological perspective. In F. M. Cox, J. Erlich, J. Rothman, & J. E. Tropman (Eds.), *Strategies of community organization* (pp. 362–373). Itasca, IL: F. E. Peacock.

McKnight, J. L. (1995). *The careless society: Community and its counterfeits.* New York: Basic Books.

McLaughlin, M. W. (1993). Embedded identities: Enabling balance in urban contexts. In S. B. Heath & M. W. McLaughlin (Eds.), *Identity and inner-city youth: Beyond ethnicity and gender* (pp. 36–68). New York: Teachers College Press.

McWhirter, J. J., McWhirter, B. T., McWhirter, A. M., & McWhirter, E. H. (1993). *At-risk youth: A comprehensive response*. Pacific Grove, CA: Brooks/Cole.

National Research Council. (1993). *Losing generations: Adolescents in high-risk settings*. Washington, DC: National Academy Press.

Rogler, L. H., & Cooney, R. S. (1984). *Puerto Rican families in New York City: Intergenerational processes*. Maplewood, NJ: Waterfront Press.

Saleebey, D. S. (Ed.). (1992). *The strengths perspective in social work practice*. New York: Longman.

Solomon, B. B. (1976). *Black empowerment: Social work in oppressed communities*. New York: Columbia University Press.

Sullivan, W. P. (1992). Reconsidering the environment as a helping resource. In D. S. Saleebey (Ed.), *The strengths perspective in social work practice* (pp. 148–157). New York: Longman.

Urban Institute. (1993). At-risk youth. *Policy and Research Report, 23*, 11–19.

The research in this chapter was funded by demonstration grant 5H86SPO2208 from the Center on Substance Abuse Prevention, Rockville, MD, to the Education Development Center, Newton, MA. The author was principal investigator.

This chapter was originally published in the July 1996 issue of Social Work in Education, *vol. 18, pp. 169–178.*

19 Strengths-Based Practice with Puerto Rican Adolescents: Lessons from a Substance Abuse Prevention Project

Melvin Delgado

S trengths-based practice offers potential for reaching underserved communities in the United States. This perspective, unlike the more commonly used deficits approach, identifies, mobilizes, reinforces, and builds on existing indigenous resources in the development of community solutions to community concerns (McKnight & Kretzmann, 1990). A strengths-based paradigm lends itself to primary prevention; a deficits approach, which is predicated on individuals, families, and communities being the source of problems and solutions being possible only if derived from and directed by external sources (Saleebey, 1992), does not lend itself to prevention.

Puerto Rican and other Latino youths are considered the fastest-growing population of young people in the United States (Aguirre-Molina & Para, 1995; Institute for Puerto Rican Policy, 1995). Puerto Rican youths, however, are also considered the most vulnerable of all Latino groups to leaving school, being under- or unemployed, experimenting with "hard" drugs, having poorer health status, and being involved with the criminal justice system (Borjas & Tienda, 1985; Institute for Puerto Rican Policy, 1995; Miranda, 1991; Morales & Bonilla, 1993; Perez & Cruz, 1994; Perez & Martinez, 1993; Rodriguez, 1991; Sullivan, 1993; Velez & Ungemack, 1989; Zambrana, Dorrington, & Hayes-Bautista, 1995). Thus, Puerto Rican youths present a high-risk profile and are worthy of special prevention and early intervention initiatives.

This chapter describes the experiences of a federally funded substance abuse prevention project—Nuevo Puente: New Bridges—focused on the development of resilience in Puerto Rican adolescents in a New England community. This initiative used cultural pride in the development of self-esteem, which is widely considered a critical domain of resilience (Brooks, 1994; Hechtman, 1991; Rutter, 1987). Cultural pride was an integral part of how Nuevo Puente helped Puerto Rican adolescents come to terms with their newly developing identities as individuals and as participants in an increasingly multicultural society while preserving essential links to their history, families, and culture. In addition, cultural pride served as a shield against the influence of risk-taking behavior involving alcohol, tobacco, and other drugs. Once the youths developed greater cultural pride, it was possible to provide content related to substance abuse, leadership, and the development of prevention activities that highlighted the youths' strengths and helped the Puerto Rican community (Delgado, 1995, 1996a, 1996b, in press; Delgado & Rosati, in press).

LITERATURE REVIEW

Nuevo Puente's conceptual foundation was informed by content from three key areas: (1) resilience, (2) self-esteem, and (3) coping strategies.

Resilience

Resilience can be defined as the result of personal and environmental factors that increase an individual's ability to resist risk-taking behavior (Newcomb, 1992). Scholars, most notably Brooks (1994), Hechtman (1991), and Rutter (1987), have extensively reviewed the literature and have identified three interrelated domains of resilience, each with multiple subcategories: (1) individual (temperament, self-esteem, self-efficacy); (2) family (affection, clarity of limits and structure, emotion, warmth); and (3) social environment (formal and informal supports). According to Brooks (1994),

> It is obvious that many factors residing within the child, in the family, and in the larger social environment interact in an on-going and dynamic way to determine whether early vulnerabilities give way to a life of productivity, success, and happiness—a life truly characterized as resilient—or whether these vulnerabilities intensify, resulting in a life punctured with disappointment, despair, envy, underachievement, and on-going failure. As these factors are articulated more precisely, increasingly effective programs can be developed and implemented for harnessing the unique strengths of individual children. (p. 547)

These three domains provide an operational framework for the use of resilience to enhance community-based strategies.

Self-Esteem

Puerto Rican and other Latino youths, especially those who are at latency and early adolescent stages of development, are particularly vulnerable to low self-esteem (Abalos, 1986; Aguirre-Molina & Para, 1995; Solis, 1995). Low self-esteem can result in youths not liking who they are, feeling incapable of controlling their destinies, and not having the ability to help themselves or others (Brooks, 1994). Lack of pride in one's ethnic background as a result of shame or lack of knowledge is widely considered a critical element in low self-esteem (Dryfoos, 1990; Fitzpatrick, 1987; Krimsky & Golding, 1992; Santiago, 1995).

McLaughlin (1993), in researching what makes youth agencies effective, stressed the importance of cultural pride–related activities:

> Many adults in these settings stressed the importance of alliance with some well-grounded cultural history as a component of general self-esteem and social competence. Youth workers understood the importance of cultural awareness and pride and of youths' development of a positive sense of this aspect of their identity. Within the broader community context, there is often little with which to ascribe value or pride to African American or Latino youths. (p. 60)

The development of an identity for Puerto Rican youths is further compounded by a search for identity by Puerto Rico itself; Puerto Rico is struggling with the formation of a positive identity as a result of its colonial history and current political status (Fitzpatrick, 1987).

Coping Strategies

Adolescents engage in risk-taking behavior as a means of coping with various stressors (Dryfoos, 1990; McWhirter, McWhirter, McWhirter, & McWhirter, 1993: Urban Institute, 1993), including those caused by entering adolescence, reduced coping, or both. Youths are less likely to engage in problematic or risk-taking behavior as a means of coping if they have high self-esteem and a positive social network and are provided with opportunities to help themselves and their community. Thus, the risk for problems can be conceptualized as a fractional equation with stress in the numerator and positive self-esteem, social competence, positive social networks, and resources in the denominator (Newcomb, 1992).

NUEVO PUENTE: NEW BRIDGES

Project Community

Holyoke, Massachusetts, located about 100 miles west of Boston, has a population of 44,000, of which 12,700 (28.9 percent) are Puerto Rican. The median age is 18 years; Holyoke has the youngest Latino population in the state.

The Puerto Rican community has the largest proportion of individuals living below the poverty level (59.1 percent), four times that of white non-Latinos. Poverty has disproportionately affected Latino children. Of families with children younger than 18, 67.6 percent had incomes below the poverty level (Gaston Institute, 1994). In addition, 60.0 percent of Latinos did not have a high school diploma. This low educational attainment translated into high levels of under- or unemployment, with Latino men and women having unemployment rates of 22.4 and 33.7 percent, respectively (Gaston Institute, 1994).

Clients and Staff

Nuevo Puente served 29 Puerto Rican boys and girls ages 12 to 14. All of the youths were from low-income households, and 60 percent of the homes were female headed. About 50 percent were children of substance-abusing parents, and 39 percent were at risk of leaving school because of academic difficulties and acting-out behavior. All had difficulty with English; some had difficulty writing and reading in Spanish as well.

All of the project staff were Puerto Rican and born in either Puerto Rico or New York City. With the exceptions of the principal investigator and the senior evaluator, all staff were residents of Holyoke. The project subscribed to the principle of hiring staff of the same ethnic group as the community it sought to serve and sought senior and field staff who were residents of the community, although this is very difficult to achieve when projects target low-income communities. Community-based staff can develop a clear and in-depth understanding of cultural issues; can decrease the likelihood of miscommunication based on socioeconomic status and cultural misunderstanding; can increase the level of trust between the community and the project; and can provide residents with role models.

Goals

According to Aguirre-Molina and Para (1995), "Community development is the ultimate goal of [substance abuse] prevention strategies employed to reduce risk factors and address the variables that contribute to their occurrence. *Community development*, as defined here, is the process of involving the community in the identification and reinforcement of those aspects of everyday life, culture, and political activity that are conducive to health" [italics added] (p. 153). Nuevo Puente had two complementary goals: (1) to increase resilience and protective factors for at-risk Puerto Rican youths and others in the community to reduce the likelihood that these adolescents would experiment with and become habitual users of alcohol, tobacco, marijuana, cocaine, and other drugs and (2) to develop a community-based intervention that enriched existing prevention efforts by highlighting cultural values and attitudes that can reduce substance abuse.

The goals were translated into a three-pronged prevention strategy: (1) psychosocial development (emphasis on cultural pride and enhancement of self-esteem); (2) peer teaching and mentoring; and (3) service to community. Much is known about increasing protective factors against substance abuse and other social problems that affect youths (Dryfoos, 1990; Lorion & Ross, 1992), and there is a growing consensus that these three strategies in combination—and predicated on a strengths perspective—are the most promising for reaching youths of color in the United States.

Interventions

Although originally funded to address substance abuse, Nuevo Puente viewed social problems as interrelated and as stemming from many of the same causes and sharing broad-based solutions. Unfortunately, most social theories attempt to view social problems as isolated from each other. Poverty, school dropout, substance abuse, and teenage pregnancy cannot be addressed in isolation from each other or at only one level of intervention.

McLaughlin (1993) stressed the importance of youth-oriented agencies, taking a broader perspective on youths and their needs:

> The needs of inner-city youth do not come in neat bundles or tidy problem definitions. Just as the identities of youth are embedded in the character and resources of the communities, neighborhoods, and families, so are their needs enmeshed and interrelated. Inner-city organizations that connect youth with larger society, promote a positive sense of purpose and personhood, and provide the resources that youngsters need to reach adulthood are not single-issue, single-purpose institutions. . . . These organizations, in short, serve as "family" for youth, meeting their needs and promoting their growth much in the inclusive way a family would. (p. 55)

Focusing on single problems and ranking them in order of importance ignores the complex causes of individual, family, and community breakdown. The responsibility for addressing social problems falls to the community and society as a whole, not to only a few individuals or institutions, and necessitates comprehensive strategies that use strengths-based approaches.

Psychosocial Approach. A psychosocial approach needs to strengthen youths' resilience through the development of intrapersonal and interpersonal skills that lead to a sense of self-worth and enhanced self-esteem; to help youths combat internal forces, such as lack of self-efficacy, that are often antecedent to substance abuse and other negative behaviors; to enable youths to decide which behaviors are in their self-interest (through development of decision-making skills, values clarification, consequential thinking skills, and information on the consequences of engaging in risk behaviors such as substance abuse); and to teach skills (for example, peer-pressure resistance, communication skills, assertiveness training) youths can use to resist social pressures to engage in negative behaviors.

These psychosocial areas were addressed through use of a formalized curriculum that involved obtaining input from all sectors of the Puerto Rican community. Major content areas for the curriculum were identified through an ethnographic survey, key informant interviews, focus groups, meetings, and discussions with community leaders, parents, and educators.

The curriculum included knowledge development and skills building that were culturally relevant for Puerto Rican youths. Participants received 72 hours of training over a seven-month period in cultural pride (Puerto Rican history, values, culture, arts, and traditions); group leadership skills (recruiting and leading groups); self-sufficiency and self-determination; communication and relationship skills (conflict resolution and identifying situations that lead to violence and other risk-taking behaviors); strategies to deal with substance abuse (increased awareness of alcohol and other drugs); and practical matters (projects that facilitate the application of knowledge learned in other parts of the curriculum).

As a whole, the curriculum had a significant impact on the participants. However, the greatest effect was achieved by the module on identity and culture, which was measured by the participants' interest and pride in speaking Spanish; awareness of Puerto Rican cuisine, history, geography, and folklore; willingness to participate in Puerto Rican folk dancing; interest in and willingness to celebrate Puerto Rican holidays; interest in learning the lyrics to the Puerto Rican anthem; and eagerness to learn about their ancestors.

Peer Teaching and Mentoring. Peer education is based on an understanding of the developmental tasks of latency and early adolescence, a time when youths must establish their own identities. Given the complexities of modern family and community life, this can be a difficult task for any adolescent. However, in the case of adolescents living in two cultures, as many Latinos do, the task becomes even more complicated, because youths must blend their more traditional heritage and values with those of the dominant culture (Felix-Ortiz de la Garza, Newcomb, & Myers, 1995; Phinney, 1995; Saldana, 1995).

Adolescents go through a process of modifying or even rejecting the identities influenced by their families. Concurrently, adolescents also maintain the basic human need for acceptance and community. To fulfill this need, youths often seek acceptance and community from peers rather than parents or other adults. This peer orientation, which can be harmful in the form of peer pressure to engage in negative behaviors, can be used to advantage. A peer education and leadership program in which adolescents teach other adolescents healthy attitudes, accurate information on and consequences of substance abuse, and the skills to turn these attitudes and information into positive behavioral outcomes offers much potential for use in strengths-based practice. In addition, while teaching others about substance abuse, participants reinforce their own attitudes, knowledge, and skills. Having learned about desirable behaviors and how to convey information to others, participants can become health proponents in their own families and communities.

A strengths-based program can attract additional resources once the reputation of a project's participants has been well established. Nuevo Puente youths participated in three trainings (minimum of 20 hours) offered by other organizations that supplemented the initial curriculum content. First, a local chapter of a nationally based organization gave 20 hours of training on how to do HIV/AIDS prevention through local media (radio). The relationship between the spread of HIV/AIDS and the sharing of needles can be felt throughout all sectors of the Latino community. Second, a local university with the goal of identifying and helping youths pursue higher education provided a six-week academic-skills enhancement training. Third, a Boston-based youth agency provided five three-hour workshops on planning and implementing communitywide prevention events that stressed empowerment principles.

Service to Community. The opportunity to serve the community places youths in a position of leadership. Youths are rarely provided with mechanisms to channel their energies and creativity in a world outside of their cohorts, because adults are not accustomed to viewing youths in this role. In addition, it is necessary to provide youths with opportunities to engage in purposeful action:

> Many aspects of program design signaled the positive value of youth and positive expectations for their future. Youth activities geared toward tangible products or performances provided a sense of accomplishment and success. These activities gave youth concrete evidence that something could be gained by sticking with an effort and provided what one youth called "visible victories" for youngsters who have had few such positive experiences in school, in their family, or in the community. (McLaughlin, 1993, p. 60)

Opportunities to serve the broader community can result in many unanticipated benefits, including reinforcing and expanding existing substance abuse programs to meet the needs of youths and other groups; increasing the number of residents involved in developing prevention strategies; decreasing the negative consequences of substance abuse; developing materials and activities that inform and unify a community around shared concerns; and helping prepare youths to assume future leadership roles in substance abuse prevention and other areas.

The youths initiated or played significant roles in several communitywide activities. They planned and implemented a 40-square-block community asset assessment that was very successful for both the 10 youth interviewers and the broader Puerto Rican community. The youths were involved in all major facets of the study and benefited from the skills and knowledge acquired from conducting a study and reinforcing a strengths perspective in the community (Delgado, 1995, 1996a, 1996b, in press).

The youths organized and participated in several teaching events. A Three Kings' Day (Puerto Rican holiday) celebration was enormously successful, attracting almost 200 community members. The youths presented traditional Puerto Rican dances in addition to speaking about substance abuse. *"Homenaje a la familia"* (homage to the family) was attended by 75 community members. The youths presented skits portraying situations in which young people encounter substance abuse in the home and community. Another event, which took place during the graduation of one of the project cohorts and was attended by 150 parents, relatives, and friends of the participants, served as a forum to present skits on substance abuse and provided the community with an opportunity to see the youths "in action" and to develop a better understanding of the project's goals. The youths undertook numerous communitywide workshops on substance abuse prevention and early intervention. These activities, which involved other youths and parents, ranged from single activities of a few hours to all-day workshops.

Nuevo Puente youths developed two community education videotapes that captured key dimensions of their experience in the program. One tape focused on substance abuse information through role-plays, skits, group discussions, and individual testimonies. Another focused on the Puerto Rican community of Holyoke, highlighting its assets and issues and discussing why there was a high incidence of substance abuse. The youths, who received training on how to operate video cameras and develop a script, were involved in all aspects of production. The videos were copied and distributed to key community-based organizations for use in in-service training of staff and youth workers.

In addition, while planning a car wash to earn money for a project field trip, the youths approached Latino community businesses to seek their financial sponsorship for cars. Donations from the owners of the washed cars totaled more than $500 (Delgado, 1996a).

Case Example

The following case example of a Nuevo Puente youth developed by a field coordinator was selected because it highlights the rewards and struggles of working with youths of color and the value of a strengths perspective. The narrative is in the coordinator's own words.

> The one who benefited the most was a young kid who came here with the attitude of the streets. . . . I think [his] parents had a lot of problems with him. They even had to go to court. . . . He was only 13 and . . . was dealing drugs when he came here. He lied. He never [admitted] he was dealing drugs. We had [problems] with him and almost decided to get rid of him. He even pushed a facilitator once. He had a lot of fights and arguments with the other participants. He always came here with a weapon . . . a stick or golf club. We had to take these away from him.
>
> [Then] he changed. He always thought that Puerto Ricans were bad because they were the only ones dealing drugs. He thought that Puerto Ricans are to be blamed for stealing . . . and he was real negative about Puerto Ricans. He was

always in the streets, and he thought the only way to make money in Holyoke was to sell drugs. He ended up having meetings with other kids about not selling drugs.

He was . . . the macho man. He was the best, until he started learning. He even cried. He let his feelings out . . . [and] talked about his problems. He actually stopped [dealing drugs].

He thought that was really bad. He thought he really ugly. He used to get suspended a lot. Then he started getting good grades. He took leadership . . . we always thought he was the best leader. He had the power to take control of the group. . . . He talked about drugs and admitted he used to deal drugs and he was ashamed. [He said], "I can't believe I did that.". . . Everybody was open mouthed. He said "I used to do that, and I don't want to deal with it." . . . [Often we] would sit down and talk.

I saw him like me when I was young. I always thought adults were against me. I thought adults were the enemy. I didn't want to deal with adults [because they] would yell at me. Everything I wanted to do was wrong. They always did it right. I had the same attitude he had, so I was always talking to him.

He graduated. He had the best attendance record. He always came. He always did his workshops. He was the one who gave the most ideas because he knew what was out there for the kids. He used to give advice. . . . I remember one time he . . . said, "You have to be careful, because when you're 13 and they put $40 in your hand just to deliver a package, and . . . your mother's on welfare and you don't get that much money, you grab it, because it happened to me." We were like . . . wow! This kid is learning about what he's going through, what is happening to him.

In the program he learned that he is Puerto Rican and that it's OK to say you're Puerto Rican. To him a Puerto Rican was a drug dealer. He didn't know that a Puerto Rican is . . . a person with culture . . . with ancestors . . . who comes from a place he can be proud of. . . . In the workshop on migration, he was the most interested. He was the one who asked the most questions . . . "Why was tobacco taken from Puerto Rico?" "Why did farmers move to the United States?" . . . He was actually looking for information and finding out who he is and why he did this. . . .

I would like for people to meet him and talk to him. He's somebody who is going to impress people.

Project Evaluation

The evaluation of Nuevo Puente involved a variety of quantitative and qualitative methods. The quantitative methods consisted of gathering data from schools (grades, attendance, participation in extracurricular activities) and administering pre- and posttests to measure knowledge acquisition. The primary qualitative methods included interviews with participants, adult facilitators, and parents and the maintenance of weekly logs by the adult facilitators.

Quantitative data indicated that school attendance increased dramatically for almost all of the participants. This may have been the result of a rule that youths could attend Nuevo Puente activities only if they had attended school that day. On average, participants increased their grades by at least one grade level during participation in the project. Six participants made the honor role. About 30 percent joined school-related clubs and teams.

The qualitative methods provided a wealth of information on how the participants benefited from Nuevo Puente. The weekly service logs maintained by the adult facilitators documented activities, observations, events, problems, and actions taken. Several major themes emerged from a content analysis of the logs: the problems and stressors encountered by the youths at home, at school, and in the community; the youths' hopes and desires as they entered and progressed through the project; the important role that facilitators played in the lives of the youths; the joys and feelings of accomplishment that the youths experienced in doing prevention activities in the community; and the frustrations experienced by the facilitators as they attempted to address the multitude of the youths' issues.

Participants were interviewed on videotape to determine how they viewed the impact of the project on them and their families. The interviews were shared with the entire group during a final exit interview and celebration. Participants raised instances in which they developed greater pride in their heritage, learned the importance of group solidarity, discovered that their relationships with adults in authority positions revealed "another side" to adults, and learned the importance of addressing all forms of substance abuse in the community. The latter was manifested in a variety of ways from the need to inform peers and family about the evils of tobacco to the importance of keeping relatives and friends from risk-taking behaviors with drugs.

IMPLICATIONS FOR SCHOOL SOCIAL WORK PRACTICE

In summarizing their experiences with a substance abuse prevention project, Aguirre-Molina and Para (1995) noted that "data support the need for primary prevention and early identification programs that target Latino children and adolescents. They also strongly underscore the principle that those who are at risk must be active participants in a process of change and community development so that empowerment can be achieved" (p. 153). The experiences of Nuevo Puente echo those of Aguirre-Molina and Para, and the following recommendations, which do not require tremendous expenditures of funds and other resources to implement, can be applicable to school social work practice in other urban areas of the country:

- School curriculum should reflect the cultural heritage of Latino youths. Material related to history, customs, and traditions can be interwoven into the fabric of a curriculum. Latino youths can play an active role in seeking out this material. Older Latino adolescents can pair with younger youths to discuss culturally related content in a way that benefits both the mentor and the recipient.
- After-school activities stressing cultural pride and skills development can be translated to other areas of a youth's life. School social workers can play an instrumental role in brokering resources and school permission for these activities.
- Sponsoring performances and celebrations stressing community life and encouraging community participation is an effective means of closing the gap between communities and schools.
- School assignments can be developed allowing Latino students to visit community institutions to obtain a picture of the community that is rarely seen.

These assignments can entail students interviewing positive role models such as business owners, social workers, and other community residents.

- Students can develop videotapes that orient teachers, school personnel, and other students to the Latino community. Creating such videos provides students with opportunities to plan, implement, and evaluate a project. These skills and knowledge areas can be transferred to other areas of their lives.

CONCLUSION

The importance of identifying, recruiting, and preparing future leaders of the Puerto Rican community cannot be overestimated. Youths who are provided with leadership opportunities not only serve as leaders among their cohorts, but also may represent their communities in the future. The use of adolescents as leaders has long been neglected in the human services field and should seriously be considered.

However, the development of Latino youth leaders can be accomplished only after they have developed a positive identity, including ethnic pride. Strengths-based practice with Puerto Rican and other Latino adolescents can reinforce a positive identity. The achievement of this goal necessitates the allocation of adequate resources and the political will to undertake a journey of self-discovery, with all the accompanying joys and pain. Such a journey is not restricted to youths and can positively affect adult staff as well.

REFERENCES

Abalos, D. T. (1986). *Latinos in the United States.* Notre Dame, IN: University of Notre Dame Press.

Aguirre-Molina, M., & Para, P. A. (1995). Latino youth and families as active participants in planning change: A community–university partnership. In R. E. Zambrana (Ed.), *Understanding Latino families: Scholarship, policy, and practice* (pp. 130–153). Thousand Oaks, CA: Sage Publications.

Borjas, G. J., & Tienda, M. (1985). *Hispanics in the U.S. economy.* New York: Academic Press.

Brooks, R. B. (1994). Children at risk: Fostering resiliency and hope. *American Journal of Orthopsychiatry, 64,* 545–553.

Delgado, M. (1995). Community asset assessment and substance abuse prevention: A case study involving the Puerto Rican community. *Journal of Child and Adolescent Substance Abuse, 4,* 57–77.

Delgado, M. (1996a). Community asset assessments by Latino youths. *Social Work in Education, 18,* 169–178.

Delgado, M. (1996b). Puerto Rican food establishments as social service organizations: Results of an asset assessment. *Journal of Community Practice, 3,* 57–77.

Delgado, M. (in press). Puerto Rican elders and merchant establishments: Natural support systems or simply businesses? *Journal of Health and Social Policy.*

Delgado, M., & Rosati, M. (in press). Religion, asset assessment and AOD: A case study of a Puerto Rican community in Massachusetts. *Journal of Health and Social Policy.*

Dryfoos, J. G. (1990). *Adolescents at risk: Prevalence and prevention.* New York: Oxford University Press.

Felix-Ortiz de la Garza, M., Newcomb, M. D., & Myers, H. F. (1995). A multidimensional measure of cultural identity for Latino and Latina adolescents. In A. M. Padilla (Ed.), *Hispanic psychology: Critical issues in theory and research* (pp. 26–42). Thousand Oaks, CA: Sage Publications.

Fitzpatrick, J. P. (1987). *Puerto Rican Americans: The meaning of migration to the mainland.* Englewood Cliffs, NJ: Prentice Hall.

Gaston Institute. (1994). *Latinos in Holyoke: Poverty, income, education, employment, and housing.* Boston: University of Massachusetts.

Hechtman, L. (1991). Resilience and vulnerability in long term outcome of attention deficit hyperactivity disorder. *Canadian Journal of Psychiatry, 36,* 415–421.

Institute for Puerto Rican Policy. (1995, August). Puerto Ricans and other Latinos in the United States: March 1994. *IPR Datanote,* pp. 1–2.

Krimsky, S., & Golding, D. (Eds.). (1992). *Social theories of risk.* Westport, CT: Praeger.

Lorion, R. P., & Ross, J. G. (1992). Programs for change: A realistic look at the nation's potential for preventing substance involvement among high-risk youth. *Journal of Community Psychology,* [Special issue], 3–9.

McKnight, J. L., & Kretzmann, J. P. (1990). *Mapping community capacity.* Evanston, IL: Northwestern University, Center for Urban Affairs and Policy.

McLaughlin, M. W. (1993). Embedded identities: Enabling balance in urban contexts. In S. B. Heath & M. W. McLaughlin (Eds.), *Identity & inner-city youth: Beyond ethnicity and gender* (pp. 36–68). New York: Teachers College Press.

McWhirter, J. J., McWhirter, B. T., McWhirter, A. M., & McWhirter, E. H. (1993). *At-risk youth: A comprehensive response.* Pacific Grove, CA: Brooks/Cole.

Miranda, L. C. (1991). *Latino child poverty in the United States.* Washington, DC: Children's Defense Fund.

Morales, R., & Bonilla, F. (1993). Restructuring and the new inequality. In R. Morales & F. Bonilla (Eds.), *Latinos in a changing U.S. economy: Comparative perspectives on growing inequality* (pp. 1–27). Newbury Park, CA: Sage Publications.

Newcomb, M. D. (1992). Understanding the multi-dimensional nature of drug use and abuse: The role of consumption, risk factors, and protective factors. In M. Glantz & R. Pickens (Eds.), *Vulnerability to drug abuse* (pp. 255–298). Washington, DC: American Psychological Association.

Perez, S. M., & Cruz, S. (1994). *Speaking out loud: Conversations with young Puerto Rican men.* Washington, DC: National Council of La Raza.

Perez, S. M., & Martinez, D. (1993). *State of Hispanic America 1993: Toward a Latino anti-poverty agenda.* Washington, DC: National Council of La Raza.

Phinney, J. S. (1995). Ethnic identity and self-esteem: A review and integration. In A. M. Padilla (Ed.), *Hispanic psychology: Critical issues in theory and research* (pp. 57–70). Thousand Oaks, CA: Sage Publications.

Rodriguez, C. E. (1991). *Puerto Ricans born in the U.S.A.* Boulder, CO: Westview Press.

Rutter, M. (1987). Psychosocial resilience and protective mechanisms. *American Journal of Orthopsychiatry, 57,* 316–331.

Saldana, D. H. (1995). Acculturative stress: Minority status and distress. In A. M. Padilla (Ed.), *Hispanic psychology: Critical issues in theory and research* (pp. 43–54). Thousand Oaks, CA: Sage Publications.

Saleebey, D. S. (Ed.). (1992). *The strengths perspective in social work practice.* New York: Longman.

Santiago, E. (1995, October 1). A Puerto Rican stew. *New York Times Magazine,* pp. 34, 36.

Solis, J. (1995). The status of Latino children and youth: Challenges and prospects. In R. E. Zambrana (Ed.), *Understanding Latino families: Scholarship, policy, and practice* (pp. 62–81). Thousand Oaks, CA: Sage Publications.

Sullivan, M. L. (1993). Puerto Ricans in Sunset Park, Brooklyn: Poverty amidst ethnic and economic diversity. In J. Moore & R. Pinderhughes (Eds.), *In the barrios: Latinos and the underclass debate* (pp. 1–25). New York: Russell Sage Foundation.

Urban Institute. (1993). At-risk youth: Identifying adolescents at risk. *Policy and Research Report, 23,* 11–19.

Velez, C. N., & Ungemack, J. A. (1989). Drug use among Puerto Rican youth: An exploration of generational status differences. *Social Science and Medicine, 29,* 779–789.

Zambrana, R. E., Dorrington, C., & Hayes-Bautista, D. (1995). Family and child health: A neglected vision. In R. E. Zambrana (Ed.), *Understanding Latino families: Scholarship, policy, and practice* (pp. 157–176). Thousand Oaks, CA: Sage Publications.

This project was funded through a demonstration grant from the Center for Substance Abuse Prevention (SP02208) to the Educational Development Center, Newton, MA. The author was principal investigator.

This chapter was originally published in the April 1997 issue of Social Work in Education, *vol. 19, pp. 101–112.*

20 Sociopolitical Antecedents to Stonewall: Analysis of the Origins of the Gay Rights Movement in the United States

Cynthia Cannon Poindexter

On Friday, June 27, 1969, shortly before midnight, New York City detectives raided the Stonewall Inn, a small gay bar in Greenwich Village. As part of his platform for re-election during the mayoral campaign, Mayor John Lindsay had agreed to another police crackdown on gay bars. At that time, the patrons of the Stonewall Inn tended to be young men of color; many were also transvestites or runaways. This routine raid did not go smoothly because the crowd did not behave in the usual passive manner (D'Emilio, 1983). Rather, the patrons of the bar erupted in violence. Rioting continued into the next three nights. Crowds gathered constantly to watch and participate. The anger was evidently not just about that night or that arrest because cries of "gay power" were frequently heard. Word of the disruption spread quickly through the mainstream media and gay press, and the modern gay rights movement in the United States was born (Duberman, 1993).

What made it possible for this social movement to spring from this particular event? Scholars from various fields have attempted to understand the timing, antecedents, and expression of social action and collective protest against oppression. For example, in his analysis of the resurgence of American Indian power in the 1960s, Cornell (1988) asked why the political uprising of American Indians occurred at that time rather than in earlier decades or centuries. Oppression, violence, and discrimination were certainly not new to these groups, so why did American Indian communities react strongly in the 1960s? Morris (1984) posed a similar question about the southern black civil rights movement, and D'Emilio (1983) did so in relation to the modern gay civil rights movement (a term used throughout to denote the actions of both gay men and lesbians).

With regard to the birth of the modern gay rights movement in 1969, perhaps the most appropriate question to consider is not "Why then?" but "How then?" As Humphreys (1972) argued, to ask why they remained unorganized for so long is to participate in a form of victim blaming, implying that gay men and lesbians are responsible in some way for their own oppression. Following Humphreys's focus on strengths rather than blame, I contend that it is important for social workers to study specific instances of successful resistance to societal discrimination to understand the genesis of social change. It is illuminating to concentrate on the processes through which the gay community mobilized power at a particular time and circumstance in the face of pervasive homophobia, stigma, and pressure.

According to both the Council on Social Work Education (1995) and the National Association of Social Workers (NASW, 1996), the profession's purpose includes political action, empowerment of groups at risk, organizational advocacy, and the pursuit of social and economic justice. Community organizing to counter oppression is a central concern of social work because this method of intervention is congruent with the profession's code of ethics (Biklen, 1983; NASW, 1996). However, social workers learn little in formal professional education about how to "assist or participate in social protest that may relate to their field of work" (Biklen, 1983, p. 103) and may be more concerned about therapy as a mode of practice than about social change (Garvin & Cox, 1995). Fisher (1995) lamented that social action occurs most frequently outside the profession. In a survey of 353 practitioners in Washington State, Ezell (1994) found that fewer than 1 percent were full-time advocates, and only a fourth of those advocates participated in class advocacy. Therefore, social workers need to understand more fully the importance and role of social action as a method of empowering constituents.

Garvin and Cox (1995) described the place of social work community organizing in a long history of community organizing against oppression in the United States since the Civil War. Their historical overview, however, only briefly mentioned such actions in the gay community. As will be evident from later discussions of the rise of the gay rights movement in the United States, the social work profession was not a catalyst or a supporter of that effort.

Rothman (1995) posited three modes of community intervention—locality development, social planning, and social action—that, although often intertwined, are separate ways of conceptualizing approaches to social change. It is social action that is addressed here, specifically, how to understand the emergence of a social action approach to community intervention in the U.S. gay community. As Rothman noted, the social action approach often has a "militant orientation" to advocacy, with a focus on empowerment of the oppressed.

This chapter addresses the emergence of a social action approach to community intervention in the U.S. gay community. Such an understanding is important to contemporary social work practice for two reasons. First, the profession was late in embracing the gay community's struggle against discrimination. Second, social workers can learn from the grassroots organizational tactics used by this population. The history of social action by gay men and lesbians needs to be fully incorporated into social work's collective understanding of the history of community organizing against oppression.

To help advance this understanding, this chapter focuses on the question of origins: how to understand the emergence of the modern gay rights movement in the United States. Because Morris's (1984) analytical framework is well developed and has received favorable attention (Edmonds, 1984; Grothaus, 1985; Woods, 1985), I use it to examine collective social action. This paradigm, developed in Morris's analysis of the emergence of the modern black civil rights movement, is applied to the emergence of the modern gay civil rights movement.

MORRIS'S PARADIGM

Morris (1984) developed a new conceptual framework for studying and under-standing collective protest—indigenous theory—after examining the limitations of three traditional models: (1) classical collective behavior theory, (2) Weber's theory of charismatic movements, and (3) resource mobilization theory. This chapter discusses Morris's views of the three traditional models and their limits in encompassing the facts of both the black and gay civil rights movements.

Three Traditional Models

Classical Collective Behavior Theory. The premise of classical collective behav-ior theory (Blumer, 1946; Lang & Lang, 1961; Park & Burgess, 1921; Smelser, 1962; Turner & Killian, 1957, all cited in Morris, 1984) is that collective behavior arises in response to unusual cultural situations, periods of rapid social change, or societal crises (such as industrialization, national disasters, and urbaniza-tion) and thus is not related to usual organizational and institutional behavior. During times of social upheaval, collective behavior is no longer guided by tra-ditional norms, customs, communication systems, and institutions; rather, it is spontaneous, unstructured, irrational, and influenced by rumor, informal com-munication networks, and generalized beliefs. Although there may be organi-zation and planning during social and political upheavals, they are thought to occur only in the later stages of the movements. This theory also assumes that these movements generate spontaneous or emotional forms of group behavior, such as mass panic, mob action, cults, crusades, revivals, and revolutions. These reactions are considered to be "tension-releasing devices for pent-up frustra-tions," even though they may result in significant societal change (Morris, 1984, p. 276).

Morris (1984) argued that this theory does not fit the events of the black civil rights movement and presented evidence of widespread deliberate, careful or-ganizing and planning early in the movement. He pointed out that the move-ment spread through existing formal and informal organized communication networks, leaders, organizations, and institutions. Rather than being mob ac-tions or fads, the activities of the early black civil rights movement were planned, rational, political phenomena.

Similarly, this theory does not fit the early gay civil rights experience in this country, because the historical record demonstrates much deliberate, structured behavior in the decades before 1969. As will be further illustrated, the resulting gay rights movement spread through pre-existing communications networks, leaders, and organizations (D'Emilio, 1983; Humphreys, 1972; Lauritsen & Thorstad, 1974; Marcus, 1992). Although the Stonewall riot appeared to be a spontaneous mob eruption, the event did not occur under what classical collec-tive behavior theory would call "unusual" circumstances. Police raids of gay bars were so frequent that they constituted business as usual. And the oppression and persecution of gay men and lesbians was commonplace and long standing.

Theory of Charismatic Movements. According to the theory of charismatic movements (Weber, 1947, cited in Morris, 1984), at certain times charismatic individual leaders mobilize a following that can cause revolutionary changes.

Weber postulated that charismatic authority occurs during periods of societal crises and is informal. Furthermore, he stated that charisma is effective only in the early stages of a political movement and must be replaced with formal power and organization if the movement is to survive. Morris concluded that Weber's analysis was limited in accounting for the dynamics of the black civil rights movement because it did not explain why charismatic movements arise or how they are mobilized. Charisma and organization existed side by side from the beginning of the movement, as is shown in the work of the black churches and leaders, such as Martin Luther King, Jr. Charisma played a vital part in the black civil rights movement, but, Morris noted, it is insufficient to explain the movement's success. With regard to the Stonewall riot, it is clear that Weber's charismatic model does not fit the profile of the black and Hispanic transvestites who were the major participants. These rioters were not charismatic community leaders, nor was there a single identifiable leader of the Stonewall uprising or of the modern gay rights movement.

Resource Mobilization Theory. Resource mobilization theory (Gamson, 1975; McCarthy & Zald, 1973; Oberschall, 1973; Tilly, 1978, cited in Morris, 1984) emphasizes the formal and informal resources necessary for the initiation and development of political movements. In this view, social protest depends on the group's success in managing resources to organize and mobilize. Behaviors are logical, grounded in existing structures and processes, and stem from actors and assets that are integrated into established community institutions. Therefore, marginal groups (those who do not possess resources) are unlikely to engage in protest. However, if individuals and groups have resources but are excluded from the traditional political processes, they are likely to participate in nontraditional social movements.

According to resource mobilization theory, dominated groups require assistance from elite advocates from outside the groups, including government leaders, attorneys and judges, political liberals, and wealthy philanthropic individuals and organizations, because they rarely have the skills and resources needed for social protest, whereas the elite outsiders typically have funds and organization. Morris (1984) showed that resource theory is an inappropriate paradigm for explaining the black civil rights movement because undue weight is given to the effect of outside elites and resources. This theory does not recognize the indigenous base, including the financial base rooted in the black church, and does not look at cultural factors, such as religion, music, and sermons, that helped mobilize the movement.

Resource theory partially illuminates the origins of the gay civil rights movement because, as will be discussed later, resources, such as existing social and political organizations and communication networks, were instrumental in the social and political mobilization of the late 1960s. However, this theory does not fully explain the Stonewall riot and subsequent movement because there were no critical outside influences or help from elites or resources; members of the gay community had the skills to mobilize on their own. Resource theory also fails to recognize the movement's indigenous base and does not acknowledge the role played by the cohesive gay culture, the collective symbols of which had existed underground for years, as well as the nonstructural factors like music, bars, drag, camp, and the insider language (Berube, 1991; D'Emilio, 1983, 1992; Duberman, 1986; Humphreys, 1972; Katz, 1976; Lauritsen & Thorstad, 1974; Marcus, 1992; Shilts, 1982).

THE INDIGENOUS MODEL

Rejecting the three traditional theories just outlined as incomplete frameworks for the analysis of the southern black civil rights movement of the 1960s, Morris (1984) proposed that the indigenous model is the more appropriate paradigm. It is argued here that the indigenous model can also illuminate the gay civil rights movement. Morris defined *dominated* and *oppressed groups* as those excluded from one or more of the decision-making processes that determine the quantity and quality of social, economic, and political rewards that groups receive from a society. Because of this exclusion, dominated groups try to mediate their own powerlessness by struggling with the power elite.

The indigenous analysis examines how these groups create the conditions that support overt power struggles. In this view, the emergence of a dominated community's sustained movement depends on whether that community has basic resources (including money, culture, communication, labor, and charisma), experienced social activists and leaders with strong ties to indigenous social institutions, communications networks, and strategies that can lessen domination and attain collective goals. Morris concluded that organizational forms that can unite the power of bureaucracies with informal structures are most appropriate for wide-scale social protest because they facilitate mass participation and rapid decision making. This hybrid is a creative way of linking formal bureaucracies, such as the National Association for the Advancement of Colored People (NAACP), with nonbureaucratic forms like those found in black churches. Morris (1984) proposed that "[political] movements are deliberately organized and developed by activists who seize and create opportunities for protest" (p. 283). In this way, Morris accounted for charisma and culture and for the fact that an indigenous social movement may be aided by outsiders. However, he offered the caveat that the presence of resources in a dominated community does not ensure that a movement will emerge. The utility of the indigenous model in understanding the gay community is discussed more fully in the next section.

Application of the Model

Although scholars and the public alike point to the Stonewall riot in June 1969 as the defining event of the gay rights movement, it is important to remember that that pivotal moment was possible only because of its strong psychological, social, organizational, and political bases. The impact of that event was intense because "at the end of the 1960s, news of a gay riot in New York could spread rapidly through the networks of communication created by the mass movements of the decade" (D'Emilio, 1989, p. 465). Over the years, gay activists had created newspapers, magazines, health clinics, churches, multipurpose social centers, social organizations, and specialized businesses. Thus, there was a fairly cohesive gay community that had identified itself as an oppressed group and claimed a shared group identity (D'Emilio, 1983; Duberman, 1986; Humphreys, 1972; Katz, 1976; Marcus, 1992). Without this structure and indigenous base, the violence at the Stonewall Inn would have been a little-noticed, isolated event.

It is clear that the self-empowerment of U.S. gay men and lesbians was rooted in their indigenous structures, collective identity and folklore, and centuries-long awareness and experience of oppression. The defining act of the modern liberation effort was an observable and dramatic point in the evolution of an oppressed group's 100-year struggle for dignity and freedom (Berube, 1991; D'Emilio, 1983, 1989; Duberman, 1986, 1993; Humphreys, 1972; Katz, 1976; Lauritsen & Thorstad, 1974; Marcus, 1992; Nardi, Sanders, & Marmor, 1994; Shilts, 1982, 1993).

Effects of Four Social Forces

Four important social forces were instrumental in creating a political and organizational structure that would later support the gay and lesbian protest movement: (1) the U.S. homophile movement, (2) treatment of gay men and lesbians in the U.S. military, (3) increased public awareness of discrimination and persecution of gay men and lesbians, and (4) the social activism of the 1960s.

The U.S. Homophile Movement. Chroniclers of gay history have demonstrated that the U.S. homophile movement had been ongoing in urban centers for a century before the violence at the Stonewall Inn (D'Emilio, 1983; Humphreys, 1972; Lauritsen & Thorstad, 1974; Marcus, 1992). From the 1870s to the 1930s, the social forces of industrialization and urbanization had created an atmosphere in the cities in which gay men and lesbians could forge distinct identities as autonomous individuals and cohesion as an oppressed and ostracized group (D'Emilio, 1983). In the first two decades of this century, there were many social and sexual gathering places for gay men and lesbians in the cities, such as clubs, bars, bathhouses, literary societies, "drag" balls, and loosely organized communities on college campuses (D'Emilio, 1983). In 1908 *The Intersexes: A History of Similisexualism as a Problem in Social Life* by Edward Stevenson (cited in Lauritsen & Thorstad, 1974) documented the existence of a gay community in the United States. In 1924, the first formally organized gay civil rights group, called the Society for Human Rights, was chartered in Chicago (Nardi et al., 1994). In the early 20th century, gay life constituted a distinctly organized community in the United States. This burgeoning subculture was to become the seed of a collective consciousness and the identity of gay men and lesbians that, in turn, provided the underlying structure and awareness that made a rebellion feasible (D'Emilio, 1983).

During this time, meetings of several small but growing gay or lesbian organizations (the Mattachine Society, Daughters of Bilitis, and ONE) allowed gay men and lesbians to discuss and address their survival in a hostile world, the nature of their orientation and identity, their political standing, opinions and writings on homosexuality, current research, available resources, their emotional burdens, their harassment by the police, their status as an oppressed group, and legal mechanisms to achieve change (Berube, 1991; D'Emilio, 1983; Duberman, 1993; Humphreys, 1972; Katz, 1976; Marcus, 1992; Shilts, 1982). The effects of these homophile groups were profoundly personal, not societal, in that the members were able to consider the revolutionary ideas of justice and living an open life (Shilts, 1982). The most important point about the U.S. homophile movement in the 1950s was that it managed to be born and survive at all. Because exposure as a gay man or lesbian could mean the loss of one's job, friends, family, home, and community, it is remarkable that these pioneers met, let alone built a structural, communication, and philosophical basis on which a massive social protest movement could grow (Marcus, 1992).

   Treatment of Gay Men and Lesbians in the U.S. Military. Military service, especially during the two world wars, is closely linked to the gradual rise of the modern gay civil rights movement and protest efforts in this century. A review of this history (Berube, 1991; D'Emilio, 1983; Shilts, 1993) leads to the following three conclusions about the uneasy relationship among the four branches of the military and gay men and lesbians in the armed forces:

1. When enlisted gay men and lesbians left the provincial restrictions of their small-town lives, saw other countries and cultures, fought for the cause of freedom for all, lived and worked with members of their own gender, became acquainted with other gay men and lesbians, and learned about gay and lesbian life in foreign and domestic cities, their expectations and perceptions changed radically and permanently.
2. The persecution and victimization that gay men and lesbians suffered at the hands of their country's military bureaucracy raised their individual and collective consciousness about inequity, injustice, maltreatment, and civil rights.
3. The psychological diagnostic screening of potential recruits that included questions about their sexual orientations, the constant worry about the thoughts and behavior of soldiers in relation to the issues of sexual orientation, and the real threat of being dishonorably discharged without benefits all brought the issue of homosexuality into the forefront of discussion. Dishonorable discharges were made not just for same-gender sexual behavior, but for the mere suspicion of homoerotic thoughts and feelings. Gay men and lesbians were often either coerced into "coming out" or "outing" others.

These three factors in tandem appear to have been major reasons for ongoing social discontent and, over time, helped form the collective identity of gay men and lesbians as an oppressed people.

   Among the earliest organized attempts to defend the rights of gay men and lesbians of all ethnic groups in the United States were the post–World War II efforts to correct the injustice of dishonorable discharges, initiated by black civil rights activists, with the support of gay and lesbian veterans. The campaign was also taken up by Congress, the U.S. Army Surgeon General's Office, the American Legion, the Congress of Industrial Organizations, the NAACP, and the military and civilian press (Berube, 1991). The gay and lesbian veterans who were fighting publicly and legally against their dishonorable discharges were helping to develop a political agenda. They were unintentionally shaping the notion that gay and lesbian taxpayers had civil rights, could engage in a fight for justice and in social protest, and were a persecuted group (Berube, 1991).

Increased Public Awareness of the Persecution of Gay Men and Lesbians.
The U.S. military's treatment of gay and lesbian citizens directly influenced their
subsequent general persecution during the Cold War. During the McCarthyism
of the 1950s, the antihomosexual hearings in the Senate began as a byproduct of
the anticommunist scare. McCarthy's House Un-American Activities Committee (HUAC) thought that gay and lesbian citizens were highly susceptible to
blackmail and thus had a propensity to betray military secrets or to join the
Communist Party. Ironically, the strongest argument presented to HUAC was
the military's continued success in emotionally breaking gay and lesbian people
during and after World War II (Berube, 1991). This systemic persecution served
to break the public silence about the topic and to begin to unite those who felt
the effects of the oppression (D'Emilio, 1983).

Social Activism of the 1960s. During the 1960s, several political and social
upheavals heavily influenced each other. A philosophy counter to the mainstream culture emerged that supported equality, freedom, choice, and peace.
The homophiles of the previous decade had inadvertently set the stage for members of the U.S. gay community to consider their place in the societal chaos of
the social protest era (D'Emilio, 1983; Shilts, 1993). The social context of choosing to be who you wanted to be had been altered. At the same time, the legal
situation began to change, and there was some movement toward the decrimi-
nalization of the private, consensual sexual acts of adults (D'Emilio, 1983).

The various liberation efforts during the 1960s had an interactive effect. Angry and disgruntled gay men and lesbians watched the tactics of and heard the
issues presented by other oppressed groups and learned from them. Black radi-
cals talked about power, structural discrimination, systematic oppression, self-
determination, liberation, community organizing, separateness, celebration of
differences, and pride. Students talked of revolution, self-preservation, and ide-
alism. The counterculture dealt with a politics of experience, celebrating the
subjective, nonconformity, new personalities, ethics, and a new style of living.
The women's movement talked of roles, sexual objectification, alienation, gender categories, and inequality. All the movements were highlighting civil rights,
equal opportunity, and fair treatment. The development of this counterculture
on U.S. streets and campuses was an essential condition for the gay and lesbian
revolution. It supplied special skills, an ideology, and the necessary reinforcement to increase autonomy (D'Emilio, 1983; Humphreys, 1972).

In the Northeast in the early 1960s, the example of the black civil rights movement inspired a militant faction of the newly emerging gay rights front. The
earlier accommodationist stance was abandoned in favor of activism (D'Emilio,
1983). As Franklin Kameny, who spearheaded this new militancy, put it: "I do
not see the NAACP and CORE worrying about which chromosome and gene
produced a black skin, or about the possibility of bleaching the Negro. . . . Why
we are Negroes, Jews, or homosexuals is totally irrelevant, and whether we
can be changed to whites, Christians, or heterosexuals is equally irrelevant"
(quoted in D'Emilio, 1983, p. 153). For the first time, those who were fighting
against the oppression of gay men and lesbians won the support of the American Civil Liberties Union (ACLU) over a court case challenging an incident of

employment discrimination. During the 1960s, there were numerous small political demonstrations by gay and lesbian people in the Northeast, although they received little media attention (D'Emilio, 1983).

In the Northeast, the movement was political and not closely connected to the social lives of gay men and lesbians. However, on the West Coast, the nascent movement grew out of the bars and the subculture that the bar scene spawned and supported. Newsletters, voter registration drives, and political campaign strategies evolved from the bar subculture (D'Emilio, 1983). The Society for Individual Rights, an outgrowth of this sociopolitical organization, borrowed a strategy from the black civil rights movement and mobilized liberal San Francisco church leaders around their cause. A new organization, the Council on Religion and the Homosexual, resulted from this alliance. With this organization, the issue went mainstream (D'Emilio, 1983; Shilts, 1982). In 1965 some heterosexual ministers who were outraged at the police harassment of attenders at a formal New Year's Eve dance called a press conference and won the support of the ACLU and the mainstream press in California. This event is considered crucial in the history of pre-Stonewall activism and had far-reaching political effects in San Francisco (D'Emilio, 1983, 1989; Duberman, 1993; Shilts, 1982).

The new leaders of the emerging gay civil rights movement considered the traditional accommodating approach of the early homophile movement slow and dated because of the less conservative approach of other movements. The massive social upheaval of the 1960s created a simmering environment, out of which the gay rights movement would spring. By 1965 the shift toward militancy was attracting more adherents (D'Emilio, 1983). In addition, the term coming out, which had been a purely personal description of an internal and sexual process, became a political concept, linked to a collective identity (Berube, 1991; D'Emilio, 1992).

Given the social discontent of the 1960s, as well as the groundwork of the early homophile pioneers in the 1940s and 1950s, there is little wonder that gay men and lesbians reacted in time. The Northeast movement had placed gay rights in a militant context, and the West Coast movement had tied gay rights to a social context. "Put all these currents of change together, and the gay liberation movement seems like an event waiting to happen" (D'Emilio, 1992, p. xviii).

After the defining Stonewall riot over 25 years ago, gay men and lesbians began making use of the techniques of the black liberation movement, the student movement, and feminism and emerged as another element in the media-covered political climate of protests against the Vietnam War and for civil rights. These new strategies were juxtaposed with the history of gay-related newsletters, organizations, political views, and the bar subculture to form a powerful and rapidly growing national force (D'Emilio, 1983).

DISCUSSION AND CONCLUSION

Morris's indigenous paradigm is a useful framework for understanding the origins of the gay rights movement because it accounts for both the radical, spontaneous nature of a pivotal event and the fact that the ramifications of that event were amplified by existing indigenous community structures. Several interacting factors contributed to the power of the Stonewall riot. First, although gay, lesbian, and transgendered people did not have formal power, they had resources, an evolving radical agenda, communications networks, a culture, and a community, all of which could be brought to bear on their fight against oppression. Second, for decades social forces and marginalized groups in the United States had been setting the stage for massive political upheaval concerning the civil rights of gay and lesbian citizens. These societal forces had a cumulative effect, contributing to conditions that supported an effective episode of protest. Third, during a routine incident, a group that had been seen as passive and acquiescent for decades surprised the authorities; therefore, a particular occurrence propelled a social action movement to new, higher levels.

There is evidence of the tremendous courage of gay and lesbian activists over decades as they balanced two opposite forces: the need to stay politically quiet for the sake of survival and their desire to be free. As Cornell (1988) posited in his examination of the American Indian civil rights movement, oppressed groups learn through painful experience how far they can go and not be killed, and they adjust to those limits. Social workers must remember that although attempts to survive may appear to some as contentment or passivity, that appearance is deceiving.

The Stonewall riot has become a powerful symbol for emancipation and should continue to be celebrated as such. Yet it should be appreciated in its full meaning: It was not actually the beginning of the modern gay rights movement; rather, it was a defining moment in a long, hard struggle.

An accurate understanding of the origins of the gay rights movement and a fuller appreciation of the arduous history of the gay community's struggle for self-determination will put social workers in a stronger position when working with gay and lesbian clients. Cultural symbols, communications networks, and leadership structures take on new meanings when seen as contemporary manifestations of the community's long history of strength and survival in the face of constant oppression. With this understanding and appreciation, social workers will also be in a stronger position when working with clients from all oppressed communities because they will have a deeper awareness of the similarities and differences in the histories of oppressed groups. Furthermore, as Fisher (1995) pointed out, social workers who seek to promote social action and community organizing need to overcome the current state of fragmentation and build coalitions among groups. Such coalition building will be strengthened by organizers' knowledge of the identities and cultures of various groups.

In addition, it would also be useful for the profession to review the history of its response to the oppression of gay men and lesbians and to acknowledge its marked absence from the early struggles of this population, as well as its more recent support of some aspects of the battle against oppression. Such knowledge is important for the profession's self-understanding and identity and deserves serious attention.

REFERENCES

Berube, A. (1991). *Coming out under fire: The history of gay men and women in World War II.* New York: Plume.

Biklen, D. P. (1983). *Community organizing: Theory and practice.* Englewood Cliffs, NJ: Prentice Hall.

Cornell, S. (1988). *The return of the native.* New York: Oxford University Press.

Council on Social Work Education. (1995). *Handbook of accreditation standards and procedures* (4th ed.). Alexandria, VA: Author.

D'Emilio, J. (1983). *Sexual politics, sexual communities: The making of a homosexual minority in the United States, 1940–1970.* Chicago: University of Chicago Press.

D'Emilio, J. (1989). Gay politics and community in San Francisco since World War II. In M. Duberman, M. Vicinus, & G. Chauncey, (Eds.), *Hidden from history: Reclaiming the gay and lesbian past* (pp. 456–476). New York: Meridian.

D'Emilio, J. (1992). Foreword. In K. Jay & A. Young (Eds.), *Out of the closets: Voices of gay liberation* (pp. vvi–xxix). New York: New York University Press.

Duberman, M. (1986). *About time: Exploring the gay past.* New York: Sea Horse.

Duberman, M. (1993). *Stonewall.* New York: Penguin.

Edmonds, A. O. (1984). [Review of the book *The origins of the civil rights movement*]. *Library Journal, 109,* 1856.

Ezell, M. (1994). Advocacy practice of social workers. *Families in Society, 75,* 36–46.

Fisher, R. (1995). Social action community organization: Proliferation, persistence, roots, and prospects. In J. Rothman, J. L. Erlich, & J. E. Tropman (Eds.), *Strategies of community intervention* (5th ed., pp. 327–340). Itasca, IL: F. E. Peacock.

Garvin, C. D., & Cox, F. M. (1995). A history of community organizing since the Civil War with special reference to oppressed communities. In J. Rothman, J. L. Erlich, & J. E. Tropman (Eds.), *Strategies of community intervention* (5th ed., pp. 64–99). Itasca, IL: F. E. Peacock.

Grothaus, L. H. (1985). [Review of the book *The origins of the civil rights movement*]. *Choice, 22,* 868.

Humphreys, L. (1972). *Out of the closets: The sociology of homosexual liberation.* Englewood Cliffs, NJ: Prentice Hall.

Katz, J. (1976). *Gay American history: Lesbians and gay men in the U.S.A.* New York: Crowell.

Lauritsen, J., & Thorstad, D. (1974). *The early homosexual rights movement (1864–1935).* New York: Times Change Press.

Marcus, E. (1992). *Making history: The struggle for gay and lesbian equal rights, 1945–1990.* New York: HarperCollins.

Morris, A. D. (1984). *The origins of the civil rights movement.* New York: Free Press.

Nardi, P. M., Sanders, D., & Marmor, J. (Eds.). (1994). *Growing up before Stonewall.* London: Routledge.

National Association of Social Workers. (1996). *NASW code of ethics.* Washington, DC: Author.

Rothman, J. (1995). Approaches to community intervention. In J. Rothman, J. L. Erlich, & J. E. Tropman (Eds.), *Strategies of community intervention* (5th ed., pp. 26–63). Itasca, IL: F. E. Peacock.

Shilts, R. (1982). *The mayor of Castro Street.* New York: St. Martin's Press.

Shilts, R. (1993). *Conduct unbecoming: Gays and lesbians in the U.S. military.* New York: St. Martin's Press.

Woods, J. M. (1985). [Review of the book *The origins of the civil rights movement*]. *Black Enterprise, 15,* 21.

The author thanks Jerry Cates, assistant dean at the Jane Addams School of Social Work, University of Illinois, Chicago, for his encouragement and assistance with this chapter. This chapter is dedicated to the memory of Bill Edens, Jr.

This chapter was originally published in the November 1997 issue of Social Work, *vol. 42, pp. 607–615.*

Part V

HOUSING INITIATIVES

21 Building Community: Principles for Social Work Practice in Housing Settings

Carol S. Cohen and Michael H. Phillips

U rban development projects have shown that it takes more than bricks and mortar to build a community. If they are to survive and flourish, communities need to have more than secure housing, available jobs, and good schools; they must also have a sense of community. This sense of community is critical in preventing housing deterioration and substandard school performance and serves as the foundation for healthy families. Feeling part of a community fosters a sense of ownership (Newman, 1972) and serves as a deterrent to alienation. This sense of belonging acts as a strong defense against environmental and social factors that prey on many residents and social work services, provided in a variety of modalities, can enhance this community-building process.

This chapter reviews the experience of Phipps Houses, a nonprofit housing developer, and its affiliate, Phipps Houses Community Development Corporation, in their attempt to foster a sense of community and family well-being in two fully rehabilitated housing developments it sponsored in a community well known for poverty and unsuccessful attempts at renewal. Three facets of Phipps Houses' identity combine to distinguish it from other projects discussed in the professional literature:

1. Phipps Houses is a private, nonprofit corporation that, with its affiliate, provides both housing and social services for tenants. Although it is not uncommon for municipal housing authorities to directly provide social services to tenants, it is very rare to find a nonprofit developer who does so.
2. Phipps Houses primarily produces permanent housing for the general public, as opposed to transitional housing or housing for a special population.
3. Phipps Houses operates within the social, political, and economic context of the 1990s. Although other programs may deal with one or two of these arenas, Phipps Houses appears to be unique in addressing all three.

With some notable exceptions, such as NASW's (1987) recommendation that the federal government consider housing as a social utility and permanently ensure services to meet the essential physical and social needs of tenants, Powers's (1979) analysis of the housing and social service linkage through history, and Morrison's (1984) study of locality development with tenants in a changing community, there have been few reports in the literature over the past 20 years that link housing and social work services. However, beginning with the work of British social worker Octavia Hill (1875), the rich literature of past community development activities provides a backdrop and professional legacy of work with programs combining housing and social services.

Social workers have struggled with the interplay of social work and housing since the reformers of the 19th century, the work of early social work theorists, the programs of the New Deal, and the initiatives of the War on Poverty and its successors. Recently, along with the development of groups such as the Association of Community Organization and Social Administration (Mizrahi & Morrison, 1993), there has come renewed dedication to social work with impoverished communities, and the profession is again looking for useful models of service (Coulton, 1995; Weil, 1996).

Phipps Houses Group is a contemporary exemplar of housing development that illustrates practice principles that can be applied in other sites in deteriorated neighborhoods. This voluntary sector model of multiple relationships with residents should become more common as direct federal housing development continues to diminish and increased attention is placed on the need for integrated social work services in housing settings.

Although the authors do not suggest that all people need supportive living services, they believe that tenants in poor and distressed communities need social work services that focus on facilitating family well-being and community development. In most neighborhoods, independent social services agencies and other providers attempt to reach out to residents, but residents are generally left to seek services on their own initiative. Unfortunately, under this system residents most in need of services have the least access to them (Rawls, 1971).

When it comes to housing advocacy and tenant organizing, residents usually become involved with self-help groups or independent social services agencies who view housing owners as targets for intervention. In rare instances these groups and agencies help establish a cooperative relationship between tenants and landlord, but commonly the relationship is adversarial. The Phipps Houses Group strikes a sensitive balance between the interests of tenants and owners, with the overriding belief that family and community well-being support family empowerment and prevent building deterioration.

The data reported in this chapter come from interviews with tenants, full-time staff members, housing managers, members of the community, and a review of workers' records. The chapter describes the community development program and the tenants and delineates six practice principles that can be drawn from the community building effort.

PHIPPS HOUSES GROUP'S PROGRAM AND SERVICES

Founded in 1905, Phipps Houses is one of the nation's oldest and largest not-for-profit developers of moderate- and low-income housing. Recognizing that its tenants in poor neighborhoods needed more than just housing, the company incorporated an affiliate, the Phipps Community Development Corporation (PCDC), to provide on-site assistance to tenants and their families to pursue their aspirations in the social, educational, and employment spheres of their lives. The PCDC mission—to build and sustain enduring communities—focuses on three core service areas: (1) family assistance, (2) community organizing, and (3) services to children and youths. Basic social work services include advocacy, community organization, recreation, education, support groups, counseling, information, and crisis intervention. In addition, referrals are made to programs sponsored by PCDC on and off site and to other community service providers.

External funding enables PCDC to extend the core services with a home-based preschool program, a youth recreation center, a teenage outreach program, summer day camps, and home management courses. An immunization and primary health care center operates on site through an affiliation with an area hospital. Staff members provide these services in the belief that families in deteriorated neighborhoods need not only well-maintained, secure housing but also services that support family life, individual growth, and community participation.

Both housing developments discussed in this chapter were previously abandoned buildings in the South Bronx section of New York City that were renovated in the early 1990s with municipal, state, and federal funds. Both are occupied by a mixture of low-income and moderate-income residents. Mapes Court, the smaller (91 units) and older of the two sites, was occupied in 1990, and Crotona Park West Cluster C (196 units) was occupied in 1992.

At Mapes Court, a single community worker provides family services to the individual households and also organizes community activities. At the considerably larger Crotona Park West, the three core areas are divided among a family worker, a community organizer, and youth program staff. Because the PCDC program at Crotona Park West also serves two additional housing clusters comprising a total of 563 apartments, the staff and their responsibilities have been distributed among three offices within a range of approximately one-third mile. The role and geographic differentiation among staff at Crotona Park West brings diversified areas of expertise, but requires more coordination and teamwork than when a single worker is charged with the PCDC mission. The overall supervision at both sites is provided by a director who reports to the social work administrator, who serves as the executive director/chief executive officer of PCDC.

Engagement Strategies

PCDC staff members use several strategies to make the service connection at each site. They first conduct an intake interview with each family, covering family composition, income status and sources, and family needs. During that interview the social services worker discusses the need for building involvement, programs available to tenants, and ways in which the staff might help the family meet their goals. Both sites help tenants in making their adjustment, through the provision of advocacy (for example, changing welfare benefits) and material assistance (for example, furnishings) to ease their transition. Given that the initial interview takes place early in their residence, families often are not ready to follow up with additional social work contacts. However, the interview serves to orient the new family to the unique structure and opportunities in this housing development. The worker gains valuable information for continuing the process of establishing a productive working relationship.

As a second strategy social services staff are provided with rent arrears lists and security reports. These reporting mechanisms, which alert workers to families who are experiencing difficulties, were put in place through the evolving relationship between the housing manager and the PCDC staff. Under this arrangement, the roles of housing manager and PCDC workers are complementary. The housing manager's function is to collect the rent and maintain a stable building. The pressure they bring to bear on the tenants can make the tenants more responsive to social services. PCDC's role is to serve as a support to tenants, with their work always focused on helping the tenant take rather than avoid responsibility in paying rent or maintaining building stability. Thus, rent arrears are explored not merely as a question of money, but in the total context of the families' lives, as shown in this excerpt from PCDC records:

> W was laid off from her job, and her husband was laid off from his job and has been on sick leave. W is unemployed and requires food stamps and Medicaid as well as SSI [Supplemental Security Income] because she is disabled because of illness. . . . W stated that she has a serious illness and does not have medical insurance; she is currently separated from her husband; she is receiving $181 through unemployment insurance every week. By the time she pays rent, telephone, clothes, home accessories, transportation, and money for her son to get to school, there is no money left for her to pay medical bills or food.

As they follow up on rent arrears, workers often find issues that extend beyond the presenting problem. The family's problems frequently trace back to low-paying, unstable jobs that make it impossible for them to set aside resources to meet contingencies. Although PCDC workers cannot change the job market, they can help tenants consider their options and help them obtain supports such as Medicaid, unemployment benefits, and public assistance. This enables families to avoid the downward spiral of increasing debt and eviction. Social services workers help tenants look at how they may gain greater security through education and improved employment opportunities. Thus, it is not surprising to find that although the most common reason for contacts with the social work staff are issues related to rent, the next most common concerns are education, employment, and public assistance.

Also, workers often find that following up on a security report provides a valuable point of entry with tenants. Security and custodial staff provide eyes and ears in the buildings and often refer tenants to PCDC. In turn, PCDC performs a similar function in the interests of the residents and community by working on problems with tenants before they require legal intervention. These contacts may lead to work around the adequate supervision of children and disputes between tenants.

Another strategy involves linking tenants to available services outside PCDC such as continuing education and general equivalency diploma (GED) programs, residential summer camps for children, job training and employment opportunities, and social services. These activities demonstrate to tenants the setting's interest in them and encourage tenants to take difficult steps to seek help with a broad range of family matters.

A final engagement strategy is for social services staff to demonstrate their usefulness to tenants by helping them advocate for apartment repairs and adequate services. Staff often mediate tenant–management conflicts, but they only intervene directly when tenants' efforts have been unsuccessful or in an emergency. Staff encourage tenants to advocate for themselves whenever possible and provide them with the tools (through education and counseling) to ensure management responsiveness.

Ironically, an increased sense of tenant ownership leads to a greater number of tenant complaints. As tenant associations and other community groups develop, tenants take an active interest in the quality of their buildings and neighborhoods. Thus, as they are empowered in other spheres of their lives, they also make greater demands on management. Rather than blaming PCDC workers for instigating tenant dissatisfaction, management recognizes that active tenants ultimately increase building security and stability.

Tenant Organizations

At both sites there is an emphasis not only on the engagement of individual families but also on more collective issues. Tenant organizing follows a fairly traditional route of developing a strong tenant association and leadership. An early entry from the worker's records illustrates the PCDC approach:

> My objective at this first meeting was to unite all the tenants to come together to establish a tenants' association with an executive committee. . . . The tenants' association had decided that their motto would be "Neighbor Looking out for Neighbor," and that if they united as one then they could overcome everything. The tenants have decided that they wanted to take back their building and have a tighter grasp on their children so that they would not be loitering in the buildings. Throughout the meeting we discussed how we can solve our main problems, what the concerns and suggestions were, and what would be the best days to hold the tenants' meeting.

Reflecting on the tenant meetings, the worker later wrote, "The tenants' meetings have a great impact on our development because there is (1) involvement, (2) support and participation, (3) understanding, (4) an even exchange always. . . . It's as if we make a joint contract, and we stick by our agreement."

Community Involvement

Community involvement beyond the physical buildings is approached somewhat differently at the two settings. At Mapes Court, community involvement is reflected in the community worker's attendance at meetings in which other groups present information on the services they provide. Mapes Court's community involvement is a vehicle for obtaining resources and program initiatives for the tenants rather than an effort to change the larger community. Although community visibility is gained, the PCDC staff plays a relatively small role in stimulating larger community change.

At Crotona Park West, the broader community involvement of PCDC staff is a more planned activity, with membership on community and school boards and the development of an active Crotona Park West Community Advisory Committee (CAC) composed of people involved in education, social services, mental health services, and other community activities. Members of the CAC were interviewed. They all felt that Phipps-sponsored buildings provided stability in a troubled area by contributing a large group of stable residents who, with the support of PCDC, affected the larger community in positive ways. An example given was how the PCDC community organizer brought together parents from the buildings to address the concern about asbestos at a local school. They noted that PCDC also provided space for school programming while the problem was being corrected and that the actions of the Phipps Houses parents provided hope and inspiration to other families living in the area.

CAC members described how feeling secure allowed tenants to feel better about themselves. This sense of security was, in turn, seen as a stabilizing influence in their environment. They felt that Phipps Houses tenants made changes in their lives as a result of the stability and security the housing provides, along with the supports given by PCDC services.

Other positive factors cited by CAC members were the clarity of vision provided by all levels of PCDC, as well as PCDC staff's willingness to serve as consultants to community agencies in seeking funding and developing proposals. They felt that these staff were invaluable in bringing additional resources into the community. Many went on to indicate that being on the CAC gave their various agencies an opportunity to network and share common concerns, making it possible to provide more efficient services and allocation of resources.

PROFILE OF PHIPPS HOUSES TENANTS

Tenants were interviewed to see how their circumstances had changed during their stay at Phipps Houses as part of a study of how residency had affected them (Phillips & Cohen, 1996). Of particular concern were the issues of employment, income support, education, perception of living situation, and dreams for the future. Data were drawn from interviews conducted with an adult member of 145 randomly selected apartments, representing 47 percent of Mapes Court and 53 percent of Crotona Park West Cluster C families. The tenants interviewed were primarily Latino (53 percent, $n = 77$) and African American (41 percent, $n = 59$). Eighty-two percent of the households were families with children ($n = 119$), of which three-quarters were headed by single women. Of families with children, 14 percent had a child one year old or younger, 38 percent had a child between two and five, and 11 percent had a youngest child who was 16 or older.

Previous Housing Experience

Because these buildings were planned as mixed-income housing, the 145 families came for a variety of reasons, including homelessness or unsafe housing (25 percent), previous housing too small or overcrowded (33 percent), and a desire for better housing or housing in a better area (20 percent). Forty-seven percent described their previous neighborhood as either somewhat or very unsafe, and 57 percent said that their new neighborhood was safer than where they previously lived. Two-thirds of the 145 families had moved at least one other time in the two years before coming to the new buildings, with 9 percent having moved three times or more. In contrast, only 23 percent of the tenants had been at Mapes Court and Crotona Park West less than two years, reflecting relative housing stability among the families. Twenty-eight percent received a Section 8 housing subsidy, limiting personal rent payment to 30 percent of their income.

Employment and Income Support

Fifty-seven percent of the 145 families had employment income, 51 percent received public assistance or SSI, and 6 percent were receiving unemployment insurance. Twenty-two percent of the families who received employment income (n = 18) also received public assistance. The lack of stability in patterns of income over time was striking. The data on receipt of public assistance and how well the families felt they were doing showed shifts; 12 families who were on public assistance when they came to the buildings no longer received public assistance, and 17 had not previously received public assistance. Thirty-four percent of families felt that their financial situation at the time of the interview was better than it was when they came to their new residences, and 25 percent felt it was worse.

Among the 44 men for whom there were data, 75 percent were currently working (24 percent at a new job). Seventeen percent had not held a job since coming to the buildings; one in five of them had been laid off and could not find employment, and three in 10 were not working because they were sick or disabled.

Seventy-two percent of the 127 women residing in the buildings had worked at some time during their stay, and 41 percent were currently working. Unfortunately, a high degree of job turnover was reflected in the fact that 42 percent of the women had looked for work during their stay. Only 41 percent of the 78 women who were working when they came currently held the same job. Although this could of course reflect upward mobility, the data on the number who were laid off suggest that the primary reason for job changes was job loss. Other than being unable to find a job, the primary reason for not being employed was the expense of child care. Given the low wages paid by the jobs these mothers could obtain, it was difficult to pay the costs of child care.

Education

Among the 127 adult females, 15 percent had less than a high school education, 19 percent had some high school, and 15 percent were high school graduates with no further education. Forty-two percent had some college, and 8 percent had completed college. Two-thirds of those with less than a high school diploma were Latino women. Of the 77 Latino women interviewed, 22 were interviewed in Spanish because they had limited facility with the English language.

Because education is a way of improving job prospects, PCDC works closely with families to increase their educational level. This focus appears to have had an effect; 22 percent of the 127 women were in school at the time of the interview, and an additional 11 percent had taken courses at some point since moving to the buildings. Because slightly more than one-third needed help in getting a GED, PCDC helped tenants enroll in GED courses. Discussion with the tenants who had dropped out of school indicated that they did so because of child care responsibilities or because they found working and schooling too difficult to handle with their family responsibilities. Twenty-three percent of the 52 working mothers, however, were also in school. Among those pursuing further education but not working, most were supported by public assistance, suggesting that public assistance support was a significant adjunct to continuing education for this population. Of the women currently in school, 53 percent had discussed educational matters with PCDC staff.

The major reasons for not attending school were as follows: needed to care for children (29 percent), long hours or other employment-related problems (25 percent), expense (8 percent), and illness or disability (10 percent). It should be noted that a number of mothers whose children were no longer young cited child care as a problem in both employment and education. They indicated that the risks presented by drugs, crime, and gangs were so high that they felt they needed to be home to provide oversight of even teenage children.

Although the adult male tenants had less formal education, fewer pursued their education while at Phipps Houses. The reasons for not pursuing further education were parallel to those cited by the women.

Use of Services

The tenant interviews showed that 84 percent of the 145 families made use of at least one service that PCDC provided or arranged for. The most common areas in which workers provided help were rent or tenant behavior issues, employment and training, education, financial assistance, health and mental health referral, and family relationships. The services provided reflected the range of problems that the families struggled with, including issues related to low income and job loss and the subsequent need to apply for financial assistance, food stamps, emergency food, and Medicaid. Also reflected in the service utilization patterns is the PCDC commitment to supporting tenant interest in employment, training, and further education.

Effects of Residence

Tenants were asked to describe the effect on their family and themselves of living in a Phipps Houses Group–sponsored building. Their responses reflected hope for the future, with 77 percent of the 145 families citing specific ways in which their employment situation was expected to improve within the next five years. Among the improvements mentioned were better pay, a better position, and having a permanent job. Twenty-one percent indicated that they saw improvement in their employment situation as a key to achieving the goals they had for their families.

Their educational aspirations were similarly high, with 22 percent of the 145 respondents indicating that they expected to have a master's or higher degree within five years and 8 percent indicating that they would have specialized training in a field such as nursing or computers. An additional 26 percent expected to have increased their education, and 6 percent indicated they expected to have completed their GED. Twenty-seven percent indicated that the key to their future goals lay in increased education.

Although it is impossible to prove that these changes resulted from living in these buildings, 17 percent of the 145 interviewed said that living there increased their motivation to better their lives and be more independent. Nineteen percent indicated that their future plans had changed because of an increased clarity on future goals achieved while in residence, and 12 percent said the services provided through the Phipps Houses Group gave them more hope for the future. Twenty-eight percent said that living in Phipps Houses increased their commitment to continuing their education, and 12 percent said that living in Phipps Houses led to a desire to participate in more programs and activities.

Tenant responses make it clear that the development of a sense of community had been an important aspect of their hope for the future. Fifty-seven percent (n = 83) said they felt safer in the current neighborhood, and 28 percent (n = 41) indicated that the best thing about Phipps Houses was the good security. Others spoke of good neighbors, the friendly atmosphere, the availability of programs, and the benefits of living in a well-maintained building.

When reviewing the findings with tenants at building meetings to verify our impressions, we found the families to be articulate in indicating that the sense of security they had in the building's community and the services available for their children were important to their being able to leave the site to pursue educational and employment opportunities. One aspect of that security was the availability of guard services at one of the sites, but equally important in the eyes of the tenants was the linkage that had been fostered between the tenants. A sense that they were in the same boat and that they needed to look out for each other prevailed. This was clearly connected to the community organizing activities designed to bring tenants together.

PRINCIPLES FOR COMMUNITY-BUILDING PRACTICE

On the basis of these detailed results and additional unreported findings (Phillips & Cohen, 1996), the authors have developed a series of practice principles. These principles were found to apply at both settings, despite the staffing differences and somewhat different approaches to service delivery with families. The six principles are intended to support innovation and freedom of choice in their application (Lewis, 1982):

1. Housing and social work services should be integrated and provided to tenants in distressed communities.
2. Staff of social work programs in housing settings should understand and subscribe to a collective vision of the program's purpose.
3. Efforts should be made to provide services on site.
4. Social work programs in housing settings should maintain a dual focus on the individual family and the collective.
5. Community development activities should be extended to the surrounding community and not be limited to the building alone.
6. The task of community building is constantly evolving and should be continually evaluated.

Integration of Housing and Social Services

Housing alone in impoverished neighborhoods will not provide the necessary level of stability to sustain either the financial viability of the buildings or the community within and around them. Developers and owners of rehabilitated urban housing should plan for social work services in a variety of modalities, just as they would plan for building maintenance and security services. This approach not only benefits residents but also serves to protect the owners' investment and assets.

The task is not to create building managers who are more sensitive or social workers who collect rent. Rather, there is a need for managers who are concerned about the welfare of the tenants and social workers who help tenants overcome whatever obstacles are preventing their payment of rent. Social work staff should serve as educators, mediators, and advocates for tenants and should expect management to help them identify tenants in need of their services and to strongly encourage tenants to accept such services if they are to remain in occupancy. Social workers must maintain their professional integrity in this system by clearly articulating their purpose and constraints to tenants and providing the maximum level possible of self-determination and confidentiality.

Just as Morrison (1984) discovered over 10 years ago, community development services are among the most cost-effective routes to housing preservation. There is a need for staff to help residents with employment, entitlements, and other income-related problems. Without such interventions and the availability of outside supports such as public assistance, families could easily slip into debt and be evicted. This pattern could in time undermine the financial base of the setting. In addition, when residents recognize that assistance will be provided to help them manage family crises and help them achieve their goals, they are more likely to engage in tenant associations and other community organizations.

Unity of Vision

Programs need a clear unity of vision. As one PCDC worker expressed, "From custodian to president, we all have a part in making it work." This is not to imply that all staff members of social work programs should do the same things, but they should be able to articulate their own role within the overall mission of building communities and strong families. This sense of collective vision is critical in bringing together a diverse group of workers with varying levels of education and areas of expertise.

Social work values, ethics, and methods should be paramount in the design and implementation of these programs. Such an approach necessitates extensive training of non–social workers, with overall supervision by a social work professional with appropriate experience in planning and administration. Social work hallmarks, such as mutuality and self-determination, must be an integral part of the program, and staff members must see themselves in partnership with tenants. This approach is evidenced in the comment "We're going to do it together" to describe PCDC staff work with tenants. As another staff member aptly put it, the program needs to "develop *with* the community—not *ahead* of it." Social services staff should convey a strong commitment to the achievement of tenants' goals in their work together, demonstrating how a clear sense of purpose can facilitate goal attainment. The clarity of vision in work with tenants also can serve as a model in their work with other staff members and representatives of the broader community.

On-Site Services

The Phipps Houses experience indicated that the best used services are those provided in the tenants' own buildings or as nearby as possible. For the large number of women with young children at home, such services are essential, but residents who found travel easier also preferred on-site services.

The greatest preferences for on-site services came in the early stages of contact with tenants. As residents became comfortable with their home community and their own abilities, they were able to more effectively connect with off-site services. Furthermore, they felt more secure about the referrals made by the on-site workers because of the relationships they had built together. On-site services also had the effect of bringing together the building community, ensuring frequent review of the facilities and engendering a sense of ownership of the social work program and housing development.

Dual Focus

A dual focus on strengthening families and communities must exist. Community development activities should be directed to enhancing residents' capacities for change and building on their own integrated view of themselves in relation to their community. This principle is related to the concept of equifinality (Germain, 1975), in which many entry points are possible in building a sense of community. For example, as a worker addresses the problems of a resident who has lost his or her job, the worker also needs to look at the broader question of how to create access systems for all tenants to increase their education or training. In the long run, only that larger effort will ameliorate the situation.

Work with an individual tenant who needs help can build a climate of trust through the demonstration of social services staff's value to them and advocating for increased access systems to address community empowerment issues. On the other hand, some tenants may want to enter the community by participating in a large tenant association meeting or a children's party. In addition, smaller groups, such as parenting programs, teen support groups, and tenant leadership committees, can engage families, enhancing the functioning of both tenant families and the community at large. Thus, activities must include community-focused activities, such as buildingwide events and smaller groups, as well as individually directed interventions with families.

Programs have many choices in allocating these functions among social service staff members. As described earlier, PCDC has used two models. In one, a single worker provides family, small group, and community organization services. In the other, functionally and geographically dispersed staffing meets the needs of a larger number of tenants. This experience suggests that the question is not, Does one use one approach or the other? Rather, it is a question of determining what the benefits and deficits of each approach are, ensuring a dual focus in the method chosen, and making ongoing adjustments accordingly.

Extension of Development Activities

The interests of tenants go beyond their building to include issues such as the schools their children attend and the safety of the area in which they reside.

Residents in surrounding buildings share their concerns. Staff can help make the broader community connection with tenants by serving as bridges to the community at large and by helping the tenants define what it is they want to do and how collectively they may work to create the changes they desire.

To effectively serve as a bridge, staff members need to become known to outside agencies through referrals and offers to help them address their concerns. These contacts both strengthen the outside organizations and make them more responsive to the needs of individuals the staff may refer to them for services. Changes in social provisions (such as changes in public assistance and Section 8 funding) can make a big difference in the lives of the tenants in marginal neighborhoods. Therefore, building-based social services efforts must maintain a dual focus on individual support and advocacy for larger community changes. This requires a vision of services that recognizes their integrated nature and the role of staff on both the individual and community change level.

Continuous Reassessment

The old adage of social workers "working themselves out of a job" is hardly applicable in today's troubled neighborhoods. It is clear that supporting families and housing in such communities needs constant redevelopment. There are always new crises, such as drug dealers moving into the area, a problematic family moving in, the discovery of asbestos in the local school, and changes in government funding and provision of services that need to be addressed.

The development of strong communities depends to some extent on the continued involvement of a critical mass of stable community residents. Yet when tenants were asked about where they expected to be living in five years, 10 percent said they expected to have moved from the city, and another 38 percent said they expected to have moved into their own home. Although some of these people may have been hoping to buy within the larger community, the flavor of many of the responses was of a dream of owning a home in the suburbs. These responses raise questions about whether housing such as Mapes Court and Crotona Park West will be transitional and in constant need of rebuilding as community residents move "up and out" and on to their own version of the American dream. Ongoing attention is needed to build a community that provides opportunities for families at many levels of educational and economic achievement.

Inevitably, some tenants will move away, and new tenants will need to be integrated into a community. In addressing each new challenge, social work program staff need to draw on their unity of vision, their past experiences, their relations with clients, and their community alliances in developing a plan to address changing needs. As one PCDC staff member stated, "We've proven we can do it, but we still have to be doing it!"

CONCLUSION

Stable, secure housing is essential but insufficient in building a sense of community. On the other hand, without a sense of community, housing will not remain stable and secure for long. Although numerous scholars have attempted to define this sense of community, it is most poignantly understood when it is lost.

As Fried (1966) pointed out in "Grieving for a Lost Home," as many as one-third of the people who left their homes and communities because of urban renewal showed signs of clinical depression two years after relocation. A sense of community can be extremely fragile in low-income, urban neighborhoods where residents have experienced steep economic decline and abandonment.

When new housing is created through rehabilitation, the stage for community renewal is set. Social workers can play a vital role in the community building enterprise, but their intervention must be planned and principled and directed toward both individual families and the community of tenants. As was true of the settings discussed in this chapter, each program will need to develop its own particular approach. The six practice principles defined in this chapter provide a foundation for efforts to expand social work programs as a viable housing and neighborhood investment strategy.

REFERENCES

Coulton, C. J. (1995). Riding the pendulum of the 1990s: Building a community context for social work research. *Social Work, 40,* 437–439.

Fried, M. (1966). Grieving for a lost home: Psychological costs of relocation. In J. O. Wilson (Ed.), *Urban renewal: The record and the controversy* (pp. 357–379). Cambridge, MA: MIT Press.

Germain, C. (1975). A theoretical view of the life model: Eco-systems perspective. In C. Germain, E. Goldstein, & A. Maluccio (Eds.), *Workshop on the ecological approach and clinical practice* (pp. 1–25). West Hartford: Connecticut Society for Clinical Social Work and University of Connecticut School of Social Work.

Hill, O. (1875). *Homes of the London poor.* London: Macmillan.

Lewis, H. (1982). *The intellectual base of social work practice.* Binghamton, NY: Haworth Press.

Mizrahi, T., & Morrison, J. D. (1993). *Community organization and social administration.* Binghamton, NY: Haworth Press.

Morrison, J. D. (1984). Can organizing tenants improve housing? *Social Development Issues, 8,* 103–115.

National Association of Social Workers. (1987, March). Board members adopt new social services, housing policy paper. *NASW News,* p. 7.

Newman, O. (1972). *Defensible space.* New York: Macmillan.

Phillips, M., & Cohen, C. S. (1996). *From tenant to neighbor: Community building at Phipps Houses* (Study report). New York: Phipps Houses/Fordham University.

Powers, M. E. (1979). *The pattern of emergence of social services in housing programs.* Unpublished doctoral dissertation, Brandeis University, Waltham, MA.

Rawls, J. (1971). *A theory of justice.* Cambridge, MA: Harvard University Press.

Weil, M. O. (1996). Community building: Building community practice. *Social Work, 41,* 481–500.

The study on which this chapter is based was supported by the Margaret T. Morris and the J. W. Kieckhefer Foundation and would not have been possible without the openness and creativity of the Phipps Group of companies, its staff, and residents.

This chapter was originally published in the September 1997 issue of Social Work, *vol. 42, pp. 471–481.*

22 Social Support and Depression among Older Adults Living Alone: The Importance of Friends within and outside of a Retirement Community

Marilyn K. Potts

Make new friends, but keep the old. One is silver and the other gold.
—*Traditional song*

The growing phenomenon of healthy older adults living independently, particularly in age-segregated retirement communities, is an important social trend. The demand for social workers in such settings is expected to grow as well. The study discussed in this chapter examined the extent to which social support from friends, both within and outside of the retirement community, was associated with depression. By focusing on this aspect of retirement community living, social workers may contribute to the well-being of this expanding segment of the older adult population.

Age-segregated retirement communities may be de jure (public and private apartment projects, planned retirement communities, and continuing care complexes) or de facto (camp grounds, mobile home parks, and certain resort areas). Estimates of the proportion of older adults living in de jure retirement communities range from 5 percent to 8 percent, and the demand for such housing exceeds its supply (Gordon, 1988). Factors contributing to growth in this demand include predicted increases in the older adult population, the desire of most older people to live independently, and medical advances that delay institutionalization. Proximity to others with shared interests and lifestyles is thought to facilitate social interaction, which is further encouraged by communal activities. On the other hand, retirement community living may result in isolation from the larger community. Interaction outside of the retirement community may be impeded by lack of proximity and the absence of structured activities.

An extensive body of research has shown that social support is an important predictor of good physical and mental health, life satisfaction, and reduced risk of institutionalization among older adults (for reviews of earlier research, see Markides & Cooper, 1989; Sauer & Coward, 1985; for examples of more recent research, see Auslander & Litwin, 1991; Bazargan & Hamm-Baugh, 1995; Forster & Stoller, 1992; Krause, Liang, & Keith, 1990; LaGory & Fitzpatrick, 1992; Pearlman & Crown, 1992; Sabin, 1993; Steinbach, 1992). In addition, social support may buffer the adverse effects of various stressors common to aging (Feld

& George, 1994; George, 1989; Krause & Borawski-Clark, 1994; Mitchell, Mathews, & Yesavage, 1993; Russell & Cutrona, 1991).

However, there is conflicting evidence about the extent to which older adults living in retirement communities are actually integrated into their immediate environment, the extent to which their needs for social support are met through their interactions with other residents, and the effects of retirement community living on emotional well-being. Three disparate views have received empirical support:

1. Retirement communities are characterized by frequent social interaction and peer interdependency, each of which contributes to increased well-being (Adams, 1985–86; Brown, 1990; Cox, 1988; Hinrichsen, 1985; Hong & Duff, 1994; Lawton, Moss, & Moles, 1984).

2. Although within-community interaction may indeed be frequent, friendships among residents tend to be superficial, limited in scope, and lacking in intimacy; retirement community living may thus have negligible or even negative effects on well-being (Fisher, 1991; Husaini, Moore, & Castor, 1991; Stacey-Konnert & Pynoos, 1992; Stephens & Bernstein, 1984; Sullivan, 1986).

3. Although some retirement community residents may engage routinely in activities with other residents, many view themselves as isolated within both their immediate environment and the larger community, particularly those who are more frail (Hunt, Feldt, Marans, Pastalan, & Vakalo, 1984; Levitt, Antonucci, Clark, Rotton, & Finley, 1985–86; Mullins & Tucker, 1992; Osgood, 1982; Sheehan, 1986).

Moreover, although considerable information exists regarding within-community interaction patterns, few studies have compared the quantity and quality of social support from friends within the retirement community with support from friends living elsewhere. These few studies have yielded contradictory findings (Hong & Duff, 1994; Stacey-Konnert & Pynoos, 1992; Stephens & Bernstein, 1984). Perhaps most important, it is unknown if social support from friends within the retirement community is equivalent to social support from friends outside of it as a predictor of well-being.

THEORETICAL CONSIDERATIONS

The view that retirement community living is characterized by a high level of social interaction with age-matched peers is compatible with the activity theory of aging, which maintains that the role losses characteristic of older age (for example, marital, parental, and occupational) are compensated for by the development of new roles and activities (Havighurst & Albrecht, 1953). Conversely, the view that retirement community living is marked by social isolation from other residents and structural isolation from the larger community is compatible with the disengagement theory of aging, which maintains that normative older age involves reduced interaction with others (Cumming & Henry, 1961). With age, fewer roles are enacted, and individuals are less active in their remaining roles. Gerontologists have long debated the relative merits of these contradictory theories of aging.

Socioemotional selectivity theory provides an alternative and possibly integrative view of aging (Carstensen, 1991, 1992). This theory suggests that reduced rates of interaction in later life are "the result of lifelong selection processes by which people strategically and adaptively cultivate their social networks to maximize social and emotional gains and minimize social and emotional risks" (Carstensen, 1992, p. 331). Social interaction is viewed as providing numerous benefits, including information and practical assistance, regulation of emotion, and maintenance of self-identity.

Social interaction also entails various costs, including expenditure of energy, risk of experiencing negative emotion, and threats to self-identity. The relative importance of these benefits and costs varies throughout the life course, as does the relative importance of various types of social partners. Earlier in life, most new information is acquired through social contact; this function is best served through interaction with a wide variety of social partners. However, with age and experience, this function becomes less important because the information gained is less likely to be novel and thus less likely to be valuable.

The functions of emotion regulation and identity maintenance, on the other hand, take on increasing importance as one ages; these functions are best served through interaction with a highly select group of social partners. Over the course of many years, emotional ties with long-term friends may have deepened, and the risk of experiencing negative emotion and threats to self-identity may have lessened. In contrast, contact with strangers and acquaintances becomes less likely to provide benefits and more likely to be costly in terms of energy expenditure and risk potential. Accordingly, "there is a reduced likelihood that interaction with casual social partners will be rewarding; yet, interaction with a select group of significant others becomes increasingly valuable" (Carstensen, 1992, p. 332).

Socioemotional selectivity theory is thus compatible with the main premises of both activity theory and disengagement theory. That is, as claimed by activity theory, older age may be characterized by high levels of social interaction with others, especially if those others are a select group of close friends or relatives. Alternatively, as claimed by disengagement theory, older age may be characterized by social isolation from others, especially if those others are more casual social partners. Furthermore, although the present study focuses on friendship patterns among older adults and their effects on depression levels, socioemotional selectivity theory encompasses a variety of types, sources, and effects of social support (for example, informational, practical, and emotional types; formal and informal sources; and physical and mental effects).

EMPIRICAL CONSIDERATIONS

Considerable empirical evidence supports the premises of socioemotional selectivity theory as applied to friendship patterns among older adults. In general, close friends tend to be long term, described as confidants, and used primarily to meet affective needs (that is, emotion regulation and self-identity maintenance). They may be seen infrequently because of lack of proximity. Casual friends tend to be short term, described as acquaintances, and used primarily to meet companionship and instrumental needs (that is, information and practical assistance). They may be seen frequently because they are readily available.

In one study of older adults living independently, Adams (1985–86) noted positive correlations between the length of the relationship and the degree of closeness. However, both frequency of interaction and physical proximity were negatively correlated with the degree of closeness, thus suggesting that many older adults are physically distanced from their long-term, most highly valued friends. Johnson and Troll (1994) found that close friends were defined by older adults as those who shared memories of the past and elicited strong sentiments, but who were seen infrequently in comparison to their more readily available but casual friends. Peters and Kaiser (1985) noted that friends were frequently identified as people met in childhood or early adulthood with whom close ties had been maintained, even in the absence of proximity, whereas neighbors were typically described as acquaintances.

Gutheil (1991) found that nursing home residents seldom interacted with former friends but that these interactions were marked by intimacy, depth, and intensity. Interactions with other residents were described as pleasant and without much emotional cost. Similarly, although some studies have documented extensive intermingling among residents of retirement communities, within-community friendships have been found to be more superficial and less valued than friendships with others in the larger community (Fisher, 1991; Shea, Thompson, & Blieszner, 1988; Stephens & Bernstein, 1984).

Several researchers have suggested that close friends are more important than acquaintances, neighbors, and relatives in promoting emotional well-being among older adults (Bazargan & Hamm-Baugh, 1995; Dykstra, 1995; Fredrickson & Carstensen, 1990; O'Connor, 1995; Sabin, 1993; Stolar, MacEntee, & Hill, 1993). Furthermore, when friends are differentiated as confidants or nonconfidants, confidant relationships appear to be related more strongly to personal adjustment (Seeman & Berkman, 1988; Simons, 1983–84).

HYPOTHESES

When applied to the context of retirement community living, the premises of socioemotional selectivity theory may be used to formulate five hypotheses:

1. Levels of social network quantity (that is, number of friends and frequency of interaction with them) will be higher for friends within the retirement community than for friends residing elsewhere. This is because the cost of interaction with friends within the retirement community is assumed to be relatively low in terms of energy expenditure. Accordingly, in terms of network quantity, it was expected that social support levels within the retirement community would be higher than those outside of it.

2. Levels of the perceived quality of social support will be higher for friends residing elsewhere than for friends within the retirement community. Although levels of social support within the retirement community may be high in a quantitative sense, residents are likely to be separated physically from most of their long-term friends. Because socioemotional selectivity theory maintains that long-term friendships with a select group of others

become increasingly valuable in older age, it was expected that the perceived quality of social support from friends would be higher outside of
the retirement community than within it.

3. Levels of confidant relationships will be higher for friends residing elsewhere than for friends within the retirement community. Long-term friendships are likely to be characterized by low risk of negative emotional experience and devalued self-identity. Because confiding in another person
typically entails self-disclosure and thus risk, it was expected that confidant relationships would be more apparent for friends living outside of
the retirement community than for those within it.

4. Social support will be more strongly associated with low levels of depression if derived from friends residing elsewhere than from friends within
the retirement community. Because social support from a select group of
long-term friends may become increasingly valuable as one ages and social support from a larger number of more casual acquaintances may take
on decreasing importance, it was expected that the former would have
greater effects on emotional well-being than the latter.

5. Social support from friends within the retirement community will be quantitatively and qualitatively greater, be characterized by higher levels of confidant relationships, and have stronger associations with low levels of depression among those who have resided there longer than among those
who have relocated more recently. With continued residence, the costs of
interaction within the retirement community may decrease, whereas the
benefits of such interaction may increase. The reverse may be true regarding interaction outside of the retirement community. Thus, duration of residence was expected to affect levels of social support from friends within
and outside of the retirement community, as well as levels of depression.

METHODS

Setting

Data were gathered in 1994 in one of the oldest and largest planned retirement
communities in Southern California, in which approximately 8,500 older adults
reside. The community provides a variety of leisure and social activities through
on-site clubs and organizations. Although an outpatient health clinic, including
social work services, is located on the grounds, in-home medical services are
not provided. Thus, the capacity for independent living is a requirement for
entry and continued residence.

Sample

A random sample of 400 households was selected using the retirement
community's telephone directory. In cases of married couples, one member of
the household was selected randomly. Sample members were asked to participate by completing a mailed, self-administered questionnaire. Seventy-three
questionnaires were returned with no forwarding address or with an indication
that the targeted individual was currently incapacitated, institutionalized, or

deceased. Of the remaining 327 potential respondents, 151 returned a completed questionnaire, a response rate of 46.2 percent. The analyses presented in this chapter were based only on residents living alone. It was believed that those living with others might have had difficulty distinguishing between within-household and within-community social support and that their living arrangements might have affected their responses regarding depression.

The final sample consisted of 99 respondents. Two were currently married but living apart from their spouses. They were included in the analyses because it was considered unlikely that their marital status would affect their responses regarding social support from friends.

Measures

Social Support. Social support is defined as a process emanating from the focal individual's location in social networks (Stahl & Potts, 1985) and operationalized in terms of network quantity, perceived quality, and confidant relationships. Two parallel sets of items were used. One pertained to social support from friends within the retirement community and the other to social support from friends outside of it.

Social networks provide structure for linkages between individuals and groups. However, the mere existence of social networks, although necessary for the provision of social support, may not be sufficient. If social networks are not used, their potentially beneficial effects will not be apparent. Thus, the network quantity measure was based on the actual use of friendship networks. The author used three items from the friend subscale of the Lubben Social Network Scale (Lubben, 1988), an instrument designed specifically for older adults. These items deal with the number of people considered friends, the number with whom contact is maintained, and the frequency of contact. The alpha reliability coefficient for the version of the scale pertaining to friends within the retirement community was .62; that for the version pertaining to friends outside of it was .88.

Qualitative aspects of social support should also be considered. Several researchers have noted that the perceived quality of social support has greater beneficial effects than its quantity (Auslander & Litwin, 1991; Feld & George, 1994; Hays, Kasl, & Jacobs, 1994; Hong & Duff, 1994; O'Connor, 1995). This aspect of social support was measured using five items based on the work of Berkman and colleagues (Berkman, 1983; Berkman & Syme, 1979). Respondents were asked to rate their satisfaction with social support from friends in these areas: the amount of time spent visiting, the extent to which personal matters were discussed, the adequacy of advice provided, and the expectation of help with daily activities and in case of illness. Alpha reliability coefficients for the versions pertaining to friends within and outside of the retirement community were .79 and .81, respectively.

Finally, access to a confidant has been documented as a critical factor in the well-being of older adults. This aspect of social support was measured using three items (Berkman, 1983; Berkman & Syme, 1979; Lubben, 1988): (1) the extent to which respondents could discuss sensitive matters with friends, (2) their satisfaction with the amount of time spent doing so, and (3) the extent to which they could turn to a friend for help in making an important decision. Alpha reliability coefficients for the versions pertaining to confidant relationships within and outside of the retirement community were .58 and .57, respectively.

Depression. Depression was measured using the Center for Epidemiological Studies Depression Scale (CES-D), developed by Radloff (1977) for use with general community samples. This instrument contains 20 items that assess the current frequency of various affective, behavioral, interpersonal, and somatic symptoms of depression. Scores can range from 0 to 60. The CES-D has been shown to have high internal consistency (alpha =.85 to .90) and moderate to high test–retest reliability (r = .45 to .70). Scores discriminate well between psychiatric inpatient and general population samples and correlate well with other depression measures. The CES-D has also been shown to be reliable and valid when used with older adults (Clark, Aneshensel, Frerichs, & Morgan, 1981; Himmelfarb & Murrell, 1983). Although its somatic subscale has been criticized for reflecting physical rather than emotional health, age and physical health do not appear to affect this subscale more than others (Davidson, Feldman, & Crawford, 1994; Kessler, Foster, Webster, & House, 1992). The alpha reliability coefficient obtained in this study was .84.

Physical Health. Physical health was measured using a single-item global scale. Others have shown that this approach is reliable and valid when used with older adults, yielding results equivalent to those based on more complex indexes (Rakowski, Fleishman, Mor, & Bryant, 1993; Thorslund & Norstrom, 1993).

Statistical Analyses

For each social support scale, the author used paired *t* tests to determine if scores pertaining to friends within the retirement community differed from scores pertaining to friends living elsewhere. Ordinary least squares (OLS) regression was used to examine the extent to which social support was predicted by duration of residence and the extent to which depression was predicted by social support. For the latter analyses, hierarchical procedures were used. Step 1 included the relevant social support scale and a variety of control variables, including duration of residence in the retirement community. Step 2 added the interaction term for social support and duration of residence. Additional analyses examined the effects of social support from friends outside of the retirement community, controlling for the effects of social support from friends within it.

The author controlled gender, age, income, and physical health in all regression analyses. Other research has shown that levels and effects of social support vary among older adults according to these factors (Antonucci & Akiyama, 1987; Connidis & Davies, 1992; Forster & Stoller, 1992; Husaini et al., 1991; Levitt et al., 1985–86; Sabin, 1993; Sheehan, 1986; Stolar et al., 1993). Gender, income, and physical health were controlled also because of their significant zero-order correlations with social support or depression. Age was viewed as a necessary control because of the potential for overlap between its effects and those of duration of residence.

RESULTS

Characteristics of Respondents

A substantial majority of the 99 respondents (80.8 percent) were women (Table 22.1). This preponderance of women is not viewed as attributable to a higher response rate among women. The percentage of women in the present sample was similar to or lower than that found in other studies of retirement community residents (80 percent by Stacey-Konnert & Pynoos, 1992; 89 percent by Shea et al., 1988; 93 percent by Stephens & Bernstein, 1984). The gender distribution may also have been a function of the age of the sample; nearly half were 80 years old or older ($M = 79.8$, $SD = 7.4$).

All but 2.0 percent of the 99 respondents were non-Hispanic white people. Over half had at least some college education. The annual household income of 19.8 percent was less than $10,000, and 8.6 percent had an annual household income of $30,000 or more. Three-fourths (76.8 percent) were widowed, 12.1 percent were divorced or separated, 9.1 percent were never married, and 2.0 percent were married but living alone. Almost three-fifths (57.6 percent) reported excellent or good physical health.

The average duration of residence in the retirement community was 12.5 years ($SD = 8.4$), and 51.6 percent had lived there for 10 or more years. Most (79.8 percent, $n = 79$) had lived within the Southern California area immediately before relocating, although only 37.4 percent ($n = 37$) had lived within the adjacent community.

Table 22.1

Characteristics of Older Adult Residents of a Retirement Community (N = 99)

Characteristic	n	%
Gender		
Female	80	80.8
Male	19	19.2
Age (years)[a]		
Younger than 70	12	12.4
70–79	31	32.0
80 or older	54	55.6
Annual household income ($)[a]		
Less than 10,000	16	19.8
10,000–19,999	42	51.9
20,000–29,999	16	19.8
30,000 or more	7	8.6
Physical health		
Excellent	16	16.2
Good	41	41.4
Fair	35	35.4
Poor	7	7.1
Duration of residence in retirement community (years)[a]		
Less than 5	18	19.4
5–9	27	29.0
10 or more	48	51.6

[a]Contained missing data.

Scores on Social Support Scales and Depression Index

Network quantity scale scores were significantly higher for friends within the retirement community than for friends living elsewhere [$t(92) = 7.41, p < .001$] (Table 22.2). In contrast, both perceived quality and confidant relationship scale scores were significantly higher for friends living outside of the retirement community than for friends within it [$t(90) = 2.40, p < .05$ and $t(90) = 3.31, p < .001$, respectively].

The mean score on the depression index was 10.0 ($SD = 7.6$), suggesting a low level of depression among the respondents as a group. However, 14.5 percent ($n = 14$) had scores of 16 or greater (the cutoff used by the CES-D to indicate significant clinical depression).

Zero-Order Correlations

Women reported higher levels of confidant relationships than men on the scale pertaining to friends living outside of the retirement community, but age and education were not associated with any aspect of social support. Respondents with higher incomes reported higher levels of both network quantity and perceived quality, but only for friends living outside of the retirement community. Respondents in poorer health reported lower levels of social support on five of the six scales (the exception was network quantity within the retirement community). Duration of residence was not significantly associated with scores on any of the social support scales.

Of the 15 zero-order correlations possible among the six social support scales, 10 were significant ($p < .05$) (Table 22.3). Higher levels of one aspect of social support tended to be associated with higher levels of other aspects, although scores on the confidant relationships scale pertaining to friends within the retirement community were not associated significantly with scores on any of the three scales pertaining to friends living elsewhere.

Only one control variable was associated with depression: Respondents in poorer health reported higher levels of depression than those in better health. Without exception, higher levels of social support were associated with lower levels of depression.

Table 22.2

Social Support Scale Scores for Older Adult Residents of a Retirement Community ($N = 99$)

	Within Retirement Community	Outside of Retirement Community
Social Support Scale[a]	M ± SD	M ± SD
Network quantity	8.56 ± 2.93	5.41 ± 3.80
Perceived quality	13.75 ± 2.93	14.67 ± 3.24
Confidant relationships	7.98 ± 2.60	9.10 ± 2.41

[a]Possible ranges were 0 to 15 for network quantity, 5 to 20 for perceived quality, and 2 to 12 for confidant relationships.

Table 22.3

Zero-Order Correlations for Variables Affecting Depression among Older Adult Residents of a Retirement Community (N = 99)

Variable	1	2	3	4	5	6	7	8	9	10	11	12
Characteristic												
1. Female												
2. Age	-.21*											
3. Income	-.29**	-.15										
4. Poor health	-.14	.08	-.16									
5. Duration of residence	.13	.00	.02	-.11								
Social support within retirement community												
6. Quantity	-.03	.15	.03	.01	.01							
7. Quality	-.06	.02	.12	-.28**	.13	.36***						
8. Confidant relationship	-.01	-.05	.17	-.24***	.09	.38**	.70***					
Social support outside of retirement community												
9. Quantity	-.11	-.01	.26**	-.20*	-.17	.27**	.14	.14				
10. Quality	.10	.04	.19*	-.22*	-.06	.12	.30**	.12	.37***			
11. Confidant relationship	-.17*	-.09	.06	-.28***	-.02	.18*	.26***	.16	.43***	.63***		
12. Depression	-.09	.11	-.17	.31**	-.03	-.09	-.35***	-.26**	-.38**	-.33**	-.39***	

*$p < .05$. **$p < .01$. ***$p < .001$.

Effects of Duration of Residence on Social Support

After using OLS regression to control for gender, age, income, and physical health, the author found that the effects of duration of residence in the retirement community on social support were nearly identical to the zero-order correlations described earlier. Thus, the length of time respondents had lived in the retirement community did not affect their reported levels of social support from friends living there or elsewhere.

Effects of Social Support and Duration of Residence on Depression

Neither the direct effects of duration of residence nor its interactive effects with social support added to the predicted variance in depression (Table 22.4). Thus,

Table 22.4

Effects of Social Support from Friends within and outside of Retirement Community on Depression ($N = 99$)

Independent Variable	Within Retirement Community		Outside of Retirement Community		Within and outside of Retirement Community	
	b	β	b	β	b	β
Network quantity						
Female	−.44	−.02	−.26	−.01	.15	.01
Age	.01	.09	.01	.08	.08	.07
Income	−.60	−.14	−.04	−.01	−.07	−.02
Poor physical health	2.42	.23	1.35	.13	1.07	.10
Duration of residence	.08	.08	−.02	−.03	−.07	−.08
Network quantity (within)	−.44	−.17	NA	NA	.12	.05
Network quantity (outside)	NA	NA	−.93	−.45***	−.98	−.47***
Adjusted R^2	.00	.18**	.17*			
Quality of social support						
Female	−1.25	−.07	−.08	−.03	−.37	−.02
Age	.00	.06	.01	.11	.18	.18
Income	−.51	−.12	.01	.00	−.20	−.05
Poor physical health	1.71	.17	2.06	.19	1.38	.13
Duration of residence	.08	.08	−.02	−.02	−.06	−.07
Perceived quality (within)	−.69	−.25	NA	NA	−.63	−.22
Perceived quality (outside)	NA	NA	−.81	−.30*	−.63	−.24
Adjusted R^2	.06	.07	.09			
Confidant relationships						
Female	−.29	−.02	−.16	−.01	.24	.01
Age	.10	.09	.00	.04	.13	.12
Income	−.57	−.14	−.31	−.08	−.39	−.09
Poor physical health	1.76	.17	1.50	.15	1.09	.11
Duration of residence	.03	.04	−.00	−.00	−.04	−.04
Confidant relationships (within)	−.54	−.17	NA	NA	−.35	−.11
Confidant relationships (outside)	NA	NA	−1.13	−.35**	−1.09	−.34**
Adjusted R^2	.00	.12*	.10			

NOTE: NA = not applicable.
*$p < .05$. **$p < .01$. ***$p < .001$.

the effects on depression of all aspects of social support measured did not vary according to the length of time participants had lived in the retirement community. No substantive differences were apparent between step 1 (without interaction term) and step 2 (with interaction term), and all changes in R^2 were .02 or less. Thus, only the results for step 1 are shown.

For all three aspects of social support measured, social support from friends within the retirement community failed to show any significant associations with depression. In contrast, higher levels of social support from friends living elsewhere were consistently associated with lower levels of depression. Thus, whether assessed in terms of network quantity, perceived quality, or confidant relationships, social support from friends was found to be predictive of low levels of depression only if those friends lived outside of the retirement community.

The third column in Table 22.4 depicts the results concerning the effects of social support from friends outside of the retirement community, controlling for the effects of social support from friends within it. For two of the three aspects of social support measured (network quantity and confidant relationships), social support from friends outside of the retirement community remained a significant predictor of low depression levels. In contrast, the perceived quality of social support from friends outside of the retirement community was no longer a significant predictor after controlling for this aspect of social support from friends within it.

DISCUSSION

Of the five hypotheses presented, four were supported by the data. In terms of network quantity, social support levels were higher for friends within the retirement community; in terms of perceived quality and confidant relationships, social support levels were higher for friends living elsewhere. Social support from friends living outside of the retirement community consistently predicted low levels of depression, whereas social support from friends within the retirement community consistently failed to do so. Moreover, in two instances (network quantity and confidant relationships), social support from friends outside of the retirement community continued to predict low levels of depression, even after controlling for social support from friends within it.

These results support the main premises of socioemotional selectivity theory and are consistent with the findings of many other studies of friendship patterns among older adults in age-segregated settings.

Frequency of Contact

Empirical evidence from a variety of age-segregated settings suggests that frequency of contact is not necessarily related to emotional closeness (Adams, 1985–86; Fisher, 1991; Gutheil, 1991; Johnson & Troll, 1994; Peters & Kaiser, 1985; Stephens & Bernstein, 1984). Given structural constraints to interaction outside of the setting, residents tend to interact more frequently with other residents, regardless of the intensity of their emotional bonds with them. As stated by Adams (1985–86), "casual friends" may be the "constant companions" of many older adults in age-segregated settings.

Duration of Residence in a Retirement Community

The data did not support the fifth hypothesis that duration of residence in the retirement community would attenuate any differences in levels and effects of social support from friends within and outside of it. Although the beneficial effects of social support from friends within the retirement community might be expected to increase over time, there was no evidence of this. Several possibilities may account for this unexpected finding.

First, the amount of time since relocation to the retirement community may have been insufficient for the development of friendships. The author views this explanation as unlikely, insofar as only 7.5 percent of the respondents had relocated within the past two years and 80.6 percent had lived there for five years or more. Second, some friends within the retirement community may actually be long-term friends who moved there coincidentally or who induced, or were induced by, the respondents to relocate. However, any mixture of long-established and newly developed relationships within the retirement community should reduce any differences between the social support derived from friends living there and elsewhere. That many such differences were observed should thus enhance, rather than detract from, one's confidence in their validity.

Finally, it is possible that the beneficial effects of maintaining ties with friends outside of the retirement community are indeed apparent, regardless of the time residents have had to develop friendships within it. Although others have shown that new friends can be made regardless of age (Gutheil, 1991; Johnson & Toll, 1994; Shea et al., 1988), such new friends may not be equivalent to longer-term friends in terms of their beneficial effects on mental health. As stated by Shea et al. (1988), new friends may be liked, but only old friends are loved.

With the exception of network quantity regarding friends within the retirement community, the bivariate associations between social support from friends both within and outside of the retirement community were significantly associated with low levels of depression. This result is consistent with the premise that social support is an important aspect of the well-being of older adults. However, only social support from friends outside of the retirement community remained a significant predictor of low depression levels after controlling for relevant demographic factors and duration of residence.

Limitations of the Study

Several limitations of this study should be noted. First, the sample was from one geographic location; thus, the findings may not be generalizable to other retirement communities, particularly those with greater ethnic diversity. Second, the response rate of 46.2 percent, although not atypical of mailed surveys, may also reduce generalizability.

Third, the design was cross-sectional; thus, causal inferences cannot be made with certainty. Depression may have had reciprocal effects on social support, insofar as depressed individuals may refrain from interacting with others or hold unduly negative views of those interactions.

Fourth, two items within the perceived quality scale concerned behaviors requiring at least some degree of proximity to the source of social support; this may have reduced the extent to which the perceived quality of social support was higher for friends living outside of the retirement community than for those within it (although a significant difference in this respect was nevertheless observed). Finally, the present application of socioemotional selectivity theory did not address social interactions solely or primarily involving concrete care or practical assistance, factors that also affect the well-being of many older adults.

CONCLUSION

Further research in this area should incorporate a wider range of settings, longitudinal designs, and continued attempts to refine the conceptualization and measurement of social support. In particular, the present results emphasize the importance of differentiating between types of friends. Following Johnson and Troll's (1994) typology, friends may be close (those with shared memories and a long-term interest in each other's lives), casual (those who are available because of proximity), club (those who are identified by the setting in which the relationships were formed), or helpers (those who provide paid or volunteer services to typically housebound or bedfast older adults). These various types of friends undoubtedly meet different needs, and the social support derived from them is undoubtedly associated with different aspects of well-being.

As researchers continue to explore the sources and effects of various types of social support among older adults, contradictory findings are likely to emerge if the definition of "friend" is not well conceptualized. Areas of inquiry that could benefit from the use of more specific definitions of "friend" include the differential effects of kin and nonkin support, the relative importance of socioemotional or expressive support and instrumental or practical support, and the relative validity of task-specific and compensatory models.

It should be emphasized that a small proportion of the variance in depression was accounted for by variables in the models presented here. Consequently, further research should incorporate additional concepts relevant to friendship patterns and mental health among older adults. Clearly, many other factors are involved, including satisfaction with social support, desire for change, barriers to interaction, and the joint or interactive effects of social support from other sources such as family members and social services professionals.

Non–social support variables are also important predictors of depression. Others who have used the CES-D as a measure of depression in older adults have obtained proportions of predicted variance ranging from 12 percent to 58 percent (Bazargan & Hamm-Baugh, 1995; Husaini et al., 1990; Phifer & Murrell, 1986; Ryff & Essex, 1992). In addition to various aspects of social support, these models have included the following predictor variables: positive views of self, perceptions of ego strength, chronic strain (particularly financial), stressful life events (particularly bereavement and residential relocation), and number of chronic illnesses or physical health problems.

Despite its limitations, the results of the present study may be useful to social workers as they intervene with residents who live alone in age-segregated settings. If we accept the premise that friends outside of the retirement community have greater beneficial effects on emotional well-being than friends within it, two types of non–mutually exclusive goals might be considered: maintaining ties with the former and strengthening ties with the latter. From an ecological perspective, interventions aimed at either goal should take into account factors inherent in the individual, the immediate retirement community, and the larger community surrounding it.

Assessment should address the individual's interest in maintaining contacts with friends living elsewhere, his or her proclivity to communicate in person or by telephone, his or her physical and financial resources, and the proximity of his or her friends. The following questions should be addressed: Is transportation affordable? Are telephone contacts limited by financial concerns? Most retirement communities provide transportation for "necessary" trips; perhaps transportation could be provided also for informal visiting. Residents should be informed of existing resources for such services; where sufficient resources are lacking, social workers might advocate for them.

In the design of interventions aimed at improving the qualitative aspects of friendships within the retirement community, additional factors should be assessed. These include historical factors relevant to the individual's desire and capacity for intimacy (Rook, 1991). A life-long pattern of social isolation and lack of gregariousness may be immutable. However, given sufficient motivation for doing so, older adults can learn social and communication skills (Husaini et al., 1991).

Several additional factors relevant to the immediate community were noted in a description of a "failed" intervention (so labeled by the authors) aimed at establishing confidant relationships among older adults (Heller, Thompson, Vlachos-Weber, Steffen, & Trueba, 1991). These authors pointed out that social norms or "display rules," as well as fear of gossip, may prevent self-disclosure. Furthermore, Parker and Parrott (1995) found that older adults tend to self-disclose more frequently to family members than to friends. Such issues should be discussed openly if interventions aimed at establishing confidant relationships are to succeed.

Carefully designed discussion or support groups might strengthen relationships among residents, which already appear to be quantitatively extensive. However, as Rook (1991) cautioned, "friendships may emerge more easily from shared activities and projects than from interactions focused overtly on friendship formation" (p. 105). In essence, close friendships cannot be forced; attempts to do so are likely to result in intense self-consciousness and the perception of penetrating scrutiny by others. On the other hand, pre-existing social and recreational activities within most retirement communities abound and may be viewed as natural contexts for nurturing deeper, more intense friendships, particularly when these activities are relevant to current concerns and interests and promote social roles perceived as meaningful. This approach is consistent with Heller et al.'s (1991) suggestion that greater attention should be given to strengthening indigenous ties before attempting to create new ones.

Regardless of whether the focus is on maintaining old friendships or on nurturing new ones, the results presented in this chapter suggest that such efforts are important. It is hoped that these findings will be put to good use by social workers as they design and evaluate interventions aimed at improving the well-being of older adults living alone in retirement communities and other age-segregated settings.

REFERENCES

Adams, R. G. (1985–86). Emotional closeness and physical distance between friends: Implications for elderly women living in age-segregated and age-integrated settings. *International Journal of Aging and Human Development, 22*, 55–76.

Antonucci, T. C., & Akiyama, H. (1987). An examination of sex differences in social support among older men and women. *Sex Roles, 17*, 737–749.

Auslander, G. K., & Litwin, H. (1991). Social networks, social support, and self-ratings of health among the elderly. *Journal of Aging and Health, 3*, 493–510.

Bazargan, M., & Hamm-Baugh, V. P. (1995). The relationship between chronic illness and depression in a community of urban black elderly persons. *Journal of Gerontology, 50*, S119–S127.

Berkman, L. F. (1983). The assessment of social networks and social support in the elderly. *Journal of the American Geriatrics Society, 31*, 743–749.

Berkman, L. F., & Syme, S. L. (1979). Social networks, host resistance, and mortality: A nine-year follow-up study of Alameda County residents. *American Journal of Epidemiology, 116*, 123–140.

Brown, A. S. (1990). The aged in changing living situations. In A. S. Brown (Ed.), *The social processes of aging and old age* (pp. 76–88). Englewood Cliffs, NJ: Prentice Hall.

Carstensen, L. L. (1991). Socioemotional activity theory: Social activity in life-span context. *Annual Review of Gerontology and Geriatrics, 11*, 195–217.

Carstensen, L. L. (1992). Social and emotional patterns in adulthood: Support for socioemotional selectivity theory. *Psychology and Aging, 3*, 331–338.

Clark, V. A., Aneshensel, C. S., Frerichs, R., & Morgan, T. M. (1981). Analysis of effects of sex and age in response to items on the CES-D scale. *Psychiatry Research, 5*, 171–181.

Connidis, I. A., & Davies, L. (1992). Confidants and companions: Choices in later life. *Journal of Gerontology, 47*, S115–S122.

Cox, H. G. (1988). Living environments in later life. In H. G. Cox (Ed.), *Later life: The realities of aging* (2nd ed., pp. 202–223). Englewood Cliffs, NJ: Prentice Hall.

Cumming, E., & Henry, W. E. (1961). *Growing old: The process of disengagement.* New York: Basic Books.

Davidson, H., Feldman, P. H., & Crawford, S. (1994). Measuring depressive symptoms in the frail elderly. *Journal of Gerontology, 49*, P159–P164.

Dykstra, P. A. (1995). Loneliness among the never and formerly married: The importance of supportive friendships and a desire for independence. *Journal of Gerontology, 50*, S321–S329.

Feld, S., & George, L. K. (1994). Moderating effects of prior social resources on the hospitalizations of elders who become widowed. *Journal of Aging and Health, 6*, 275–295.

Fisher, B. J. (1991). *It's not quite like home: Illness, career descent and the stigma of living at a multi-level care retirement facility.* New York: Garland.

Forster, L. E., & Stoller, E. P. (1992). The impact of social support on mortality: A seven-year follow-up of older men and women. *Journal of Applied Gerontology, 11*, 173–186.

Fredrickson, B. L., & Carstensen, L. L. (1990). Choosing social partners: How old age and anticipated endings make people more selective. *Psychology and Aging, 5*, 163–171.

George, L. K. (1989). Stress, social support, and depression over the life course. In K. S. Markides & C. L. Cooper (Eds.), *Aging, stress, social support, and health* (pp. 241–267). London: John Wiley & Sons.

Gordon, P. A. (1988). *Developing retirement facilities.* New York: John Wiley & Sons.

Gutheil, I. A. (1991). Intimacy in nursing home friendships. *Journal of Gerontological Social Work, 17*, 59–73.

Havighurst, R., & Albrecht, R. (1953). *Older people*. New York: Longman, Green.

Hays, J. C., Kasl, S., & Jacobs, S. (1994). Past personal history of dysphoria, social support, and psychological distress following conjugal bereavement. *Journal of the American Geriatrics Society, 42*, 712–718.

Heller, K., Thompson, M. G., Vlachos-Weber, I., Steffen, A. M., & Trueba, P. E. (1991). Support interventions for older adults: Confidante relationships, perceived family support, and meaningful role activity. *American Journal of Community Psychology, 19*, 139–146.

Himmelfarb, S., & Murrell, S. A. (1983). Reliability and validity of five mental health scales in older persons. *Journal of Gerontology, 38*, 333–339.

Hinrichsen, G. A. (1985). The impact of age-concentrated, publicly assisted housing on older people's social and emotional well-being. *Journal of Gerontology, 40*, 758–760.

Hong, L. K., & Duff, R. W. (1994). Widows in retirement communities: The social context of subjective well-being. *Gerontologist, 34*, 347–353.

Hunt, M. E., Feldt, A. G., Marans, R. W., Pastalan, L. A., & Vakalo, K. L. (1984). *Retirement communities: An American original*. New York: Haworth Press.

Husaini, B. A., Castor, R. S., Linn, J. G., Moore, S. T., Warren, H. A., & Whitten-Stovall, R. (1990). Social support and depression among the black and white elderly. *Journal of Community Psychology, 18*, 12–18.

Husaini, B. A., Moore, S. T., & Castor, R. S. (1991). Social and psychological well-being of black elderly living in high-rises for the elderly. *Journal of Gerontological Social Work, 16*, 57–78.

Johnson, C. L., & Troll, L. E. (1994). Constraints and facilitators to friendships in late late life. *Gerontologist, 34*, 79–87.

Kessler, R., Foster, C., Webster, P., & House, J. (1992). The relationship between age and depressive symptoms in two national surveys. *Psychology and Aging, 7*, 119–126.

Krause, N., & Borawski-Clark, E. (1994). Clarifying the functions of social support in later life. *Research on Aging, 16*, 251–279.

Krause, N., Liang, J., & Keith, V. (1990). Personality, social support, and psychological distress in later life. *Psychology and Aging, 5*, 315–326.

LaGory, M., & Fitzpatrick, K. (1992). The effects of environmental context on elderly depression. *Journal of Aging and Health, 4*, 459–479.

Lawton, M. P., Moss, M., & Moles, E. (1984). The suprapersonal neighborhood context of older people: Age heterogeneity and well-being. *Environment and Behavior, 16*, 89–109.

Levitt, M. J., Antonucci, T. C., Clark, M. C., Rotton, J., & Finley, G. E. (1985–86). Social support and well-being: Preliminary indicators based on two samples of the elderly. *International Journal of Aging and Human Development, 21*, 61–77.

Lubben, J. E. (1988). Assessing social networks among elderly populations. *Family and Community Health, 11*, 42–52.

Markides, K., & Cooper, C. (Eds.). (1989). *Aging, stress, social support, and health*. London: John Wiley & Sons.

Mitchell, J., Mathews, H. F., & Yesavage, J. A. (1993). A multidimensional examination of depression among the elderly. *Research on Aging, 15*, 198–219.

Mullins, L. C., & Tucker, R. D. (1992). Emotional and social isolation among older French Canadian seasonal residents in Florida: A comparison with the English Canadian seasonal residents. *Journal of Gerontological Social Work, 19*, 83–106.

O'Connor, B. P. (1995). Family and friend relationships among older and younger adults: Interaction motivation, mood, and quality. *International Journal of Aging and Human Development, 40*, 9–29.

Osgood, N. J. (1982). *Senior settlers: Social integration in retirement communities*. New York: Praeger.

Parker, R. G., & Parrott, R. (1995). Patterns of self-disclosure across social support networks: Elderly, middle-aged, and young adults. *International Journal of Aging and Human Development, 41*, 281–297.

Pearlman, D. N., & Crown, W. H. (1992). Alternative sources of social support and their impacts on institutional risk. *Gerontologist, 32,* 527–535.

Peters, G. R., & Kaiser, M. A. (1985). The role of friends and neighbors in providing social support. In W. J. Sauer & R. T. Coward (Eds.), *Social support networks and the care of the elderly: Theory, research, and practice* (pp. 123–158). New York: Springer.

Phifer, J. F., & Murrell, S. A. (1986). Etiologic factors in the onset of depressive symptoms in older adults. *Journal of Abnormal Psychology, 95,* 282–291.

Radloff, L. (1977). The CES-D scale: A self-report depression scale for research in the general population. *Applied Psychological Measurement, 1,* 385–401.

Rakowski, W., Fleishman, J. A., Mor, V., & Bryant, S. A. (1993). Self-assessments of health and mortality among older persons. *Research on Aging, 15,* 92–116.

Rook, K. S. (1991). Facilitating friendship formation in late life: Puzzles and challenges. *American Journal of Community Psychology, 19,* 103–110.

Russell, D. W., & Cutrona, C. E. (1991). Social support, stress, and depressive symptoms among the elderly: Test of a process model. *Psychology and Aging, 6,* 190–201.

Ryff, C. D., & Essex, M. J. (1992). The interpretation of life experience and well-being: The sample case of relocation. *Psychology and Aging, 7,* 507–517.

Sabin, E. P. (1993). Social relationships and mortality among the elderly. *Journal of Applied Gerontology, 12,* 44–60.

Sauer, W. J., & Coward, R. T. (1985). *Social support networks and the care of the elderly: Theory, research, and practice.* New York: Springer.

Seeman, T. E., & Berkman, L. F. (1988). Structural characteristics of social networks and their relationship with social support in the elderly: Who provides support? *Social Science and Medicine, 26,* 737–749.

Shea, L., Thompson, L., & Blieszner, R. (1988). Resources in older adults' old and new friendships. *Journal of Social and Personal Relationships, 5,* 83–96.

Sheehan, N. W. (1986). Informal support among the elderly in public senior housing. *Gerontologist, 26,* 171–175.

Simons, R. L. (1983–84). Specificity and substitution in the social networks of the elderly. *International Journal of Aging and Human Development, 18,* 121–139.

Stacey-Konnert, C., & Pynoos, J. (1992). Friendship and social networks in a continuing care retirement community. *Journal of Applied Gerontology, 11,* 298–313.

Stahl, S. M., & Potts, M. K. (1985). Social support and chronic disease: A propositional inventory. In W. A. Peterson & J. Quadagno (Eds.), *Social bonds in later life: Aging and interdependence* (pp. 305–323). Beverly Hills, CA: Sage Publications.

Steinbach, U. (1992). Social networks, institutionalization, and mortality among elderly people in the United States. *Journal of Gerontology, 47,* S183–S190.

Stephens, M.A.P., & Bernstein, M. (1984). Social support and well-being among residents of planned housing. *Gerontologist, 24,* 144–148.

Stolar, G. E., MacEntee, M. I., & Hill, P. (1993). The elderly: Their perceived supports and reciprocal behaviors. *Journal of Gerontological Social Work, 19,* 15–33.

Sullivan, D. A. (1986). Informal support systems in a planned retirement community: Availability, proximity, and willingness to utilize. *Research on Aging, 8,* 249–267.

Thorslund, M., & Norstrom, T. (1993). The relationship between different survey measures of health in an elderly population. *Journal of Applied Gerontology, 12,* 61–70.

An earlier version of this chapter was presented at the Annual Program Meeting of the Council on Social Work Education, February 1996, Washington, DC. This work was supported in part by the following: Affirmative Action Faculty Development Program, California State University, Long Beach; University Scholarly and Creative Activity Award, California State University, Long Beach; and Chancellor's Mini-Grant, Office of the Chancellor, California State University. The author thanks Julie Mack for her assistance with data entry and analysis and Richard Serpe, Raymond Berger, Catherine Goodman, and James Kelly for their review of an earlier draft.

This chapter was originally published in the July 1997 issue of Social Work, *vol. 42, pp. 348–362.*

Part VI

Schools and Community Development

23 Community Practice and Policy Issues Revisited

Edith M. Freeman

The director of an early childhood program in an urban midwestern community was explaining to a colleague of mine the reason he would not be attending an upcoming coalition meeting. He had been called to Washington, DC, to testify before a congressional committee charged with developing legislation for block grant funding to the states. In sharing the conversation with me, my colleague pointed out that her friend was taking a risk because what he planned to include in his testimony could be construed as admitting that his program has not completely resolved the problems of the families it serves. Would Congress understand and respond to his message, or would his testimony fuel the assumptions of some lawmakers that social programs do not work?

He planned to testify that more funding is needed for programs that can help communities develop themselves. His reasoning was that no matter how well his early childhood program serves the children and their families, they are confronted daily with adverse environmental and community conditions that overwhelm their gains and resources. By the time many children enter public school, their gains in cognitive and social skills from the early childhood program begin to erode. He believes more community partnership grants might be an important empowerment strategy when combined with other approaches.

SCHOOL–COMMUNITY PRACTICE

Two recent patterns echo this helping professional's perspective: One is the growing frustration voiced by school social workers around the country; the other is a trend toward school–community practice. Many school social workers, especially those in districts experiencing financial cutbacks, are frustrated by barriers that prevent them from following the problems affecting students' school adjustment into the community. Some administrators will not allow school social workers to refer students for community services because districts could be required to pay for those services. School social workers are not allowed to coordinate and collaborate with community services on mutual cases because those activities take time away from direct services. Even in the direct services area, some practitioners must help students with no home visits, no family counseling, no preventive or other services for students in regular education, and no focus on areas of students' problems that are not directly related to their school functioning.

Despite this pattern, other school districts are working to develop more community-based practice models or strategies. School-linked, wraparound, and integrated service models attempt to concentrate a broad array of comprehensive services in the school or another central site for "one-stop shopping" (Aguirre, 1995). One strategy is to develop mobile or community-based units to serve high-risk populations such as homeless families and people with HIV/AIDS or those needing preventive health services (for example, well-baby services) (Freeman & Pennekamp, 1988). The philosophical and conceptual underpinnings of these programs emphasize the physical and psychological accessibility of services, cultural sensitivity, and the person-in-environment perspective. Attention is focused on service organization and placement in terms of environmental and community dynamics.

These programs are different, however, from community-centered programs. The latter programs embody concepts such as community development, planning, capacity building, and empowerment, which are experiencing a rebirth in the literature. Until now, there has been a movement away from the philosophy and organizational framework of the community-centered model of practice, an implicit aspect of the settlement house movement and the War on Poverty (Gulati & Guest, 1990). This model requires structural components that make programs accountable to community members by involving advisory boards and citizen review boards in planning, implementing, and monitoring programs. This type of community involvement, along with the use of peer-led services, increases a community's sense of ownership and agency accountability and also encourages power sharing and involvement of program participants and community residents in policy-making with agency staff consistent with social work values of self-determination and social justice (Figueira-McDonough, 1993).

Concerns about social justice have, at least in part, been a factor in helping professionals' and policymakers' renewed interest in community practice. The current focus on this model places even greater emphasis on examining and changing social structures within and outside communities that may impede efforts toward self-sufficiency and capacity building. Expanding on Freire's (1983) and Solomon's (1987) efforts to operationalize the term "community empowerment," Gutiérrez (1990) explained that empowerment can occur only when people identify how the roots of their individual and common problems are embedded in the social structure. Then successful collective action must be taken over time, risking mistakes and revising plans, to change systems based on information from power analyses.

Communities can discover forgotten or unacknowledged sources of power as well as sources of disempowerment. Leadership can be enhanced by discovering existing leadership skills and gaps among residents. This perspective implies that simply facilitating a community in improving its mutual helping process and strengthening its resources for managing internal problems is not empowerment. In fact, Isreal (1985) cautioned that many such communities may still not have the power to affect negative environmental conditions that are controlled by the social structure outside the community. Isreal's assumptions are supported by other authors who believe that the target of change must be the existing social structure rather than people's ways of coping with that structure (Wallerstein & Bernstein, 1988; Yeich & Levine, 1992).

IMPLEMENTING A PARTNERSHIP

Given this perspective about community-centered programs and the current limitations on some school social work roles in the community, what changes are needed? What information from our early childhood program directors and other key informants could affect the congressional policy-making process? In spite of recent legislation for early childhood education and related services and funding for community partnership grants in various areas (child welfare, substance abuse, community violence, and community enterprise zones), many policy- and practice-related tasks have yet to be undertaken. School and community practitioners should be alerted to numerous opportunities and responsibilities to influence community policy.

Opportunities exist to influence school- and community-related policy at multiple levels through membership on committees, advocacy and expert testimony about successes in increasing self-sufficiency, and data collection around specific problems or needs. Involvement may occur at the school level (crisis management and special education reintegration committees), at the community level (citizen review committees or community planning boards), at the local level (city boards and committees on funding policy), at the state level (departments of education, public health, and public welfare advisory committees and state legislature committees), and at the national level (congressional committees and networking with lobbyists) (Figueira-McDonough, 1993; Florin & Wandersman, 1990; Freeman & Pennekamp, 1988; Jansson, 1990; O'Donnell, 1993).

American society has had opportunities to help communities develop themselves in the past, for example, during the War on Poverty. Although gains were made all over the country, many problems were not resolved. Today this country is confronted with another opportunity to help communities build on and expand their human and material resources. School and community practitioners have an essential role to fulfill in this complex recovery process. If we get it right this time by addressing issues of structural change, we can then focus our attention and resources on other problems. If we do not, we will be confronted continually with the responsibility for revitalizing our communities.

REFERENCES

Aguirre, L. M. (1995). California's efforts toward school-linked, integrated, comprehensive services. *Social Work in Education, 17*, 217–225.

Figueira-McDonough, J. (1993). Policy practice: The neglected side of social work intervention. *Social Work, 38*, 179–188.

Florin, P., & Wandersman, A. (1990). An introduction to citizen participation, voluntary organizations, and community development: Insights for empowerment through research. *American Journal of Community Psychology, 18*, 41–54.

Freeman, E. M., & Pennekamp, M. (1988). *Social work practice: Toward a child, family, school, community perspective.* Springfield, IL: Charles C Thomas.

Freire, P. (1983). *Education for critical consciousness.* New York: Seabury Press.

Gulati, P., & Guest, G. (1990). The community-centered model: A garden-variety approach or a radical transformation of community practice? *Social Work, 35*, 63–68.

Gutiérrez, L. M. (1990). Working with women of color: An empowerment perspective. *Social Work, 35*, 149–154.

Isreal, B. (1985). Social networks and social work: Implications for natural helper and commu-
    nity-level interventions. *Health Education Quarterly, 12,* 65–80.
Jansson, B. S. (1990). Blending social change and technology in macro-practice: Developing
    structured dialogue in technical deliberations. *Administration in Social Work, 14,* 13–28.
O'Donnell, S. (1993). Involving clients in welfare policy-making. *Social Work, 38,* 629–635.
Soloman, B. (1987). *Empowerment: Social work in oppressed communities.* New York: Columbia
    University Press.
Wallerstein, N., & Bernstein, E. (1988). Empowerment education: Freire's ideas adapted to
    health education. *Health Education Quarterly, 15,* 379–384.
Yeich, S., & Levine, R. (1992). Participatory research's contribution to a conceptualization of
    empowerment. *Journal of Applied Social Psychology, 22,* 1894–1908.

This chapter was originally published in the January 1996 issue of Social Work in
Education, *vol. 18, pp. 3–5.*

24 Alternative Stories and Narratives for Transforming Schools, Families, Communities, and Policymakers

Edith M. Freeman

The dictum "Do no harm" has assumed greater importance in recent years as the social work profession has articulated much more clearly its responsibilities in regard to social justice issues (Allen-Meares, 1996; Burstow, 1991; Chapin, 1995; Hardy-Fanta, 1986; Knitzer, Steinberg, & Fleish, 1990; Solomon, 1987; Wyers, 1991). Social justice issues can limit people's control over their lives by limiting important rights and benefits, affecting their survival and quality of life. The impact of social justice issues is often expressed in people's stories about their lives, including their perspectives about how things are and how they ought to be. To avoid doing harm, school social workers and other practitioners and administrators should tune into these stories from two different but related perspectives: personal stories and cultural narratives.

STORIES AND NARRATIVES

Consideration of both personal and societal perspectives is essential, because both individuals' and society's (socially constructed) meanings "can get people into trouble, get them stuck, or embroil them in crisis" (Saleebey, 1994, p. 356). From a personal perspective, Borden (1992) recommended that practitioners not only hear the facts of clients' stories, but also tune into their subjective realities and meanings and the consequences those meanings have in their lives for good or ill. Thus, *stories* are defined as people's expressions of their ideas, feelings, lived experiences, and meanings, as well as events and people of significance to them (Sluzki, 1992). Stories can focus on ordinary or dramatic and manageable or unmanageable experiences. By listening to clients tell their stories, social workers can help them make sense of those experiences in terms of current problems and help them create continuity in their lives (Borden, 1992).

From a societal perspective, Saleebey (1994) suggested that it is important for social workers to tune into and acknowledge how cultural and societal narratives and meanings may dictate what clients do and how they live. He defined *narratives* as prototypical discourses that are grounded in and essential to the culture, in contrast to people's more "idiosyncratic" stories. Trouble can develop when there is a scarcity of solution-focused stories or narratives that can help people obtain problem-solving resources. In some situations, available narratives are "composed by and imposed from the outside" (Saleebey, 1994, p. 356). Imposed narratives may be oppressive and without real meaning in people's daily lives. Moreover, such narratives are thought to be political in nature because they maintain societal customs and conventions while limiting some individuals' possibilities and power (Sands & Nuccio, 1992).

EXPLORING ALTERNATIVE STORIES AND NARRATIVES

Countering oppressive narratives and seemingly unresolvable stories requires an exploration of alternative truths and realities, or, as Hartman (1990) pointed out, an appreciation for many ways of knowing. Alternative stories and narratives can help clients transform their lives and influence systems that compromise their survival and growth (Saleebey, 1994; Sluzki, 1992). Transformations occur in clients' situations when their experiences, symbols, and meanings are restoried, reclaimed, or renamed. Further transformations and new possibilities may develop when the perspectives of schools, families, communities, and policymakers change regarding children's strengths and needs. The transformation process causes a shift toward more equitable distribution of power and respect in each of these systems, as reflected in the alternative stories and narratives the key actors generate collaboratively.

Transforming Schools

Alternative stories and narratives in schools can occur through restorying procedures such as the one discussed in this issue's [April 1997, *Social Work in Education*'s] Practice Highlights column. "The Getting Better Phenomenon" describes the use of videotape to help at-risk youths analyze their process of change over time from problem student to successful student. By reflecting on their process of change before a video camera, including what helped and hindered their successes, these students have an opportunity to develop and share alternative stories. Whereas the students' "old" stories are typically problem saturated and regressive (Borden, 1992), the "new" stories reflect ownership of new empowerment experiences, a renaming and restorying of old experiences and meanings, and new identities as worthwhile individuals.

Such a restorying would not be possible, however, if oppressive school or institutional narratives about students and staff did not change simultaneously. The project's videotapes have been shown to teachers and administrators to help them restory their own processes of working with students, creating alternative stories and narratives about the role and identity of the school and staff in facilitating the getting better phenomenon. Moreover, the videotapes provide a means for influencing the school's culture, and thus its narratives, regarding the needs, values, resilience, and growth potential of at-risk students. The videotaped narratives highlight students' rights to and benefits from an effective education, because they provide feedback about institutional supports for and barriers to their change process. The project described in the column is one method social workers can use to transform school stories and narratives that maintain students' problems.

Transforming Families

Family mapping procedures are useful for helping families generate alternative stories for resolving problems that affect their children's school adjustment. Using genograms and life history grids, for example, social workers can help families identify and share stories about intergenerational and societal prescriptions that affect how they handle family and school issues (Anderson & Brown, 1980; Hartman & Laird, 1983). Intergenerational patterns of family violence and school failure, as well as of accomplishments, may be revealed by such stories.

Sluzki (1992) recommended the use of circular questions and reframing when families are "stuck" to identify alternative views and stories about the same events and new interpretations of old family rules. Circular questions highlight covert barriers and supports to change within a family (what is going on in the family when the problem is not occurring?), and reframing offers alternative ways of viewing or restorying family problems (a child's school problems may reflect his loyalty to the family and his effort to assist the family in getting the help it needs). Giving a child's problems a positive connotation or transforming the family story about the child's problems provides alternative solutions and sources of power for the unit.

Families may be stuck, too, because of biased narratives about them in schools and communities. Biased narratives about families living in poverty; families of color; families of children with disabilities; and families experiencing divorce, homelessness, violence, and chronic illnesses such as HIV/AIDS are examples of what Saleebey (1994) described as narrative adversities. Social workers can help generate alternative, transforming narratives by writing about families' resilience and accomplishments in school newsletters, supporting families in presenting their stories to influence school boards and other decision makers, and encouraging families to share their problem-solving stories with other families in peer support groups.

Transforming Communities

In disempowered and hopeless communities, and in others affected by the current era of diminishing federal responsibility, residents face incredible challenges. They are being given more local control, but they are also being asked to "do more with less" (Weil, 1996). Narratives about ineffective and dying communities relying on "the dole" are likely to increase. And when people lose faith in their communities, often they have lost faith in themselves and in their control over their environments. In contrast, empowerment ideals and narratives focus attention on resources within communities, on community assets and community building (Delgado, 1996).

A tool for generating alternative, empowerment-oriented narratives about communities is community assets mapping or assessment. According to Delgado (1996), assets mapping involves identifying indigenous resources; developing community goodwill, capacity, and leadership; and establishing collaborative activities. In regard to community building in particular, Gardner (1994) observed that two main ingredients are the participation and the development of young people. Delgado (1996) provided evidence that youths can be a valuable resource in community assets assessments and other activities. Schools and youth organizations that do not consider using the strengths of youths in improving community narratives are contributing to the very bias that has led to many school and community narratives about uninvolved, violent, and hopeless youths.

What can school social workers do to facilitate the development of alternative stories and narratives about communities and youths? They can work with other social services agencies to undertake community assets assessments involving youths to actively uncover hidden resources; educate school staff about communities' strengths, support networks, and indigenous leaders; help natural supports and informal organizations work collaboratively with schools; and have students participate in school-focused assessments that can improve in-school supports (Delgado, 1996).

Transforming Policy

Transformations at the school, family, and community levels lay a strong foundation for transforming the perspectives and decisions of policymakers. For example, Wallerstein and Bernstein (1988) demonstrated that youths can be trained to deconstruct negative media messages and narratives that encourage substance abuse and to write position papers, based on those deconstructions, to influence policy affecting the availability of alcohol to youths.

School social workers can encourage youths, families, and communities to use their natural resources to influence policy and social justice issues by collecting and disseminating success stories and other alternative stories as widely as possible. There is a danger, however, in treating such stories superficially. Discussions of image making as a device for changing perceptions are one example of a superficial approach. What is needed is a genuine appreciation for people's stories as an opportunity to hear and share in their experiences, accomplishments, and hopes for change. Such stories can humanize policymakers by transforming their own self-stories from claims of eliminating the drain on our national resources to accounts of supporting and enhancing our most important human resources.

REFERENCES

Allen-Meares, P. (1996). The new federal role in education and family services: Goal setting without responsibility. *Social Work, 41,* 533–540.

Anderson, M., & Brown, R. A. (1980). Life history grid for adolescents [Notes for Practice]. *Social Work, 25,* 321–322.

Borden, W. (1992). Narrative perspective in psychosocial intervention following adverse life events. *Social Work, 37,* 135–141.

Burstow, B. (1991). Freirian codifications and social work education. *Journal of Social Work Education, 27,* 196–207.

Chapin, R. K. (1995). Social policy development: The strengths perspective. *Social Work, 40,* 506–514.

Delgado, M. (1996). Community asset assessments by Latino youths. *Social Work in Education, 18,* 169–176.

Gardner, J. W. (1994). *Building community for leadership studies program.* Washington, DC: Independent Sector.

Hardy-Fanta, C. (1986). Social action in Hispanic groups. *Social Work, 31,* 119–123.

Hartman, A. (1990). Many ways of knowing [Editorial]. *Social Work, 35,* 3–4.

Hartman, A., & Laird, J. (1983). *Family-centered social work practice.* New York: Free Press.

Knitzer, J., Steinberg, Z., & Fleish, B. (1990). *At the schoolhouse door.* New York: Bank Street College of Education.

Saleebey, D. (1994). Culture, theory, and narrative: The intersection of meanings in practice. *Social Work, 39,* 351–359.

Sands, R. G., & Nuccio, S. (1992). Postmodern feminist theory and social work. *Social Work, 37,* 489–493.

Sluzki, C. E. (1992). Transformations: A blueprint for narrative changes in therapy. *Family Process, 31,* 217–230.

Solomon, B. (1987). *Empowerment: Social work in oppressed communities.* New York: Columbia University Press.

Wallerstein, N., & Bernstein, E. (1988). Empowerment education: Freire's ideas adapted to health education. *Health Education Quarterly, 15,* 379–394.

Weil, M. O. (1996). Community building: Building community practice. *Social Work, 41,* 481–500.

Wyers, N. L. (1991). Policy-practice in social work: Models and issues. *Journal of Social Work Education, 27,* 241–250.

This chapter was originally published in the April 1997 issue of Social Work in Education, *vol. 19, pp. 67–71.*

25 School-Linked Services in Action: Results of an Implementation Project

Terry Saunders Lane

Since the mid-1980s, interest has re-emerged in the integration of human services with education, specifically in linkages between social work services and schools. This theme has been one goal in numerous school reform efforts. It has been argued that if children and families are overwhelmed with social and economic difficulties, the task of learning becomes difficult. Because the schools reach every child and family, integration of services with schools can help to enhance educational performance. School-linked services are valued as a means to provide direct services to children and families; connect children and families with community services; coordinate services within schools; and facilitate communication among teachers, children, and families (Allen-Meares, 1996; Allen-Meares, Washington, & Welch, 1986; Comer, 1980; Levy & Shepardson, 1992; MacDowell, 1989, cited in Bailey 1992).

Great hopes and promises have accompanied efforts to implement school-linked services. Research about interventions with youths at risk of "rotten outcomes," such as school failure, early childbearing, illiteracy, criminal behavior, and lack of job skills, has shown that successful programs are comprehensive, flexible, and have multiple components that link educational enrichment with social supports (Schorr, 1989). However, although experts have called for increased collaboration among social services providers, families, and educators, the actual experiences of such efforts are not widely understood (Davies, Burch, & Palanki, 1993; Quaranta, Weiner, Robison, & Tainsh, 1992).

This chapter documents the experiences of one effort to apply the theories and experiences of past school-linked services programs to a school reform partnership between a university and a public school system. It describes the major factors that contributed to the success of the project, the techniques for reducing and avoiding expected barriers, and the new lessons that emerged over a seven-year period. For the purposes of this chapter, *school-linked services* include the following dimensions: "(a) services are provided to children and their families through a collaboration among schools, health care providers, and social service agencies; (b) the schools are among the central participants in planning and governing the collaborative effort; and (c) the services are provided at, or are coordinated by, personnel located at the school or a site near the school" (Larson, Gomby, Shiono, Lewit, & Behrman, 1992).

UNIVERSITY/PUBLIC SCHOOL PARTNERSHIP

Background

The University/Public School Partnership began in 1989 as a unique arrangement in which the university manages the public school system through a 10-year contract. A management team from the university handles all the functions of the locally elected policy-making body, the School Committee, although the committee retains the power to cancel the contract with the university. The city government is expected to maintain the base budget for the school system, and the university offers expertise from among its faculty, staff, and students and raises new funds from government, corporate, and foundation sources.

This arrangement is in place in a small city of 30,000 people, with a school population of about 4,000 in seven schools (one high school, one middle school, four elementary schools, and one preschool). The community is adjacent to a large urban area, and it has long been a destination for new immigrants in the United States. During the past two decades, the area increasingly has become the home of Latin American, Puerto Rican, and Southeast Asian families. It is one of most economically impoverished cities in the state.

At the beginning of the partnership, the university's School of Social Work (SSW) was asked to help the school system strengthen its organizational capacity to help children function more effectively in academic settings. At that time, there were limited social services programs and few formally trained human services providers in the schools. The school system employed only one master's-level human services worker and no master's-level social workers. None of the staff were bilingual or bicultural, although almost two-thirds of the school population was of Latino background. Linkages to community-based services also were weak. The goal was to craft a program that would fit the administrative and financial requirements of the school system and to establish an effective social services unit with stronger linkages to community-based services within the time frame of the partnership.

By 1996 the school system had hired seven full-time master's-level and one bachelor's-level social services staff members who were bilingual or bicultural to provide services in all of the schools. The school system also created a position for a director of outreach services to supervise the human services staff and provide leadership to the service program throughout the school system. All of the schools had begun to develop mechanisms for tapping and coordinating community-based services, such as coordinating committees, contracting for service delivery, and placing community agency staff in the school buildings. As the public school system institutionalized the service program, the SSW continued its collaboration with the school system through internships for master's-level social work students throughout the schools. The SSW therefore achieved its major objectives and accomplished its task two years before the deadline.

Five essential factors contributed to the success of this organizational development effort: (1) development of a specific action agenda in response to ongoing assessments of the strengths and needs of the school system and community services agencies; (2) availability of skilled, ethnically diverse social services personnel who provided consistent leadership and clinical services throughout the project; (3) availability of new funding and contributed resources, which supported program development and implementation; (4) understanding the political context of school-linked services; and (5) a long-term commitment to implementation of school-linked services from within the SSW and the school system.

Action Agenda and Assessment

As the project got underway in 1989, the planners turned to the literature for advice about how to begin. The usefulness of needs and assets assessments was promoted; specifically, the project should fit the special interests and require-ments of each community and school. It should use natural strengths of the setting while addressing the needs articulated by local actors from the commu-nity (Delgado, 1996; Levy & Shepardson, 1992; Mintzies, 1993). The project also should keep in mind recognized standards of "good" practice (NASW, 1992).

With this guidance in mind, two staff members from the SSW learned through a series of interviews that a small, dedicated human services staff worked in the school system and that a wide array of service agencies was in place in the com-munity. Representatives from several agencies wanted to strengthen service delivery in the schools. Coordination and utilization of community programs in the schools needed improvement. This assessment helped articulate the over-all goal of the SSW strategy: to demonstrate the ways in which a school system can use social services to promote and enhance the education of children. The services should help create a climate in which children can feel safe and ready to learn and in which they can seek help with problems that interfere with learning. The services also should facilitate connections between schools and families.

Specific objectives emerged through regular discussions with the major par-ticipants (principals, teachers, children, and families). The priorities shifted throughout the partnership as problems were tackled and new issues emerged. The objectives were to

- strengthen the social services capacity of the school system by providing high-quality, culturally appropriate services, without financial or adminis-trative barriers
- improve access to community services for children and families through better coordination of on-site services and referrals for off-site service
- strengthen knowledge and skills of teachers and administrators regarding child and adolescent development issues in the context of various cultures
- reduce verbal and physical conflicts in the high school, so that all students can focus on learning activities
- provide opportunities for SSW students to participate in program devel-opment and service delivery activities through field work internships.

Although the assessment process was useful for identifying areas of program focus, it was not adequate to help the partnership participants specify an action agenda. The literature suggested that many problems could be tackled through school-linked services—for example, high dropout rates and low school attendance (Dupper, 1993), violence in schools (Schmitz, 1994), poor coordination of services (Buetens & Kern, 1991), prevention of teenage pregnancy (Weatherley & Semke, 1991), poor access to physical and mental health care (Balassone, Bell, & Peterfreund, 1991), and lack of parent involvement (Comer, 1980; Davies et al., 1993). All of these problems were present in the school system when the partnership began.

Two risks were always present. First was the temptation to tackle as many problems as possible, thereby reducing significant progress in any one area. Second, the development of "special projects" could isolate the social services staff from the mainstream activities of the school and create a separate unit, which would disappear once program-based funding had ended (Gardner, 1992). Therefore, the ongoing challenge was to select appropriate and specific programs that were important to the core staff of the school (principals, assistant principals, and teachers), so that progress could be achieved and then used to provide ongoing rationales for systemic change.

An implementation model emerged that allowed for selection of strategic activities that responded to the top priorities of the school system. The model included mechanisms for the program to be adapted over time. The program phases were start-up and demonstration, assessment and adaptation, and expansion.

Start-up and Demonstration—Years 1 and 2. The SSW hired a full-time social worker who was bilingual in English and Spanish. She began her work in the high school because of the need for improved services to Latino adolescents. However, the principal was not convinced that the addition of a social workers to the school would be helpful. She indicated that the value of social services in the school must become evident. Nevertheless, the principal asked for assistance to address an increasing number of fights and arguments, especially among the Latino high school girls. The program's focus on the immediate crisis included individual meetings with each student involved in a fight to explore immediate reasons for the conflict, as well as health, emotional, or family problems that might have contributed to the situation; joint meetings with all participants; meetings with parents; preparation of contracts specifying the expectations of the future behavior of participating students; referrals for additional health or social services, if appropriate; and follow-up sessions with each student to track progress on the behavioral contract, school performance, and so forth. This program complemented other activities: the presence of security officers in the halls and strengthened disciplinary actions, such as in-school suspensions administered by the assistant principals. The social worker not only was a key link to the Latino students and families, but she also advocated for and explained their concerns to school personnel.

The incidence of conflicts declined dramatically, and teachers and students began to contact the social services staff with information about rumors of upcoming arguments so that preventive efforts could be used. The success of this work helped persuade school personnel that social services could address problems that interfered with the functioning of the school and could provide valuable assistance to students. It also persuaded students that the social worker could be helpful to them.

Assessment and Adaptation—Years 3 and 4. After the initial program year, the social worker discussed the results of her efforts with other high school personnel, students, and the staff at the superintendent's office. Together they considered options for meeting new requests for assistance and explored ways to integrate violence prevention activities into a more comprehensive service program. They selected an on-site model, with the recognition that there were advantages and disadvantages to the approach. On the one hand, integration of service staff into the daily life of schools can enhance the acceptance and use of school-linked services by school officials and personnel. However, exclusive control by school authorities may lead to decision making that discourages participation by a wide range of community actors, and it may undermine efforts to try unconventional program strategies or to use programs provided in locations other than school buildings (Chaskin & Richman, 1992; Levy & Shepardson, 1992).

In this situation the on-site strategy seemed appropriate, because programs in community agencies often had lengthy waiting lists or presented barriers such as distance and cost. Some students refused to go elsewhere for services but agreed to meet with the school-based social worker because she was familiar to them, spoke their native language, and knew their families and community. In addition, it seemed that a high-quality social services capability was important within the school system, so that outside services could be effectively tapped and coordinated.

The core of the program was counseling services for individual children and families by social workers who were housed at the schools. Teachers and administrators referred students with behavior and attendance problems to the social work staff and interns. In addition, students could seek assistance on their own. Common were family problems, difficulties with friends, isolation, or cultural misunderstandings with other students or teachers. Most cases required two or three meetings with the student and parents. In the few cases in which students continued to have difficulty at school, the social work team provided ongoing service.

Over a five-year period, the number of counseling visits increased fourfold for several reasons. First, the number of staff available to provide services increased, and the number of graduate MSW students assigned to the program for field placements increased. Second, the referral process in the school was strengthened. Teachers and administrators gained familiarity with the capabilities of the team and also noticed that desirable outcomes were being achieved. Students sought assistance on their own when their peers reported that the social worker was a good resource for them. Serious incidents of violence in the high school became more infrequent when the violence intervention and prevention program was implemented. The focus of the social services staff on addressing family and student problems that contributed to school dropout and poor school attendance complemented the efforts of other administrators and teachers. Between 1989 and 1996 the annual dropout rate fell in the high school from 20 percent to

8 percent. Thus, educators began to seek assistance for students more quickly and frequently.

The on-site model did not preclude linkages to community-based services, however. Whenever possible the team made referrals for long-term services to community agencies, and the social work staff worked closely with a local hospital, which opened an on-site clinic at the high school. To strengthen program development and service coordination throughout the school system, several committees were developed. For example, a "student support team" included all school personnel and community agency staff (about 15 people) who provided health and human services to high school students. The team met weekly to develop and coordinate service plans for high-risk students, discuss difficult cases, prepare treatment plans that included school and community resources, and plan activities to fill service gaps. The group discussed issues of common concern, such as client confidentiality, crisis intervention procedures, and the filing of child abuse and neglect reports. Occasionally, members of the team provided in-service training to each other, based on individual areas of expertise.

Another component of the program was the organization of groups for students, widely noted for their effectiveness in school settings (Franklin & Streeter, 1991; LeCroy, 1982; Levinsky & McAleer, 1994), which provided opportunities for activities as well as time for discussion of topics of interest and concern to students. The major group work projects included socialization and life skills. At the high school these groups engaged in time-limited discussions about issues such as friendships and dating, dealing with conflict, alcohol and drug abuse, family relationships, and adjusting after arriving from another country. Programs included the Violence Prevention Group, the Newcomers Group, the Substance Abuse Prevention Group, and the African American Club. Among younger students, programs focused on socialization skills and the reduction of behavior problems and were organized and conducted by MSW students with guidance from the SSW social worker and faculty consultants.

Expansion—Years 5, 6, and 7. As the program developed, outcomes of importance to the schools occurred, (for example, violence was reduced, the dropout rate was reduced, and individual students with discipline and attendance problems received assistance). Teachers and administrators throughout the school system requested assignment of permanent staff and social work interns to their individual schools. The superintendent supported these requests and approved the creation of seven new social work positions and a position for a director of the entire program. In spite of this success, however, some challenges remained. The SSW social worker had to take on the tasks of hiring and supervision in addition to program development and implementation. These constantly escalating demands were often difficult to balance.

Skilled Leadership

Both the community assessment process and the literature indicated that the planning and implementation of the program should be carried out by skilled staff (Ingram, Bloomberg, & Seppanen, 1996; Monkman, 1982). In addition, strong leadership is considered essential (U.S. General Accounting Office, 1993).

To teachers and administrators in this school system, the first priority was to add new social services staff with clinical skills in services for adolescents. Also needed were bilingual personnel to better serve students of Spanish-speaking backgrounds. Therefore, the SSW hired a licensed clinical social worker who was bilingual and had experience in service to Latino families and the treatment of substance abuse. She was present in the school system four days per week, taught courses in the SSW, and developed and supervised a field unit of graduate MSW students. In this "staff model," because she had a regular presence in the school system, she could develop day-to-day relationships with school and community staff, as well as with children and families.

It was expected that a "consultant model" would not be successful in this particular situation, because consultants visiting periodically could not demonstrate how an integrated service program could function on a daily basis (Gardner, 1992). However, the staff social worker invited consultants from the SSW to carry out specific assignments, such as training workshops or assistance with writing grant proposals. She was careful to ensure that these tasks fit into the overall goals of the social services program.

The staff model also was helpful for overcoming distrust of and competition with outsiders. These problems often occur when school reform and operational changes begin to take place (Gardner, 1992; Mintzies, 1993). With the introduction of a new policy-making body (the "management team") from the university, teachers and administrators feared that they would be reassigned to different positions or, even worse, lose their jobs. They expected that the university's experts might tell them how to organize and deliver human services without asking for their recommendations. Because the school system had never hired social workers, they did not know what such individuals could do. They worried that social services staff would "take the children away from the classroom for counseling" without addressing matters of educational importance, such as poor attendance, inappropriate classroom behavior, or poor academic performance.

Over time, the social worker was able to deal with each of these barriers. Because the social worker was at the schools almost every day, she could develop relationships that supported collaborative work, and she could quickly adapt the social services program to effectively address the concerns and priorities of the school system. In addition, her consistent presence over a period of years deflected the expectation that the outsiders from the university would disappear in a short time.

Funding and Resources

For school-linked services to be successful, adequate funding is needed. If efforts are promoted within a context of declining or stagnant resources, competition and turf battles can make implementation impossible. Other problems can emerge if funding is fragmented and available only for categorical programs. New services can be "added on" without any coherent connection to an overall strategy of providing coordinated services and education for all children (Farrow & Joe, 1992). Projects also can begin in a climate of suspicion that the reformers will be present only for a short term and will disappear as their funding fades (Larson et al., 1992).

For this partnership the salary of the social worker was supported initially by the university as well as by foundation grants. Therefore, the social worker represented new resources brought into the school system, and her presence did not require the elimination of another job. Several years into the partnership, state-level education reform legislation passed, and implementation brought new state funds to the poorest local school districts. With this infusion, some new positions could be created. Thus, when the superintendent decided to institutionalize the school-linked services program by creating new positions for professional-level human services staff, consolidation of other positions was not necessary.

Political Context

Although program, staffing, and funding are important features of the school-linked services, these efforts also must consider the complexities of their political and organizational environments. The technical "nuts-and-bolts" components must fit into and respond to the life cycle, the insecurities, and the leadership and power dynamics of the organization (Gardner, 1992). In the school setting, the dominant profession is that of the educator, and the primary goals of the school are educational. Thus, the social worker must be aware of the sources of power in the school system, weigh alternative strategies to avoid disruptive power struggles, and determine how to gain power to achieve service goals on behalf of students and their families. Typically, school principals and the senior staff in the superintendent's office have major decision-making responsibilities about service priorities and the ways in which integration of services with education can proceed (Allen-Meares, 1993; Lee, 1983). Advocacy, negotiation, and political action within the school system are components of the task of implementation of school-linked services: "educating those in charge of school social work services of their breadth and effectiveness was fundamental to the expansion of such services and equally important to the development of new roles for service providers" (Allen-Meares, 1993, p. 4).

Long-Term Commitment

The development and implementation of school-linked services requires intensive and long-term efforts and cannot succeed without persistence and flexibility. This dimension is often underestimated or overlooked by those who begin the task of linking services and schools (Gaston & Brown, 1995). In the partnership described here, the school personnel with power wanted the social services program to proceed, for they argued that social services could contribute to the goals of the school system. The major champions of this position were the superintendent and the principals and assistant principals at several schools. The recognition, status, and power accorded to social services providers therefore came from members of the school system's power structure. Thus, the social worker had to build alliances with key actors in the school system and continually create a positive image of the abilities and contributions of the human services providers.

However, because the status of the social services program was dependent on others in the school system, it was undermined when personnel turnover took place. The school system had four superintendents, three high school principals, and eight assistant high school principals in seven years. With every change came redefined goals, objectives, and programming. Because the SSW had made a commitment to continue with the partnership, these shifts were handled as the inevitable challenges of a long-term process. Consistent delivery of high-quality service, flexible programming, and continuous, respectful dialogue with actors in the school system helped overcome barriers along the way.

DISCUSSION AND CONCLUSION

The experiences of this partnership suggest some lessons and raise additional questions for others struggling with planning and implementing school-linked services. One implication is that multiple factors were necessary for the program to proceed to the point at which services were linked permanently. In the early stages, the educators in the school system distrusted the potential of competition from the social services providers and also perceived the social services initiatives as ancillary to the main business of the school system—just another set of projects that could easily disappear. In this case, the intertwined dynamics of effective programming, skilled and consistent staffing, adequate funding, and political support seemed to be connected to the long-term success of establishing an in-house professional social work program with strong linkages to the educational programs. However, the results came only after years of persistence.

Another implication is that the efforts to integrate services with schools required considerable time and energy along with a wide range of clinical, political, administrative, and leadership skills. The demands for such breadth of expertise can be overwhelming for those thrust into leadership roles. In this partnership, the social worker from the SSW could turn to her colleagues at the university for expertise, advice, and support as she developed the program. This connection meant that she did not have to handle all of the demands alone. For example, she could arrange for training and consultation for teachers and administrators on various topics. In addition, this role allowed her to be an "outsider within," and she had the advantages of some intimacy and distance at the same time (Collins, 1991; Riessman, 1995). That is, she was part of the day-to-day world of the school system, but she also could rely on her connections to the university to help her reflect on the situation, explore her frustrations, and develop strategies for how to proceed at crucial decision points.

The tentative conclusions suggested by the results of this partnership need to be compared to results in other communities that are experimenting with school-linked services. For example, it is not clear from recent evaluations whether there are common definitions of success across school-linked service efforts. In addition, limited evidence exists to indicate that what is tried is effective. It also is not clear whether the same essential factors are always present in successful programs or whether common factors are absent in unsuccessful efforts.

REFERENCES

Allen-Meares, P. (1993). Pull and push: Clinical or macro interventions in schools [Editorial]. *Social Work in Education, 15,* 3–5.

Allen-Meares, P. (1996). Social work services in schools: A look at yesteryear and the future. *Social Work in Education, 18,* 202–208.

Allen-Meares, P., Washington, R. O., & Welsh, B. L. (1986). The design of social work services. In *Social work services in schools* (pp. 211–231). Englewood Cliffs, NJ: Prentice Hall.

Bailey, D. (1992). Organizational change in a public school system: The synergism of two approaches. *Social Work in Education, 14,* 94–105.

Balassone, M. L., Bell, M., & Peterfreund, N. (1991). School-based clinics: An update for social workers. *Social Work in Education, 13,* 162–175.

Buetens, K. K., & Kern, T. L. (1991). Comprehensive systems collaboration: A model for coordinating services for alcohol- and drug-affected students. *Social Work in Education, 13,* 105–117.

Chaskin, R. J., & Richman, H. A. (1992). Concerns about school-linked services: Institution-based versus community-based models. *Future of Children, School-Linked Services, 2*(1), 107–117.

Collins, P. H. (1991). *Black feminist thought: Knowledge, consciousness, and the politics of empowerment.* Boston: Routledge.

Comer, J. (1980). *School power: Implications of an intervention project.* New York: Free Press.

Davies, D., Burch, P., & Palanki, A. (1993). *Fitting policy to practice: Delivering comprehensive services through collaboration and family empowerment.* Boston: Boston University, Center on Families, Communities, Schools and Children's Learning.

Delgado, M. (1996). Community asset assessments by Latino youths. *Social Work in Education, 18,* 169–178.

Dupper, D. R. (1993). Preventing school dropouts: Guidelines for school social work practice. *Social Work in Education, 15,* 141–149.

Farrow, F., & Joe, T. (1992). Financing school-linked, integrated services. *Future of Children, School-Linked Services, 2*(1), 56–67.

Franklin, C., & Streeter, C. L. (1991). Evidence for the effectiveness of social work with high school dropout youths. *Social Work in Education, 13,* 307–327.

Gardner, S. L. (1992). Key issues in developing school-linked, integrated services. *Future of Children, School-Linked Services, 2*(1), 85–94.

Gaston, M., & Brown, S. (1995). *School restructuring and school-linked services: Working together for students and families.* San Francisco: Stuart Foundation.

Ingram, D., Bloomberg, L., & Seppanen, P. (1996). *Collaborative initiatives to develop integrated services for children and families: A review of literature.* Minneapolis: University of Minnesota, Center for Applied Research and Educational Improvement.

Larson, C. S., Gomby, D. S., Shiono, P. H., Lewit, E. M., & Behrman, R. E. (1992). Analysis. *Future of Children, School-Linked Services, 2*(1), 6–18.

LeCroy, C. W. (1982). Teaching social skills to children in the schools. In R. T. Constable & J. P. Flynn (Eds.), *School social work: Practice and research perspectives* (pp. 29–37). Homewood, IL: Dorsey Press.

Lee, L. J. (1983). The social worker in the political environment of a school system. *Social Work, 28,* 302–307.

Levinsky, L., & McAleer, K. (1994). Listen to us! Young adolescents in urban schools. In A. Gitterman & L. Shulman (Eds.), *Mutual aid groups: Vulnerable populations and the life cycle* (pp. 151–162). New York: Columbia University Press.

Levy, J. E., & Shepardson, W. (1992). A look at current school-linked service efforts. *Future of Children, School-Linked Services, 2*(1), 44–55.

Mintzies, P. M. (1993). The continuing dilemma: Finding a place for the social work profession in the schools. *Social Work in Education, 15,* 67–69.

Monkman, M. M. (1982). The contribution of the social worker to the public schools. In R. T. Constable & J. P. Flynn (Eds.), *School social work: Practice and research perspectives* (pp. 13–28). Homewood, IL: Dorsey Press.

National Association of Social Workers. (1992). *NASW standards for school social work services.* Washington, DC: Author.

Quaranta, M. A., Weiner, M., Robison, E., & Tainsh, P. (1992). *Collaboration for social support of children and families in the public schools.* New York: Fordham University.

Riessman, C. K. (1995). Locating the outsider within: Studying childless women in India. *Reflections, 1*(3), 5–14.

Schmitz, R. (1994). Teaching students to manage their conflicts [Practice Highlights]. *Social Work in Education, 16,* 125–128.

Schorr, L. B. (1989). *Within our reach: Breaking the cycle of disadvantage.* New York: Anchor Books.

U.S. General Accounting Office. (1993). *School-linked human services: A comprehensive strategy for aiding students at risk of school failure* (Report to the Chairman, Committee on Labor and Human Resources, U.S. Senate, GAO/HRD-94-21). Washington, DC: Author.

Weatherley, R. A., & Semke, J. I. (1991). What chance for school-based health clinics? Lessons from the field. *Social Work in Education, 13,* 151–161.

This chapter was originally published in the January 1998 issue of Social Work in Education, *vol. 20, pp. 37–47.*

26 Portrait of a School-Based Health Center: An Ecosystemic Perspective

Linwood H. Cousins, Kai Jackson, and Michael Till

Human services providers are increasingly taking advantage of opportunities to provide an array of nonacademic services to children and families under the rubric of school-based, full-service, or school-linked human services (Dryfoos, 1994; Levy & Shepardson, 1992; Newton-Logsdon & Armstrong, 1993; Pennekamp, 1992). Along with the dividend of improved outcomes in such areas as medical, psychological, and social functioning, many school-based human services programs provide the additional benefit of improved academic performance. Yet these programs face challenges that are most readily exposed by an examination of both the foundation on which they are built and the daily activities of professionals such as social workers who are central to the delivery of services.

This chapter presents a portrait of the Edison School-Based Health Center (ESBHC) in Kalamazoo, Michigan, as an example of an effective and viable school-based service provider. By presenting an administrative profile of the program and of the activities of a social worker who is a primary service provider, this chapter shows how defining health services in a political, cultural, psychological, and social context can improve the effectiveness of school-based medical services. The ESBHC defines health services in this way to fit more compatibly with the needs and vision of the community it serves. Consequently, the center has grounded itself in an ecosystemic perspective, a core element in community-based social work practice (Adams & Nelson, 1995; Fine & Carlson, 1992; Germain & Gitterman, 1980; Longres, 1995).

ECOSYSTEMIC RATIONALE

Levy and Shepardson (1992) suggested that the most important and obvious reason for school-linked services "is that the school is where children can be found and, in fact, is the only institution with which virtually every child and family has contact" (p. 46). As such, schools cannot avoid interfacing with social, psychological, economic, and even political problems that children experience in their families and communities (Aponte, 1994; Dryfoos, 1993, 1994; Fine & Carlson, 1992; Lee, 1983). Thus, schools are cultural sites in which school personnel and students engage in carving out socialization norms and values, particularly in terms of competing definitions of problems and adequate social functioning (Allen-Meares, 1993; Giroux, 1992; Giroux & Simon, 1989; Spindler & Spindler, 1994). These actions reflect also the interests of competing segments in community life and society at large (Longres, 1995; Moriarty & McDonald, 1991; Pinderhughes, 1989; Wall, 1996). Competing interests can undermine school-based collaborations, yet also provide fertile ground for the kind of collaborations that are familiar to social workers and necessary to their overall mission (Allen-Meares, Washington, & Welsh, 1996; Duttweiler, 1995; Hepworth & Larsen, 1993; Reid & Popple, 1992).

The ecosystemic rationale that drives community-based services in general drives school-based human services as well: namely, provision of services where clients live, taking into account the complex, but often ignored, human ecology of their neighborhoods and communities (Adams & Nelson, 1995; Fisher, 1994). The ecosystemic perspective suggests a multifaceted approach to both the interpretation of social functioning and the delivery of human services in institutions such as schools (Allen-Meares et al., 1996; Fine & Carlson, 1992; Longres, 1995). The ESBHC provides an important example of the application of the ecosystemic perspective to the delivery of school-based health services in a community setting characterized by an increasingly diverse yet racially and economically divided citizenry.

DEVELOPMENT OF THE ESBHC

Background

A headline in the *Kalamazoo [Michigan] Gazette* on February 25, 1996, broke the story to an unsuspecting community in the following manner: "Flunked!" (Walters, 1996a, p. 1). The head caption of one of 12 later, related articles read, "Where Are the Parents?" (Walters, 1996b, p. 7). The stories reported that the fourth-grade students at Edison Elementary School had failed the Michigan Education Assessment Performance Test (MEAP).

The articles also revealed that in December 1994 the State Board of Education, in response to a gubernatorial crackdown on academic outcomes, had notified the local school district that Edison Elementary School did not meet accreditation standards. This news was quite a shock and a disappointment to local public school officials, staff, parents, and the community at large, who had not been notified. Edison was one of the first learning institutions in the history of the Kalamazoo public school system to face possible loss of state funding because of inadequate academic performance.

In 1995–96 Edison enrolled between 470 and 518 students ages four to 13 in grades kindergarten through six. The student body was almost equally divided by gender. Ethnic groupings included 250 white students, 225 African Americans, 28 Hispanics, 14 American Indians, and one Asian American. A 1994 survey sponsored by the Kalamazoo Integrated Service Alliance (KISA) found that a disproportionate number of Edison students experienced behavior problems, high absenteeism, psychological problems, inconsistent academic performance, and lack of parental support. Parents' responses in the survey indicated that they lacked access to community resources and transportation and, very interestingly, that they perceived a lack of support services for teachers. KISA comprised focus and problem-solving groups consisting of invited and self-selected human services providers and consumers in the local community, all of whom shared a concern about the multifaceted welfare of children.

Edison serves one of the lowest socioeconomic areas in the county (Kalamazoo Public Schools, Office of Demographics, 1996). As a result of court-ordered busing in the 1970s, the school also enrolls students from a division of Section 8 housing and a low-income trailer park. Hence, in 1996 two-thirds of Edison neighborhood residents under age 18 lived below the federal poverty level; the median annual household income was approximately $11,000, or 30 percent below the rest of the city of Kalamazoo; and about 91 percent of the students qualified for free or reduced-price lunches. During the 1995–96 academic year, the school experienced a 96 percent turnover or mobility rate (that is, 279 students transferred out and 253 transferred in, for a total of 532 moves), indicating that as many as half of the students were homeless, lived in overcrowded family situations, or moved two or more times during the school year to a different school and family residence. Edison is also the designated site for local homeless and domestic violence shelters.

Overall, Edison neighborhood residents expressed anger and betrayal at how they were characterized in the *Kalamazoo Gazette* articles. By the time the ESBHC opened for services in April 1995, the school and community had been besieged with additional media images that largely construed the community, the students, and their families as multidysfunctional. The most common concern residents expressed to ESBHC staff was that their children were viewed differently—because of their poverty and academic status—by the school, the state, and the city at large. The ESBHC was forced by these circumstances to define "primary health services" in a manner that considered the needs of the parents and residents and the sociopolitical circumstances of the students and their school.

Origins

The ESBHC is the first of its kind in Kalamazoo County. It evolved in 1994 from a partnership between an existing federally funded family health center in another low-income community in Kalamazoo and the local school district. In the spring of 1994 KISA, a key mobilizer, facilitated collaborative agreements with two hospitals, a local university, a medical teaching facility, and the county health department. Later that year, an outreach committee was formed of 30 neighborhood residents and parents and local human services agency representatives. Key participants from most of these partnerships formed the management team for the ESBHC. By the end of spring 1994, the management team had applied for and was awarded a $270,000 three-year grant under the federal program called Healthy Schools, Healthy Communities.

The original objectives of the ESBHC were
- to increase access to health care for Edison Elementary School students who request services, with an emphasis on dental, medical, mental health, pharmaceutical, and health education services
- to provide access to community primary health resources for Edison students and their families, with case management follow-up

- to create an infrastructure where parents, community members, school staff, and health care providers can work closely together in the design, implementation, governance, and evaluation of the health care programs
- to categorize student health visits, diagnosis, and treatment to determine demographic trends related to causality and treatment and to include a holistic team approach that performs and supports, for example, lead screening and neighborhood efforts to test water in dwellings
- to identify the high-priority health needs of Edison students that can be addressed through health education and promotion.

Organization and Staff

The operational foundation of the ESBHC is anchored in a multidisciplinary team concept (Figure 26.1). Ongoing funding for the ESBHC is derived from an annual federal grant, grants from local community foundations, and reimbursements from Medicaid and private insurers for medical services to students. Selection of staff was based on the desire to have professionals who were competent in working in a culturally and racially diverse pediatric environment. Successful functioning of the center depended on the following additional elements: respect for and understanding of practitioners in different disciplines; commitment to a holistic perspective for service delivery; and willingness and training to identify social, cultural, political, and psychological issues that may underlie medical or health issues and vice versa.

Eighty-eight percent of the 517 students who became registered patients used ESBHC services at least once during the 1995–96 school year. In addition, 30 of 36 Edison preschool students were registered patients. Any Edison student can be referred to the ESBHC by school staff or community human services providers; however, students become registered patients only after a parent or guardian has completed the ESBHC registration process. Medicaid covered the greatest percentage of health care costs for these students (60 percent), followed by commercial insurance (21 percent) and nonidentifiable insurance (19 percent). Typical low-cost services at the ESBHC are health screenings, immunizations, and follow-up visits. The ESBHC offers services that are preventive and that are not available simultaneously in most pediatric and general medical practices: Mental health, dental, and case management services are located under one roof at the ESBHC. These are important factors for a school population designated as medically at risk but underserved.

During the 1995–96 school year, half of the 548 mental health encounters resulted from interoffice referrals that originated in the medical–dental department (Table 26.1). Many children came to the health center with headaches and upset stomachs. Biopsychosocial assessments indicated that these children were experiencing high amounts of stress related to family lifestyles and community life and issues related to separation from parents; transient lifestyles; school performance anxiety; and parent–child, teacher–child, and parent–teacher conflicts.

Turf Issues

School-based health services are often obscure and underrated among subspecialties in public health (Igoe, 1995). No matter how sound an organizational

Figure 26.1
Staffing of the Edison School-Based Health Center

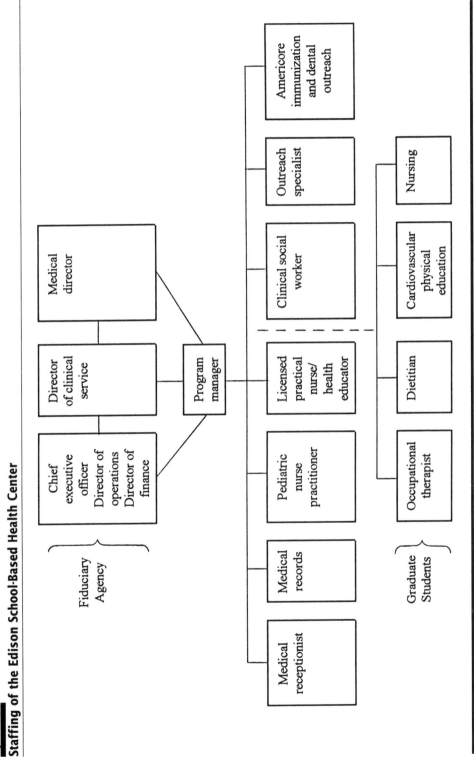

Table 26.1

Visits to the Edison School-Based Health Center: August 1995 to August 1996

Variable	Medical	Dental	Mental Health	Occupational Therapy
Start date	8-25-95	11-1-95	10-30-95	1-6-96
No. of encounters	2,197	664 331 oral exams 321 cleanings 12 restorations	548	171
Top five concerns	Immunizations Ear infections Trauma (lacerations, burns, and sprains) Asthma Head lice	Lack of dental education Failure to brush, floss, and rinse No primary dental visits for over a year Dental disease or cavity pattern high for Latino, African American, and lower socioeconomic white students Shortage of area dentists who will accept Medicaid or new pediatric patients	Stress and anxiety Conflict resolution Parental substance abuse Transitory lifestyle patterns Sexual abuse or child neglect	Not available

structure and plan of execution, interpersonal and organization politics often interrupt effective service delivery. Among other things, such factors set the tone for a health center and color the realities that professionals in school-based health centers must contend with on a daily basis (Dryfoos, 1994). The ESBHC has forged alliances with neighborhood residents and parents, but it still faces the daily challenge of mediating between these community entities and the school, while also attempting to manage its own strained relationship with the school and primary health care providers such as physicians.

Medical Community and Managed Care Issues. Embedded in medical service delivery are issues that affect the overall climate of care. Specifically, the decisions of primary physicians regarding services performed at school-based health centers are frequently driven by type of insurance reimbursement, which in turn creates pressure related to quality assurance standards, strict managed care mandates, and a tradition of practice that is often closed to midlevel medical practitioners. These issues influence the objective quality and composition of health care as well as the subjective climate of a health center.

For example, out of 20 identified primary providers to ESBHC patients, only four consistently authorized the center to bill for treatment. And although managed care mandates push primary physicians to take an active role in directing the overall care of patients, it is generally understood that there are definite financial advantages for doctors rather than allied health practitioners to see assigned patients. Hence, midlevel medical and mental health practitioners are underutilized, although they are essential for reduction of cost and for continuity of the broad range of services needed by Edison children.

School–Center Relations. The key to the overall effectiveness of school-based health centers is their ability to collaborate and compromise within a multidisciplinary, ecosystemic context. That this has to occur in the context of the school system is itself a challenge; although it is true that schools are the crossroads of our communities, school systems often operate in an institutional vacuum (Dryfoos, 1994; Duttweiler, 1995). The desire to retain control over services in schools can result in decisions that appear to be dictatorial and exclusionary in nature. Thus, in the case of the ESBHC, it took an entire year for the fiduciary lead agency of the health center project (the Family Health Center) and school representatives to move beyond the initial planning stage. Other administrative challenges included navigating layers of authority regarding hiring staff with the subjective and objective qualifications necessary to the mission of holistic services; negotiating physical maintenance of the space used by the center; developing contracts between primary partners in the project that did not restrict activities that meet the basic needs of center staff and patients; and sharing power in a way that attended to the sensitivities of parents, with whom the school has had a tradition of strain.

Parents. Many Edison parents were angry about the negative media portrayals of their children, families, and neighborhood. However, many were able to separate their perceptions of the school system and the media from their perception of the ESBHC. From the beginning, parental support for the center has been strong. And the tension that existed among these parents, the school system, and media representatives created a need that could be met by the holistic services of the center.

Parents' approval of the center is also related to direct support offered to them by the center's outreach workers. Center staff often mediate between the school, community, and the service needs of children. Outreach workers and social workers allow parents to vent their frustrations; at the same time, these professionals offer parents personal support and encourage them to follow through in meeting the health needs of their children. This kind of interaction generates mutual respect and support and makes meaningful interpersonal relationships possible between school staff and parents and community residents. In a parent satisfaction survey conducted in March 1996, 70 percent of 232 respondents said the center assisted them in four important areas: (1) The parents missed less time from work because of their children's dental and medical appointments, (2) their children missed less time from class because medical and dental care is on site, (3) their prescription needs were addressed, and (4) Spanish-speaking parents noted that bilingual outreach services assisted them in locating appropriate health services for their children.

The survey also highlighted inconsistent parent attendance at educational events sponsored by the ESBHC. Inconsistent attendance seemed to be related to poor weather and the parents' tendency to get involved in a specific educational activity. (Health education often involves helping parents understand the impact of preventive and follow-up care.) Second, although parental presence was not required during health and dental screenings, many parents expressed the desire to attend anyway, but they had difficulty doing so because of their work schedules. A follow-up survey in the summer of 1996 found that 90 percent of 50 parent respondents were satisfied with the medical and mental health services of the center.

Neighborhood. Health care was an important issue in the Edison neighborhood, and several community activists made it known that they were not interested in a "quick fix." Many neighborhood residents had witnessed the rapid rise and fall of human services programs in their community. In addition, the media's monolithic, low-income portrait of the Edison neighborhood concealed the presence of working- and middle-class families living there. Knowing these factors before the development of the ESBHC, the challenge for the center was not only to transcend the current images of human services provision, but also to consider the interests of working- and middle-class segments of the Edison neighborhood.

The ESBHC successfully marketed their services to all segments of the Edison neighborhood. At first, many parents who had insurance through their place of employment did not register their children with the center. Center team members approached these parents and successfully persuaded them to participate. Many working-class parents with limited health care benefits found the center's services very helpful.

Human Services Agencies. The center was the first of its kind in the county. Although many human services providers were invited and decided to participate in this venture during early developmental stages, interagency cooperation still emerged as an issue. Some factors were duplication of services and therefore strain over a billable client base, authority for overall case management and decision making, and turf issues related to ESBHC professionals who delivered services that extended beyond the traditional definitions of their professional titles. One result is that some community agencies took a cautious approach to the center. And like neighborhood residents, they questioned the center's longevity in light of the limitations of federal funding. Still, several mental health and community social services providers have worked successfully with the center to provide a range of services.

SOCIAL WORK AND THE ESBHC: A CASE STUDY

Social workers and outreach workers are the most contacted center professionals after the pediatric nurse practitioners and physician assistants. Furthermore, social workers occupy a crucial role in mediating interpersonal and social politics that loom large among and between parents and residents, entities in the city at large, and the school system.

The social worker, an employee of the ESBHC rather than Edison, directs the mental health component of the center, coordinates referrals, conducts psychosocial assessments, and provides on-site and home-based counseling. He generally arrives at school 30 to 40 minutes before the start of school breakfast and is available to students who seek the nurturance and compassion that generally accompany his style of interaction with them. Some students are often hurried out of their homes because of their parents' work schedule or because home is just not the most nurturing place for them to be on a particular day. The social worker may be joined by the outreach specialist, who also is an employee of the ESBHC. The outreach specialist works in tandem with the social worker, nurse practitioner, program manager, parents, and school staff to provide a range of support services that complement intervention efforts and goals for a child and his or her family.

Together they walk through the school, encountering along the way the normal routine of interpersonal conflicts among students and between students and teachers or staff. The social worker tries not to intervene without an invitation. Not only does he want to give students a chance to resolve their own conflicts, but he has also learned that other professionals—teachers, staff, and so forth—are very sensitive about being interfered with and made to feel incompetent. Frustration and distrust seem to be the common feelings expressed in the school, where helplessness and hopelessness are all too common.

Background

Jimmy, a student at Edison, is the youngest of two children in his family. His mother is a 32-year-old single parent with a 10th-grade education. She has a history of substance abuse (primarily crack cocaine and alcohol) and has undergone four incomplete attempts to participate in rehabilitation programs. She has numerous health problems, including cervical cancer, depression, and hepatitis C. Her cancer is said to be related to the fact that she was raped and molested at various times during childhood in foster care and in early adulthood. Jimmy's family has been involved with the Department of Social Services (DSS) for at least two years, largely as a result of child abuse and neglect related to his mother's substance abuse problem.

Jimmy's mother is not married to his father. The man Jimmy identifies as his father lives in Kalamazoo; however, according to DSS, Jimmy's biological father is a 65-year-old resident of Chicago. Jimmy's adopted father is also a substance abuser and provides neither sustained nurturance nor support to Jimmy.

Jimmy's sister is 13 years old. Her situation is unstable as well. She voluntarily lives with the family of a police officer who offered his home to Jimmy's sister after interceding in a domestic assault situation at Jimmy's home. The court approved this temporary foster care arrangement.

Jimmy's family has lived in the Edison neighborhood for the past three years, and Jimmy has attended Edison for the past two years. He has been retained in the second grade as a result of attendance problems related to frequent relocations. School attendance problems notwithstanding, Jimmy has proved to be academically talented, which has raised the question of interschool politics regarding his retention in the second grade.

Jimmy's mother has held numerous jobs but has lost them as a result of her substance abuse problems. She is, in one sense, a professional client who is persevering through problems of enormous depth; although she has not been totally successful with the social services system, she has used it to meet some of her needs and those of her children. In another sense, she is a woman who is out of control, desperate, scared, and confused; she has not been able to fully capitalize on her limited opportunities to fully recover from the scars that have afflicted her from childhood to the present. In the meantime, her children share her lifestyle, which includes cycles of economic, psychological, social, and biological dysfunction. To be sure, she loves Jimmy, but she is in the grips of many problems that limit her capacity to adequately care for herself or her children.

Crisis Intervention

The social worker was paged by his program manager, who asked him to meet her in the hall as she escorted Jimmy, who was sobbing and anxious, to the health center. Jimmy had been observed shaking and crying profusely in class. After they arrived at the health center, Jimmy calmed down. During his examination by the physician's assistant, Jimmy began to have an asthma attack. The professionals used relaxation techniques to reduce his anxiety, and his asthma attack subsided. Afterward, Jimmy was cooperative and pleasant in his interactions with those around him. He tried to show humor from time to time, but his affect was too flat to pull it off. Otherwise, he discussed quite a bit of domestic violence in which he was hit as a result of trying to help his mother. He denied sustaining any injuries, and the evaluation revealed none. The events in Jimmy's home life, his behavior at school, and his stress-induced asthma attack led the social worker and outreach specialist to do a home visit; center protocol is to contact family members when a student is seen at the ESBHC.

On arriving at Jimmy's apartment building later that day, they were met by an elderly woman who refused to answer their questions about which apartment Jimmy's mother lived in. She was verbally abusive. (Later they learned that this woman was mentally ill.) They were still able to accompany her to an adjoining apartment, where a man about 35 years old came to the door and said that Jimmy's mother was not home and that he had no idea when she would return. After unsuccessfully trying to engage this man in a conversation, they left and returned to the center.

The social worker and outreach specialist did not consider the outreach effort very successful in terms of their goal of speaking with Jimmy's mother. On the other hand, the visit did provide additional information about the subjective circumstances surrounding Jimmy's home and community life. They also knew that to make an impact in this case, they would have to return to Jimmy's home under more planned circumstances.

Follow-up Activities

In the days following their unsuccessful visit to Jimmy's home, the social worker and outreach specialist continued to collaborate with other service providers involved in this case: the YWCA Domestic Assault Program, who had provided temporary shelter and counseling; DSS, who provided financial support for substance abuse interventions and foster care services; a community substance abuse treatment center; and another social worker, who provided ongoing counseling to the family. The school made adjustments to Jimmy's academic plan in light of his other needs. The ESBHC monitored Jimmy's health and provided case management. During one of Jimmy's routine follow-up visits to the center, staff learned that his nebulizer was no longer at home. Thus, Jimmy's prescribed routine of health care could not be followed and was limited to the treatment he received at the center. Jimmy's mother told staff that the machine had been in the closet a week previously but had since been missing.

These and other issues Jimmy faced figured into a larger scenario of problems affecting Edison students that span the spectrum of care from psychological issues to safety issues to community circumstances to basic health needs. Consequently, interventions are carefully constructed, inclusive of professionals from different disciplines, and considerate of the overarching environment in which services are delivered and in which clients such as Jimmy and his family live. Therefore, the ESBHC embraces a conceptualization of and attitude toward intervention consistent with the broad interdisciplinary and ecosystemic needs of children like Jimmy (Aponte, 1994).

IMPLICATIONS FOR SCHOOL-BASED HEALTH CENTERS

The ESBHC has continued to have a positive impact on the delivery of health and psychosocial services and on the academic performance of Edison students. In April 1996 Edison obtained interim accreditation. Standardized test scores and daily attendance (96 percent) have improved dramatically. The percentage of students scoring satisfactory on the MEAP math test rose from 23.8 in 1994–95 to 42.5 in 1995–96, and the percentage scoring satisfactory in reading rose from 12.5 in 1994–95 to 31.0 in 1995–96. Mutual efforts toward mutual goals and challenges have positively affected Edison, the ESBHC, and the children they serve.

Nonetheless, we do not believe that we have charted any new ground in the ESBHC. The center is in its beginning stages and currently is in the process of evaluating its effectiveness. Still, we believe that our program offers important empirical evidence of the role an ecosystemic perspective can play in school-based health centers. To apply an ecosystemic perspective, such centers must pay attention to the interplay among the political, psychosocial, economic, and cultural elements of the lives of children and must be aware of the ways these elements may undermine or exacerbate health issues, which in turn may undermine or exacerbate psychosocial and educational issues (Dryfoos, 1993, 1994).

Social workers have long advocated for ecosystemic perspectives and need look no further than their own work in school-based health centers as an example of their application. When this kind of practice knowledge is kept from public and professional view, social workers in human services research, education, and practice can easily lose focus on the interdependence and interconnectedness of all of life's processes. Likewise, increasing specialization of knowledge and practice in social work and the human services in general, although necessary, can contribute to a dangerous and artificial isolation of human processes and can lead to myopia in the name of expertise and high-intensity intervention. The need to develop specialized knowledge while remaining in touch with the reality of all life processes is a dilemma and a challenge that social workers must embrace.

Program planners and administrators face a formidable task in educating primary physicians and negotiating with managed care organizations so that school health programs can benefit from social workers' expertise. The outcomes of such tasks directly affect program funding, which affects the quality and range of services a school-based health clinic can provide. To achieve some level of success in this area, we recommend that school-based programs continually collect data that document both the existence of biopsychosocial and ecosystemic problems and the services that are having the greatest impact on them. The ESBHC is currently undergoing such an evaluation.

Maintaining functional relationships among health centers, residents, schools, and other human services providers is also a challenging task. Social workers must identify, assess, and directly confront competing interests by reaching out to all stakeholders and attending to their perceptions, needs, and goals. This task also requires consideration of the political, social, economic, and cultural factors forming the overall ecology in which stakeholders exist.

Finally, we believe that one of the most effective ways of improving the training of professionals who provide services in school-based health centers is to engage in collaborations with colleges, universities, and medical institutions. As one example, the authors—a university professor, a program administrator, and a social work practitioner—collaborated to produce this chapter and present at conferences. Such collaborations can include internships for social workers, physicians, teacher aides and teacher interns, allied health professionals, and the like. These activities address training needs before professionals become engaged in the delivery of services. Collaborative activities combined with ongoing research and evaluation approach an ecosystemic ideal, even in indirect service and knowledge development. At the ESBHC we are evaluating and adjusting our program to improve the effectiveness of services. We continue to learn that the needs of children and the families and communities to which they belong can be the beacon that ultimately guides how services are conceptualized and delivered.

REFERENCES

Adams, P., & Nelson, K. (Eds.). (1995). *Reinventing human services: Community- and family-centered practice.* New York: Aldine de Gruyter.

Allen-Meares, P. (1993). Pull and push: Clinical or macro interventions in schools [Editorial]. *Social Work in Education, 15,* 3–5.

Allen-Meares, P., Washington, R. O., & Welsh, B. L. (1996). *Social work services in schools.* Boston: Allyn & Bacon.

Aponte, H. J. (1994). *Bread and spirit: Therapy with the new poor: Diversity of race, culture, and values.* New York: W. W. Norton.

Dryfoos, J. (1993). Schools as places for health, mental health, and social services. *Teachers College Record, 94,* 540–567.

Dryfoos, J. (1994). *Full-service schools. A revolution in health and social services for children, youth, and families.* San Francisco: Jossey-Bass.

Duttweiler, P. (1995). *Effective strategies for educating students in at-risk situations.* Clemson, SC: Clemson University Press.

Fine, M., & Carlson, C. (1992). *The handbook of family-school intervention: A systems perspective.* Boston: Allyn & Bacon.

Fisher, R. (1994). *Let the people decide.* New York: Twayne.

Germain, C. B., & Gitterman, A. (1980). *The life model of social work practice.* New York: Columbia University Press.

Giroux, H. (1992). *Border crossings: Cultural workers and the politics of education.* New York: Routledge.

Giroux, H., & Simon, R. (1989). *Popular culture, schooling, and everyday life.* Granby, MA: Bergin & Garvey.

Hepworth, D., & Larsen, J. (1993). *Direct social work practice: Theory and skills.* Pacific Grove, CA: Brooks/Cole.

Igoe, J. (1995). Designing the policy environment through understanding. *Nursing Policy Forum, 1,* 1–33.

Kalamazoo Integrated Service Alliance. (1994). *Community needs assessment.* Kalamazoo, MI: Kalamazoo Public Schools Foundation.

Kalamazoo Public Schools, Office of Demographics. (1996). *Edison School information, 1995–96: Report of the Office of Demographics.* Kalamazoo, MI: Author.

Lee, L. (1983). The social worker in the political environment of a school system. *Social Work, 28,* 302–307.

Levy, J., & Shepardson, W. (1992). A look at current school-linked service efforts. *Future of Children, 2,* 44–55.

Longres, J. F. (1995). *Human behavior in the social environment.* Itasca, IL: F. E. Peacock.

Moriarty, A., & McDonald, S. (1991). Theoretical dimensions of school-based mediation. *Social Work in Education, 13,* 176–184.

Newton-Logsdon, G., & Armstrong, M. (1993). School-based mental health services. *Social Work in Education, 15,* 187–191.

Pennekamp, M. (1992). Toward school-linked and school-based human services for children and families. *Social Work in Education, 14,* 125–130.

Pinderhughes, E. (1989). *Understanding race, ethnicity, and power.* New York: Free Press.

Reid, P., & Popple, P. (Eds.). (1992). *The moral purposes of social work: The character and intentions of a profession.* Chicago: Nelson-Hall.

Spindler, G., & Spindler, L. (Eds.). (1994). *Pathways to cultural awareness.* Thousand Oaks, CA: Corwin Press.

Wall, J. C. (1996). Homeless children and their families: Delivery of educational and social services through school systems. *Social Work in Education, 18,* 135–144.

Walters, B. (1996a, February 25). Flunked! *Kalamazoo Gazette,* p. 1.

Walters, B. (1996b, May 26). Where are the parents? *Kalamazoo Gazette,* p. 7.

This chapter was originally published in the July 1997 issue of Social Work in Education, *vol. 19, pp. 189–202.*

Public Schools and the Revitalization of Impoverished Communities: School-Linked, Family Resource Centers

David R. Dupper and John Poertner

Substance abuse, juvenile delinquency, crime and violence, gangs, unsafe sexual practices, teenage pregnancy, single parenthood, limited health care, slum housing, and homelessness are problems frequently experienced by families living in poverty-stricken urban areas. A sense of hopelessness and despair pervades the lives of these poor children and children of color, "who see their parents and loved ones succumb to the pressures of poverty and see for themselves no chance of doing better" (Lerner, 1996, p. 8). In this budget-deficit era it is less likely that income transfer programs are a way out of poverty. Education, which increases a youth's skills and employment opportunities, is an important route out. Unfortunately, schools in impoverished communities often have been part of the problem rather than part of the solution. Too often these schools have become as impoverished as their surrounding communities. According to a recent U.S. General Accounting Office (GAO) report, the most physically decrepit school buildings are located in central cities and have student populations that are predominantly poor children or children of color (Richards, 1996).

Poverty in the inner cities has a profoundly negative impact on children's educational success. Resnick and colleagues (cited in Hendrickson & Omer, 1995) found that more than 70 percent of children born into poverty experienced severe academic problems during their early elementary grades. These problems include poor cognitive development, decreased language ability, inadequate social skills, reduced abstract-reasoning ability, deficient problem-solving skills, reduced self-esteem, shortened attention spans, and little impulse control. Kirst (1991) powerfully portrayed the impact of poverty and its related problems on school performance:

> Johnny can't read because he needs glasses and breakfast and encouragement from his absent father. Maria doesn't pay attention in class because she can't understand English very well, and she's worried about her mother's drinking, and she's tired from trying to sleep in the car. Dick is flunking because he's frequently absent. His mother doesn't get him to school because she's depressed because she lost her job. She missed too much work because she was sick and could not afford medical care. (p. 615)

These problems result in higher-than-average dropout rates (Condition of Education, 1996). It has been estimated that almost half of all students in New

York City, Chicago, and Detroit drop out of school (Schorr, 1989). The personal and social consequences of dropping out are devastating to the individual who leaves school and to society. Compared to high school graduates, school drop-outs are three and a half times more likely to be arrested, six times more likely to be unwed parents, and twice as likely to be unemployed and live in poverty (Schorr, 1989).

Fortunately, there is a growing recognition of the impact of nonacademic factors on children's school performance (Hare, 1995) and that to "rescue children, whole families must [be] rescued along with them" (Hornblower, 1996, p. 37). This is particularly crucial in the severely distressed, impoverished, inner-city communities. A movement is underway in a number of communities across the United States to make schools "hubs" for community development. A number of communities are designing programs that link many services to schools through the establishment of school-linked, family resource centers. This chapter discusses the rationale behind this movement, describes several exemplary programs already developed, and focuses on the promise the movement holds for being a major social work strategy for revitalizing impoverished communities.

SCHOOL-LINKED, FAMILY RESOURCE CENTER MOVEMENT

The school-linked, family resource center movement is being driven largely by the seemingly intractable problems with the current network of social services for children and families. The current social services system has been characterized as disempowering, fragmenting, and confusing for families (Lerner, 1996). Far too many high-risk children and families, particularly in the inner cities, lack access to needed services. Too many of these children slip through the cracks in the social services system and receive little or no assistance. Even when they have access to services, services are fragmented and often fail to be culturally relevant (Pennekamp, 1992). The current social services system is generally composed of a series of targeted programs with overlapping or conflicting eligibility requirements and a complicated web of rules and regulations overseen by a bewildering array of seemingly autonomous bureaucracies (Koppich & Kirst, 1993).

Chang (1993) described the unique problems experienced by low-income parents, parents of color, and recent immigrants and the challenges these problems pose for social workers and other service providers in impoverished communities:

> Low-income and minority parents have traditionally found it extremely difficult to obtain needed services and supports. Services are often offered at inconvenient times or inaccessible locations. Many families do not even realize that services are available or are confused by the fragmented service delivery system. Maneuvering through this complex system can be even more difficult for families who are new to the United States and do not speak English fluently, particularly if their immigration status means that they are eligible for only some services. . . . This nation's demographic shifts pose tremendous challenges for service providers unaccustomed to this new client population. (pp. 212–213)

A common goal of the movement is for all children in the community to grow and develop in a safe family home, acquire essential education in a normal school setting, and become productive members of the community. To achieve these goals, children must receive the full range of services they need to be ready to learn and be successful in school, and poor parents and parents of color must receive the assistance they need to support their child's education, health, growth, and development. The essence of a family resource center is the pursuit of these common goals with shared resources through the collaboration of schools and human services agencies. The school provides a logical organizational setting for providing access to high-risk families and children and has the potential of becoming a "community hub" (Dryfoos, 1996) and a "welcome light" (Coltoff, 1996). School-linked, family resource centers cannot be peripheral to the academic mission of schools but rather must be an essential component of the school and the community. These programs all involve "concentrated efforts to integrate services with school, and heavy involvement with the parents and the community" (Dryfoos, 1996, p. 13).

Adler (1994) described a number of characteristics common to the school-linked, family resource center movement:

- Families and children can access all services at a center located at a school or other facility in their neighborhood.
- A wide variety of services is available such as health, mental health, recreation, job development, child development and care, education, and housing.
- Service providers work collaboratively to meet all of the needs of children and their families in a holistic way.
- Services stress community development and family support that prevents problems rather than being crisis driven.
- Both families and the frontline workers who provide direct services are empowered through their participation in planning to meet the needs of the community.
- There is more flexibility in how categorical funding can be used or, ideally, new funding streams are created to support collaborative services on an ongoing basis.
- Professionals who work in community and family services will need training and preparation to develop new skills.
- Systemwide changes will be necessary to achieve these goals.

EXEMPLARY PROGRAMS

A rich array of school-linked, family resource centers is evolving across communities, as is necessary for any successful community development model. Each program is unique in its configuration, emerging from the needs of children and families and building on the strengths of the particular community to meet those needs (Dryfoos, 1996). Many programs reach out to those at greatest risk and mobilize resources to reduce and prevent school dropout, substance abuse, juvenile delinquency, and teenage pregnancy. Outcomes of the more comprehensive programs are encouraging. For example, attendance and graduation rates are significantly higher than in comparable schools; reading and math scores have shown some improvement; and "students are eager to come to schools that are stimulating, nurturing, and respectful of cultural values" (Dryfoos, 1996, p. 14).

The following descriptions of several exemplary programs reflect the various forms that these centers can assume in communities with a high percentage of poor children and children and families of color.

St. Louis

The Walbridge Caring Communities program in St. Louis is based in an inner-city school and a nearby church. The program expands the use of school buildings to create opportunities for life-long learning and to incorporate Afrocentric culture. Family crisis intervention, substance abuse counseling, afterschool tutoring and recreational activities, and other family services are available. The goals of the program are to keep children in school, in their families, and out of the juvenile justice system. A school facilitator helps families navigate the services available to them, and all providers collaborate in the scheduling and day-to-day program operation. An advisory panel and an interagency team facilitate the division of funds pooled from four state agencies and oversee the day-to-day operation of the program. Teachers serve as the frontline staff in identifying children and their families who may be in need of services using a set of 14 criteria to determine risk status (U.S. Department of Education, 1994; Zalenski, 1994).

New York City

The Children's Aid Society, a private, nonprofit organization, formed a partnership with a middle school (I.S. 218) in New York City to provide extended day and Saturday services at the school. A decision-making team of administrators, teachers, and parents has developed a number of academic and human services programs that include reading and math tutoring for new immigrants in their native language; a health clinic, including mental health consultation; and a resource center for parents (U.S. Department of Education, 1994).

Bowling Green, Kentucky

James P. Comer, a Yale professor and psychiatrist, has over the past three decades "helped to convert 600 mostly inner-city schools to a cooperative management in which parents, teachers, and mental health counselors jointly decide policy and focus on building close-knit relationships with children" (Hornblower, 1996, p. 37). Comer most recently collaborated with Edward Zigler, another Yale professor and one of the founders of Head Start, to implement "Cozi" schools in several communities. One of the most successful Cozi schools is located in Bowling Green, Kentucky, a community that is overwhelmingly African American and low income.

One of the keys to success in Bowling Green was parent involvement, which was accomplished by school representatives visiting the parents' homes and asking them what they needed. As a result of this parental feedback, Bowling Green now offers adult education courses and exercise classes and a once-a-month Family Breakfast Club. Another successful strategy is the "adoption" of students by school staff members. Students are targeted whose parents have died or gone to prison, whose siblings are involved in drug dealing, or whose single parent is neglectful. School staff members take their "adoptees" out to eat, to get a haircut, or home for a weekend. Bowling Green's success can be measured in higher test scores, a 97 percent attendance rate, and an increase in the number of parents coming into the school.

Minneapolis

The Family Resource Center at Anderson Elementary School, the multicultural, gender-fair demonstration site for Special School District 1 in Minneapolis, is an example of how a school can successfully build linkages with the surrounding community (Wattenberg & Pearson, 1996). Parent involvement is the foundation of the center. Parents were asked to serve on the Site Council and were paid through state grant money. Parents also were given gift certificates for doing volunteer work. This recognition of parent participation was critically important. According to the project director,

> [Money and gift certificates] recognize the importance of their work. They get other parents involved, and now we've got the whole school talking about the things that the Family Resource Center does. We've got parents working in the Clothes Closet getting donations, sorting, washing, and giving [clothes] to kids and families; parents searching out the food shelves that really deal with basic needs; parents working on empowerment, setting up leadership training for other parents; parents working on community policy, doing the community newsletter, working on systems issues. (pp. 26–27)

The project director measures success by the smile of a child "who comes in and gets that jacket or the clean pair of jeans that fit, . . . when we can get a family committed to coming to Family of Readers, . . . when a parent says 'you know it's never been important to me to have my GED but since I've been involved here, I think I should do that'" (p. 27).

Kentucky

The Kentucky system of Family Resource and Youth Service Centers is an example of a statewide movement targeted at poor communities and linked to educational reform. In 1989 the Kentucky Supreme Court ruled that the state's public school system was unconstitutional because of an inequitable funding structure. As a result, the governor and the general assembly formed the Task Force on Educational Reform, which ultimately resulted in the Kentucky Educational Reform Act of 1990 (Doktor & Poertner, 1996). This act created Family Resource Centers aimed at families with young children and Youth Service Centers aimed at middle and high schools. The centers are targeted at schools in which 20 percent or more of the student body is eligible for free school meals.

A minimal core of six services is required for each Family Resource Center: (1) full-time preschool for children ages two and three; (2) afterschool care for children ages four to 12; (3) parent education, including home visiting; (4) monitoring of child development; (5) support and training for child day care providers; and (6) health services. The minimum core of services for Youth Service

Centers is health and social services referrals; employment counseling, training, and placement; summer and part-time job development; drug and alcohol abuse counseling; and family crisis and mental health counseling. As of 1993, 134 Family and Youth Service Centers had been established in Kentucky (GAO, 1993).

ESTABLISHING SCHOOL-LINKED, FAMILY RESOURCE CENTERS IN IMPOVERISHED COMMUNITIES

A number of challenges await the establishment of school-linked, family resource centers in any community. These include funding, inadequate space in schools, the decision over who is to be served, confidentiality issues, and opposition from community members (for a further discussion of these challenges, see Behrman, 1992; Koppich & Kirst, 1993).

Parental Involvement

Perhaps the most important of these challenges is involving poor parents and parents of color in program design. Parent involvement is a critical factor in ensuring school success; it results in better attendance, more positive attitudes about school (Henderson, 1989), and higher student achievement (Epstein, 1983). Parent participation is a key ingredient common to all the exemplary programs described earlier in this chapter. Working to meaningfully involve parents in the design of school-linked, family resource centers affords social workers an opportunity to assume a leadership position, because they possess considerable training and expertise in working with families.

Quinn (1995) stated that "parental involvement in the school is strengthened when school personnel enlist parental participation in decision-making and problem resolution" (p. 251). However, actively involving and engaging poor parents and parents of color from impoverished communities in making decisions and resolving problems is problematic for several reasons.

> One of the major problems we have in poor, disadvantaged, urban communities is that we have "client communities." They're not producers of jobs, they're not producers of the solutions to their own problems, partly because the system has created that. Poor and minority families in these communities are used to being "clients" in a public social service system. They are now being asked to be "partners." (Salinas cited in Wattenberg & Pearson, 1996, p. 43)

Another factor precluding parental involvement is a long history of negative relationships between parents and the school staff. These schools have already failed these parents. A 1988 study of low-income parents found that they stayed away from their child's public school because they saw no role for themselves, felt they had little to offer academically (as a result of their own poor school performance), were intimidated by administrators and teachers, or found the schools unapproachable or "hard to reach" (Davies, 1994). This same study also found that low-income parents cared as much as middle-class parents about having their child succeed in school. However, despite these findings, many school personnel continue to blame these parents for their children's failure in school and perceive them as being both indifferent to their child's education and hard to reach. This situation has both policy and practice implications. If the school is not viewed as a friendly and supportive institution, families and children will not readily turn to it for help and support. It is also difficult to convince entrenched bureaucrats in schools and community agencies to share authority and decision making with parents, who are blamed for their children's school failure and perceived as indifferent toward their children's academic success.

A number of other barriers also may preclude the active involvement of parents in impoverished communities. Because of problems associated with poverty, such as lack of adequate resources, many poor parents do not have the time or energy to actively participate as partners (Dunst, Trivette, & Cross, 1986). Cultural differences also may pose a substantial challenge. Chang (1993) pointed out that building and maintaining trust can be difficult in situations that bring together individuals from diverse ethnic and linguistic backgrounds. For example, Hispanic families often value informal (for example, extended family) over formal networks (Salend & Taylor, 1993). Collaboration in impoverished communities poses a significant challenge because the majority of professionals working in schools and agencies in those communities are of a different race, economic background, and lifestyle than the children and families they serve.

Practice Skills

The opportunity to engage parents from impoverished communities calls on practice roles and skills that reflect the historical roots of social work. Perhaps most importantly, social workers must conceptualize their relationship with parents as a "partner role," empowering them to become active advocates involved in the shaping of parent-driven services. Professionals must shift from a child-centered, individualistic approach to a more family-centered and community-centered approach. Social workers have long operated from a deficit approach with families and must shift to an empowerment, family-strengths model within this new service paradigm. However, this shift cannot be accomplished by merely providing social workers with "pertinent information and a new repertoire of skills" (Cohen & Lavach, 1995, p. 268). In working with poor, ethnically diverse, and non-English-speaking parents, social workers from a different culture must gain the trust of these parents and engage them in a respectful partnership.

Social workers and other professionals working in impoverished communities must become more culturally competent by examining their own attitudes and expectations and ensuring that they are sensitive to diversity issues. According to Cohen and Lavach (1995), this conversion to a family-centered approach to practice must include a process of self-examination and relearning and an honest assessment of factors that contribute to maintaining a distant, judgmental relationship with families. One critical step in this process is the acknowledgment of diversity as a strength rather than a problem. To accomplish this, Cohen and Lavach (1995) proposed that parents "be used as teachers to help professionals understand more fully how their behavior impacts family members' attitudes and willingness to work collaboratively" (p. 268). The implications of these shifts are provocatively stated by Salinas (cited in Wattenberg & Pearson, 1996): "Families who receive services are the only solution . . . it's not social workers, it's not educators. . . . We can help, but it is really the people who receive the services. Somehow we have got to change our paradigm of thinking from doing for people. We have got to get people to work with us to solve all of our problems together" (p. 43).

Several suggestions have been made for involving poor parents and parents of color who may be distrustful of the school. For example, the family resource center can be located close to the school; a storefront may be more welcoming to parents who have not had success in school. Parents can be recruited to become members of advisory councils. They can be hired as outreach workers to help build cultural understanding on the part of new workers or take part in the initial training for staff. Parents can be remunerated with money or gift certificates for their participation (Wattenberg & Pearson, 1996).

Sustaining Programs

Another critical challenge facing social workers who establish these new service models is sustaining programs for the long term. Many programs are tied to the energy and enthusiasm of the one or few individuals who created them; it is important to build the foundation necessary to sustain these efforts with or without those individuals. Two essential activities are required to sustain school-linked service efforts. First, social workers have to show that programs are doing what they were intended to do (that is, process evaluation) and prove that they are effective (that is, outcome evaluation). A process evaluation of school-linked, family resource center programs in impoverished communities should include an assessment of the extent to which children receive the full range of services they need to be ready to learn and be successful in school and an assessment of the extent to which poor parents receive the help and assistance they need to support their child's education, health, growth, and development. To determine whether a program is effective, program outcomes should include measures of school achievement, including grades, attendance, and school behavior (Gomby & Larson, 1992).

Second, social workers must organize a constituency that demands that these programs are maintained in the community. As Wattenberg (cited in Wattenberg & Pearson, 1996) stated, "you have to have lots of people who want, need, and require it and won't go away until they have it. An important question is whether parents who are poor, beleaguered, struggling can really mount such pressure" (p. 40). This is an important consideration because poor families historically have had little or no political clout.

CONCLUSION

The school-linked, family resource center movement is a promising model for improving results for children and families through reshaping the service delivery system in impoverished communities. Although this movement is relatively new, the concept is deeply rooted in social work. The movement toward school-linked, family resource centers "represents a rediscovery of, and giving new shape to, tools that were once part of the social worker's standard repertoire" (Ooms & Owens cited in Hare, 1995, p. 2106).

The challenges surrounding the school-linked, family resource center movement in impoverished communities are those familiar to social work; they are the same or similar challenges surrounding community development. Although social workers have not always been successful in solving these problems, their knowledge and experience is well beyond that of others involved in this movement. As a result of their training and expertise, social workers have the opportunity to take the lead in involving poor parents and parents of color in the design of school-linked, family resource centers, thereby contributing to the creative solutions needed to address the dire and entrenched problems confronting impoverished communities.

REFERENCES

Adler, L. (1994). Introduction and overview. In L. Adler & S. Gardner (Eds.), *The politics of linking schools and social services: The 1993 yearbook of the Politics of Education Association* (pp. 1–16). Washington, DC: Falmer Press.

Behrman, R. E. (Ed.). (1992). School-linked services [Entire issue]. *Future of Children.*

Chang, H. (1993). Serving ethnically diverse communities. *Education and Urban Society, 25,* 212–221.

Cohen, R., & Lavach, C. (1995). Strengthening partnerships between families and service providers. In P. Adams & K. Nelson (Eds.), *Reinventing human services: Community- and family-centered practice* (pp. 261–277). New York: Aldine de Gruyter.

Coltoff, P. (1996). Community schools: The next stage. *Conversations: Supporting Children and Families in the Public School, 3*(1–2), 4–7.

Condition of Education. (1996). *Dropout rates* (Indicator 5). Washington, DC: National Center for Education Statistics. Available online at http://www.ed.gov/NCES/pubs/ce/index.html.

Davies, D. (1994). IRE's international league of schools reaches out to hard-to-reach parents. *Family Resource Coalition Report, 13*(1–2), 9–10.

Doktor, J. E., & Poertner, J. (1996). Kentucky's Family Resource Centers: A community-based, school-linked services model. *Remedial and Special Education, 17,* 293–302.

Dryfoos, J. G. (1996). How to implement full-service schools: Observations from the field. *Conversations: Supporting Children and Families in the Public Schools, 3*(1–2), 1, 13–15.

Dunst, C., Trivette, C., & Cross, A. (1986). Mediating influences of social support: Personal, family, and child outcomes. *American Journal of Mental Deficiency, 90,* 403–417.

Epstein, J. L. (1983). Longitudinal effects of family–school–person interactions on student outcomes. *Research in Sociology of Education and Socialization, 4,* 101–127.

Gomby, D. S., & Larson, C. S. (1992). Evaluation of school-linked services. *Future of Children, 2*(1), 68–84.

Hare, I. (1995). School-linked services. In R. L. Edwards (Ed.-in-Chief), *Encyclopedia of social work* (19th ed., Vol. 3, pp. 2100–2109). Washington, DC: NASW Press.

Henderson, A. (1989). *The evidence continues to grow: Parent involvement improves school achievement.* Columbia, MD: National Committee for Citizens in Education.

Hendrickson, J. M., & Omer, D. (1995). School-based comprehensive services: An example of interagency collaboration. In P. Adams & K. Nelson (Eds.), *Reinventing human services: Community- and family-centered practice* (pp. 145–162). New York: Aldine de Gruyter.

Hornblower, M. (1996, June 3). It takes a school: A new approach to elementary education starts at birth and doesn't stop when the bell rings. *Time,* pp. 36–38.

Kirst, M. W. (1991). Improving children's services: Overcoming barriers, creating new opportunities. *Phi Delta Kappan, 72,* 615–622.

Koppich, J. E., & Kirst, M. W. (Eds.). (1993). Editors' introduction. *Education and Urban Society, 25,* 123–128.

Lerner, R. M. (1996). Creating caring communities: Building university–community partnerships to enhance youth and family development. *Conversations: Supporting Children and Families in the Public Schools, 3*(1–2), 8–12.

Pennekamp, M. (1992). Toward school-linked and school-based human services for children and families. *Social Work in Education, 14,* 125–130.

Quinn, W. H. (1995). Expanding the focus of intervention: The importance of family/community relations. In P. Adams & K. Nelson (Eds.), *Reinventing human services: Community- and family-centered practice* (pp. 245–259). New York: Aldine de Gruyter.

Richards, N. (1996, July 10). Schools in all states need repair, report says. *Education Week,* p. 8.

Salend, S., & Taylor, L. (1993). Working with families: A cross-cultural perspective. *Remedial and Special Education, 14,* 25–32.

Schorr, L. (1989). *Within our reach: Breaking the cycle of disadvantage.* New York: Anchor Books.

U.S. Department of Education. (1994). *Strong families, strong schools: Building community partnerships for learning.* Washington, DC: Author.

U.S. General Accounting Office. (1993). *School-linked human services: A comprehensive strategy for aiding students at risk of school failure.* Washington, DC: Author.

Wattenberg, E., & Pearson, Y. (Eds.). (1996). *Defining excellence for school-linked services: A summary of the proceedings of the conference held September 14, 1995, at the University of Minnesota.* Minneapolis: University of Minnesota, Center for Urban and Regional Affairs.

Zalenski, J. (1994). *Creating cultures of family support and preservation: Four case studies.* Iowa City, IA: National Resource Center on Family-Based Services.

This chapter was originally published in the September 1997 issue of Social Work, *vol. 42, pp. 415–422.*

Creating Family-Centered Integrated Service Systems and Interprofessional Educational Programs to Implement Them

Dean Corrigan and Kathleen Kirk Bishop

As education, social services, and health care concerns have expanded and grown in complexity, many agencies are serving the same families (Hodgkinson, 1992), and the professional responsibility for specific services is often uncoordinated and dysfunctional. An increasing number of federal and state policymakers and legislators now recognize that new organizational relationships at the family and community level must be developed among schools, universities, health agencies, and other human services organizations; a systemic, collaborative approach is imperative.

Calls to put the pieces together have come from policy analysts and practitioners as well as politicians. Fifteen states have passed legislation fostering collaboration across state agencies and local communities (Education Commission of the States, 1994).

Starting from the premise that families must be at the center of any system designed to serve them, this chapter focuses on a reconceptualization of service delivery systems and interprofessional training programs to prepare a new generation of interprofessionally oriented service providers who possess the knowledge, skills, and values to create family-centered, community-based, integrated education, social services, and health systems. Family–interprofessional collaboration is no longer an option; it is a necessity and an obligation of professional leadership. This chapter presents case descriptions and the results of feedback to the National Commission on Leadership in Interprofessional Education (NCLIE) from families, practitioners, and trainers currently involved in designing and implementing collaborative family-centered, community-based programs.

CONDITIONS OF CHILDREN AND THEIR FAMILIES

The starting point in designing family-centered integrated service delivery systems and the interprofessional development programs to support them must be the needs, problems, and conditions facing children and their families. Children are the nation's fastest growing poverty group (National Commission on Children, 1993). Poverty among children has reached such critical proportions that the future of the nation is at stake. In 1994 more children were living in extreme poverty than in any year since 1975, when such data were first collected (Children's Defense Fund, 1994). The increase in poverty was particularly dramatic for the youngest children. Twenty-five percent of children younger than six were poor, as were 27 percent of all children younger than three. African American and Hispanic children are two to three times more likely to live in poverty than white children. Poverty is not restricted to people of color; among white people the level rose from 9.7 percent in 1973 to 15.6 percent in 1992, the highest rate of increase for any racial group (National Center for Health Statistics, 1993).

Schools see more and more children who are doomed to fail before they ever start. One of three six-year-olds is not ready for formal education (Boyer, 1991). Once in school, untold numbers cannot learn adequately because they come to school hungry, suffer neglect or abuse at home, or have birth defects or are ill. The children of poor families are the victims of "savage inequalities" (Kozol, 1991, 1995).

America's schools are set up to produce winners and losers. Through inequities in financing and an outmoded organizational structure that emphasizes labeling, tracking, ranking, and categorization, American schools and society lock poor children into poverty and later blame them for the state they are in.

Boyer (1991) charged that America is losing sight of its children. In decisions made every day, the needs of children are placed at the very bottom of the public agenda, despite the evidence that such decisions have grave consequences for the future of the nation. "It is intolerable that millions of children are physically and emotionally disadvantaged in ways that restrict their capacity to learn, especially when we are aware of the terrible price that will be paid for such neglect, not just educationally, but in tragic terms as well" (p. 3).

As Douglas Nelson, director of the Annie E. Casey Foundation, stated, "It may well be that the nation cannot survive—as a decent place to live, as a world class power or even as a democracy—with such high rates of children growing into adulthood unprepared to parent, unprepared to be productively employed, and unprepared to share in mainstream aspirations" (Gleick, 1996, p. 33). These conditions signal the need for changes in our service delivery systems and in professional practices.

CHARACTERISTICS OF FAMILY-CENTERED INTEGRATED SERVICES SYSTEMS

In response to the conditions children and families are facing, integrated services programs that foster collaboration among professional partners and with families are being designed and implemented. Progress has been made toward articulating the kinds of service delivery systems that families want and need when they are seeking services for themselves and their children. In fact, there is considerable agreement among families and a growing cadre of education, social work, and health care professionals that approaches that are family centered, community based, and coordinated (Brewer, McPherson, Magrab, & Hutchins, 1989; Dunst, Trivette, & Deal, 1988; Koop, 1987; Shelton & Stephanek, 1994) and culturally competent (Cross, 1988; Hayes, 1993; Lieberman, 1990) create the conditions for the development of high-quality integrated services. An increasing number of professionals also believe that families must be involved in family–professional, interprofessional, and interorganizational collaborative processes (Bishop, Woll, & Arango, 1993; Briar & Lawson, 1994; Haas, Gray, &

McConnell, 1992). Bishop, Weaver, Vohs, Taylor, and Kilburn (1997) suggest a paradigm for practice that encompasses all of these elements.

Collaborative programs vary in emphasis depending on the profession designing and implementing them and the level of family involvement, but all models place children and families at the center. Professionals learn through this collaborative program development that no single profession, no single agency alone can meet the multiple and varied needs of children and families. In doing so they have increased the need for professional partners to link. As professionals begin to serve families' education, health, social, and economic needs, service providers discover that their roles interlock.

For example, Lawson (1994), in reporting lessons learned from his journey throughout the United States studying schools, universities, and communities involved in interprofessional collaboration, pointed out that family-centered, community-based, culturally competent schools are not engaged just in structural changes. The changes go much deeper. Purpose and substance are changed by actually developing schools as family-friendly support environments.

Schools designed and used as hubs of a network of family-centered, community-based integrated services programs as well as centers of inquiry for preservice and in-service training and research become interprofessional development schools. As Dryfoos (1994) noted, an increasing number of school sites have social workers, psychologists, child care workers, nurses, pediatricians, adult job trainers and placement advisers, legal assistants, tutors, mentors from business and industry, adult literacy and parenting specialists, and more. The full-service school concept cultivates community involvement by expanding activities during the nonschool hours in school facilities. In fact, it changes the facilities, too. A child- and family-friendly community development approach involves the reimaging and reinventing of schools, social services, and health services and their relationships.

CASE EXAMPLES

The following case descriptions provide examples of family-centered integrated services programs initiated by different professions but involving professional partners serving the same families. However, the creation of integrated service centers is not confined to school sites. Project Unity uses a school site. The Healthy and Ready to Learn Center does not; it links with schools and other agencies. Location is determined by the purposes of the program and the uniqueness of the community it serves. (For additional descriptions of family-centered collaborative programs, see Additional Resources after the reference list.)

Project Unity

As described by Bowen (1996), Project Unity's guiding principles are that groups are more effective if they work together rather than separately and that the best way to improve conditions in a community is by including neighborhood residents themselves. Community Voices is a key component of Project Unity, a grass-roots coalition of citizens, businesses, charitable groups, and government agencies working at the neighborhood level to strengthen families in Bryan, Texas.

The program receives assistance from the Bryan Independent School District, St. Joseph Regional Health Center, the City of Bryan, Junior League of Bryan/College Station, Texas A&M University's College of Education, the Danforth Foundation, Columbia Medical Center, and other agencies. What makes this program different from other neighborhood revitalization efforts is that these groups are working with the people who actually live in the community.

Project Unity had its beginnings in 1993 with Jeannie Heller, who was a social worker and coordinator of the Parent Education Partnership Program at the Bryan school district. Heller noticed that although the community had dozens of agencies dealing with poverty, unemployment, and other problems, many people were not getting the aid they needed.

As a parent educator, Heller often had to help residents seek aid from various agencies. She saw that although some services were duplicated, others were lacking. People in crisis did not know where to turn to get quick, effective help. Many agency workers were themselves unaware of what was available just down the street.

In addition, the various requirements of each individual agency often discouraged potential clients from getting the aid they needed and were eligible for. Organizations required applicants to fill out stacks of paperwork that would be difficult to complete even for people with college degrees. Also, many applicants had to take time off from work to apply for aid. Some had to borrow cars to get to the agency and then wait for hours to be seen, only to find that they needed some document they had not known to bring and would have to come back another day. The risk of losing their jobs, and in turn their homes, was too great for many residents struggling to stay afloat, so they did not return.

To try to remedy the problem, in 1992 Heller applied for and received a $9,000 grant from the Danforth Foundation to form the Children's Partnership Board, originally a group of eight (now 30) agencies coordinating services to families. In two years of quarterly meetings, board members streamlined paperwork and learned about each other's services for families. Agencies worked together to create a single form to replace the many used by the 30 agencies; they formed a communications network so that anyone entering one Children's Partnership Board member organization could be linked to aid from any of the other agencies with minimal effort.

The Children's Partnership Board consists of people working on the front lines with families. From it arose another group, the Interagency Coalition, which includes a broader range of representatives of city government, health care providers, criminal justice professionals, and university and public school officials. Created in 1994, this group tries to help families by changing policies on the administrative level.

The Children's Partnership Board and the Interagency Coalition wanted to take services directly to the community where the needs were and to involve the residents in problem solving. They envisioned a center located in a high-needs neighborhood, where residents could have easy access to family services and participate in family-based education and recreational activities. The coalition also wanted to send a van into the neighborhood to deliver services such as immunizations and health screenings. In 1995 the coalition received a $113,000 grant from the Texas Department of Protective and Regulatory Services to create Project Unity, a three-tiered partnership that includes the Children's Partnership Board, the Interagency Coalition, and the newly created neighborhood-based Family Center and Mobile Unit.

The Mobile Unit is a van equipped with a computer and fax machine to allow health and social services providers to communicate with their home agencies. Children's Partnership Board members use it to go into the neighborhood to offer such services as immunizations, diabetes screening, and tuberculosis and HIV/AIDS testing.

The Family Center is located in the former Carver Elementary School on Martin Luther King Jr. Street, where stable families as well as those with high needs live. According to 1990 census information, the 774 households in that area have an average annual income of $12,900. Project Unity members cleaned out the school's basement, then being used for storage, to house the center, which opened weekdays and some evenings beginning in June 1995. At the center neighborhood residents learn about services available to help them. Program staffers talk with residents to determine which agency or agencies can best assist them and coordinate the services. The center also offers parenting and other classes and family activities to educate citizens and foster a feeling of community. Graduate and undergraduate interns and student volunteers from the departments of education, health, sociology, psychology, medicine, architecture, and agricultural extension work with staff at the center. The center has become a site for training as well as service delivery.

To inform residents about new programs, Project Unity staff walked door to door explaining the Mobile Unit and Family Center services. Also, to introduce the new program to the community and to recruit residents to become involved in identifying and solving problems in the neighborhood, Project Unity organizers called a town meeting on June 20, 1995. Citizens were invited to voice their concerns to government officials about community issues.

The residents readily admit they were suspicious about the city's and school district's seemingly new-found interest in their community. For years North Bryan residents had watched as their neighborhood slowly deteriorated, to the apparent indifference, from their standpoint, of government leaders. Next to neat, well-kept residences and lawns sat deteriorating, abandoned houses whose owners the city seemed unwilling or unable to force to make renovations. Junk cars and trash heaps multiplied.

When new schools were to be built, the Carver-Kemp area was passed over in favor of more affluent parts of town. Broken water lines went unrepaired for years, undermining streets and creating hazards for drivers. Gangs and prostitutes made parts of the neighborhood unsafe and unappealing. The safe, clean neighborhood in which many residents remembered growing up had become infested with crime and urban decay.

More than 100 families attended the first town meeting, and this meeting was used to recruit community members for the new leadership program. Ten community members volunteered for the program called Community Voices. The initial training for the members of Community Voices was a 10-week leadership program. However, because the volunteers already possessed many of the leadership skills necessary to be Community Voices, the participants quickly moved to address some of the community's concerns. Before long, Community Voices had 40 members addressing problems such as placing a crossing guard at a busy school intersection where a child had been hit by a car, organizing community voter registration, and creating safe havens for children to play and work.

After one year, Community Voices was able to share numerous success stories. A crossing guard now works at the busy intersection, a new elementary school located in the community will be completed by 1998, and the family center now occupies the basement of Carver Elementary School. Also, a mobile unit supplied by St. Joseph's Hospital makes door-to-door preventive medicine trips in the community. Finally, Community Voices has begun publicizing town meetings over the radio, and some members have become deputized voter registrars who sign up residents who have never voted and provide transportation to the polls.

Today, the Family Center and Project Unity host many programs for the neighborhood. Every Friday and Saturday night 150 to 200 children participate in Family Fun Night in the Carver gymnasium. The food for this event is supplied by the Brazos Food Bank. Other programs, including Girl Scouts, have been incorporated, and a local drill team has been created by community members. In addition, a neighborhood quilt has been completed, and parenting and prenatal care programs are in place.

Currently, Community Voices is involved in a community engagement process that will survey 800 homes in the community. During this survey phase, Community Voices and other volunteers go into homes in the community and ask residents to share their concerns and to suggest possible solutions to ongoing problems. This part of the process allows neighborhood residents to identify what they already know, what they need to know, and what they are going to do now that they know. The results of the survey will be formulated into comprehensive graphs and charts, which will then be reported to the community and used in designing and implementing community programs. The data will be used as a benchmark for progress. As well as sparking enthusiasm, Community Voices has become a vehicle for getting direction from the community.

Making decisions to do what once seemed impossible has become the norm. Heller says, "We have learned that leaders must let go of the process and have faith in families in order for collaboration to occur at the grass roots level" (Project Unity & Texas A&M University, 1996, p. 7).

Healthy and Ready to Learn Center

The Healthy and Ready to Learn Center (Sia & Taba, 1993) in Honolulu was incorporated as part of several pre-existing programs including Hawaii's child abuse and neglect prevention program, Healthy Start; the Medical Home and Physician Involvement Projects, which heighten awareness among primary care physicians of the psychosocial problems of children and families as they relate to community and child health; federal funds under Part H of the Education of the Handicapped Act of 1965 (P.L. 99-457); and the Hawaii Zero to Three Project with early intervention services for at-risk infants and toddlers. The center, initiated and directed by Cal Sia, a pediatrician, and Sharon Taba, an early childhood educator, is the educational component of a system of programs and services that integrates health and family support addressing the need for school readiness. A central concern is to promote healthy children who are ready for school.

The Healthy and Ready to Learn Center collaborative is composed of practicing professionals from health care, social services, and education. Members of the operating foundation, private social services agencies, Tertiary Maternal and Children's Medical Center, professional physicians organizations, and the College of Medicine at the University of Hawaii work together to overcome barriers, solve problems, and take best advantage of available resources.

Program organizers believe that interprofessional collaboration in small groups using individual case scenarios facilitates problem solving and promotes a team-oriented response to meeting the needs of families and children. The concept of organizing as a collaborative is a strong cultural force that influences decisions about center staffing, structure, service delivery, client identification, need identification, and goal formulation. The values held by the center collaborative drive goal identification, whereas the synergy created by the collaborative itself increases the likelihood of goal attainment.

Some of the major goals of the center include encouraging family-centered, community-based, coordinated, and culturally competent care; ensuring use of basic health care, social support, and education by all family members, with a special focus on mothers and infants; promoting primary prevention and early identification of health problems; fostering collaboration among families' medical home care, quality early education, and family support services; encouraging new dimensions in providing health care services, professional education, and training; and promoting fiscally responsible programs that will endure a changing health care system. In addition to interprofessional collaboration, the center is committed to the active participation of children and families in program evaluation and problem solution. Family empowerment and the creation of conditions that allow children and families to reduce their immediate stresses and start to positively invest in their own lives are goals of the collaborative process.

Center coordinators have recognized the need for a training and staff development function that orients the Healthy and Ready to Learn Center staff to interprofessional collaboration. The center operates a training program titled Pediatrics and the New Morbidity. The program includes three modules: (1) community-based care, (2) coordinated care, and (3) family-centered care. All were designed and are taught by an interprofessional team of specialists from medicine, social work, and education. Past training sessions have sparked many questions about the kinds of skills interprofessional teams need, how collective information is obtained and maintained without duplication, how teams deal with jargon unique to a particular profession, and how teams deal with patterns existing in the participating professional cultures (ways of behaving, rituals, rites of passage, status symbols) that clash with the values of collaboration.

By taking advantage of profamily legislation, multiple funding sources, and a generally favorable environment, the Healthy and Ready to Learn Center placed families in the center of the health, education, social services, and the medical home care systems. The philosophy of the center and its leaders placed a priority on child health problems because of the inherent vulnerability of children in this particular population in Hawaii and because it is in early childhood that positive and negative conditions have the greatest effect on conditions in later life.

FAMILIES AND THE NCLIE

Families, practitioners, trainers, and policymakers involved in interprofessional education programs have organized at the national level to network across the professions and share lessons learned about the development of family-centered integrated services and family–interprofessional development programs.

In 1993 the Maternal and Child Health Bureau of the U.S. Department of Health and Human Services awarded three interprofessional development grants to the Western Oregon State College Teaching Research Division, the University of Vermont Department of Social Work, and the Hawaii Medical Association. These grants were linked with the goals and activities of the NCLIE. The commission was initiated and sponsored by the Association of Teacher Educators in its first two years; association officials appointed the first members of NCLIE. It now links with professional associations through its 55 members. The commission took its guidelines from discussions with C. Everett Koop, former Surgeon General of the United States, and the document *Principles to Link By: Integrating Education, Health, and Human Services for Children and Families* (American Academy of Pediatrics, 1994). The basic criterion for membership in the NCLIE is active involvement as a policymaker, practitioner, trainer, or family partner in the implementation and evaluation of integrated services and interprofessional education.

As the work of the NCLIE progressed, it became clear that partnerships with families were central to all of the activities of the commission and the three grant recipients and therefore essential to fully implementing a family-centered approach to interprofessional collaborative practices and training. Therefore, the commission developed and ratified the following purpose statement:

> Through a family/professional partnership, the Commission will support the preparation of a new generation of interprofessionally oriented leaders in health, education, and social work, who possess the knowledge, skills and values to practice in new community-based integrated service delivery systems.
>
> The National Commission will focus on interprofessional preparation in both pre-service and continued professional development. The best community-based practices with children and families will serve as knowledge bases by which changes are made in university missions and service programs. (Corrigan, 1995, p. 12)

Since 1993 NCLIE meetings have been held the day before the national conferences of the participating professions (for example, Association of Teacher Educators, American Academy of Pediatrics, NASW, and others). At these conferences, multidisciplinary teams have presented their ideas and case studies using a panel format. Dialogue has been established with the various networks in each of the professions, and concept papers and articles on integrated services and interprofessional education have appeared in the publications of the professional associations of the commission members. An extensive library including 50 case studies, newsletters, and other descriptive materials of programs has been compiled (Corrigan & Udas, 1996).

Bibliographies and a newsletter, *Service Bridges* (Searcy, 1996), have been published by the Western Oregon State College project. The University of Vermont Partnerships for Change (Bishop, 1996) has produced newsletters and a bibliography on interprofessional education and practice (published by the Council on Social Work Education) and is at work on the development of interprofessional seminar materials and teaching modules with a special focus on family–professional collaboration. Both groups' newsletters provide up-to-date descriptions of programs and meetings related to integrated services and interprofessional development programs.

The most recent meeting of the NCLIE was held in Albuquerque, New Mexico, from May 28 to May 29, 1996, in conjunction with the International Parent to Parent Conference. This event provided the opportunity to strengthen the linkage with many organizations representing children and families and to share lessons learned from specific programs that involve families as partners. Discussion focused on what is meant by "family-centered" education, health, and social services systems.

Families defined very clearly the expectations they had for collaborative, family-friendly education, health, and social services systems, and from their personal experiences they described the essential characteristics of effective providers of services. For example, one parent gave the educators this advice regarding her children: "If they can't learn the way you teach, then you'd better learn to teach the way they learn."

The NCLIE planning committee, which included family members and professionals, worked with the International Parent to Parent Committee to ensure that families directly involved in programs, not just professional practitioners, trainers, and policymakers, shared their ideas with the commission. Five programs demonstrating best practice in collaboration with families were presented, including Project Unity. Also, through a premeeting survey of the commission members, the family–professional planning group collected ideas about the roles of families in implementing interprofessional training programs as well as community-based integrated services systems from the current commission members. A forthcoming monograph, *Partnerships at Work*, produced by the Vermont Social Work Project will disseminate the proceedings of the meeting (Bishop, 1996).

Criteria for Family-Centered Practice

The NCLIE discussions with families generated five positions:

1. Families are needed as partners in improving the preparation programs that train service providers and as partners in improving service delivery systems.

2. Each program is unique and must emerge from the cultural setting in which it will operate and be planned by the people who will make it work.
3. Families must be involved in developing the plans to improve their neighborhoods to have a sense of ownership in these plans and sustain them over time.
4. The primary job of service providers is to create the conditions for change. Their primary goal is to enable families to act on their own behalf.
5. A shared vision of the future is what will bring families and professionals together.

Perhaps the greatest barrier to change is "learned helplessness." Hopes have been dashed so many times that ordinary human beings give up. The "cultivation of optimism" must replace the "spiral toward futility." We must build on a strengths model, not a deficit model.

Training for Family-Centered Practice

Families and NCLIE members agreed that helping professionals need to ask themselves some key questions before an integrated approach to family-centered practice and training can occur. Bishop (1994) suggested some beginning questions for social work, education, and health care professionals:

- What are my beliefs about families?
- Do I see families as people with strengths and resources, or as people in dysfunction needing help from the experts?
- Do I see families as potential colleagues who bring specialized knowledge, skills, and experience to the table?
- Am I willing and prepared to work with family members as partners in developing integrated services systems and interprofessional training and research programs?

As Witkin and Weaver (1993) pointed out,

> Underlying the concept of family-centered services is a set of values and beliefs. These include the fundamental beliefs that families are benevolent—they seek to act in the best interest of their children, families are experts on their own children, families can be trusted, families must be supported in ways that allow them to maintain their integrity, and families should be equal partners in their relationships with professionals. (p. 2)

Survey data from 34 NCLIE members and ideas emerging from dialogue with families at the meeting produced the following suggestions on ways in which families might participate in preprofessional training at universities and in continuing education in communities:

- Invite family members as colleagues into classes to discuss the implications of proposed legislation, particularly those family members who will be affected by a particular policy proposal (for example, welfare, housing, health, family leave, school vouchers).
- Develop assignments that support family members and trainees in working collaboratively, such as preparing testimony to support a bill before the legislature.

- Begin field-based experiences by inviting family members to assist with the introduction and orientation to the community setting (for example, in a community agency, family center, school, or family home).
- Develop a consultant list of family members who would be willing to mentor trainees on the meaning and practice of family-centered approaches.
- Seek suggestions from families on required readings that reflect parent or family concerns.
- Include assignments in course syllabi that bring families and trainees together in community projects; such tasks need to be negotiated with families to ensure that they are respectful of family schedules and situations.
- Invite families to participate in the review and evaluation of course goals, content, and activities and to serve on curriculum committees and advisory councils as full partners.
- Engage community agency and school personnel and trainees in discussions of ways to implement a family-centered philosophy, including the ways families help each other.
- Discuss with field instructors and trainees ways to integrate a family-centered philosophy into all aspects of the field experience.
- Join agency personnel in a review of agency missions, goals, and objectives and ways to deliver services within the framework of the principles of family–professional collaboration.

The following publications provided additional descriptions of interprofessional education programs: *Expanding Partnerships: Involving Colleges and Universities in Interprofessional Collaboration and Service Integration* (Lawson & Briar, 1994), *Interprofessional Education for Family-Centered Services: A Survey of Interprofessional/ Interdisciplinary Training Programs* (Jivanjee, Moore, Schultze, & Friesen, 1995), *Higher Education Curricula for Integrated Services Providers* (Lehman & Searcy, 1995), and the *Proceedings of the National Conference on Interprofessional Education and Training* (Brandon, 1995).

Although family-centered, community-based, integrated service systems are emerging throughout the United States, university family-centered interprofessional training and research programs to support them are in the early stages of development. Most of the university professors currently engaged in developing integrated service systems and interprofessional education programs are pioneers on their campuses. They are often more closely linked to their community partners than to the traditional decision makers in their institution. Largely dependent on foundation grants or other sources of outside financing, they are extremely concerned about long-term university financial support for the difficult task of revising professional preparation in education, health, and social work. Unless commitment is reflected in the missions, budgets, and reward systems of universities, their efforts cannot be sustained.

University professors, family partners, and students need opportunities to learn the new knowledge and skills necessary to make the required changes. Professional development in forming linkages between universities and their family and community partners is a key reform strategy. Change in professional practice in education, health care, and social services agencies and change in the training and research arm of each participating profession in universities must take place simultaneously. Reform in one part of the system without reform in the other will fail.

The education, social work, and health professions must identify the particular knowledge, skills, values, and commitments needed to be effective collaborators. They must ensure that such knowledge, skills, values, and commitments become part of the curriculum in each field of specialization and are appropriately included in interprofessional programs where family members and students and professionals from a variety of disciplines have opportunities to train and work together. Also, creative ways must be developed to make appropriate knowledge and related skills and values a part of continuing education efforts for career professionals working in community-based training sites and centers.

In addition to interprofessional education at the introductory preservice and in-service level, advanced preparation programs are also needed for leaders at the doctoral and postdoctoral level who represent expertise in each of the participating professions. This cadre of professionals, already licensed in their own fields of specialization and highly respected by their colleagues, will have special training in interprofessional collaboration, policy development, and the design and implementation of preservice and in-service interprofessional programs.

It is important to note that the development of collaborative family-centered, community-based systems has special implications for faculty who work in the professional colleges that serve as the training and research arms of their professions. In addition to discovering new knowledge and integrating knowledge from the various disciplines, faculty in professional colleges have a responsibility to inform practice. Professors who educate practitioners to work in collaborative systems and interprofessional partnerships must confront reality: If they do not model collaborative behavior in the training and research arm of the education, health, and human services professions, it is unlikely that future providers will understand the importance of such collaboration or be prepared to function in the new family-centered integrated services systems.

COLLABORATION: A CHALLENGE

Society and the professions charged with the delivery of education, health care, and social services have a common stake in the health and welfare of children and families. We must accept this common concern, and we must profess it to others. Collaboration with families and each other is a necessity and an obligation of professional leadership.

The social work, education, and health professions constitute the largest workforce in the nation. Guided by a new family-centered interprofessional ethic and driven by a common mission—child and family advocacy—together we can create education, social services, and health systems that provide services in ways that families find helpful, nonintrusive, and supportive.

We must mobilize the profession's resources and political power, and we must develop ways to work together to place the well-being of children and families at the top of the social and political agenda where it belongs. In the process we will rediscover the common purpose of our professions.

REFERENCES

American Academy of Pediatrics. (1994). *Principles to link by: Integrating education, health and human services for children and families* (Final report of more than 50 organizations concerned with children, youths, and families). Washington, DC: Author.

Bishop, K. K. (1996, Summer). *Partnerships for Change: Information Exchange*, pp. 1–4 [Newsletter published by the Department of Social Work, University of Vermont, 228 Waterman Building, Burlington, VT 05405.]

Bishop, K. K., Weaver, P., Vohs, J., Taylor, M. S., & Kilburn, J. (1997). *A new paradigm for the delivery of high quality services to children and families.* Manuscript in preparation. [Available from Partnerships for Change, Department of Social Work, University of Vermont, Burlington, VT 05405.]

Bishop, K. K., Woll, J., & Arango, P. (1993). *Family/professional collaboration for children with special health needs and their families.* Burlington: University of Vermont, Department of Social Work.

Bowen, D. B. (1996, September). Neighbors in action. *Insite*, pp. 22–27. [Available from Insite Publishing, P.O. Box 1387, Bryan, TX 77806.]

Boyer, E. L. (1991). *Ready to learn: A mandate for the nation.* Princeton, NJ: Carnegie Foundation for the Advancement of Teaching.

Brandon, R. (Ed.). (1995). *Proceedings of the National Conference on Interprofessional Education and Training.* Spokane: University of Washington, Human Services Policy Center.

Brewer, E. J., McPherson, M., Magrab, P. R., & Hutchins, V. L. (1989). Family-centered, community-based, coordinated care for children with special health care needs. *Pediatrics, 83,* 1055–1060.

Briar, K. H., & Lawson, H. (1994). *Serving children, youth and families through interprofessional collaboration and service integration: A framework for action.* Oxford, OH: Miami University, Danforth Foundation and the Institute for Educational Renewal.

Children's Defense Fund. (1994). *The state of America's children yearbook 1994: Leave no child behind.* Washington, DC: Author.

Corrigan, D. (1995). Interprofessional education. *Human Service Education, 15*(1), 3–16.

Corrigan, D., & Udas, K. (1996). Creating collaborative, child- and family-centered education, health and human service systems. In J. Sikula (Ed.), *Handbook of research on teacher education* (2nd ed., pp. 893–921). New York: Macmillan.

Cross, T. (1988). Services to minority populations: What does it mean to be a culturally competent professional? *Focal Point, 2*(4), 1–7. [Available from Regional Research Institute for Human Services, Portland State University, P.O. Box 751, Portland, OR 97207-0751.]

Dryfoos, J. G. (1994). *Full service schools: A revolution in health and social services for children, youth, and families.* San Francisco: Jossey-Bass.

Dunst, C. J., Trivette, D. M., & Deal, A. G. (1988). *Supporting and strengthening families.* Cambridge, MA: Brookline Books.

Education Commission of the States, Governors' Commission. (1994). State policy makers play key role in interagency collaboration (Special issue on interagency collaboration). *State Education Leader, 13*(1), 1–15. [Newsletter available from the Education Commission of the States, 707 17th Street, Suite 2700, Denver, CO 80202-3427.]

Education of the Handicapped Act of 1965, P.L. 99-457, 100 Stat. 1145 to 1170.

Gleick, E. (1996, June 3). The children's crusade. *Time Magazine*, pp. 31–35.

Haas, D. L., Gray, H. B., Jr., & McConnell, B. (1992). Parent/professional partnerships in caring for children with special health care needs. *Issues in Comprehensive Pediatric Nursing, 15,* 39–53.

Hayes, M. D. (1993). Cultural diversity. In S. L. Hostler (Ed.), *Family centered care: An approach to implementation* (pp. 329–348). Charlottesville: University of Virginia, Children's Medical Center, Kluge Children's Rehabilitation.

Hodgkinson, H. L. (1992). *A demographic look at tomorrow.* Washington, DC: Institute for Educational Leadership. (ERIC Document Reproduction Service No. ED 359 087)

Jivanjee, P. R., Moore, K. R., Schultze, K. H., & Friesen, B. J. (1995). *Interprofessional education for family-centered services: A survey of interprofessional/interdisciplinary training programs.* Portland,

OR: Portland State University, Research and Training Center on Family Support and Children's Mental Health.

Koop, C. E. (1987). *Surgeon General's report: Children with special health needs—Campaign '87.* Rockville, MD: U.S. Department of Health and Human Services.

Kozol, J. (1991). *Savage inequalities: Children in America's schools.* New York: Harper & Row.

Kozol, J. (1995). *Amazing grace: The lives of children and the conscience of a nation.* New York: Crown.

Lawson, H. (1994). Toward healthy learners, schools, and communities. *Journal of Teacher Education, 45*(1), 62–70.

Lawson, H., & Briar, K. H. (1994). *Expanding partnerships: Involving colleges and universities in interprofessional collaboration and service integration.* Oxford, OH: Miami University, Danforth Foundation and the Institute for Educational Renewal.

Lehman, C. M., & Searcy, J. A. (1995). *Higher education curricula for integrated service providers: Annotated bibliography.* Monmouth: Western Oregon State College, Teaching Research Division.

Lieberman, A. F. (1990). Culturally sensitive intervention with children and families. *Child and Adolescent Social Work, 7,* 101–119.

National Center for Health Statistics. (1993). *Child health* (Report compiled by Office of Public Affairs). Washington, DC: U.S. Department of Health and Human Services.

National Commission on Children. (1993). *Just the facts: A summary of recent information on America's children and their families.* Washington, DC: Author.

Project Unity, & Texas A&M University. (1996). *Action plans: Responding to community voices* (Report of the Institute on Leadership in Interprofessional Collaboration). College Station, TX: Author.

Searcy, J. (1996). *Service bridges.* [Quarterly newsletter available from the Teaching Research Division, Western Oregon State College, 345 North Monmouth Avenue, Monmouth, OR 97361.]

Shelton, T. L., & Stephanek, J. S. (1994). *Family centered care for children needing specialized health and developmental services* (3rd ed.). Bethesda, MD: Association for the Care of Children's Health.

Sia, C., & Taba, S. (1993). *Health and Education Collaboration Project.* Honolulu: Hawaii Medical Association.

Witkin, K., & Weaver, M. (1993). Challenges to collaboration. *Family–Professional Collaboration News, 2*(1), 2.

ADDITIONAL RESOURCES

Bishop, K. K. (1994). Family-centered education for social workers. In S. L. Hostler (Ed.), *Family centered care: An approach to implementation* (pp. 372–387). Charlottesville: University of Virginia, Children's Medical Center, Kluge Children's Rehabilitation.

Bishop, K. K., Kilburn, J .G., & Flaherty, B. A. (1996). *Interprofessional education and practice: A selected bibliography.* Alexandria, VA: Council on Social Work Education.

Harvard Family Research Project. (1995). *Raising our future: Families, schools and communities working together.* Cambridge, MA: Author.

Melaville, A. I., & Blank, M. J. (1992). *What it takes: Structuring interageny partnerships to connect children and families with comprehensive services.* Washington, DC: Education and Human Services Consortium.

Office of Educational Research and Improvement. (1993). *Together we can: A guide for crafting a profamily system of education and human services.* Washington, DC: U.S. Government Printing Office.

Office of Educational Research and Improvement. (1995). *School-linked comprehensive services for children and families: What we know and need to know.* Washington, DC: U.S. Government Printing Office.

Schorr, L. B., & Schorr, D. (1988). *Within our reach: Breaking the cycle of disadvantage.* New York: Doubleday.

This chapter was originally published in the July 1997 issue of Social Work in Education, *vol. 19, pp. 149–163.*

29

An Interagency Collaboration Strategy for Linking Schools with Social and Criminal Justice Services

Donna Tapper, Paula Kleinman, and Mary Nakashian

Many schools in deteriorating inner-city neighborhoods are overwhelmed by the number of students who have multiple extracurricular problems. These problems—poverty, parental substance abuse and mental illness, substandard housing, and neighborhood drug dealing and violence—interrupt children's ability to learn and confront schools with a range of needs that the educational system has neither the funding nor the personnel to provide. At the same time, in severely distressed neighborhoods schools are often the only institutions that remain involved with most school-aged children and their families (Morrill, Reisner, Chimerine, & Marks, 1991). Under these difficult circumstances, schools can do their job more successfully only when they develop structural linkages to other systems that can help them provide support and guidance for the children under their care (Kirst, 1993; Levy, 1991; Shepardson, 1994).

The history of provision of social services through the schools goes back to the early years of the 20th century (Tyack, 1992). Although early efforts relied on staff from settlement houses and other outside organizations to provide social work services to schools, in 1913 the Board of Education in Rochester, New York, first placed "visiting teachers" under the control of the superintendent of schools. The primary function of these school social workers was to act as home–school liaisons to mitigate external problems that inhibited a child's educational development (Allen-Meares, Washington, & Welsh, 1996).

Over the years, school reformers succeeded in expanding the range of nonacademic services offered in schools, so that vocational counseling, health services, and nutritional supplement programs became common in many schools (Morrill & Gerry, 1990). However, multiple providers working in isolation from one another may waste resources by duplicating efforts, may not reach children most in need of services, or may work at cross-purposes. These points often are cited as reasons for undertaking the interagency collaborative efforts known as "services integration" (Agranoff, 1991).

In the past few decades, there has been an enormous increase in efforts at services integration with schools as the focus. Kahn and Kamerman (1992) described a number of such attempts. For example, as of 1992 there were 28 "one-stop-shopping" schools in New Jersey run by the state Department of Human Services. In addition, there were three Family Resource Centers in Connecticut

331

that offered full-time child care for preschoolers and before- and afterschool programs for children through the sixth grade; these centers also offered parent education and training classes, general equivalency diploma classes, and general information and referral services for parents. Joining Forces, a joint initiative of the American Public Welfare Association and the Council of Chief State School Officers, assisted this kind of school collaboration for several years and reported at least 800 such attempts in 47 states (Kahn & Kamerman, 1992).

Three models of school-focused social services provision have been proposed by Corbett and Farber (1990): (1) role expansion—the teacher counsels, helps, and serves as a liaison with home and social services agencies; (2) organizational expansion—various professionals, such as counselors, school social workers, and nurses, are hired as part of school staff; and (3) system supplementation—the school supplies referrals to outside agencies and specialists. To these models Kahn and Kamerman (1992) added a fourth, which they referred to as a variation on the role expansion model. In this model, the "school opens itself to a variety of community-based agencies by offering space and a degree of endorsement, perhaps making referrals, but the agencies retain their autonomy and community allegiances" (p. 25).

The Children at Risk (CAR) program, the subject of this chapter, suggests that a fifth model needs to be added to the conceptualizations already listed. This addition, the system partnership model, provides a structure for a more equal partnership, closer collaboration, and more integrated service delivery among several concerned institutions or agencies. CAR was designed to prevent delinquency and drug use among especially high-risk 11- to 15-year-olds living in decaying inner-city neighborhoods. The central focus of the program is on the high-risk student, and this focus results in inclusion of the school, social services agencies, the police force, and the juvenile justice system in efforts to help these youths. This chapter describes the implementation of the CAR program in Bridgeport, Connecticut. In Bridgeport the CAR project is known locally as SIHRY (Strategic Intervention with High Risk Youth); however, this chapter refers to it by the more general term "CAR" to facilitate future comparisons with other CAR sites.

CAR MODEL

Theoretical Basis

The CAR project was developed by the National Center on Addiction and Substance Abuse (CASA) at Columbia University and was run as a partnership between CASA and the U.S. Department of Justice. A consortium of private foundations and the Department of Justice provided funding for the demonstration program, which operated in one or more schools in each of six cities from 1992 through 1995. After the end of the demonstration period, three of the programs were able to continue operating for varying periods of time by securing local funding.

The CAR model is based on the integrated theoretical explanation of drug use and delinquency proposed by Elliott, Huizinga, and Ageton (1985). This explanation integrates three prominent theories: strain theory (Cloward & Ohlin, 1960; Merton, 1957), social control theory (Hirschi, 1969), and social learning theory (Akers, Krohn, Lanza-Kaduce, & Radosevich, 1979; Bandura, 1977). *Strain theory* identifies the discrepancy between socially approved goals and inadequate legitimate means for achieving those goals as a major source of delinquency. In *social control theory*, attachment to conventional norms and values and commitment to conventional individuals, groups, and institutions inhibit deviant behavior. *Social learning theory* highlights the importance of the social situation in all learning: This integrated theory assumes that both conventional and deviant behaviors are socially learned and that the learning process is governed by exposure to social learning role models and experiences and the anticipated or real rewards and punishments of various behaviors (Elliott et al., 1985).

Through a coordinated and intensive program based on the integrated theory, the CAR model seeks to reduce risk factors for delinquency and drug use by

- improving the youths' attachment to prosocial individuals and institutions
- reducing their bonds to deviant norms and groups
- increasing their opportunities to achieve positive goals
- decreasing their opportunities for exposure to negative experiences.

Implementation of the CAR Project

The CAR project joined community-based preventive social, educational, and health services with juvenile and criminal justice system intervention through the creation of a multiagency collaboration. Agencies participating in the collaboration worked toward common goals, shared responsibility for program activities, and coordinated their services. The CAR project was implemented in a somewhat different manner in each of the sites.

CAR is a tightly focused program in terms of geographic area, target population, and services. To participate in the program, youths must live in a geographically defined neighborhood and attend the target school. CASA and the Department of Justice selected the target neighborhoods on the basis of a concentration of problems that included high crime rates, neighborhood deterioration, poverty, and a lack of available services for youths.

In addition to living in the target neighborhood and attending the target school, youths have to meet age, grade, and "risk factor" requirements to be eligible for participation. Requirements were set at 11 to 13 years of age and grade six or seven at time of recruitment. Risk-factor requirements related to school, family, or personal characteristics. School risk criteria included a combination of performance problems—poor grades, grade retention, or placement in special education—and behavior problems—truancy, tardiness, out-of-school suspension, or disruptive behavior in school. Family risk criteria included a history of family violence, child abuse or neglect, and gang membership or criminal behavior. Personal risk criteria included drug use or sales, other delinquent behavior or arrest, mental illness, gang membership, history of abuse or neglect, and pregnancy. Youths meeting at least one of these risk criteria were identified in a joint effort in which case management, school, law enforcement, and juvenile court personnel participated.

On the basis of considerations suggested by the integrated theory of delinquency, the CAR program model incorporates eight core services with intensive case management as the centerpiece. The other seven services are education services, afterschool and summer activities, mentoring, incentives (monetary and gift), family services, community policing and enhanced enforcement, and juvenile justice intervention.

Case managers, who are responsible for caseloads of 15 to 18 youths and their families, prepare comprehensive service plans and work closely with the youths and their families to implement them. Case managers become familiar with the youths and families through frequent contacts at school and home. Education services include tutoring or homework assistance and referrals for educational testing and remediation. The youths also are offered the opportunity to participate in afterschool and summer recreational, life skills, and leadership development activities and other positive individual and peer group experiences. Through arrangements with local organizations, mentors for youths in need of a caring relationship with an adult are provided. Programs reward youths who regularly attend program activities and adhere to program rules with gifts, special events, and stipends.

Family services include referral to individual, group, and family counseling; parenting skills training; treatment for substance abuse; assistance with health care, education, employment, and training; and assistance in obtaining income support and other concrete services.

The police participate directly in CAR programs through community-policing efforts, by patrolling safe corridors around the school, by developing relationships with community residents and program participants, and by trying to keep drug dealers off the streets. Juvenile court personnel also work on behalf of program participants who are involved with the juvenile justice system.

BRIDGEPORT CAR PROGRAM

Target School and Neighborhood

The target school for the Bridgeport CAR program is the Luis Munoz Marin School. Opened in 1992, the school has nearly 1,000 students in kindergarten through eighth grade. It offers a bilingual elementary program and is the receiving school for three feeder elementary schools ending at grade six. The student body is predominantly of Puerto Rican descent (75 percent). In addition, 19 percent of students are African American, 4 percent are Southeast Asian, and 2 percent are white. Eighty-six percent of the students are eligible for the free lunch program.

As a full-service school, the staff of the Luis Munoz Marin School includes a social worker and a psychologist, each of whom work three days a week, and a guidance counselor. It houses a year-round health clinic operated by the city health department and staffed by a nurse practitioner, social worker, and outreach worker. The school also has an afterschool program that operates every day from 3 P.M. to 6 P.M. Two neighborhood police officers spend four to six hours a week in the school on several different days teaching Drug Awareness and

Resistance Education to fifth-grade and Gang Resistance Education and Training classes to seventh-grade students.

The Luis Munoz Marin School is located at the edge of the target neighborhood for the program, a distressed 10-block area in the northern half of Bridgeport known as the East Side. The area's open-grid street pattern and easy automobile access from Interstate 95 contributed to an active illegal drug trade, and drive-by shootings were common. Burned out, abandoned, and boarded-up houses were scattered through the target area. Although earlier in its history the East Side included a mix of factories and residential housing, as manufacturing and assembly plants left the region and employment opportunities declined, prosperity was replaced by decay and neglect. About one-third of the households in the neighborhood received public assistance (U.S. Bureau of the Census, 1990), although more than two-thirds of CAR families received public assistance.

Concomitant with economic decline, the East Side has experienced a marked change in the racial and ethnic composition of the neighborhood during the past 25 years, although the population size has remained constant at about 13,000. In 1970 the population was 80 percent white and 15 percent Latino, whereas in 1990 the white population had declined to 17 percent, the Latino population had increased to 57 percent, and the African American population was 21 percent (Urban Institute, 1993).

In response to the deterioration and drug trafficking in the neighborhood, in 1992 the Bridgeport Police Department implemented a number of initiatives including the installation of a system of concrete barriers to disrupt traffic flow and enhanced enforcement against drug dealing and gang activity. In collaboration with the CAR project, the department opened a storefront office staffed jointly by designated neighborhood police officers and the CAR case managers (Hirota, 1995; Institute for Law and Justice, 1996).

Program Partners

The CAR program is sponsored by the Child Guidance Center of Greater Bridgeport, which as lead agency employs and coordinates case managers for the program. During the three-year demonstration period, the sponsor and lead agency was the Bridgeport Futures Initiative; Family Services Woodfield supervised the case managers for the first two years. The Child Guidance Center assumed responsibility for case management during the third year of the program, and when the demonstration period was over and the program continued operation with local funds, the Child Guidance Center became sponsor and lead agency. In addition to the Child Guidance Center and the Luis Munoz Marin School, the partners in the collaboration were the Bridgeport Police Department, the Bridgeport Health Department (which has an office in the school), the State of Connecticut Superior Court–Juvenile Matters, the state Department of Social Services, and Garfield Elementary School.

The Bridgeport program built on and extended the lead agency's relationships with its partner organizations, including the school system. As part of the proposal for the demonstration program, the directors of the collaborating organizations signed a memorandum of understanding outlining shared goals and objectives and a commitment to secure long-term funding. Thus, the program had the support of top-level executives from its inception.

Along with the agreement at the executive level, a trusting relationship among the partners at the program level was critical to success. For all of the partners, trust was developed by participating in discussion and planning for overall program goals and individual child–family goals and by working together over an extended time. The process of developing trust and confidence in fellow team members began at program start-up. At that time, a committee consisting of representatives of the police department and the juvenile justice system, the school principal, and a parent of a child in the school interviewed finalists for the two case manager positions and made hiring decisions jointly. The process gave each institution a stake in the program and also served to bond individual team members to one another. It also laid the foundation for more-direct communication among team members throughout the life of the project; for example, the school principal said that because she had been involved in selecting the case managers, she felt comfortable calling them directly, rather than following protocol and first calling their supervisors as she would have felt constrained to do otherwise.

Case Management

In Bridgeport the case managers are called "family mentors." They are the line staff who connect participants and their families to program services. Family mentors are not required to have MSW degrees but are chosen because of their previous experience and ability to relate to children and families served by the project. The family mentors fulfill all of the responsibilities of traditional case managers—identification and outreach, assessment, planning, monitoring, linking, and advocacy (Ridgely & Willenbring, 1992). They also assume some nontraditional roles. They serve as personal mentors to both the youths and their caregivers. In addition, they plan and lead group activities for program participants.

Through regular home visits, family mentors become familiar with the families with whom they work. On call 24 hours a day, they are available to families at times of crisis—for example, if the family is about to be evicted or if the youth has a serious problem at school. Family mentors supplement the school's own staff, by being a regular, even daily, presence at the school and checking on participants during lunch or at other times of the day. If necessary, they call or visit students early in the morning to make sure they attend school. As a result of this close relationship, family mentors are often able to provide a link between the youths' home life and school, for example, by providing the school with information and insights about problems the youths face at home.

Colocation Meetings

The innovative colocation team meetings, which take place weekly, are the primary mechanism for coordination of services among school, social services, and health agencies and criminal juvenile justice agencies. The term "colocation" has been used in the field to refer to the delivery of multiple services at one location. Bridgeport adapted the term to refer to the regular meeting of representatives of several organizations. Representatives of all of these organizations, including the two police officers, who teach classes at the school and spend most of their day policing the target neighborhood, attend these meetings.

As a major partner in the collaboration, the Luis Munoz Marin School allocates the time of several top administrators and staff to the colocation meetings. A neighboring elementary school, attended by some of the younger children enrolled in the program, sends its principal or social worker as well. Before each colocation meeting, the school's Student Assistance Team (SAT), made up of school personnel only, meet to review their own information and to raise concerns about students who are program participants or who are being considered for recruitment into the program.

Colocation meetings begin with reports on overall CAR and school activities, but most of the time is devoted to case presentations by family mentors. These discussions include regular reviews of cases and unmet service needs, identification of new resources, and development of new program activities.

Because they represent different sectors of the service community, each colocation team member has a different piece of information or can obtain additional information that adds to a collective understanding of each case. For example, from their knowledge of community residents, the police officers are aware of family members who are or have been involved with the criminal justice system. The welfare worker, who understands complex public assistance requirements, can determine family eligibility for benefits. The school social worker may have unconfirmed information on family problems, such as domestic violence, which a family mentor can clarify through home visits.

By using the family mentors' understanding of specific families and family dynamics, as well as the school's knowledge of the youths' classroom and school experience, the team develops service plans (individual or family counseling or therapy, psychological evaluation, afterschool recreation, tutoring, referral to other services) appropriate to their needs. In one case, information provided by a family mentor (that a participant's mother had left home the night before) resulted in the school's decision not to suspend the youth from school. Instead, the mitigating circumstances described by the family mentor led the school to address his school behavior problems in alternative ways. At other times, school administrators seek advice from family mentors about appropriate teacher assignments for troubled students.

Colocation meetings eliminate the need for each institution to gather information and act separately. Although the amount of time the school devotes to the SAT and colocation meetings can be substantial (several hours a week for multiple staff), school administrators believe that it is worthwhile. Because all of the information is consolidated and interagency communication and feedback are immediate and because school and agency responses are coordinated, problems can be addressed before they escalate. The range of providers participating in the meetings greatly facilitates resource identification and problem solving. The school credits the CAR program with contributing to a more peaceful school environment, because the program addresses the needs of especially high-risk students, many of whom have serious school behavior problems.

Case Study

Peter was having problems at Luis Munoz Marin. The family mentors learned from school staff that he was often truant and that when he did come to school, he was late. The school social worker felt that he might have a learning disorder, because he seemed to have trouble concentrating in his classes. Eventually, he began attending school less frequently, and the school was forced to take disciplinary action and place him in an alternative school. When Peter continued to be truant and tardy at his new school, his family mentor began to search for previously unnoticed problems at home that might account for his behavior.

The mentor discovered that Peter's mother, who was mentally ill, was not receiving adequate treatment. Presenting the case at a colocation meeting, the family mentor learned from clinically trained colleagues that the mother was not receiving appropriate medication. Her illness was proving extremely disruptive to Peter's home life. She would wake him up in the middle of the night, make him sleep in her bed, and turn off his alarm clock so that he would not wake up in time for school. The mother's behavior was preventing Peter from getting enough sleep, so that when he did make it to school, he was too tired to concentrate.

When this information was shared at the colocation meeting, clinicians present were able to tell the family mentor what kind of treatment was required as part of the mother's health care plan. With this information, the mentor was better able to advocate for the woman and secured the appropriate services for her. Clinicians at colocation also were able to describe the medication that the woman would be likely to need and to prepare the mentor to help the mother deal with side-effects of the medication. The welfare department staff were able to obtain funding to pay for the mother's transportation to the hospital for treatment.

After the treatment and medication began to take effect, the family mentor was able to get Peter and his mother to agree on a set of rules of conduct in the home. Peter had to be in bed by a certain time, and the mother promised not to disrupt his sleep. Peter's attendance record improved dramatically, and he was re-enrolled at the Luis Munoz Marin School.

Police Involvement

A particularly noteworthy element of the program is the strong relationship that has developed between the Bridgeport Police Department and the CAR program. As part of both CAR and the police initiative to reduce crime and drug trafficking in the neighborhood, the police department opened the East Side Police Officer Sector Terminal ("the POST"), a storefront police outpost on the main business street of the CAR target area. The family mentors and two neighborhood police officers share space at the POST, serve both CAR families and other neighborhood residents who come into the office, and often join forces.

Stationing police officers and family mentors together has "forced them to walk in each other's shoes," as one family mentor commented. Family mentors have learned some policing basics, and police officers have gained a better understanding of the needs and problems of the neighborhood and its residents. The police officers often make joint home visits with the case managers, so that situations that might otherwise lead to arrest lead instead to other resolutions.

On other occasions, it has been possible to implement an innovative criminal justice approach that involves the combination of official sanctions with counseling and participation in prosocial activities.

The strength of police involvement is also evident in the extent to which the two police officers have become engaged in school activities. They teach classes in the school on a regular basis and also lead youth trips and chaperone youths at CAR program activities. These police officers have become so involved in the welfare of the neighborhood youths that they have even volunteered their time to provide security at evening program events held at the school.

Juvenile Justice Involvement

The juvenile justice agency in Bridgeport is an equal partner in CAR and regularly attends the weekly colocation team meeting, even though it does not, of course, deal with all CAR youths. A designated probation officer to work with the program and with youths in the target neighborhood has been assigned by the juvenile justice agency. The officer has a smaller than usual caseload to provide time for participation in colocation and other community meetings. As part of a state initiative to decentralize services, she is based at the POST.

The involvement of the juvenile justice agency further increases the resources of the program, providing access to additional information on the youths and to the probation officer's expertise in counseling youths whose behavior has brought them into juvenile court. It also allows colocation members to use the authority of the juvenile court to mandate services to youths whom the program finds difficult to engage. For example, as part of the service plan, colocation members may ask the probation officer to require a youth to attend counseling or to participate regularly in afterschool or other program activities. The probation officer can then monitor the behavior and activities of the youth, thereby extending the resources of the family mentor. In this model, the supervision of youths on probation is closely coordinated with, rather than isolated from, the provision of other prevention and intervention services.

Bridging Bureaucratic and Professional Boundaries

Individual institutions and agencies have their own rules and regulations for providing services. Two areas that affect the provision of comprehensive, coordinated services are restrictions on information (case confidentiality) and restrictions on providing services (categorical services). In addition, personnel in each institution reflect the culture of the service sector with which they are affiliated and speak the language of their own professional discipline. Services integration provides a means of cutting through these restrictions and boundaries.

CAR addressed the issue of case confidentiality at the program's inception. Each institution that is a member of the CAR collaborative is bound by its own rules. School, police, juvenile probation, mental health agency, and health clinic all have legal and regulatory requirements outlining the type of information that is confidential and what may be shared.

To eliminate this barrier to the sharing of information among colocation team members, caregivers of participants sign a release form at time of recruitment into the program and agree to allow all agencies participating in the collaborative access to information. (However, if the caregiver wants a particular agency to be excluded from the colocation meeting, that wish is respected.)

The structure of the program and the relationships that the program established have motivated team members to cut through red tape, use their agencies' resources collectively on behalf of the program, and extend their efforts beyond the traditional boundaries imposed by their agency or professional disciplines. Reciprocally, having agency representatives at the colocation table provides family mentors with easier access to information and services than case managers who work in less comprehensive programs. The family mentors know whom to call to resolve problems and so can devote more of their time to proactive efforts on behalf of the youths and their families. These shared human and financial resources benefit program youths as well as the larger school community.

As a program based in the community, the CAR program uses its ties to benefit the broader student population. On many occasions, the program's responses have met real needs and provided significant services to the community's youths. For example, when they realized that some of the school's eighth-grade girls could not afford dresses for the graduation dance, family mentors asked the local newspaper to publicize a request for donations of dresses. These efforts led the program to open a boutique in the school's health clinic after school hours that gave 90 dresses to students. Then neighborhood merchants offered free cleaning and alterations, a florist offered corsages at half-price, and several teachers at the local high school contributed funds to purchase them so that every girl would have one.

Another collaboration resulted in the opportunity for both program participants and other students from the school to attend summer camp. A local day camp offered scholarships to many students, but the youths still needed transportation to get there. Because program funds to cover the cost of bus transportation to the camp were not available, school administrators used their own transportation funds for this purpose. As a result, 60 students at the school were able to attend summer camp.

The involvement of professionals from a variety of disciplines in colocation meetings and in the program as a whole provides critical support and direction to family mentors, who are selected for their individual strengths, personal life experiences, and field experience rather than educational or professional credentials. Colocation meetings offer family mentors access to the expertise of professionals who understand the stresses of the mentors' job and can help them grapple with the role boundary conflicts that may arise as a result of the close relationships that they form with program participants.

CHALLENGES AND OPPORTUNITIES OF THE CAR MODEL

The very barriers that collaborative programs seek to eliminate are the ones that make these programs a challenge to implement. The sometimes conflicting roles of the organizations involved in the collaboration create tension between staff who must enforce the regulations of their agencies and staff who are attempting to engage families in a voluntary service. This tension was evident when a school health clinic worker, repeatedly required to enforce a regulation barring a student with lice from school, attempted to have the case manager assist in this enforcement. The adversarial relationship between health clinic staff and family became a barrier to the case manager's recruitment of the family into the program. These tensions may sometimes be resolved at the colocation meetings, when the roles of staff members are clarified and a plan that integrates competing goals with the best interests of the family can be developed and facilitated.

Another challenge involves funding issues. Separate education, health, social services, mental health, and criminal justice funding streams make consolidation of funds for program operation and for the core case management component difficult to achieve. Agencies willing to allocate staff time to a collaborative program may be unwilling or unable to designate a portion of their funds for a program that crosses traditional boundaries.

Because the program involves collaboration across traditional organizational boundaries, it is particularly susceptible to changes in the political climate. A new mayor, a new police chief, or even a change in the local crime rate may affect the operation of the program. The innovative nature of the collaboration also means that for the program to be successful, there must be cooperation at multiple levels: Both managers and front-line workers need to be committed to the program.

CONCLUSION

In reviewing the barriers to services integration, Agranoff (1991) identified system fragmentation, inaccessibility, discontinuity, and unaccountability. To this list, we might add confidentiality issues and professionals' differing frames of reference. This chapter describes one program in which many of these obstacles were surmounted. To the degree that it was successful, the CAR program achieved services integration by building trust and communication across agencies and across hierarchical levels through a long period of development and by holding regular meetings in which staff in different professions became a source of support and education rather than friction to each other. The Bridgeport CAR program used colocation of key service providers, which led to cross-discipline understanding and fertilization; obtained the commitment and flexibility of key school personnel; and developed a high level of esprit de corps, which provided the glue that made it easier for all participants to deal with the frustrating circumstances that life in distressed neighborhoods regularly provides.

REFERENCES

Agranoff, R. (1991). Human services integration: Past and present challenges in public administration. *Public Administration Review, 51*, 533–542.

Akers, R. L., Krohn, M. D., Lanza-Kaduce, L., & Radosevich, M. (1979). Social learning and deviant behavior: A specific test of a general theory. *American Sociological Review, 44*, 635–655.

Allen-Meares, P., Washington, R. O., & Welsh, B. L. (1996). *Social work services in schools* (2nd ed.). Boston: Allyn & Bacon.

Bandura, A. (1977). Self-efficacy: Toward a unifying theory of behavioral change. *Psychological Review, 84*, 191–215.

Cloward, R., & Ohlin, L. E. (1960). *Delinquency and opportunity: A theory of delinquent gangs.* Glencoe, IL: Free Press.

Corbett, T., & Farber, N. (1990). *Schools, families, and social services: An exploration of the emerging relationship between the education and the welfare systems* (Draft of a research proposal). Madison: University of Wisconsin–Madison, Institute for Research on Poverty.

Elliott, D. S., Huizinga, D., & Ageton, S. S. (1985). *Explaining delinquency and drug use.* Beverly Hills, CA: Sage Publications.

Hirota, J. M. (1995). *Children at risk: An interim report on organizational structure and dynamics.* New York: Columbia University, Center on Addiction and Substance Abuse.

Hirschi, T. (1969). *Causes of delinquency.* Berkeley: University of California Press.

Institute for Law and Justice. (1996). *Children at Risk Program: Review of policing activities* (Report prepared for National Institute of Justice, U.S. Department of Justice, and the Urban Institute). Alexandria, VA: Author.

Kahn, A. J., & Kamerman, S. B. (1992). *Integrating services integration: An overview of initiatives, issues and possibilities.* New York: National Center for Children in Poverty.

Kirst, M. D. (1993). Changing the system for children's services: Building linkages with schools. In Council of Chief State School Officers (Ed.), *Ensuring student success through collaboration: Summer Institute papers and recommendations of the Council of Chief State School Officers* (pp. 9–15). Washington, DC: Council of Chief State School Officers.

Levy, J. (1991). Schools and social services: A nascent partnership. *Families in Society, 72,* 310–313.

Merton, R. K. (1957). *Social theory and social structure.* New York: Free Press.

Morrill, W. A., & Gerry, M. H. (1990, February). *Integrating the delivery of services to school-aged children at risk: Toward a definition of American experience and experimentation* (Paper prepared for the Conference on Children and Youth at Risk sponsored by the U.S. Department of Education and the Organization for Economic Cooperation and Development, Washington, DC). Washington, DC: U.S. Department of Health and Human Services, Office of the Assistant Secretary for Planning and Evaluation.

Morrill, W. A., Reisner, E. R., Chimerine, C., & Marks, E. (1991). *Collaborations that integrate services for children and families: A framework for research.* Princeton, NJ: Mathtech; Washington, DC: Policy Studies Associates.

Ridgely, M. S., & Willenbring, M. L. (1992). Application of case management to drug abuse treatment: Overview of models and research issues. In R. S. Ashery (Ed.), *Progress and issues in case management* (Research Monograph 127, pp. 12–33). Rockville, MD: U.S. Department of Health and Human Services, Public Health Service, and National Institute on Drug Abuse, Alcohol, Drug Abuse, and Mental Health Administration.

Shepardson, B. (1994). Beyond books. *Spectrum, 27,* 6–14.

Tyack, D. (1992). Health and social services in public schools: Historical perspectives. *Future of Children, 2*(1), 19–31.

Urban Institute. (1993). *Underclass database constructed using census data from 1970 STF4-A and 1980 and 1990 STF3-A.* Washington, DC: Author.

U.S. Bureau of the Census. (1990). *1990 U.S. census data: Database C9OSTF3A* [online]. http://www.census.gov.

This chapter was originally published in the July 1997 issue of Social Work in Education, *vol. 19, pp. 176–188.*

30 School-Linked Comprehensive Services: Promising Beginnings, Lessons Learned, and Future Challenges

Katharine Briar-Lawson, Hal A. Lawson, Connie Collier, and Alfred Joseph

As a growing number of children, youths, and families develop problems related to learning, development, health, and well-being, their concerns increasingly affect the various helping professions (for example, social work, education, health, and recreation and leisure) and work organizations (for example, child protective services, public schools, health education organizations, and recreation and leisure agencies) that serve children and families. This interdependence compels innovative strategies that depart from traditional ways of defining and solving problems.

Social workers are assuming leadership roles in innovations involving schools, social and health services agencies, and families (Denham, 1996; Franklin & Streeter, 1995; Hare, 1995). In these innovations, families and helping professionals are working together (U.S. General Accounting Office, 1992). If the dire needs of children, youths, families, neighborhoods, and communities are interdependent, then the helping professions and their work and other relevant organizations must become more interdependent.

Because the needs and challenges of children serve as an early-warning system for many other societal needs and challenges and because schools are children's only universal entitlement, schools are being redesigned to help address interdependent problems. Several states are allocating special resources to these initiatives (for example, New Jersey, Kentucky, California, Florida, and Missouri). A growing number of schools are colocating social and health services providers onsite and are establishing communication and organizational partnerships with others in the community. The label "school-linked services" has been applied to these collaborations and partnerships, although some prefer the term "full-service schools" (Dryfoos, 1994).

These initiatives vary considerably, from minimal parent involvement to redirected school missions for family support (Epstein, 1995; Hooper-Briar & Lawson, 1996). Some schools have chosen to concentrate on children and youths by establishing youth centers while restricting parent involvement to Parent–Teacher Associations. Others combine the two, seeking to involve parents and youths in service delivery and educational support. Still others are revitalizing the community-schools concept, many using the model of the settlement house

(Harkavy & Puckett, 1994; Lawson, Briar-Lawson, & Lawson, 1997; Tetleman, 1996). These schools offer day, week, and full-year programs for children, youths, parents, and other community members. Some also promote economic and community development.

Needs exist for across-site information sharing, learning, development, and evaluation. Drawing on site visits in 36 states, interview data, and a literature review (Hooper-Briar & Lawson, 1996; Lawson & Briar-Lawson, 1997), this chapter identifies lessons learned from past and present work. We view innovations involving collaborative practices, organizational partnerships, and school-linked services as having different generations. We assess the first generation and offer a primer for a second generation of partnerships (Hooper-Briar & Lawson, 1996).

FIRST-GENERATION PARTNERSHIPS

School-linked services are one of three changes under way in many schools (community schooling and parent involvement are the other two). It is helpful to frame these changes against a historical backdrop (Harkavy & Puckett, 1994; Tyack, 1992; Tyack & Cuban, 1995).

Legacies of Jane Addams and John Dewey

Today's priorities for community-responsive and integrative practices are not new to social work or education. Schools have always had some kind of services even if these have not been provided by social workers (Tyack, 1992). Social work pioneer Jane Addams and her work at Hull House deeply influenced John Dewey and the thinking, writing, and practices that led to the promotion of community-based schooling. Hull House promoted family-centered education and supports along with occupational opportunities and cultural preservation activities (Harkavy & Puckett, 1994).

Unfortunately, Addams's holistic, family-supportive, and community-based strategies gradually declined as more specialized, categorical schools and service systems evolved. The expressed purposes of public schooling were to stop the exploitation of child labor and nurture children as future citizens in the democracy. A hidden purpose was to compensate for perceived problems in parents and families. Schools were expected to perform as local parents, reflected in the legal doctrine in loco parentis.

During this century, many schools and child-serving agencies became increasingly disconnected from families. In fact, both have alienated those whom they serve. For example, today's families may confront as many as 14 service providers, each with different conceptions of family needs and problems and with different language systems and intervention strategies. In addition to these providers, the most vulnerable families also must navigate a maze of organizations including but not limited to schools, social services agencies, health agencies, and recreational agencies. Unfortunately, even though they are involved in the lives of the same families, these organizations often do not communicate with each other, let alone coordinate or collaborate. No one benefits under these circumstances.

Lessons Learned

Today's school reform strategy—parent involvement—is an effort to reconnect with parents and families. Similarly, the school-linked service movement is a hybrid designed to help reconnect children and, in many cases, their families to schools and other recreational, social, and health services agencies.

Key Concepts for Change. The key words for change reveal leaders' thinking and action strategies. Four related concepts have been used nationally and internationally to identify, describe, and explain first-generation work. *Interprofessional collaboration* describes efforts to get specialized helping professionals to work together. *Service integration* refers to efforts to coordinate and blend the intervention and improvement strategies professionals offer to children, youths, and families. *Systems change* involves revisions in job descriptions, leadership structures, accountability requirements, resource allocation, work cultures, and policies needed to facilitate interprofessional collaboration and service integration. *School-linked comprehensive services* colocate and link educators with service providers—a strategy that connects the other three concepts.

These key concepts are derived from three assumptions. First, colocating professionals at schools and expanding communication will stop duplication of efforts, and families will make greater use of services, in part because the services will be more accessible. Accessibility of services and service providers is the main need; their quality is less of an issue. By coordinating conventional service strategies, outcomes for children, youths, and families will improve. Needy children will be helped, and the school's work will be facilitated. Second, school professionals, especially teachers, need not be directly involved in planning and decision making about services. Schools need not change appreciably, because the needs and problems reside in the children, youths, and families, and service providers have the responsibility to address these needs and problems. Third, social workers have access to a knowledge base that allows them to critically evaluate these assumptions.

Understanding Alienation and Vulnerability. Many service systems designed to promote improved functioning among children and families are failing them (Bruner, 1996). This failure has been attributed to a number of factors, including lack of cultural competence, lack of family-centered practice, excessive specialization, use of categorical approaches, and insufficient resources. Calabrese (1990) suggested that some school practices "generate high minority dropout rates and disproportionately high numbers of minority student suspensions and placements in mentally or emotionally retarded classes" (p. 148). He also found that parents of color felt more alienated from schools than white parents. The parents of color had greater feelings of isolation and powerlessness and felt that teachers were unfriendly, that they were not invited to the school as often as they should be, that school policies were arbitrary, and that they were seldom consulted when there was a policy change. Some had grave doubts about the welfare of their children while at school.

These findings and others challenge some of the assumptions of the first-generation partnerships. It is highly unlikely that people who feel alienated and who fear for the emotional and academic well-being of their children will use many school-linked services. Both schools and social and health services agencies must reach out to alienated parents and youths. Similarly, few school-linked initiatives have involved classroom-based services, which are responsive to teachers' needs as well as students'. At best, most schools have had schoolwide or targeted services serving a special population, such as teenage mothers, child abuse victims, truant children, suspended students, or dropouts.

Beyond Child-Centered Coordinated Services. Many schools have framed their work as "coordinating services for children" (Cibulka & Kritek, 1996). While focusing attention on individual children, educators have hoped to improve their schools, so much so that their work is overly school centered. Beyond these initiatives, ecological thinking compels simultaneous change strategies that support and strengthen families, neighborhoods, and community organizations. In this perspective, although the characteristics of individual children and school performance are important priorities, they are not the only ones.

After families gain equal priority, all organizations and helping professions face the challenges of family-centered practice. Conventional service strategies are an important component of family-centered practice, but services alone will not address all the needs and problems. In this sense, "services" and "comprehensive services" are important but are insufficient to improve results. Families also need supports (for example, neighborhood networks, barter systems, occupational development) and resources (for example, transportation assistance, flexible dollars for child care). As families are enfranchised as joint designers of strategies intended to help them, school-linked service providers will face increasing demands for these social supports and resources in addition to services.

Moreover, once families and neighborhoods are targeted, school-linked service configurations alone are not likely to mobilize all needed stakeholders. New community-based and -led coalitions are required. Schools are key members, and so are the social, justice, and health services providers linked to them. However, even the best school-linked service configuration cannot do it all alone. School–family–community consortia need to be convened so that root causes such as evictions, poverty, marginalization, and racism can be addressed.

Beyond Colocation. Service systems that are ineffective in the community are not likely to become effective merely because they have been colocated at the school. First, the service must be adapted to the school setting. For example, one author found that renaming school-based child protection workers "family support workers" and assigning them new functions helped encourage families to seek help at the school. Second, leaders must integrate their services with others. For example, relationships with educators have not been firmly established on many sites. Third, accountability structures need to be more flexible. For example, changes in one worker's name, functions, and roles will not amount to much if the supervision of staff remains with the loaning agency.

Many of these challenges have not been well understood. For example, teachers, principals, counselors, and school nurses may wonder why service providers are not more responsive to their referrals, needs, and requests to serve on problem-solving teams. In addition, most service providers have eligibility requirements for their services, which often means that children must be in crisis before providers can help them. Thus, children and families referred by teachers will not benefit from primary prevention and early intervention, a chief aim of relocating services at the school.

In addition, services need to be more flexible and responsive to the first indications of need in children and families as identified by referring teachers and other school personnel. For example, a high-risk child abuse referral made by a teacher may be deemed a low-risk referral by a child protection worker. If service providers fail to respond to teachers, the aims for school-linked services are not achieved. There should be agreed-on, integrated risk detection, assessment, referral, and follow-up systems that allow close collaboration between teachers and service providers. As these are developed, school-linked services will double as teacher and family support strategies.

Shared Accountability for Outcomes. Outcomes accountability is a reality in school communities. At the same time, a child's learning and academic achievement are inseparable from indicators of health status, family well-being, and characteristics of local neighborhoods. Ideally, this means that a teacher's success is also the success of a social worker or health professional. Unfortunately, real shared accountability for child and family outcomes is difficult to find.

A youth who has successfully used a school-linked substance abuse counseling program but continues to fail in school will be impeded both in his or her overall occupational goals and in potential long-term sobriety. A youth performing well in school but arrested for theft and drug dealing so he or she can put food on the table may not be able to move out of the conditions that led to stealing and drug dealing. Although teachers, social workers, health professionals, and law enforcement providers cannot be expected to forgo their formal roles and responsibilities, collaboration requires that all attend to the social, health, and familial impact of their work while service providers attend to the educational implications and success of their children and families.

In the future, shared accountability for outcomes may be a requirement. For example, new policies from the U.S. Children's Bureau require that child welfare services become accountable for more than child safety, especially in cases of abuse and neglect. In addition, school outcomes will be assessed as a measure of child protection and welfare (Williams, 1996). Moving toward "shared or collaborative accountability" will be a key challenge of the next generation of initiatives (Young, Gardner, Coley, Schorr, & Bruner, 1994). Without it, children, youths, and families may not improve and succeed.

Despite notable exceptions, such as California's Healthy Start and New Jersey's School-Based Youth Services Program (Tetleman, 1996; Wagner & Golan, 1996), comprehensive and integrative evaluations have not been undertaken. Although the majority of sites have data on the number of people they have served, most do not have evidence in support of improvements in the quality of services and supports offered. Some data are encouraging and merit follow-up evaluations. For example, reductions have been documented in out-of-home care, detention, juvenile justice involvement, teenage pregnancy, substance involvement, truancy, suspensions and dropouts, and behavioral disruptions (Lawson & Briar-Lawson, 1997; Tetleman, 1996). With minor exceptions (Wagner & Golan, 1996), these improvements are not linked to improvements in academic achievement in school. Service provision has not been closely integrated with school reform (Gaston & Brown, 1995; Lawson & Briar-Lawson, 1997).

Problems of Replication. Even the most promising demonstration projects are difficult to replicate and institutionalize. "Going to scale" is a major challenge across the nation because the developmental progression of these initiatives is not well documented, technical assistance and capacity-building help are in short supply, and the human and fiscal resources needed to launch these projects are unavailable. Some social workers and educators estimate that more than 80 percent of their students and families are "at risk." There will never be enough service providers to meet the needs of every vulnerable child, youth, family, and community. Some well-intentioned initiatives have mobilized community service providers for work in schools yet have ignored the student support and services professionals (school social workers, nurses, counselors, psychologists) already working there (Adelman, 1996). In fact, some of the turf wars and boundary problems associated with school-linked services occur because of the exclusion of existing school professionals.

Social and health services professionals and pupil support professionals already onsite need to be redeployed (Adelman, 1996; Smith, 1995). Moreover, parent outreach and training can generate additional services and supports while creating occupational ladders for parents. Parents can play key roles as paraprofessional educators and service providers by working with at-risk children, youths, and families at school and helping with home visits and family supports in the community. In addition, children and youths can deliver services to each other. They can be effective in truancy outreach and in providing support groups as peer mediators and natural helpers for those who feel misunderstood at home and at school. Mobilizing these untapped resources helps to integrate separate change initiatives and recasts the role of school social workers in several ways: Social workers can help the highest risk families, a job for which they are uniquely prepared; can play lead roles as parent and youth mobilizers, trainers, coordinators, and supervisors (Alameda, 1996); and can become conveners and mobilizers of expanded resource networks and community consortia.

SECOND-GENERATION PARTNERSHIPS

Demonstration Projects

A second generation of partnerships can build on the promising beginnings and lessons learned from the first. Our thinking about these partnerships is informed by our demonstration projects, in which we have tried to integrate separate change strategies. Likewise, some authors (Alameda, 1996; Foree, 1996; Lipscomb, 1996) have reported that several parent groups in southern Florida and Cincinnati have had a positive impact on children's learning, attendance, and aspirations.

RAINMAKERS. In RAINMAKERS in Florida, low-income volunteers challenged by language barriers and even hostility from some of the helping institutions mobilized services, supports, and outreach. The group's school, along with social services and teacher supports, now regularly wins awards and ranks in the top of Title I schools in the state. The group, which has achieved its own independent status as an agency within the school and the community so it can receive its own grants, opened a child care center, a source of jobs for other low-income parents.

West End Philadelphia Improvement Corps. University, school, and community advocates in the West End Philadelphia Improvement Corps developed a "wraparound" service and teaching strategy for youths and their families. Working with a group of 21 of the most challenged eighth graders who had repeated several previous grades and had failed eighth grade, the corps designed a special summer school involving parents, teachers, and service providers that focused on the strengths and aspirations of the youths. The need for more comprehensive, tailored supports was evident; for example, two youths were teenage mothers, and several others had cases pending in juvenile court. When the youths were asked about their greatest fear, many said they were afraid that they would be killed before they reached adulthood.

The 21 students had two teachers who had high expectations for them and balanced these expectations with individual attention and support. In addition, an on-site parent advocate and social services student intern acted as academic tutors on some days and on others spent their time redirecting disruptive behaviors and repairing the youths' fragile self-esteem. The parent advocate worked with the youths' parents and caregivers, enlisting contractual agreements from them in concert with their children.

The results surprised everyone. All 21 youths in the summer school project completed eighth-grade requirements in the summer term and were promoted to ninth grade. Most important, the support spilled into their personal lives. Having professionals invest time and energy in caring about their success was a foreign notion to many students. One young woman recalled her previous experience with schooling: "In eighth grade they just give us it [assignments] and tell us to do it, they ain't gonna care if we pass. . . . In summer school, they did [care], 'cause we all passed. . . . I won't say they made me do it [school work], but they pressured me to do it, they, like, kept on my back to make sure I did it." The teachers and social services staff provided enough support that these students overcame their negativity about school.

By the end of the term, all of the students expressed an interest in attending college. In looking back a year later on their summer school experience, the students were aware of their poor behavior and achievement. One student who described herself as she was during her eighth-grade year said, "[I was] gloomy and disruptive. I ain't listening. I ain't gonna do what I was told. I just did what I wanna do." The same student had much different views of schooling after the project: "I don't wanna be in school for the rest of my life. . . . I want to get an education. I would like to go to college and everything."

The interplay between teachers and service providers was key to the success of the project. When stressed or upset during class, instead of walking out and spending the day on the streets, the youths had the parent advocate and student intern with whom to discuss their learning barriers, levels of frustration, or worries over a court appearance or being a young parent. After the discussions, the students were able to become motivated again to learn and succeed in school.

Two of the authors recently completed follow-up interviews with the youths after the ninth-grade year (Collier & Joseph, in press). The youths were again failing. The two authors provided intensive supports during summer school but could not during the students' high school years because their grant covered interventions only with middle school students. Although most of the youths continued to have some contact with the parent advocate and student intern, they did not have the immediate supports of the demonstration project that had penetrated their lives and classrooms. Even with on-site school counselors and social workers in their high schools, the students lacked the more intensive supports that seemed to be key to their success in summer school.

This experience compares with others' (Lawson & Briar-Lawson, 1997). Classroom-based services and supports that help teachers as well as children need to be built in across an entire school. A one-year, one-class intervention will not provide lasting supports for vulnerable children and youths.

Responsive, Enfranchising Practices

More services may not include the right or enfranchising services children, youths, and families need to become more successful in their functioning and problem solving. Regardless of the numbers of service providers linked to a collaborative, families, youths, and children sometimes report that they do not feel well treated by the service providers or teachers (Alameda, 1996).

Effective collaborative practices must be enfranchising and empowering. For example, teachers will have a much greater likelihood of using school-linked services if they have helped design them. Parents will react differently if they are partners and not just clients or cases needing to be managed. If all stakeholders see the services as responsive and tailored to their needs, there is a greater likelihood of more timely and appropriate service use. Top-down, mandated change strategies are not likely to produce these necessary conditions.

Children, parents, families, and professionals often feel like they are under siege and blamed. Some children and parents claim they are being maltreated, and others feel they are discriminated against because they are poor or ethnically or racially different and because service providers are culturally insensitive or hurtful. Teachers and service providers may have encountered such negativity from some clients that they adopt a protective shield, carrying mace and separating themselves from those they serve with armored reception areas, locked school and classroom doors, and police-based hallway patrols.

Working agreements about blame-free problem-solving strategies, bills of rights written by parents about how they are to be treated, and codes of conduct or rights that students write with their teachers in their interactions with each other are examples of culture building that reinforces the service enhancements in the school. In parent groups delivering support services to one another, a first act is to seek more positive interactions with service providers and educators. Bills of rights and mediation skills are part of the work to improve the maltreatment syndromes that have developed over time.

Addressing School Failure as a Social Work Issue

Social workers need to show how dropout, teenage pregnancy, depression, sub-stance abuse, and other problems can be averted if teachers empower students to learn and achieve in ways similar to the summer school demonstration project. This empowerment involves getting help into classrooms, recasting the work of teachers, and supporting them. Classroom-based social workers, parent para-professionals, volunteers from businesses, and university students can help re-verse cycles of failure.

School policies, especially curricular tracking, can negatively affect the lives of children, youths, and families. There is a wealth of evidence that tracking alienates children, racially segregates classrooms, increases antisocial behavior, and leads to student dropout (Broussard & Joseph, 1996). Social workers are obligated by the *NASW Code of Ethics* (NASW, 1996) to challenge any policy that interferes with clients having access to opportunities and resources. Schools should be places where services and resources are available to everyone.

BUILDING SCHOOL, FAMILY, AND COMMUNITY CAPACITIES

Facilitating second-generation, advocacy-based work requires expanded roles and practices for school social workers. To advance these, social workers need to be freed from some current work responsibilities. Some social workers have found that this can be accomplished when they form partnerships with parents and youths. For example, as social workers build parent-run family resource and youth support centers, parents and youths themselves can address issues such as truancy with outreach efforts and can help others find the appropriate information and referral services. As social workers build new roles for chal-lenged youths and parents, they simultaneously refocus their own job descrip-tion on capacity building and resource mobilization. When school social work-ers move into roles of facilitators of family resource centers and collaboratives, they also maximize supports for teachers, parents, and others. A collaborative of service providers linked to classrooms can place school social workers in the role of advocating for the needs of the teachers, youths, and families rather than trying to meet all the needs themselves.

School social workers have pivotal roles to play in helping educators and other professionals understand poverty and develop culturally responsive, fam-ily-centered practice and root cause problem-solving strategies. For many schools, reform cannot be effectively achieved without school-linked services, parent empowerment, and community development, because the children and youths schools hope to better educate are often besieged by the challenges of poverty, family and community stress, trauma, and neglect. The crisis created by welfare reform will only aggravate these conditions. Social workers can help others develop cultural competence, empathy, high expectations, and strengths-based teaching and service strategies. In their facilitative role, school social workers can help all who serve children, youths, and families adopt shared codes of ethics and can help agencies and schools adopt enfranchising missions, policies, and practices. This work may require designing and implementing cross-system training and ongoing staff development to ensure more cohesive practices across agencies and organizations.

School social workers can advocate for parent stipends and jobs linked to the school and community. It is expected that the welfare reform crisis will become a child welfare crisis because more children will be in foster care. School social workers can help protect some of the most challenged parents from losing their children to foster care because they are jobless and have no welfare grant. School social workers can help child protection workers relocate to the school to focus on placement prevention and occupational development for poor, jobless parents. For example, in one community, child protection workers located at a school developed an estimated diversion rate of 87 percent among families that would have been charged with neglect (Tanoury, Saunders, & Lusk, 1996).

Even when community professionals are recruited into the school, there will never be enough professionals to address unmet needs because most eligibility criteria require families to be in crisis before they can obtain help. To fill the prevention gap, school social workers can promote among agencies and the community the need to build prevention and early intervention occupational ladders into the school and other organizations. Microenterprise development also is needed; neighborhood child care and family resource centers can be promoted and financed though local and state investments in the poor. Community members can advocate for such change through a community–school consortium. School social workers can help convene such consortia and reframe what are now "student outcome" problems as "community development" issues. Moreover, the consortia may help the school address and change such practices as tracking and suspensions.

Rising poverty and inequality are predictably spawning educational and school improvement agendas among politicians across the nation. School social workers are in key positions to help others understand the relationship among poverty, marginalization, welfare terminations, racism, and educational outcomes. Because educational reform agendas are top concerns among many elected officials, the social work profession must inform policy reform debates with its longheld knowledge about poverty and its effects on children's life chances.

CONCLUSION

School-linked services can be transformational tools, especially when tied to other local family and community development efforts. The challenges facing children, families, and school communities will not be addressed without schools and families shaping the community problem-solving agenda. Reminiscent of the work of Jane Addams and John Dewey, this is a way for school social workers and school-linked services to move forward to the future while looking back.

REFERENCES

Adelman, H. (1996). *Restructuring education support services: Toward the concept of an enabling component.* Kent, OH: American School Health Association.

Alameda, T. (1996). The Healthy Learners Project: Bringing the community into the school. In K. Hooper-Briar & H. Lawson (Eds.), *Expanding partnerships for vulnerable children, youth and families* (pp. 46–56). Alexandria, VA: Council on Social Work Education.

Broussard, C. A., & Joseph, A. (1996). Tracking: A child welfare issue? In K. Hooper-Briar & H. Lawson (Eds.), *Expanding partnerships for vulnerable children, youth and families* (pp. 121–132). Alexandria, VA: Council on Social Work Education.

Bruner, C. (1996). *Realizing a vision for children, families and neighborhoods.* Des Moines, IA: National Center for Service Integration, Child and Family Policy Center.

Calabrese, R. L. (1990). The public school: A source of alienation for minority parents. *Journal of Negro Education, 14,* 148–153.

Cibulka, J., & Kritek, W. (Eds.). (1996). *Coordination among schools, families and communities.* Albany: State University of New York Press.

Collier, C., & Joseph, A. (in press). *Evaluating impacts and challenges for 91 youth in the WEPIC Summer School Program.* Oxford, OH: Miami University, Departments of Physical Education, Health, and Sport Studies and Family Studies and Social Work.

Denham, C. H. (1996). A report from the National Center for Social Work and Education Collaboration. In K. Hooper-Briar & H. Lawson (Eds.), *Expanding partnerships for vulnerable children, youth and families* (pp. 107–112). Alexandria, VA: Council on Social Work Education.

Dryfoos, J. (1994). *Full-service schools: A revolution in health and social services for children, youth and families.* San Francisco: Jossey-Bass.

Epstein, J. (1995). School/family/community partnerships: Caring for the children we share. *Phi Delta Kappan, 76,* 701–712.

Foree, S. (1996). Who is this lady called "Mrs. G" and why does everyone call her for help? One community's story on parent advocacy. In K. Hooper-Briar & H. Lawson (Eds.), *Expanding partnerships for vulnerable children, youth and families* (pp. 41–45). Alexandria, VA: Council on Social Work Education.

Franklin, C., & Streeter, C. L. (1995). School reform: Linking public schools with human services. *Social Work, 40,* 773–782.

Gaston, M., & Brown, S. (1995). *School restructuring and school-linked services: Working together for students and families.* San Francisco: Stuart Foundations.

Hare, I. (1995). School-linked services. In R. L. Edwards (Ed.-in-Chief), *Encyclopedia of social work* (19th ed., Vol. 3, pp. 2100–2109). Washington, DC: NASW Press.

Harkavy, I., & Puckett, J. (1994). Lessons from Hull House for the contemporary university. *Social Service Review, 68,* 299–321.

Hooper-Briar, K., & Lawson, H. (Eds.). (1996). *Expanding partnerships for vulnerable children, youth and families.* Alexandria, VA: Council on Social Work Education.

Lawson, H., & Briar-Lawson, K. (1997). *Connecting the dots: Progress toward the integration of school reform, school-linked services, and community schools.* Oxford, OH: Danforth Foundation and Institute for Educational Renewal at Miami University.

Lawson, H., Briar-Lawson, K., & Lawson, M. (1997). Mapping challenges for vulnerable children, youth and families: Implications for university-assisted community schools. *Universities and Community Schools, 5*(1), 80–95.

Lipscomb, A. (1996). Going the distance: A journey. In K. Hooper-Briar & H. Lawson (Eds.), *Expanding partnerships for vulnerable children, youth and families* (pp. 57–64). Alexandria, VA: Council on Social Work Education.

National Association of Social Workers. (1996). *NASW code of ethics.* Washington, DC: Author.

Smith, A. (1995). School-based case management: An integrated service model for early intervention with potential drop-outs. In *A series of solutions and strategies* (Vol. 10). Clemson, SC: Clemson University, National Dropout Prevention Center.

Tanoury, T., Saunders, M. A., & Lusk, M. (1996). Partnership with families, schools and communities: Using Title IV-A emergency assistance funds in expanding partnerships for vulnerable children, youth and families. In K. Hooper-Briar & H. Lawson (Eds.), *Expanding partnerships for vulnerable children, youth and families* (pp. 83–91). Alexandria, VA: Council on Social Work Education.

Tetleman, E. (1996). Implications for national policymakers. In K. Hooper-Briar & H. Lawson (Eds.), *Expanding partnerships for vulnerable children, youth and families* (pp. 298–304). Alexandria, VA: Council on Social Work Education.

Tyack, D. (1992). Health and social services in schools: Historical perspectives. *Future of Children, 2*(1), 19–31.

Tyack, D., & Cuban, L. (1995). *Tinkering toward utopia: A century of public school reform.* Cambridge, MA: Harvard University Press.

U.S. General Accounting Office. (1992). *Integrating human services: Linking at-risk families with services more successful than system reform efforts.* Washington, DC: U.S. Government Printing Office.

Wagner, M., & Golan, S. (1996). *California's Healthy Start school-linked services initiative: A summary of evaluation findings.* Menlo Park, CA: SRI International.

Williams, C. (1996, September). *Opening address.* National Child Welfare Conference, Southern Illinois University School of Social Work, Memphis.

Young, N., Gardner, S., Coley, S., Schorr, L., & Bruner, C. (1994). *Making a difference: Moving to outcome-based accountability for comprehensive service reforms.* Falls Church, VA: National Center for Service Integration.

The authors acknowledge support from the Danforth Foundation, the U.S. Department of Health and Human Services, the Dewitt Wallace Foundation, and the University of Pennsylvania West End Improvement Corps. However, the views expressed in this chapter are those of the authors.

This chapter was originally published in the July 1997 issue of Social Work in Education, *vol. 19, pp. 136–148.*

31

Establishing School-Based, Collaborative Teams to Coordinate Resources: A Case Study

Cynthia Lim and Howard S. Adelman

The need for integrating and linking education, social, and health services to better serve the multiple needs of students and families is well documented (Dryfoos, 1995; Kirst, 1991; Levy & Shepardson, 1992; Uphold & Graham, 1993). Although a school's primary purpose is to attend to the education needs of students, school and community personnel realize that noneducational needs pose significant barriers to learning. In the past decade, various school-based and school-linked service integration models have been demonstrated to integrate and coordinate school and community resources. Simultaneously, reform movements aimed at restructuring education have highlighted the need to expand traditional school services to provide comprehensive, coordinated services to students and families.

An important component of establishing school–community linkages is organizing existing school-owned and -operated support programs and services. Before establishing links and collaborating with outside agencies, schools need to organize the delivery of their internal services so that additional services are woven into the school's current system rather than just becoming another added-on program (Adelman, 1996).

A model using an enabling component has been proposed to help schools restructure the delivery of their internal support programs and services and establish collaborations with community resources (Adelman, 1996; Adelman & Taylor, 1994). A central element is the establishment of a school-based mechanism (for example, a resource coordinating team) to coordinate and enhance programs and resources, and the key mechanism for adapting the model to a new site is a change agent—the organizational facilitator (Rosenblum, DiCecco, Taylor, & Adelman, 1995). Although conceptualization of such mechanisms appears straightforward, actual implementation raises a multitude of complications. This chapter extends previous studies of the enabling component by describing the implementation process at two schools. The roles of the organizational facilitator are explored, as are the perceptions of the participants about the nature of the collaborative process. This chapter also provides an example of how school social workers can become involved in school reform activities and offers recommendations for how school social workers can be prepared to assume these roles.

ENABLING COMPONENT

Current school reform discussions center around changes in instruction, such as teaching activities and curriculum, and management, such as increased participation in decision making. Missing from the discussions is a comprehensive, integrated approach to addressing barriers to learning in ways that enable students to experience the benefits of instructional reform. From this perspective, it becomes essential that school restructuring agendas encompass three primary and complementary components: (1) instruction, (2) management, and (3) enabling (Adelman, 1996; Adelman & Taylor, 1994).

The concept of the enabling component is formulated around the proposition that a comprehensive, integrated continuum of enabling activity is essential to addressing the needs of the many students who encounter barriers to learning and performing satisfactorily at school. The enabling component stresses efforts to address specific problems students and their families experience, including establishing programs to promote healthy development and to foster positive functioning as the best way to prevent many learning, behavioral, emotional, and health problems and as a necessary adjunct to corrective interventions. To accomplish all this requires meshing school and community enabling activity.

One key element of the enabling component is the creation of a school-based collaborative mechanism—the resource coordinating team (Rosenblum et al., 1995)—that includes all school personnel involved in education support programs and services (for example, psychologists, counselors, school social workers, nurses, bilingual and Title I coordinators, and special education staff, as well as representatives of the administrative or governing body such as principal or assistant principal). The support personnel on the team typically are assigned to schools through a variety of funding sources.

A resource coordinating team is designed to facilitate coordination; ongoing enhancement; and, where feasible, integration of all enabling activity at a school site. Among the main tasks are mapping and analyzing existing school-owned and relevant community activity with a view to improving resource use and efficacy. As an aid in moving toward a comprehensive, integrated approach, programs and services are clustered into six programmatic areas: (1) classroom-focused enabling, (2) student and family assistance, (3) crisis assistance and prevention, (4) support for transitions, (5) home involvement in schooling, and (6) community outreach for involvement and support (including a focus on volunteers). Existing programs are charted according to these areas to foster a programmatic vision, to help team members visualize how enabling activities can be woven together, and to help clarify which areas need strengthening. After analysis of existing activity and resources, team members identify ways to improve resource use and enhance the school's overall approach to addressing barriers to learning.

Organizational facilitators can facilitate the establishment of an enabling component at schools. This professional facilitates change in three overlapping phases: The first stage is creating readiness—the facilitator introduces the model to the school and attempts to build interest and consensus for developing the component. The second stage is phasing in—the facilitator helps the site build an infrastructure for systemically addressing barriers to learning (including a resource coordinating team). In the third phase, institutionalization, the facilitator ensures that there are plans for maintenance and evolution of the component's infrastructure.

PILOT PROJECT

As part of a pilot project, the enabling component model was introduced to a group of about 50 schools (elementary, middle, and senior high schools) in the Los Angeles Unified School District (LAUSD). School social workers were used as organizational facilitators because their training in consultation and collaboration with school personnel made them well suited as change agents. At the initiation of the pilot project, several overlapping school reform efforts were under way in the school district. The administrative structure governing all schools in LAUSD had become decentralized, with administrative control, decision making, and accountability being shifted to local clusters of schools. In addition, some schools were participants in a voluntary restructuring movement called LEARN (Los Angeles Educational Alliance for Restructuring Now) aimed at improving educational outcomes by increasing parent participation, creating a school-based planning process, and adopting performance standards. Although restructuring support services is mentioned in each reform movement, the main focus is on instruction and management practices. The enabling component was piloted as a viable mechanism for restructuring support services in the hopes that it would be replicated in the future at schools in conjunction with ongoing reform efforts.

The difficulty of implementing systemic change in organizations is well documented (Beer, 1980; Hall & Hord, 1987; Hasenfeld, 1983; Zaltman & Duncan, 1977). Numerous barriers arise, such as lack of commitment from the leadership of the school or resistance to change from other stakeholder groups. For example, creation of mechanisms such as a resource coordinating team does not guarantee that services will be coordinated or that school personnel will work collaboratively. Team members must value such coordination and learn to establish effective working relationships, share information, and communicate freely with each other.

Two elementary schools were selected for the case study because they were farthest along in the implementation process of the enabling component and were being assisted by the same organizational facilitator. Information on the implementation process was gathered in a variety of ways to provide multiple perspectives and to enhance validity and reliability (Miles & Huberman, 1984; Spradley, 1980; Yin, 1984). The organizational facilitator's detailed notes of meetings and interactions with school personnel were content analyzed, the organizational facilitator was interviewed, and participant observations were conducted at resource coordinating team meetings at both schools over a three-month period. Near the end of the school year, each member of the team was interviewed, yielding 16 interviews. A semistructured instrument was used that covered topics such as the team member's vision of how the enabling component should

work, how the school dealt with support services before adoption of the enabling component and what changes had occurred, satisfaction with their school's
effort to change support services, appealing aspects, perceived strengths and
weaknesses, and potential impact. Interviews were about 30 minutes in duration, moving from general to more specific questions. (A copy of the interview
instrument is available on request.)

School A

School A, located in an urban suburb in northeastern Los Angeles, enrolled about
1,100 students in kindergarten through sixth grade on a year-round schedule.
Nearly 80 percent of the students were eligible to receive free or reduced-price
lunches based on family income, and 68 percent spoke Spanish as their primary
language. The student population was 87 percent Latino, 6 percent white, and
the remainder Asian or African American.

The support personnel assigned to the school were a full-time resource specialist teacher, a coordinator of bilingual programs, a dropout prevention consultant, a part-time nurse, and a part-time psychologist. The dropout prevention consultant's position was funded by a state dropout prevention program,
but the consultant was accountable to the principal. The nurse and psychologist
reported to offices centrally administered in the school district.

The support personnel characterized their service delivery system as fragmented and disconnected from the overall educational program before they
began resource coordination efforts. Service provision reflected the individual
efforts of separate professionals working independently of each other. According to one team member, "the right hand didn't know what the left hand was
doing." The principal recalled, "You didn't feel empowered. It didn't feel like
the support services people were part of our program. They were just sort of an
add-on—a convenience—and when you could get them to do what you wanted
them to do, that was great, and if you didn't, then that's just the way it was."

Before the enabling component was introduced to the principal in September
of the 1994–95 school year, the school had been involved in the LEARN school
reform process for a year. During that year, the principal and a teacher attended
training sessions on management, budgeting, strategic planning, and team building. After the presentation of the enabling component by the organizational facilitator, the principal agreed to its adoption because it was consistent with and
expanded on the reforms under way. She said, "it's not going to do any good to
have a wonderful curriculum if [we] don't have any way to impart it to the
children." The principal initiated a process for eliciting the involvement of potential members for a resource coordinating team and allocated time and space
for team meetings.

A variety of strategies were used to build interest and consensus among potential team members. The principal personally approached and invited some
team members to a meeting where they were introduced to the concept. The
organizational facilitator approached other team members by asking for their
input on how a resource coordinating team should operate at their school. A
majority of the team members conveyed an interest in improving strategies for

addressing barriers to learning. When asked, "How worthwhile do you think it is to make changes in the way support services operate at your school?" using a six-point response scale (6 = very worthwhile), the mean response was 5.9. Team members cited the lack of coordination of current resources as reasons why changes were needed. One team member commented, "We're talking about all these resources and going out and getting resources, but we have a lot going on now that's not coordinated." Other factors cited by team members were the changing demographics of families and the difficulties in disseminating information to families.

The resource coordinating team held its first meeting in November. The team consisted of the nurse, psychologist, resource specialist teacher, coordinator of bilingual programs, dropout prevention consultant, two classroom teachers, and two parent volunteers as well as the principal and assistant principal.

One of the first team tasks was to map existing resources in the school into the six programmatic areas of enabling activity. Under the facilitator's guidance, team members catalogued all of the current programs at the school and determined which programmatic areas were addressed (for example, classroom-focused enabling, student and family assistance). A listing of current and desired resources was recorded on a wall chart. Team members then analyzed where gaps existed in current activity and proposed programs or services that were needed. With assistance from the facilitator, team members developed plans to obtain desired resources.

In general, team members reported little or no difficulty in getting people involved on the team and did not feel it was difficult for them personally to participate. Part of the ease in participating on the team was because of such aspects of the enabling component as the ability to take a holistic, integrative view of interventions to address barriers to learning. One team member stated, "the format, the charts that showed an overall look of our school, which included our crisis team, classroom enabling, student transitioning, and parent involvement—all these things together, globally, made up our school." Another team member cited the advantages of teamwork or "philosophy of collaboration" in getting various disciplines to plan activities together. Other appealing aspects mentioned were the potential for greater community and parent involvement.

Follow-up meetings focused on topics such as instituting parent education classes, providing support for transitions, writing a school safety plan, and conflict resolution training. Discussion of individual programs allowed team members to see how well various activities were coordinated or integrated. For example, the dropout prevention consultant presented an overview of conflict resolution training she was providing for children on the student council. As she described how students were using skills to resolve peer conflicts on the play yard, other team members pointed out the need for similar training for all adult personnel in the school to cut down on the number of student discipline referrals to the office. Interactive discussions among team members resulted in plans to extend conflict resolution training to lunch duty personnel, teaching assistants, and teachers.

Because the school was interested in acquiring more volunteers, the organizational facilitator invited a county public health nurse to speak about community outreach activities. During the meeting team members agreed that immunizations were needed for a large number of families, and the public health nurse offered the services of her office. This exchange resulted in plans for a health fair during which immunizations and medical and dental screenings could be offered. Team meetings focused on obtaining community resources for the health fair and coordinating planning duties among team members. Contacts were made with a dental school to provide screenings, local businesses were approached to cover printing and refreshment expenses, and resources from within the district were solicited to provide referral information. The health fair, held at the end of the school year, was attended by many families. Although the health fair did not represent an institutional change in the delivery of services, the success of this one-time event demonstrated the power of the team's collaborative efforts.

Team meetings were well attended. The principal demonstrated commitment by providing time for teachers to attend meetings, setting aside classroom space, and participating as an active facilitator of meetings. The principal led the meetings with action-oriented questions such as "How can we incorporate more interaction with older and younger kids in the classroom meeting time?" which generated much interactive discussion and brainstorming among team members. Members conveyed respect for the opinions of others and freely offered suggestions.

To explore how resource coordination efforts changed the use of resources at their school, team members were asked what changes had occurred as a result of adopting the enabling component. Although the work of the various support personnel did not change, team members reported a greater awareness of the resources available in the school and community. One team member explained, "What the resource coordinating team has done is enable us to see what we've done and what we are doing with our . . . resources. And we also know what we'd like to get from them. It's enabled us to go out and get those things." Another change was the ability to view support services in a more holistic manner, or "looking at all the things we do as part of a program, rather than just a piece that needs fixing. [Our work] is part of a program; there are overall goals to it. Our support services people are really involved in being integral members, being leaders in our school."

One team member perceived a difference in the delivery of support services at the school as compared to other schools she worked with that did not have a resource coordinating mechanism. When asked how her role differed, she replied, "it's much more difficult to communicate [at the other school]. Everyone is doing things with the same student, and you'd never know about it because everyone is working in isolation. . . . This school feels more organized, and everybody knows what's going on. There are systems set up already to provide the proper referrals for parents and teachers, whether it has to do with academics or behavior."

When asked what they thought were the strengths of the resource coordinating team, members reported better coordination of resources and an ability to communicate with each other. A strength for one team member was "all your resources coming together for one purpose, and everyone is kept updated on what's going on within the school with the resources." Another team member stated, "it focuses the school. It helps people understand that we need to be more than just a place where children come to learn to read and write."

When team members were asked about the perceived weaknesses of the enabling component, time was a major constraint. The teachers who regularly participated on the team generally had available out-of-classroom time. Increasing teacher participation on the team would require more flexible scheduling arrangements.

Language barriers were also mentioned as a constraint. Team members at both schools acknowledged that more parent and community involvement was needed and that translators were required for non-English-speaking parents. A team member explained the dilemma as follows: "Community people . . . often don't speak English. [But] we can't conduct our meetings all in Spanish. We have to conduct them in English and Spanish, and that loses something in the translation."

Although most team members expressed a high level of satisfaction with their school's current efforts at restructuring (mean rating of 5.0 using a six-point scale, with 6 = very satisfied), team members felt there was still more to be done. Members also felt that resource coordination would have a strong impact on enabling students to learn (mean rating of 4.8 using a six-point scale, with 6 = strong impact). Some team members felt the commitment from the leadership and other team members was important, fearing that if the leadership or team membership changed, resource coordination would become more difficult.

School B

School B, located a few miles from School A, enrolled about 1,270 students in kindergarten through sixth grade on a year-round schedule. Nearly 95 percent of the school population was Latino, with the remainder Asian or white. About 80 percent of the students were eligible for reduced-price or free lunches based on parental income; about 75 percent had limited proficiency in English.

Support personnel assigned to this school consisted of a full-time nurse, a resource specialist teacher, a categorical programs coordinator, a part-time psychologist, and a part-time pupil services and attendance counselor. Although support personnel described their work as fragmented and individually focused before resource coordination, they did meet together as the guidance committee to discuss individual student cases.

When the enabling component was introduced to the principal in September of the 1994–95 school year, some members of the school staff had just completed extensive training in management, budgeting, strategic planning, and team building. The school adopted the LEARN program in 1994–95 and was in the midst of instituting various changes. The principal was reluctant to proceed with the enabling component because she did not want to overwhelm her staff.

She arranged for individual meetings between the organizational facilitator and several potential team members to gauge their interest level. When she was satisfied there was sufficient interest, she made an initial commitment to resource coordination and appointed the assistant principal to head the enabling component.

One deciding factor in considering implementation of the enabling component was the growing conviction that instructional reforms were insufficient to address barriers to learning. The principal explained that children were not learning "in spite of all these teaching strategies and all these materials." "We've done everything we can as educators, and the traditional educator role isn't enough—it's not working. We need to expand our description of what we need to do and how we need to do it within the course of a school day so that we meet the needs of the child, so he [or she] can benefit."

The organizational facilitator explained the model to potential team members individually or in small groups. Team members felt it worthwhile to make changes related to enabling activities (mean of 5.6 on a six-point scale, with 6 = very worthwhile) to enhance resources and improve services for children. Most team members reported that motivation to join the team was high because of a strong commitment among school personnel to improve student achievement.

The resource coordinating team held its first meeting in November. The team consisted of the nurse, psychologist, resource specialist teacher, categorical programs advisor, pupil services and attendance counselor, office manager, principal, and assistant principal. One of the first tasks accomplished was the mapping of existing resources and programs into the six programmatic areas of enabling activity and identifying desired programs to meet needs. A list of internal and external resources was produced. This activity provided the impetus to focus on programs related to support for transitions. The office manager had many ideas on how to improve their programs to welcome new families and volunteered to organize orientation materials for them. The result was a comprehensive welcoming booklet.

Other team meetings highlighted the need for information on availability of outside resources. The organizational facilitator helped arrange speakers from the school district's suicide prevention unit and the state-administered child health and disability prevention program; team members perceived these activities as very informative. In April the assistant principal folded various planning activities into the work of the resource coordinating team. One activity involved writing a school safety plan. Portions of meetings for the remainder of the school year were spent formulating objectives for the plan. This activity focused the team's attention on clarifying current resources and how they could be improved; the discussions also highlighted the complexities of developing systems for referral to outside agencies. Ironically, only a few decisions were made for meeting the specific objectives formulated for the school safety plan. However, the activity resulted in greater clarification and appreciation of the value of having a resource coordinating team.

The assistant principal kept the meetings on task and productive. She began each meeting with an update of accomplishments from the previous meeting, and she continually praised the efforts of team members. Meetings were characterized by feelings of warmth and empathy among team members. Early success with the organization of welcoming activities provided the team with tangible results and maintained momentum for change efforts. In addition, presentations from outside speakers provided a foundation for community linkages.

When team members were asked what changes had occurred as a result of adopting the enabling component, most team members cited better communication among support staff and increased awareness of individual efforts. Team members did not mention changes in their individual roles at the school but felt that the creation of the resource coordinating team produced a forum for team members to "meet, exchange ideas, and make suggestions." One team member commented, "there's a greater understanding and appreciation for all the work that we are all doing individually. We are certainly more aware of all the services that we are providing."

However, perceptions of change were not all positive. Several team members felt that the functioning of support services within their school was no different than before resource coordination efforts. One team member explained, "The efforts are more focused, more coordinated, but other than that, I don't know what to say. I can't really differentiate because of LEARN, and before that, we did all of this with this principal. It's hard to say what has changed. . . . It's hard to tell what all these changes are."

When asked what were the strengths of the resource coordinating team, team members reported better coordination of resources, an ability to communicate and share ideas with each other, and a sense of strong commitment from other team members. When asked about perceived weaknesses, time constraints were most often cited. Some team members felt frustrated spending so much time in meetings when there were children needing direct services. Others felt frustrated with the amount of time spent writing plans rather than implementing programs. One team member reported, "so far we have just been brainstorming, not implementing. . . . There has been nothing tangible or concrete." Other weaknesses included team members feeling uncomfortable with new roles and responsibilities. One team member mentioned that some support personnel did not feel comfortable assuming leadership roles for which they were not trained.

When team members were asked how satisfied they were with their school's current efforts at restructuring, most team members expressed a high level of satisfaction (mean rating of 5.0 using a six-point scale, with 6 = very satisfied). Several team members felt satisfied because of the commitment level of other team members. However, members felt there was still more to be done and expressed frustration at the slow pace of change. One member felt the team wanted to do more but was confined by the everyday needs in running the school.

Role of the Organizational Facilitator

The organizational facilitator played an important role in creating readiness for reform and helping phase in the resource coordinating team. In describing strategies used to create readiness, the organizational facilitator said she began her efforts with schools that expressed interest in the change process; she tailored her presentations to fit the circumstances and perceived expertise at the school. The facilitator took great care to emphasize that the enabling component was a model that could be adapted to and integrated with the educational program to comprehensively address barriers and enable learning, as well as to improve delivery of specific services.

This strategy worked well at the two schools studied. When asked what factors were considered before proceeding, both principals said the fit with their current activities was a big factor. The principal at school B stated, "One of the big considerations as I talked to [the organizational facilitator] was, 'does this fit?' If this is part of the integral whole, if this is what we are trying to do, then the help sounds wonderful. . . . But if it's another program, . . . then I wasn't interested. It took a little explanation on her part for me to see this was . . . help for us in getting to where we want to go educationally."

In phasing in the resource coordinating teams, the organizational facilitator helped maintain the commitment and motivation of team members by meeting periodically with individuals to provide ongoing support. She assisted team members in setting priorities and agendas for meetings, coordinated community contacts, and arranged visits to other sites. She also gained trust and respect by offering assistance in areas outside of the team's sphere of activity (for example, translating a letter or photocopying documents).

The organizational facilitator also contributed to building effective working relationships within teams by providing problem solving and ongoing support during meetings. She clarified and guided the work of the teams. In some instances, she steered the group toward more manageable tasks when their plans seemed too encompassing or overreaching. In other instances, she provided anecdotes from other schools about similar topics or offered referrals to resources.

LESSONS LEARNED

Although this study focused on only two schools, several factors can be identified that helped the adoption of resource coordination efforts. First, part of the schools' success in establishing resource coordinating teams was due to the strong commitment of the leadership and team members to the change process. They viewed coordination of enabling activities as a valuable and attainable endeavor and were motivated to bring about change. The commitment of the teams and culture of informal support also contributed to smooth functioning of the teams. At both schools, the leadership demonstrated commitment by allocating time for teachers to attend meetings and by personally attending meetings.

Second, successes leading to tangible results were important to validate team efforts and to continue the momentum for change. At school A, the implementation of a health fair demonstrated a measure of success. At school B, the production of a welcoming booklet presented tangible results.

Finally, the organizational facilitator played a key role by mobilizing and directing the energy of the teams. She assessed the level of readiness in the school; incorporated the capabilities of the school in her introductory presentations; and used interactive, individual contacts with team members to personalize explanations of the model. The facilitator also offered guidance and direction during team meetings and provided technical assistance and support to individual members between meetings.

The preliminary findings suggest that members perceived the creation of the collaborative team positively and valued the outcomes of their efforts. Whether the teams continue to work together in a collaborative manner to coordinate services remains to be seen. Examination of the efforts at these two schools in the second year will illuminate the extent to which momentum for change is maintained.

IMPLICATIONS FOR SOCIAL WORK PRACTICE

Restructuring movements in education and social services, in progress throughout the nation, have important implications for the role of school social workers. Social workers in schools must function as "case managers, chairs of transdisciplinary assessment teams, interdisciplinary team builders, technical training advisors, program planners, policymakers, and policy influencers" (Aguirre, 1995, p. 222). School social workers need to become more active in leadership and policy-making roles to highlight the need to expand traditional school services (Allen-Meares, 1994). Clearly, reform efforts in schools and communities provide an excellent opportunity for school social workers to take a leadership role in restructuring systems to better address barriers to learning.

In this pilot project, school social workers were used as organizational facilitators because their training makes them well suited for a role as change agents. The types of skills needed encompass traditional community organization skills, such as consensus building, problem solving, and acting as a catalyst for change (Rothman & Tropman, 1987). As change agents, school social workers can expand their role beyond provision of direct services to become team leaders, advocates, and capacity builders at macro levels of practice in school systems.

School social workers are also spending increasingly more time working in interdisciplinary teams, which suggests that they should become knowledgeable about the "orientation and values of other professionals in educational settings" (Radin, 1989, p. 223) such as psychologists, nurses, and special education staff. School social workers and other professionals need to engage in active dialogue with school and community leaders about new directions and models. In times of limited resources for education, health, and social services, collaboration is essential.

How well prepared are school social workers to assume these expanded roles? Those participating on school-based resource coordinating teams generally had not been trained to carry out the roles and functions involved in restructuring their programs and services. Universities and professional development programs are just beginning to explore the value of interprofessional collaborative programs that cross-train practitioners from disciplines such as social work, psychology, education, and public health (Lawson & Hooper-Briar, 1994). At a minimum, schools of social work offering a school social work specialization need to emphasize community organization methods designed to develop change agent and policy advocacy skills. To survive and grow as a profession, school social workers must gain expertise in instituting and coordinating systemic change and learn to maneuver among interdisciplinary collaborative teams.

REFERENCES

Adelman, H. S. (1996). *Restructuring education support services: Toward the concept of an enabling component.* Kent, OH: American School Health Association.

Adelman, H. S., & Taylor, L. (1994). *On understanding intervention in psychology and education.* Westport, CT: Praeger.

Aguirre, L. M. (1995). California's efforts toward school-linked, integrated, comprehensive services. *Social Work in Education, 17,* 217–225.

Allen-Meares, P. (1994). Social work services in schools: A national study of entry-level tasks. *Social Work, 39,* 560–565.

Beer, M. (1980). *Organizational change and development: A system's view.* Santa Monica, CA: Goodyear.

Dryfoos, J. (1995). Full-service schools: Revolution or fad? *Journal of Research on Adolescence, 5,* 147–172.

Hall, G. E., & Hord, S. M. (1987). *Change in schools: Facilitating the process.* Albany: State University of New York Press.

Hasenfeld, Y. (1983). *Human service organizations.* Englewood Cliffs, NJ: Prentice Hall.

Kirst, M. (1991). Improving children's services: Overcoming barriers, creating new opportunities. *Phi Delta Kappan, 72,* 615–618.

Lawson, H. A., & Hooper-Briar, K. (1994). *Expanding partnerships: Involving colleges and universities in interprofessional collaboration and service integration.* Oxford, OH: Danforth Foundation & Institute for Educational Renewal at Miami University.

Levy, J. E., & Shepardson, W. (1992). A look at current school-linked service efforts. *Future of Children, 2,* 44–55.

Miles, M., & Huberman, A. M. (1984). *Qualitative data analysis.* Beverly Hills, CA: Sage Publications.

Radin, N. (1989). School social work practice: Past, present and future trends. *Social Work in Education, 11,* 213–225.

Rosenblum, L., DiCecco, M., Taylor, L., & Adelman, H. (1995). Upgrading school support programs through collaboration: Resource coordinating teams. *Social Work in Education, 17,* 117–124.

Rothman, J., & Tropman, J. E. (1987). Models of community organization and macro practice perspectives: Their mixing and phasing. In F. M. Cox, J. L. Erlich, J. Rothman, & J. E. Tropman (Eds.), *Strategies of community organization* (pp. 3–26). Itasca, IL: F. E. Peacock.

Spradley, J. P. (1980). *Participant observation.* Fort Worth, TX: Harcourt Brace Jovanovich.

Uphold, C. R., & Graham, M. V. (1993). Schools as centers for collaborative services for families: A vision for change. *Nursing Outlook, 41,* 204–211.

Yin, R. K. (1984). *Case study research.* Beverly Hills, CA: Sage Publications.

Zaltman, G., & Duncan, R. (1977). *Strategies for planned change.* New York: John Wiley & Sons.

This chapter was originally published in the October 1997 issue of Social Work in Education, *vol. 19, pp. 266–278.*

Part VII

COMMUNITY HEALTH PARTNERSHIPS

32 Building Community Capacity to Promote Social and Public Health: Challenges for Universities

Dennis L. Poole

There is a sudden renewal of interest in community capacity building to achieve broad social and public health goals. Part of it stems from the healthy cities movement launched in the late 1980s (Hancock, 1993), from more recent innovations in public health and primary care (Human Resources and Services Administration [HRSA], 1996; Suen, Christenson, Cooper, & Taylor, 1995), and from the need to replace fragmented systems with coordinated community networks of managed care (Berkman, 1996). Cutbacks in federal spending for scores of social programs have sparked interest as well, along with the "new federalism" that gives states and communities greater control over and responsibility for these programs through block grants (Weil, 1997). Another source of renewal is civic distrust of large public institutions and, with it, popular outcry for localism, decentralization, and greater reliance on local mediating structures in the provision of community care (McKnight, 1995). Although many policy analysts (for example, Davis, 1997; Jansson & Smith, 1997; Keigher, 1996; Lehman & Danzinger, 1994; Poole, 1996) fear that a return to the "lost world of community" could harm people of color and other politically vulnerable groups, few question the urgent need for community capacity building in social and health services.

Earlier we discussed the need for community capacity building in primary care and prevention (Poole & Van Hook, 1997). After examining several successful projects in the national Models That Work campaign (HRSA, 1996), we concluded that some retooling in our field will be necessary for social workers to build and participate in community health partnerships. Specifically, social workers need to enlarge their professional tool kit to include a repertoire of skills in community practice.

Here the discussion continues, this time focusing on the need for universities to become effective participants in the community capacity-building movement. At this stage of the movement, there appears to be a great divide between what faculty are teaching students in academia and what practitioners are doing in the field.

COMMUNITY CAPACITY BUILDING

McLeroy (1996) defined *community capacity* as the characteristics of communities that affect their ability to identify, mobilize, and address social and public health problems. The purpose of capacity building, therefore, is to foster conditions that strengthen the characteristics of communities that enable them to plan, develop, implement, and maintain effective community programs (for example, Cottrell, 1977; Fawcett et al., 1996). Critics (for example, Funiciello, 1993; Illich, 1975; Lasch, 1977, 1995; McKnight, 1995) argued that professionals, and the programs they administer, often weaken community potential to address local needs—hence, their call for community capacity building in the provision of social and health services.

In December 1995 the Centers for Disease Control and Prevention, Division of Chronic Disease Control and Community Intervention convened a symposium on community capacity. On the basis of the findings of the symposium, an expert panel (Speers et al., 1997) reached initial agreement on the dimensions of community capacity. These include participation and leadership, access to and prudent application of resources, social and interorganizational networks, sense of community, community history of collective action, community power, shared core values, and capacity to engage in critical reflection.

Numerous examples of community capacity building for health promotion can be found in the literature. Some of the most frequently cited ones are the Pennsylvania County Health Improvement Project (Stunkard, Felix, Yopp, & Cohen, 1985), the Minnesota Heart Health Program (Carlaw, Mittelmark, Bracht, & Leupker, 1984), the Stanford Five-City Projects (Farquhar et al., 1985), and the Planned Approach to Community Health (PATCH) programs (Steckler, Orville, Eng, & Dawson, 1989). Other less known but promising efforts include the Cure/ Heart, Body and Soul program in Baltimore; Project Vida of the Comprehensive Community Health and Services program in El Paso, Texas; and the Community Health Advisory program in Mississippi (HRSA, 1996).

Recent examples of community capacity building published in *Health & Social Work* include an array of local health promotion projects designed to address issues of at-risk pregnant women (Balsanek, 1997), to create an empowerment-centered, church-based asthma education program for African American adults (Ford, Edwards, Rodriguez, Gibson, & Tilley, 1996), to prevent the spread of sexually transmitted diseases among high-risk adolescents (Sullivan, 1996), to promote supportive behaviors in natural support networks of people with serious mental illness (Walsh & Connelly, 1996), and to develop culturally responsive strategies to prevent heart disease (Mokuau, Hughes, & Tsark, 1995).

COMMUNITY ACTION STRUCTURES

A pressing need at this time is for the development or revitalization of community action structures. Most of the projects mentioned earlier rely heavily on these structures; their utility in community health promotion is widely recognized in public health (for example, Bracht & Gleason, 1990; Green, 1986; World Health Organization [WHO], 1986).

To initiate and sustain local reforms in health promotion, community action structures must be in place. As noted elsewhere (Poole, in press), community action structures

> provide channels through which responsible citizens can take part in commu-
> nity health decision making through local planning and voluntary social ac-
> tion. Usually these channels are called councils, commissions, committees, and
> task forces. To qualify as *action* structures, they must be citizen-driven, and
> their membership must include the top political, economic, and social welfare
> leadership of the community. [They] must also have the capacity to make deci-
> sions which promote shared responsibility for local problems, which confront
> and prompt behavioral change in individuals and institutions, and which ini-
> tiate and sustain reform efforts over a long period of time.

The challenge now is to provide the external and internal supports these structures need to function effectively. Regarding external support, it is important to
recognize that community action structures are not a cure-all for national social
and health problems. With proper support, these structures can forge partnerships within communities, provide vehicles for citizens and professionals to
engage in health decision making through voluntary social actions, and help
federal and state officials achieve top-down reforms in social and health services (for example, Bracht & Gleason, 1990; Thompson & Kinne, 1990; WHO,
1986). But community action structures are not a substitute for federal- and state-
level policy actions. Their success at the local level depends, in part, on technical, financial, and other supports from the broader economic and social environment, including federal and state agencies and institutions of higher learning
(Green, 1986; Pilisuk & Minkler, 1985; Poole, in press).

It is important to recognize that community action structures need internal
support as well. Their capacity to function as the local nexus of innovation depends on several internal factors: the ability of their members to work effectively together, available skills and knowledge for defining and addressing local problems, decision-making processes, leadership characteristics, formalized
rules and procedures, and member–staff relationships (McLeroy, Steckler, Kegler,
Burdine, & Wizotsky, 1994). Equally important is access to professionally trained
staff who can perform internal maintenance functions for these structures
(Goodman, Steckler, Hoover, & Schwartz, 1993; Theilen & Poole, 1985).

CHALLENGES FOR UNIVERSITIES

The community capacity-building movement and the support needs of community action structures present challenges to academic departments involved
in the training of professionals for community-based practice. Dramatic changes
in the financing and delivery of professional services, coupled with the sudden
demand for community ownership of social and health problems, sound the
alarm for curriculum changes in professional education. Two challenges relate
to the transmission of theoretical knowledge and applied research and the development of practical reason for effective community-based practice.

Transmission of Theory and Applied Research

Social work is in a good position to meet the challenge of transmitting theory
and applied research. For years students have been taught ecological or systems
approaches to understanding human and community behavior (Longres, 1995),
which are similar to the host–agent–environment model taught in public health

(McLeroy, Bibeau, Steckler, & Glanz, 1988). Social workers recognize, therefore, that individual and social health affects and is affected by multiple levels of influences. These are commonly referred to as micro-, meso-, and macrosystem influences.

Despite limitations (Falck, 1988), ecological and systems approaches give students a broad theoretical framework for understanding the "big picture" of capacity building in community health. Community health promotion requires multiple levels of intervention: individuals, families, social networks, organizations, neighborhoods, communities, and extra-community systems including public policy. Students also learn that no single theory can predict health behavior, nor can any single discipline solve community health problems. Multiple social science theories and multiple practice disciplines are needed to tackle this complex task.

Nevertheless, to prepare students for effective practice within the community capacity-building paradigm, adjustments must be made in how we transmit theoretical knowledge and applied research. On the basis of personal observation, our students usually experience difficulty in choosing among the great constellation of theories needed to understand a community health problem and to design an appropriate intervention. In the absence of a good conceptual framework to organize these theories, students take the easy way out: They limit the scope to one theory—for example, social learning theory, conflict theory, or family resource theory—and ignore the others that also explain health behavior. It is extremely difficult for them to recall all levels of intervention at one time *and* to select theories within and across these levels to guide them in their analysis of the problem and in the formulation of a solution.

Fortunately our colleagues in health education offer a solution. McLeroy, Steckler, Goodman, and Burdine (1992) have developed a social ecology framework that organizes and synthesizes knowledge about a community health problem and its solution across levels of intervention and disciplines. The framework has four components: (1) It starts with a social or health problem for which ecological levels of interventions are needed; (2) it identifies the social sciences most appropriate for understanding the social processes through which social or health problems are produced with attendant theories or models; (3) it identifies potential points of intervention or targets of change; and (4) it contains information about which interventions are successful with which populations under which conditions (Table 32.1). Thus, the framework helps students develop a comprehensive "theory of the problem" based on the interactive effects of intrapersonal, interpersonal, organizational, community, cultural, and public policy factors *and* a comprehensive "theory of intervention" with potential points of intervention and appropriate strategies.

Students (and faculty) involved in community capacity-building projects can use the framework as a tool to aid lay and professional leaders in analyzing a community health problem across all levels of influence and disciplines as well as in designing interventions across the spectrum of community resources. It is difficult to overstate the importance of the transmission of theory and applied research at the community level. My personal experience in community

Table 32.1

A Social Ecology Framework for Theories Related to Health Promotion and Health Education

Ecological Level	Change Processes	Theories or Models	Targets of Change	Strategies and Skills
Intrapersonal	Psychological	Value expectancy Attitude change Social learning theory Control theories Personality theories Attribution theories	Developmental processes Knowledge Attitudes Values Skills Behaviors Self-concept, self-efficacy, self-esteem	Tests and measurements Program planning Educational approaches Mass media Social marketing Skills development Resistance to peer pressure
Interpersonal	Psychosocial	Network theory Social support theories Role theory Social influence models Social comparisons	Social networks Social support Families Work groups Peers Neighbors	Enhancing social networks Changing group norms Enhancing families Social support groups Increasing access to normative groups Peer influence
Organizational	Organizational	Diffusion of innovations Stage theories Leadership theories Organizational climate Organizational culture Leadership	Norms Incentives Organization culture Management styles Organization structure Communication networks	Organizational development Incentive programs Process consultation Coalition development Linking agents
Community	Cultural and social	Cultural change theories Social change theories Community development Diffusion of innovation Community power Community decision making	Area economics Community resources Neighborhood organizations Community competencies Social and health services Organizational relationships Folk practices Governmental structures Formal leadership Informal leadership	Change agents Community development Community coalitions Empowerment Conflict strategies Mass media
Public policy	Political	Policy development theories Political change theories Political parties Citizen participation Bureaucracies	Legislation Policy Taxes Regulatory agencies	Mass media Policy analysis Political change Lobbying Political organizing Conflict strategies

Reprinted by permission of Oxford University Press. McLeroy, K., Streckler, A., Goodman, R., & Burdine, J. N. (1992). Health education research: Theory development indicates that a major barrier to local service reform is limited access to theoretical knowledge on factors affecting community health problems and to applied research studies on interventions preventing them. In the absence of this information, communities often waste scarce local resources on "reinventing the wheel" or, worse yet, implementing solutions that have no chance of success. The social ecology framework can help communities avoid both pitfalls.

To illustrate the usefulness of the framework, let us consider the problem of welfare dependence, which has profound implications for social and public health. One goal of the Personal Responsibility and Work Opportunity Reconciliation Act of 1996 (P.L. 104-193) is to reduce long-term welfare dependence by requiring unmarried teenage mothers to attend school and live with an adult to receive federal public assistance benefits. Families headed by teenage mothers account for almost half of families receiving welfare (U.S. General Accounting Office [GAO], 1995). There is considerable national debate about how to prevent long-term dependence among this group, but communities are strapped with the responsibility for finding a solution now. In its comprehensive investigation of the problem, the GAO reported that low-income teenage mothers stand a better chance of avoiding long-term dependence if they obtain a high school diploma. It also reported that active monitoring and follow-up of school attendance, along with financial incentives and sanctions, seem to increase high school or general equivalency diploma completion rates—hence, the welfare reform ruling that teenage mothers must attend school and live under adult supervision to receive benefits. Child care was identified as a critical factor as well, so an additional federal appropriation of $14 billion was attached to the new law.

In this case, the federal theory of the problem neglects a host of other ecological factors that affect welfare dependence, such as low self-esteem, learning disabilities, weak family support networks, lack of affordable transportation, domestic violence, unemployment, low wages, and school policies on teenage pregnancy (for example, Maternal and Child Health Bureau, 1996). Because national policymakers did not consider these factors in formulating their theory of the problem, communities must develop their own comprehensive theory—or pay the consequences when the federal approach reveals its shortcomings. Communities will need to identify additional targets of change (for example, self-concept, social networks, peers, families, community economic resources, school management styles and policies) and select interventive strategies for each of them (for example, resistance to peer pressure, alternative educational approaches, enhancing families, changing group norms, job training and development, transportation to work, and policy analysis).

Communities throughout the nation have begun to grapple with the ripple effects of welfare reform. Many are in the process of developing community action structures to deal with the opportunities and shortcomings of the new law. Students and faculty can use the social ecology framework to help local citizens and professionals involved in these structures understand the full theoretical scope of the problem, the multiple levels of intervention and targets needed to change the situation, and the tested strategies to prevent long-term dependence among teenage mothers.

Development of Practical Reason

Another challenge for universities is to foster the development of practical reason in students so they can participate effectively in the community capacity-building movement. It is one thing to develop a theory of a problem and a theory of intervention but quite another to understand the problem within the context of a particular community and to match the intervention with local norms and practices. Failure to do so spells early defeat for many community health projects and weakens the capacity of communities to solve their own problems (McLeroy, Steckler, Goodman, Burdine, & Gottlieb, 1993; Steckler, Goodman, McLeroy, Davis, & Koch, 1992).

What is practical reason? Buchanan (1994), drawing on Aristotle's classic distinction between theoria and praxis, pointed out that no two social situations are the same. Recognizing and responding to the differences require the ability to engage in practical reason:

> Given that each social situation is in certain respects unlike any other (e.g., a new cast of characters, a fresh context, a peculiar set of circumstances, unforeseen challenges, surprises, etc.), practical reason is the ability to recognize, acknowledge, pick out and respond to the singular salient features of a complex and unique situation. [It] is the thinking process involved in deciding what to say or how to do that which best suits the particular situation at hand. Practical reason is involved in weighing which of the available courses of action is most appropriate given the specific circumstances. . . . [Because] of the complexity and distinctiveness of each social situation, this can never be reduced to a general formula. (p. 279)

Practical reason is the sine qua non in community capacity building. As Buchanan further explained, one must be sensitive and perceptive about each local situation, including "the history of the community, the demographic composition of the community, the players and personalities involved, the history of working together, the issue at hand (especially as it is related to other community concerns), potential political resistance from different stakeholders and a host of other considerations" (p. 279). There is little room for formula or "cookie-cutter" thinking in community capacity building. What works well in one community may not work well in another. Recognizing the difference, then creating a unique response to each local situation, demands the exercise of judgment.

How can faculty foster the development of practical reason for effective community practice? First, students must engage in research activities that develop sensitivity to the complexities of community life. Research courses using hypothesis-testing designs are inadequate for the task; they usually focus on only one or two theories to explain, predict, control, and produce a desired outcome. Fostering the development of practical reason requires student immersion in the more flexible research designs of ethnologies, case studies, and qualitative and participatory research, which deepen sensitivity to the complexities of local situations (Buchanan, 1994; McLeroy et al., 1992).

Another way to cultivate practical reason is through the development of knowledge and skill in community practice. To become sensitive and tactful participants in the community capacity-building movement, students must learn to perform several internal support functions in community action structures:

- facilitate the process of forming community action structures to address broad social and public health needs
- sustain these structures by developing productive lay leadership, and securing broad-based participation in decision-making processes
- create new organizational arrangements that span professional disciplines and agency domains
- perform mediating functions that lead to productive linkages among civic leaders, client groups, business organizations, faith communities, nonprofit agencies, and public agencies
- strengthen the problem-solving capabilities of communities by assisting community action structures in identifying and analyzing social and public health problems, setting goals, considering alternative interventive possibilities and their consequences, and making decisions on courses of action
- perform activities necessary to implement decisions, evaluate outcomes, and sustain commitment toward solving community health problems.

Cultivating practical reason could require additional changes in universities. One persistent challenge in professional education is bridging the gap between theoretical knowledge and practical knowledge. Isolation of academic programs from the community undoubtedly contributes to the problem, as does excessive pragmatism in community agency planning. Both impede the development of practical reason by disengaging faculty from the real training and research needs of communities, creating a mismatch between the training needs of practitioners in agencies and the training provided by faculty in academic departments, and failing to transfer theoretical knowledge from the university to practice contexts of community (Burdine & McLeroy, 1992).

Meeting this challenge may require a major realignment of resources to support faculty-based field instruction or, at the very least, the development of laboratory-type learning centers where faculty, students, and practitioners can work together on community capacity-building projects. It is interesting that social work, a practice discipline, moved away from these powerful modes of instruction but now is beginning to revisit them. Another solution is to establish community capacity-building institutes. Many state agencies in health and social services are searching for ways to redirect staff and other agency resources to community development. Universities can partner with these agencies by forming joint institutes that would

- train agency staff to form and sustain community action structures
- train students from relevant disciplines to provide support services to staff and lay leaders involved in community development
- transfer theoretical knowledge and applied research to communities
- monitor and evaluate community health outcomes
- disseminate findings to local, state, regional, and national audiences
- advise policymakers on ways to achieve broad social goals through community action structures.

CONCLUSION

We have now entered the era of community renewal in the United States. Although there is reason to fear a return to the "lost world of community," it is urgent that we find ways to strengthen those characteristics of communities that enable them to care for their members, especially those who are most vulnerable to dramatic shifts in national policy. For social work practitioners this will require a repertoire of community practice skills and involvement in community action structures. For faculty it will require adjustments in the transmission of theory and applied research as well as in the development of practical reason for effective community-based practice. Faculty-based field instruction, laboratory-type learning centers, and community capacity-building institutes can help social workers meet the challenges of community renewal.

REFERENCES

Balsanek, J. (1997). Addressing at-risk pregnant women's issues through community, individual, and corporate grassroots efforts. *Health & Social Work, 22,* 63–69.

Berkman, B. (1996). The emerging health care world: Implications for social work practice and education. *Social Work, 41,* 541–551.

Bracht, N. F., & Gleason, J. (1990). Strategies and structures for citizen partnerships. In N. F. Bracht (Ed.), *Health promotion at the community level* (pp. 109–124). Newbury Park, CA: Sage Publications.

Buchanan, D. R. (1994). Reflections on the relationship between theory and practice. *Health Education Research, 9,* 273–283.

Burdine, J., & McLeroy, K. (1992). Practitioners' use of theory: Examples from a workgroup. *Health Education Quarterly, 19,* 331–340.

Carlaw, R. W., Mittelmark, M., Bracht, N., & Leupker, R. (1984). Organization for a community cardiovascular health program: Experiences from the Minnesota Heart Health Program. *Health Education Quarterly, 11,* 243–252.

Cottrell, L. (1977). The competent community. In R. Warren (Ed.), *New perspectives on the American community* (pp. 535–545). Chicago: Rand McNally.

Davis, K. (1997). *Welfare reform, states' rights and managed care: Impact on social work philosophy, education and practice.* Paper presented at the annual meeting of the National Association of Deans and Directors of Schools of Social Work, Chicago.

Falck, H. (1988). *Social work: The membership perspective.* New York: Springer.

Farquhar, J., Fortmann, S., Maccoby, N., Haskell, W. I., Solomon, D. D., & Hulley, S. (1985). The Stanford five-city project: Design and methods. *American Journal of Epidemiology, 122,* 323–334.

Fawcett, S. B., Paine-Andrews, A., Francisco, V. T., Schultz, J. A., Richter, K. P., Lewis, R. K., Harris, K. J., Williams, E. L., Berkley, J. Y., Lopez, C. M., & Fisher, J. L. (1996). Empowering community health initiatives through evaluation. In D. M. Fetterman, S. J. Kaftarian, & A. Wandersman (Eds.), *Empowerment evaluation: Knowledge and tools for self-assessment and accountability* (pp. 161–187). Thousand Oaks, CA: Sage Publications.

Ford, M. E., Edwards, G., Rodriguez, J. L., Gibson, R. C., & Tilley, B. C. (1996). An empowerment-centered, church-based asthma education program for African American adults. *Health & Social Work, 21,* 70–75.

Funiciello, T. (1993). *Tyranny of kindness.* New York: Atlantic Monthly Press.

Goodman, R. M., Steckler, A., Hoover, S., & Schwartz, R. (1993). A critique of contemporary health promotion approaches: Based on a qualitative review of six programs in Maine. *American Journal of Health Promotion, 7,* 208–221.

Green, L. W. (1986). The theory of participation: A qualitative analysis of its expression in national and international health policies. *Advances in Health Education and Promotion, 1,* 211–236.

Hancock, T. (1993). The evolution, impact and significance of the healthy cities/healthy communities movement. *Journal of Public Health Policy, 14*, 5–18.

Human Resources and Services Administration. (1996). *Models that Work campaign.* Washington, DC: Author. Available online at http://www.bphc.hrsa.dhhs.gov/mtw/mtw.html.

Illich, I. (1975). *Medical nemesis: The expropriation of health.* London: Calder & Boyars.

Jansson, B. S., & Smith, S. (1997). Articulating a "new nationalism" in American social policy. In P. L. Ewalt, E. M. Freeman, S. A. Kirk, & D. L. Poole (Eds.), *Social policy: Reform, research, and practice* (pp. 5–18). Washington, DC: NASW Press.

Keigher, S. (1996). Speaking of personal responsibility and individual accountability [National Health Line]. *Health & Social Work, 21*, 304–311.

Lasch, C. (1977). *Haven in a heartless world.* New York: Basic Books.

Lasch, C. (1995). *Revolt of the elites and the betrayal of democracy.* New York: W. W. Norton.

Lehman, J., & Danzinger, S. (1994, October). *Ending welfare as we know it: Problems and prospects.* Paper presented at the fall meeting of the National Association of Deans and Directors of Schools of Social Work, Myrtle Beach, SC.

Longres, J. (1995). *Human behavior in the social environment* (2nd ed.). Itasca, IL: F. E. Peacock.

Maternal and Child Health Bureau, Office of Adolescent Health. (1996). *Adolescent health report, 1995–1996.* Arlington, VA: National Center for Education in Maternal and Child Health.

McKnight, J. (1995). *The careless society.* New York: Basic Books.

McLeroy, K. (1996). *Community capacity: What is it? How do we measure it? What is the role of the Prevention Centers and CDC?* Paper presented at the Sixth Annual Prevention Centers Conference, National Centers for Disease Control and Prevention, National Center for Chronic Disease Prevention and Health Promotion, Atlanta.

McLeroy, K., Bibeau, D., Steckler, A., & Glanz, K. (1988). An ecological perspective for health promotion programs. *Health Education Quarterly, 15*, 351–378.

McLeroy, K., Steckler, A., Goodman, R., & Burdine, J. N. (1992). Health education research: Theory and practice—Future directions. *Health Education Research: Theory and Practice, 7*, 1–8.

McLeroy, K., Steckler, A., Goodman, R., Burdine, J. N., & Gottlieb, N. (1993). Social science theories in health education: Time for a new model? *Health Education Research: Theory and Practice, 8*, 305–312.

McLeroy, K., Steckler, A., Kegler, M., Burdine, J., & Wizotsky, M. (1994). Community coalitions for health promotion: Summary and further reflections. *Health Education Research: Theory and Practice, 9*, 1–11.

Mokuau, N., Hughes, C. K., & Tsark, J. U. (1995). Heart disease and associated risk factors among Hawaiians: Culturally responsive strategies. *Health & Social Work, 20*, 46–51.

Pilisuk, M., & Minkler, M. (1985). Supportive ties: A political economy perspective. *Health Education Quarterly, 12*, 93–106.

Poole, D. (1996). Welfare reform: The bad, the ugly, and the maybe not too awful [Editorial]. *Health & Social Work, 21*, 243–246.

Poole, D. (in press). Achieving national health goals in prevention with community organization: The "bottom-up" approach. *Journal of Community Practice.*

Poole, D., & Van Hook, M. (1997). Retooling for community health partnerships in primary care and prevention [Editorial]. *Health & Social Work, 22*, 2–4.

Speers, M., Goodman, R., McLeroy, K., Fawcett, S., Kegler, M., Parker, E., Smith, S., Sterling, T., & Wallerstein, N. (1997). *An initial attempt at identifying and defining the dimensions of community capacity to provide a basis for measurement.* Unpublished manuscript.

Steckler, A., Goodman, R., McLeroy, K., Davis, S., & Koch, G. (1992). Measurement of the diffusion of health promotion programs. *American Journal of Health Promotion, 6*, 214–225.

Steckler, A., Orville, K., Eng, E., & Dawson, L. (1989). *Patching it together: A formative evaluation of CDC's planned approach to community health (PATCH) program.* Chapel Hill: University of North Carolina, School of Public Health, Department of Health Behavior and Health Education.

Stunkard, D., Felix, M., Yopp, P., & Cohen, R. Y. (1985). Mobilizing a community to promote health for the Pennsylvania County Health Improvement Program. In J. C. Rosen & L. J.

Solomon (Eds.), *Prevention in health psychology* (pp. 143–190). Hanover, NH: University of New England Press.

Suen, J., Christenson, G. M., Cooper, A., & Taylor, M. (1995). Analysis of the current status of public health practice in local health departments. *American Journal of Preventive Medicine, 11*(Suppl. 6), 51–54.

Sullivan, T. R. (1996). The challenge of HIV prevention among high-risk adolescents. *Health & Social Work, 21,* 58–65.

Theilen, G., & Poole, D. (1985). Educating leadership for effecting change through voluntary associations. *Journal of Social Work Education, 22,* 19–29.

Thompson, B., & Kinne, S. (1990). Social change theory: Applications to community health. In N. Bracht, (Ed.), *Health promotion at the community level* (pp. 45–65). Newbury Park, CA: Sage Publications.

U.S. General Accounting Office (1995, September 29). *Welfare to work: Approaches that help teenage mothers complete high school* (GAO/HEHS/PEMD-95-20). Washington, DC: U.S. Government Printing Office.

Walsh, J., & Connelly, P. R. (1996). Supportive behaviors in natural support networks of people with serious mental illness. *Health & Social Work, 21,* 296–303.

Weil, M. (1997). Community building: Building community practice. In P. L. Ewalt, E. M. Freeman, S. A. Kirk, & D. L. Poole (Eds.), *Social policy: Reform, research, and practice* (pp. 35–61). Washington, DC: NASW Press.

World Health Organization, Office of Health Promotion. (1986). *Health promotion: Concept and principles in action.* Copenhagen: Author.

This chapter was originally published in the August 1997 issue of Health & Social Work, *vol. 22, pp. 163–170.*

33

The SAFE Project: Community-Driven Partnerships in Health, Mental Health, and Education to Prevent Early School Failure

Dennis L. Poole

T he complex interplay of forces that put children at risk of early school failure has been well documented. Children of alcoholics and drug users, for example, often experience headaches, depression, and other symptoms that erode their self-esteem and trigger disruptive behaviors in school (Tharinger & Koranek, 1988). Children of divorced parents sometimes suffer anxiety and confusion, cognitive and behavioral disorders, and deficits in communication and social skills in the classroom (Stolberg & Mahler, 1994). And children who suffer from abuse, neglect, violence, and stress frequently display symptoms of hyperactivity, distractibility, and impulsiveness that can impair academic performance (Phelps & Jarvis, 1994; Wenckstern & Leenaars, 1993). School failure eventually affects the community through higher rates of crime, substance abuse, teenage pregnancy, and dependence on welfare (U.S. Office of Technology Assessment, 1991; Zigler & Styfco, 1994).

Studies have shown that the prevention of early school failure requires support at four levels: family, school, community, and public policy. Families can help children receive feedback and validation, master emotional burdens, and obtain resources to reach their potential in school (Bronfenbrenner, 1979; Caplan, 1976). Recognition of this crucial role led to the family support movement in education, which calls on teachers to develop partnerships with families and for school-based professionals to attend to the more complex needs of students (Fairchild, 1986; Weissbourd & Kagan, 1989). Communities also can help by bringing health and mental health services to schools, forming alliances with civic clubs and neighborhood groups, and mobilizing public support for needed services (Capper, 1994; Dryfoos, 1993). Public policy officials can give support by providing stable funding and technical assistance to communities seeking to prevent early school failure (U.S. Department of Health and Human Services, 1992).

This chapter presents a case study of an innovative project that prevents early school failure in Garfield County, Oklahoma. The project's success is attributed to the development of broad-based partnerships involving families, schools, communities, and public policy officials.

SAFE PROJECT

The School and Family Enrichment (SAFE) Project, a joint effort of the Enid Metropolitan Area Human Service Commission, Enid Public Schools, and the eight rural school districts of Garfield County, targets its services to children and youths who are at risk of early school failure in Garfield County. The county's population base is roughly 50,000 residents, slightly less than a tenth of whom are African American, Native American, and other ethnic and racial minorities. Enid, the county seat, serves as the metropolitan hub of northwest Oklahoma, a vast 13-county region situated in the Great Plains. The economic infrastructure of Garfield County rests mainly on revenues from agricultural and petroleum production, service industries, and Vance Air Force Base.

Community–Public Policy Partnerships

Critical incidents in the SAFE Project have demonstrated the need for community partnerships in health, mental health, and education to prevent early school failure. These partnerships must be driven by community action structures that provide opportunities for responsible citizens to play leadership roles in planning and implementing prevention projects (Poole, 1997). Critical incidents have also shown that a community acting alone cannot prevent complex social problems; partnerships with public policy officials outside the community are needed as well.

The SAFE Project has always depended on two community action structures for its survival—the Enid Metropolitan Area Human Service (Metro) Commission and the SAFE Local Advisory Council—both of which historically have been staffed by professional social workers. The Metro Commission is a voluntary, citizen-driven planning organization that identifies unmet human services needs, initiates communitywide pilot projects to address them, and advocates for attendant changes in public policy. Its 25-member board consists of 15 influential leaders from the community at large and two representatives from each of the five major service funding entities in the county: the City of Enid, Garfield County, the United Way, the Enid public school system, and the Oklahoma Department of Human Services. The SAFE Local Advisory Council is a community action structure of the Metro Commission. Leading citizens, teachers, parents, school administrators, counselors, and agency professionals serve on this council, which has met regularly since 1987 to monitor the SAFE Project.

The SAFE Project began in 1987, shortly after a community needs-assessment committee, organized by a professional social worker with skills in community development, identified early school failure as a major problem in Garfield County. Although only anecdotal evidence from teachers, parents, and students was available on the scope of the problem, there was a strong consensus among key leaders that up to a third of the children in area public schools were not performing to their potential. There were good reasons for their concern. At the time, Garfield County was still reeling from the oil bust of the early 1980s that crippled the economic infrastructure of the area and devastated thousands of families. Hardest hit were neighborhoods on the east side of Enid, the site of the Champlin oil refinery, which provided 1,000 jobs to area residents before the industry relocated to Texas in the mid-1980s. Eastside public schools, where the SAFE project was first implemented, were in neighborhoods that suffered the most. Between 1979 and 1989, single-parent households in these neighborhoods increased nearly 300 percent, and dilapidated and boarded-up housing units soared 1,200 percent. Juvenile delinquency, abuse and neglect, poverty, teenage pregnancy, and other conditions associated with the poor academic performance of students increased dramatically as well (Enid Metropolitan Area Human Services Commission, 1993).

The Metro Commission responded to the committee's report by appointing a citizen-led task force to study the problem of early school failure and to recommend a solution. Through a series of community meetings, the task force found that an escalating number of children were going to school with complex personal and family problems that made teaching and learning increasingly difficult in the classroom. It also found that possibly as many as a fourth of the students in the school system were being "written off" as early school failures. Startled by these findings, the task force then directed its attention to the more difficult job of identifying a solution to the problem. A consensus eventually was reached that school–family partnerships were needed to bridge the gaps among students, teachers, parents, and agency professionals. The task force recommended that the Metro Commission initiate a pilot project to test a new school–family partnership model of intervention called SAFE. The commission adopted the recommendation, then established the SAFE Local Advisory Council to implement the project during the 1987–1988 school year.

The need to expand the SAFE Project's partnership base to public policy officials outside the community became evident early in the project. SAFE initially was financed entirely by local contributions of the Junior Welfare League, the local community action agency, a school drug education grant, and private benefactors. Although these contributions were difficult for the Metro Commission to raise, they were enough to pay the salary of one school–family counselor, who served two Enid elementary schools for the first two years of the project. The commission soon recognized, however, that local voluntary contributions would not be adequate to meet the long-term needs of the project. Larger, more stable sources of public funding outside the community would be needed to sustain the project and to extend its services to other schools in Garfield County.

The opportunity to expand the project's partnership into the public policy arena came in 1989 when the Enid public schools and the Metro Commission won a highly competitive, three-year demonstration grant through the state department of education, funded by a special appropriation from the state legislature, to test five model dropout prevention projects in Oklahoma. The SAFE Project used the first-year grant of $180,000 to employ five more school–family counselors and to expand the delivery of services to seven rural school districts in Garfield County, as well as to three additional elementary schools and the high school in Enid. These dramatic changes caused growing pains for the SAFE Project, but gained it policy partners in the state legislature and the state department of education.

The partnership base expanded again in 1992, when a severe funding crisis nearly ended the SAFE Project. The state dropout prevention grant had one major flaw: it stipulated a local "cash match" contribution of 25 percent in the first year of funding, 50 percent in the second year, and 75 percent in the third year. Early in the second year of funding, it became clear that the 50 percent cash match would be too much for the local community to bear. Faced with the prospect of a large budget shortfall, the superintendent of the Enid public schools notified SAFE Project counselors in September that their employment contracts would end in November if local cash commitments to match the state grant were not secured in the interim.

The Metro Commission and the SAFE Local Advisory Council responded by calling an emergency community meeting, to which they invited civic leaders, parents, students, teachers, school administrators, and agency professionals, along with state and federal Medicaid officials. The turnout was substantial, and testimonials from parents and students were dramatic and powerful. The Medicaid officials responded with a proposal of their own to end the crisis by using funds from the Early and Periodic Screening and Diagnosis and Treatment (EPSDT) program to reimburse SAFE Project counselors for preventive health services provided to Medicaid-eligible children. Their proposal included three conditions: (1) a physician had to determine that these services were "medically necessary"; (2) non–Medicaid eligible children had to have equal access to SAFE Project services; and (3) the local community had to pay the 30 percent cash match needed by the state to draw down federal EPSDT dollars. Both the Metro Commission and the SAFE Local Advisory Council immediately endorsed the proposal. It complemented the preventive goals of the SAFE Project, offered a source of long-term funding for school–family counselor services, and cut the local cash-match requirement well below the amount set in the state dropout prevention grant.

The fiscal crisis ended when Enid public schools signed a contract with the state department of human services and the community mental health center to provide EPSDT services through the SAFE Project. This contract remains in effect, except that the community mental health center no longer acts as a conduit for the funds, now that Enid public schools are a state-certified EPSDT provider. Enid public schools receive fee-for-service reimbursement for mental health assessments and individual and family therapy services provided by SAFE counselors to Medicaid-eligible children in Garfield County. The county board of health, Enid public schools, rural school districts, and the area community action agency contribute the 30 percent cash match. Managed care does not affect funding for the project, because rural service providers remain exempt from managed care under the state's Medicaid plan.

SAFE Project staff consist of six school–family counselors who are employed by the Enid public schools, which administers the EPSDT contract. Although a professional social worker helped design, implement, and monitor the project— and continues to provide community development support services—none of the six counselors has a graduate degree in social work because of the scarcity of clinical social workers in rural northwestern Oklahoma. Five of the counselors have graduate degrees in counseling or a related field, and one has a bachelor's degree in mental health. Three counselors serve five elementary schools and the high school in the Enid public school district, and two counselors work on an itinerant basis at seven rural elementary schools. Referrals come mostly from teachers and principals. The average caseload is about 35 students, most of whom face difficult challenges in life—poverty, family breakdown, abuse and neglect, domestic violence, and trauma—that erode their self-esteem and diminish their academic performance.

School–Family Partnerships

Partnerships between schools and families are also needed to prevent early school failure. The SAFE Project model is similar to the traditional school-based helper model described by Fairchild (1986). School-based helpers include "a wide range of professionals who work in schools and promote the mental health of students" (p. 3). Their services are often in great demand, and they must respond quickly with assessments of problems and intervention plans. Because school-based helpers work in proximity to teachers and students, they usually can develop home–school partnerships more easily, monitor service outcomes more closely, and adjust intervention plans more quickly than professionals based in community agencies.

But the SAFE Project school–family partnership model differs from the traditional school-based helper model in three important ways. First, the services provided by SAFE Project counselors are comprehensive, covering eight major support functions:

1. early identification and assessment—Work closely with teachers, parents, administrators, and other professionals in the early identification and assessment of social, emotional, and health problems that affect student performance in school and in the development of an intervention plan to address these problems.
2. counseling—Provide individual, family, and group counseling to help children and families deal with problems and mobilize resources to promote better school functioning.
3. consultation—Offer practical information and advice to parents and teachers.
4. advocacy—Act as advocates for students and families as they interact with schools and community organizations.
5. referral and follow-up—Refer students and families to community agencies for EPSDT, mental health care, and other services as needed and follow up on the provision of these services.
6. service coordination—Coordinate the delivery of school and community services to students and their families.
7. resource development—Assist the community in developing other programs needed to prevent school failure and underachievement.
8. performance monitoring—Monitor and record outcomes (such as grades, self-esteem scores, attendance, classroom conduct, and achievement scores) for children who have been targeted by the project.

Second, the SAFE Project model puts emphasis on prevention and early intervention, rather than on crisis intervention. The goal of the SAFE Project is to help parents, students, and teachers identify and address problems early, before they fester and get more difficult and costly to treat. SAFE Project counselors help schools manage crisis situations, but on a limited basis. Providing early and ongoing support to a small caseload of students and families is their primary job, not crisis intervention.

Finally, the SAFE Project model differs from the traditional school-based helper model in that the project's counselors must develop other resources in the community that families need to help their children succeed in school. One example is the Self-Esteem through Art program started by SAFE Project counselors in 1988, which helps students who are at risk of school failure demonstrate their feelings, break through emotional barriers, and experience success in a nonacademic setting. About 80 students participate in this program during the school year. Another example is the Steve Sheik Memorial Tutoring program, developed in 1991, which coordinates 70 trained volunteers who provide tutoring services to more than 200 students every year. Before this program was started, free tutoring services were not available to needy students in Garfield County.

Thus, the SAFE Project school-based partnership model pivots on a broad understanding of family and school support. The project's counselors must support students, parents, and teachers with direct services, such as assessment and counseling, and indirect services like advocacy and the development of resources.

Services and Outcomes

Annual statistics on services (School and Family Enrichment Project, 1995) show that the SAFE Project's counselors deliver a broad range of support services to students, parents, and teachers. For example, during the 1994–1995 school year, five counselors provided clinical services—including 220 mental health assessments, 4,257 individual therapy sessions, and 156 group therapy sessions—to 170 elementary school students and 33 high school students. The counselors also conducted 231 home visits, made 847 additional contacts with parents, provided counseling to 123 families, arranged parenting groups for 31 families, delivered in-service training workshops to 65 teachers, and made 2,879 additional contacts with teachers. In addition, they provided 241 short-term crisis interventions, participated in 606 clinical staffings, completed 190 referrals to community agencies, and enrolled 150 children in the EPSDT program.

Regarding outcomes, the Oklahoma Technical Assistance Center (OTAC) conducted an independent evaluation of the project from August 1989 to June 1993. OTAC compared random samples from two sites—a SAFE Project site and a comparison site in south-central Oklahoma. Both sites were similar in economic infrastructure, per capita school expenditures, student ethnicity, participation rates in the free or reduced school lunch program, dropout rates, and student scores on the Iowa Test of Basic Skills. OTAC conducted annual pre- and posttest group comparisons between students at the two sites on six predictors of early school failure: self-esteem, grade point average, achievement, absences, disciplinary referrals, and classes failed.

OTAC's final report to the state department of education (McKean, 1993) concluded that since 1989 SAFE Project students had improved significantly (at the $p \le .05$ level) on several variables that were introduced into a multiple analysis of covariance (MANCOVA). That is, in comparison to the other group, SAFE Project students scored higher in self-esteem on the Piers-Harris (1984) Children's Self-Concept Scale, had a higher mean grade point average on a 4.0 grading scale (2.47 versus 1.96), and had a higher mean composite normal curve equivalent (NCE) score on the Iowa Test of Basic Skills (Hieronymus, Linquist, & Hoover, 1986) (47.14 versus 39.61). The report noted that although the demonstration site had more programs for at-risk students operating at the time of the evaluation, the magnitude of difference in NCE scores was "impressive."

OTAC's report (McKean, 1993) also concluded that absences, disciplinary referrals, and classes failed were significantly lower for SAFE Project students during the first two years of the evaluation. The evaluator hypothesized that the students did not improve on these variables again in the third year because their total absences, disciplinary referrals, and classes failed were already well below the levels reported when they entered the project.

The report's findings paralleled those reported earlier (Poole, 1991) in an annual survey of 20 parents and 20 teachers, who found consistently high levels of satisfaction with the project's services and outcomes. Qualitative data presented in the survey added richness to the quantitative data gathered by OTAC. Consider the following comments of teachers:

- "I have seen some definite changes in behavior and self-esteem. The SAFE counselor gives teachers and students strategies for solving problems."
- "I work as a team with the SAFE counselor. I've seen improvement in grades and behavior of several students."
- "SAFE is a bridge between home and school, between school and outside referral agencies. Parents hesitate to use agency services. SAFE helps with that. When parents feel comfortable with the SAFE counselor, they trust her advice and begin using other community services."

Parents' responses to the survey were enlightening as well. Typical comments included the following:

- "I've seen improvement in my child at school. I think it is due to the SAFE counselor, teachers, and me. We're working as a team. The SAFE counselor helped us through a tough time."
- "Last year our son had a lot of trouble in school. This year he only sees the counselor once a week. His grades have gone up, and his behavior has improved."
- "My son has been in kindergarten once and prekindergarten twice. He's been in three different schools. Now it's working. Because of the SAFE counselor help, he's getting better in speech, counting, writing, and self-esteem. The SAFE counselor is more than a teacher; she's a friend to him. He needed a winter coat and she found him one."

LESSONS LEARNED

The project reported in this chapter has been tested only in a rural area. Further research is needed, therefore, to test the SAFE Project model in other states and communities. In the meantime, five lessons learned during the model's implementation in Garfield County may help guide replication efforts elsewhere:

1. The SAFE Project works best when school–family counselors stay focused on the two primary goals of the model: prevention and early intervention. At the beginning of the project, school principals called on SAFE Project counselors to handle crisis situations so often that putting out fires for school principals became the major responsibility of several counselors. Teachers' requests for project services soared as well, so the counselors quickly became overburdened with large caseloads. To correct both situations, the SAFE Local Advisory Council limited the clinical caseloads of the counselors to 35 students each, restricted crisis management to 15 percent of the counselors' service activity time, and established a policy of referring acute cases to highly skilled professionals in the community. These decisions helped the counselors return to the primary goals of the project and protected them from demands that often dilute the effectiveness of school-based helpers (Lear, Gleicher, St. Germaine, & Porter, 1991; National Center for Education Statistics, 1990; Prout, Alexander, Fletcher, Memis, & Miller, 1993).

2. The SAFE Project model works best when counselors use a social work model of practice rather than the medical model that emphasizes individual diagnosis and treatment, not prevention, and intervention with multiple social support systems (Northen, 1982). The deficits of the medical model became obvious early in the SAFE Project. Most counselors worked well with individual students, but neglected the equally important task of involving parents, teachers, and community professionals in the problem-solving process. After reviewing the mission statement of the SAFE Project, the counselors corrected the oversight by adding home visits to their job duties and by developing a service activity form to track collateral contacts with parents, teachers, and community professionals. These changes incorporated an understanding of students as individuals whose performance in school depended largely on their interactions with a network of social support systems.

3. School-based helper programs alone cannot prevent early school failure. Supports from other programs, such as the tutoring and art programs developed by the SAFE Project, are also needed to prevent this complex social problem. In this regard, it is interesting that when the art program began in 1988, only anecdotal evidence was available on the utility of art therapy in prevention (McNiff, 1987; Moore, 1983; Rubin, 1982). Empirical research later conducted by Springer, Phillips, Cannady, and Kerst-Harris (1992) confirmed that this modality can reduce behavioral problems and increase competence among children who are at risk of early school failure.

4. School-based projects like the SAFE Project inevitably raise questions about the primary mission of schools and community agencies (Bruininks, Frenzel, & Kelly, 1994; Dryfoos, 1994), a debate usually sparked by funding difficulties. For school administrators the question is, Why should schools, strapped

with tight budgets, bear fiscal responsibility for prevention projects when schools receive funding only for education? Agency directors pose a similar question: Why should agencies, strapped with tight budgets, give money to schools to help them do what they already should be doing, providing a broad range of educational programs to ensure that all children experience success in school? The Metro Commission's answer to both questions proved compelling in the SAFE Project: Preventing early school failure is a shared responsibility, and every community institution must contribute its fair share to the solution. In this case, the resources of community health and mental health agencies had to be joined with those of local educational institutions to solve the complex biopsychosocial problems associated with early school failure.

5. Citizen-driven community action structures are important to the success of such programs, as has been widely recognized in the field of prevention (Bracht & Gleason, 1990; Davies, 1991; Epstein, 1992; McKnight, 1994; O'Callaghan, 1993; Poole, 1997; Theilen & Poole, 1986). Community action structures are neither a cure-all for social problems nor a substitute for centralized public funding and technical support. But they can promote shared responsibility for local problems, prompt behavioral changes in individuals and community institutions, and initiate and sustain projects such as the SAFE Project for a long time.

REFERENCES

Bracht, N., & Gleason, J. (1990). Strategies and structures for citizen partnerships. In N. F. Bracht (Ed.), *Health promotion at the community level* (pp. 109–124). Newbury Park, CA: Sage Publications.

Bronfenbrenner, U. (1979). *The ecology of human development: Experiments by nature and by design.* Cambridge, MA: Harvard University Press.

Bruininks, R. H., Frenzel, M., & Kelly, A. (1994). Integrating services: The case for better links to schools. *Journal of School Health, 64,* 242–248.

Caplan, G. (1976). The family as a support system. In G. Caplan & M. Killilea (Eds.), *Support systems and mutual help* (pp. 19–36). New York: Grune & Stratton.

Capper, C. A. (1994). We're not housed in an institution, we're housed in the community. *Educational Administration Quarterly, 30,* 257–277.

Davies, D. (1991). Schools reaching out: Family, school, and community partnerships for student success. *Phi Delta Kappan, 72,* 376–382.

Dryfoos, J. G. (1993). Schools as places for health, mental health, and social services. *Teachers College Record, 94,* 540–567.

Dryfoos, J. G. (1994). *Full-service schools.* San Francisco: Jossey-Bass.

Enid Metropolitan Area Human Service Commission. (1993). *Residential housing and homeless report.* Enid, OK: Community Development Support Association.

Epstein, J. (1992). *School and family partnerships* (Report No. 6). Baltimore: Center on Families, Communities, Schools, and Children's Learning.

Fairchild, T. N. (1986). *Crisis intervention services for school-based helpers.* Springfield, IL: Charles C Thomas.

Hieronymus, A., Linquist, E., & Hoover, H. (1986). *Iowa test of basic skills.* Lombard, IL: Riverside.

Lear, J., Gleicher, H., St. Germaine, A., & Porter, J. (1991). Reorganizing health care for adolescents: The experience of the school-based adolescent health care program. *Journal of Adolescent Health, 12,* 450–580.

McKean, K. (1993). *Alternative approaches grant projects: Final evaluation report.* Cushing: Oklahoma Technical Assistance Center.

McKnight, J. (1994). Two tools for well-being: Health systems and communities. *American Journal of Preventive Medicine, 10*(Suppl. 1), 23–25.

McNiff, S. A. (1987). Research and scholarship in the creative art therapies. *The Arts in Psychotherapy, 14,* 285–292.

Moore, R. W. (1983). Art therapy with substance abusers: A review of the literature. *The Arts in Psychotherapy, 10,* 251–260.

National Center for Education Statistics. (1990). *National education longitudinal study of 1988: User's manual* (NCES-464). Washington, DC: U.S. Department of Education.

Northen, H. (1982). *Clinical social work.* New York: Columbia University Press.

O'Callaghan, B. (1993). *School-based collaboration with families: Constructing family–school–agency partnerships that work.* San Francisco: Jossey-Bass.

Phelps, S., & Jarvis, P. (1994). Coping in adolescence: Empirical evidence for a theoretically based approach to assessing coping. *Journal of Youth and Adolescence, 23,* 359–371.

Piers, E., & Harris, D. (1984). *The Piers-Harris Children's Self-Concept Scale.* Los Angeles: Western Psychological Services.

Poole, D. L. (1991). *School and family enrichment (SAFE) project annual assessment report.* Enid, OK: Enid Metropolitan Area Human Service Commission.

Poole, D. L. (1997). Achieving national health goals in prevention through community organization: The "bottom up" approach. *Journal of Community Practice, 4,* 77–92.

Prout, H. T., Alexander, S. P., Fletcher, C.E.M., Memis, J. P., & Miller, D. W. (1993). Counseling and psychotherapy services provided by school psychologists: An emphasis of patterns in practice. *Journal of School Psychology, 31,* 309–316.

Rubin, J. A. (1982). Art therapy: What it is and what it is not. *American Journal of Art Therapy, 21,* 752–760.

School and Family Enrichment Project. (1995). *Annual statistics report.* Enid, OK: Enid Public Schools.

Springer, J. F., Phillips, J. L., Cannady, L. P., & Kerst-Harris, E. (1992). CODA: A creative therapy program for children in families affected by abuse of alcohol or other drugs. *Journal of Community Psychology* (OSAP special issue), 55–74.

Stolberg, A. L., & Mahler, J. (1994). Enhancing treatment gains in a school-based intervention for children of divorce through skill training, parental involvement, and transfer procedures. *Journal of Consulting and Clinical Psychology, 62,* 147–156.

Tharinger, D. J., & Koranek, M. E. (1988). Children of alcoholics—At risk and unserved: A review of research and service roles for school psychologists. *School Psychology Review, 17,* 166–191.

Theilen, G. L., & Poole, D. L. (1986). Educating leadership for effecting community change through voluntary associations. *Journal of Social Work Education, 2,* 19–29.

U.S. Department of Health and Human Services. (1992). *EPSDT: A guide for educational programs* (HCFA Publication No. 02192). Washington, DC: Health Care Financing Administration.

U.S. Office of Technology Assessment. (1991). *Adolescent health—Volume I: Summary and policy options* (Publication No. OTA-H-468). Washington, DC: U.S. Government Printing Office.

Weissbourd, B., & Kagan, S. (1989). Family support programs: Catalysts for change. *American Journal of Orthopsychiatry, 59,* 20–31.

Wenckstern, S., & Leenaars, A. (1993). Trauma and suicide in our schools. *Death Studies, 17,* 151–171.

Zigler, E., & Styfco, S. J. (1994). Head Start: Criticisms in a constructive context. *American Psychologist, 49,* 127–132.

This chapter was originally published in the November 1997 issue of Health & Social Work, *vol. 22, pp. 282–289.*

34

Partnerships for Improved Service Delivery: The Newark Target Cities Project

M. Katherine Kraft and Janet E. Dickinson

Despite the many efforts at improving treatment for chemically dependent individuals, people undergoing treatment still relapse. The tendency to relapse is exacerbated by fragmentation of services, lack of coordination among treatment providers and social service agencies, duplication of services, insufficient access to primary health care, long waiting periods for treatment, inconsistent case follow-up, and inadequate case management. This situation is magnified in the inner city. Problems in service delivery reduce client access, diminish program quality, increase costs, and impair efficiency. Many professionals believe that recovery rates and treatment outcomes would improve if these many problems with service delivery were eliminated (Couch, 1991; Gillies, Shortell, Anderson, Mitchell, & Morgan, 1993; Halvorson, Pike, Reed, McClatchey, & Gosselink, 1993; Shortell, Gillies, Anderson, Mitchell, & Morgan, 1993; Shortell & Morrison, 1990).

Many communities have been experimenting with models of substance abuse treatment service delivery that address these threats to treatment effectiveness. Some of the experiments with alternative designs for health care delivery have found that creative and cooperative models can remove obstacles to service delivery and can promote high-quality, accessible care (Adelman, 1993; Crowson & Boyd, 1993; Fennel & Alexander, 1993; Gaines, Rice, & Carmon, 1993). In addition, many funding sources are requiring applicants to develop consortium models of service delivery to avoid duplication of services and to maximize resources.

This chapter describes the Newark Target Cities Project (NTCP), which was developed to address service delivery problems and to improve the outcomes of people admitted to substance abuse treatment programs by creating a seamless treatment network. This chapter describes the NTCP, the problems it addressed, and the issues that arose in implementing the program. The chapter discusses implications for other communities seeking to create a coordinated system of care.

PROBLEMS WITH SERVICE DELIVERY IN NEWARK

Newark, the largest city in New Jersey, is located in one of the largest metropolitan regions (between New York and Philadelphia) in the United States. The majority of Newark's 275,221 residents are people of color, and the city has high rates of poverty, unemployment, illiteracy, and substance abuse. In 1993 Newark's substance abuse treatment programs served over 4,000 Newark residents (New Jersey Department of Health, 1993). The majority (51 percent) of individuals in treatment reported using heroin as their drug of choice.

Newark's citizens suffer disproportionately from health care risks. New Jersey is fifth in the nation for reported AIDS cases and has a tuberculosis rate five times higher than New York City, and more individuals with these health problems reside in Newark. Sixty-six percent of the AIDS cases in Newark are among intravenous drug users (New Jersey Department of Health, 1993), and the rate of drug abuse–related hospital emergency room visits is second only to San Francisco (National Institute on Drug Abuse, 1991).

In 1993 substance abuse treatment services in Newark were fragmented, duplicated services, and used resources inefficiently. Ten independent agencies provided substance abuse treatment services. Individuals had to contact directly any one of these agencies to obtain treatment. Each program had its own unique intake protocol and assessment instruments. Admission criteria were independently determined by each service provider. There was no uniform policy for dealing with clients who did not meet an agency's admissions criteria and no guarantee that an individual applying for treatment would be referred to the most appropriate service.

In addition, clients receiving substance abuse treatment were routinely served by other health and human services programs. Large caseloads and severe personnel shortages made it difficult for these agencies to communicate with each other about shared clients. As a result, clients were often shuttled between various agencies, wasting time repeating similar intake interviews at each stop. Health care clinics required at least a two-week wait for an appointment, so most substance-abusing clients used emergency rooms for their health care.

Clients needing substance abuse treatment were faced with various barriers to access, including insufficient substance abuse treatment capacity, oversubscribed public health services, lack of reliable transportation, and geographic inaccessibility of services. Substance abuse treatment agencies were possessive of clients and distrustful of each other.

Social services providers and clients were equally frustrated by the substance abuse treatment system. The complexity of client problems and the limited resources to deal with them had been a constant challenge for Newark's social services system.

SOLUTIONS TO SERVICE DELIVERY PROBLEMS

The city of Newark developed an innovative service delivery model to address service delivery problems. The model created a network of service providers with a single point of entry, standardized assessment and placement procedures, and electronic client–treatment matching. A Centralized Intake Unit (CIU) was opened, and a case management function was developed to coordinate client care. A systemwide staff development initiative was implemented to enhance treatment quality, and links with primary care providers were established to improve access to health care.

Single Point of Entry

The CIU was designed to provide comprehensive psychosocial and medical assessments for all clients seeking substance abuse treatment. An assessment of
support service needs, the development of a case management plan, and the
addition of case managers to maintain contact with clients and follow up on all
service referrals make up the core of the CIU operations. The unit provides complete medical care assessment, including blood and urine tests (including a drug
screen), gynecological exams, and screening for infectious diseases (hepatitis A,
B, and C; tuberculosis; sexually transmitted diseases; and HIV), and nurses provide follow-up to ensure that clients receive needed medical treatment. To address geographic burden, transportation is provided during the assessment period. A comprehensive treatment record, including a health profile, substance
abuse history, and service needs, follows clients and is made available to the
appropriate substance abuse treatment provider.

Management Information System and Case Management

The complete assessment record is maintained on a networked, computerized
management information system (MIS) that matches clients' needs to available
substance abuse treatment programs. Daily reporting by programs makes it
possible for the MIS to track treatment-slot capacity at the different programs.
This real-time information increases CIU case managers' ability to develop realistic plans for clients. Case managers assist clients in obtaining services and developing plans for treatment aftercare. Particular attention is given to clients
moving from detox to treatment or returning to the community after attending
a residential rehabilitation program. Case managers provide clients with added
support during these vulnerable periods of the early recovery process.

Computer tracking is used to monitor individual client progress while in the
treatment network. CIU case managers can receive regular reports through the
MIS from substance abuse counselors. Potential dropouts can be identified so
that case managers can try to re-engage them in treatment.

Quality of Care

The model aims to enhance the quality of care through several mechanisms.
First, an ongoing clinical skills development program was implemented. Direct
service workers from the substance abuse treatment agencies receive advanced
clinical skills training throughout the year. To ensure the relevance of this training, direct line staff participate in designing and conducting the training and
receive certification credits for all sessions attended. Second, funds are available
for substance abuse treatment providers to hire workers who serve as liaisons
with the CIU. Most clients who drop out of treatment do so on completion of
outpatient detoxification (a pretreatment service). The liaison from each treatment agency connects clients with their designated treatment program. This
relationship is used as a strategy to bridge the gaps in service between the CIU
and the substance abuse treatment agency. The treatment agency liaison, along
with the case managers, is an important strategy for coordinating care and preventing treatment dropout.

SYSTEMS CHANGE PROCESS

The effort at coordinating a long-standing fragmented, proprietary system began during the development of a Center for Substance Abuse Treatment (CSAT) Systems Improvement grant. In April 1993 under the auspices of CSAT Systems Improvement Branch, the U.S. Department of Health and Human Services, Public Health Service, Substance Abuse and Mental Health Services Administration made grants available to 10 metropolitan areas. These grants were designed to facilitate the CSAT program known as Target Cities; the initiative was designed to establish a coordinated effort to address some of the problems in the delivery of substance abuse treatment in urban areas. The state of New Jersey was awarded a Target Cities grant in September 1993 to establish the program in Newark.

The grant development team worked with service providers in Newark to solicit their guidance on local needs and system capability. The developers hoped the service providers that assisted in the project design would be willing to participate in the project implementation.

Planning

The systems change began with a series of planning meetings hosted by the state to which local treatment agencies and other health and human services providers were invited. At the meetings, the project mission was marketed, and ideas for and adjustments to the project were developed. Providers who had participated in several coordination initiatives in Newark in the past provided valuable historical perspectives. Past failures had left agencies skeptical of future changes and hostile toward outside influences. However, these planning meetings helped develop a clear vision of the proposed project that incorporated lessons learned from past coordination attempts and failures. This vision was to prove instrumental in developing the treatment network.

Unlike some changes within health care delivery systems that are promulgated from inside the system, the Newark project was imposed by an outside funding source. The changes were developed with local input but proposed and funded by an external entity. Without this outside pressure, change may not have occurred.

Interagency Agreements

Once the project was funded, the relationships that developed during the grant-writing phase were formalized with interagency agreements. Once again, external pressure from the state initiated this effort toward coordination by requiring the development and execution of written agreements. All of the substance abuse treatment agencies and other involved health and human services agencies signed the agreements. The agreements specified referral processes between the agencies and the CIU and facilitated a smooth transition when the service delivery changes were implemented.

Over a six-month period, these independent service providers formed a network of substance abuse treatment delivery. The changes made took a largely proprietary system of individual agencies and created a client-focused network of care. However, change did not occur without conflicts and difficulties.

IMPLEMENTATION OF THE MODEL

The implementation of the changed service delivery system took place in phases. The first six months of the project consisted largely of planning activities. Federal requirements for submission of reports were met, the CIU staffing pattern was designed, an advisory committee was established, and contacts were made with the numerous service agencies in Newark. During this time, the state provided leadership in educating the system service providers about the evolving service delivery model. The first step was outlining the pros and cons of the new centralized intake system and assuring providers that they would survive.

Focused Leadership and Decision Making

An understanding of how the new system would affect each individual agency had to be developed by listening and attending to service providers' fears and concerns. Key to negotiating these steps was strong and focused leadership. This leadership came from state and federal officials, who made difficult decisions while demonstrating an understanding for the concerns of all parties. One example of this leadership was the plan to provide outpatient detoxification to CIU-referred clients.

Before the network developed, two agencies provided outpatient opiate detoxification. Initially they competed to be the single provider of outpatient methadone detoxification services in the new network. One agency was located at the CIU site, and the other was across town. It was concluded that the idea of seamless service delivery at the CIU would be better realized if a client could receive everything from intake through detoxification at one site. In addition, one-site service provision would also meet the project's goal of minimizing the geographic burden on clients caused by multiple service sites. Yet each detox unit would lose revenue if not selected for the network.

State officials had to make a difficult choice. They chose to follow the project mandates and awarded the detox contract to the agency located within the CIU. Although the losing agency openly voiced its discontent, the argument for seamless service delivery and the strong, focused leadership made it possible to make the change within this political environment.

Start-Up

During the second six months, the CIU opened, and the network was ready to serve clients. Staff were hired and trained; space and furnishings were arranged; supplies and materials were purchased; and client assessment components, detoxification providers, and service referral processes were finalized. Providers' input into the specific design of the CIU was elicited both to take advantage of their expertise and to facilitate their "buy in" for the new system.

The provision of funds was an initial incentive for agencies to participate in network development. However, as the first grant year and planning process drew to a close, service providers still had not received any of the funds. In fact, they were informed of a possible decrease in the promised allocations. Without these funds, the incentive for ongoing involvement of the substance abuse treatment providers was unclear. In fact, attendance at advisory and planning meetings had declined, yet participation in core CIU operations remained constant.

The reasons that most agencies still participated, given the limited financial incentives for project involvement, are unclear. It is possible that even with service delivery systems that had been built through competition, providing appropriate client treatment, minimizing obstacles to care, and improving quality remained top priorities. Ultimately, it appears that the service delivery changes that resulted in improved quality transcended agency self-interest or self-preservation, resulting in cooperation without financial gain. What seemed critical for the successful implementation of this project was the articulation of project goals so that administrators, practitioners, and government officials understood the benefits to clients and the compromises each had to make.

The treatment organizations were often critical of the changes, their project participation was sometimes low, and agency staff members sometimes refused to follow protocols. Nevertheless, the new system was implemented, and comprehensive client services were delivered. The struggles encountered during these changes were turned into challenges, and the vision of improved client care was a guiding force.

FACTORS THAT CONTRIBUTED TO SUCCESSFUL CHANGE

The service delivery change effort was assisted by four factors that contributed to its successful redesign: (1) focused leadership, (2) a clear vision of the objective, (3) phased-in change, and (4) formal interagency agreements.

Focused Leadership and Clear Vision

As was demonstrated by several key decisions that were necessary to keep the project moving, leaders who made swift decisions and stuck to them were important. Leadership that was focused on outcome and listened to various points of view but in the final analysis made decisions that would result in the most efficient and effective service delivery was critical. The decisions reached were considered fair by most, even when not in their best interest. Such decision making was made easier by a clear vision.

In the initial phases of this project, the ability to articulate the advantages and gains for clients and treatment agencies that would result from the new system was important in gathering project participation. The coordinating agency projected a vision of a system that would provide additional support to clients and staff that would lead to improved quality of care and decreased treatment dropout. This vision of benefits for clients seemed to prompt ongoing participation from all players, even when individual organizations stood to lose.

When a vision includes improved services to clients, social workers are morally inclined and ethically bound to uphold and support such services. When the vision is clear and feasible, leadership can use it to guide decision making. Difficult decisions, such as the closing of a service, must be made with the utmost integrity. It is much easier for those who are hurt by proposed changes to deal with and support them when they can trust that such decisions were necessary for the vision to be accomplished. This has been true for the NTCP.

Phased-in Change and Formal Interagency Agreements

The NTCP benefited from a phased-in start-up. The step-by-step implementation provided organizations with the time necessary to train staff and make the organizational culture adjustments needed to support coordinated service delivery. It also allowed time to learn the processes necessary for collaboration within an integrated system. The new model was tested slowly, whereas problem correction was addressed quickly.

For a system to be integrated and coordinated, the individuals within that system must communicate with each other. They must understand what needs to be communicated and know how best to do that. The treatment agencies had to learn a common treatment language, they needed to accept standardized decision-making models, and they needed to trust that all participants would fulfill their obligations. The phased-in implementation allowed time for these developments.

The formal interagency agreements helped clearly define the obligations and expectations of all participants. The agreements communicated the tasks and duties to be performed, so that lines of accountability were clear. The specification of obligations, tasks, oversight, and lines of accountability resulted in smoother, more efficient service delivery.

CONCLUSION

Implementation of change is never easy. However, consultation with others who have made similar changes can prepare planners for a potentially arduous experience. This outline of the development of the NTCP is meant to provide insight into individuals and agencies attempting to implement change in fragmented systems of substance abuse treatment. The NTCP created a seamless, coordinated treatment delivery system for residents of the City of Newark. Through a single-point-of-entry system, the provision of ongoing case management, service monitoring and patient tracking, and clinical training for treatment agency staff, the outcomes of individuals completing treatment are expected to improve.

In system change experiments such as this one, it is important to evaluate whether the goals of the change (specifically, improvement in substance abuse treatment outcomes) are actualized. Studies are currently under way at the NTCP to evaluate the accomplishment of the project's goals and objectives. These studies will touch on the efficacy of the single-point-of-entry model.

The results will be particularly useful in this age of managed care and gatekeeper models of service delivery. Without the results of these studies in hand, it is difficult to delineate the client outcomes related to the new system that has been developed in Newark. The one clearly documented result is that an increased number of Newark residents who are substance abusers can obtain primary medical care. More specific results are yet to come.

REFERENCES

Adelman, H. S. (1993). School-linked mental health interventions toward mechanisms for service coordination integration. *Journal of Community Psychology, 12,* 309–319.

Couch, J. B. (1991). *Health care quality management for the 21st century.* Tampa, FL: American College of Physician Executives.

Crowson, R. L., & Boyd, W. L. (1993). Coordinated services for children: Designing arks for storms and seas unknown. *American Journal of Education, 101,* 140–179.

Fennell, M. L., & Alexander, J. A. (1993). Perspectives on organizational change in the United States medical care sector. *Annual Review of Sociology, 19,* 89–112.

Gaines, S. K., Rice, M. S., & Carmon, M. C. (1993). A model of health care delivery in a child day care setting. *Public Health Nursing, 10,* 166–169.

Gillies, R. R., Shortell, S. M., Anderson, D. A., Mitchell, J. B., & Morgan, K. L. (1993). Conceptualizing and measuring integration: Findings from the health systems integration study. *Hospital & Health Services Administration, 38,* 467–489.

Halvorson, H. W., Pike, D. K., Reed, F. M., McClatchey, M. W., & Gosselink, C. A. (1993). Using qualitative methods to evaluate health services delivery in three rural Colorado communities. *Evaluation & the Health Professions, 16,* 434–447.

National Institute on Drug Abuse. (1991). *Annual emergency room data: Data from the Drug Abuse Warning Network (DAWN)* (Series 1, Number 11-A). Bethesda, MD: Author.

New Jersey Department of Health. (1993). *Target Cities Project.* Trenton: Author, Division of Alcoholism, Drug Abuse, and Addiction Services.

Shortell, S. M., Gillies, R. R., Anderson, D. A., Mitchell, J. B., & Morgan, K. L. (1993). Creating organized delivery systems: The barriers and facilitators. *Hospital & Health Services Administration, 38,* 447–466.

Shortell, S. M., & Morrison, E. M. (1990). *Strategic choices for American hospitals: Managing change in turbulent times.* San Francisco: Jossey-Bass.

This chapter was originally published in the May 1997 issue of Health & Social Work, *vol. 22, pp. 143–148.*

35

An Empowerment-Centered, Church-Based Asthma Education Program for African American Adults

Marvella E. Ford, Gloria Edwards, Juan L. Rodriguez, Rose C. Gibson, and Barbara C. Tilley

Asthma, a chronic inflammatory condition of the airways, is a major health problem in the United States, affecting about 12 million people (Bailey et al., 1992; British Thoracic Society, 1990; Huss et al., 1992). People with asthma experience on average more than 100 days of restricted activity annually (Bailey et al., 1992). Mortality and morbidity due to asthma are increasing, particularly among African Americans (Buist & Vollmer, 1990; Wilson, 1993).

The costs for treating asthma in African Americans are exceptionally high because members of this population tend to use the emergency department as a primary source of care (Baker, Stevens, & Brooks, 1994; Kellerman, 1994). It is important that African Americans learn, through asthma self-management programs, what they need to manage their asthma and how to meet these needs through the health care system and increase their access to health services. As African Americans with asthma increase their access to and use of primary care and their use of inhaled corticosteroids as appropriate, they will better manage their asthma, thus maintaining their activity levels and reducing asthma-related mortality and morbidity and emergency department use (Bauman et al., 1989; Clark & Starr-Schneidkraut, 1994; Sly, Cahill, Willet, & Burton, 1994).

ASTHMA SELF-MANAGEMENT

Two central components of most asthma education programs are asthma attack prevention and attack management (Clark & Starr-Schneidkraut, 1994). Asthma education and skills training in self-management help individuals draw from a base of asthma knowledge and make appropriate decisions and take corrective actions (Bauman et al., 1989; Clark & Starr-Schneidkraut, 1994). The knowledge gained by participants in educational programs, such as accurate use of peak flow meters and asthma inhalers, may positively affect their perceptions of asthma; these perceptions have been found to play a major role in how well patients adhere to medical treatment regimens (Acker, 1992; Taytard, 1992). As individuals become more proficient at managing their asthma and are able to function better in their daily lives, their asthma-related quality of life should improve (Juniper, Guyatt, Ferrie, & Griffith, 1993; Rowe & Oxman, 1993). Researchers agree that for behavioral changes to be long lasting, they must become sufficiently integrated into aspects of individuals' daily lives (Bauman et al., 1989; Bolton, Tilley, Kuder, Reeves, & Schultz, 1991).

Empowerment Principles

To help individuals integrate asthma management into their daily lives, asthma self-management courses must teach principles of empowerment. *Empowerment* refers to the development of the personal resources (social, psychological, intellectual, and spiritual) individuals need to give them control and mastery over their lives (Feste, 1992; Kalyanpur & Rao, 1991). Developing these personal resources is especially critical for African Americans with asthma, a disease in which much of the burden of day-to-day management and recognition of symptoms rests with the individual. In addition, African Americans have traditionally held a disempowered political, economic, and social position in U.S. society and have thus been prevented from exercising control and mastery over their environments (McKinney, Harel, & Williams, 1990; Thomas & Quinn, 1991). Empowerment-centered asthma education can help African Americans with asthma better manage this chronic condition.

Church Setting

Asthma education programs can be offered in the local church, a context central to many African Americans. Taylor and Chatters (1986) described the African American church as functioning as an "omnipresent and important institution" (p. 637) for African Americans of all ages. Historically, churches have provided for the educational, nutritional, psychological, and employment needs of African Americans and been focal points for community activities (Taylor, Thornton, & Chatters, 1987; Walls & Zarit, 1991). Given the ability of African American churches to organize people within communities, they are viable alternative sources of support for the provision of formal services (Morrison, 1991).

In the church setting, members can function as both recipients and providers of services and resources. It is expected that although health professionals will initially conduct the program described here, church members with asthma who have successfully completed the program will present the program to other adults with asthma in their communities.

DEMONSTRATION PROJECT

The authors have designed a seven-week demonstration project consisting of an empowerment-centered, church-based asthma self-management education program for African American adults. The project is scheduled to start in the spring of 1996. The asthma education program is based on a program designed by Bailey and Manzella (1989) and incorporates principles of empowerment (Feste, 1991). The asthma education and empowerment materials used in this demonstration project have been designed to make them culturally relevant for African Americans with asthma (Table 35.1). One hour of each three-hour class will be spent on the asthma self-management component, and the other two hours will be spent emphasizing empowerment principles.

Table 35.1

The Empowerment-Centered Asthma Self-Management Program

Session No.	Asthma Self-Management Component (1 hour)	Empowerment Component (2 hours)
1	Making introductions, selecting an asthma control partner	Goal setting: living with everyday stressors and chronic illness; eight major stressors experienced by many African Americans
2	Learning about asthma	Problem solving
3	Learning how to get help from professionals (including a resource list documenting locations where individuals without insurance can receive health care and medication)	Reactions to health care providers: common perceptions of health care providers among African Americans; exploring African Americans' cultural patterns that affect health care management; problem-solving techniques to receiving good medical care
4	Learning about asthma medication options; using asthma inhalers. Placebo inhalers will be distributed	African American health care beliefs and practices: blending African and European American health beliefs, values, and practices; health-seeking behaviors of African Americans; thinking through the implications of many cultural health care beliefs and practices to appropriate management of asthma
5	Learning more about asthma medications	Reactions to the health care system (including assisting individuals with asking for and obtaining what they need from the health care system); issues related to fear of unethical treatment and lack of trust in health care providers; discussion of issues relating to African Americans' interaction with formal health care providers
6	Learning how to prevent an asthma attack; using peak flow meters. Peak flow meters will be distributed	Coping with illness: exploring feelings related to perceptions of asthma; identifying common coping skills associated with the African American culture
7	Learning how to treat an asthma attack	Staying motivated

Session 1

In session 1, the asthma self-management component entails conducting introductions and selecting an asthma control partner. The importance of communicating regularly with an asthma health care team and with family members, friends, and coworkers about the condition is stressed. Participants are encouraged to select a physician to head their health care team and to answer their questions about asthma.

The empowerment component emphasizes the fact that individuals often confront major socioeconomic stressors that can interfere with well-being. Eight major stressors experienced by many African Americans are racial discrimination, poverty and economic instability, feelings of being trapped, feelings of worthlessness and rage, the weakening of traditional community and family ties, the lack of accessible and quality health care, the cost of health care, and poor health. In addition to these stressors, participants are asked to identify major personal stressors, to discuss which of these stressors interferes the most with their well-being, and to consider ways to reduce or resolve each stressor.

Session 2

The asthma self-management component of session 2 involves learning about asthma. In this session, the physiology of asthma is discussed. The events occurring during an asthma attack, the signs of an impending attack, and the causes of attacks are described. Also, in this session the empowerment component focuses on problem solving. Participants are encouraged to identify obstacles interfering with reaching the goals they set in session 1. Personal problem-solving techniques that have proved effective in the past are considered, and participants are asked to think of additional problem-solving techniques they could use to tackle obstacles. Participants are encouraged to apply appropriate techniques to handling obstacles in the coming week and to evaluate the effectiveness of their plan of action.

Session 3

In the asthma self-management component of session 3, participants learn how to work with a primary care physician to find an asthma specialist in their area. The importance of finding a second medical opinion if they think their asthma condition is not being effectively controlled is stressed to the participants. Successful communication with the health care team is emphasized. Participants are reminded that they are the most important members of their health care team, that they should help to develop their own asthma care plan, and that they have the right and the responsibility to question their asthma treatment. Area emergency care services for asthma and information to be shared over the telephone with emergency medical personnel are also discussed.

In the empowerment component of session 3, participants explore common anticipated reactions from mainstream health care providers regarding African Americans. These reactions include indifference to patients' waiting time; overidentification of non–African American health care providers with African American patients, which may be seen by these patients as paternalistic and condescending; and stereotyping. In this session, participants also explore African American patients' cultural patterns that may affect their health care encounters. These cultural patterns include communication styles, the meaning of time, dietary customs, the use of home remedies and medications, and the use and importance of religion. Problem-solving techniques geared toward improving communications between patients and providers are also discussed in this session.

Session 4

In session 4, participants learn about the generic and brand names of various asthma medication options and their functions. Participants also learn the proper steps for using an inhaler correctly. To assist in this process, placebo inhalers can be distributed. The empowerment component of this session focuses on African American health care beliefs, values, and practices. In this session, participants discuss their perceptions about illness and health; the blending of African American and European American health beliefs and practices; and health care–seeking behaviors, such as the use of home remedies, delay in obtaining formal health care, and the use of indigenous healers. Participants are encouraged to think through the implications of many of their cultural health care beliefs and practices for the appropriate management of asthma and to develop skill in determining which cultural health care practices can be applied in certain situations and which should be discarded.

Session 5

The asthma self-management component of session 5 involves learning more about asthma medications. Participants are encouraged to keep a record of their medication schedule and are given tips to help them maintain a proper medication treatment plan. Information is provided on over-the-counter drugs, the effects of other drugs on asthma medications, and asthma and pregnancy. The empowerment component involves common reactions to the health care system on the part of African Americans. These reactions include problems with the accessibility, availability, affordability, and appropriateness of health care and the fact that hospitals are perceived by some African Americans as a place to die. Problem-solving techniques addressing these reactions are explored.

Session 6

The asthma self-management component in the sixth session focuses on learning how to prevent an asthma attack. Peak flow meters are distributed to participants, and the proper use of these meters is demonstrated. A list of common asthma triggers is presented. General health practices such as learning to deal with stress, relaxing, joining an asthma support group, and exercising are discussed.

The empowerment component focuses on coping with illness. In this session, participants discuss their feelings about what caused their asthma, the severity of their asthma, the types of treatment they think they should receive, the most important results they hope to receive from the treatment, what they fear most about their asthma, whether having asthma has affected their sense of self-worth, and the effects of asthma on their nuclear and extended family systems and their social lives. Customary means of coping with illness are explored and assessed for their constructive and destructive consequences. Common coping skills associated with the African American culture are identified, including the use of religion, nuclear and extended family systems, perseverance, "making do with little," and the use of humor.

Session 7

In session 7, participants learn how to treat an asthma attack. Participants are encouraged to relax during an asthma attack, to take their medications, and to try to breathe as normally as possible. Proper breathing techniques are illustrated. Tips for controlling coughing, which can aggravate an asthma attack or be the primary symptom of one, are presented. Seeking medical attention for an asthma attack and the aftereffects of an attack are discussed.

In the empowerment component, participants learn how to stay motivated in managing their asthma. Specifically, participants are encouraged to focus on the personal benefits they gain from taking charge of their own health care, to develop a plan of action for their health care management, to recognize and be proud of their own strengths, to identify major sources of support, and to take advantage of current opportunities to be in charge of making wise decisions to achieve good health.

STUDY METHODOLOGY

Design

The seven-week demonstration project will be offered to 20 randomly assigned individuals (the intervention group) in a church setting. Twenty other individuals will be randomly assigned to a control group and will receive the demonstration intervention after a six-month follow-up period has been completed and comparisons between the intervention and control groups have been made. This randomization procedure is expected to produce two groups with similar baseline demographic characteristics. The control group is necessary to control for seasonal variation in the occurrence of asthma attacks.

Participants

The goals of the demonstration project and the need for investigators to identify potential participants from church congregations have already been discussed with ministers in a local African American Baptist Ministers' Council. A short questionnaire designed by the investigators has been distributed as a church bulletin insert to congregational members of some churches in the local Ministers' Council and will be completed by the members and returned to the investigators. The questionnaire assesses the prevalence of asthma among congregational members, their families, and their friends and their willingness to participate in the demonstration project. The questionnaire also requests that respondents provide their telephone numbers. From the list of potential participants, a sample of 40 eligible and consenting individuals will be identified and recruited by telephone. Individuals will be considered eligible if they are 18 years or older and report that they have been diagnosed with asthma. We estimate that we will need to contact 80 potential participants to recruit the necessary 40 respondents for the demonstration project.

Program Evaluation

The authors plan an evaluation of the education program. The anticipated outcomes they will assess are reduced emergency department use, accurate use of

peak flow meters and asthma inhalers, increased asthma knowledge, more positive perceptions of asthma, and a higher asthma-related quality of life. Emergency department use will be based on self-report. The accuracy with which
peak flow meters are used will be measured by a health professional using the
peak flow self-management plan adapted by Beaseley, Cushley, and Holgate
(1989). Use of inhalers will be measured by a 10-item observational checklist
documenting inhaler use and skill developed by Manzella et al. (1989).

Asthma knowledge can be measured by the asthma knowledge questionnaire
developed by the National Heart, Lung, and Blood Institute (1992). Individuals'
perceptions of their asthma will be measured using the Meaning of Illness Questionnaire (MIQ), which contains 33 items rated on three- and seven-point scales
(Browne et al., 1988). Asthma-related quality of life will be measured using a
questionnaire developed by Juniper et al. (1993) that contains 32 questions covering four domains of daily life: activities, asthma symptoms, emotional functioning, and environmental exposure.

Other data to be collected include participants' medical histories, history of
asthma attacks, general health status, age, gender, and zip codes. Information
pertaining to outcomes will be collected from all intervention and control group
members before the beginning of the demonstration project and monthly for six
months following the conclusion of the project. In addition, an evaluation will
be completed by participants at the end of each demonstration project session.

CONCLUSION

Mortality and morbidity rates due to asthma are rising among African Americans. Through the use of this empowerment-centered, church-based program,
it is hoped that participants will increase their knowledge of asthma, learn to
better manage their asthma-related needs, and gain a more positive perception
of this chronic condition, resulting in reduced mortality and higher quality of
life.

REFERENCES

Acker, K. V. (1992). Lessons from diabetes education? *European Respiratory Journal, 5,* 129–132.
Bailey, W. C., Clark, N. M., Gotsch, A. R., Lemen, R. J., O'Connor, G. T., & Rosenstock, I. M.
(1992). Asthma prevention. *Chest: The Cardiopulmonary Journal, 102,* 216S–231S.
Bailey, W. C., & Manzella, B. A. (1989). *Learn asthma control in seven days: A step-by-step guide
using principles proven effective in research studies conducted at the University of Alabama Hospital,
UAB.* Bethesda, MD: National Heart, Lung, and Blood Institute, Division of Lung Diseases.
Baker, D. W., Stevens, C. D., & Brooks, R. H. (1994). Regular source of ambulatory care and
medical care utilization by individuals presenting to a public hospital emergency depart-
ment. *Journal of the American Medical Association, 271,* 1909–1912.
Bauman, A., Craig, A. R., Dunsmore, J., Browne, G., Allen, D. H., & Vandenberg, R. (1989).
Removing barriers to effective self-management of asthma. *Individual Education and Counseling, 14,* 217–226.
Beaseley, R., Cushley, M., & Holgate, S. T. (1989). A self-management plan in the treatment of
adult asthma. *Thorax, 44,* 200–204.
Bolton, M. B., Tilley, B. C., Kuder, J., Reeves, T., & Schultz, L. R. (1991). The cost and effectiveness of an education program for adult asthmatics. *Journal of General Internal Medicine, 6,*
401–407.

British Thoracic Society, Research Unit of the Royal College of British Physicians of London, National Asthma Campaign. (1990). Guidelines for management of asthma in adults, I. Chronic persistent asthma. *British Medical Journal, 301,* 651–653.

Browne, G. B., Byrne, C., Roberts, J., Streiner, D., Fitch, M., Corey, P., & Arpin, K. (1988). The Meaning of Illness Questionnaire: Reliability and validity. *Nursing Research, 37,* 368–373.

Buist, A. S., & Vollmer, W. M. (1990). Reflections on the rise of asthma morbidity and mortality. *Journal of the American Medical Association, 264,* 1719–1720.

Clark, N. M., & Starr-Schneidkraut, J. (1994). Management of asthma by individuals and families. *American Journal of Respiratory and Critical Care Medicine, 149,* S54–S56.

Feste, C. (1991). *Empowerment: Facilitating a path to personal self-care.* Tarrytown, NY: Miles Diagnostics Division.

Feste, C. (1992). A practical look at patient empowerment. *Diabetes Care, 15,* 922–925.

Huss, K., Squire, E. N., Carpenter, G. B., Smith, L. J., Huss, R. W., Salata, K., Salerno, M., Agosthelli, D., & Hershey, J. (1992). Effective education of adults with asthma who are allergic to dust mites. *Journal of Allergy and Clinical Immunology, 89,* 836–843.

Juniper, E. F., Guyatt, G. H., Ferrie, P. J., & Griffith, L. E. (1993). Measuring quality of life in asthma. *American Review of Respiratory Diseases, 147,* 832–838.

Kalyanpur, M., & Rao, S. S. (1991). Empowering low-income black families of handicapped children. *American Journal of Orthopsychiatry, 61,* 523–532.

Kellerman, A. L. (1994). Nonurgent emergency department visits: Meeting an unmet need. *Journal of the American Medical Association, 271,* 1953–1954.

Manzella, B. A., Brooks, C. M., Richards, J. M., Windsor, R. A., Soong, S., & Bailey, W. C. (1989). Assessing the use of metered dose inhalers in adults with asthma. *Journal of Asthma, 26,* 223–230.

McKinney, E. A., Harel, Z., & Williams, M. (1990). Introduction to the black aged. In Z. Harel, E. A. McKinney, & M. Williams (Eds.), *Black aged: Understanding diversity and service needs.* Newbury Park, CA: Sage Publications.

Morrison, J. D. (1991). The black church as a support system for black elderly. *Journal of Gerontological Social Work, 17,* 105–120.

National Heart, Lung, and Blood Institute. (1992). *Check your asthma "I.Q."* (National Institutes of Health Publication No. 92-1128). Bethesda, MD: Author, National Asthma Education Program.

Rowe, B. H., & Oxman, A. D. (1993). Performance of an asthma quality of life questionnaire in an outpatient setting. *American Review of Respiratory Diseases, 148,* 675–681.

Sly, P. D., Cahill, P., Willet, K., & Burton, P. (1994). Accuracy of mini peak flow meters in indicating changes in lung function in children with asthma. *British Medical Journal, 308,* 572–574.

Taylor, R. J., & Chatters, L. M. (1986). Church-based informal support among elderly blacks. *Gerontologist, 26,* 637–642.

Taylor, R., Thornton, M. C., & Chatters, L. M. (1987). Black Americans' perceptions of the sociohistorical role of the church. *Journal of Black Studies, 18,* 123–138.

Taytard, A. (1992). Assessing compliance in asthma patients. *European Respiratory Journal, 5,* 125–126.

Thomas, S. B., & Quinn, S. C. (1991). Public health then and now: The Tuskegee Syphilis Study, 1932 to 1972: Implications for HIV education and AIDS risk education programs in the black community. *American Journal of Public Health, 81,* 1418–1504.

Walls, C. T., & Zarit, S. H. (1991). Informal support from black churches and the well-being of elderly blacks. *Gerontologist, 31,* 490–495.

Wilson, S. R. (1993). Individual and physician behavior models related to asthma care. *Medical Care, 31,* MS49–MS60.

This work was supported by Agency for Health Care Policy and Research Grant No. B10450.

This chapter was originally published in the February 1996 issue of Health & Social Work, *vol. 21, pp. 70–75.*

36 Retooling for Community Health Partnerships in Primary Care and Prevention

Dennis L. Poole and Mary Van Hook

Major changes in medical care challenge health care professionals to discover new ways to address health needs in primary care and prevention (Berkman, 1996). Replacing fragmented systems with coordinated networks of care is one of the greatest challenges. Ensuring that underserved and vulnerable populations have access to comprehensive care is another. Both call for the development of creative partnerships among traditional health care providers, social services professionals, and members of the community. Building and participating in partnerships will require retooling for many professionals.

MODELS THAT WORK

Recognizing the urgent need for partnerships, the Human Resources and Services Administration's (HRSA, 1996) Bureau of Primary Health Care in the U.S. Department of Health and Human Services is leading a partnership of 36 national foundations, associations, and nonprofit organizations in a Models That Work campaign. The campaign seeks to increase access to primary and preventive health care for underserved and vulnerable populations by encouraging communities to establish comprehensive primary health care programs that are creative, responsive to the community, and transferable to other communities. The following six examples are partnerships that communities have developed to achieve these objectives in a variety of settings.

First, the partnerships involve community members in the design and delivery of services. The Cure/Heart, Body and Soul program in Baltimore uses trained neighborhood health workers to carry out prevention efforts in urban African American communities. Workers complement traditional systems of primary care by providing preventive screening, health education, referral, follow-up, advocacy, and community organization. Similarly, the Camp Health Aide Program in Michigan enlists migrant farmworkers to provide culturally appropriate health education, advocacy, outreach, referral, and follow-up services. The Community Health Advisor program in Mississippi uses trained natural helpers who live and work in rural communities to provide health information and advice; organize self-help action projects; and connect neighbors, families, and friends to needed services. This program has reduced infant mortality in one county by 16 percent.

Second, the partnerships identify people at risk for health problems during crisis events. In a poverty-stricken neighborhood of St. Paul, Minnesota, HouseCalls identifies families at risk of homelessness through referrals from housing inspectors, outreach workers, and traditional service providers. A staff social worker and the family develop a crisis intervention plan to identify housing priorities as well as health needs related to inadequate prenatal care, delayed immunizations, and overdue well-child checks. Home visits, transportation, and other support services are provided to facilitate access to housing and health services. The Adolescent Community Services project in Binghamton, New York, provides reproductive health services, health education, counseling, and transitional housing supports to pregnant, parenting, and high-risk adolescents and their families. Intervention during this crisis-prone stage of life reduces teenage pregnancy rates, lowers foster care placements, and increases high school completion rates.

Third, the partnerships reach out to people by providing coordinated health services in accessible community sites or in the homes of families. For example, Enloe Hospital in Chico, California, offers a wide array of health and social services at a community center for migrant farmworkers and their families. This approach decreases pediatric visits to emergency rooms by increasing access to primary and preventive care. In the Arkansas Delta Community Integrated Service System, a family care coordination team uses a home-visiting model to improve access to services, pregnancy outcomes, and infant health in rural areas. The Healthy Homes Program in Lincoln, Nebraska, reduces infant mortality rates through outreach, home visits, and culturally appropriate health care services to low-income, uninsured pregnant women, infants, and families. Outreach workers at St. Mary's Breast Cancer Education and Detection Program in Rochester, New York, give home parties and visit sites where low-income women congregate (for example, laundromats, churches, homeless shelters, soup kitchens, beauty parlors, and senior citizen centers).

Fourth, the partnerships emphasize community ownership of health problems and solutions. Project Vida of the Comprehensive Community Health and Services Program in El Paso, Texas, includes a "community congress" in which community members meet annually to review and evaluate programs, suggest new directions, and propose priorities. In Philadelphia, tenant council members from the public housing communities hold a majority of the seats on the health center management board of the Abbottsford and Schuylkill Falls Community Health Centers. Community members in the Cure/Heart, Body and Soul program offered several helpful suggestions to professionals seeking community ownership of health problems and solutions:

- Understand our ways and beliefs. We have a different history and a culture that is based on our heritage as well as our struggle to survive.
- Keep in mind that agencies and institutions and their representatives are the "foreigners" in our communities. Adapt to our ways; don't automatically expect us to adapt to yours.
- Look at our people as equals and worthy of your respect.

- Don't start with the notion that you have to "empower" us. Recognize that we are in power. This is our community, and when your program is gone, we'll still be here. If you want something to last, understand that we must own it eventually.

Fifth, the partnerships develop training mechanisms that cut across traditional professional boundaries to help health professionals and community members provide holistic and coordinated care. Ke Ola O Hawaii in Honolulu uses a multidisciplinary, problem-based curriculum to train practitioners in real-life community health issues. Students from schools of medicine, nursing, public health, and social work learn to assess community needs together and to understand the importance of partnerships with communities. Cure/Heart, Body and Soul takes this training concept one step further; indigenous community leaders receive faculty appointments at John Hopkins University to teach in the schools of medicine, nursing, and public health. Similarly, the Camp Health Aide Program relies on community members to educate health professionals about the culture and lifestyle of migrant farmworkers.

Sixth, the partnerships usually create new structures to integrate traditionally fragmented systems of care. A coalition of hospitals, insurance companies, schools, local providers, and community groups formed the Consortium for Latino Health in Philadelphia to reduce barriers to primary and preventive health. Churches and community agencies joined forces to establish a nonprofit corporation to run the one-stop service center of the Adolescent Community Services Project. Community partners in Marion County, Florida, established the Indigent Care Oversight Board to oversee implementation of the county's comprehensive primary health care system for low-income residents. The Cure/Heart, Body and Soul partnership created "coordinated community–medical care system task forces" to develop and monitor neighborhood-based prevention programs.

PROFESSIONAL RETOOLING

Building and participating in community health partnerships will require retooling for many professionals. In the case of social workers, the soundness of their involvement in primary and preventive health care has been accepted for years in many other countries (Hokenstad, Khinduka, & Midgley, 1992). Not until recently have opportunities for such involvement expanded dramatically in the United States. To seize these opportunities, many social workers in direct practice must enlarge their tool kit to include a repertoire of skills in community practice.

Skills in grassroots organization and constituency building are needed to weld coalitions among diverse community groups to mobilize support and secure funding for partnerships. These skills can help social workers develop a constituency base for the unique direct service contributions they can make in primary and preventive health care.

Skills in creative resource packaging and budgeting also are critical. No longer can programs rely on a single source of funding. To earn a place at the bargaining table, social workers must display skills in packaging and budgeting the full range of resources needed to fund a community health partnership: government sources (municipal, county, state, and federal), voluntary sources (civic organizations, United Way, churches, and foundations), and consumer sources (in-kind and fee-for service).

Training and consultation skills are needed as well. Partnerships need professionals to perform direct services in primary and preventive care. However, current realities are such that professionals also must train and consult with community members to deliver some of these services. Conversely, professionals must be competent in devising ways for community members to train and consult with them. This reciprocal arrangement can help professionals deliver more efficient, culturally effective services.

The current drive toward accountability and efficiency in health care also demands skills in outcome evaluation and cost analysis. Social workers must be able to calculate the contributions they make in achieving outcomes in primary care and prevention. Identifying the unit cost of their services, comparing these costs with other ways to provide similar services, and recommending strategies to deliver services more efficiently are highly valued competencies in community health partnerships.

Marketing skills are essential as well. The unique contributions social workers can make in primary care and prevention are sometimes overlooked. Getting consumers to understand and request social work services and planners to appreciate and value psychosocial interventions require skills in marketing. Without them, social workers will have difficulty conveying what they can contribute to community health partnerships.

Finally, skills in building and sustaining new structures are needed to integrate previously fragmented systems of care. Familiarity is needed with a variety of structural alternatives—councils, commissions, committees, advisory groups, and task forces—that communities can use to forge public–private partnerships in primary and preventive health. Being capable of facilitating group task performance once these structures are formed is another skill. It is interesting that no professional group now performs this critical leadership function in community health partnerships. Social workers have the edge; they can use their generalist training to build new structures through community organization and sustain them by using group work skills to help community groups achieve objectives in primary care and prevention.

REFERENCES

Berkman, B. (1996). The emerging health care world: Implications for social work practice and education. *Social Work, 41,* 541–551.

Hokenstad, M. C., Khinduka, S. K., & Midgley, J. (Eds.). (1992). *Profiles in international social work.* Washington, DC: NASW Press.

Human Resources and Services Administration, Bureau of Primary Health Care, U.S. Department of Health and Human Services. (1996). *Models that work campaign.* http://www.bphc. hrsa.dhhs. gov/mtw/mtw.html; e-mail: models@hrsa.ssw. dhhs.gov. Washington, DC: Author.

This chapter was originally published in the February 1997 issue of Health & Social Work, *vol. 22, pp. 2–4.*

37 Addressing At-Risk Pregnant Women's Issues through Community, Individual, and Corporate Grassroots Efforts

Judy Balsanek

P renatal care is crucial to the health and well-being of our youngest children. Yet millions of children are coming into the world without the benefit of this care, and their numbers are increasing. About one-fourth of pregnant women do not receive the recommended level of prenatal care. The percentage of pregnant women who receive virtually no prenatal care (no more than a visit or two in the last few weeks of pregnancy) has increased in recent years. Mothers are less likely to obtain adequate or prompt prenatal care if they are young, poor, unmarried, relatively uneducated, uninsured, or living in inner cities or rural areas (Carnegie Task Force on Meeting the Needs of Young Children, 1994).

Pregnant women, new mothers, and families are often ill informed or misinformed about the need for preventive health care and the process of actually getting care. Even if people have the necessary information, they may lack the motivation, friendly guidance, ability to pay, or means of transportation necessary to get to care. Services are provided in different places, and eligibility forms are varied, complex, and designed to frustrate (National Commission to Prevent Infant Mortality, 1989).

Mothers who do not receive prenatal care are more likely to have low-birthweight infants (2,500 grams or less). These babies are significantly more likely to have neurodevelopmental handicaps, congenital anomalies, and more frequent respiratory tract infections. Over 40 percent of these infants are rehospitalized more than once in their first year of life (Carnegie Task Force on Meeting the Needs of Young Children, 1994). Consequently, pregnant women who do not receive prenatal care and thus have less chance of delivering healthy, full-term, normal-weight babies are referred to in this chapter as "at risk."

In spite of considerable investment of resources and the highly skilled and well-equipped medical system, by most measures the overall health status of Americans lags behind that of many other nations' citizens. Among the nations of the world, the United States ranks 19th in infant mortality, 21st in deaths of children under five, and 29th in the percentage of low-birthweight babies. The low childhood immunization rates in the United States are a national disgrace (Children's Defense Fund, cited in Hartman, 1992). Zuravin (1989) defined refusal or delay in providing health care as one subtype of parent behavior resulting in child neglect. Social work studies provide overwhelming evidence that extreme poverty is significant in the etiology of neglect, especially chronic neglect. At the micro level, the multiplicity of problems facing chronically neglecting caregivers requires interventions that are comprehensive, in-home, and longer term. Social services agencies have long been unable to provide the concrete and paraprofessional services necessary to increase household management and parenting skills (Nelson, Saunders, & Landsman, 1993).

The crises in health care—the new demands and the need for answers—clearly point to the need for a redefinition of services. Although social work emphasizes the importance of family involvement, research indicates that the actual number of encounters with families is a relatively small percentage of the many interventions provided by social workers in health care settings (Bergman et al., 1993). Society cannot afford to ignore the increasing blight of child maltreatment perpetuated by economic inequities and by the failure of the human services system to adequately meet the needs of families and children (Nelson et al., 1993).

Shared Beginnings was established in 1994 to address the needs of "high-risk" pregnant women in Denver, specifically women enrolled for health care at Provenant Family Medicine Centers. The program involved the collaboration of the medical, social services, and business communities; philanthropic sectors; and community members. This chapter describes the nature of this program and the steps taken to initiate and maintain such a grassroots program.

GENESIS OF SHARED BEGINNINGS

Poverty is growing in the Denver area at a more dramatic rate than in most other western cities. Children in particular are becoming poorer—about 27 percent of the city's children now live in poverty. The increase in female-headed, single-parent households in Denver is one of the reasons for these findings. Female-headed households in Denver had a poverty rate of 46 percent, whereas the poverty rate of married couples with children was just 10.2 percent. In 1992, 36 percent of births in Denver were to women under 25. Denver leads the metropolitan area in births to women with less than a high school education, almost one in three. Almost 1,200 babies are born each year to women who are young (under 25) and unmarried and have less than a high school education. These children face the double jeopardy of a life in poverty and an increased risk for child abuse and neglect (Piton Foundation, 1994).

A report by the Piton Foundation (1994) identified important needs in the Denver community that formed the basis of a collaborative community program to improve health services to at-risk pregnant young women and their babies. The report stressed the family as society's basic unit for raising children to become productive adults. Every child deserves to grow up in a family capable of providing for his or her physical, intellectual, emotional, and spiritual development. This can be a difficult responsibility for those carrying the added burden of poverty. Strong families include adults who have developed a network of personally supportive relationships through associations with friends, family, church, and community and civic organizations. People in these networks help each other get through tough times. Consequently, all segments of the community, both public and private, must be involved in meeting the unique challenges of raising children in poor families.

The Piton Foundation (1994) report stressed that people must believe that they make a difference and must see opportunities to make positive contributions to their communities. Every business must see itself within the context of the community in which it does business. The philanthropic community must take the lead in demonstrating commitment to tackling poverty-related issues and showing how individuals and businesses can become involved.

Identifying a Need for Services

Newspaper and television coverage heightened awareness in the Denver community of isolated single parents and increasing numbers of pregnant teenagers and young mothers. Within the Provenant Mercy Medical Center, residents in the family medicine department expressed concerns to attending physicians regarding low-income pregnant teenagers and young mothers who had high rates of prenatal appointment "no shows." Many adolescent patients were receiving no prenatal care before presenting to deliver at the emergency room. Unkept well-baby appointments resulted in poor rates of immunization for these newborns.

A concerned community volunteer philanthropist contacted Provenant Health Partners Foundation to offer assistance in creating a special program to meet the needs of Denver's pregnant teenagers. The challenge was to change community attitudes toward preventive prenatal health care by involving the community in a partnering process including community residents, social services professionals, financial supporters, project participants, and an established health care system. Because of necessary medical center budget constraints, the pilot program had to be financed entirely through philanthropy, medical center foundation fundraising activities, and community partnership.

Volunteers conducted initial research and on-site visits to examine existing nationwide programs that support pregnant adolescents and young mothers. They visited key program models such as Zeta Phi Beta's Stork's Nest in Washington, DC, and the Phoenix Birthing Project in Arizona. They contacted program models such as Resource Mothers in Norfolk, Virginia, and Baby Amigo in Albuquerque, New Mexico. (Additional programs and resources found in the literature review are listed in the reference section of this chapter.) There were two primary approaches that appeared to have success with this population—mentoring and incentive programs. After research and site visits were completed, a three-page program prospectus was developed that included mentoring and incentives.

Mobilizing Financial Support for Services

The initial fundraising goal was to obtain funding for the first 18 months of service delivery. A luncheon program was held with concerned Denver community members including Bea Romer, Colorado's first lady; a city council representative; key philanthropists; Provenant Mercy Medical Center staff; and potential individual and corporate donors. At this event, strong support for the program prospectus generated a desire to continue pursuit of funds for program start-up. Initial financial donations were received. The program prospectus was next presented throughout the community for fundraising, targeting corporate foundations and private donors. These funding efforts took two years. The medical center also donated space and utilities. A community bank donated used furniture.

Program Goals

The program goals of Shared Beginnings for at-risk pregnant women are as follows:

- change community attitudes toward preventive health care by involving the community in a partnering process, including community residents and resources, financial supporters, project participants, and an established health care system.
- enlist volunteer Sharing Partners (mentors) from the community to provide informal community perinatal paraprofessional outreach, home visitation, telephone support, and education. Sharing Partners encourage their partners to make health-promoting lifestyle choices.
- provide a program infrastructure on-site consisting of a program director, secretary, and volunteer services coordinator to provide personal support, professional health education, research implementation, and resource and referral information.
- provide an incentive program for at-risk pregnant women by creating a Baby Store in the hospital where coupons could be redeemed for new baby care items to reinforce health care appointment attendance before the baby is born and immunizations after the baby is born.
- create a research evaluation component to document program effectiveness for the purpose of program refinement and replication.

The outcome goals for the Shared Beginnings program are to increase the birthweight and gestational age of infants, improve perinatal risk, improve health care utilization practices of pregnant women and the infants they deliver, and improve family functioning.

Program Objectives

The program objectives of Shared Beginnings included

- improve health indicators of infants at birth, specifically birthweight. The goal is to approximate the overall rate of low-birthweight babies at Provenant Mercy Medical Center (5.7 percent, compared with 8.5 percent for Colorado in 1992 and 7.1 percent for the United States in 1991) (Colorado Department of Public Health and Environment, 1992).
- improve family functioning over time, from the first prenatal appointment through the infant's six-month well-child visit.
- improve perinatal risk scores for program participants.
- improve health care utilization for pregnant women, as indicated by earlier initiation of prenatal care and better attendance at prenatal appointments. In Colorado in 1992, 79 percent of mothers reported beginning

prenatal care in the first trimester, and 21 percent reported initiating pre-natal care after the first trimester. Nationally, 79 percent of non-Hispanic white women and 58 percent of Hispanic women begin prenatal care in the first trimester (Moore & Hepworth, cited in Clarke, 1993). Both statewide and nationally, late prenatal care is more prevalent among Hispanic and African American mothers (Colorado Department of Public Health and Environment, 1992; Moore & Hepworth, cited in Clarke, 1993).
- improve health care utilization for infants, as indicated by increased atten-dance at well-child clinics and completed immunizations.

INITIAL PROGRAM ACTIVITIES

In September 1994 the program was staffed with a full-time paid project direc-tor and a secretary to oversee daily activities and a part-time research consult-ant to develop an evaluation component. Affiliation with the medical center residency program and a corporate foundation provided continued guidance. Future plans included the formation of a community advisory board composed of program volunteer mentors and community supporters to maintain commu-nity linkages.

An initial planning session involving medical center clinic personnel, the re-search consultant, and project staff identified the prenatal clinic patients to tar-get for program enrollment: patients under 18 years of age. Women over 18 would be enrolled on the basis of individual circumstances. All women would be on financial medical assistance; reside near the bus line located close to the clinic; and be at high risk of poor pregnancy outcome from social, developmen-tal, behavioral, and environmental factors.

Volunteer recruitment began by educating the community and the medical center regarding the new program. An article on the front page of the *Denver Catholic Register* on December 14, 1994, entitled "Young Women Need Support on the Nativity Journey," resulted in 25 inquiries from potential volunteers (Droege, 1994). Internal communication, including an article in the medical cen-ter newspaper entitled "Shared Beginnings Is Born" and staff group presenta-tions for the obstetrics (OB) floor, family medicine clinic, social work depart-ment, and pastoral care, resulted in several medical center staff expressing interest in becoming mentors.

Two program brochures were created using pictures of mothers and infants from various ethnic and cultural backgrounds and easy reading vocabulary. One brochure was designed to use for patient program enrollment at the clinic. A second brochure used for volunteer recruitment was distributed to churches, neighborhood group meetings, and agencies located near the clinic. Additional brochures were given at the monthly meeting of Denver agencies serving preg-nant and parenting teenagers, as well as Denver organizations involved in vol-unteer recruitment. Another key source for brochure distribution was SHARE—an organization where volunteers obtained reduced-price food items from a food warehouse. A one-page program information fact sheet written on a higher read-ing level was created for ongoing fundraising promotional activities and infor-mation outreach to the professional community.

Liaison and integration with the Family Medicine Center clinic was critical in developing necessary relationships for program implementation. The Family Medicine Center social worker became a communication liaison, meeting weekly with the program staff for program planning and information updates, which in turn were communicated to the clinic staff. Several meetings were held with clinic office and nursing staff to lay groundwork for program implementation. The office staff would be involved with scheduling new and return OB patients, critical to enrolling and monitoring Shared Beginnings patients. Nursing staff would help orient new OB patients to the program. A resident physician with a keen OB interest volunteered to be the physician liaison to provide necessary information to family medicine resident physicians. Family medicine staff also volunteered to participate as mentor trainers. All program information and communication activities emphasized education regarding program goals and objectives.

Volunteer Screening and Training

Recruited volunteers completed a written volunteer application and an hour-long interview. Basic qualities screened for included ease in building a new relationship; sensitivity toward others; nonjudgmental attitude; previous pregnancy and parenting experience; and ability to share stories of hardship, survival, and hope. Mentors needed to express their desire to build on the strengths of young pregnant women—survivors in very tough situations—providing a "hand up, not a hand out." Volunteer mentors had to agree to an 18-month commitment, initial training session participation (before patient assignment), and monthly volunteer group meeting attendance for ongoing support and education. The volunteer and program director signed a written letter of commitment.

In February 1995 a 40-hour training program for eight volunteers was held on weekdays. Volunteer feedback resulted in shortening the second training program to three Saturdays from 9:00 A.M. to 3:00 P.M. to meet the needs of parents and working women. Feedback from this training resulted in the creation of a four-Saturday training program to enable additional role playing and more time for discussion. Topics for training included prenatal care; teen pregnancy; adolescent behavior; labor and delivery; postpartum care; nutrition; infant care; child growth and development; positive parenting; emotional, physical, and sexual abuse; substance abuse; depression; home visitation; safety; community resources; symptoms of infant illnesses; infant stimulation problem solving; mentoring; case management; confidentiality; and case documentation. Resource speakers were obtained from community agencies, such as Catholic social services, as well as the medical center staff.

Baby Store

A 140-page coupon booklet was developed to be given to each new enrollee by her Sharing Partner at the first home visit. Included in the booklet were key medical center and community telephone numbers and important information regarding topics such as prenatal care, fetal development, child growth and development, and immunization. Information was arranged to correspond with each prenatal and well-baby physician visit. Coupons were provided for each visit to be redeemed for new items for mother and infant at the Baby Store.

To obtain items for the Baby Store, a Provenant corporatewide baby shower was jointly held with the Colorado National Bank's 60 Denver branches. Donations for the Baby Store were collected during a week-long campaign culminating in the "World's Largest Baby Shower" with cake, games, streamers, balloons, and a guest appearance by the first lady of Colorado, who donated a hand-knit sweater to be given from "Grandma Bea" to the first baby born in Shared Beginnings. Over $5,000 in in-kind and cash donations were obtained to stock the Baby Store. Provenant donated a room for the Baby Store, which was painted, carpeted, shelved, and decorated with balloons, kites, and infant wall hangings—a cheerful place with rocking chairs, books, pamphlets, videos, and infant items. The aim was to create a true "baby boutique" where patients would come and be rewarded for positive health care behaviors.

PROGRAM STATUS

The first enrollments began after six months of program preparation. A volunteer core of 15 Sharing Partners from all ethnic groups were trained and ready to begin. Many had been teenage parents. Many "loved being mothers" and wanted to share their parental expertise. As of this writing, 20 patients have enrolled. Home visits vary from weekly to bimonthly. Sharing Partners make at least one telephone contact a week. Mentors and patients develop goals for the visitation process. Volunteers create a home visit plan and record goals met.

Patients express appreciation that the volunteer Sharing Partner "comes to my place and saves me a trip to clinic." Initial feedback from physicians is positive; one physician stated, "I wish all my patients could be in Shared Beginnings." Sharing Partners provide transportation to clinic appointments for ultrasound and other tests. They help patients preregister and tour the medical center before labor and delivery. Sharing Partners report improved prenatal nutrition behavior. Program enrollees are excited about redeeming their coupons for infant care items. Our monthly volunteer group support meetings are well attended and facilitated by the volunteers. A part-time volunteer coordinator has been hired, and volunteers are being recruited for our third training.

Plans are in progress for the research program to expand to a second Family Medicine center. A strategic planning committee composed of key medical center staff has met four times to plan for the program's future. Activities for securing additional funding for ongoing program implementation and Baby Store items include a boxed-lunch information program for eight potential community individual donors and program presentations for directors and board members of corporate foundations. A fall community luncheon targeted at potential community donors, philanthropists, and volunteers is planned in the home of the chief executive office of Boston Market (the corporate headquarters are located in a suburb of Denver). Shared Beginnings is off to a strong collaborative start.

PROGRAM EVALUATION

To determine the effectiveness of Shared Beginnings, the program design included a research component for program refinement and replication. Research recruitment will be concluded when 120 study participants and 120 comparison participants are recruited. Eligible program enrollees will be assigned randomly to the study or control group, enrolled in the study at the time of their first prenatal visit, and continue in the study until their infant is six months old. Study participants will be assigned a Sharing Partner and will participate in the Baby Store incentive component. The control group will receive no Shared Beginnings services. Both groups will agree to provide information and complete forms for data collection. Variables measured will include demographic information, family functioning using the family APGAR (Adaptation–Partnership–Growth–Affection–Resolve) (Smilkstein, 1978), infant gestational age and birthweight, perinatal risk using the Hobe, Hyvarinin, O'Kada, and Oh (cited in Clarke, 1993) perinatal risk assessment, health care utilization of women based on the number of prenatal health care visits from each woman's clinic record, and health care utilization of infants assessed by the number of well-child appointments, completeness of immunization, and number of inappropriate emergency room visits. Additional budget allocation will be needed to provide salary reimbursement for research data collection and information processing.

CONCLUSION

Shared Beginnings represents a grassroots approach to providing the community support that poor and at-risk families need to raise healthy children. The model can be replicated in other communities as an approach that challenges traditional approaches by government and society.

REFERENCES

Bergman, A., Wells, L., Bogo, M., Abbey, S., Chandler, V., Embleton, L., Guirgis, S., Huot, A., McNeill, T., Prentice, L., Stapleton, D., Shekter-Wolfson, L., & Urman, S. (1993). High-risk indicators for family involvement in social work in health care: A review of the literature. *Social Work, 38,* 281–288.

Carnegie Task Force on Meeting the Needs of Young Children. (1994). *Starting point.* New York: Author.

Clarke, L. (1993). *Provenant Shared Beginnings research prospectus.* Unpublished manuscript, Graduate School of Nursing, University of Colorado at Denver.

Colorado Department of Public Health and Environment. (1992). *Colorado vital statistics, 1992.* Denver: Author.

Droege, P. J. (1994, December 14). Young women need support on the nativity journey. *Denver Catholic Register,* p. 1.

Hartman, A. (1992). Health care: Privilege or entitlement? [Editorial]. *Social Work, 37,* 195–196.

National Commission to Prevent Infant Mortality. (1989, July). *Home visiting: Opening doors for America's pregnant women and children.* Washington, DC: Author.

Nelson, K. E., Saunders, E. J., & Landsman, M. J. (1993). Chronic child neglect in perspective. *Social Work, 38,* 661–671.

Piton Foundation. (1994). *Poverty in Denver: Facing the facts.* Denver: Author. (Available from Piton Foundation, 370 17th Street, Suite 5300, Denver, CO 80202).

Smilkstein, G. (1978). The family APGAR: A proposal for a family function test and its use by physicians. *Journal of Family Practice, 6,* 1231–1239.

Zuravin, S. (1989). *Suggestions for operationally defining child physical abuse and neglect*. Paper presented at the meeting on Issues in the Longitudinal Study of Child Maltreatment, Toronto.

PROGRAMS AND RESOURCES FOR AT-RISK PREGNANT WOMEN

Healthy Mothers Healthy Babies: A Coalition for Public Education to Improve Maternal Infant Health, 409 12th Street, SW, Washington, DC 20024.

March of Dimes Birth Defects Foundation, Community Services Department. (1990, April). *Lessons learned from the Better Babies Project*. White Plains, NY: Author.

National Center for Education in Maternal and Child Health, Maternal and Child Health Bureau. (1993, July). *Comprehensive adolescent pregnancy services—A resource guide*. Arlington, VA: Author.

National Commission to Prevent Infant Mortality. (1991, April). *One-stop shopping: The road to healthy mothers and children*. Washington, DC: Author.

New Mexico Prenatal Care Network, Maternity and Infant Care Program: "Baby Amigo." University of New Mexico, School of Medicine, Department of Obstetrics and Gynecology, Health Sciences and Services Building, Room 125, Albuquerque, NM 87131.

Phoenix Birthing Project, 1201 South 7th Avenue, Phoenix, AZ 85007.

Resource Mothers, Mother Net—A program of INMED, 45449 Severn Way, Suite 1161, Sterling, VA 20166.

Stork's Nest, The Hunt Place Clinic, 431 Hunt Place, NE, Washington, DC 20019 (a project of Zeta Phi Beta).

Teen Pregnancy Prevention 2000 Initiative (Colorado Trust Report). (1995, April). *Teens speak out about teen pregnancy*. Denver: Author.

The author thanks the Provenant Shared Beginnings staff and volunteers, Provenant Family Medicine Center personnel, Provenant Foundation, and Denver community supporters for their assistance.

This chapter was originally published in the February 1997 issue of Health & Social Work, *vol. 22, pp. 63–69.*

38 Social Support Networks of Confidants to People with AIDS

Stephen Jankowski, Lynn Videka-Sherman,
and Karen Laquidara-Dickinson

There is mounting evidence that social support is positively related to good health. Furthermore, social support buffers the negative effects of stress and health problems (Cohen & Syme, 1985; Gottlieb, 1983), including AIDS. Social support has been found to be associated with better health outcomes, better morale, and more successful coping with the physical and emotional demands of a health crisis (Cohen & Syme, 1985).

Less is known about the effects of social support on the family members and friends of the person who is ill. There is considerable stress associated with caring for a person with a serious health problem. Research on caregivers has indicated that social support can buffer the stresses of caring for the ill person. However, little is known about the specific effects of AIDS on family members and close friends of the person with AIDS (PWA). In this study, we investigated the effects of AIDS on the social support available to confidants who provide care and support for PWAs.

SOCIAL SUPPORT

Social support is defined as resources provided by people. Members of support networks provide tangible, material support and expressions of affection and acceptance to the individual (Cohen & Syme, 1985). Social support networks include kin and nonkin and professional and nonprofessional relationships as well as both instrumental and socioemotional support (Gottlieb, 1983; Wellman, 1981). House and Kahn (1985) showed the importance of using multiple indicators of social support, including quantity of support (number, type, and amount of contact of the social relationship); the structure of social relationships (density, homogeneity, range, content, reciprocity, dispersion, and intensity); and the functional content of relationships (degree to which the relationship involves flow of affect or emotional concerns, instrumental or tangible aid, and information).

Many studies of social support focus on confidant relationships. In the social support literature, *confidant* is defined as the person to whom one can turn for any and every problem under any circumstances (Abbey, Abramis, & Caplan, 1985; Blazer, 1982; Brown, Bhrolchain, & Harris, 1975; Cobb, 1976; Northouse, 1988). Confidant relationships can diminish the impact of life stress and promote well-being. Confidant relationships can also decrease vulnerability to disease, emotional distress, and psychological symptoms during crises (Miller & Ingham, 1976; Pearlin & Lieberman, 1979).

Only a few studies of social support and AIDS have focused on the family and friends of the PWA. Most of these studies are anecdotal case reports that discuss the impact of AIDS on the confidant relationship (Rowe, Plum, & Crossman, 1988). In one study (Grief & Porembski, 1988), researchers conducted interviews with 11 significant others of deceased PWAs to explore the factors that helped or hindered the significant others' ability to cope with their loss. Grief and Porembski concluded that "significant others have many needs that have to be addressed so that significant others can continue to function as a valuable resource to the person with AIDS" (p. 264).

RESEARCH QUESTIONS

This chapter focuses on the impact of AIDS on both the person closest to the PWA (the confidant) and the confidant's social support network. We were interested in the help provided by the support network and both the structural and functional content of the relationships. We examined the amount, type, and purpose of contacts as indicators of the social interaction between the confidants and their own networks as well as between the confidant and the PWA. The breadth and types of support, both before and after diagnosis, were investigated.

The major research questions addressed in this study were as follows: How does AIDS affect the social lives of those closest to the PWA? What is the impact of AIDS on the number and types of social contacts of confidants of PWAs? What is the impact of AIDS on the amount and type of social support received by the confidant?

METHOD

This study used a qualitative, semistructured interview methodology to gather information about the social networks of PWAs' confidants. Qualitative research methodology is naturalistic and oriented to discovery rather than hypothesis testing. We attempted to learn about social networks and social lives from the perspective of the person being interviewed, a phenomenological approach (Patton, 1986; Ruckdeschel, 1985).

PWAs and confidants were interviewed separately in their homes for one to two hours. The semistructured interview protocol was based on the theoretical literature and on research on social support and AIDS. Interviews were conducted by graduate social work students.

Sample

The PWA sample of 14 people was drawn from the AIDS clinic rosters of two hospitals, one a Veterans Affairs medical center and the other a regional AIDS treatment center. Quota sampling across risk groups (men who have had sex with other men, injection-drug users of any sexual orientation, and men and women who have engaged in male–female sex with infected partners) was used. Adults (men and women, 20 to 50 years old, mean age = 35) who were in the middle stages of AIDS and who were currently ambulatory and successfully medically managed at the time of the study were included. Middle-stage AIDS PWAs were individuals who had been diagnosed with AIDS at least six months ago, were primarily caring for themselves, and had been out of the hospital for several months since their diagnosis. Mentally impaired PWAs, asymptomatic HIV-positive individuals, and newly diagnosed people were excluded from the sample.

The confidant, the person who had been most helpful to the PWA since the diagnosis and to whom the PWA felt closest, was identified by the PWA during the interview. "Confidant" was used rather than "caregiver" or "supporter" to connote the intimate nature of the relationship between the PWA and the primary supporter. Caregivers and supporters may be acquaintances, paraprofessionals, family, or friends but are not necessarily confidants. Miller and Ingham (1976) identified intimacy (not necessarily sexual), utmost trust, availability, and confidence in a personal relationship as qualities that define a confidant relationship.

Interview Protocol

The evaluation and measurement of social networks is controversial. In a review of methodologies, House and Kahn (1985) stated, "We are unable to find a single measure that is so well validated and cost effective that it is to be preferred above others; various measures may be appropriate for various purposes and circumstances" (p. 94). Pagel, Erdly, and Becker (1987) supported using the confidant approach: "How to define the inclusion criteria for social networks is important theoretically and empirically. . . . There seem to be three general approaches used. . . . The simplest, and in some ways most theoretical, is the confidant approach, in which the individual is asked to list his or her confidants" (p. 795).

The purpose of interviewing confidants was to obtain their perspectives on the impact of the illness on their relationships with the PWAs and on their other social relationships. Also, it allowed us to obtain a different perspective, second to the PWAs, on the impact of AIDS on the PWA, the impact on the confidant, and the support they received. Confidant interviews permitted us to investigate reciprocity between confidants and PWAs, the ways support was perceived and used by each, and the types of support received by the confidant. Wortman (1984) spoke of the need to interview those who receive support and those who provide support to gain a better understanding of particular kinds of support. Areas of inquiry included feelings the confidant had about the AIDS diagnosis; changes that occurred in the relationship before and after the diagnosis; support used, received, and perceived by the confidant; type, amount, and breadth of support; evaluation of support; gaps in support; barriers to receiving support; burden experienced by the confidant; and support that was not helpful to the confidant.

Analysis

To facilitate analysis using the grounded theory qualitative content analysis method (Glaser & Strauss, 1976), all interviews were tape-recorded and transcribed. A coding inventory was developed. Each interview was independently coded by two investigators (triangulation) to reduce bias. Interview content segments (sections that addressed themes in the interview) were identified. Each interview was coded using the Ethnograph computer program (Seidel, Kjolseth, & Clark, 1985). Interview segments were then grouped by theme and analyzed to discover the content of PWAs' and confidants' experiences, subthemes, and other issues.

FINDINGS

Eleven of 14 PWAs named a confidant. The three PWAs without confidants were from the injection-drug user (IDU) risk group. Confidants included cohabiting partners ($n = 4$), sisters ($n = 3$), mothers ($n = 2$), and friends ($n = 2$). Of the four cohabiting partners, one was the spouse of a PWA from the IDU risk group and three were gay lovers or former lovers. Of the sisters, one was named by an IDU PWA and two were from the heterosexual sample. Of the mothers, both were named by homosexual PWAs; of the friends, both were named by IDU PWAs.

Emotional Impact of AIDS

In another article, we described the emotional impact of AIDS on the PWA (Jankowski, Videka-Sherman, & Laquidara, 1995). The primary emotional impact of AIDS on the PWA included loneliness, isolation, and depression. PWAs universally experienced guilt. Their anger focused on why they were saddled with the disease. A primary fear of PWAs was that they might expose (or might already have exposed) another person, especially the confidant, to the disease. These themes also related to the shame and stigma associated with AIDS.

The stigma associated with AIDS drove confidants' emotional responses, too. Anger was a common emotional theme. Many spoke of the unfairness of the disease. One sister said, "Why did it happen to her?" Others displaced their anger. One mother stated, "So I was very angry at them [other family members]. One of the emotions that comes from time to time in dealing with this has been anger. And I have directed it at different directions, and generally being mad at somebody for a time."

Anger toward the PWA was especially difficult for the confidants to manage. Eight confidants discussed guilt about their anger toward the PWA. Confidants feared that the PWA would die and that the confidant would have to live with the knowledge that he or she was resentful or angry with the PWA while he or she was ill. One former lover stated,

> Sometimes it makes me angry; I don't know why it should. Yeah, I watch it—in fact very consciously watch—trying not to get him ticked because I can always, you know, just envision. . . . You know, it could be next week he will wind up in the hospital and never get out again. I don't want things to end that way between us.

Confidants also expressed the emotional burden imposed on them by the secrecy surrounding the diagnosis. One sister stated, "I wish I had someone to talk to before, but I did not want to betray M's trust or confidence." Another stated, "It has been a strain, I think, on my relationship with my family. Because still, to this day, my mom does not know what the situation with K is." The stigma and secrecy surrounding AIDS compounded the emotional demands of AIDS for confidants.

Most confidants found some positive changes that resulted from AIDS. Three confidants explained in great detail their increased spirituality gained from the illness. One mother stated,

> Boy, are my prayers being answered. Unbelievably so. I can't believe how God is working in my life and changing me and turning me around and taking what's happening to F to turn me around and go in my faith in the Lord. And it's doing it in the same way for my husband. We're growing in our faith together.

Other positive changes occurred in the meaning of life for or existential concerns of confidants. Another mother reported the changes AIDS had on her and her husband: "This has just made us be more compassionate and understanding and tolerant and less critical and judgmental about everything in general." One sister stated,

> I think that I have a better perspective; little things don't mean anything anymore. . . . Things that used to be so big have become so little now. I just look at my kids differently. God, thank you. They're healthy, they don't have AIDS, and God willing, they have normal, healthy lives. I took my own health for granted before. I don't worry so much about that it isn't the way things are supposed to be, but that's the way it is. It's really made me appreciate my family and made me realize that there is nothing that is as important than life.

Structural Characteristics of Confidants' Social Networks

Confidants' social networks were constricted in both contact and size. Most confidants reported having lost contact with acquaintances and friends. Confidants had diminished "weak social ties" (Granovetter, 1973)—that is, fewer contacts with acquaintances, coworkers, and neighbors. Confidants relied primarily on a limited number of "strong social ties," usually family members or very close friends. Because many confidants assisted PWAs in obtaining concrete services and visited the PWA while he or she was hospitalized, social services and health care professionals became central figures and sources of socioemotional support.

Role changes and uncertainty over the course of the illness constricted the confidants' social networks. One aspect of the confidant's relationship with the PWA was caregiving. Caregiving placed constraints on available free time and increased commitment to the relationship. Nine confidants reported being unable to plan social events and having their lives "on hold." Thus, less social contact (and resulting support) was available to them. Limiting contacts also resulted in fewer questions asked about the PWA, which reduced the likelihood of divulging the diagnosis. In a sense, network constriction shielded confidants from potential rejection and stigma.

Secrecy and Stigma

Maintaining secrecy about the AIDS diagnosis was a powerful motivator for confidants' interpersonal behavior that exerted dramatic effects on their social lives. Four confidants guarded against disclosure by deliberately misrepresenting the PWA's diagnosis. One stated, "They think he had a heart attack." Another, who was asked by a friend about her husband, stated, "My husband has been sick and he's been in the hospital a lot. He has a blood disease. Sometimes things are good and sometimes things are bad. . . . It's not easy to talk about." Misrepresentation limited the available support for confidants. Confidants who misrepresented the diagnosis typically tried to minimize their discussion of the illness with others. Some confidants minimized their social contacts to maintain the secret of the AIDS diagnosis.

Seven confidants spoke of the "veil of pretense" or a "diagnostic charade" with those individuals with whom they did have contact. Social interaction became more stressful over time. Sometimes the confidant was directly constrained by the PWA's wish to maintain secrecy about the disease.

The presence of at least one other person with whom the PWA and confidant could share the truth of the AIDS diagnosis served as a valve to release the confidant's emotional burdens. Three confidants spoke of encouraging the PWA to disclose the diagnosis to a friend: "I just kind of gave him, I guess, permission . . . to go ahead and be open about it [the diagnosis]." Self-disclosure by the PWA broke the secrecy and in turn gave the confidant permission to tell another person. One sister stated,

> You can speak with the person [PWA], but sometimes you need to talk to someone else. I get frustrated and don't like to think of somebody I love dying, and I really can't tell anyone, no one. My husband and I are separated by miles since I came up here to help, so I can't tell him. Even though you may want to . . . it puts a real, real strain on you. J [the PWA's other sister] knew, and we could actually talk about it. How free I felt that someone else knew. I think you need at least one other person to talk to.

Six confidants selected their own confidants (with or without the knowledge and permission of the PWA) to help ease the burden of the illness. Other confidants relied on professionals for their support.

Confidant Support Provided to the PWA

Confidants clearly saw themselves in a help-giving rather than help-receiving role. Confidants talked extensively and with a great deal of pride about the ways that they tried to support the PWA.

Confidants rallied to support the PWA. In this sample, two confidants (a mother and sister) moved from their homes in different states to be closer to the PWA. A former lover renewed his relationship with the PWA after a two-year separation and moved into the PWA's apartment after learning of the diagnosis. These confidants all shared a sense of increased responsibility for the PWA, even though the PWA was not yet physically dependent on them. A mother spoke of her son, "I feel that he doesn't have as many friends and people are not as supportive of him, and I just want to make sure that he knows someone is. I wouldn't see him half as much if he wasn't sick."

Unconditional availability, which PWAs stated was very important, was described by confidants as the fundamental support that they provided to their friend or family member with AIDS. One friend described the support she provided in this way: "And if she needs something from me, money-wise, wants to have me be here at a certain time because she wants me to talk . . . just because she wants me to be here, she can count on it. And she knows it. She knows it." Another mother described the ways that she and her husband tried to be available for their son who had AIDS: "My husband does, too. Just to be there with him. Whether it's emotional support or financial support, to just have him know that we are there in the background and he doesn't have to worry about anything, that whatever he needs, we'll be there."

Confidants made sure that they maintained regular contact with the PWA. This was especially important for former IDU PWAs whose lifestyles were socially isolated. One friend of an IDU PWA stated,

> So I told her, "After two days, all right, two days." Three days in a row I don't hear from her, she knows. You know, I give her those two days to be depressed, to come out of it, to know that she's got some other things that she's got to deal with. And on the third day, I'm calling or I'll come to her house.

Other instrumental help provided by confidants to PWAs included physical care, monetary loans, transportation, assistance with financial management, in-kind financial help (such as handing down furniture), or grocery shopping and preparing meals. They also gave PWAs advice on health and other life issues such as parenting.

Another important support provided by confidants was as a source of hope and motivation for the PWAs. Sometimes this was accomplished by diverting attention from the disease. One mother of a gay PWA described her role with her son: "He wouldn't have made it if I hadn't come up. He would have just said, 'The hell with it,' you know. Because there isn't another soul that could have gone in . . . they couldn't . . . nobody could go in without . . . without giving him the sympathy thing. Now sick people don't need that." Confidants described how they went out of their way to accommodate the PWA's needs. One gay partner stated,

> I try to work my schedule around his, 'cause usually late in the evening, he'll rest. So then when he's resting, I'll go downstairs and do whatever I have to do, and while he's awake I'll try to be upstairs and do stuff that I can do upstairs, so it's like you're in the room or in the next room. . . . He doesn't like to be alone, and he doesn't like other things to take my attention away.

Social Support Available to Confidants

Reciprocity in the PWA–Confidant Relationship. Balanced exchange is the hallmark of a stable, intimate relationship. What do the confidants get from their relationship with the PWA? Three confidants, all partners of gay men, reported that they got nothing from the PWA. In only one relationship, a female-to-female friendship, did the confidant report mutuality. In this case, the confidant described how she could turn to the PWA for her needs as well as vice versa. One formerly drug-addicted confidant talked about the role of the PWA as a primary source of social support during the confidant's own recovery. This confidant spoke of altruism and "giving something back."

Although a lack of reciprocity is to be expected given the current needs of PWAs, only in a few cases had there been a history of reciprocity. We believe that this imbalance puts the confidant at risk for emotional isolation and stress. Given the limited support available to confidants due to factors such as physical relocation and the secrecy and stigma associated with AIDS, confidants may themselves be at risk for physical and mental deterioration.

Other Sources of Support. Confidants' social support needs differed from those of PWAs in several ways. Confidants were not focused on the instrumental help that PWAs reported as indispensable. Rather, confidants, like PWAs, needed help obtaining information concerning AIDS. They relied primarily on health care and social services professionals and, to a lesser extent, on mass media to supply this information.

Although a lack of reciprocity in the confidant–PWA relationship was noted, confidants reported receiving support from others. Given the constricted social networks available to confidants, professionals played an especially important role in providing support to the confidant, even when professionals had not intentionally focused supportive interventions on the confidant. One confidant reported that it was important to talk to a neutral person. She went on to describe the following unplanned interaction with a home health aide:

> A funny thing happened. The home health girl rang up my phone by mistake, instead of G's apartment, and we talked for a while on the phone. And it was good to be able to be that open with somebody about the entire problem, the entire situation, and not to have to play a charade with somebody about [it] . . . "Well, he's very ill but he's better" type of thing. So I think to have neutral parties that are not in a relation or linked, tied closely to you in some way, but who understand the problems of this disease, is good.

The knowledge that professionals have about the disease is an important aspect of their helpfulness. It relieves the confidant of the dual burdens of having to explain the disease and of having to present the disease course in an optimistic manner to save face and to avoid raising uncomfortable feelings in the listener.

Spirituality also provided comfort to confidants. One confidant described the solace she got from a sermon: "We had a guest speaker at the church that my husband and I belong to. And the theme of the man's talk was walk with God. And I thought, that's just what [the PWA] does: he walks with God."

Of course, confidants sometimes used people from their own primary networks, such as family members or friends, as sources of emotional support and as someone to talk to about their experiences. But family and friends—typically the first line of support in any crisis—often were not available to many confidants because of the secrecy surrounding the diagnosis, the stigma associated with AIDS, and the geographical separation due to the relocation of the confidant to be with the PWA. As a result, many confidants endured high stress and did not have adequate supports available to them.

Unsupportive Responses from Network Members. The stigma associated with AIDS resulted in very real social support consequences for these confidants. Several were rejected outright by friends and acquaintances when the diagnosis was disclosed. One wife of a PWA stated, "Some people they find out and they never talk to you. . . . One of my friends doesn't talk to me anymore." Some family members disappointed confidants by not being sufficiently attentive to the PWA. One described the following response by family members:

> His family makes me mad. They haven't even come to see him since. . . . I think his father and his brother came once. His brother came up at Christmas time and his father came up once. . . . [W]e needed money for the rent one time. His father is pretty well off and so is his brother. They wouldn't give us the money.

The role of caregiver often required having to appear strong. One sister of a gay PWA stated, "If I could just sometimes talk to somebody who is going through the same thing. And I don't get that from my family. Because, as I said, when they come, I'm supposed to be the strong one for them. I just can't let it all down." Surprisingly, few confidants were involved in support groups or in other types of formal supports such as seeing a counselor.

IMPLICATIONS FOR PRACTICE

Findings from this study have several implications for social work practice. First, there are genuine constraints in support available to the PWAs' confidants. Factors perpetuating inadequate support were vividly described by confidants as secrecy, stigma, burden, lack of reciprocity in relationships, increased responsibility, geographic relocation, and fear of rejection. Health care and social services professionals can play a critical role in providing necessary support to the confidant because they are viewed as knowledgeable and emotionally accepting.

Social support can play a central mediating role in preventing disease, maintaining health, and insulating people from stressors (Gottlieb, 1983). Confidants who remain unsupported during the illness process of the PWA may be placed at further risk for psychological and physical complications. Factors constricting support may be sustained after the death of the PWA, thereby complicating the bereavement process and adaptation to the loss.

A major focus of social work intervention with confidants should be bolstering supportive ties, especially for confidants who relocate to be closer to the PWA. Openly discussing disclosure issues with the PWA and confidant together, role-playing how a trusted individual could be told, and using community resources for networking—all of these interventions help the confidant and PWA feel less restricted and better able to use others for support. Confidants and PWAs who have successfully disclosed and established supportive networks may be willing to discuss their experiences and strategies with other confidants and PWAs individually or in a group setting.

Leading confidant support and bereavement groups can be another important role for social workers. Because patterns of disclosure may be established during the illness, a supportive group setting may allow confidants to express their apprehensions more openly and to normalize their feelings, especially the anger, resentment, and shame related to stigma. This support can reduce the stress of secrecy, promote psychological well-being during the illness, and assist with adaptation during bereavement.

IMPLICATIONS FOR FURTHER RESEARCH

Investigating the role of reciprocity and the obstacles to mutuality as part of exchanges during the crisis of AIDS are important areas for future research. Reciprocity between confidants and their family and friends should be studied to explain how friendship and family supports provide nurturance or promote isolation for confidants during HIV/AIDS illnesses.

Much more needs to be learned about the role of secrecy in the lives of PWAs and their confidants. Decisions about disclosure of the PWA's diagnosis to others in the confidant's network is another important focus for future research. Developing strategies to evaluate secrecy during the illness may assist social workers and other professionals in reducing the need for secrecy, thereby broadening support for both the confidant and the PWA.

Longitudinal studies that capture the dynamic process of support needs and the types of support that are beneficial to confidants during the PWA's illness are needed. Are the support needs and types of support required by confidants dictated by the stages of the illness? Now that the course of AIDS can be prolonged, identifying support requirements may help sustain and bolster confidants' sense of well-being as well as their coping abilities.

REFERENCES

Abbey, A., Abramis, D. J., & Caplan, R. D. (1985). Effects of different sources of social support and social conflict on emotional well-being. *Basic and Applied Social Psychology, 43*, 315–323.

Blazer, D. G. (1982). Social support and mortality in an elderly community population. *American Journal of Epidemiology, 115*, 684–694.

Brown, W., Bhrolchain, R., & Harris, T. (1975). Social class and psychiatric disturbance among women in an urban population. *Sociology, 9*, 225–254.

Cobb, S. (1976). Social support as a moderator of life stress. *Psychosomatic Medicine, 38*, 300–314.

Cohen, S., & Syme, S. K. (1985). *Social support and health.* Orlando, FL: Academic Press.

Glaser, B. J., & Strauss, A. K. (1976). *The discovery of grounded theory: Strategies for qualitative research.* New York: Aldine.

Gottlieb, B. (1983). *Social support strategies: Guidelines for mental health practice.* Beverly Hills, CA: Sage Publications.

Granovetter, M. (1973). The strength of weak ties. *American Journal of Sociology, 78*, 1360–1380.

Grief, G., & Porembski, E. (1988). AIDS and significant others: Findings from a preliminary exploration of needs. *Health & Social Work, 13*, 259–264.

House, J., & Kahn, R. (1985). Measures and concepts of social support. In S. Cohen & S. L. Syme (Eds.), *Social support and health* (pp. 83–108). Orlando, FL: Academic Press.

Jankowski, S., Videka-Sherman, L., & Laquidara, K. (1995). *The social support networks of persons with AIDS.* Unpublished manuscript, University at Albany, State University of New York, School of Social Welfare.

Miller, P. M., & Ingham, J. G. (1976). Friends, confidants and symptoms. *Social Psychiatry, 11*, 51–58.

Northouse, L. (1988). Social support in patients' and husbands' adjustment to breast cancer. *Nursing Research, 37*(20), 20–30.

Pagel, M. D., Erdly, W. W., & Becker, J. (1987). Social networks: We get by with (and in spite of) a little help from our friends. *Journal of Personality and Social Psychology, 53*, 793–804.

Patton, M. Q. (1986). *Qualitative evaluative methods.* Beverly Hills, CA: Sage Publications.

Pearlin, L. I., & Lieberman, M. A. (1979). Social sources of emotional distress. In R. Simmons (Ed.), *Research in community mental health* (pp. 217–248). Greenwich, CT: JAI Press.

Rowe, W., Plum, G., & Crossman, C. (1988). Issues and problems confronting the lovers, families and communities associated with persons with AIDS. *Journal of Social Work and Human Sexuality, 6*(2), 71–88.

Ruckdeschel, R. A. (1985). Qualitative research as a perspective. *Social Work Research & Abstracts, 21*(2), 17–20.

Seidel, J. V., Kjolseth, R., & Clark, J. A. (1985). *The ethnograph.* Littleton, CO: Qualis Research Associates.

Wellman, B. (1981). Applying network analysis to the study of support. In B. Gottlieb (Ed.), *Social networks and social support* (pp. 171–200). Beverly Hills, CA: Sage Publications.

Wortman, C. (1984). Social support and the cancer patient: Conceptual and methodological issues. *Cancer, 53*(10), 2339–2360.

A previous version of this chapter was presented at NASW's annual conference, November 1988, Philadelphia.

This chapter was originally published in the March 1996 issue of Social Work, *vol. 41, pp. 206–213.*

About the Editors

Patricia L. Ewalt, PhD, *is dean and professor, School of Social Work, University of Hawaii, Honolulu. She has a master's degree in social work from Simmons College School of Social Work and a PhD in health care policy, research, and administration from the Florence Heller School for Advanced Studies in Social Welfare, Brandeis University, Waltham, Massachusetts. She was the editor of* Social Work *from 1993 to 1997.*

Edith M. Freeman, PhD, *is professor, University of Kansas School of Social Welfare, Lawrence. She has an MSW from the University of Kansas School of Social Welfare and a PhD from the Departments of Psychology and Human Development and Family Life. She was the editor of* Social Work in Education *from 1993 to 1997.*

Dennis L. Poole, PhD, *is professor, University of Central Florida, Orlando. He has an MSW from West Virginia University and a PhD from the Florence Heller School for Advanced Studies in Social Welfare, Brandeis University, Waltham, Massachusetts. He is the editor of* Health & Social Work.

About the Contributors

Howard S. Adelman, PhD, LCP, is professor, Department of Psychology, University of California–Los Angeles.

Ellen B. Ames, PhD, LCSW, is project coordinator, Interdisciplinary Training Project, Department of Social Work, California State University, Long Beach.

Judy Balsanek, ACSW, LCSW, is family services coordinator, Clayton/Mile High Early Head Start, Denver.

William H. Barton, PhD, is associate professor, School of Social Work, Indiana University, Indianapolis.

Tony Bell, MSW, is director of social services, Trinity Resources Unlimited Head Start Program, Chicago.

Kathleen Kirk Bishop, DSW, is associate professor and director, Partnerships for Change, Department of Social Work, University of Vermont, Burlington.

Katharine Briar-Lawson, PhD, is professor, Graduate School of Social Work, University of Utah, Salt Lake City.

Mark Cameron, MSSW, ACSW, is research associate, Columbia University School of Social Work, New York.

Iris Carlton-LaNey, PhD, is associate professor, School of Social Work, University of North Carolina at Chapel Hill.

Robert J. Chaskin, PhD, is research fellow, Chapin Hall Center for Children, University of Chicago.

Selma Chipenda-Dansokho, MPA, is research associate, Chapin Hall Center for Children, University of Chicago, Chicago.

Carol S. Cohen, DSW, ACSW, is assistant professor and program director, BA Program in Social Work, Fordham University, New York.

Connie Collier, PhD, is assistant professor, School of Exercise Leisure and Sport, Kent State University, Kent, OH.

Dean Corrigan, EdD, holds the Harrington Chair in Educational Leadership, Department of Educational Administration, Texas A&M University, College Station.

Linwood H. Cousins, PhD, CSW, is assistant professor, School of Social Work and Anthropology, Western Michigan University, Kalamazoo.

Melvin Delgado, PhD, is professor of social work and chair of the macro practice sequence, School of Social Work, Boston University.

Janet E. Dickinson, PhD, is former deputy director, Newark Target Cities Project, New Jersey Department of Health and Senior Services, Trenton.

Dennis Dooley, MA, is writer and editorial consultant, Cleveland.

David R. Dupper, PhD, is assistant professor, School of Social Work, University of Illinois at Urbana–Champaign.

Gloria Edwards, PhD, ACSW, is associate director, Office of Multicultural Health, University of Michigan Health Systems, Ann Arbor.

Holly R. Ford, MSW, is human resources manager, Kryptonics, Louisville, CO.

Marvella E. Ford, PhD, is associate staff investigator, Center for Medical Treatment Effectiveness Programs, Henry Ford Health Sciences Center, Detroit.

Rose C. Gibson, PhD, is faculty associate, Institute of Gerontology, faculty associate emerita, Institute for Social Research, and professor emerita, School of Social Work, University of Michigan, Ann Arbor.

Susan F. Grossman, PhD, is assistant professor, Loyola University School of Social Work, Chicago, and former research director, Gang Violence Reduction Project, School of Social Service Administration, University of Chicago.

Neil B. Guterman, PhD, MSW, is assistant professor, Columbia University School of Social Work, New York.

Kelly J. Haughey, MSW, is a full-time at-home parent, Blanco, TX.

Joy Howard, MSW, is foster care specialist, Illinois Department of Children and Family Services, Sycamore.

Kai Jackson, BS, is program manager, Edison School-Based Health Center, Kalamazoo, MI.

Sondra Jackson, MSW, LCSW, is deputy receiver for programs, Child and Family Services, Washington, DC.

Stephen Jankowski, PhD, ACSW, BCD, is director, Mental Health Outpatient Services, Veterans' Affairs Medical Center, Albany.

Roger Jarjoura, PhD, is assistant professor, School of Public and Environmental Affairs, Indiana University, Indianapolis.

Casey Johnson, MSW, is program manager, Aunt Martha's Youth Agency, Aurora, IL.

Alfred Joseph, PhD, is assistant professor, Department of Family Studies and Social Work, Miami University, Oxford, OH.

Mark L. Joseph, MA, is research associate, Chapin Hall Center for Children, University of Chicago.

Paula Kleinman, PhD, is senior research associate, CASA, Columbia University, New York.

M. Katherine Kraft, PhD, is program officer, Robert Wood Johnson Foundation, Princeton, NJ.

Terry Saunders Lane, MSS, is associate dean for professional education and sponsored projects, Boston University School of Social Work.

Karen Laquidara-Dickinson, MSW, is director, AIDS Services, Catholic Charities of the Diocese of Albany, NY.

Hal A. Lawson, PhD, is professor, Graduate School of Social Work, University of Utah, Salt Lake City.

Marceline M. Lazzari, PhD, ACSW, is chair, Social Work Department, University of Southern Colorado, Pueblo.

Cynthia Lim, MSW, is doctoral student, Department of Social Welfare, School of Public Policy and Research, University of California–Los Angeles.

Lou Matheson, MA, is a counselor and consultant, Spokane, WA.

Elizabeth A. Michalak, MA, is lecturer, Department of Social Work, California State University, Long Beach.

John D. Morrison, DSW, ACSW, is professor and MSW program chair, George Williams School of Social Work, Aurora University, Aurora, IL.

Elizabeth A. Mulroy, PhD, is associate professor, School of Social Work, University of Hawaii at Manoa.

Mary Nakashian, MA, is vice president and director of program demonstration, CASA, Columbia University, New York.

Arthur J. Naparstek, PhD, is Grace Longwell Coyle Professor of Social Work, Mandel School of Applied Social Sciences, Case Western Reserve University, Cleveland.

Francisco J. Navarro, MSW, is public service administrator, Illinois Department of Children and Family Services, Aurora.

Julie O'Donnell, PhD, is associate professor, Department of Social Work, California State University, Long Beach.

Deborah Page-Adams, PhD, is assistant professor, School of Social Welfare, University of Kansas, Lawrence.

Michael H. Phillips, DSW, ACSW, is professor, Graduate School of Social Service, Fordham University, New York.

Beth Plachetka, MSW, LSW, is youth minister, Aurora Central Catholic High School, Aurora, IL.

John Poertner, DSW, is professor and associate dean, School of Social Work, University of Illinois at Urbana–Champaign.

Cynthia Cannon Poindexter, MSW, PhD, is assistant professor, School of Social Work, Boston University.

Marilyn K. Potts, PhD, ACSW, is professor, Department of Social Work, California State University, Long Beach.

Salome Raheim, PhD, ACSW, is associate professor, School of Social Work, University of Iowa, Iowa City.

Juan L. Rodriguez, MD, is allergy specialist, Henry Ford Health Sciences Center, Detroit.

Maria Scannapieco, PhD, LMSW, is associate professor and director, Center for Child Welfare, School of Social Work, University of Texas at Arlington.

Sharon Shay, PhD, is executive director, Family Nurturing Center, Department of Pediatrics, Boston University.

Michael Sherraden, PhD, is Benjamin E. Youngdahl Professor of Social Development, George Warren Brown School of Social Work, Washington University, St. Louis.

Irving A. Spergel, PhD, is George Herbert Jones Professor, School of Social Service Administration, University of Chicago.

Donna Tapper, MA, is senior associate, Metis Associates, New York.

Michael Till, MSW, CSW, is clinical social worker, Edison School-Based Health Center, Kalamazoo, MI, and PhD student in counseling psychology, Western Michigan University.

Barbara C. Tilley, PhD, is director, Center for Medical Treatment Effectiveness Programs, and department chair, Biostatistics and Research Epidemiology, Henry Ford Health Sciences Center, Detroit.

Mary Van Hook, PhD, is associate professor, School of Social Work, Grand Valley State University, Grand Rapids, MI.

Lynn Videka-Sherman, PhD, is dean, School of Social Welfare, University at Albany, State University of New York.

Marie Watkins, PhD, CSW, ACSW, is research associate, School of Social Work, Indiana University, Indianapolis.

Gautam N. Yadama, PhD, is associate professor, George Warren Brown School of Social Work, Washington University, St. Louis.

Index

Academic achievement. *See also* School failure
   dropout rate and, 31
   poverty and, 306
   risk factors affecting, 380
Accountability, 347–348
Activity theory of aging, 253, 254
Addams, Jane, 344
Adolescent Community Services project
   (Binghamton, New York), 408
Adolescent pregnancy prevention programs,
   31
Adolescents. *See also* Children; Youth
   development
   with AIDS, 185
   asset assessment by Latino, 202–210. *See*
    also Asset assessment
   community violence affecting. *See*
    Community violence
   coping strategies in, 215
   delinquency and violence among, 32–33,
    333
   juvenile justice system and, 33–34
   as mentors, 193–200. *See also* Collabora-
    tive Afterschool Prevention Program
   peer orientation of, 217–218
   pregnancy among, 30–31, 374
   problems affecting, 29–30
   resilience in, 214, 216
   as resource, 202–203
   risk factors for, 191
   school dropout rate and, 31–32
   self-esteem in, 214–215
   substance abuse and, 32
   substance abuse prevention and Puerto
    Rican, 213–222. *See also* Substance
    abuse prevention project
   youth development approaches for, 35
Adoption Assistance and Child Welfare Act
   of 1980, 182
African Americans
   asthma in, 398. *See also* Asthma education
    program
   community violence effecting, 117. *See*
    also Community violence
   current challenges for, 185–186
   current response to separation and loss
    and, 186–187
   discriminatory lending practices and, 9
   historical response to separation and loss
    by, 184–185

kinship bond in, 183
kinship care and, 183, 187–188
poverty among, 185, 317
resilience and, 182–183
role of churches for, 399
"womanist" perspective of female, 152
Agenda for Children Tomorrow (ACT), 19
Aging theories, 253–254. *See also* Elderly
   individuals
Aguirre-Molina, M., 216, 221
AIDS/HIV
   African Americans with, 185
   children and adolescents with, 185
   emotional impact of, 423–424
   prevention training and, 218
   secrecy and stigma attached to, 424–425,
    429
   substance abuse and, 391
AIDS social support networks
   confidants' social networks and, 424
   implications for further research on, 428–
    429
   implications for practice and, 428
   previous studies of, 420, 421
   research questions regarding, 423
   study findings for, 423–428
   study method for, 421–423
Aid to Families with Dependent Children
   (AFDC), 73–78, 187
American Civil Liberties Union (ACLU),
   232–233
American Indians
   federal policy toward, 178–179
   foster placement of, 177–181
   Indian Child Welfare Act and, 179–181
AmeriCorps VISTA, 45
Anderson Elementary School (Minneapolis),
   310
Andrade, S. J., 165
Annie E. Casey Foundation, 37
Antigang education programs, 112
Arkansas Delta Community Integrated
   Service System, 408
Asset assessment
   description of, 204–205
   empowerment and, 203
   facilitating factors in, 206–207
   hindering factors in, 207–209
   Latino youths as field interviewers in, 204
   review of literature and, 202–203

Community Building: Renewal, Well-Being, and Shared Responsibility

Cover design by Beth Schlenoff

Interior design by Bill Cathey

Typeset in Lucida Sans and Palatino by Bill Cathey

Printed by Graphic Communications, Inc. on 60# Windsor